MW00757499

POPULAR PSYCHOLOGY
AN ENCYCLOPEDIA

POPULAR PSYCHOLOGY
AN ENCYCLOPEDIA

Luis A. Cordón

Greenwood Press
Westport, Connecticut • London

Library of Congress Cataloging-in-Publication Data

Cordón, Luis A.
 Popular psychology: an encyclopedia / Luis A. Cordón.
  p. cm.
 Includes bibliographical references and index.
 ISBN 0-313-32457-3 (alk. paper)
1. Psychology—Encyclopedias. I. Title.
 BF31.C715 2005
 150'.3—dc22   2004017426

British Library Cataloguing in Publication Data is available.

Library of Congress Catalog Card Number: 2004017426
ISBN: 0-313-32457-3

First published in 2005

Greenwood Press, 88 Post Road West, Westport, CT 06881
An imprint of Greenwood Publishing Group, Inc.
www.greenwood.com

Printed in the United States of America

The paper used in this book complies with the
Permanent Paper Standard issued by the National
Information Standards Organization (Z39.48-1984).

10 9 8 7 6 5 4 3 2 1

To Joanne, with appreciation and love

Contents

Preface

The mysteries of the human mind and human behavior have been a source of fascination and speculation throughout recorded history, and surely, for a long time before that. Attempts to explain human thoughts, emotions, and behavior, especially when they are disordered, go back just as long; and have often involved magic, evil spirits, invisible entities, and such unusual ideas as stones in the head and memories of previous lives. The scientific field of psychology is less than 150 years old. Most textbooks date its beginning to the establishment of Wilhelm Wundt's laboratory in Leipzig, Germany, in 1879. Since that time the field has grown rapidly, and the application of scientific method has led to many remarkable discoveries about how the human brain and mind actually work, along with what actually determines human behavior.

Unfortunately, magical thinking and superstition had a head start of 20,000 years on the scientific method, and so their elements still permeate the popular presentation of psychology, or "pop" psychology. We in the academic world probably should not be as surprised as we are that people are still willing to believe in a wide array of bizarre causal mechanisms for mental illness and in the treatments those beliefs inspire, despite a complete lack of empirical evidence supporting them. The realm of pop psychology certainly overlaps the science of psychology, but there are large areas of the two that rarely meet. A central purpose of this book is to explore key areas of both, in hopes of finding what is good science in the popular presentation of psychology, while providing some of the necessary tools for detecting those parts that are unworthy of serious attention.

Since I began my career as a psychology professor, the need for a book like the *Popular Psychology: An Encyclopedia* has become increasingly clear to me. First, most people don't know what psychology actually is. When I was a psychology major at Louisiana State University, I had a frightful experience that is well known to most students of psychology. I was at a party, and someone asked me what I was majoring in. Upon hearing "psychology," this person suddenly looked wary, then said, with a suspicious gleam in his eye, "I bet you're analyzing me right now!" Despite the popularity of psychology as a college major, and the enormous research literature in the field, the popular image of psychology remains locked in a Victorian-era psychoanalyst's office, complete with couch and Viennese accent. There is little understanding among the general public that psychological scientists even exist, or that there is a difference between psychology and psychiatry. This confusion is only increased by the mass media.

Like the general public, bookstore chains don't know what psychology is either. I am always fascinated, and more than a bit appalled, at what the bookstores put in the "psychology" (now frequently called "psychology and self-help") section. A handful of works of real scholarship is usually surrounded on all sides by the banal platitudes of self-help "pop" psychologists like John Gray, books of alleged "personality tests" that have never actually been validated with real people, and outright pseudoscientific junk like the works of L. Ron Hubbard and Deepak Chopra.

As a result of this mass-media bombardment of the public with poorly supported theories and treatments, I get asked a lot of questions by my students. Some of these questions are fairly innocuous, like, "Do subliminal messages in movies really make people buy more popcorn?" (The answer is "no"—details can be founding the Subliminal Perception entry in this volume.) Over time, however, I came to realize that some of these questions involved much more serious issues, like people's lives, health, and safety. A student once asked me the following question: "My cousin is autistic, and my aunt's doctor wants to try this thing called facilitated communication. It sounds pretty promising. What do you think?" My reply was that she absolutely should *not* try it, and that if her doctor were recommending it, she should change doctors immediately (my reasons appear in the Autism and Facilitated Communication entries). In the ensuing conversation, in which I explained the process thoroughly, the student stopped me to ask, "If all this is true, why haven't I heard about it?" I had no good answer for that. I tried, of course, to blame an irrational culture, the media, parents' willingness to try anything, and a whole array of other factors, but I knew the real answer: The people who know better are not saying what they know loudly enough.

This, then, is the real reason I undertook this book: To try to counteract the tide of misinformation about the field of psychology with a concise guide to some things that the well-informed student of psychology and the interested general public ought to know.

The *Encyclopedia* requires no specialized knowledge or training. I have written all entries assuming the reader is reasonably intelligent, but relatively uninformed about psychology, or indeed about science. The organization of this book is a simple encyclopedia-style alphabetical listing, with further readings listed at the ends of entries to provide more helpful information resources, and a bibliography of useful general works at the end of the volume. Cross-references within the text of an entry to other entries in the book are highlighted in small capital letters upon their first mention. A "Guide to Related Topics" provides a separate listing of categories of related topics to help readers quickly find multiple entries with similar themes. Concluding the volumes is a detailed subject index that provides access to information within entries.

This *Encyclopedia* is by no means a complete guide to everything there is to know about psychology, but it will serve as a starting point for those who wish to find out more. I have included entries on important historical figures in the development of psychology, along with further information on them within many of the other entries, so the reader can get a sense of where the field has come from and where it is going. I have attempted to cover a broad range of topics about which the average non-psychologist may have heard something but not had enough information on which to judge validity. My goal is to provide that information and to clear up some of the mystery surrounding the topics so beloved of pop psychologists.

Acknowledgments

Thanks are due to many people: to Alfred Kornfeld, without whom I wouldn't have undertaken this project in the first place; to the colleagues whose frequent hallway conversations about the topics in this book kept me fired up, especially Calvin Saxton, Charlie Wynn, Wendi Everton, Sue Boney-McCoy, Margaret Letterman, Deirdre Fitzgerald, John Kilburn, Jeff Danforth, and Peter Bachiochi; to Gus Allo, who is responsible for this book without realizing it—the world needs more great high school science teachers; to Joanne, Tomás, and Anna for putting up with me while I wrote it; to my parents, Carlos and Sylvia, without whom neither this book nor its author would be possible; and to Carlos and Paty—many of my conversations with you pointed me in this direction, too.

List of Entries

List of Entries

Guide to Related Topics

Biological Bases of Behavior
Addiction
Aphasia
Biofeedback
Brain
Brain Imaging Techniques
Chemical Imbalance
Electroconvulsive Therapy (ECT)
Epilepsy
Imprinting
Mad Cow Disease
Nervous System
Prefrontal Lobotomy
Premenstrual Dysphoric Disorder (PMDD)
Sleep and Dreaming
Split-Brain Surgery
Stroke
Ten Percent Myth

Disorders
Addiction
Alzheimer's Disease
Amnesia
Aphasia
Asperger's Disorder
Attention-Deficit/Hyperactivity Disorder (ADHD)

Autism
Chemical Imbalance
Down Syndrome
DSM-IV
Epilepsy
Learning Disability
Mad Cow Disease
Mental Retardation (MR)
Mood Disorders
Multiple Personality Disorder (MPD)
Munchausen Syndrome
Narcolepsy
Nervous Breakdown
Paraphilias
Pervasive Development Disorders
Phobias
Posttraumatic Stress Disorder
Premenstrual Dysphoric Disorder (PMDD)
Schizophrenia
Seasonal Affective Disorder (SAD)
Tourette Syndrome
Williams Syndrome

Drugs and Chemicals
Addiction
Chemical Imbalance

Guide to Related Topics

Depressants
Gingko Biloba
Kava
Opioids (Opiates)
Psychedelic Drugs
St. John's Wort
Stimulants

Historic Figures/Associations in Psychology
American Psychological Association (APA)
Chomsky, Noam (1928–)
Erikson, Erik (1902–1994)
Freud, Sigmund (1856–1939)
Galton, Francis (1822–1911)
James, William (1842–1910)
Jung, Carl Gustaf (1875–1961)
Kinsey, Alfred (1894–1956)
Masters, William H. (1915–), and Johnson,
    Virginia E. (1925–)
Neo-Freudians
Pavlov, Ivan (1849–1936)
Piaget, Jean (1896–1980)
Skinner, B. F. (1904–1990)
Vygotsky, Lev Semenovich (1896–1934)
Watson, John B. (1878–1958)
Wundt, Wilhelm (1832–1920)

Popular "Gurus" and Movements
Chopra, Deepak (1947–)
Dianetics/Scientology
Gray, John (1951–)
McGraw, Phillip ("Dr. Phil") (1950–)
Transcendental Meditation

Pseudoscience
Acupuncture
Alien Abduction
Aromatherapy
Astrology
Body Type
Chopra, Deepak (1947–)
Cold Reading
Craniosacral Therapy
Dianetics/Scientology
Eye Movement Desensitization and
    Reprocessing (EMDR)
Facilitated Communication (FC)
Gray, John (1951–)

Homeopathy
Parapsychology
Past-Life Regression
Pseudoscience
Randi, James (1928–)
Rebirthing
Rolfing
Satanic Ritual Abuse
Self-Esteem
Subliminal Perception
Ten Percent Myth
Therapeutic Touch
Thought Field Therapy
Transcendental Meditation

Psychological Assessment
"Big Five" Personality Factors
Brain Imaging Techniques
Gardner, Howard (1943–)
Intelligence
Projective Tests of Personality

Psychological Research Methods
Brain Imaging Techniques
Correlation
Hawthorn Effect
Nonspecific Effects
Obedience to Authority
Parapsychology
Psychology, Research Methods in

Psychological Theories and Ideas
Attachment
Bilingualism
Birth Order
Body Type
Brainwashing
Chemical Imbalance
Cognitive Dissonance
Diffusion of Responsibility
Emotional Intelligence
Gestalt
Humanistic Psychology
Insanity Defense
Media Violence and Its Effects on
    Children
Memory
Moral Development

Mozart Effect
Obedience to Authority
Parapsychology
Parenting Styles
Sapir-Whorf Hypothesis
Savants and Prodigies
Self-Esteem
Stockholm Syndrome
Subliminal Perception
Ten Percent Myth

Psychology and the Law
Education for All Handicapped Children
    Act (P.L. 94-142)
Insanity Defense

Treatments
Acupuncture
Aromatherapy
Biofeedback
Cognitive-Behavior Therapy
Craniosacral Therapy
Depressants

Electroconvulsive Therapy (ECT)
Eye Movement Desensitization and
    Reprocessing (EMDR)
Facilitated Communication (FC)
Gestalt
Gingko Biloba
Homeopathy
Humanistic Psychology
Hypnosis
Kava
Opioids (Opiates)
Past-Life Regression
Prefrontal Lobotomy
Primal Therapy
Psychiatry
Rebirthing
Rolfing
St. John's Wort
Split-Brain Surgery
Stimulants
Therapeutic Touch
Thought Field Therapy
Transcendental Meditation

A

ACUPUNCTURE Acupuncture is one of several treatment approaches widely used in traditional Chinese medicine (TCM). Like much of TCM, it is based on the idea that a vital energy, or life force, flows throughout the body along channels called *meridians*. Illness, both physical and psychological, is attributed to imbalances or disturbances in the flow of this energy, often referred to as *chi* or *qi*. Treatment, therefore, consists of adjusting the balance and flow of qi through such practices as *qigong* (similar to the discredited American practice of THERAPEUTIC TOUCH) and acupuncture.

In acupuncture, flow of qi is adjusted via the insertion of very thin stainless-steel needles into various "acupuncture points" along meridians throughout the body. In modern practice, weak electrical currents are sometimes applied to the needles to enhance the effect (this is known as electroacupuncture). Over the course of the approximately 2,000 years of Chinese acupuncture practice, the number of these identified points has increased from the original 365 (one point to correspond to each day of the year) to about 2,000. Unfortunately, practice is not especially standardized—some practitioners place needles near the location of the injury or illness, others choose locations based on the ancient belief of symptoms corresponding with particular meridians, and many engage in some combination of these two methods.

Acupuncture advocates claim that it is helpful in treating a wide range of physical and psychological ailments, including but not limited to stress and anxiety, depression, smoking, overeating, drug addiction and alcoholism, gastrointestinal complaints, hypertension, chronic pain, migraines, impotence, and deafness. These are remarkably broad claims, based on remarkably narrow

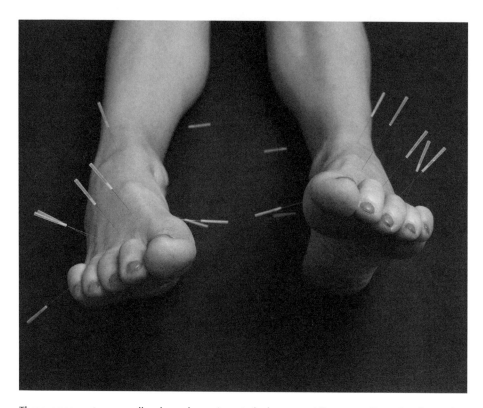

These acupuncture needles have been inserted along meridians to adjust the flow of qi through the body.

evidence. Most advocates cite only their own observations and poorly controlled studies as evidence of the treatment's effectiveness. Large-scale examinations of acupuncture's effectiveness (*see* Ter Reit et al., 1990) tend to conclude that acupuncture is neither more nor less effective than a placebo, suggesting the palliative properties may be due to NONSPECIFIC EFFECTS rather than acupuncture. Double-blind placebo-controlled research on acupuncture is rare in any case, due to the very real difficulties of designing a realistic placebo condition that will not be distinguishable from real acupuncture by the research participants (*see* PSYCHOLOGY, RESEARCH METHODS IN).

Probably the most-researched effect of acupuncture is its alleged utility in the treatment of pain, both in cases of chronic pain and as an anesthetic measure. How such pain relief might actually occur is unclear. Advocates mostly adhere to either the gate-control hypothesis or the endorphin hypothesis. According to the gate-control advocates, acupuncture somehow diverts pain impulses in such a way that they do not reach the spinal cord or the brain, in effect shutting the "gate" to those areas. The other major theory is that acupuncture somehow stimulates the release of endorphins, opiate-like neurotransmitters that reduce pain in exactly the same way as prescription painkillers (*see* NERVOUS SYSTEM).

Within the medical world, opinion has been strongly divided as to whether or not these effects exist, as well as regarding whether the effects are unique to acupuncture, even if it can be shown to work. A 1981 American Medical Association report, for example, concluded that pain relief does not occur consistently or reproducibly in most patients, or at all in some of them. In 1991 the National Council Against Health Fraud went further, publishing a paper that concluded that acupuncture is an unproven treatment based on concepts of health and disease that bear no relationship to present scientific knowledge, and that recent research has failed to show the effectiveness of acupuncture against any disease. Despite this, a National Institutes of Health panel convened in 1997 concluded that the government and insurers should expand coverage of acupuncture to increase the number of people with access to its benefits. This panel and its conclusions have lent acupuncture a new aura of scientific respectability in the popular media, but they have been roundly disparaged by the scientific community as the result of loading the committee with acupuncture proponents rather than with more objective scientific minds (Sampson, 1998).

The inconsistency of research results, even when reported by advocates, is not surprising given the physiological improbability of the alleged mechanism involved in acupuncture. The meridians do not correspond with any known structures in the body (they do not, for example, correspond to the nervous or circulatory systems), and so it is unclear exactly how the qi flows along them. The vital force itself has also proven remarkably elusive when attempts have been made to measure it. Acupuncture is therefore a mechanism by which a healer attempts to affect the flow of a force that cannot be measured along pathways that don't exist (*see also* THOUGHT FIELD THERAPY).

Further Reading: Barrett, S. *Acupuncture, Qigong, and "Chinese Medicine."* www. quackwatch.org, 2002; Beyerstein, B. L., and Sampson W. "Traditional Medicine and Pseudoscience in China: A Report of the Second CSICOP Delegation (Part 1)." *Skeptical Inquirer,* 20(4) (1996): 18–26; Melzack, R., and Katz, J. "Auriculotherapy Fails to Relieve Chronic Pain: A Controlled Crossover Study." *Journal of the American Medical Association,* 251 (1984): 1041–1043; Sampson, W. "Acupuncture: The Position Paper of the National Council Against Health Fraud." *Clinical Journal of Pain,* 7 (1991): 162–166; Sampson, W. "On the National Institute of Drug Abuse Consensus Conference on Acupuncture." *Scientific Review of Alternative Medicine,* 2(1) (1998): 54–55; Skrabanek, P. "Acupuncture: Past, Present, and Future." In D. Stalker and C. Glymour, eds. *Examining Holistic Medicine.* Amherst, NY: Prometheus, 1985; Ter Reit, G., Kleijnen, J., and Knipschild, P. "Acupuncture and Chronic Pain: A Criteria-Based Meta-Analysis." *Clinical Epidemiology,* 43 (1990): 1191–1199; Ter Reit, G., Kleijnen, J., and Knipschild, P. "A Meta-Analysis of Studies into the Effect of Acupuncture on Addiction." *British Journal of General Practice,* 40 (1990): 379–382.

ADDICTION   When a pattern of substance abuse results not just in a craving for the substance but also in an actual physiological need for the substance, the person is said to have an addiction. Substance abuse simply refers to a pattern of use that causes serious social, legal, or interpersonal problems for the user.

Clearly, what is defined as substance abuse is therefore at least somewhat dependent on cultural change. In the late nineteenth century, for example, cocaine was widely available in nonprescription medications in the United States, including toothache drops for children. Conversely, alcoholic beverages were illegal in this country for nearly a decade in the twentieth century.

Not all substance abuse results in addiction, of course. When an addiction is present, a pattern of physiological dependence (characterized by both tolerance and withdrawal) develops, along with, usually, a pattern of psychological dependence (a pattern of compulsive use, along with a feeling of being unable to function without the substance). Tolerance means that the effective dose of the substance increases over time—there is a physiological need for larger and larger doses of the substance to achieve the same effect, or a significantly reduced effect from continued use of the same amount. The amount of tolerance that develops varies wildly from substance to substance and from individual to individual. Abusers of OPIOIDS and STIMULANTS, for example, may develop levels of tolerance that would kill a nonuser. Heavy smokers may consume a number of cigarettes daily that would have made them very ill when they first started.

Where there is tolerance, withdrawal usually follows. Withdrawal is a set of physiological, behavioral, and cognitive changes that results when a person who has been using a substance heavily goes without it for long enough that blood or tissue concentrations of the substance decline significantly. Withdrawal symptoms associated with different drugs vary substantially but can include becoming very ill, to the point of the user's life being in jeopardy, as with alcohol and some opiates. Alcohol withdrawal can cause a syndrome known as delirium tremens, or the DTs, which includes serious illness and hallucinations. The substance-dependent person's logical response to this is to recognize that the illness is caused by the absence of the substance, and so the solution is clear: get some more. In some cases of substance dependence, the individual's entire life comes to revolve around getting the substance, using it, recovering from its use, and going to find more.

The most widely abused categories of drugs are opioids (or opiates), stimulants, and DEPRESSANTS. Contrary to popular belief, there is no evidence of either marijuana or PSYCHEDELIC DRUGS producing a physiological dependence, though psychological dependence certainly develops in many users, especially marijuana users.

Although the popular image of drug abuse involves such illegal substances as heroin and cocaine, abuse of prescription drugs is on the rise in the United States, and now constitutes a major public health problem. According to the National Institute on Drug Abuse (NIDA), in 1999 about 2 percent of the population aged 12 and over (4 million people) were using the following prescription drugs nonmedically: 2.6 million were using painkillers (opioids), 1.3 million were using sedatives and tranquilizers, and .9 million were using stimulants.

Further Reading: National Institute on Drug Addiction. *NIDA Research Report—Prescription Drugs: Abuse and Addiction.* NIH Publication No. 01-4881, www. drugabuse. org, 2004.

ADHD *See* ATTENTION-DEFICIT/HYPERACTIVITY DISORDER

ADLER, ALFRED *See* NEO-FREUDIANS

ALIEN ABDUCTION In one of the most unusual developments to ever come to the attention of psychologists, tens of thousands of Americans currently believe they have been kidnapped by alien creatures from outer space. Furthermore, most report similar experiences. Common features of the experience include capture by the aliens, usually from bed in the middle of the night; transportation to a spaceship, usually through the air, and frequently through solid walls or windows; a brief tour of the spaceship; a medical examination; and not infrequently, a sexual assault of some sort. Many victims also claim to have been examined internally, and to have had some sort of device implanted, either under the skin or internally—most commonly in the nose or rectum. Many victims further claim to have been involved in human-alien hybrid breeding programs and to have seen either embryos or live children resulting from these experiments. Abduction accounts are also typically marked by a complete absence of both physical evidence and other witnesses to the incident.

Many of the classic features of the alien-abduction experience date back to the first widely publicized modern abduction claim, the alleged 1961 abduction of Betty and Barney Hill. A married couple traveling through the White Mountains of New Hampshire, they saw a bright light in the sky that seemed to be following them. They assumed it was a helicopter or other aircraft until it appeared to come much closer and descend very rapidly. Barney got out of the car to get a better look. He came to believe it was a spacecraft, and glimpsed occupants behind its windows. After this, the couple drove home, seeming to have lost about an hour of time that they couldn't account for. After Betty had a series of nightmares involving alien creatures, she and Barney saw a psychiatrist, who hypnotized them both. Following repeated hypnotic sessions, they both came to remember having been taken aboard a spacecraft and given medical examinations by strange aliens with "wraparound" eyes (a description that doesn't match that given by the majority of abductees).

Apart from a few isolated incidents in the intervening years, aliens appear to have left humanity alone until the early 1980s, when a huge upsurge in reports of alien abduction occurred, coinciding with the publication of a book called *Missing Time* by Budd Hopkins. According to Hopkins, a virtual epidemic of alien abductions was occurring, but the victims were unaware of what had happened to them. Under HYPNOSIS, by a therapist who knew the experience was real, they could be helped to recover the memory of their experiences and confront the reality of what had happened.

The bulk of the book is devoted to describing several cases in great depth, along with the signs that could let a person know that he or she is a possible abductee. Chief among these signs is missing time; that is, the sense of having lost several hours without being able to account for them. This, along with various types of anxiety, mysterious scars, and the experience of having woken up

This depiction of an alien abduction is drawn from common descriptions, which also indicate that a thorough physical exam for the victim is probably imminent.

and been unable to move, with a sense of foreboding and a mysterious presence in the room, are all believed by Hopkins to be signs that a person may have been abducted. On the final page of the book, the following sentence appears: "If you believe you may have had the kind of experience dealt with in this book, you may wish to write your recollections in detail to:" followed by a contact address for Hopkins; and then: "As time permits, an investigator will be in touch with you. All letters will be kept strictly confidential."

After an abductee contacted Hopkins, he began hypnotic sessions, and after a series of these, Hopkins reported that most of his subjects report very similar experiences, a fact Hopkins insists confirms the reality of the phenomenon. This is neither surprising nor convincing evidence of anything save the fact that they were all hypnotized by someone who believes in alien abduction. As the primary defining feature of hypnosis is a heightened susceptibility to suggestion, attempts to "recover" memories via hypnosis are notorious as a source of vivid false memories. Unfortunately, memories created through suggestion under hypnosis are indistinguishable from real ones to the person experiencing them. Indeed, as they are so vivid, the person experiencing them may actually feel more confident about them than about things that actually happened. This effect is even more likely when the hypnotist lacks training in either the proper use of hypnosis or the working of human MEMORY, so Hopkins's training is relevant: not a therapist of any sort, his background is in sculpture.

To really bring Hopkins's message to the masses required a far more gifted writer. Whitley Streiber, a successful author of horror and fantasy novels, was among the readers who recognized himself in the experiences described by Hopkins. Following hypnosis, Streiber published his so-called recollections in *Communion: A True Story*, a nonfiction volume marketed very much like his novels. Like his earlier books, *Communion* sold quite well and was adapted for a film. In the wake of *Communion* and its sequels, many more people came forward believing they may have been abducted. Streiber and Hopkins also got the attention of John Mack.

Mack, a Harvard-affiliated psychiatrist, had several patients referred to him by Hopkins for further evaluation. After examining them thoroughly, and apparently engaging in further hypnotic sessions, he eventually came to what struck him as a logical conclusion: it's really happening. His book, *Abduction: Human Encounters with Aliens*, followed the path blazed by Hopkins and Streiber and became a major best seller. Unlike Hopkins and Streiber, however, Mack was already a highly respected scholarly author (his biography of T. E. Lawrence won a Pulitzer Prize) with a connection to a prestigious university, and thus his equally outlandish claims were accorded a far more respectful reception by the press. His reception by the scientific community was far less positive, however, and the dean of the Harvard Medical School went so far as to form a committee to investigate Mack's methods, resulting in a report sharply critical of Mack's research.

This negative reception did not stop Mack. He collaborated with other abduction researchers (including Hopkins) on a sixty-four-page report mailed to nearly 100,000 psychotherapists, encouraging them to keep watch for signs of alien abduction in their patients. The report further estimated that nearly 4 million Americans have been abducted, a number that was subsequently reported widely by the media. This estimate demands further explanation. In 1991, the Roper organization conducted a survey of less than 6,000 people, in which they were asked whether they had undergone any of the following experiences:

- Waking up paralyzed with a sense of a strange person or presence *or something else* in the room. (Author's italics)
- Experiencing a period of time of an hour or more, in which you were apparently lost, but you could not remember why, or where you had been.
- Seeing unusual lights or balls of light without knowing what was causing them or where they came from.
- Finding puzzling scars on your body and not remembering how you received them or where you got them.
- Feeling that you were actually flying through the air although you didn't know why or how.

Most reasonably healthy and honest adults will answer "yes" to at least some of these. The authors, however, regarded as probable abductees all respondents who answered yes to at least four of these five symptoms. Only 119 people in the original sample fit this criterion, but the survey authors simply extrapolated that proportion to the adult population represented by the sample (about 185 million at the time) to arrive at the 3.7 million estimate. Although this estimate sounds incredible, the statistical procedures involved are actually fairly legitimate. The real problem lies in the assumption that the experiences listed are so extraordinary that they must be signs of alien abduction.

The set of experiences associated by these writers with abduction isn't as special as their readers have come to believe—it just involves phenomena that most people, including most psychologists who don't study SLEEP, don't know about. Sleep paralysis, for example, is experienced by all of us on a nightly basis. As we are usually asleep at the time, however, we are not generally frightened by it. When the body is in REM sleep, the brain actively prevents the body from acting on the content of dreams. In an occurrence that, while unusual, is not especially rare, sleep paralysis does not always go away immediately upon waking up.

Two other phenomena combine with sleep paralysis to produce the portion of the abduction experience that is usually remembered prior to hypnosis: hypnagogic hallucinations and hypnopompic hallucinations. A hallucination is any sensory experience unaccompanied by an actual sensory stimulus—hearing, seeing, smelling, tasting, or feeling something that isn't actually there. A hypnagogic hallucination is simply a hallucination which occurs while a person is in the process of falling asleep—if you've ever been startled back awake because you thought you were suddenly falling, you've experienced a hypnagogic hallucination.

Hypnopompic hallucinations are a more crucial part of the abduction experience, as they occur at the moment of waking up from a sound sleep and are sometimes accompanied by sleep paralysis. Most hypnopompic hallucinations involve a familiar person or other strange presence in the room, and the person having the hallucination typically goes back to sleep afterward. As sleep paralysis often includes a feeling of tightness in the chest, it is not unusual for hypnopompic hallucinations to include the feeling that the strange presence is either holding down the sleeper or actually sitting on his or her chest. This sort of experience has been well known in previous centuries, in which it was interpreted in terms of then-current beliefs.

The old European stories of demons that would assault people in the night (incubi and succubi), or of an old hag who would enter people's bedrooms and steal the breath from their lungs, have at their core the experience of waking up paralyzed with a strange presence in the room. In modern America, demons and hags are almost never reported, but in a culture in which some of the most lucrative movies ever made center on alien visitors, it comes as no great surprise that these sleep experiences are now primarily interpreted in those terms instead.

Consider again the case of Betty and Barney Hill. Their description of the aliens they saw differs from almost every other abductee account, because of their mention of "wraparound eyes." Several different authors have now pointed out that an episode of *The Outer Limits*, a science-fiction television show that often depicted alien visitors, titled "The Bellero Shield," featuring an abduction by aliens fitting that description perfectly, aired twelve days prior to their experience. The show was very popular and highly publicized. As for the experience of missing time, which the Hill case also helped establish as central to abductions, it is also rather commonplace and has probably been experienced by everyone reading this. It is not unusual on a long trip by road or airplane, or during periods of deep concentration or fatigue, for a person to discover that far more time has passed than it seemed. Like the other experiences that convinced John Mack to warn the nation's psychotherapists of a large-scale invasion, missing time is an ordinary, if somewhat intriguing, phenomenon. Nonetheless, some people have taken the report seriously, as exemplified by a whole new area of publishing: self-help books on how to avoid getting abducted by aliens (*see also* MEMORY).

Further Reading: Baker, R. "The Aliens Among Us: Hypnotic Regression Revisited." *The Skeptical Inquirer* (Winter 1987–88); Druffel, A. *How to Defend Yourself Against Alien Abduction.* New York: Three Rivers Press, 1998; Klass, Philip J. *UFO-Abductions: A Dangerous Game.* Buffalo, NY: Prometheus Books, 1988.

ALZHEIMER'S DISEASE Alzheimer's disease is the most common cause of senile dementia, accounting for about 70 percent of all cases. Although the symptoms of dementia have been widely (and inaccurately) viewed by the public as a standard part of the aging process for a very long time, Alzheimer's only gained broad recognition as the primary cause of dementia rather recently—the Alzheimer's Association was formed in 1980.

The symptoms and signs of senile dementia generally, and Alzheimer's disease more specifically, include a decline in memory, learning, attention, and judgment, as well as disorientation and increased difficulties in communication. Alzheimer's disease often makes it more difficult to think of the right word, for example. Behavioral manifestations of Alzheimer's disease include a decline in personal hygiene, as when a person who has a prior history of fastidiousness stops bathing; inappropriate social behavior; and apparent changes in personality. Wandering and forgetting what one is doing can become serious problems also, as this can create a genuine danger. As the disease progresses, the patient eventually becomes incontinent and incapable of self-care. A common pattern in Alzheimer's patients involves the worsening of symptoms at night—this is known colloquially among care providers as *sundowning*. It is important to note, however, that Alzheimer's disease, like most age-related syndromes, follows a widely variable course in different individuals. It has been estimated, for example, that fewer than 10 percent of patients who show the mild impairment characteristic of the early stages will actually deteriorate further.

The visible symptoms of Alzheimer's disease, as described above, are almost all symptoms of other psychological problems as well, which until recently made definitive diagnosis only possible after death, as the changes created by Alzheimer's disease are directly related to changes that occur in the brain. New, noninvasive BRAIN IMAGING TECHNIQUES such as fMRI, CT scans, and PET scans are now on the way to making it easier to see the distinctive brain features of Alzheimer's. The primary cellular changes associated with Alzheimer's disease are neurofibrillary tangles and neuritic plaques, along with atrophy, or the simple death of neurons.

A neurofibrillary tangle is an abnormal set of twisted threads of protein found inside nerve cells. Neurofibrillary tangles appear to interfere with nerve cell functioning by impairing the transmission of impulses down the axon to the next neuron. The distribution of neurofibrillary tangles spreads through the brain as the disease progresses, starting with subcortical structures such as the hippocampus but eventually spreading throughout the cortex. Neuritic plaques are hard, spherical deposits outside the cell walls, formed from proteins that would ordinarily be metabolized. The degeneration of the cells around them leaves spaces called vacuoles, which fill with fluid and granular material.

Without an autopsy and a thorough examination of the brain, it is still possible to diagnose the disease. This process involves noting the history of the impairment, documenting cognitive impairments, and conducting a physical exam, a neurological exam, and a psychiatric evaluation. It is very important to obtain the medical history from a family member, rather than just from the patient. The psychological/psychiatric assessment always includes a mental status exam, which consists of questions tapping the patient's orientation, memory, math ability, direction-following, motor skills, and other general information. Orientation refers to the patient's sense of location in space and time and is tested by asking such questions as "Where are you right now?" "What day is it?" and "Where were you born?"

The etiology, or cause, of Alzheimer's disease is still a subject of considerable debate, but several possibilities have been considered. One possibility is that a virus is involved. This hypothesis receives consideration because another disease involving serious physical deterioration of the brain, Creutzfeldt-Jakob disease (the human version of bovine spongiform encephalopathy, widely known as mad cow disease) is known to definitely involve a virus. No clear evidence of such a virus involved with the onset of Alzheimer's has been found yet, however.

Another hypothesis that has received considerable media attention despite scant evidence is the possibility that aluminum exposure is responsible. In support of this hypothesis, unusually high levels of aluminum have been found in the brains of some Alzheimer's patients. Note, however, that most Alzheimer-affected brains that have been examined have *not* followed this pattern. Other research, however, suggests that rates of Alzheimer's disease may be elevated in people with unusually high levels of aluminum exposure. Contrary to some media claims, the evidence does not indicate that all cooks should get rid of their aluminum pans just yet.

The most promising area of research into the causes of Alzheimer's disease involves the possibility of a genetic cause. One possible source of the problem is a protein known as apoliprotein E, which occurs in several subvarieties. The kind a particular brain produces is genetically controlled, and those who have the gene for the type called E4 have a much higher risk for Alzheimer's disease than those who do not have it. The gene is inherited with an autosomal dominant pattern, meaning it is inherited much like brown eye color—if either parent passes along the gene for E4, the child *will* have that variety. This may explain why Alzheimer's disease seems to run in families. Another promising piece of genetic evidence comes from research on Down syndrome. Until the last several decades, persons with Down syndrome rarely lived past childhood or early adulthood, but medical advances have made life past 35 much more common. As this has happened, an interesting pattern has emerged: virtually everyone with Down syndrome who lives long enough eventually develops early onset Alzheimer's disease. Physiologically, this seems to be because people with Down syndrome develop neurofibrillary tangles much earlier than other people do. The fact that most cases of Down syndrome are caused by mutations to the twenty-first pair of chromosomes, usually an extra chromosome, or a trisomy, hence the term trisomy 21, suggests an obvious place to look for a genetic cause to Alzheimer's. Sure enough, people without Down syndrome who develop very early onset Alzheimer's also seem to have abnormalities to the twenty-first chromosome pair.

At present, no cure is known for Alzheimer's disease. Treatment largely consists of drugs intended to improve blood flow or to increase levels of the various neurotransmitters affected by the abnormal cells and cell atrophy associated with the disease. No drug regimen has so far emerged as the clearly preferred approach, but various drug and nondrug treatments continue to appear (*see* Gingko Biloba). Treatment also usually involves full-time nursing care in the more advanced stages of the disease.

Further Reading: Moore, E. A. *Encyclopedia of Alzheimer's Disease.* Jefferson, NC: McFarland & Company, 2003.

AMERICAN PSYCHOLOGICAL ASSOCIATION (APA) The American Psychological Association (APA) held its first organizational meeting in 1892, at which G. Stanley Hall was elected president. Annual dues were set at three dollars, and the first annual meeting, the first major psychological conference in the world, was held in December of the same year. The establishment of the organization was a major milestone in the history of psychology, marking its coming of age as a distinct academic discipline, separate from physiology and philosophy, the disciplines from which many of its early researchers were drawn. The APA's annual meetings gave psychologists an opportunity to meet with other psychologists from all over the country and discuss their work, as well as finding out the latest information about what others were doing. These meetings, and others like them, continue to serve this very important function for the field of psychology.

The APA grew rapidly, and it has especially expanded its membership rolls in recent years, as the popularity of psychology as an academic discipline has continued to grow. The APA was the first major scholarly society in America to extend full membership to women. In 1892 the APA had thirty-one registered members. As of 2004 the APA claimed more than 150,000 members. It is the largest organization of psychologists in the world, and its influence on the way both research and clinical practice is conducted has been profound. Articles in professional journals, as well as most other publications by psychologists, along with college papers for psychology classes, follow the style and format guidelines of the *Publication Manual of the APA*, now in its fifth edition.

Psychological research at virtually all educational and research institutions in the United States is required to comply with the APA's *Ethical Standards for Psychologists*.

Within the APA, there are 53 divisions: organizations devoted to a particular subfield or area of interest within psychology, numbered from 1 to 55. The odd numbering occurs because, for historical reasons, there is neither a Division 4 nor a Division 11. Division 4 was originally to be the Psychometric Society, but they chose not to become an APA division after Division 5 (Evaluation and Measurement) had been formed with a very similar purpose. Division 11 was originally devoted to Abnormal Psychology and Psychotherapy but by 1946 it had joined forces with the original Division 12 (Clinical Psychology) to become the Division of Clinical and Abnormal Psychology, which changed its name again in 1998 to the Society for Clinical Psychology. Reflecting the huge growth in the field of psychology in the last couple of decades, Divisions 39 to 55 all date from 1980 or later—Division 55, added in 2000, is the American Society for the Advancement of Pharmacotherapy.

Despite its attempts to be all things to all psychologists, however, the APA's uncritical promotion of unscientific therapies (such as accepting advertising for SUBLIMINAL PERCEPTION self-help tapes and continuing-education credit for THOUGHT FIELD THERAPY) and its increasing advocacy of specific political positions, along with its advocacy of prescription privileges for clinical psychologists, alienated some of its prominent members sufficiently that they started a new, independent organization, the American Psychological Society (APS) in 1988. The APS is explicitly devoted to the advancement of scientific psychology and the representation of psychology as a science on the national level. This is taken seriously enough that a proposal to change the name of the organization to the Association for Psychological Science was narrowly defeated in 2002. The APS started by signing up over 5,000 members in its first six months and had more than 13,500 members by 2003 (a number the APA took about fifty years to reach). Its membership includes most of the leading American psychological scientists and academics, as well as many prominent clinicians. Despite its origins, the APS has maintained a cordial relationship with the APA, and many people are members of both organizations, seeing them as serving different purposes. Indeed, APS members get discounted rates on several APA journals.

Further Reading: Cattell, J. M. "The Founding of the Association." *Psychological Review,* 50 (1943): 61–64.

AMERICAN PSYCHOLOGICAL SOCIETY (APS) *See* AMERICAN PSYCHOLOGICAL ASSOCIATION (APA)

AMNESIA   Amnesia is simply the standard term for a loss of MEMORY, whether partial or complete. The condition is usually temporary, and it usually affects only a small part of a person's experience, such as memory of the immediate past. Amnesia can be produced by a range of causes, including both psychological trauma and brain damage that may be caused by a blow to the head; but can also be due to such varied causes as STROKE, BRAIN tumor, encephalitis, or long-term damage by alcohol.

There are several distinct types of amnesia:

- *Anterograde amnesia* is the most common type to result from brain damage. Anterograde amnesia is an inability to form new memories, usually caused by damage to the temporal lobes and/or the hippocampus, a small structure located beneath the cerebral cortex. The person with anterograde amnesia has no difficulty remembering the past, or who he is; but may not be able to remember anything that happened after the injury. This can result in the victim's permanently living in the present moment, and having to be re-introduced to people met since the injury, since no memory of them remains.

- *Retrograde amnesia* is a difficulty retrieving memories prior to an incident in which a head injury occurred. Contrary to the cliché presented on television, loss of memory is often limited to the seconds, minutes, or sometimes hours, leading up to the trauma. This is common in people who have been involved in serious automobile accidents: they frequently have no memory of either the accident or the moments leading up to it. Memory often returns eventually, though it is not unusual for the person to never recover the final seconds leading up to the injury.

- *Korsakoff's syndrome* is special kind of memory loss caused by large-scale, long-term alcohol abuse and often includes features of both anterograde and retrograde amnesia. The disorder is often accompanied by neurological symptoms, such as loss of feeling in the extremities. This is a progressive disorder, in the sense that it will continue to get worse if drinking continues. The damage tends to be irreversible; once symptoms occur, it is too late for the effects to be reversed, if one were to stop drinking.

Research on patients with anterograde amnesia and Korsakoff's syndrome has led researchers to discover some interesting things about memory that might otherwise have remained poorly understood, specifically the differences between declarative and procedural memories. A declarative memory (also called semantic memory) is one that can be put into words—this would cover most of what we "know," and most of our personal experiences (also called episodic or autobiographical memory). These are the memories that appear to be affected by anterograde amnesia. There is another category, however, of procedural (or implicit) memories—these are the things we know but cannot express verbally, and may not even have a clear, conscious awareness of knowing. The amnesic patient rarely forgets how to speak, or walk, or use silverware, for example.

In a famous experiment with HM, perhaps the best-known anterograde amnesia patient in the psychological literature, a psychologist introduced a new, difficult task one day: mirror writing. This involved a simple hinged apparatus that set up so that the subject could only see his own hand and the writing paper in a mirror. The task is to write something neatly, which is very challenging for most people the first time they try it. HM was no exception; he was extremely frustrated the first time he tried it, and remained agitated every time it was introduced to him for the next two weeks (since it was, in his view, *always* the first time). After two weeks, however, he did the task extremely well, showing a clear practice effect. With no explicit memory of ever encountering the task, he nonetheless improved steadily in his performance.

A similar effect was discovered with Korsakoff's patients by Clarapéde, a physician who greeted a patient one day with a handshake. Unknown to the patient, there was a pin concealed in the proffered hand, which of course resulted in pain and unpleasantness. The next day, Clarapéde again offered a handshake, but the patient hesitated. When asked why, the patient offered only a vague suspicion that "sometimes, people conceal sharp things in their hands." This suspicion was unaccompanied by any explicit memory of it having actually happened. These and similar cases make up a fairly clear body of evidence suggestive of different neurological systems in the brain handling the different types of memory—damage that affects formation of declarative memories leaves implicit memories unaffected.

One other type of amnesia deserves some mention here: *dissociative amnesia*, also known as psychogenic amnesia or fugue amnesia. This refers to the extremely rare phenomenon of amnesia produced by psychological trauma rather than physical injury to the brain. Although the rarest form of amnesia, this is the type favored by television writers as a plot device, in which the primary symptom is a pervasive loss of memory of significant personal information, including identity. What the television writers usually get wrong is the fact that dissociative amnesia, unlike other types of amnesia, does not result from medical trauma, such as a blow to the head. Dissociative amnesia is often confused with a related disorder, dissociative fugue, which can be succinctly described as "dissociative amnesia plus travel." An individual with dissociative fugue suddenly and unexpectedly sets off on a journey, which may only last hours, but may also last days, weeks, or even months. In the fugue state, the individual becomes confused about his identity, and may actually assume a new identity in a location thousands of miles from home (some psychologists are skeptical about the authenticity of such extreme cases of fugue, especially when the person involved is conveniently absolved, by the fugue, of serious responsibilities and accountability for his actions).

Further Reading: Parkin, A. J. *Memory and Amnesia: An Introduction.* 2nd ed. Malden, MA: Blackwell, 1997.

ANIMAL MAGNETISM *See* HYPNOSIS

APHASIA Aphasia is a disruption of language functions caused by BRAIN damage. There are many different forms of aphasia, with specific symptoms largely dependent on the particular location of the brain damage. The study of aphasia has led to the discovery of the specific functions of many brain areas involved in language comprehension and production. The best-known pattern of aphasia is known as Broca's aphasia, named for the French physician Paul

Broca, who first identified the brain area primarily responsible for language production. Located in the left frontal lobe just in front of the primary motor cortex, this area has since been known as Broca's area.

In 1861 the young surgeon had a fifty-one-year-old patient transferred to his ward with a gangrenous leg. When he attempted to question the patient, Broca discovered that his only response to any question was the nonsense syllable *tan*. Although he could communicate adequately with gestures, the only sound that would emerge was *tan*. Broca investigated Tan's (the patient's nickname in the hospital) background, discovering that he had first been admitted to the asylum twenty-one years earlier, having lost the ability to speak. The loss occurred gradually, until it finally reached the point where only *tan* came out when he tried to speak. He clearly understood language, and remained intellectually normal otherwise for his entire hospitalization, though he did eventually develop a paralysis of his right limbs. It should be noted, however, that if he became sufficiently agitated and frustrated by people who failed to understand his gestures, clearer speech would briefly emerge, but only in the form of angry curses.

Tan passed away a mere six days after coming into Broca's care. Broca, as the chief of surgery, performed the autopsy, during which he discovered that an area about the size of a large chicken egg had been destroyed in Tan's left frontal lobe. The tissue at the center of the damaged area was completely destroyed, and it was very soft around the edges, suggesting that damage continued to spread. Broca hypothesized that the original lesion had begun at the center of the damaged area and slowly spread, eventually affecting areas in control of the right side of the body. Tan's pattern of symptoms has since been called Broca's aphasia, or production aphasia, in which patients show good language comprehension but have disrupted production. Tan was not the first well-documented case of production aphasia, however. The seventeenth century Irish author, Jonathan Swift, also developed the problem late in life, following a very similar pattern, including the ability to curse fluently when angry enough. Tan's was, however, the first case in which the brain was examined.

Within thirteen years of Broca's discovery, a German physician discovered the brain area responsible for a different form of aphasia. Carl Wernicke had patients who spoke fluently but made little sense, and they had great difficulty understanding language directed at them. Whereas Broca's patients had production aphasia, Wernicke's patients had receptive aphasia, soon to be known as Wernicke's aphasia. Wernicke discovered that his patients had damage to a small area of the left temporal lobe, a few inches behind Broca's area. Whereas Broca's area primarily governs production of language, and smaller lesions there produce difficulties with syntax, Wernicke's area is responsible for semantics, or comprehension of the meanings of words. Since many head injuries affect more than one area, many aphasic patients have elements of both varieties.

Testing for aphasia often involves a variety of informal language tasks. Spontaneous language production is tested through simple interviewing; if the patient doesn't spontaneously say anything, this suggests problems with Broca's area. Simple questions are usually a part of an aphasia interview as well. If the patient fails to answer but appears frustrated by his/her inability to do so, Broca's aphasia is indicated. If the patient answers, but the responses are incorrect or nonsensical, Wernicke's aphasia is indicated. One last common element of aphasia assessment involves giving very simple spoken directions, e.g. "Stand up and clap your hands." The person whose damage is confined to Broca's area will understand the directions and will comply, whereas damage to Wernicke's area may cause a failure to understand the directions, resulting in either inaction or the performance of an action other than the one requested.

Further Reading: Gregory, R. J. *Psychological Testing: History, Principles, and Applications.* 4th ed. Boston: Allyn & Bacon, 2004.

AROMATHERAPY Aromatherapy is a scientifically unproven alternative medicine practice involving the use of aromatic oils from plants to affect mood or to promote health. The oils are administered in small quantities through inhalation, massage, topical application, bathing in water to which the oils have been added, and/or ingesting them. Aromatherapy has become big business in the United States, with widely available products including bath soaps, candles, pottery, jewelry, moisturizers and other personal products, massage devices, and massage oils, all promising various aromatherapy-related benefits. The makers of most of these products simply claim aesthetic effects: they smell nice and that helps people to feel relaxed and comfortable.

Of concern here is another aspect of the practice, a field sometimes referred to as "medical aromatherapy" or "aromatic medicine." The plant substances, known as essential oils, are alleged by aromatherapy practitioners to contain hormones, antibiotics, and antiseptics, or to act in the same manner as those substances. Some go further and add a spiritual dimension, suggesting that the oils contain and impart the "life force," "spirit," or "soul" of the plant. Aromatherapy is presented as a complete medical system that can revitalize cells, strengthen defense mechanisms, and cure the cause of disease.

On the psychological front, oil of bergamot (the added flavor in Earl Grey tea) is said to balance and normalize emotions and fight depression; lavender oil is said to relieve anxiety and promote relaxation; rose oil and sandalwood oil are favored for boosting confidence. There are many more claims, covering a wide range of physical and mental health problems, and some have surfaced in mainstream marketing. In 2001, for example, Johnson & Johnson began national promotion of lavender-scented baby bath soap, with commercials that strongly suggested that the lavender would promote relaxation in a way that other baths would not.

The essential fact which is often absent from essential oil testimonials is a simple one: although pleasant odors of rose and lavender may help a person to relax, and oil of bergamot can help a nice relaxing cup of tea to smell more interesting, there is no scientific evidence that they can alter the course of any disease or alleviate the symptoms of any psychological disorder. Furthermore,

Plant oils may smell nice, but the medical benefits of their aromas are unproven.

essential oils are not without unpleasant side effects. Some people are allergic to aromatherapy products, and some essential oils used in aromatherapy (including cinnamon, clove, nutmeg, ginger, and various peppers) can cause chemical burns. Other oils can cause serious health problems if ingested. Pennyroyal, for example, can cause miscarriage. In the absence of controlled experimental research confirming the health-related effects of essential oils, aromatherapy should be considered a way of adding nice smells to the atmosphere, but nothing more.

Further Reading: Berwick, A. *Holistic Aromatherapy: Balance the Body and Soul with Essential Oils.* St. Paul, MN: Llewellyn Publications, 1994; Feller, R. M. *Practical Aromatherapy: Understanding and Using Essential Oils to Heal the Mind and Body.* New York: Berkley Publishing Group, 1997; Sweet, C. A. "Scents and Nonsense: Does Aromatherapy Stink?" *Priorities for Health (American Council on Science and Health),* 9(4) (1997); Worwood, V. A. *The Complete Book of Essential Oils and Aromatherapy: Over 600 Natural, Non-Toxic and Fragrant Recipes to Create Health, Beauty, and a Safe Home Environment.* New York: New World Library, 1991.

ASPERGER'S DISORDER   Asperger's disorder, also known as Asperger's Syndrome, is a developmental disorder first described by Hans Asperger, a Viennese psychiatrist, in 1944. The disorder did not enter the general psychiatric lexicon for another fifty years; the *DSM-IV* (1994) is the first edition to include it.

Until recently most people who would now receive an Asperger diagnosis either were undiagnosed or classified as high-functioning individuals with autism. The disorders do share some important features in common, but the differences between them are quite striking.

Asperger's disorder is listed in the *DSM-IV* as an autism spectrum disorder and is distinguishable from AUTISM primarily by the lack of a delay in language development and the absence of any clinically significant delays in either cognitive functioning or adaptive behavior, other than social interaction. In other words, unlike a majority of the autistic population, people with Asperger's disorder are not mentally retarded. To the contrary, these individuals are usually extremely good on rote memory skills (facts, figures, dates, times, etc.), and many do especially well in math and science (a 2001 *Wired* article dubbed Asperger's "The Geek Syndrome"). Like autistic children, children with Asperger's disorder demonstrate a severe and sustained impairment in social interaction, as well as the development of restricted, repetitive patterns of behavior, interests, and activities—what Asperger, in his original description, referred to as "typical autistic behaviors."

Since it only became well-known recently, many adults with Asperger's disorder have had the experience of finally understanding why they've always felt different and been regarded as a bit odd. People with Asperger's disorder are typically regarded as socially awkward and stiff, self-centered, inflexible, and lacking in empathy and understanding. Children are therefore usually socially isolated and are often easily agitated. Unlike normal children, however, they do not reveal this agitation and anxiety in the usual ways (tone of voice, body language, facial expression), and so their agitation may escalate to a crisis point before anyone, including the children themselves, is aware of it. As a consequence, these children are easy targets for teasing, and they grow up aware that they are different but unsure of what to do about it. SELF-ESTEEM problems and a self-deprecating attitude are often the result.

Since recognition of the disorder is so recent, information on its prevalence is limited and inconsistent. What is known thus far is that, like autism and other developmental disorders, Asperger's disorder is more frequently diagnosed in boys than in girls. It is almost certainly more common than classic autism. Age of onset may be later than for autism, or at least it tends to be diagnosed later, usually after age five. This doesn't necessarily mean that the disorder takes longer to manifest itself, however, but rather that the absence of language delays makes it more challenging to detect than autism.

As with autism, the cause of Asperger's disorder is unknown, but genetics appear to play a powerful role. In studies of identical twins, it appears that if one twin has autism, the other twin has about a 90 percent probability of having it as well. Although epidemiological research on Asperger's disorder is in its infancy, similar figures will likely be found. Also as with autism, treatments that emphasize a behavior-modification approach to eliminating problematic behaviors and increasing desired behaviors have proven far more effective than other approaches (*see also* PERVASIVE DEVELOPMENTAL DISORDERS).

Further Reading: Myles, B. S., and Simpson, R. L. *Asperger Syndrome: A Guide for Educators and Parents.* Austin, TX: Pro-Ed, 1998; Silberman, S. "The Geek Syndrome." *Wired,* 9(12) (2001).

ASTROLOGY Of the many systems of personality description and prediction that predate modern psychology, the most popular by far is astrology. The basic hypothesis underlying astrology is quite straightforward: it is based on the notion that the positions and movements of celestial bodies, including sun and moon as well as the stars and planets, at the moment of birth exert a profound influence on personality and the course of one's life. This idea dates to the early days of astronomical observation, a time when nothing was known of interstellar distances or of the actual nature of the stars. The recorded history of astrological divination dates back at least 3,000 years to the Chaldeans and Assyrians. The twelve-sign zodiac, so familiar to modern newspaper readers, was already in use in Babylon by about 450 BCE.

That twelve-sign zodiac, also known as sun-sign astrology, remains the most popular form of traditional western astrology, distinct from various Asian astrological systems such as the one often encountered by Americans on Chinese restaurant placemats, which bear little relationship to the western form. A horoscope is simply a map of the skies over Earth at the time of one's birth, divided into twelve zones, or signs of the zodiac. Horoscope is also the name given to a forecast based on that map. Each sign represents the approximate location in the sky (in ancient times) of each zone's namesake constellation. The paths of the sun, moon, and major planets are then traced through the zodiac, and their locations at the exact moment of birth noted. According to astrologers, this information determines important aspects of an individual's personality and can be used to make predictions about that person's future.

Of the many objections that can be made to astrology, perhaps basic astronomy and physics are the best place to start. As every junior-high science student knows, the universe is in constant motion, with celestial bodies forever moving further apart from each other. The resulting changes in bodies' positions relative to each other are slow and subtle, but they add up over time. Because of a phenomenon known as precession of the equinoxes, for example, key elements of the position of the constellations in the sky have moved westward approximately 30 degrees in the last two millennia. What this means in layman's terms is that the constellations of the zodiac no longer correspond to the regions of the map named for them. Thus, an ancient Babylonian born on the same day of the year as the reader of this book was born under a different sign, but basic sun-sign astrology has not changed to reflect this. Some astrologers are, of course, aware of this and draw their charts according to the sidereal year rather than the solar year, which takes these changes into account.

A further problem arises when other changes in astrological knowledge are considered. By the twenty-first century man had discovered several more planets in the solar system that were unknown to the ancient Babylonians, including

The signs of the Zodiac, shown here, are named for the shapes the ancients perceived in the stars.

Pluto, one that was discovered more than two thousand years after the sun signs were designated. Some astrologers have come to include Pluto in their calculations, but they still fail to take into account the many other celestial phenomena that have been discovered in the intervening millennia.

Physics is no more likely to support the basic premises of astrology: gravitational pull, the only logical way for a star to exert an influence on other bodies, decreases proportionally with distance. It is a matter of fairly simple calculation to demonstrate that smaller objects, including the people present at the delivery, would exert a gravitational pull on the newborn child several orders of magnitude greater than that provided by even the nearest stars. If the physical influence of the constellations is the basis for astrology, therefore, a system of divination based on the different body types of obstetricians would make at least as much sense.

Another basic objection comes from psychology: given the current state of knowledge about human personality, the suggestion that everyone belongs to one of twelve distinct types seems dubious.

Despite the logical problems, however, astrology remains hugely popular among adults in the United States, with most daily newspapers running a horoscope column. In the late 1980s the Committee for the Scientific Investigation of Claims of the Paranormal (CSICOP) sent a letter, endorsed by many top scientists, to approximately 1,200 newspapers asking them to add a small disclaimer to their horoscope column simply pointing out that its purpose was entertainment; only eighty papers complied with the request.

The most obvious reason for astrology's popularity is the fairly common feeling that it "works." Many people, including those who disdain the newspaper sun-sign columns, believe professional horoscopes to be very accurate and point to their own horoscope, which was astonishing in how well it described them, as evidence of this. The problem is a well-documented phenomenon sometimes called the Barnum effect, named for the circus entrepreneur who famously observed, "There's a sucker born every minute"; given a sufficiently vague, positive personality description, most people will fit it to their own preconceived notions about themselves. This has been demonstrated experimentally many times, and actually makes an excellent classroom demonstration. The class is told that a professional horoscope has been drawn up for each of them, and each student is given a written personality description. The students are then asked to rate how accurately it describes them, on a scale of one to five. Most students give the profile a five, often including comments about what a classic Virgo, Taurus, and so on, profile they are. They are then somewhat chagrined to discover that they all received the same vague, generic personality profile.

More solid empirical evidence exists, of course. Professional astrologers believe firmly in their work and their ability to use charts to understand individual personalities, and so they have sometimes been willing to undergo empirical tests of their skills. In an experimental design that has now been used several times by different research teams, and which astrologers have agreed is a fair test, the astrologers are given thorough horoscope charts for a sample of volunteers, along with the results of psychological personality tests for each of them. Their task is to match up the horoscopes to the correct personality profiles, a job which should be very easy for them if the horoscope really provides predictable information about personality. The result is always the same: the professional astrologers can't reliably pick out a correct horoscope reading.

Despite the fact that there is scarcely a shred of scientific evidence in its favor, however, astrology continues to be enormously popular. Nowhere was the gap between evidence and practice clearer than in the Reagan White House, where, apparently, Ronald Reagan's schedule was partly determined via the First Lady's consultations with an astrologer.

Further Reading: Carlson, S. "A Double-Blind Test of Astrology." *Nature*, 318 (1985): 419–425; Clarke, D., and Gabriels, T. "Astrological Signs as Determinants of Extroversion and Emotionality: An Empirical Study." *Journal of Psychology*, 130(2) (1996): 131–141.

ATTACHMENT Attachment is an emotional bond, usually between child and parent, characterized by the child's tendency to seek and maintain proximity to the parent, especially under stressful conditions. John Bowlby, a British psychoanalyst, developed attachment theory in the 1950s and 1960s as a way of explaining certain elements of personality and of psychopathology that were not already accounted for by other psychoanalytic theorists. Specifically, the genesis of the theory comes from Bowlby's work with juvenile delinquents in pre-World War II England. He was impressed by how often the young criminals' early experiences included severe disruptions in their relationships with their mothers. At the time, most psychoanalytic theory concerning childhood experiences was based on retrospective interviews with adults, and so Bowlby's plan to study children via direct observation was nothing short of revolutionary. The result was an interesting and rather surprising blend of traditional Freudian psychoanalysis (*see* FREUD, SIGMUND) and evolutionary theory.

Influenced by Konrad Lorenz's ethological studies of IMPRINTING among animals, Bowlby believed that humans might also be biologically predisposed to form a powerful, long-lasting bond to a specific individual. Such a bond would certainly serve a survival function, especially given the extreme helplessness of human infants, and so the idea fit right in with an evolutionary perspective. Bowlby was also influenced by Harry Harlow's work with rhesus monkeys. In a classic experiment, Harlow presented infant monkeys with a choice of two surrogate mothers, both made of chicken wire. One was made of bare wire but was equipped with a nipple that dispensed milk. The other provided no food, but had a soft covering and was warm. Harlow found that contact comfort (access to the warm, cloth-covered "mother") was more important to infants than the food. This discovery upset the then-dominant view that the physiological need for food assured attachment.

Combined with the psychoanalytic belief in the power of early experiences to either produce lifelong psychological adjustment or lifelong psychological problems, the result of Bowlby's evolutionary thinking was a theory in which failure to form a healthy mother-child attachment could serve as an explanatory mechanism for many developmental problems later in life. (As with so much of psychoanalytic thinking, mothers are central to the theory, whereas fathers barely rate a mention at all.) According to Bowlby, the mother-child bond is formed during a sensitive period in childhood and is carried forward through the rest of the lifespan in the unconscious mind.

Unlike most other theories rooted in psychoanalysis, however, attachment theory has proven fairly popular among more scientifically oriented developmental psychologists (although they tend to discard the notion of the

unconscious influence on all other psychological development), largely because of its roots in actual observational research on children. The primary
laboratory technique used to measure the attachment relationship is the
"Strange Situation," developed by Mary Ainsworth, which has now been
used in thousands of studies. In the Strange Situation, a mother and child (or,
in some recent research, father and child) are brought into a laboratory space,
typically containing two chairs and a pile of toys in the middle of the floor.
The room is usually equipped with a two-way mirror to allow for unobtru-
sive observation and/or videotaping. The only other participant is a stranger,
usually a woman, for whom the primary selection criterion is that she must
genuinely be completely unfamiliar to the baby. The Strange Situation typically consists of the following eight phases, though some variations have
been occasionally used:

- Parent and infant are introduced to the experimental room.
- Parent and infant are alone. Parent places infant on the floor near the toys
  and sits in a chair. Parent does not participate while infant explores.
- Stranger enters, sits in chair, converses with parent. Stranger then approaches
  infant and engages in play with infant. Parent then leaves inconspicuously.
- First separation episode: stranger's behavior is responsive to that of
  infant—if infant is comfortable with stranger, play continues. If infant is
  distressed, stranger attempts to soothe infant. The timing of this episode is
  quite variable—if the baby is highly distressed, the next phase begins
  immediately.
- First reunion episode: parent greets and comforts infant. Stranger leaves.
  Once infant is calm, parent leaves again.
- Second separation episode: Infant is alone.
- Continuation of second separation episode: stranger enters and gears
  behavior to that of infant. As with the first separation episode, the second
  separation episode may be brought to an end prematurely if the infant is
  highly distressed—the goal is to make accurate observations of the parent
  and child, not to traumatize the baby.
- Second reunion episode: parent enters, greets infant, and picks up infant;
  stranger leaves inconspicuously.

The child's behavior during the reunion episodes is the primary basis for
classifying the infant's attachment. The Strange Situation is usually used with
children who are one year of age or older, for several reasons. First, mobility is
necessary, and most children are at least crawling by that age, if not actually
attempting to walk. Second, there are crucial developmental milestones, usually reached by that age, which are necessary for the attachment relationship to
be evaluated.

For at least their first half-year, many infants appear fairly undiscriminating
in their affections, showing equal levels of comfort with most adults, whether
friend or stranger. By the first birthday, however, most have started showing

signs of stranger anxiety (also called stranger distress), as well as separation distress (crying and general emotional upset in response to the departure of the mother or other primary caregiver). Both of these are among the signs sought as evidence of the quality of attachment in the Strange Situation, along with such things as proximity-seeking behavior and body language and eye contact upon reunion.

Based on infant behaviors in the Strange Situation, Ainsworth has identified three distinct patterns of attachment responses, resulting in three attachment classifications: Secure, Anxious/Avoidant, and Anxious/Resistant. Secure infants explore freely while the mother is in the room, making frequent eye contact and returning to the mother's side from time to time—this behavior is frequently described as using the mother as a "home base" for exploration. These infants show some distress when left with the stranger, but they reunite with the mother enthusiastically and calm down very quickly. Anxious/avoidant infants sometimes show little distress when the mother leaves, and they actively avoid the mother when reunited. Anxious/resistant infants are distressed throughout the procedure.

Attachment classifications appear to result from the interaction of several variables, including both maternal responsiveness and infant temperament. Mothers who are sensitive to infant needs and adjust their behavior to that of their child have securely attached infants. Secure attachment has been found to impact positively other characteristics of the infant's life as he or she grows up. Among other things, securely attached infants, unlike other infants, may grow up to be more curious and more comfortable with exploration of new situations, as well as better problem solvers. They also tend to be more socially competent and less likely to experience emotional problems.

Attachment has become a popular outcome variable in child development research, as the positive or negative impact of various childhood experiences on development is often assessed through attachment classifications. One of the more controversial uses of such data has been in the study of the impact of day care on child development. As more families switch from a single income to dual income, requiring more and more non-parental child care, developmental psychologists have become concerned over the impact this might have on the children's social and emotional development. A large-scale review of research by Jay Belsky and David Eggebeen created a tempest when it came out in 1991, due to its conclusion that children who were placed in full-time day care during the first six months of life were less likely to be securely attached to their mothers (though the article argued persuasively that the relative quality of care was a major confounding factor). The primary criticism of the use of attachment data in research on day care, and to a lesser extent in research on children of divorce, is that the American family, and the behavior society expects of it, has changed dramatically since Bowlby first identified the importance of the attachment bond. Specifically, the behaviors sought as evidence of a secure attachment (moderate distress upon mother's departure, stranger anxiety) may not be appropriate to expect in a child whose mother drops him off, sometimes to a stranger, on a daily basis. That child may appear insecure to some observers simply because he doesn't react with distress.

Attachment has also been shown to vary according to different national and cultural contexts. Compared to American children, more German children are insecure/avoidant, more Japanese children are insecure/resistant, and Israeli children raised on a kibbutz (a communal, collective farming community in which children are not reared by their own parents) are more insecure/resistant. Within the United States, attachment classifications vary widely according to ethnicity. African American infants, who often have multiple caregivers, are less reactive than white children to the Strange Situation. Hispanic mothers intervene more with their children to maintain suitable public behaviors. Similarly to the international samples, this can lead to large numbers of children being classified as, respectively, insecure/avoidant or insecure/resistant. As with children in day care, these differences may reflect secure attachment consistent with cultural norms rather than suggesting unhealthy developmental outcomes.

Some researchers have attempted to extend research on parent-child attachment to adult populations, using a retrospective questionnaire called the Adult Attachment Interview. It classifies adults' childhood attachments into four categories (labeled differently than the established infant-attachment categories): autonomous, dismissing, preoccupied, and unresolved. This has allowed researchers to classify mothers' childhood attachments and explore the relationship between their bond with their own parents and the caregiving style they adopt with their children. This research has found that maternal memories of and feelings about their own parents have an impact (either positive or negative) on the mothers' own behaviors and beliefs as parents.

Further Reading: Ainsworth, M. D. S., Blehar, M. C., Waters, E., and Wall, S. *Patterns of Attachment: A Psychological Study of the Strange Situation.* Hillsdale, NJ: Erlbaum, 1978; Belsky, J., and Eggebeen, D. Scientific Criticism and the Study of Early and Extensive Maternal Employment. *Journal of Marriage & the Family,* 53(4) (1991): 1107–1110.

ATTENTION-DEFICIT/HYPERACTIVITY DISORDER (ADHD) Attention-deficit/hyperactivity disorder (ADHD) is a childhood disorder, usually classified as a learning disability, in which the child has great difficulty concentrating on anything for more than a few moments at a time, and also has great difficulty sitting still or controlling physical activity levels. Their impulsiveness and lack of self-control, combined with inattentiveness, frustrate and annoy those around these children, and can lead to serious problems in school. In fact, the diagnosis of ADHD is usually made in response to school-related problems. Epidemiological studies suggest that approximately five percent of U.S. schoolchildren have the disorder, a majority of whom are boys.

According to the *DSM-IV*, there are three subtypes of ADHD: impulsive type, inattentive type, and combined type. For each of the impulsive and the inattentive types, the *DSM-IV* lists nine symptoms, at least six of which must be present for at least six months to a degree that is maladaptive and inconsistent with developmental level. For the combined subtype, criteria for both types must be met. The criteria for impulsive types is:

a. Often fails to give close attention to details or makes careless mistakes in schoolwork, work, or other activities
b. Often has difficulty sustaining attention in tasks or play activities
c. Often does not seem to listen when spoken to directly
d. Often does not follow through on instructions and fails to finish schoolwork, chores, or duties in the workplace (not due to oppositional behavior or failure to understand instructions). Often has difficulty organizing tasks and activities.
f. Often avoids, dislikes, or is reluctant to engage in tasks that require sustained mental effort (such as homework)
g. Often loses things necessary for tasks or activities (toys, school assignments, pencils, books, or tools)
h. Is often easily distracted by extraneous stimuli
i. Is often forgetful in daily activities

The criteria for inattentive types is:

a. Often fidgets with hands or feet or squirms in seat
b. Often leaves seat in classroom or in other situations in which remaining seated is expected
c. Often runs about or climbs excessively in situations in which it is inappropriate (in adolescents or adults, may be limited to subjective feelings of restlessness)
d. Often has difficulty playing or engaging in leisure activities quietly
e. Is often "on the go" or often acts as if "driven by a motor"
f. Often talks excessively
g. Often blurts out answers before questions have been completed
h. Often has difficulty awaiting turn
i. Often interrupts or intrudes on others (such as butting into conversations or games)

The diagnostic requirements are rather stringent because of the risk of misdiagnosis and overdiagnosis. The symptoms listed, such things as "does not seem to listen when spoken to directly," "often has difficulty organizing tasks or activities," and "often talks excessively," are not particularly unusual in children, at least on occasion, and do not individually provide cause for alarm.

The underlying problem in ADHD appears to be neurological, as evidenced by the remarkable success of psychoactive medication in treating the symptoms of the disorder. For reasons which are still not fully understood, drugs which act as central nervous system stimulants seem to have the *reverse* effect on many children with ADHD. The most widely used of these drugs is methylphenidate, mostly sold under the trade name Ritalin, an amphetamine-like drug that can have remarkable effects, allowing children to sit still and concentrate on their work for the first time. Its apparent effectiveness has led to very widespread use. In 1999, 9.9 million prescriptions for Ritalin were written in the United States alone, most of them for children.

It is important to note, however, that stimulants are not a cure for ADHD; they merely help to control the symptoms. A combination of drugs and psychotherapy, preferably involving applied behavior analysis, is necessary to produce real, lasting improvement. Furthermore, in the absence of proper diagnosis and follow-up care, the drugs can do more harm than good. Stimulants do not produce improvement in all cases, and overmedication may actually make the problem worse or produce lethargy and lack of interest in learning. Overmedication is a fairly common problem, since the effective dose of methylphenidate varies from individual to individual. Also, given the effectiveness of behaviorally based treatments in the absence of drugs, there are many who feel that prescribing amphetamines to children is inappropriate when alternative treatments exist without the side effects associated with amphetamine use. The drugs are used because they work, however, and such use is therefore appropriate as long as their primary purpose is controlling symptoms in order to make use of other techniques, such as behavior modification and family therapy, more feasible.

Further Reading: American Psychiatric Association. *Diagnostic and Statistical Manual of Mental Disorders,* 4th ed. Washington, DC: American Psychiatric Association, 1994; Krusch, D. A., Klorman, R., Brumaghim, J. T., Fitzpatrick, P. A., Borgstedt, A. D., and Strauss, I. "Methylphenidate Slows Reactions of Children with Attention Deficit Disorder during and after an Error." *Journal of Abnormal Child Psychology,* 24 (1996): 633–650; Rapport, M. D., Loo, S., Isaacs, P., Goya, S., Denney, C., and Scanlan, S. "Methylphenidate and Attentional Training: Comparative Effects on Behavior and Neurocognitive Performance in Twin Girls with Attention-Deficit/Hyperactivity Disorder." *Behavior Modification,* 20 (1996): 428–450.

AUTISM   In the *DSM-IV* autism is classified as a PERVASIVE DEVELOPMENTAL DISORDER (PDD), meaning the affected child has a severe impairment in several areas of development: reciprocal social interaction skills, communication skills, or the presence of stereotyped behavior, interests, and activities. Autism appears in the first three years of life, although it may be diagnosed much later, usually after school attendance has made the symptoms more obvious. There is no single pattern of symptoms common to all autistic children, since the disorder encompasses a wide spectrum of behavior patterns and a wide range of levels of functioning. There are some fairly standard features, however, including impaired social interactions, impaired verbal and nonverbal communication, and restricted and repetitive patterns of behavior (or stereotyped behaviors). The symptoms may vary from quite mild to quite severe. Some autistic children never develop spoken language and are classified as severely or profoundly mentally retarded (*see* MENTAL RETARDATION), while others have normal or above-average intelligence and can achieve high levels of education. All have in common a deficiency in social interaction accompanied by social withdrawal, often first evident in a failure to make normal eye contact or to respond positively to social contact, especially physical contact, like hugs, which is ordinarily highly reinforcing to children. This is usually accompanied by stereotyped behavior (or repetitive movements without an immediately apparent purpose, such as rocking back and forth, spinning, tapping hands or feet, waving hands, etc). as well as varying degrees of language delay.

Leo Kanner (1894–1981) first identified the syndrome as Early Infantile Autism in a 1943 paper, asserting that he had worked with such children since 1938. He argued that children with autism had of course existed prior to that time, but they had been misdiagnosed as mentally retarded or emotionally disturbed up to that point. Hans Asperger made similar discoveries at the same time, but the patients he worked with had all developed speech, so the term Asperger's Syndrome or ASPERGER'S DISORDER is frequently used to refer to higher-functioning autistic people who are able to speak. Prior to Kanner, the word "autism" had already been used by Bleuler to mean "escape from reality." Indeed, the bizarre behavior patterns associated with autism once led to the use of terms like "psychosis" and "childhood schizophrenia" to refer to individuals with this condition, but more recent research has shown clearly that autism and other PDDs are distinct from SCHIZOPHRENIA.

After Kanner provided a label for the syndrome, clinicians attempting to treat it began to notice a common pattern among parents of children with autism. They seemed not to show the warmth and affection characteristic of the normal positive parent-child relationship. As Freudian theory (*see* FREUD) was then very much in vogue, this information pointed to a clear causal relationship: autism in a child is the result of being raised by cold, rejecting parents. Furthermore, in keeping with the sexism inherent in many psychoanalytic ideas, it was the mothers who bore the lion's share of the blame. In the 1950s and through the 1960s, the theory that autism was caused by "refrigerator mothers" was immensely popular in the United States, largely due to the efforts of Bruno Bettelheim, an Austrian emigré who presented himself as a student of Freud and a survivor of the Dachau and Buchenwald concentration camps. Bettelheim established the Orthogenic School at the University of Chicago, where he treated (and frequently "cured") hundreds of autistic children with a regimen that began with separating the children from their parents and forbidding their families from further contact with them. In his influential 1967 book, *The Empty Fortress*, Bettelheim asserts that "the precipitating factor in infantile autism is the parent's wish that his child should not exist." He goes on, in that book as well as in later work, to compare the mothers of autistic children to concentration camp guards.

The major source of this line of reasoning is a simple observation that was wildly and irresponsibly misinterpreted: parents of autistic children often do show them less warmth and affection than parents of non-autistic children. Consider, however, the fact that most autistic children do not enjoy social contact, especially physical contact, in the way that ordinary children do. Temple

Grandin, an autistic adult who obtained a PhD and is renowned as an expert on animal behavior, recalls experiencing hugs from adults as painful, along with other sensory stimuli such as ordinary speech. Although direct first-person descriptions such as Grandin's are still rare in the literature, because her level of educational attainment is also rare, they tend to concur on this point. The sensitive parent will, of course, learn quickly that the child does not enjoy this sort of contact and will thus refrain from it. Ironically, the behavior of such sensitive and devoted parents became the source of a theory blaming them for their children's problems.

By the time Bettelheim published *The Empty Fortress*, most of the psychological and psychiatric communities had already begun to accept that autism is a biologically based disorder with possible genetic factors, and that blaming the disorder on parents was ludicrous. No less ludicrous was Bettelheim's claim to have cured the vast majority of the children left in his care. This claim was partly made possible by the fact that it was Bettelheim who diagnosed the children and determined when a cure had occurred. No outside observers were involved, nor were any clear objective criteria. Subsequent evidence has emerged to suggest that most of the children Bettelheim worked with were never autistic at all. This is not surprising, given that evidence has also emerged suggesting that Bettelheim grossly misrepresented his past and his credentials. Among many other things, he had no formal training in psychoanalysis.

Current thinking on the causes of autism continue to blame the parents, but only in an indirect, impersonal way: the disorder may have a genetic basis. As with schizophrenia, if one identical twin has autism, the other is much more likely to have it than a person without an identical twin. Because of this, researchers have spent the last twenty-five years hunting for genes that cause autism. As with most human characteristics, autism is unlikely to be caused by a single genetic defect. Some researchers suggest that the person with autism might have mutations in several genes; thus two people with the disorder might have completely different sets of mutations. The discovery of such genes has been hampered by the complex nature of autism. Because the symptoms of people with autism vary dramatically in degree and form, researchers believe the condition might involve two or more of a large number of genes. In fact, a person with autism may have mutations in several of perhaps twenty suspect genes. Although no clear genetic pattern has emerged yet, there are several promising hypotheses, and the research continues.

The clear presence of a genetic influence has, of course, not stopped people from continuing to look in unlikely places for a clear-cut cause of the disorder. In 1998 for example, a study of autistic children raised the question of a connection between the MMR (measles, mumps, rubella) vaccine and autism. This quickly resulted in panic among parents in the United Kingdom, thousands of whom chose not to get their children vaccinated. The original study was based on only twelve children, who allegedly were diagnosed with autism within a very short time of receiving the vaccine. In the United States, additional data have fueled the concern initiated by that study: there has been a substantial increase in the number of cases of autism diagnosed since the vaccine became widely used. This has created concern substantial enough that the Centers for Disease Control and Prevention (CDC) has created a special Web page (www. cdc.gov/nip/vacsafe/concerns/autism/autism-mmr.htm#5) to address MMR worries.

In fact, much larger studies have found no relationship between MMR vaccine and autism. For example, the CDC reports that researchers in the UK studied 498 children with autism born between 1979 and 1998 and found that the percentage of children with autism who had received the MMR vaccine was the same as the percentage of unaffected children in the region who had received the MMR vaccine, and that there was no difference in the age of diagnosis of autism in vaccinated and unvaccinated children. Furthermore, the onset of symptoms of autism did not occur within six months of receiving the vaccine. As for the increase in diagnoses, experts are in agreement that it has nothing to do with the use of the MMR vaccine.

The diagnostic criteria for autism are much better known among those who work directly with small children than they used to be, thanks in part to federal laws mandating that all children with disabilities must be provided with an education. Also, psychologists are learning to recognize early signs of autism in infants and toddlers, whereas in the past the diagnosis usually didn't occur until at least the age of three. Improved diagnostic techniques have inevitably led to an increase in the number of cases identified, which has coincided with increased use of the MMR vaccine. The two developments have occurred simultaneously but appear to be unrelated.

Just as research on causes has ceased blaming the parents' behavior, treatment has also progressed. There is no cure for autism, but the most effective approach to treatment of symptoms has been behavior modification techniques (also known as behavior therapy or applied behavior analysis), perhaps because they focus in on particular problem behaviors rather than attempting to treat underlying causes. Behavioral techniques have been successful in increasing language use, eye contact, instruction following, self-care skills, letter, number, and word recognition, and many other desired behaviors; as well as helping to decrease stereotyped behavior, self-injury, social withdrawal, tantrums, and many others.

A disorder as mysterious and misunderstood as autism, however, has unfortunately also attracted a number of therapies with little or no scientific basis. Practitioners of FACILITATED COMMUNICATION, for example, claim to help autistic persons who have never learned the alphabet to type complex messages to their parents. Others have suggested that autism is actually caused by diet, and that autistic children's behavior is much improved by removal of all gluten (grain protein) and casein (milk protein). Evidence suggesting improvement as a result of diet is inconsistent, almost entirely anecdotal, and ignores the clear role of genetics. Music therapy and play therapy have also been widely advocated for autistic children, despite a lack of controlled experiments indicating that they confer any benefit (see also PERVASIVE DEVELOPMENTAL DISORDERS).

Further Reading: Azar, B. "The Development of Tools for Earlier Diagnosis of Autism Is Moving Quickly." *APA Monitor,* 29(11) (1998); Bettelheim, B. *The Empty Fortress: Infantile Autism and the Birth of the Self.* Chicago: The Free Press, 1967; Finn, M. "In the Case of Bruno Bettelheim." *First Things,* 74 (1997): 44–48; Grandin, T. *Thinking in Pictures: And Other Reports from My Life with Autism.* New York: Vintage Books, 1996; Kanner, L. "Autistic Disturbances of Affective Contact." *Nervous Child,* 2 (1943): 217–250; McIntosh, H. "Autism Is Likely to Be Linked to Several Genes." *APA Monitor,* 29(11) (1998); Pollak, R. *The Creation of Dr. B: A Biography of Bruno Bettelheim.* New York: Simon & Schuster, 1996.

B

BEHAVIORISM *See* Skinner, B. F. (1904–1990)

"BIG FIVE" PERSONALITY FACTORS   Personality theory has been dominated by two different forces. On one side, psychoanalysts and humanistic psychologists; and on the other, trait theorists. Trait theorists have largely devoted themselves to administering tests to uncover personality traits. J. P. Guilford, a prominent personality test designer, produced the 1959 definition of trait that remains the standard: a trait is "any relatively enduring way in which one individual differs from another."

This has left room for many different personality theories based on traits. An early trait theorist, Gordon Allport, attempted to make a list of all trait terms in the English language and came up with many thousands. One reason for this has to do with our tendency to have several labels for a single trait (shy, timid, and introverted, for example). According to Allport, when trait terms are distilled down to a set of nonoverlapping adjectives that describe reasonably distinct traits, the remaining set still consists of several hundred. For this reason, trait theorists have come up with very different sets of traits when attempting to describe human personality.

- Raymond Cattell, for example, has identified sixteen source traits, which are the basis for his popular 16PF (Sixteen Personality Factors) personality inventory.
- Another trait theorist, Eysenck, on the other hand, produced a similarly popular personality test (the Eysenck Personality Questionnaire, or EPQ) based on

the notion that personality consists of just two basic dimensions: introversion-extraversion and emotional stability-instability.

- The Comrey Personality Scales measure eight dimensions of personality.
- Several different personality tests (including the Edwards Personal Preference Schedule and the Personality Research Form) are based on Henry Murray's description of personality as being determined by a set of twenty basic needs.

To sort out this confusion, personality psychologist L. R. Goldberg proposed the *fundamental lexical hypothesis*: that the most important individual differences between humans will come to be single terms in the world's languages. This means that any term that has endured for describing differences between people could theoretically represent a trait that someone might be able to measure. This would unfortunately result in potentially thousands of possible traits, but in 1981 Goldberg came up with a solution that has caught on with surprising speed among personality theorists and researchers. In his examination and analysis of the entire research literature on personality traits, he identified five traits that frequently and consistently appeared in most attempts to define the basic human factors. Although researchers have used many different words for them, the five most commonly identified personality factors are: neuroticism, extraversion, openness to experience, agreeableness, and conscientiousness. Those factors are now known as the Big Five. These labels, each a continuum, rather than a characteristic a person either does or does not have, represent the following:

- *Neuroticism*—Now frequently referred to as emotional stability or instability. At one extreme of the continuum, a person would be calm, secure, and self-satisfied, whereas at the other extreme are those who are anxious, insecure, and self-pitying.
- *Extraversion*—This trait originated with CARL JUNG and was also central to Eysenck's model. Jung chose the words introversion and extraversion because they mean, respectively, inner-directed and outer-directed. At one end of the continuum are people who are sober, reserved, and withdrawn, while those at the other end are sociable, fun-loving, and affectionate.
- *Openness to Experience*—At one end of the continuum are people who are independent and imaginative, with a preference for variety, while those at the other extreme are practical conformists who prefer a set routine.
- *Agreeableness*—This continuum has people who are excessively trusting, helpful, and soft-hearted, arrayed against the ruthless, suspicious, and uncooperative people on the other side.
- *Conscientiousness*—The highly conscientious person is organized, careful, disciplined, and reliable, whereas the other end of the continuum includes people who are disorganized, careless, and impulsive.

These traits all represent a broad spectrum of personality and behavior. Few people are at either extreme; most are located somewhere in the vast middle ground between the extremes. A team of psychologists and historians once attempted to retrospectively assign all U.S. presidents to scores on the Big Five. Not surprisingly, Richard Nixon scored high in neuroticism and fairly low on the other traits, whereas Bill Clinton scored very high in extraversion and openness to experience.

A well validated personality test based on the Big Five, the Neo-Personality Inventory-Revised (NEO-PI-R), has come into very wide use, allowing extensive research to be done on the Big Five, and so quite a bit is already known about these personality dimensions. For one thing, scores on the Big Five appear to be quite stable over time, with three of them tending to wane somewhat in adulthood (neuroticism, extraversion, and openness), while the other two (conscientiousness and agreeableness) increase during the same period. It also appears that about 50 percent of the variability in the five dimensions may be inherited. A frequent criticism of personality theories is that they can be somewhat culture-specific, but the Big Five appear to describe personality pretty well in a variety of cultures. The real test for a personality theory, however, is whether it can predict any other areas of psychological functioning. Here again, the Big Five show promise. In a study of people with different circadian rhythm patterns, highly conscientious people were more likely to be "morning people," while "night people" were found to be more extraverted. Much research remains to be done, but the Big Five has brought back to life the study of trait conceptions of personality.

Further Reading: Goldberg, L. R. "The Structure of Phenotypic Personality Types." *American Psychologist*, 48 (1993): 26–34; McCrae, R. R., and Costa, P. T. Jr. "The Stability of Personality: Observations and Evaluations." *Current Directions in Psychological Science*, 3 (1994): 173–175.

BILINGUALISM Bilingualism simply refers to fluency in two languages (more than two would be multilingualism). Within the field of educational psychology, the major debate over bilingualism has concerned a simple question: Should bilingualism be regarded as an asset or as a handicap? Over the last century two very different answers have emerged, depending on the era. Like many other debates within psychology, clear answers to this question have tended to become clouded by politics.

Early studies of bilingualism, in the first half of the twentieth century, took place in a highly charged atmosphere of isolationism and xenophobia. Recent immigrants were looked upon with suspicion in a nation suffering the effects of the Great Depression, as well as the aftermath of World War I. This suspicion took a variety of forms, with the most obvious example of prejudice against foreign languages occurring in 1923, when the case of *Meyer vs. Nebraska* was heard by the U.S. Supreme Court. The suit was brought by German Lutherans, who had been educating their children in German-language schools, at least until the state of Nebraska made non-English schools illegal.

In this atmosphere, some educators sought to determine whether bilingualism among immigrant children was a hindrance to their education (frequently with the initial assumption that it was). The usual method involved entering the public schools of a large city and giving intelligence and/or achievement tests, then comparing the results for monolingual speakers of English to the scores of bilingual children. Most of these studies found that the monolingual children outperformed the bilingual children, often by a great deal. This was then explained by the researchers (and associated politicians) as indicating that bilingualism interferes with cognitive development and that schoolchildren should be made to speak only English. These early studies made little effort to control for some fairly obvious confounding factors, however, such as differences in socioeconomic status, how long the children had actually lived in the country, or even actual proficiency in English; also no effort was made to test children in their primary language.

A new picture began to develop in Wallace Lambert's studies of the emerging French-Canadian middle class in the 1960s, however. When such factors as socioeconomic differences were controlled, Lambert found no shortcomings among bilingual children at all. The French/English bilingual children of Montréal actually outscored monolingual children of both language groups in both verbal and nonverbal measures of intelligence. He further identified a greater cognitive flexibility in the bilingual children: since they know more than one language, they are far more aware of the arbitrary nature of words. For example, they understand that there is nothing intrinsic about a hat that requires *that* word to be used—it could just as easily be a *chapeau* or a *sombrero*. It bears one name rather than another only because the community has agreed to call it that. These findings have since been confirmed by studies of bilingual children in many other multilingual locations around the world, including South Africa, Israel, Singapore, Switzerland, and the United States.

This has led to some interesting educational experiments in Montréal, in which parents from an English-speaking suburb have requested French immersion schooling for their children, meaning most classes are conducted entirely in French. Results have been quite positive: the Anglophone children are somewhat behind at first, like the American children in the early studies; they haven't become truly bilingual yet at that point, but by sixth grade they have completely caught up and score higher on some measures than monolingual controls.

Research over the last several decades has continued to further affirm the advantages of bilingualism. The positive cognitive gains associated with learning a second language in childhood include classification skills, concept formation, creativity, and even visual-spatial skills. Lambert and his associates also documented a very interesting side effect of the immersion training: the bilingual children, whether of French or English background, became more tolerant of members of the other group than monolingual children were. Indeed, the only disadvantage that has been found consistently in bilinguals is a very slight decrease in processing speed on certain language tasks, probably because there is a larger vocabulary and set of rules to search through for an answer. It is important to note, however, that these cognitive advantages all assume true bilingualism—mastery of both languages. Many of our immigrant children lack this at first, so education that ensures fluency in both languages is very important.

The positive cognitive findings have been successfully replicated repeatedly in the United States, including some highly successful attempts at full-immersion education, yet the English-only movement continues to be strong. Lambert's distinction between positive and negative bilingualism may be relevant here. There are two ways to regard bilingualism. Positive bilingualism is a view of bilingualism that involves no loss of the first language and in which both languages are associated with prestige and respect. Negative bilingualism is the view that something is lost when a new language is learned and that the new language will replace the old language to some degree. The U.S. educational establishment and certain legislators seem to accept negative bilingualism as the proper attitude where elementary schoolchildren are concerned but switch to positive bilingualism at the high school level. When young children come to school already speaking a language other than English, they are discouraged from using it, but U.S. high school students are almost universally required to study a foreign language. A well-documented shift in difficulty of language learning occurs in adolescence as compared to early childhood. Young children usually find learning a second language extremely easy, but after puberty language acquisition can be quite difficult. Thus, saving bilingualism for high school may not be the most sensible approach.

Further Reading: Lambert, W. E. *Bilingual Education of Children: The St. Lambert Experiment*. Montreal: Newbury House, 1974.

BIOFEEDBACK Biofeedback training is a method of coping with stress and anxiety that involves monitoring and trying to exert voluntary control over involuntary physiological processes such as heart rate, blood pressure, galvanic skin resistance, and muscle tension. The idea originated in animal research conducted in the 1960s that demonstrated, among other things, that rats could alter their heart rate if given pleasurable BRAIN stimulation when their heartbeat increased or decreased. The idea that completely involuntary physiological processes could be altered by classical conditioning was hardly new; Pavlov had demonstrated it long before, with the salivation of his dogs. Recognizing the potential therapeutic application of that principle for anxious humans was new, however, and required new equipment.

To use biofeedback to help control chronic headaches, for example, a person would wear a sensor in a headband, to record actual forehead muscle tension. A computer converts that information into an easily understood signal, perhaps a light that grows brighter with more tension and dimmer as tension is reduced. The patient must then learn to control the indicator, thus learning also to control the tension and the resulting headaches. Initial claims for biofeedback, based on a large number of studies conducted during the 1970s and 1980s, were a bit optimistic, suggesting that people could easily learn to control heart rate, finger temperature, blood pressure, and various other physiological functions.

A more sober appraisal of the research indicates that some people can slightly increase blood flow to the fingers and relax forehead-muscle tension. In 1995 the National Institutes of Health concluded that biofeedback can be an effective treatment for tension headaches, however, the technique works due to the patient's relaxation, which does not necessarily require specialized biofeedback equipment.

Further Reading: National Institutes of Health. Press Release: *NIH Panel Encourages Wider Acceptance of Behavioral Treatments for Chronic Pain and Insomnia.* consensus.nih. gov/news/releases/017ta_release.htm, 1995.

BIPOLAR DISORDER   *See* Mood Disorders

BIRTH ORDER   The idea that birth order exerts an influence on personality has been popular throughout the history of psychology. Psychologists have developed a variety of theories regarding birth order effects. Firstborns have been considered more likely than their later-born siblings to be high achievers, later-born children are supposed to be more popular than their first-born siblings, and later-born siblings have been alleged to be overrepresented among contact-sport athletes. These ideas have also flourished outside the academic community. Pop psychologist John Bradshaw, for example, claims that firstborn children are either conservative, holding values and making decisions consistent with the father; or rebellious, holding and acting on values in opposition to him. He also echoes a long line of writers in assuming that the firstborn child will have self-esteem problems, that middle children are better able to pick up on "hidden agendas" and tend to operate as intermediaries in family conflicts, and that third children feel ambivalent and have trouble making choices.

Certainly the early environment of the first child is a different one from that experienced by later siblings. The firstborn gets all the parental attention for at least the first year or so, then has to become accustomed to competing with a rival, whereas the later children have competition from the beginning. The parents are certainly less experienced with the first child than they are with later children. It is often claimed that parents give firstborns more responsibility and less independence. Given all this, it might not be surprising if there are some differences based on birth order.

Most recently, Frank Sulloway resurrected the idea that birth order has a big influence on almost everything in his book *Born to Rebel.* He proposes that innovations in scientific, religious, and political thought tend to be more readily accepted by later-born children, while firstborn children tend toward conservative opposition to such innovations. He relies on his own reading of history as much as on psychological research, arguing that throughout history, firstborns have tended to support, and later-born siblings have tended to challenge, the status quo. Focusing on both intellectual and political revolutions, he claims, with little scientific evidence, that revolutionaries and their supporters were disproportionately likely to be later-born children.

According to Sulloway, within the family, first-born children tend to either wholeheartedly embrace or fully reject their parents' values and beliefs, whereas later-born children are more likely to rebel against their parents' (and siblings') ways of doing things. First-born children have first shot at their parents' attention, so they have less motivation to rebel than the later children do. The later-born children have to find other ways to get attention, so they are more likely to adopt what Sulloway calls heterodox views—in other words, views that deviate from their parents' accepted beliefs.

In fact, over the last fifty years, the validity of birth-order effects has been debunked by hundreds of studies; no consistent birth-order effects have been documented. The Swiss researchers Ernst and Angst examined nearly forty years of birth-order research and found that some studies found birth-order effects, some did not, and most were inconclusive. Most of the studies that did find birth-order effects had serious methodological flaws, including failure to control for other important factors like socioeconomic status and sibship size (the number of children in the family). The positive studies also tended to use much smaller samples, whereas the studies with large groups failed to find anything. This in itself argues against the birth-order effects. Statistically, positive results are much easier to detect with larger sample sizes, so an effect that is actually occurring in the population is more likely to turn up with a larger sample than with a smaller one.

To avoid relying purely on their meta-analysis of other people's data, Ernst and Angst undertook a study of their own, with a sample that was gigantic by psychological-research standards (7,582 people). Their subjects took personality tests that measured twelve different traits, and the results turned up no differences at all between first- and second-born children, and only trivial effects in larger families. Ernst and Angst concluded that birth order is simply not a predictor of personality or behavior and that "this kind of research is a sheer waste of time and money."

Despite this, birth-order ideas continue to flourish. Sulloway is aware of Ernst and Angst's conclusions, and he addresses their review of the literature in his book, but he dismisses their conclusions and arrives at some different ones based on his own reading of their data. Sulloway's rejection of their methods has drawn a fair amount of criticism within the social sciences.

Further Reading: Ernst, C., and Angst, J. *Birth Order: Its Influence on Personality*. Berlin: Springer-Verlag, 1983; Spitzer, A. B., and Lewis-Beck, M. S. "Social Science Fiction." *Journal of Interdisciplinary History*, 30(2) (1999): 259–272; Sulloway, F. J. *Born to Rebel: Birth Order, Family Dynamics, and Creative Lives*. New York: Pantheon, 1996; Townsend, F. "Rebelling against *Born to Rebel*." *Journal of Social and Evolutionary Systems,* 20(2) (1997): 191–205; Wrage, S. "Rebelling against Research Methods? Using Frank Sulloway's *Born to Rebel* to Teach Research Methods." *International Studies Perspectives*, 1(2) (2000): 161–164.

BODY TYPE One of the wider detours off the scientific path that personality theory has taken is that the characteristics of a person's body determine personality. Sometimes known as physiognomy, the idea that facial features and body shape are accompanied by certain personality traits dates back at least to the ancient Greeks, with nineteenth-century echoes in the criminal anthropology of Cesare Lombroso (1835–1909). According to Lombroso, the criminal type is less evolved and can be detected by his atavistic simian (apelike) features, which Lombroso called stigmata. We have Lombroso to thank for every literary villain with a heavy brow, low forehead, long arms, large ears, thick hair, or shifty, deep-set eyes.

A German psychiatrist named Ernst Kretschmer (1888–1964) gave such ideas a scientific patina in a 1921 book called *Physique and Character*. In the book, he claimed that people with short limbs, round faces, and thickset bodies tended to have mood fluctuations and to be manic or depressed, thin people with long limbs and narrow faces were introverted, shy, cold, and antisocial, and people with more balanced physiques (at neither extreme) were energetic, aggressive, and cheerful. The problems with this theory were quickly pointed out by other scientists: many people violate the rules. Short, overweight people who are shy are fairly easy to find, as are tall, thin manic-depressives. The idea did not die, however, and it soon had a new champion in Harvard physician/psychologist William Sheldon (1899–1977).

Inspired by Kretschmer's book, Sheldon spent several decades collecting information on body types, which he called somatotypes, and personality. In the course of his research, Sheldon photographed at least 4,000 male college students and recorded their physical measurements. Based on his data, he decided, exactly like Kretschmer before him, that there were three basic body types: the endomorph (soft, rounded, plump), the mesomorph (hard, square, big-boned, muscular), and the ectomorph (tall and thin with a large head). He named them for the three layers of cells, which are the first to differentiate in the human embryo, each of which forms a different body system eventually. In addition to taking all those measurements, Sheldon also gave personality tests to some of his subjects, and he interviewed and observed many more. Based on this, he concluded that each somatotype is associated with a particular personality pattern.

According to Sheldon, the endomorph is social, talkative, relaxed, and hedonistic; whereas the mesomorph is energetic, assertive, courageous, optimistic, and devoted to sports. The ectomorph is introverted, shy, and intellectual. Sheldon's theory aroused a great deal of public and professional interest when first published in the 1940s, but both his ideas and methodology quickly came under attack by psychologists who noted that his theory completely ignored such environmental factors as socioeconomic status, health, and nutrition, all of which might have a fairly large effect on body type. Another problem had to do with the CORRELATIONS between the three body types and the three personality types. The numerical relationships he found were much stronger than are usually found in psychological research, which may have been due to the fact that Sheldon, expecting certain results, conducted all the data collection on both sets of variables himself. Although Sheldon's theory was popular into the 1950s, it has since faded into near-complete obscurity, yet the words he created—mesomorph, ectomorph, and endomorph—are still in use occasionally to describe different body types.

Further Reading: Sheldon, W. H., and Stevens, S. S. *The Varieties of Temperament: A Psychology of Constitutional Differences.* New York: Harper and Brothers, 1942.

BOVINE SPONGIFORM ENCEPHALOPATHY *See* MAD COW DISEASE

BRAIN
The brain is the main organ involved in consciousness, thought, emotion, motivation, learning, memory, judgment, control of basic biological functions, and almost everything else that makes a person human. Structurally, it is more complex than any other natural object yet discovered; the difficulty of even approximating the complexity and the sheer number of connections in the brain is one of the major obstacles to the creation of artificial intelligence.

For purposes of discussing structure and function, it may be useful to think of the brain in sections: the hindbrain (or brain stem), the midbrain, and the forebrain. These terms are based on vertebrate biology in general rather than on humans specifically, which is why the lowest portion is called the hindbrain (because in creatures that do not walk upright, it is located further back than the rest of the brain rather than beneath it).

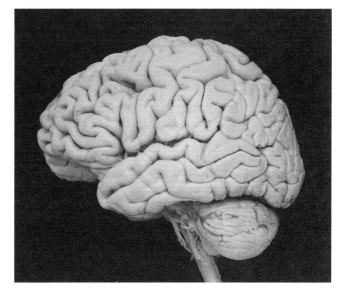

The cerebral cortex of the human brain, with the cerebellum (lower right) and the medulla visible underneath.

The Hindbrain (Brain Stem)— The brain stem is the oldest, most primitive part of the brain and is responsible primarily for the body's automatic survival functions. At its base, it is simply a swelling of the spinal cord as it enters the skull. There are three crucial structures here: the medulla oblongata, the reticular formation, and the cerebellum. The medulla is responsible for what are sometimes called the vegetative functions, involuntary actions required to keep the body alive. The medulla entirely controls heart rate and largely controls breathing, swallowing, and digestion. While it is possible to exert some control over breathing, that control is quite limited. Barring any serious respiratory problem, for example, a person is capable of holding his or her breath, but not capable of holding it indefinitely. Eventually the person will lose consciousness, at which point the medulla will carry on doing its job and start up the breathing again. The medulla is also the place where neurons from the right side of the body cross over to the left side of the brain, in the well-known phenomenon of contralaterality. Because of this crossing over, sensory information from the left side of the body is processed in the right hemisphere of the cerebral cortex (in the forebrain), and vice versa; and the two sides are controlled by contralateral signals from the brain as well.

The reticular formation (or reticular activating system) is a network of neurons that extends from the spinal cord all the way up to the thalamus. Its primary function is the regulation of overall level of brain activity, and so it is also somewhat involved in regulation of sleeping and wakefulness.

Cerebellum means "little brain," inspired by the cerebellum's resemblance to the whole brain. Its primary function is the coordination of voluntary movement and gross motor function, especially things that are done automatically. Any finely coordinated movements that require following a certain sequence with a certain timing, such as playing a sport, dancing, or playing a musical instrument, require the help of the cerebellum. Damage to the cerebellum can result in difficulty walking, difficulty with balance, and an inability to use the hands without shaking, among other problems.

The Midbrain—The midbrain is the area immediately above the brainstem but below the forebrain, and it is the home of some nuclei, clusters of cell bodies, that govern reflexive behaviors. Two important structures are here: the superior and inferior colliculi. There are two of each, one in each hemisphere, with the superior colliculi located on top of the inferior colliculi.

The inferior colliculi are involved in integrating auditory input with automatic movement; they are responsible for the tendency to automatically jerk the head around in the direction of a sudden, unexpected noise.

The superior colliculi serve a similar function, associated with visual input. They are the reason for turning quickly in response to sudden light or movement at the corner of the visual field.

The Forebrain—The forebrain includes both the cerebral cortex and a number of very important smaller structures located beneath it, known collectively as the limbic system. The various elements of the limbic system are involved in regulation of emotion, motivation, learning, and memory formation, among other things. The key structures in the limbic system are:

- *Hippocampus*—was named because an early dissector felt that it resembled a seahorse (the Greek meaning of the name). The hippocampi, like all limbic system structures, come in pairs, one for each hemisphere. They serve a vital function in the consolidation of new memories. Loss of the hippocampus to injury or surgery can result in a permanent case of anterograde amnesia in which the person is unable to form any new long-term memories.
- *Amygdala*—An almond-shaped cluster of neurons beneath each hemisphere, the amygdala appears to be involved primarily in regulation of anger, aggression, and fear. Early animal studies using cats indicated that electrical

stimulation of one area of the amygdala would cause the cat to prepare for attack. Stimulation of a slightly different area of the same structure will cause that same cat to cower in fear when placed in a cage with a mouse.

- *Thalamus*—Its extremely important primary job involves relaying sensory input to the correct areas of the cortex to be processed. Information from the inner ear, for example, must be sent to the area of the cortex that processes auditory information, whereas visual input must go to the cortical area responsible for visual processing. The importance of this function becomes very clear when it ceases to operate properly, as can sometimes happen under the influence of psychedelic drugs. It is not unusual for a person who has taken LSD to claim to be "seeing" sounds, or "hearing" colors. Oddly enough, in a sense they really are because the thalamus has relayed the sensory information to the wrong place, a phenomenon known as synesthesia. "Smelling" sounds or colors is never reported because the sense of smell does not pass through the thalamus.

- *Hypothalamus*—Its name means "below the thalamus," and that is where it is located. Although tiny, this structure is known for its involvement in a wide range of human activities, partly due to its close proximity to the pituitary gland, which governs the activities of all hormone systems in the body. Through selective lesioning, scientists have identified neural clusters that influence or regulate hunger, thirst, body temperature, sexual behavior, and emotional reactions, as well as pain and pleasure.

Above the limbic system is the heavily convoluted outer surface of the brain, known as the cortex. If any area of the brain can be said to be the part that truly distinguishes human brains from all others, it would be the cortex (also called the cerebrum, neocortex, or cerebral cortex). All of what are considered the higher mental functions, reasoning, MEMORY, language processing, musical ability, judgment, etc., emanate from the cortex, which makes up some 80 percent of the total tissue mass of the brain. It is widely believed by the general public that it is the size of the human brain that makes us so advanced, but in fact it is the convolutions themselves that allow our high degree of intelligence. Brain size is closely allied to body size, so certainly there are brains larger than man's (consider a blue whale, for example); but none are more complex. The convolutions allow a much larger surface area to exist than would otherwise be possible, given the size of a human head. From an evolutionary perspective, as human brains got more complex, there was a firm upper boundary on how large they could grow, given that a skull still has to fit through a pelvis for birth to occur. Therefore, the cerebral cortex became more wrinkled, allowing more surface area to fit into the same space, in much the same way as a large piece of paper folded up small enough to fit in a shirt pocket still has the same amount of writing on it as it did before.

The cortex is sometimes referred to as gray matter, because the cell bodies that make up most of it are that color. Much of the other brain tissue, as well as NERVOUS SYSTEM tissue in the body, looks white instead, due to the myelin covering on the axons of neurons.

The gray matter is divided into two separate hemispheres, which communicate with each other via a thick bundle of nerve fibers called the corpus callosum. Each hemisphere is further subdivided into four lobes:

- The frontal lobes appear to be the primary seat of judgment, reasoning, motivation, and decision-making; and they are also the location of the primary motor cortex, or motor strip. This is the cortical area that controls all aspects of fine motor movements.

- The parietal lobe, located directly behind the frontal lobe, is home to the primary somatosensory cortex, which represents touch sensations from all parts of the body. More sensitive areas of the body have a larger amount of cortex devoted to them than less sensitive areas.

- The temporal lobe is located directly beneath the parietal lobe, and is the home of auditory processing, as well as a large proportion of verbal long-term memory storage. The temporal lobe is also responsible for modulation of fear, aggression, and sexuality (along with the limbic system).

- The occipital lobe, behind the parietal lobe, is where visual information is processed, and thus also where visual thoughts and memories occur and are stored. Damage to specific areas in the occipital lobe can produce visual agnosia, a failure to recognize familiar objects. In some cases a more specific form, prosopagnosia, can occur, in which the person loses the ability to recognize or distinguish between faces.

There are some clear functional differences between the left and right hemisphere, starting with language functions, which are largely localized to the left hemisphere. Language production (the ability to speak), for example, is controlled by Broca's area, a small region of the left frontal lobe adjacent to the primary motor cortex. Language comprehension, along with memory of word meanings, is largely confined to the left temporal lobe (*see* APHASIA). The left hemisphere also appears to be responsible for logical thought, along with singing and writing. Visual and spatial processing, along with perception of rhythm and abstract thought, appear to be primarily right-hemisphere functions. Contrary to the spate of popular books arguing that some people primarily use their right hemisphere ("right-brained") while others rely primarily on the left ("left-brained"), both hemispheres are active in all people at all times, barring serious head injuries. Smooth communication between the hemispheres is a result of the corpus callosum (*see* SPLIT-BRAIN SURGERY).

The pop-psychology notion that there are gender differences in the brain does have some truth to it. It has long been observed that men's brains tend to be slightly larger, for example, a difference that a number of nineteenth- and twentieth-century thinkers took to indicate the clear intellectual superiority of men. In fact, the difference can be accounted for entirely by the larger average size of men's bodies. When all other factors are accounted for, however, researchers have found evidence that a small area of the parietal lobe, which is intimately involved in spatial processing and mathematics, tends to be larger in male brains. Other recently documented differences tend to be far subtler, involving different overall response patterns to similar stimuli. When men are shown visual stimuli, for example, emotional centers in the amygdala are activated that are not activated when women view the same images. Pain responses also involve activation of different cortical areas across the two genders. This sort of research, made possible by the availability of PET and MRI scans (*see* BRAIN IMAGING TECHNIQUES), is still in its infancy; there is much more to learn about the brain and its functioning (*see also* BRAINWASHING; CHEMICAL IMBALANCE; PREFRONTAL LOBOTOMY).

Further Reading: Johnson, K. A., and Becker, J. A. (2004). *The Whole Brain Atlas*. www.med.harvard.edu/AANLIB/home.html, 2004.

BRAIN IMAGING TECHNIQUES   After more than a century of trying to infer BRAIN function by looking at behavior or the effects of brain damage, we now have an array of tools that allows researchers to pinpoint the location of various functions as they happen. The first modern technique to be developed is computer-assisted tomography (CT or CAT scan), which takes a series of X-ray pictures of the brain, treating it as a series of layers. The pictures are fed into a computer that enhances the pictures with color to make various brain structures easier to see.

CT scans have actually been rendered nearly obsolete for purposes of studying brain function by the development of positron-emission tomography (PET scan). This technique provides a live view of brain activity as it happens, rather than static photographs. The technique is fairly simple in theory. Radioactive glucose is injected into the bloodstream. When it reaches the brain, more of the radioactive glucose enters cells that are highly active (therefore metabolizing more glucose) than will enter relatively inactive ones. When the brain is viewed in the scanning device, with computers enhancing the image by using different colors for different areas of activity, the areas that are more active will be easily visible due to the presence of the radioactive substance. Such imaging has allowed researchers to identify exactly which regions of the brain, enhanced with different colors, are stimulated by different activities.

Although colorful PET pictures can give a clear idea of the level of activation of various brain areas, they do not show details of the brain's physical structure. Magnetic resonance imaging (MRI, sometimes also called nuclear magnetic resonance or NMR) uses a radically different technique to do just that. The MRI exposes the brain to a powerful magnetic field and measures the resulting radio-frequency wave pattern to provide astonishingly clear pictures of the anatomical details of the brain.

The newest player, functional magnetic resonance imaging (fMRI), combines the best features of MRI and PET scans, by monitoring changes in blood flow that reflect changes in the activity level of the neurons in different parts of the brain. This allows a real-time picture of the activity in the brain, like the PET scan, but with the added photorealism of the MRI.

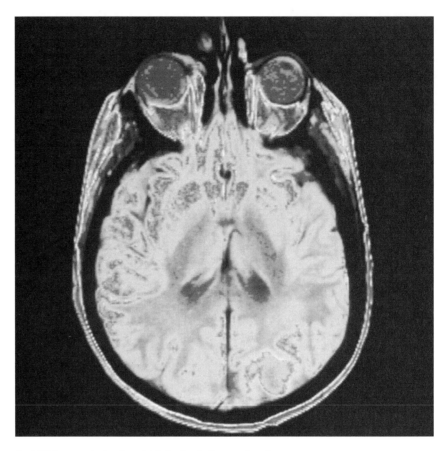

An MRI image of a horizontal "slice" of a human head.

Further Reading: Engel, S. A. "Using Neuroimaging to Measure Mental Representations: Finding Color-Opponent Neurons in Visual Cortex." *Current Directions in Psychological Science*, 8 (1999): 23–27.

BRAINWASHING Brainwashing is a term frequently used in the popular media to refer to a phenomenon known among psychologists as coercive persuasion. Essentially, the term refers to a set of strategies used to forcibly change someone's belief system, so they will adhere to a new set of beliefs and obligations. In the public mind, the term often has been associated with the change of perspective and abandonment of family and values often seen in members of religious cults. Some of the techniques described below, however, have also been standard tools in the interrogation of uncooperative prisoners throughout human history.

Major elements of coercive persuasion include:

- Application of physical or emotional stress. Physical stress would include deprivation of sleep, food, light, or exercise. Emotional stress would include isolation with no stimulation, constant repetitive chanting, or sleep deprivation to the point of entering a trancelike state.

- Attribution of all of the person's problems to one simple explanation, which is repeated over and over. This technique worked well for the Nazis, but it works equally well for today's financial self-help gurus and fringe religious groups.

- Unconditional love, acceptance, and attention are provided by the group leader, who ignores any and all faults, if the subject will come to him.

- Creation of a new identity. This frequently includes a name change and special clothes, as with the practices of the Hare Krishna movement, who all dress identically and sport distinctive haircuts. This makes group membership far more important than individual identity, thus rendering members easier to control.

- Entrapment: also known as the foot-in-the-door technique. The member agrees to a few small changes but then demands begin to gradually increase. Once the demands become unreasonable, it's too late, and COGNITIVE DISSONANCE is reduced by continuing to go along with the demands.

- Access to information is severely controlled. The group may require a severing of preexisting social ties, including ties to family. Doubts about the group or its leader are mocked, along with attempts at critical thinking. Any distress caused by this is attributed to a lack of sufficient faith in the group or its leader.

The implementation and effectiveness of these techniques are readily seen in the activities of several of the more notorious cults of recent years. The members of Marshall Applewhite's small Heaven's Gate community, for example, were all highly intelligent by most measures, yet all of them, including their leader, after dressing identically, lay down and committed suicide in anticipation of being taken aboard a spaceship hidden in the tail of the comet Hale-Bopp. In Tokyo the members of Aum Shinrikyo, who all wear identical clothing and masks of their leader's face, injured thousands by releasing nerve gas in a subway system.

Contrary to what many believe, these techniques work on everyone, not just the ignorant or unintelligent. Mohamed Atta, a 9/11 pilot, was well-educated and wealthy, with no apparent psychopathology, a description which equally well suits the followers of Marshall Applewhite, as well as those of Jim Jones, the People's Temple leader whose followers, over 900, including many children, committed suicide together in the jungles of Guyana.

Further Reading: Ofshe, R. J., and Watters, E. *Making Monsters: False Memory, Psychotherapy, and Sexual Hysteria.* New York: Scribner's, 1994; Zimbardo, P. G., and Leippe, M. R. *The Psychology of Attitude Change and Social Influence.* New York: McGraw-Hill, 1991.

BYSTANDER EFFECT *See* DIFFUSION OF RESPONSIBILITY

C

CHEMICAL IMBALANCE As we have gained more knowledge about the functioning of the BRAIN and the key role played by neurotransmitters in that functioning, it has become clear that a variety of psychological disorders, including depression, SCHIZOPHRENIA, various anxiety disorders, and many others, are associated with abnormal levels of specific neurotransmitters. This has led to some remarkably effective treatments that target receptor sites and reuptake mechanisms for specific neurotransmitters. Selective serotonin reuptake inhibitors such as Prozac and Zoloft, for example, have proven to be very effective in the treatment of depression as well as several other disorders, simply by increasing the levels of serotonin in key areas of the brain. Psychotic symptoms of schizophrenia are now often controlled quite effectively with antipsychotic medications that alter levels of various neurotransmitters, obviating the need for such old-fashioned tools as the straitjacket, the padded cell, and the lobotomy.

This increased understanding of the role of crucial brain chemical levels has led to widespread use of the term "chemical imbalance" as a sort of short-hand term for the knowledge that a particular person's disorder may be due primarily to improper neurotransmitter levels. Chemical imbalance is not actually a diagnosis, but the term has become popular among nonspecialists, who find it a convenient way to quickly explain that a particular person's problem behaviors are due to a medical cause rather than anything deliberate. The trouble with this is that establishing a cause-and-effect relationship based on correlational data (*see* CORRELATION) is difficult. We know, for example, that lower serotonin levels are found in depressed people than in non-depressed people, but this could be interpreted in either of two ways: low serotonin levels produce depression, or depression causes serotonin levels to drop (solid experimental evidence supports both interpretations). Regardless of the causal direction, clearly raising serotonin levels back up relieves depression, but the effectiveness of cognitive-behavioral therapy with depression suggests that the same result can also be achieved through non-medical means. Attributing mental illness to chemical imbalances may lead to exclusively medical treatment, whereas seeing the imbalance as a symptom leaves us open to examining the effectiveness of a wider range of treatment options. The downside of drug treatment is that no change occurs in behaviors that may be contributing to the disorder, and the person becomes dependent on the drug to keep the symptoms away, so our recognition of the role of chemical imbalances is a bit of a double-edged sword.

Further Reading: Jensen, J. "Let's Not Medicate Away Student Angst." *Chronicle of Higher Education*, 49(40) (2003): B5.

CHOMSKY, NOAM (1928–) Arguably the best-known linguistics professor in the world, Massachusetts Institute of Technology professor Noam Chomsky has become better known in his later years as a political commentator and dissident. In 1957, at the age of 29, he published a monograph entitled *Syntactic Structures*, which radically altered the study of human language. Two central ideas lie at the core of his revolution: universal grammar and the language acquisition device, or LAD. Universal grammar refers to Chomsky's observation that, despite the many superficial differences in the surface structure of the world's languages, they all share a very similar deep structure. To explain how this was possible, he proposed that there is an innate component to human language, a "language organ" pre-wired to absorb linguistic input and decipher the rules of language. This came to be known as the LAD. Chomsky offered as further evidence of this the fact that children tend to develop various components of language in a set order, for example, being able to form possessives before learning to form past tense. Indeed, before any formal instruction in language use has occurred, children show by their errors that they have already learned some of the formal semantic and syntactic rules. Over-regularization errors occur when the child applies a rule to an irregular word for which the rule is inappropriate (e.g., "I runned," "two foots," "the bird flied," etc.).

At the time, the dominant perspective on language acquisition was a fairly solid, tabula rasa empiricist view, dominated by B. F. SKINNER's behaviorist approach. Skinner argued that operant conditioning could explain verbal behavior just as well as it did other kinds of behavior, with the combination of imitation, positive reinforcement, and punishment entirely explaining children's language acquisition. Chomsky insisted that such an explanation could not account for over-regularization errors, as they involve the child stubbornly producing utterances that are not being reinforced and which cannot be explained by imitation, as the child has never heard them before.

Chomsky's influence on the field of linguistics has been huge, in that his ideas are now central to the field. Even so, most linguistic theorists since the 1960s have set out to prove him wrong. His is still the theory from which they begin, the theory to beat. Chomsky himself has long since become better known for his long opposition to U.S. foreign policy, from the Vietnam war through to the occupation of Iraq. He has presented his political views in over thirty books and innumerable articles, and lectures far more frequently on politics than on linguistics.

Further Reading: Allen, J. P. B, and Van Buren, P., eds. *Chomsky: Selected Readings.* New York: Oxford University Press, 1971.

CHOPRA, DEEPAK (1947–) Dr. Chopra is the leading advocate of ayurvedic medicine, also known simply as ayurveda, a healing system said by its followers to be the ancient medicine of India and to represent practices that are over 5,000 years old. In fact, most of it appears to date back only to the early 1980s, to the writings and teachings of the Maharishi Mahesh Yogi, founder of TRANSCENDENTAL MEDITATION. In fact, much of what Chopra has advocated belongs to a trademarked product line called Maharishi Ayurveda. Chopra started his medical career in a fairly orthodox, science-based manner, even briefly teaching at Tufts University Medical School, but then he joined the Transcendental Meditation organization, eventually placed in charge of the Maharishi Ayurveda Health Center for Stress Management in Lancaster, Massachusetts, and running the Maharishi's herbal-supplement business.

Since going out on his own, Chopra has become an industry unto himself, making millions of dollars from the sales of ten million copies of at least nine books, along with more than thirty audio and video programs. He has also produced several programs for PBS and runs seminars from time to time at the Chopra Centers at the La Costa Resort and Spa in La Costa, California, and the Doral Golf Resort and Spa in Miami, Florida. He has recently addressed the needs of a large and previously untapped senior market with the publication of *Golf for Enlightenment.*

It is easy to see why retirees might be interested in what he has to say. He has recently suggested that following his regimens can, among other things, reverse biological age by fifteen years, as well as fight the cognitive effects of aging by "eliminating toxins" (a usually undefined phrase in the alternative-medicine community). It is convenient for Chopra to claim that his methods are over 5,000 years old because that removes the requirement that they fit in with modern science and what is now known about how the physical world and the body work. Otherwise, some of his statements and claims might sound illogical: "Illness and aging are an illusion. We can achieve an ageless body and a timeless mind by the sheer force of consciousness"; "If you could live in the moment you would see the flavor of eternity, and when you metabolize the experience of eternity your body doesn't age"; and "If you have sad thoughts, and angry thoughts, and hostile thoughts, then you make those molecules which may depress the immune system and make you more susceptible to disease," for example.

Most ayurvedic treatments consist of dietary recommendations and herbal remedies. There are three prakriti, or body types, based on the relative proportions of the three doshas, which govern mind-body harmony (much like traditional Chinese medicine's chi, only there are three components rather than just *Yin* and *Yang*). Sickness is caused by imbalances among the doshas, so treatment consists of restoring harmony to the doshas. The doshas are as follows:

- *Vata,* made of air and space, responsible for movement in the mind and body. Two kinds of imbalance can occur: an excess leads to anxiety and insomnia, as well as intestinal difficulties including gas, cramps, and constipation. Vata is also in control of the other two doshas.

- *Pitta* is made of fire and water, and it is in charge of both mental and physical metabolism, in other words, not only our digestion and our "metabolism of sensory perceptions," but also our ability to distinguish between right and wrong. Conditions caused by an excess of pitta include anger and stress, ulcers, skin problems, and hair loss.

- *Kapha* is made of earth and water. It is apparently responsible for much of the body's physical structure, including strength, healing, immunity, joint lubrication, skin moisture, and healthy heart and lung function. This dosha, apparently, gives us greed and envy (though it is also claimed to be a source of peace, forgiveness, and love). An excess can cause lethargy and weight gain, along with congestion and allergies.

Given the Ayurvedic emphasis on digestive processes, the sort of treatments recommended is not especially surprising. An excess of Pitta, for example, is treated via the consumption of sweet foods and avoidance of the spicy. Nuts and dairy products are good for reducing Vata. Treatments available through Chopra's organization have also included special gems, semi-religious ceremonies to appease angry gods, and an elixir that he recommends taking twice a day (at over $1,000 for a year's supply). How the Ayurvedic physician determines which dosha is the problem remains unclear, but Chopra claims that an Ayurvedic physician can diagnose illness and prescribe the proper remedies simply by feeling the patient's pulse. There's no evidence of this, or a testable scientific hypothesis, but Chopra has tried to tie his ideas in with modern science anyway. However, the connection is with subatomic physics rather than human physiology and medicine: "Our bodies ultimately are fields of information, intelligence and energy. Quantum healing involves a shift in the fields of energy information, so as to bring about a correction in an idea that has gone wrong."

Apparently, Chopra believes that quantum physics teaches that the physical world, including our bodies, is a creation of our own minds, and therefore we get the body (and overall health) that we choose to create for ourselves. Poor mental or physical health, stress, aging, senility, and so on, are all therefore completely preventable by our own free will—though it is unclear where nutrition fits into this—we create our universe but can't choose the state of our doshas.

Further Reading: Chopra, D. *Quantum Healing: Exploring the Frontiers of Mind/Body Medicine.* New York: Bantam, 1989; Chopra, D. *Ageless Body, Timeless Mind: The Quantum Alternative to Growing Old.* New York: Random House, 1993; Skolnick, A. A. "The Maharishi Caper: Or How to Hoodwink Top Medical Journals." *Science Writers: The Newsletter of the National Association of Science Writers,* Fall 1991; Stenger, V. J. "Quantum Quackery." *Skeptic,* 4(3) (1996): 12–21.

CINGULOTOMY *See* PREFRONTAL LOBOTOMY

CLAIRVOYANCE *See* PARAPSYCHOLOGY

CLASSICAL CONDITIONING *See* PAVLOV, IVAN (1849–1936)

CLINICAL PSYCHOLOGY *See* PSYCHIATRY

CNS DEPRESSANTS *See* DEPRESSANTS

CNS STIMULANTS *See* STIMULANTS

COERCIVE PERSUASION *See* BRAINWASHING

COGNITIVE-BEHAVIOR THERAPY Although behavior therapists tend to focus attention on external stimuli and consequences as causes of maladaptive behavior, they also recognize that many disorders, including depression and anxiety, can be rooted in how clients perceive themselves and the world around them. As cognition (thinking) is a form of behavior, it should be possible to alter problematic thoughts just as it is possible to change other kinds of behavior by manipulating stimuli and consequences. Cognitive-behavior therapy (CBT) focuses on using learning principles to change the way clients think and, consequently, how they behave as a result of that thinking.

Aaron Beck, a hugely influential cognitive therapist, has had great success in the treatment of depression via cognitive restructuring. His approach assumes that mental disorders originate in false beliefs and errors of logic, called cognitive distortions (not to be confused with COGNITIVE DISSONANCE). Over time, these false beliefs (such things as "I can't do anything right," "I'm a total loser," "If I say anything, they'll all think I'm an idiot") begin to occur automatically, so that the client never stops to consider whether they are even true. Therapy therefore consists of identifying the false beliefs and distortions, and then treating them as hypotheses to be tested. In addition to helping people examine their false beliefs through gentle questioning, therapy therefore often also involves designing empirical tests of these beliefs. As homework, a client who fears meeting new people may be required to introduce himself to a stranger. Success at this task without any negative consequences will help to reduce his anxiety in such situations, and further success may eventually eliminate the fear and anxiety entirely, or at least to a sufficient extent that the anxiety is no longer a problem.

Another influential approach to cognitive-behavior therapy is Albert Ellis's rational-emotive behavior therapy (REBT). In Ellis's view, mental distress is produced not so much by upsetting events as it is caused by rigid and maladaptive ways in which we interpret those events. The person with depression, for example, may interpret a suggestion as criticism, friendliness as pity, or enter all situations with the belief that "I must be perfect at everything I do." Like Beck's approach, REBT consists of helping the client zero in on these irrational beliefs and then challenging them. Unlike Beck's relatively gentle approach, however, REBT involves a rather blunt, confrontational approach. Beck has expressed his ultimate goal with a client as "making him work his ass off, cognitively, emotionally, and behaviorally, to profoundly change." Like Beck's therapy, this approach involves homework. A very shy client, for example, may be encouraged to sing loudly in a subway or flirt with men she finds attractive, so that she may come to realize that her life does not fall apart as a result. Success in challenging false beliefs ultimately eliminates them, perhaps eliminating the resultant psychological disorder as well. Research on both Ellis's and Beck's therapy has generally shown positive results.

Further Reading: Beck, J. S., and Beck, A. T. *Cognitive Therapy: Basics and Beyond.* New York: Guilford Press, 1995; Ellis, A. "Reflections on Rational-Emotive Therapy." *Journal of Consulting and Clinical Psychology*, 61 (1993): 199–201.

COGNITIVE DISSONANCE Leon Festinger (1919–1990) believed that individuals strive for internal consistency, with thoughts, beliefs, and feelings matching one's actions. In everyone's life, however, there will inevitably be occasions when actions are not consistent with beliefs. On these occasions, according to Festinger, an individual experiences cognitive dissonance, or discomfort, caused by the inconsistency between beliefs and actions. The greater the personal responsibility felt for a troubling action, the greater the dissonance felt. This tension can only be relieved by making changes to bring the actions and beliefs into line with each other. This discomfort will often lead to a change in beliefs rather than changing actions, explaining it away: "Since I did that, I must believe that it's acceptable."

Cognitive dissonance has been confirmed in many experiments that follow a common pattern: make people feel responsible for behavior that violates their attitudes or beliefs and for which no clear justification is at hand, and then measure their attitudes again. A classic example (which has been replicated dozens of times, with minor variations) involves paying research participants to write a short essay, or participate in a short debate, arguing for a position that they personally oppose, and for which there will be foreseeable consequences. In one variation on this theme, subjects are asked to write a short essay favoring a change in university policy that they oppose and are told that the resulting essay will be seen by university administrators.

As it turns out, the amount of cognitive dissonance (and, consequently, attitude change) that emerges appears to depend directly on the amount of money paid to subjects. If they are well compensated, little attitude change occurs. If they receive a mere pittance, they come around to genuinely supporting the position they have argued for. Subjects who have been well paid can easily justify the dissonance between their views and the position being presented ("I did it for the money"), whereas those who have received the smaller payment cannot use the same justification and are thus confronted by real discomfort regarding the argument they've just made. They often reduce the uncomfortable dissonance by starting to believe their own disingenuous words.

The idea of cognitive dissonance has had a broad impact in social psychology, influencing opinion and research on everything from advertising to the Stockholm syndrome. Into a world in which we tend to assume (or at least tell ourselves) that our actions are firmly grounded in our beliefs and values, Festinger introduced the notion that in fact the reverse is frequently true: our actions and behaviors influence our beliefs and attitudes far more than we are usually willing to admit.

Further Reading: Festinger, L. *Theory of Cognitive Dissonance*. Palo Alto, CA: Stanford University Press, 1957.

COLD READING Cold reading is a technique used by mediums, psychics, faith healers, and fortune-tellers to persuade complete strangers that they know all about them. Doing a cold reading does not require any advance information about the person, as opposed to a hot reading. A hot reading involves finding out information about the person ahead of time and then presenting it as though it is simply "popping" into your mind or is being delivered by the spirits of the dead. Information used in this way may make the person more receptive to information produced in a subsequent cold reading.

The simplest approach to cold reading is to rely on what psychologist Ray Hyman calls a stock spiel—a set of vague, general statements that can fit almost anyone. A skilled reader will have memorized an assortment of spiels, tailor-made for particular categories of people. The true cold reading, however, starts off with no prepared information other than acute powers of observation. The best cold readers are good at noticing subtle signs, including details of clothing, jewelry, hands, gestures, and manner of speech. The skillful reader will then produce a few tentative hypotheses intended to zero in on the issue the client wishes to hear about, to then say what he or she came to hear. The result of this technique is that the reader tends mostly to ask questions rather than actually give information, usually instructing the client to simply say "yes" or "no" regarding whether each hypothesis is meaningful or not. Some readers become remarkably adept at asking many questions; according to skeptical paranormal investigator James Randi's estimates, television medium John Edward (host of a show called *Crossing Over*) sometimes asks more than seventy questions per minute. The result is that people will often remember the correct guess and forget about the dozens of wrong statements that were made.

The people who seek a reading with Mr. Edward or others (to allegedly contact the dead) are desperate for some news from beyond and are therefore highly motivated to believe that this contact has occurred. Consequently, although a successful reading usually involves very few affirmative statements (rather than questions) by the reader, except for what the client said first, they will usually marvel later at the things the medium knew without being told. In a 60-minute reading by James Van Praagh, filmed by CBS for *48 Hours*, for example, Van Praagh asked 260 questions but made only two independent statements, both of which were wrong. The woman appeared impressed that he had known her husband's name, partly because she didn't appear to remember the 26 wrong guesses which preceded the correct guess (and if they are in touch with the deceased, Why must they always guess the spirit's name?). John Edward has been accused of using television editing to his advantage as well—in a 1999 *Time* magazine article, a man who had been "read" on the show accused him of improving the reading by attaching some of his "yes" answers to questions to which he had actually responded "no." Unlike the séances of ages past, these psychic readings do not rely on phony table movements or apparitions, but today's mediums often use equally dishonest trickery to earn their money by taking advantage of the grief of others. Edward and Van Praagh deny using cold reading, and it can't be proved that they never hear from the deceased, but their techniques, genuine or not, are indistinguishable from cold reading (*see also* PARAPSYCHOLOGY, PSEUDOSCIENCE).

Further Reading: Hyman, R. "Cold Reading: How to Convince Strangers That You Know All about Them." *Skeptical Inquirer*, 2(1) (1977): 18–37; Jaroff, L. "Talking to the Dead." *Time*, March 5, 2001: 52.

COMPETENCY TO STAND TRIAL   *See* INSANITY DEFENSE

CORRELATION   "There are three kinds of lies: Lies, *damned* lies, and statistics." That famous quotation is frequently attributed to Mark Twain but was actually (according to Twain himself, anyway) the work of British prime minister Benjamin Disraeli. Whoever said it, it remains familiar because it captures a widespread suspicion of the extent to which statistics can be made to support any position, with sufficient manipulation. This is an especially big public-relations problem for psychological scientists, who use statistical analysis to reach most of their research conclusions.

Of the various available statistical techniques, probably none is more frequently and egregiously abused than the correlation coefficient, which is also the most common way of handling the data from observational (non-experimental) studies in psychology. A correlation coefficient is a single number that indicates the nature and the strength of the relationship between two sets of numbers. Values can range between −1.0 and 1.0.

A positive number means high scores on one factor accompany high scores on the other factor being studied—as one goes up, so does the other. A negative correlation indicates an inverse relationship—as one goes up, the other goes down. The closer the correlation gets to an absolute value (positive or negative) of 1.0, the stronger the measured relationship is. For example, there is a strong positive correlation between shoe size and pants size, at least during childhood—as one number goes up, so does the other. There is a negative correlation between the air temperature and the number of layers of clothing that people wear—as the temperature rises, fewer clothes are worn.

Unfortunately, a common error, in regular life as well as in statistical analysis, is to assume that a correlation represents a causal relationship. Sometimes this is a reasonable assumption—the strong positive correlation between total number of cigarettes smoked and the likelihood of getting lung cancer, for example—and sometimes it is not. Take, for example, the strong positive correlation between the number of churches in a city and the number of bars. Internationally, as one number increases, so does the other. A causal interpretation may tempt us: religion drives people to drink, or conversely perhaps the consumption of alcohol leads to greater religiosity. Note that there is nothing in the data themselves to indicate either a causal relationship or the direction of such a relationship (which variable causes which), if one were to exist. In fact, the relationship between the two numbers is again explained by a third variable, in this case population expansion. Larger towns and cities have both more churches and more bars.

A cause-and-effect relationship would clearly be an inappropriate interpretation of the foregoing example. An important warning: cause-and-effect interpretations are *always* inappropriate for correlational data. Sometimes the data may actually represent a causal relationship, but there is no way of telling from the correlation coefficient alone. The only type of psychological research that allows causal inferences to be drawn is the experiment.

Despite this, causal inferences are made all the time. Politicians are major offenders. The last five presidents (and probably all their predecessors as well), for example, have all seized credit for improvements in certain economic indicators by correlating the figures with their months in office. The government keeps track of many economic indicators, and in any given period some will rise and others will fall. It's a simple matter to examine the statistics for the first hundred days in office and pick one that has gone up, and to then point out that this has occurred while the president has been in office. As with other correlational data, however, there is not enough information contained in the correlation to assume a causal connection. Be alert for this sort of thing—it's everywhere, and it's a clever way of lying.

The tendency to confuse correlation with causation is a perfectly natural one, and one which serves an adaptive function, despite sometimes being wrong. Recognizing that two things that occur consecutively may share a causal relationship is not a bad thing—consider the survival value of noticing that a certain type of cloud often precedes a dangerous thunderstorm or that a certain type of activity by birds often precedes the arrival of a tiger by a few seconds. It can also lead us to see such relationships where none exist, however, a phenomenon known as illusory covariation. This may explain the popularity of many unproven cold remedies. Although several clinical trials have now demonstrated that *Echinacea purpurea* has no effect either on the immune system or on cold symptoms, it remains hugely popular for such alleged effects. A cold usually lasts about a week, maybe a little less, maybe a bit more. If we take a remedy for several days and begin to feel better after taking it, it seems fairly obvious that the remedy caused the improvement. As scientists, however, we must be wary of the obvious—the cold would probably have gotten better anyway, with or without the remedy.

Correlation remains an extremely useful statistical technique despite these flaws, as the problem is with the interpretation rather than with the numbers themselves. The real purpose of correlation is to indicate whether two variables are related in some way and how strong that relationship is—it cannot tell us anything else about the nature of that relationship. When we get promising results from correlations, we can then use these data to plan experiments to test whether a causal relationship of any sort actually exists (*see also* PSYCHOLOGY, RESEARCH METHODS IN).

Further Reading: Dewdney, A. K. *200 Percent of Nothing*. New York: Wiley, 1993; Huff, D. *How to Lie with Statistics*. New York: W.W. Norton, 1954, 1993.

CRANIOSACRAL THERAPY Craniosacral therapy (also known as cranial therapy) is a fringe approach whose advocates claim that it is effective as a treatment for ATTENTION-DEFICIT/HYPERACTIVITY DISORDER (ADHD), chronic fatigue, disorders of the central nervous system, and a variety of physical illnesses. Craniosacral therapy purportedly involves the gentle movement of the bones of the skull to adjust the flow of the cerebrospinal fluid (CSF) beneath. Advocates claim that the CSF pulses with its own rhythm, independent of heart rate and breathing, and that disruption of this rhythm and blockage of CSF flow are the underlying causes of many illnesses. This disruption is said to be due to restriction of movement of the cranial sutures (the lines of contact between the skull bones). What is most fascinating about all of this is the extent to which it contradicts basic biological knowledge of human growth; the bones of the skull fuse together early in life to form a solid surface and cannot be moved independently. Under no circumstances, outside of a very serious head injury, would the bones in an adult human skull move at all. As its underlying theory is demonstrably false, craniosacral therapy is unlikely to possess any value as a treatment (*see also* BRAIN).

Further Reading: Barrett, S. "Craniosacral Therapy." *Quackwatch Home Page, www. quackwatch.com,* 2001; Wirth-Pattullo, V., and Hayes, K. W. "Interrater Reliability of Craniosacral Rate Measurements and Their Relationship with Subjects' and Examiners' Heart and Respiratory Rate Measurements." *Physical Therapy,* 74 (1994): 908–916.

CT/CAT SCAN *See* BRAIN IMAGING TECHNIQUES

D

DEMAND CHARACTERISTICS *See* Hawthorn Effect

DEPRESSANTS Any substance that slows down normal BRAIN function and reduces overall central nervous system (CNS) arousal is a depressant. Most depressants appear to act on the brain by affecting levels of the neurotransmitter gamma-aminobutyric acid (GABA), a neurotransmitter that serves a primarily inhibitory function in the brain (meaning its main action is to decrease the level of brain activity). Depressant medications principally treat anxiety and sleep disorders.

There are two broad categories of depressant medications: benzodiazepines and barbiturates. Benzodiazepines (also widely known as tranquilizers) are primarily prescribed to treat panic attacks, anxiety, and stress; the best-known examples are Valium (diazepam), Librium (chlordiazepoxide HCl), and Xanax (alprazolam). Some benzodiazepines have a greater sedating effect, including Halcion (triazolam) and ProSom (estazolam), which are prescribed for short-term treatment of sleep disorders. Barbiturates generally have a greater sedating effect than benzodiazepines, and less of an impact on anxiety, so they are used primarily to treat sleep disorders, though they are also sometimes prescribed for anxiety and stress. The best known of the barbiturates include phenobarbital, pentobarbital sodium (Nembutal), and mephobarbital (Mebaral). In high doses, these are sometimes used to produce general anesthesia.

Beyond these prescription drugs, the most widely used depressant in the world is alcohol. Like other depressants, it reduces CNS arousal and has a sedative effect. With all depressants, this translates into slower reaction time, poor judgment, and impaired decision-making, which is why driving under the influence of alcohol is illegal. That is also the reason why other depressants, including the prescription drugs listed above, as well as milder substances such as antihistamines, usually bear warnings regarding the inadvisability of operating heavy machinery.

At first, the person taking a prescription depressant will feel sedated, but within several days that person will become accustomed to the drug and develop a tolerance, needing more of the drug to achieve the same effect. It can therefore be quite dangerous to use barbiturates and benzodiazepines for more than a very short period of time. Once a physical dependence has developed, removal of the drug will lead to withdrawal, which can be especially dangerous with depressants. Since the primary action of a depressant is to slow down the brain's activity, the brain's reaction when the individual stops taking it may be a bit of a rebound, with activity racing out of control and possibly causing seizures (this is more likely with barbiturates than with benzodiazepines—withdrawal from the latter is rarely life-threatening). It is important not to take depressants while already taking any other substance that depresses CNS activity, including painkillers, alcohol, or even many over-the-counter allergy medicines. Combining these medicines, especially with alcohol, can slow down breathing or heart rate enough to lead to death (*see also* SLEEP AND DREAMING; STIMULANTS).

Further Reading: Brecher, E. M. *Licit and Illicit Drugs; The Consumers Union Report on Narcotics, Stimulants, Depressants, Inhalants, Hallucinogens, and Marijuana— Including Caffeine.* New York: Little, Brown & Co., 1974.

DEPRESSION *See* MOOD DISORDERS

DIAGNOSTIC AND STATISTICAL MANUAL OF MENTAL DISORDERS, FOURTH EDITION See DSM-IV

DIANETICS/SCIENTOLOGY In 1950, a pulp science-fiction writer named L. Ron Hubbard created the most successful psychotherapy-themed cult of all when he published a book called *Dianetics: The Modern Science of Mental Health.* In it, he claims to have done extensive research into the human mind, resulting in the discovery of therapeutic techniques that can cure all psychological ills. The use of the word "science" in the title is a curious choice, since what he describes within it is not science at all but rather an emphatic claim to have discovered the single source of insanity and psychosomatic ills, as well as a completely effective way to cure them. He claims to have made these discoveries on his own, but no evidence is provided regarding when or where his claimed 11 years of research may have been done. He also claims, rather unscientifically, to have already worked out all the details—missing are any testable hypotheses to guide further research, as apparently none is needed.

The mind has three parts, according to Hubbard: the analytical mind, the reactive mind, and the somatic mind. The analytical mind appears to be the thinking part of the mind, which processes perceptions, processes experience, and handles judgment and problem solving. The reactive mind, the really important part in Dianetics, files away and retains physical pain and painful emotion, and it responds unthinkingly to stimuli. The somatic mind is the portion of the mind that acts on the directions of the analytical or reactive mind to take physical action. (The astute reader may note some powerful similarities, despite the jargon, to Freud's 3-part model of the self.)

According to Hubbard, the source of all insanity is the engram (a legitimate term among cognitive psychologists who study MEMORY—it isn't used correctly here, however). An engram appears to be a unit of memory of some sort, found in a part of the reactive mind called the engram bank. As to the engram, Hubbard defines it as "a definite and permanent trace left by a stimulus on the protoplasm of a tissue. It is considered as a unit group of stimuli impinged solely on the cellular being." These engrams are recorded only at times of physical or emotional suffering, and they are recorded directly on the cells of the body. Hubbard argues that the individual cells of the body actually have a rudimentary consciousness—their thoughts influence the body's thoughts, and the reactive mind is simply made up of all the impressions stored by the cells. Meanwhile, the analytical mind, possessed of a memory that is perfect and error-free, records everything that is seen or heard while the engram is laid down on the tissues.

Hubbard presents all this as scientific fact, based on careful research, but he provides no actual evidence of this, just anecdotes about how engrams might work. It is disturbing to note that many of his examples seem to involve violence against women, which he treats as though it is an ordinary part of a relationship. In the following frequently reprinted example: "A woman is knocked down by a blow. She is rendered 'unconscious.' She is kicked and told she is a faker, that she is no good, that she is always changing her mind" (Hubbard, 1950). While she lies on the floor, a car goes by, and water is running in the sink. All this is recorded in the engram. In the future, any element that recurs (she hears running water, a car goes by, someone else hits her) will trigger the engram, causing her to feel like a no-good fickle faker.

Hubbard viewed the womb as a very frightening, dangerous place in which the worst engrams were recorded (as many as 200 before birth). The prenatal experiences he focuses on especially are the mother's constipation (which apparently makes the fetus feel cramped and uncomfortable), sexual activity by the parents (same problem), the mother being hit or kicked in the belly while abusive things are said to her, and attempted abortions (which he seems to have seen as a very common experience). Some of these engrams may be recorded at an early stage of fetal development, even by the single-celled zygote.

A modern science of mental health would be nothing without a treatment technique, and Hubbard proposed a radical new idea: talking about problems with another person! He calls it auditing, which eventually came to require an electronic device called an e-meter, essentially a galvanic skin response monitor with two wired cans for a person to hold, as a way of monitoring the extent to which the truth is being confronted sufficiently. The book sold well from the beginning, and people began auditing each other all over the country. Confronted with such a fad, Hubbard took what seemed to him a logical next step. In 1952, claiming he had discovered incontrovertible scientific proof of the existence of the human soul, he established the Church of Scientology, with himself at its head.

As head of a religious movement, Hubbard of course needed an impressive personal history, and his organization has over the years claimed, among many other things, the following:

- He was trained as a nuclear physicist. [He attended George Washington University for two years, made poor grades, and left without earning a degree.]
- He was the youngest Eagle Scout in the history of the Boy Scouts. [The Boy Scouts of America do not agree.]
- His family owned a ranch one-third the size of Montana. [No, they did not.]
- During World War II, he served in all five theaters of the war, winning many medals, and in 1944 he was severely wounded and was taken crippled and blinded to Oak Knoll Naval Hospital. [The U.S. Navy says that he saw no combat.]

Hubbard built Scientology into a successful moneymaking machine, in part by making it into what is surely the world's costliest religion. Where other religions make their scriptures and teachings freely available to all, Hubbard's followers are required to purchase training, which becomes more expensive as one advances through the various levels (at times costing more than $1,000 per hour of additional auditing). Under both the old Dianetics name as well as under Scientology, the ultimate goal is rid oneself of all engrams, thus becoming a person with no stress, anxiety, or psychological difficulties at all (a "clear"). In Scientology, there are higher levels than that, known as OT (operating thetan) levels. The highest levels of Scientology teaching appear to have been written only as people achieved the levels right below them, necessitating some additional writing by Hubbard. The theology of the upper levels sounds very much like Hubbard's early pulp science fiction, including a bizarre alternate history of Earth involving the exile of trapped spirits here by an evil space tyrant. As people approach the highest levels of training, these spirits (thetans) are freed.

Scientology has been quite successful at luring high-profile celebrities into its ranks, in part by treating them like, well, celebrities. In Hollywood, Scientology runs a luxurious, expensive gathering place for the famous (and the gawkers who hope to spot them) called the Celebrity Center. High-profile Scientologists include movie stars Tom Cruise and John Travolta, actress Kirstie Alley, musicians Edgar Winter and Chick Corea, and cartoon voices Nancy Cartwright and Isaac Hayes, all of who have provided the Church of Scientology with invaluable publicity.

Scientology has found many other ways to recruit new adherents, including a number of front groups: organizations that are run by Scientology but which do not publicize this fact. Narconon, for example, runs drug-rehabilitation programs internationally, without explicitly presenting itself as a Scientology organization. As Narconon's methods are based on non-physician Hubbard's ideas about drug addiction, it has unsurprisingly come under fire from a variety of medical organizations, including direct criticism by the Surgeon General of the United States. Applied Scholastics, another front, is an organization that runs schools and distributes teaching materials, again all based on Scientology.

The front group that should be of greatest concern to the psychological community is the Citizens' Commission on Human Rights (CCHR), which claims to help people who have been abused or mistreated by psychology, psychiatry, and/or mental institutions. A major goal of Scientology from the beginning, perhaps as revenge for the failure of psychology and psychiatry to embrace Dianetics, has been to discredit and destroy the fields of clinical psychology and PSYCHIATRY. Scientology has long fought the use of drugs in psychiatric treatment, claiming that psychiatrists frequently kill patients, among other things. The CCHR was responsible for the wave of lawsuits attempting to discredit Prozac in the early 1990s, for example. The claim was that Prozac actually made people behave in a violent, psychotic manner, rather than curing their depression. In fact, virtually no empirical evidence supports this claim. Most press coverage, however, failed to mention the Scientology connection.

Scientology's most egregious offense using a front group, however, concerns a group called the Cult Awareness Network (CAN). This organization was, for twenty years, devoted to helping parents whose children had joined religious cults by providing information and advice about those groups (including Scientology). Unfortunately, legal action by several groups, most notably the Church of Scientology, eventually forced the CAN into bankruptcy court, where their name, logo, and toll-free number were sold. The organization, previously a resource for parents concerned about their children's involvement with Scientology, is now run by the Foundation for Religious Freedom, yet another Scientology organization.

Further Reading: Gardner, M. *Fads and Fallacies in the Name of Science*. New York: Dover, 1957; Miller, R. *Bare-faced Messiah: The True Story of L. Ron Hubbard*. New York: M. Joseph, 1987.

DIFFUSION OF RESPONSIBILITY   At approximately 3 a.m. on March 13, 1964, in New York City, thirty-eight people watched from their apartments as a young woman named Kitty Genovese was stabbed to death outside. None of them moved to help her, despite the fact that her murder was a slow one, in which she actually escaped and was recaptured at least twice. The first call to police was finally made at 3:50 a.m., at which time the victim was already dead. The incident sparked a lot of outrage and a fair amount of pop psychology media speculation as well. Nobody was sure why her neighbors did nothing, but explanations ranged from secretly held hostile impulses caused by the frustration of living in the city to simple apathy.

Rather than simply blaming the bystanders, two social psychologists, John Darley and Bibb Latané, decided to experimentally examine the social factors involved in such situations. In a series of experiments, they simulated emergencies with varied conditions and observed what happened. In one study, for example, participants filled out questionnaires either alone or in groups of three. While they worked, white smoke was pumped into the room through a vent. Left alone, most participants quickly reported the smoke to the experimenter. In groups, however, most did not seek help, even when the smoke became so thick that participants rubbed their eyes and waved smoke away from their faces while working. In a variation on this, participants sat in cubicles and interacted with other college students over an intercom (for confidentiality, they were told). Some were assigned to two-person discussions, while others were put in larger groups, but all sat alone and only communicated with others over the intercom. Early in the discussion, an accomplice of the experimenter casually mentioned that he had a seizure disorder. When his turn to speak came again, he proceeded to fake a seizure, including choking sounds and the stuttered phrase "I'm gonna die." The results were similar to those found in the white-smoke study. Virtually all participants who believed they were in a two-person discussion left the room immediately to seek help, whereas in the larger groups, participants were far less likely to intervene, and those who did take action waited substantially longer before doing so. In these and many follow-up studies, a clear pattern emerged: the more bystanders there are, the less likely any individual is to offer help. In other words, the mere presence of other people inhibits helping behavior. This pattern of results became known as the bystander effect.

Darley and Latané described the conditions under which bystanders *will* give help as follows:

   a. they must notice the event

   b. they must interpret the event as an emergency

   c. they must take responsibility for helping

   d. they must decide to intervene

   e. they must act on that decision

The presence of others can act to interfere with any of these conditions, but the overall effect of other people is *diffusion of responsibility*—the tendency, in groups, for individual bystanders to assume that someone else will help. When the bystander is alone, and therefore feels solely responsible for the welfare of the person in trouble, action is far more likely. In a group, each member's self-perceived responsibility decreases steadily as the size of the group increases.

The man pictured in the center shows the classic facial features associated with Down syndrome.

Further Reading: Latané, B., and Darley, J. M. *The Unresponsive Bystander: Why Doesn't He Help?* New York: Appleton-Century-Crofts, 1970.

DISSOCIATIVE IDENTITY DISORDER (DID) *See* MULTIPLE PERSONALITY DISORDER

DOWN SYNDROME   Of the various known organic (as opposed to social) causes of mental retardation, the genetic mutation known as Down syndrome is second only to fetal alcohol syndrome in prevalence and incidence. Ordinarily, the gametes (ovum and sperm) each possess 23 chromosomes, which results in the usual human complement of 23 pairs, or 46 chromosomes total, in every cell of the body. In Down syndrome, however, one of the gametes brings extra genetic material along, resulting in an extra chromosome, or at least a portion of one, in the twenty-first pair. For this reason the syndrome is also known as trisomy 21. In 95 percent of cases, this results from an error in cell division called nondisjunction, in which prior to conception a pair of number 21 chromosomes, in either the sperm or the egg, fails to separate. The extra chromosome is then replicated in every cell of the developing embryo.

Two other types of chromosomal abnormalities, mosaicism and translocation, are also sometimes implicated in Down syndrome. Mosaicism occurs when the nondisjunction of the twenty-first chromosome occurs in one of the initial cell divisions after fertilization. This results in a mixture of two types of cells, some containing 46 chromosomes and some containing 47. Mosaicism is rare, being responsible for only 1 to 2 percent of all cases of Down syndrome. There is some evidence suggesting that individuals with mosaic Down syndrome are less affected than those with nondisjunction, but broad generalizations are not possible due to the wide range of abilities that people with Down syndrome possess. Translocation occurs when part of the number 21 chromosome breaks off during cell division and attaches to another chromosome. While the total number of chromosomes in the cells remains 46, the presence of an extra part of the number 21 chromosome causes the features of Down syndrome. As with nondisjunction trisomy 21, translocation usually occurs prior to conception. Regardless of the specific cause, all people with Down syndrome have an extra, critical portion of the number 21 chromosome present in all, or some, of their cells, and this additional genetic material alters the course of development and causes the characteristics associated with the syndrome.

Many of the physical characteristics commonly found in people with Down syndrome are also found, to some extent, in the general population. It is the combination of traits that is characteristic of the syndrome, rather than any one feature. The most common visible traits include the following:

- Flat, broad face with small ears and nose
- Unusually short stature
- Muscle hypotonia (poor muscle tone)
- Upward slanting eyes with epicanthic folds (small skin folds on the inner corner of the eyes)
- Short, broad hands with incurving fingers and a single deep crease across the center of the palm
- Hyperflexibility (an excessive ability to extend the joints)
- Excessive space between large and second toe
- Small mouth with enlarged tongue, making articulation difficult
- Incomplete or delayed sexual development

Most of these signs are obvious to the casual observer, but there are also some rather serious effects that are less evident. Prior to the last several decades, a large proportion of children with Down syndrome died before reaching adulthood, due primarily to congenital heart problems (most commonly in the form of holes) and bowel obstructions. Surgery in infancy to correct these problems is now fairly routine, and so people with Down syndrome regularly live well into adulthood, which has led to another interesting discovery: people with Down syndrome who live past their midthirties seem almost universally to develop early-onset ALZHEIMER'S DISEASE. This lends a strong boost to the hypothesis that a genetic component is involved in that syndrome as well, and researchers are currently examining the role of the twenty-first chromosome pair in Alzheimer's disease as a result.

Down syndrome also invariably results in MENTAL RETARDATION, though it is usually of the mild to moderate variety rather than severe or profound. Because most cases are only mildly or moderately retarded, a majority of people with Down syndrome are able to live in community settings and lead productive lives, including earning a living, though even the highest functioning continue to need some help and support.

Much has been made of the role of maternal age in Down syndrome, and indeed the incidence of the disorder increases dramatically as maternal age increases. The probability of having a baby with Down syndrome rises, for example, from 1 in 885 at age thirty to 1 in 32 at age forty-five. What these widely reported numbers tend to obscure, however, is that more than 80 percent of babies with Down syndrome are born to women under thirty-five, as fertility rates are much higher for younger women. The more intriguing fact usually overlooked, however, is that most women over thirty-five who become pregnant do so in the company of men who are even older. The extra genetic material can be contributed by either parent and indeed can be shown to have come from the father in as many as 20 to 25 percent of cases. This of course still leaves the mother as the source in a majority of cases. There are several reasons for this, but the main one is the simple fact that the father produces new sperm cells throughout adulthood, whereas the woman's ova are all present from birth and are thus subject to the effects of aging. It may be that the woman in her forties has simply been exposed for a longer time to environmental hazards that can affect the ova than a woman in her twenties. Research so far, however, has failed to find a consistent relationship between nondisjunction and any particular environmental agent.

The signs and symptoms of Down syndrome have been observed and reported for many centuries, but they were not accurately described as making up a distinct syndrome until J. Langdon Down did so in 1866. In keeping with the casual racism of the time, however, the epicanthic fold around the eyes that is typical of the syndrome led him to call the pattern "Mongolism," as it gave a vaguely Asian appearance. Individuals with the disorder were therefore known as Mongoloids, suggesting that their problems stemmed from somehow having been born in Asia. Perhaps there is some poetic justice, therefore, in the fact that the syndrome now bears Down's own name instead (*see also* AUTISM).

Further Reading: Abroms, K. K., and Bennett, J. W. "Current Genetic and Demographic Findings in Down's Syndrome: How Are They Represented in College Textbooks on Exceptionality?" *Mental Retardation,* 18 (1980): 101–107; Eyman, R. F., Call, T. E., and White, J. F. "Life Expectancy of Persons with Down Syndrome." *American Journal of Mental Retardation*, 95 (1991): 603–612; Patterson, D. "The Causes of Down Syndrome." *Scientific American,* 52 (1987): 112–118; Zigman, W. S., Schupf, N., Lubin, R. A., and Silverman, W. P. "Premature Regression of Adults with Down Syndrome." *American Journal of Mental Retardation,* 92 (1987): 161–168.

DREAMING   *See* SLEEP AND DREAMING

DR. PHIL   *See* MCGRAW, PHILLIP ("Dr. Phil") (1950–)

DRUGS AND CHEMICALS *See* Chemical Imbalance; Depressants; Opioids; Psychedelic Drugs; Stimulants

DSM-IV Published by the American Psychiatric Association, the *Diagnostic and Statistical Manual of Mental Disorders, Fourth Edition* (*DSM-IV*) is the standard reference book used by American psychiatrists and clinical psychologists for classifying and diagnosing mental disorders. The current edition, the *DSM-IV*, was published in 1994 and revised slightly in 2000 and renamed the *DSM-IV-TR*— the TR stands for text revision, indicating that the most recent changes involved the addition of current research and clarification of some portions, rather than any large-scale changes in the classification system within. Given the book's history, this is an important distinction to make. The first edition, published in 1952, was only 86 pages long and contained only 60 diagnoses. The *DSM-IV*, by comparison, is 900 pages long and contains nearly 400 diagnoses (see the following Table for the major categories, along with some of the disorders within each).

This tremendous expansion in the number of disorders has some interesting implications for the apparent prevalence of mental illness in our society. With so many disorder categories, one recent national survey indicates that nearly 30 percent of American adults meet the criteria for at least one psychiatric disorder. Why are there so many more categories now than in the past? Supporters of the *DSM-IV*'s expansion point out that this simply allows clinicians to diagnose clients more precisely, and thus treat them properly. There is an underlying reason that is less noble but more practical, however: health insurance companies require a *DSM* diagnostic code on their forms before they will pay for therapy. This puts pressure on the manual's writers to add more diagnoses so that clinicians can be sure of being paid. This pressure to increase the number of categories has led to some confusion regarding what is a serious mental disorder versus what constitutes an ordinary problem. The latest version of the *DSM*, for example, includes Mathematics Disorder (not doing well in math) and Caffeine-Induced Sleep Disorder. This last one has the unusual virtue, at least, of being very easy to cure—just have the client switch to decaf. Critics are wary of these changes because they seem to imply that minor everyday problems are as likely to require treatment as serious disorders such as schizophrenia. The continuing evolution of the *DSM* is necessary to reflect changes in the psychiatric and psychological professions and their accumulated knowledge, however, and has removed as many people from the ranks of the diagnosable as the new disorders have added them.

As social norms change, what is classified as a disorder must change with them. The *DSM-III*, for example, still listed homosexuality as a disorder. Desiring to have sex too often (nymphomania, a term only applied to women) is no longer considered a disorder, but the *DSM-IV* does list not wanting it often enough (hypoactive sexual desire disorder). The *DSM-IV* continues to include a category for emotional problems associated with menstruation, despite having never included any mention of behavioral problems associated with testosterone. This is consistent with psychiatric history, given that one of the founders of the discipline, Sigmund FREUD, formulated his theories based largely on observations of female patients suffering from hysteria, which was believed to occur only in women, possibly as a result of being female (note that the root of the word is the Greek term for the uterus, just as in hysterectomy). Clearly, cultural changes and biases have always played a part in psychiatric diagnosis, and they continue to do so today. The *DSM* continues to be a work in progress, which serves the very important purpose of providing psychiatrists, psychologists, and other therapists a common language to communicate clearly regarding the symptoms and causes of various disorders.

Major Diagnostic Categories in the *DSM-IV*

1. Disorders usually first diagnosed in infancy, childhood, or adolescence	Mental retardation, attention-deficit disorders, pervasive developmental disorders (including autism and Asperger's disorder), tic disorders (including Tourette's disorder), and other disorders of childhood.
2. Delirium, dementia, and amnestic and other cognitive disorders	Alzheimer's type dementia, delirium (a disturbance of consciousness), memory impairments in the absence of other cognitive impairments, and other cognitive disorders.
3. Mental disorders due to a general medical condition not elsewhere classified	As the category name suggests, this category includes a range of symptoms (including catatonic disorder, personality change, delirium, dementia, amnesia, psychosis, mood or anxiety disorder, sexual dysfunction, and sleep disorder) where evidence suggests the disturbance is a direct consequence of a general medical condition.
4. Substance-related disorders	Abuse, dependence, intoxication, withdrawal, and various symptoms caused by various chemical substances, including alcohol and the various categories of psychoactive drugs.
5. Schizophrenia and other psychotic disorders	Schizophrenia, schizophreniform disorder, schizoaffective disorder, delusional disorder, and other disorders with psychotic symptoms.
6. Mood disorders	Major depressive disorder, dysthymic disorder, bipolar disorder, cyclothymic disorder, and variations on each.
7. Anxiety disorders	Panic disorder, agoraphobia, specific phobia, social phobia, obsessive-compulsive disorder, posttraumatic stress disorder, and generalized anxiety disorder.
8. Somatoform disorders	Generally, these disorders involve physical symptoms without a clear physical cause, including somatization disorder, conversion disorder, pain disorder, hypochondriasis, and body dysmorphic disorder

(continued)

9. Factitious disorders	The primary feature of factitious disorder is the intentional production of physical or psychological symptoms (the disorder is commonly known as Munchausen syndrome).
10. Dissociative disorders	A dissociation is a major disruption in memory, consciousness, identity, or perception, as well as the usual smooth integration of those functions. Disorders include dissociative amnesia, dissociative fugue, and dissociative identity disorder (formerly multiple personality disorder).
11. Sexual and gender identity disorders	These include sexual dysfunctions (disturbances in sexual desire or physiological responses), paraphilias (sexual urges, fantasies, or behaviors involving unusual objects, activities, or behaviors),and gender identity disorders (strong cross-gender identification and discomfort with one's own sex).
12. Eating disorders	Severe disturbances in eating behavior, including anorexia nervosa and bulimia nervosa.
13. Sleep disorders	This category includes insomnia, narcolepsy, hypersomnia, sleep apnea, nightmare disorder, night terrors, and sleepwalking.
14. Impulse-control disorders not elsewhere classified	Failure to resist an impulse, drive, or temptation to perform a harmful (to self or others) act—this category includes kleptomania, pyromania, pathological gambling, and intermittent explosive disorder.
15. Adjustment disorders	This is the development of clinical significant symptoms (either emotional or behavioral) in response to a specific event or stressor. The symptoms must occur within three months of the onset of the stressor, and must include either marked distress in excess of what would be expected, or significant impairment in social or occupational functioning.
16. Personality disorders	These are enduring patterns of "inner experience" and behavior that violate cultural expectations. They begin by adolescence or early adulthood and are pervasive and continuous. There are ten, including antisocial personality disorder (formerly known as sociopaths or psychopaths), borderline personality disorder, and narcissistic personality disorder.

Further Reading: American Psychiatric Association. *Diagnostic and Statistical Manual of Mental Disorders.* 4th ed. Text revision. Washington, DC: American Psychiatric Association, 2000; Houts, A. C. "Discovery, Invention, and the Expansion of the Modern *Diagnostic and Statistical Manuals of Mental Disorders.*" In L. E. Beutler and M. L. Malik, eds. *Rethinking the DSM: A Psychological Perspective.* Washington, DC: American Psychological Association, 2002.

E

ECT   *See* Electroconvulsive Therapy

EDUCATION FOR ALL HANDICAPPED CHILDREN ACT (P.L. 94-142)

Public Law 94-142 (P.L. 94-142), the Education for All Handicapped Children Act, is the only piece of federal legislation widely known among psychologists and their students by its numerical designation, perhaps because its impact on the nation's educational practices and on the profession has been so profound. Prior to the passage of this law, which took effect in the 1976–1977 academic year, school systems were legally free to turn away students whose disabilities they were poorly equipped to handle, causing the availability of special education services to vary widely. Furthermore, without a standard approach to the provision of those services, the quality and the appropriateness of the resulting education varied widely as well.

P.L. 94-142 set out to rectify the situation by mandating that appropriate special education services be made available to all school-age children, and by providing federal funds to help meet that goal. The law also includes the first federal legal definitions of both MENTAL RETARDATION and LEARNING DISABILITIES. Many standard practices in the psychological assessment of disabled children followed directly from the provisions of this law, especially its provisions to ensure that every child receives an education that is appropriate for that particular child. The law requires that every disabled student receives an Individual Educational Plan (IEP) based on a thorough assessment by a multidisciplinary team (a psychologist, educational professionals, and the child's parents, among others). The IEP describes both short-term and long-term goals,

Thanks to the Education for All Handicapped Children Act (P.L. 94-142), no U.S. child can be denied a free education on the basis of any disability.

as well as clear plans for achieving them. It also specifies how progress toward those goals will be assessed. The approval of the child's parents is required before the IEP may be implemented. The law also includes a due process clause that guarantees an impartial hearing to resolve any conflicts that may arise between the parents and the school system.

The law requires that the child must be placed in the least restrictive environment possible. This is the clause that led to the widespread mainstreaming of mentally and physically disabled children, allowing them the greatest possible opportunity to interact with nondisabled children. Separate schooling is now allowed only when the level of disability renders achievement of the child's educational goals impossible in the regular classroom.

In 1986, P.L. 99-457 amended P.L. 94-142 by including the provision that the original law should also apply to preschool children. Children aged three to five are now also entitled to a free and appropriate public education. As an incentive, the law also provides federal funds to states that provide educational services to disabled infants and toddlers and their families. The 1997 revision of the law, known as the Individuals with Disabilities Education Act (IDEA), reaffirms the provisions of the earlier laws and extends the provision of special accommodations for students with learning disabilities to college-level education.

P.L. 94-142 and its progeny have so altered the American educational landscape in so brief a time that it is very difficult for today's students to grasp how different things used to be. The media often reminds us of the ugly old days of racial segregation, but people seem to have forgotten as a nation that there was a time when a handicapped child could be refused an education by a public school—a clear sign of how much progress has been made.

Further Reading: Salvia, J., and Ysseldyke, J. *Assessment in Special and Remedial Education.* 4th ed. Boston: Houghton Mifflin, 1988.

ELECTROCONVULSIVE THERAPY (ECT) Electroconvulsive therapy (ECT) is one of the most controversial treatments in psychiatry, and perhaps it deserves to be. It has a long history of abuse and unfavorable media presentation, and there are clearly significant side effects, especially acute confusion and memory deficits. ECT, however, is also the most effective treatment currently known for severe depression, even though patients tend to prefer drugs because of their fear of ECT. On the other hand, drugs and traditional therapy take far longer to work, and some drug treatments offer more serious side effects. Widely viewed by the general public as a relic of a bygone age, ECT is actually still practiced in a majority of psychiatric units in hospitals and mental institutions. The actual story of ECT differs dramatically from the horror tales presented in the media.

ECT involves the induction of a grand mal seizure, similar to those experienced in EPILEPSY, by the brief (usually one second or less) presentation of an electrical current across the BRAIN. Evidence that the seizure is occurring can include twitching toes, an increased heart rate, clenched fists, or a chest heave. Clinically effective seizures generally last from about thirty seconds to just over one minute. Because of the use of muscle relaxants and intravenous anesthesia, the patient's body does not convulse and the patient feels no pain. Seizure activity is monitored on an electroencephalogram (EEG). As the patient awakens, there may be headache, nausea, temporary confusion, and muscle stiffness. Contrary to popular belief, it is the convulsion (seizure) activity, and not the electricity, that cures the depression. Inpatient treatment is often given three times weekly for six to twelve treatments, depending on how rapidly the depression improves. ECT can be either unilateral or bilateral, meaning it can involve one or both hemispheres of the brain. One-sided treatment and brief-pulse, instead of continuous, electrical impulse have decreased side effects without interfering with the anti-depression effect.

ECT is given annually to over 100,000 patients in the United States alone. ECT is generally used in severely depressed patients for whom psychotherapy and medication have not worked. It is also indicated when there is an imminent risk of suicide or the patient is otherwise in danger due to other depressive symptoms, such as refusal to eat, because ECT often has much quicker results than antidepressant drug remedies. In patients for whom antidepressants have failed (approximately 20 percent of all who try them), ECT is successful in at least 60 percent of them. More generally, after two to four weeks of treatment, 80 percent of patients show marked improvement, with no evidence of brain damage. Although the mechanism by which ECT actually works remains a mystery, it clearly can be very effective.

Some of ECT's negative image has to do with the early days of the treatment. The earliest use of electricity as a cure for mental illness dates back to early sixteenth century attempts to treat headaches using electric eels. ECT originates from research in the 1930s on people with schizophrenia. These earliest attempts induced the seizures with drugs, especially high doses of camphor. Attempts were also made that involved insulin. The first electrical induction of a seizure in a schizophrenic patient was accomplished by two Italian researchers—Ugo Cerletti and Lucio Bini in 1938—via a technique which was therefore known for a while as the Cerletti and Bini method. After eleven treatments, they described the man as fully recovered, which led to a rapid spread of the use of electricity to induce convulsions in the mentally ill. This was not without its risks. Prior to the development of effective muscle relaxants, for example, it was not unusual for patients to suffer broken bones. The negative image of ECT was not helped by Ken Kesey's very grim and widely read portrayal of ECT as a tool for controlling difficult patients, in *One Flew over the Cuckoo's Nest*—although this is no longer done, it is unfortunately true that in the 1940s and 1950s the treatment was in fact occasionally used in this way.

Today the American Psychiatric Association has strict guidelines that must be followed in the application of ECT. It is to be used only to treat severe, debilitating mental disorders and never to control behavior. Written informed consent is also required, or a legal guardian must consent in cases where the patient is unable to do so. The procedures, and the reasons for their being considered, are always explained in detail to the patient and/or the patient's family, along with the potential side effects.

The best-documented side effect of ECT, and surely the most worrisome to potential patients, is memory loss. There are varying opinions as to how ECT affects the memory. In most cases, the only memory loss reported is for events that occurred in the hours or days surrounding the ECT. More rarely, the span involved is weeks or even months. This is an effect common to events that disrupt memory consolidation and is often reported by accident or crime victims as well. As in those cases, many of these memories may return, although not always. Some patients have also reported that their short-term memory continues for months to be affected by ECT, although they may be blaming the wrong thing, as this type of AMNESIA is not infrequently associated with severe depression, whether ECT has been used or not.

Testimony of patients who have benefited from ECT differs rather dramatically from the media portrayals. In one survey, 54 percent of elderly patients reported that a visit to the dentist induced more anxiety than ECT treatment did. Perhaps the negative image will eventually be dispelled by the introduction of a kinder, gentler variation on ECT. A painless procedure performed while the patient is fully awake, repetitive transcranial magnetic stimulation (rTMS) also seems to improve depressed moods. It is performed by administering repeated pulses from a magnetic coil held close to the skull, above the right eyebrow. Unlike ECT, it produces no memory loss and does not require a seizure. As more research is performed on rTMS, it may supplant ECT, while bringing along none of the historical baggage (*see also* CHEMICAL IMBALANCE; MOOD DISORDERS).

Further Reading: Bergsholm, P., Larsen, J. L., Rosendahl, K., and Holsten, F. "Electroconvulsive Therapy and Cerebral Computed Tomography." *Acta Psychiatrica*

Scandinavia, 80 (1989): 566–572; Coffey, C. E., ed. *Clinical Science of Electroconvulsive Therapy*. Washington, DC: American Psychiatric Press, 1993.

EMDR *See* EYE MOVEMENT DESENSITIZATION AND REPROCESSING

EMOTIONAL INTELLIGENCE Emotional intelligence (sometimes referred to as EQ) is the ability to perceive, understand, express, and control emotions. The concept was popularized in a 1995 book by Daniel Goleman, in which he argues that emotional intelligence counts more for success in life than IQ does. The book was specifically driven by the observation that people with high IQ scores sometimes fail to accomplish much, while people with less impressive intellectual gifts prosper. Goleman argues that one of the reasons IQ tests fail to predict success is that they do not measure emotional competence.

The term *emotional intelligence* was coined by Peter Salovey and John Mayer in 1990, who described it as consisting of five traits:

- *Emotional Self-Awareness:* The ability to monitor your own feelings and recognize emotional states as they occur.
- *Self-Management:* The ability to control impulses, ensure that emotional reactions are appropriate, and understand what underlies those feelings.
- *Self-Motivation:* The ability to channel emotions towards the achievement of personal goals. This includes the ability to delay gratification and stifle impulses.
- *Empathy:* The ability to read other people's emotional cues and to take their perspective, being sensitive to how their feelings may be different.
- *Managing Relationships:* The ability to react appropriately to the emotions of others as well as manage one's own; social competence.

As with the sorts of intelligence measured by standard IQ tests, emotional intelligence is clearly a set of traits on which large individual differences exist in the human population.

As often happens with popular books in psychology, Goleman's *Emotional Intelligence* has generated a whole industry devoted to spreading the gospel of emotional intelligence, little of it driven by science. The educational profession has wholeheartedly embraced the concept, with many elementary schools providing lessons designed to increase children's EQ. Many books have followed in the wake of Goleman's initial offering, including at least two by Goleman himself, concerning the applicability of his ideas to the workplace. In *Working with Emotional Intelligence*, Goleman asserts that EQ is a better predictor of success than IQ for any job and that it is essentially the only useful determinant of leadership ability. As Robert Sternberg has pointed out, this statement may be true, but that is only because Goleman has expanded the definition of emotional intelligence to the point of including within it essentially every measurable human trait other than IQ; including such things as confidence, conscientiousness, service orientation, and trustworthiness, typically classified as personality traits rather than as elements of intelligence.

At present, little empirical research exists by which to evaluate the claims made for emotional intelligence, and no valid, reliable test has surfaced to measure it.

The concept of emotional intelligence is promising, nevertheless, and it has echoes in many other theories of intelligence. Howard GARDNER's theory of multiple intelligences, for example, incorporates the concepts of interpersonal and intrapersonal intelligences as something beyond the scope of traditional IQ; but even Gardner, whose theory postulates seven or more different varieties of intelligence, has criticized Goleman for stretching the definition of emotional intelligence too far. Much more research is needed before the validity and usefulness of this intriguing new theory may be properly judged (*see also* INTELLIGENCE).

Further Reading: Goleman, Daniel. *Emotional Intelligence: Why It Can Matter More than IQ*. New York: Bantam, 1995; Goleman, Daniel. *Working with Emotional Intelligence*. New York: Bantam, 1998; Sternberg, R. J. "Review of *Working with Emotional Intelligence*." *Personnel Psychology*, 52(3) (1999): 780.

EPILEPSY Epilepsy is a BRAIN disorder in which the primary symptom is the experience of seizures. In a seizure a cluster of neurons in the brain begins to signal abnormally; frequently this involves a synchronous pattern of firing by cells that would not normally be firing in unison. This disturbed pattern of neuronal activity creates a variety of symptoms, including, but not limited to, odd sensations, emotional states, and behaviors; as well as, in the more serious seizures, convulsions, muscle spasms, and loss of consciousness.

The major convulsive seizures are sometimes called grand mal (French for *big bad*) seizures; the small ones, petit mal. A seizure can be caused by anything that disrupts the usual pattern of brain activity, including drugs, brain damage, abnormal brain development, fever, or altered levels of neurotransmitters. Simply having a seizure does not mean that a person has epilepsy. Only when a person has had two or more seizures is a diagnosis of epilepsy made. PET scans and fMRI (*see* BRAIN IMAGING TECHNIQUES) have made diagnosis of epilepsy far more precise than it used to be.

Modern treatment of epilepsy usually involves drugs, which are effective in controlling seizures in about 80 percent of cases. Brain surgery was far more common as a treatment in the past, prior to the advent of better drugs; and now when surgery is done, it is much less invasive than some of the past procedures, which included completely severing the connection between the hemispheres (*see* SPLIT-BRAIN SURGERY).

For those patients whose epilepsy hasn't responded well to drugs, another treatment has recently become available. In 1997 the FDA (Food and Drug Administration) approved an electronic device called the vagus nerve stimulator (VNS) for use in epileptic patients. About the size and shape of a thin hockey puck, the VNS is implanted in the chest and connected to the vagus nerve, one of the major nerves that allows the brain to communicate with various parts of the body. The VNS works by periodically stimulating the vagus nerve. How it achieves an anti-epileptic effect is unclear, but it may be that it interrupts the production of the synchronous discharges that create seizures, scrambling them before they can become seizure activity. Since some people with epilepsy can feel when a seizure is about to start, the device can be programmed with a special sequence of impulses that can abort a seizure before it really gets going. This function can be activated by passing a magnet over the VNS. For patients who can't detect an impending seizure, this function can allow caretakers to shorten the seizure. This device has allowed many patients to reduce their medication and improve their quality of life, both by preventing seizures and by significantly reducing their recovery time after a seizure.

Some patients have also been helped by a ketogenic diet, which is extremely low in carbohydrates and high in fat. This is actually similar to the low-carb diets that are popular for weight loss, except that protein intake is also restricted. How the diet helps is unclear, but it may alter levels of various neurotransmitters, including GABA (gamma-aminobutyric acid), which is known to be involved in some seizure activity.

Further Reading: Kossof, E. H., and Pyzik, P. L. "Improvement in Alertness and Behavior in Children Treated with Combination Topiramate and Vagus Nerve Stimulation." *Epilepsy & Behavior*, 5(2) (2004): 256–259.

EQ *See* EMOTIONAL INTELLIGENCE

ERIKSON, ERIK (1902–1994) Erik Erikson is often credited as the father of lifespan developmental psychology. He was the first psychologist to propose a theory that followed development throughout life, rather than treating everything beyond adolescence as a single stage. Erikson was a Freudian ego-psychologist, meaning that he accepted Sigmund FREUD's ideas as essentially correct. Rather than focus on the instincts and unconscious conflicts over sexuality, however, Erikson was much more interested in the relationships between the individual and society and culture, and how these relationships influence the development of identity.

Freud proposed that development of the self occurs in a series of stages, but the final stage begins in adolescence. Erikson refined and expanded on all previous stage theories (including PIAGET's) by recognizing that psychological development does not stop at age twelve or thirteen. Erikson proposed eight separate stages, extending from birth to old age. According to Erikson, everyone proceeds through the stages in a universal and invariant sequence; the timing will vary, but everyone goes through them in the same order.

At each stage, a developmental crisis must be resolved, and success or failure in that resolution will influence what occurs in the later stages. Each stage is named by indicating both what must be learned in that stage and what the result of not learning it will be. If a stage is managed properly, in other words, a certain virtue or psychological strength will be carried away from it which will help in later stages. Failure to resolve the crisis in a particular stage will lead to a weakness or maladaptation that will endanger a person's progress in all later stages. The infant's task, for example, is known as *trust versus mistrust.* In this stage the child will either learn to mostly trust people and circumstances, or will instead become untrusting.

The various stages are as follows (age ranges, especially in adulthood, are just approximations and can vary dramatically):

I. *Age 0–1 (infancy). Trust vs. Mistrust:* The task is to develop trust without completely losing the capacity for mistrust; to be completely trusting could be maladaptive and lead to being taken advantage of by others. It is up to the parents to help the infant to develop the feeling that the world is a safe place to be, and that people are reliable. If the parents are unreliable or neglectful, or if they reject or harm the child, then the result will be mistrust: the infant will become anxious and suspicious of people. The resulting social withdrawal could eventually result in depression or even psychosis. Note however that Erikson also believed that parents who were overprotective could also cause harm, by producing an overly trusting, gullible child.

II. *Age 2–3 (toddler). Autonomy vs. Shame and Doubt:* If parents and caregivers permit the toddler to explore and act upon his or her environment, the child will develop a sense of autonomy and independence. If the parents are discouraging of the child's attempts to explore, however, the child may feel incapable of acting on his or her own, or will feel ashamed of having tried to do so. Giving children either too much help rather than letting them learn to do it themselves or unrestricted freedom to try things for themselves can result in their thinking too little of their own capabilities or believing themselves capable of anything, and developing no shame and doubt at all.

III. *Age 3–6 (preschool). Initiative vs. Guilt:* Initiative is simply feeling purposeful and able to try out new skills and responsibilities. Parents should encourage children to try out their ideas and use their imaginations. At this stage the children are also able to begin imagining the consequences of their actions, however, and so the capacity for guilt also appears. As with other stages, the goal is to develop a proper amount of guilt rather than either an excess or too little. Since Erikson is a Freudian, he also considers the role of the Oedipal conflict in this stage. In Erikson's view the Oedipal crisis involves the child's reluctance to give up his or her closeness to the opposite-sex parent. The parent's responsibility is to encourage the child to become more mature but not too harshly because if it is done improperly, the child learns to feel guilty about those feelings. Too much initiative and too little guilt produces ruthlessness—the person has the initiative to pursue goals, but doesn't care about the consequences for anyone else. Left unchecked, this tendency can eventually develop into sociopathic behavior. Too much guilt and too little initiative results in a person so inhibited that he or she will not try new things. On the sexual front, due to the Oedipal conflict, this person may grow up to be incapable of achieving sexual satisfaction.

IV. *Age 7–12 (school age). Industry vs. Inferiority:* Here the key players include teachers and peers, not just parents. Depending on the encouragement and acceptance provided by each, the child will either learn to enjoy the feeling of success, and thus become more industrious, or will instead develop feelings of inferiority or incompetence. Erikson consistently sees too much of a good thing as bad, and industry is no exception. Children with too much industry develop a maladaptive tendency called narrow virtuosity. These are children who have been pushed hard into a single area of competence, without being allowed to develop other interests or even to "just be a kid." This is frequently seen in prodigies.

V. *Age 12–18 (adolescence). Ego-Identity vs. Role Confusion*: This is probably the best known of Erikson's stages, as the phrase "identity crisis" has since passed into common usage. The adolescent's task is to achieve ego-identity, which is nothing less than deciding who or what kind of person he or she really is, and how he or she will fit into the rest of society. The adults' role is to provide a society and role models worthy of respect. Erikson especially emphasized the importance of rites of passage in providing a clear demarcation line between childhood and adulthood. In a society that does not clearly provide these, the result may be uncertainty about one's place in the world, which Erikson saw as related to the high rate of suicide among teens. Some adolescents deal with the identity crisis by taking a psychosocial moratorium, a break from growing up. This could be taking a year off to work before going to college, for example, or traveling for a summer before getting a job or going to school. Erikson thought this was healthy, since too many young people in modern society become obsessed with achieving success before they have adequately identified what would actually constitute success. As with other virtues, however, there is such a thing as too much identity. Some people become so involved with a particular role or a particular subculture that they become very intolerant of everyone else. This is fanaticism. Worse is the lack of identity, however. Some adolescents repudiate their need for identity and their membership in the world of adults, taking refuge in a group that will provide the identity for them, such as gangs, religious cults, hate groups, and so on.

VI. *Late teens–about 30 (young adulthood). Intimacy vs. Isolation*: The task here is to find intimacy with another person to spend the rest of life with, rather than remaining in isolation. The ability to do this is heavily influenced by the results of the prior stage. If someone has no clear sense of who they are, it is difficult to achieve intimacy with someone else. Too much intimacy— becoming intimate too freely and easily—results in promiscuity, in which relationships with others remain very shallow. Too little intimacy results in exclusion, which can result in developing hatefulness as a way of dealing with loneliness. Successful negotiation of this stage will of course result in love, here defined as "mutuality of devotion," by which Erikson refers not just to marital love but also to friendship and good relationships with co-workers.

VII. *Late 20s–early 50s (middle adulthood). Generativity vs. Self-Absorption*: This is the period during which people are actively raising children as well as pursuing careers. Generativity refers to the extension of love into the future by the things done today. This can be achieved by raising children well; or via teaching, art, social activism, music, or anything that may contribute to the welfare of future generations. Insufficient generativity leads to extreme self-absorption or stagnation. The stagnant person is no longer a productive member of society. It is at this stage that a midlife crisis may arise, in which the person looks around at his or her life and wonders about the purpose of it all. If he or she has not accomplished enough in life, there may be a misguided attempt to recapture one's youth. The person who is sufficiently generative, however, can usually weather such a crisis. Too much generativity causes a person to become overextended by trying too hard to be generative, leaving no time for rest and relaxation.

VIII. *50s and beyond (older adulthood). Integrity vs. Despair:* The last stage begins around the age of retirement, after the children have moved away to pursue their own adult lives. The task is to develop ego integrity without an excess of despair. At this age people may come to feel less useful and more detached from society, accompanied by an increasing sense of biological obsolescence, as the body is no longer capable of all the things that it used to do. With the coming of menopause, this can be an especially trying time for women. There are also fears of things that were not so frightening at younger ages. Simply falling down can now be especially dangerous, for example. In addition to greater fear of illness (concerns about diabetes, heart disease, and various cancers are inevitably greater than they used to be), death becomes more familiar as others of the same generation begin to die. A certain amount of despair is to be expected, but too much can lead to paranoia, depression, hypochondriasis, and a preoccupation with regrets of the past. Being able to look back and come to terms with the life lived and the choices made, and thus become less fearful of death, is to achieve ego integrity; and Erikson calls wisdom the ability to face death without fear.

Erikson in many ways embodied the crises about which he wrote. Take the matter of his identity, for example: born in Germany to a Danish mother in 1902, his name growing up was Erik Homburger. He never knew his biological father, who left before Erik was born. His mother subsequently married Dr. Homburger, who had treated her during her pregnancy. Erikson was part Jewish, but his appearance, blonde hair, blue eyes, was very Nordic, and so he had a difficult time fitting into either subculture in the Germany of the early twentieth century. After training in psychoanalysis with Anna Freud, he emigrated to the United States, where he took the opportunity to rename himself. The message buried in that new name is difficult to interpret, but Erikson translates as "son of Erik," suggesting he considered himself solely responsible for his identity, having overcome the influence of his parents.

Further Reading: Erikson, E. H. *Identity and the Life Cycle.* New York: W. W. Norton, 1994.

ESP   *See* PARAPSYCHOLOGY

EUGENICS   *See* GALTON, FRANCIS (1822–1911)

EXHIBITIONISM   *See* PARAPHILIAS

EXISTENTIAL PSYCHOLOGY   *See* HUMANISTIC PSYCHOLOGY

EYE MOVEMENT DESENSITIZATION AND REPROCESSING (EMDR)

As she walked in a park in 1988, Francine Shapiro noticed that the anxious thoughts that were troubling her became less of a burden when her eyes spontaneously shifted back and forth. Based on this experience, she developed an unusual treatment for anxiety. Eye movement desensitization and reprocessing (EMDR), the technique she developed, has been heavily promoted as an unusually effective treatment for anxiety and stress produced by traumatic memories, especially as seen in POSTTRAUMATIC STRESS DISORDER (PTSD).

EMDR involves recalling the particular traumatic memory, along with negative thoughts associated with it, then maintaining awareness of the thoughts while following the therapist's finger back and forth in front of the patient's eyes. In addition to PTSD, EMDR advocates also have proposed its use for other disorders, including but not limited to depression, panic disorder, phobias, alcoholism, sexual dysfunction, LEARNING DISABILITIES, and eating disorders.

Though the first publication concerning the treatment only dates back to 1989, published reports now indicate that as many as 25,000 to 40,000 therapists have been trained in its use. This is a remarkably rapid spread for a new and largely untested therapy, but then the claims supporting it are also quite remarkable. Shapiro (and Forrest, 1997) reported that the aversive impact of persistent and traumatic memories could be eliminated for between 84 and 100 percent of clients, often in as few as three therapy sessions. This is a much higher cure rate, with much faster results, than proponents of any other technique claim for PTSD, or for any other psychological disorder for that matter. The treatment has accordingly been greeted with great enthusiasm by the therapeutic community, but the scientific literature has been quite critical.

Criticism of the technique has focused on several issues, but probably the greatest of these is that there is no known physiological process by which eye movements could, or should, have any effect on the anxiety produced by a traumatic memory. Various possibilities have been proposed, most noteworthy among them the idea that by moving the eyes back and forth, the client duplicates the brain state of rapid eye movement sleep (REM), thus entering a sort of waking dream state, during which it is easier to experience the traumatic memory without stress. It should be noted that no empirical support whatsoever exists for this explanation.

The second major criticism is the absence of empirical support for the effectiveness of EMDR in the form of controlled experiments showing it to work better than other treatments. Though some studies show that EMDR works better than doing nothing, this is true for virtually all treatments due to NONSPECIFIC EFFECTS such as the placebo effect and the simple fact of receiving therapeutic attention. Furthermore, much of the published evidence for EMDR takes the form of case studies and single-subject trials with few experimental controls in place. Many of the studies that have compared EMDR to other treatments have found EMDR equally effective as, but no better than, other treatments.

It is now acknowledged by Shapiro that the actual eye movements are not even a necessary part of the treatment. This is the source of the third major criticism of EMDR: apart from the eye movements, it offers nothing new. Indeed, the process of focusing attention on the traumatic memory for a prolonged period of time is already a central part of flooding and exposure, two therapies that EMDR's proponents claim that it outperforms. Other elements of EMDR seem to be borrowed from cognitive-behavioral therapy, which is already well established as a treatment for anxiety.

The many studies which have failed to show a difference in outcomes between EMDR and control conditions are interpreted by EMDR advocates, however, as actually supportive of EMDR. In one study that compared EMDR to a control condition in which subjects simply tapped their fingers rather than moving their eyes, a null result (no difference) was reported. Rather than the usual interpretation, which would be that EMDR was no more effective than the placebo treatment, the authors saw this as evidence that both EMDR *and* finger tapping are useful treatments.

Given that its only unique element appears to be unnecessary for its therapeutic efficacy, its extremely rapid spread seems to be in part due to the same sort of successful marketing and almost cult-like atmosphere that have accompanied other highly successful psychological PSEUDOSCIENCES such as FACILITATED COMMUNICATION and THOUGHT FIELD THERAPY (Herbert et al., 2000). Furthermore, despite the therapy's relative newness, it already possesses a central governing body, the EMDR Institute, Inc., which is the sole provider of training in this therapy, following which therapists are invited to join the EMDR Network and the EMDR International Association. Despite these scientific-sounding trappings, however, the evidence for EMDR remains very inconclusive, while its claims continue to grow.

Further Reading: Herbert, J. D., Lilienfeld, S. O., Lohr, J. M., Montgomery, R. W., O'Donohue, W. T., Rosen, G. M., and Tolin, D. F. "Science and Pseudoscience in the Development of Eye Movement Desensitization and Reprocessing: Implications for Clinical Psychology." *Clinical Psychology Review*, 20(8) (2000): 945–971; Shapiro, F. "Efficacy of the Eye Movement Desensitization Procedure in the Treatment of Traumatic Memories." *Journal of Traumatic Stress*, 2 (1989): 199–223; Shapiro, F., and Forrest, M. S. *EMDR: The Breakthrough Therapy for Overcoming Anxiety, Stress, and Trauma.* New York: Basic Books, 1997.

F

FACILITATED COMMUNICATION (FC) Facilitated communication (FC) is a technique that allegedly allows a person with severe developmental disabilities, especially AUTISM, to communicate at a much higher level than was previously believed possible for that individual. In FC the facilitator supports and steadies the client's hand over a computer keyboard, thus allowing the client to type messages which reveal "unexpected literacy" (Biklen, 1993) in the form of syntax, fluency, and content which are age-normative or even indicative of superior INTELLIGENCE. On the surface, the technique can appear to provide nearly miraculous results, with previously nonverbal clients typing poems and carrying on high-level conversations. The technique's appeal to parents is fairly straightforward: an adolescent who has never developed language skills is suddenly able to tell his parents that he loves them. In addition to the obvious emotional reward of such an experience, the parents are also grateful to discover that their child who was previously found to have severe MENTAL RETARDATION is actually highly intelligent.

With such fantastic results, especially with a disorder so notorious for its poor prognosis, the rapid spread of the technique is unsurprising. FC started with Rosemary Crossley in Australia, and was introduced in the United States in 1990 by Douglas Biklen. By 1994 FC had become widely accepted and used in special education and adult services for the disabled, despite an almost total lack of scientific evidence of its efficacy. In addition to the absence of evidence that FC actually works, there are major logical difficulties with the technique and the theory behind it. FC practitioners believe that a large proportion of people with serious developmental disabilities actually possess normal or superior intelligence that has been hidden by the "prison" of the body (though the technique is used in cases where no physical disabilities exist as well). Furthermore, FC requires believing that a person who has never learned the alphabet, much less the layout of a computer keyboard, could type complicated and coherent messages in the absence of any assistance other than hand support.

The messages are clearly coming from somewhere, however, and experimental studies have almost without exception agreed on the actual source of what is being typed: the facilitator. The basic experimental design used in most of these studies is very simple: the facilitator and client are seated in their usual fashion at a computer keyboard and are shown pictures, which the client is expected to identify via typing. Conditions are set up, however, such that the facilitator and patient each see separate screens, and the facilitator cannot see what the patient sees. Under such conditions, FC works extremely well as long as both participants are seeing the same stimulus. When the pictures are different, however, the answer typed is almost always what was shown to the facilitator. The results of a large number of controlled studies are quite consistent in concluding that FC is communication by the facilitator rather than by the client.

The dangers of FC go well beyond its simple worthlessness, however. By the mid-1990s there was widespread reporting in the media and at professional conferences of allegations of sexual abuse being made through FC. In a review of legal cases involving facilitated communication (Margolin, 1994), legal action had already resulted from FC allegations of sexual abuse in at least five dozen cases in the United States. Recognizing the dangers to patients and their families, as well as the remarkable body of evidence against its usefulness, the American Psychological Association, American Academy of Pediatrics, Ameri-can Academy of Child and Adolescent Psychiatry, and American Academy of Speech and Hearing have all issued official position papers opposing FC as a treatment modality (Campbell et al., 1996).

As with most instances of PSEUDOSCIENCE in psychotherapy, unfortunately, the story does not end there. The Facilitated Communication Institute at Syracuse University, which has trained most of those using FC in the United States, continues to advocate for the use of FC and provide training in the method, as well as selling promotional materials and training videos on its Web site (*http://soeweb.syr.edu/thefci/*).

Further Reading: Biklen, D. "Communication Unbound: Autism and Praxis." *Harvard Educational Review*, 60 (1990): 291–314; Biklen, D. *Communication Unbound: How Facilitated Communication Is Challenging Traditional Views of Autism and Ability/Disability.* New York: Teacher's College Press, Columbia University, 1993; Campbell, M., Schopler, E., Cueva, J. E., and Hallin, A. "Treatment of Autistic Disorder." *Journal of the American Academy of Child & Adolescent Psychiatry*, 35(2) (1996): 134–143; Crossley, R. "Getting the Words Out: Case Studies in Facilitated Communication Training." *Topics in Language Disorders*, 12(4) (1992): 46–59; Jacobson, J. W., Mulick, J. A., and Schwartz, A. A. "A History of Facilitated Communication: Science, Pseudoscience, and Antiscience: Science Working Group on Facilitated Communication." *American Psychologist*, 50(9) (1995): 750–765; Margolin, K. N. "How Shall Facilitated Communication

Be Judged? Facilitated Communication and the Legal System." In H. C. Shane, ed. *Facilitated Communication: The Clinical and Social Phenomenon.* San Diego: Singular Press, 1994, pp. 227–258;Wheeler, D. L., Jacobson, J. W., Paglieri, R. A., and Schwartz, A. A. "An Experimental Assessment of Facilitated Communication." *Mental Retardation,* 31 (1993): 49–60.

FALSE MEMORY   *See* MEMORY

FC   *See* FACILITATED COMMUNICATION (FC)

FETISHISM   *See* PARAPHILIAS

fMRI   *See* BRAIN IMAGING TECHNIQUES

FREUD, SIGMUND (1856–1939)   Though his influence on the current generation of child and clinical psychologists is small, Sigmund Freud casts a giant shadow on the history of psychology and psychiatry and remains the psychological thinker whose work is most likely to be familiar to non-psychologists. Both his admirers and his detractors would agree that his impact on the way Americans and Europeans think of themselves has been greater than that of anyone else in the field. This is evident even in popular entertainment, as television and movie portrayals of psychotherapists continue to heavily favor psychoanalysis as the method of choice, though most actual therapists now follow other approaches.

Born in Freiberg, Moravia, then part of the Austro-Hungarian Empire, in 1856 to a poor and uneducated Jewish trader, Freud was the eldest of seven children. Although they moved to Vienna when he was four years old, his family never lived a life of privilege or even comfort. The first member of his family to attend a university, Freud specialized in physiology and neuroscience and graduated with his M.D. in 1881. His training as a neurologist, however, would soon be left behind, beginning with his introduction to his first hysteric patient.

Hysteria refers to a general, nonspecific set of ailments consisting of psychological and physical symptoms with no apparent physical cause. Several of his patients, for example, experienced glove anesthesia, in which a loss of sensation in the hand occurs that is inconsistent with known nerve pathways. The name given to hysteria is emblematic of the sexism that was rampant in nineteenth-century science: the root of the word refers to the uterus, and hysteria was believed to

Sigmund Freud. © CORBIS.

affect only women. Josef Breuer, who brought Freud his first hysterical patient, also introduced Freud to the idea of the "talking cure," that is, the idea that hysterical symptoms are due to unresolved conflicts and that a cure can be effected by helping the patient to think and talk about the events that generated the symptoms.

Although he specialized in neurological and BRAIN disorders, Freud spent more time with hysterical patients who were referred to him by Breuer. Through his work with these patients, which often included HYPNOSIS as an aid to uncovering buried thoughts and memories, Freud began to formulate both the theory and the technique that would become known as psychoanalysis.

Working with hysterics whose physical symptoms had no apparent physical cause led Freud to reason that the cause must be psychological, and the fact that the patients were unaware of this cause led directly to the most basic and most influential insight of Freud's psychoanalytic theory: the existence of the unconscious mind. Freud argued that the psychologists (such as Wilhelm WUNDT, for example) who attempted to study the human mind through introspection were mistaken in assuming that the mind's contents were available for that sort of examination in the first place.

Freud believed instead that much of what motivates a person's actions is unknown to them. This is partly because of instinct. Humans, in Freud's view, are driven by two sets of instincts, which he labeled Thanatos (death instincts) and Eros (life instincts). Though humans are driven instinctively to do good, positive, constructive things, we are also equally driven by destructive impulses, and the conflict between these two sets of drives is a source of psychological problems. Freud explored this conflict further by dividing the personality or mind—psychoanalysis does not clearly distinguish between them—into three structures: the id, ego, and superego.

The id is the only structure a person is born with and in later life is the most inaccessible portion of the mind. The id is entirely unconscious, and it can only be known indirectly through dream contents and through the symptoms, such as anxiety, that it helps to cause. The id is the location of the instincts, including such basic needs as food, water, sexual gratification, and avoidance of pain. The id exists to satisfy these needs in accordance with the "pleasure principle," the impulse to seek pleasure and satisfaction that is pursued without regard for values or morality. The id is irrational and has no concept of time, meaning that experiences of frustration stored by the id may be preserved unconsciously for decades, where they may continue to create trouble behind the scenes.

Clearly possession of only the id would make survival unlikely, and so the ego begins to develop soon after birth. Its purpose is to serve as a mediator between the id and reality, by consciously seeking realistic and safe ways of releasing the tensions that are constantly arising from the instinctual pressures of the id. Since it acts upon the demands of the real world rather than simply seeking pleasure, the ego is said to follow the "reality principle." Later psychodynamic theorists have frequently used ego interchangeably with "self." In addition to the id, however, the ego must also deal with the demands of the superego, the ethical portion of the personality that is roughly synonymous with conscience, which begins to emerge during the first five years of life.

The superego develops as children internalize the societal standards of right and wrong presented by their parents. Though partly conscious, the superego is also largely unconscious, and its main job is to restrict the attempts of the id to obtain gratification. The ego is therefore constantly mediating between the demands of the id and the often equally irrational superego. Failure to find a morally acceptable way of satisfying the id will result in punishment by the superego, usually in the form of guilt.

While attempting to satisfy all three (id, reality, and superego), the ego will inevitably fail with some frequency, resulting in anxiety. Failure to resolve inner conflicts effectively is the source of psychological problems in general, so it is important that the ego has some tools available to prevent anxiety from getting out of hand. Freud proposed a set of such tools, a group of mental strategies known as defense mechanisms. These mechanisms, although they are controlled by the ego, operate unconsciously and reduce anxiety by distorting reality to some degree. The following are some example of these mechanisms in operation:

- *Repression*: Anxiety-arousing thoughts and feelings are banished from consciousness. Repression underlies the other defense mechanisms, as they all serve the purpose of protecting the mind from unwelcome thoughts and impulses. This is the source of Western society's widespread belief in buried memories of trauma (*see* MEMORY).

- *Regression*: A person retreats to an earlier, more infantile state of development, as when a child reverts to thumbsucking during the first few days of school.

- *Reaction formation*: The ego unconsciously makes unacceptable impulses look like their opposites. This is often seen on school playgrounds, where information that one is "liked" by another child is often greeted by exaggerated revulsion.

- *Projection*: Threatening impulses are disguised by being attributed to others. The individual sees his/her fault very clearly—in someone else. "He hates me!" may, in other words, be the projection of the actual feeling "I hate him!"

- *Rationalization*: Self-justifying explanations are generated unconsciously to conceal from oneself the actual reasons for one's actions, as when the habitual heavy drinker says that he or she drinks "just to be sociable."

- *Displacement*: Sexual or aggressive impulses are diverted onto a safer target than the one that aroused the feelings in the first place. A child upset with his parents may kick a pet, for example.

Another way that the unconscious mind releases the tension created by intrapsychic conflict is by allowing the forbidden content to surface in dreams. Dream interpretation is an important part of psychoanalytic theory, as our dreams, which are beyond conscious control, allow the expression of impulses and feelings that the conscious ego cannot. Even in dreams, however, the controversial content must be disguised to cause as little anxiety as possible. Freud defined two levels of content to every dream: manifest content is the actual surface content of the dream, whereas latent content is the hidden, buried stuff, concealed by the symbols that make up the surface content. For example, a dream involving a journey by train, past a waterfall, and into a tunnel has only the train, the waterfall, and the tunnel as manifest content, but the latent content would be of a sexual nature—Freud wrote about all three items as symbols of sexual impulses. Freud explained this in great detail in *The Interpretation of Dreams*, which remains his best-selling book, though it was considered a failure when first released.

Possibly the most controversial portion of Freud's theory is his view of child development. Freud saw personality development as proceeding through an orderly, invariant set of five stages, each named for the primary source of sensory pleasure for the id at the time. Freud believed that if conflicts that arise are not resolved in a satisfactory manner, it is possible to become fixated on the particular stage, resulting in an abnormal preoccupation with that stage's source of pleasure later in life. A heavy smoker or gum-chewer, for example, might be regarded as fixated at the oral stage, during which the primary focus of sensual pleasure is the mouth. The stages are as follows:

- *Oral stage*: It occupies approximately the first two years of life, during which casual observation reveals that children do indeed use their mouths to explore new objects and enjoy putting things in their mouths. Freud explained that this occurs in part because the child's first contact with the mother in feeding is via the mouth and that the child's bond with the mother is therefore inextricably bound up with oral contact. He further speculated that oral fixation might be a result of either insufficient time or too much time spent nursing, depending on the case.

- *Anal stage*: Between ages two and four, the child gains control over his/her bowels, making the act of defecation one of the very few things the child can control in an environment which is almost entirely determined by the whims and preferences of adults. How parents handle the task of toilet training can therefore influence subsequent development, including the creation of two different types of fixation. The anal-retentive person learned as a child to exercise control and get what he wants by refusing to excrete; and as an adult is excessively concerned with neatness and organization, controlling his environment by keeping everything in its place. The anal-expulsive type may have instead controlled his parents by excreting freely and liberally, and as an adult may attempt to control others through sloppiness.

- *Phallic stage*: This is the period, roughly from four to six years old, during which a boy discovers his penis and derives pleasure from contact with it. Some boys also fear that they may lose theirs as a punishment; Freud called this castration anxiety. As with the oral stage, the evidence that boys go through something like this is easily obtained; getting little boys to understand that they mustn't sit with their hands in their pants is a major concern in preschools and day-care centers. Not to leave anyone out, Freud would point out that girls are also concerned with penises during this stage, specifically with the question of why they don't have one. Observing that boys have penises and girls do not, a little girl may wish that she did and suspect deep down that she had one at one time and that it was removed. Freud called this penis envy. This is also the stage in which Freud suggested the existence of the Oedipal conflict or complex, named for the Greek protagonist Oedipus, who inadvertently kills his father and marries his mother. During the phallic stage, boys go through a period in which they bond strongly with their mothers and show less interest in their fathers. According to Freud, the boys fantasize about growing up and marrying their mothers. Only one thing stands in the way: Dad. Recognizing his powerlessness against his father, who might take away the penis if he finds out, the boy resolves this conflict by identifying strongly with the father instead of competing with him for Mother's affection. When the same essential conflict occurs in girls (substitute Father for Mother in the above), it is called the Electra complex. Freud, like much of the psychological community until the early 1970s, regarded homosexuality as a disorder and believed it had its roots in a failure to properly resolve the Oedipal conflict.

- *Latency period*: This period follows the phallic stage with several years of concentration on schoolwork until sensual concerns blossom again with the coming of adolescence.

- *Genital stage*: This period begins with the onset of puberty, when the id turns its attention outward in the direction of contact with others, usually of the opposite sex.

Much of the controversy over this portion of the theory may have been exacerbated by the name by which the stages have become known: stages of psychosexual development. While Freud's concern was indeed the id's quest for sensual pleasure, most of what he was suggesting about children was not at all sexual in nature. It also should be noted that this was the first fairly comprehensive view of child development based on stages, an idea which Jean PIAGET would later use to further revolutionize the study of child development.

Freud's impact on the field of psychology, and indeed on the world as a whole, has been full of contradictions. This most influential of psychologists was judged by no less than Nobel Laureate Sir Peter Medawar to be the perpetrator of "the most stupendous intellectual confidence trick of the century." Indeed, modern empirical research has not been kind to Sigmund Freud. A large body of research on human memory suggests that repression of traumatic or uncomfortable memories, a centerpiece of psychoanalysis, is extremely rare and may not be a normal part of memory function at all. As for the unconscious mind, modern cognitive research is a bit gentler on Freud, showing that there are many mental processes of which people are unaware as they happen. The type of unconscious processes that go on, however, largely concern automation of information processing (see example below), not buried conflicts and repressed feelings and memories.

Here's an example of non-Freudian unconscious information processing: A subject is asked to think of his/her mother. What's her middle name?

If they're like most people, the answer "popped" into their head without any effort, certainly without any apparent search of memory. Modern cognitive psychology suggests that a search certainly occurred, but the person was unaware of it because it occurred automatically and involuntarily. Here's another example: A subject is asked *not*, under any circumstances to imagine a black-and-white spotted dog wearing a multi-colored, striped party hat and a name tag that says, "Hi, My Name Is Bob." Most subjects can't resist the suggestion, and picture exactly that.

The larger problem with Freud's theory, at least from the point of view of those who prefer to regard psychology as a science, is that his ideas are simply not scientific. Where the goal of scientists is usually to use observations to make predictions about future events, psychoanalysis excels at providing post hoc explanations, but doesn't produce testable hypotheses. His defenders point out, correctly, however, that Freud was not aiming at empirical precision in the first place. He was seeking a better explanation for normal and abnormal human behavior than existed at the time. In this he was successful, especially if success is to be measured by the number of his terms and concepts that remain part of the modern lexicon. In the words of Drew Westen: "Many aspects of Freudian theory are indeed out of date, and they should be: Freud died in 1939, and he has been slow to undergo further revisions."

Further Reading: Freud, S. *The Interpretation of Dreams (Reissue edition)*. New York: Avon, 1980; Gay, P. *Freud: A Life for Our Time*. New York: W. W. Norton, 1988; Westen, D. "The Scientific Legacy of Sigmund Freud: Toward a Psychodynamically Informed Psychological Science." *Psychological Bulletin*, 124 (1998): 333–371.

FROTTEURISM   *See* PARAPHILIAS

FUNCTIONALISM   *See* JAMES, WILLIAM (1842–1910)

G

GALTON, FRANCIS (1822–1911) Francis Galton's influence on modern psychology, and on scientific inquiry in general, cannot be overstated. His research, discoveries, and inventions included modern meteorology, as he discovered high and low pressure systems and fronts and invented the weather map, the use of fingerprints for identification, CORRELATION analysis, the normal distribution, also known as the "bell curve," twin studies, survey research, word-association tests, mental testing, and the nature-nurture distinction. Like many scientists in nineteenth-century Europe, Galton was fascinated by the advances that had been made in the physical sciences, especially regarding new means of objectively and precisely measuring natural phenomena, but he focused his attention on human traits.

At the 1884 International Health Exhibition in London, visitors to Galton's Anthropometric Laboratory paid three pence each to be tested and measured for thirteen characteristics: reaction time, keenness of sight and hearing, height, weight, color discrimination, ability to judge length, strength of pull and squeeze, strength of blow, arm span, breathing power, and breathing capacity. Over 9,000 visitors were tested, and the exhibit proved so popular that it was installed in the South Kensington museum for an additional six years, eventually providing raw data on over 17,000 people. This enormous data set allowed the observations that led to the discovery of normal distribution. Examining his data, Galton discovered that with a large enough number of scores, no matter what was being measured, the data would form a roughly symmetrical, bell-shaped distribution, with most scores clustered around the mean and fewer and fewer scores appearing at either end. This fact is of vital importance in

Sir Francis Galton. © Bettmann/CORBIS.

statistics and in the design and scoring of psychological tests of all types, but especially intelligence tests.

Indeed, though Galton's subjects were unaware of it, they had participated in a trial of the very first intelligence test battery. While a modern observer would not recognize the tasks listed above as measures of intelligence, they reflect Galton's ideas on intelligence quite well. He believed that people of higher intelligence had faster reactions, keener senses, greater strength, and better health, and that it ought to be possible to measure intelligence indirectly by measuring these physical traits. He also believed that intelligence was entirely inherited, as he argued in the book *Hereditary Genius*.

His method was to examine the genealogy of 286 English judges. He found that about one in nine was the father, son, or brother of another judge, and that the judges were also related to many other eminent men in the arts, government, military, science, and clergy. The eminent men were hundreds of times more likely to be related to other eminent men than were members of the general population. Galton's own family ties to the more-famous Darwins certainly influenced him here as well. Failing to consider any environmental explanations or even such simple factors as nepotism, wealth, and the rigidity of the English class system, Galton concluded that he had proven his thesis that men's abilities are derived entirely from heredity. On the heels of this research, he developed the idea for eugenics.

His cousin Charles Darwin's ideas about natural selection and survival of the fittest fascinated Galton. He became convinced that many of society's problems were the result of the irresponsible activities of the least intelligent, and that it might be possible to improve the human species through selection, in much the same way that a horse breeder produces winners by only allowing the swiftest and strongest to interbreed. Galton argued that if the most fit, that is, intelligent members of the species reproduce together, the general level of human intelligence will be raised, eliminating the many social problems brought about by those of low intelligence.

Galton's ideas took hold in the United States in a big way, where others took them considerably further than Galton ever intended; for instance, he did not explicitly advocate preventing the less fit from reproducing, although that follows logically enough. Eugenics became a popular perspective, leading eventually to widespread implementation of state laws allowing involuntary sterilization of those judged to be feeble-minded. A challenge to the Virginia law eventually made it to the U.S. Supreme Court (*Buck vs. Bell, 1927*), which upheld the law with the following chilling language (the majority opinion was written by Oliver Wendell Holmes):

> We have seen more than once that the public welfare may call upon the best citizens for their lives. It would be strange if it could not call upon those who already sap the strength of the state for these lesser sacrifices.... The principle that sustains compulsory vaccination is broad enough to cover cutting the Fallopian tubes.... Three generations of imbeciles are enough. (quoted in Gould, 1996)

At the time of this decision, similar laws were on the books in twenty-three states. The sterilization law passed in Germany in the early 1930s was modeled on the U.S. laws. Though Galton was responsible for many important developments in psychology, he is best remembered today for his ideas on eugenics and the consequences of those ideas.

Further Reading: Fancher, R. *The Intelligence Men: Makers of the IQ Controversy.* New York: W.W. Norton & Company, 1985; Galton, F. *Hereditary Genius: An Inquiry into its Laws and Consequences.* Chicago: University of Chicago Press, 2001; Gould, S. J. *The Mismeasure of Man.* Rev. ed. New York: W.W. Norton & Company, 1996; Hunt, M. *The Story of Psychology.* New York: Doubleday Anchor, 1993.

GARDNER, HOWARD (1943–) Disenchanted with the testing industry's focus on INTELLIGENCE as a single, unitary quality that can be captured in a single number, Harvard psychologist Howard Gardner proposed in 1983 a radically different view of intelligence: the theory of multiple intelligences. Gardner's theory is based loosely upon what is known so far about brain-behavior relationships, and argues for the existence of several relatively independent kinds of human intelligence. Although he proposed seven of them to begin with, he acknowledges that the total number of intelligences has not been established, nor has their exact nature, so there may be more.

For an ability or aptitude to qualify as intelligence, it must fulfill several criteria, including the following:

- *Potential isolation by brain damage*: It must be localized somewhere in the brain, in such a way that it could conceivably be destroyed, or spared while other abilities are destroyed, by brain damage.
- *Existence of savants and prodigies*: The faculty is distinct enough to be spared under circumstances that render other areas of intelligence subnormal or to stand out among otherwise average performance.
- *Distinctive developmental history*: It follows a distinctive developmental progression, complete with milestones and critical periods.
- *Evolutionary plausibility*: It should serve some sort of plausible survival function, and/or share evolutionary antecedents with other organisms.
- *Can be encoded in symbols*: It should be possible to communicate the ability to others via symbols (such as mathematical formulas, words, musical notation, etc.).

Of the seven basic types of intelligence that Gardner initially proposed, three are well known even to traditional intelligence theorists: linguistic intelligence (the verbal intelligence that is a key part of the standard IQ tests), logical-mathematical intelligence, and spatial intelligence. There are many well-established tests to measure those, unlike the remaining four intelligences:

- Interpersonal intelligence is the kind found in great political and spiritual leaders, along with all people who are skilled at understanding the intentions and desires of others, with the ability to influence and gain trust. Certainly, the large individual differences among people in this area are fairly easy to observe.
- Bodily-kinesthetic intelligence comprises the skills and abilities used by dancers, athletes, hunters, and others who rely on their ability to use their body to make a living. The evolutionary plausibility of this one is pretty straightforward: People who could hunt effectively and skillfully avoid predators certainly had an evolutionary advantage in humanity's early days.
- Intrapersonal intelligence is essentially self-understanding, of the sort possessed by the great novelists and artists who are able to express feelings in a way that is universally understood.
- Musical intelligence is possessed by people who can easily learn to play an instrument or to compose music.

Gardner has recently added three more tentative candidates to his list of intelligences: naturalistic intelligence, spiritual intelligence, and existential intelligence. Naturalistic intelligence involves an ability to discern patterns in nature, such as was possessed by Charles Darwin and other great naturalists. Spiritual intelligence is a concern with religious and cosmic issues as they relate to one's own development. Existential intelligence is simply a concern with the meaning of existence.

Many objections can be raised to the theory of multiple intelligences, on both practical and scientific grounds. Gardner's critics frequently have difficulty seeing the difference between intelligence and an aptitude or ability. If any potentially isolatable ability is intelligence, is there any real limit to the number of intelligences that can be proposed? Does the concept of intelligence begin to lose its meaning as this happens? The list of aptitudes on which people can differ is potentially quite long. Also, several of the intelligences, especially the most recent three, are defined so nebulously as to make them virtually impossible to study further. In a practical sense, even if one agrees, for example, to consider bodily-kinesthetic intelligence as a real thing, what implications does this have for the world of intelligence testing? Would it be possible to come up with a test that would be fair to both Michael Jordan and Mikhail Baryshnikov? Their areas of physical specialty are quite different from each other.

The real impact of Gardner's theory has been in the educational profession. Many elementary schools are implementing curricula that are explicitly based on the idea of multiple intelligences, and this is probably a good thing. In a world where both the schools and their students are increasingly being judged against the narrow criterion of a standardized achievement test, an approach that respects and seeks to nurture a wider range of abilities can only be positive. Solid psychometric theory or not, Gardner's multiple intelligences are a useful tool for reestablishing that there is more to human performance than is measured by standardized tests (*see also* SAVANTS AND PRODIGIES).

Further Reading: Gardner, Howard. *Frames of Mind: The Theory of Multiple Intelligences.* New York: Basic Books, 1983.

GESTALT One of the most influential movements in psychological history, the Gestalt school of psychology was born when a group of German researchers described the principles that govern human perception of familiar stimuli. At the time, psychologists such as Wilhelm WUNDT were focusing on attempts to break down human cognitive and perceptual experiences into their component parts, following the lead of chemistry and physiology. The Gestalt psychologists, however, argued that people perceive sights and sounds as organized patterns rather than as discrete components, and the perception of that whole pattern becomes more than the mere sum of its parts.

The German word *gestalt* can be roughly translated as "whole object" or "whole pattern," thus these researchers became known as Gestalt psychologists. The best known among them were Max Wertheimer, Kurt Koffka, and Wolfgang Köhler. They proposed several principles that describe how the perceptual system makes sense of raw sensory information, which they frequently tested and demonstrated through the use of optical illusions, a few of which are illustrated here:

- *Proximity*: Objects or events that are close to each other are perceived as belonging together. For example, the following pattern is usually described as 3 pairs of Xs, rather than as 6 Xs (although that would also describe it accurately): XX XX XX.

- *Similarity*: Similar elements are automatically perceived as belonging to a group. The pattern below is usually described in terms of columns of Xs and Os, rather than as mixed rows. The Xs seem to belong together, as do the Os.

    X O X O

    X O X O

    X O X O

    X O X O

- *Continuity*: Sensations that appear to create a continuous form are perceived as doing so. In the drawing on the next page, for example, most people will perceive a straight line crossed by a curving line, rather than two curving lines which both contact the straight line at the same point.

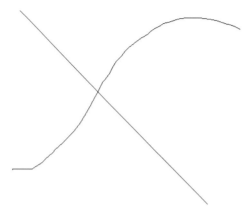

- *Closure*: We mentally fill in the missing parts of incomplete objects—we may mentally fill in gaps that appear in a picture. In the figure below, for example, most people will perceive a triangle, even though what is actually depicted is a set of three incomplete circles.

Figure adapted from an example in Mullet, K. & Sano, D., *Designing Visual Interfaces: Communication Oriented Techniques*, Englewood Cliffs, NJ: Prentice Hall, 1995.

- *Common Fate*: Stimuli that move together in the same direction, at the same speed, are perceived together. This is why doing "the wave" in stadiums is so popular; to observers across the field, it is seen as a single smooth motion by a large object, the crowd, rather than a large number of people moving individually.

The name *Gestalt* has also been applied to a type of therapy, which has little in common with the perception and cognition research of the same name. Gestalt therapy is an amalgam of ideas from psychoanalysis, HUMANISTIC PSYCHOLOGY, and the work of Gestalt psychologists. Its focus is on the idea that people create their own internal reality, and psychological growth requires perceiving, remaining aware of, and acting on true feelings.

Symptoms of mental disorder are said to be the result of people not being aware of all aspects of themselves, and so Gestalt therapy is designed around creating conditions that allow clients to become more self-aware and self-accepting, thus able to grow again. This often requires confrontation, with the therapist pushing the clients to acknowledge uncomfortable feelings or pointing out inconsistencies in what they say, with an emphasis on the importance of body language in revealing feelings that the client hasn't acknowledged.

Further Reading: Köhler, W. *Gestalt Psychology: An Introduction to New Topics in Modern Psychology.* New York: Liveright, 1992; Perls, F. S., and Wysong, J. *Gestalt Therapy Verbatim.* Highland, NY: Gestalt Journal Press, 1992.

GILLES DE LA TOURETTE'S SYNDROME   *See* TOURETTE SYNDROME

GINGKO BILOBA   Gingko Biloba (also spelled ginkgo) is the world's best-selling herbal dietary supplement, primarily because of the widespread claim that it will enhance MEMORY and ward off the effects of senile dementia. The supplement is an extract from the leaves of the plant that has been used in Asia for thousands of years to treat cardiovascular problems and lung complaints. Its use for these purposes is unsurprising, since gingko is known to act as a vasodilator, causing the dilation of blood vessels, especially capillaries and microcapillaries. This, along with its anticoagulant effect, could well make it useful for improving circulation, although very little well designed research exists to confirm this. Its claimed effects on memory and cognitive performance appear to follow logically enough: if blood flow to the brain areas involved in memory is improved, this could legitimately be expected to improve memory function.

Numerous studies have been undertaken to examine gingko's potential as a treatment for ALZHEIMER'S DISEASE, but results have been mixed, and some serious flaws limit the interpretability of the results. A 1997 study published in the *Journal of the American Medical Association*, for example, found a slight improvement in cognitive functioning and mood in Alzheimer's patients given daily doses of gingko. Only about 60 percent of the participants completed the study, however, which could distort the findings significantly. Furthermore, the effect observed was quite small, and this study and others like it have dealt only with improvement of functioning, not the exaggerated claims about delay of onset and prevention that are found in many locations on the Internet.

Given the data supporting a slight improvement in functioning in Alzheimer's patients, the marketers of herbal supplements have been quick to present gingko biloba as a useful memory aid for healthy younger adults as well. In studies on these effects, the results are less impressive. Paul Solomon and his colleagues recently conducted a trial in which 230 adults aged sixty or over received either gingko or a placebo three times daily for six weeks. The dose used was that recommended by the supplement manufacturer, and a six-week period was chosen because the same manufacturer promised results within four weeks. The results showed no difference between gingko and the placebo on fourteen different measures of cognitive function and memory. Furthermore, there was no difference found in the participants' own subjective self-report of memory improvement.

Although it may have a small effect on functioning in patients with senile dementia, the claim that gingko biloba will in any way enhance memory in healthy adults is simply not supported by evidence. More troubling are the possible side effects of gingko, especially in elderly patients who already take daily doses of aspirin or other anti-coagulants or have a prior history of high blood pressure or STROKE. The modest improvement in memory function may not be worth the slightly increased risk of cerebral bleeding or stroke.

Further Reading: Le Bars, P. L., Katz, M. M., Berman, N., Itil, T. M., Freedman, A. M., and Schatzberg, A. F. "A Placebo-Controlled, Double-Blind, Randomized Trial of an Extract of Ginkgo Biloba for Dementia." *Journal of the American Medical Association,* 278 (1997): 1327–1332; Solomon, P. R., Adams, F., Silver, A., Zimmer, J., and DeVeaux, R. "Ginkgo for Memory Enhancement: A Randomized Controlled Trial." *Journal of the American Medical Association,* 288 (2002): 835–840.

GRAY, JOHN (1951–)   John Gray, a best-selling pop-psychology author of the 1990s and onward, sold over 15 million copies of his first book, *Men Are from Mars, Women Are from Venus,* which he then followed up with additional books, most featuring Mars and Venus prominently in their titles, a Mars and Venus newspaper column, a Mars and Venus television talk show, a Mars and Venus board game, and even a Mars and Venus stage musical. He also has trained a large coterie of "MarsVenus Workshop Facilitators" at the MarsVenus Institute, who provide a sort of "name-brand" relationship counseling.

The basic premise underlying Gray's work is extremely simple: men and women are different from each other, so different that they might as well be from different planets. Resolving relationship difficulties, therefore, requires understanding and respecting those differences. These differences (according to Gray there are seven big ones), drawn in broad strokes, conveniently mirror current American cultural clichés about men and women. For example, men don't listen or share their feelings. Reflecting Robert Bly's *Iron John,* Gray says that men feel better by "going into their caves," and women try to change men rather than accepting them as they are.

A central theme of all Gray's books concerns male-female differences in sense of self. A man's sense of self "is defined through his ability to achieve results," whereas a woman defines herself through "her feelings and the quality of her relationships." Gray's materials present these somewhat caricatured gender roles as universal and as the key to resolving any male-female relationship troubles.

Gray has recently moved beyond psychological self-help into the next great frontier of the best-seller list: *The Mars and Venus Diet and Exercise Solution* was published in 2003. In keeping with his other work, the focus is once again on the idea that men and women are fundamentally different, this time in how diet and exercise affect their bodies and minds. Claims in this book range from the merely bizarre, like "men require more sex to experience healthy brain chemistry," to the irresponsible, "most people who take drugs like Prozac or children who are prescribed with [sic] drugs like Ritalin … are just nutritionally deficient," and "once the brain is fed the proper food through amino acid supplementation, the symptoms of mental illness immediately begin to disappear, sometimes in just days."

Despite his great financial success and his genius for self-promotion, his books have not been taken seriously by the psychological profession as a whole, for two primary reasons. Not only has Gray not engaged in any scientific research to support his claims, but also his assertions and advice about relationships frequently contradict actual research findings. This caveat also applies to his newer statements regarding nutrition, exercise, and brain chemistry.

His credentials are also suspect. The Ph.D. that appears after his name on the covers of all his materials was apparently obtained from Columbia Pacific University, a now-defunct, unaccredited California institution that granted degrees via correspondence. In 1999 the school was ordered to permanently cease operations in California, and a final appeal of this order was denied in 2001. The state suit that led to the order called the school "a phony operation" granting "totally worthless degrees." The order was accompanied by a requirement that former students receive a refund of their tuition.

The self-proclaimed "leading authority in communication and relationships," whose "teachings have helped to enrich the lives of countless men and women" (*marsvenus.com*), therefore remains a major force in American popular culture, yet wields very little influence among scientifically minded psychologists.

Further Reading: Barrett, S. "Court Orders Columbia Pacific University to Cease Operating Illegally in California." www.quackwatch.org, 2002; Gray, J. *Men Are from Mars, Women Are from Venus: A Practical Guide for Improving Communication and Getting What You Want in Your Relationships.* New York: HarperCollins, 1992.

H

HALLUCINOGENIC DRUGS *See* PSYCHEDELIC DRUGS

HAWTHORN EFFECT A nearly universal problem in research with human subjects is the impossibility, from both a practical and an ethical standpoint, of keeping research subjects unaware that they are participating in a research project. Unfortunately, the mere recognition that they are being observed can exert a profound influence on the behavior of research participants. Whereas the usual goal of observational research is to describe behavior as it occurs naturally, it is actually quite difficult to get people to "act naturally" when they know they are being observed. Also, recognition of various features of an experimental design, known as demand characteristics, can cause research participants to form hypotheses regarding what the experimenter is hoping to observe and to alter their behavior accordingly.

This phenomenon is widely known as the Hawthorn effect, named for an industrial-engineering study conducted in 1926 at Western Electric's Hawthorn works, a telephone assembly factory in the Chicago suburb of Cicero, Illinois. The researchers were investigating the effect of different levels of ambient light on worker productivity. The experiment was performed by reducing the amount of light in the factory over a period of several days. The unexpected result was that the women working in the factory continued to work at the same high level of productivity even when lighting was reduced to the point where they were assembling telephones in near-total darkness. Rather than conclude erroneously that lighting levels were completely irrelevant for productivity, the researchers realized that the women, knowing they were being closely watched but unaware of the research hypotheses, formed their own ideas about what was going on and worked extra hard to make a good impression, rather than acting naturally.

Whereas the Hawthorn effect applies primarily to the experimental group in a study, subjects for whom a condition is changed to observe the effects of the change, some observers have also identified a related effect that applies to the control group: the John Henry effect. Named for the folk hero who worked extra hard to show his superiority to the new steam-powered hammer, the John Henry effect is the tendency for persons in a control group to attempt to outperform the members of the experimental group to whom a treatment has been applied. This would of course invalidate the purpose of including the control group, and the need to avoid this effect is a major reason for the popularity of single- and double-blind experiments.

The Hawthorn study has achieved near-mythic status among both social scientists and industrial productivity consultants, to a point at which tracking down the true story is a bit challenging. Books and Web sites variously attribute the study to both General Electric and Western Electric, and the location is variously cited as Ohio, New York, Pennsylvania, and only occasionally Illinois. The Hawthorn effect is now frequently cited by so-called experts in business productivity as an example, not of research bias, but rather of the role of a caring management style in improving productivity. The explanation offered is usually that the study showed that when employees feel that management cares enough about them to watch them closely, they reward the positive attention by working harder.

Further Reading: Lehner, Philip N. *Handbook of Ethological Methods.* New York: Cambridge University Press, 1998.

HITE, SHERE   *See* KINSEY, ALFRED (1894–1956)

HOMEOPATHY Homeopathy, or homeopathic medicine, is an early nineteenth-century system of diagnosis and treatment that predates the modern germ theory of disease. At the time, medicine was still quite primitive, and it was largely based on the humoral theory of disease that dated back to Galen and Hippocrates. Many diseases were believed to be caused by "bad blood," for example, and were thus treated through the removal of some of the offending substance. Quite a few toxic substances were used as medicines as well; for instance, the use of mercury as a prescription for syphilis was responsible for at least some of the mental deterioration associated with the later stages of the disease. In that era a treatment approach that was guaranteed to do no harm was certain to prove popular, and so German physician Samuel Hahnemann (1755–1843) found a ready audience for homeopathy.

According to homeopathic theory, sometimes referred to as the Law of Similars, a physical or psychological symptom can be cured by administering an ingredient that causes that symptom in a healthy person. Hahnemann was apparently inspired in this by the use of quinine to treat malaria. It helps, but it also produces fevers in a healthy individual. In the world of homeopathy, "like cures like," and so treatment consists of identifying the person's symptoms, identifying an ingredient that would cause those symptoms, and administering that ingredient as a medicine. On the surface, this sounds absurd: treating a poisoned person by administering more poison, for example, could lead to the patient's immediate death, rather than a cure. Dr. Hahnemann believed, however, that a medicine's curative effect actually increases as the medicine becomes more dilute. In fact, most homeopathic remedies, by definition, are so dilute that they usually don't actually contain the active ingredient—many are diluted so far that they do not contain even a single molecule of the original substance. These are the medications that homeopaths often consider their most potent cures.

On the packaging of homeopathic remedies, the amount of dilution involved is indicated by a number followed by a multiplication sign (X). A 10X dilution (not uncommon) means the process starts with a 10:1 dilution in water: five ounces of water to a half-ounce of the active ingredient, for example. This is to be shaken thoroughly. Next 1/10 of solution is diluted 10:1 in water. Then 1/10 of *that* solution is diluted in 10 parts water. After following these steps eight more times, the result is a solution of 1 part in 10 million. Again, basic chemistry indicates that at those levels of dilution it is possible that not a single molecule of the original substance remains. This is not the only system of dilution used, however; some medications use a *C* (as in 5C, for example), to denote dilution steps of 100:1 rather than 10:1.

This is a classic example of PSEUDOSCIENCE because for these remedies to work, the currently well-established laws of chemistry would have to be completely wrong. Most homeopathic manuals don't bother to explain how this might work, though some propose that the water retains a "memory" of the substance that it once contained. The basic homeopathic claim is not that the original ingredient effects a cure, but rather that the "memory" of it in the water will somehow stimulate the body to heal itself. Not only do homeopaths not deny that their medications contain no active ingredients, but this is actually a central tenet of their theory. Unfortunately, many of the people who buy these remedies are unaware of the theory behind them, simply lumping in homeopathic remedies with herbal remedies and assuming that it's all the same thing.

There are many customers: homeopathic medicines are a $200 million a year industry in the United States alone, and they enjoy far greater popularity in India and in Great Britain and Germany, where state-funded health care plans will pay for them.

Given the unscientific basis of homeopathy, the reader may wonder why the FDA allows these remedies to be marketed. The answer is simple: the FDA has authority over the sale of drugs, but none over the sale of plain water or sugar pills. As long as the homeopathic "medicines" contain no actual medicine, the FDA is powerless, and the manufacturers can continue to claim that their products are completely safe and have no side effects; there are very few substances about which that statement may be made, but pure water is certainly one of them. Recent developments in supplement regulation have led to full disclosure on the labels of one category of homeopathic remedy, however: those in which the diluted ingredient is ephedra (or ma huang), the herbal stimulant that was banned for U.S. sales in the spring of 2004. It is now illegal to sell any preparation that contains ephedra, even highly diluted ephedra. A recent perusal of labels on a grocery-store shelf turned up a homeopathic anti-snoring spray in which the special substance was ephedra. On the back label, where the dilution information appeared, it was accompanied by a fine-print disclaimer noting that, due to dilution, this product contained no ephedra.

Further Reading: Carroll, R. T. *The Skeptic's Dictionary*. New York: Wiley, 2003; Gardner, Martin. *Fads and Fallacies in the Name of Science*. New York: Dover, 1957.

HORNEY, KAREN   *See* NEO-FREUDIANS

HOT READING   *See* COLD READING

HUBBARD, L. RON   *See* DIANETICS/SCIENTOLOGY

HUMANISTIC PSYCHOLOGY   Humanistic psychology, now also widely known as phenomenological psychology, is much more a therapeutic approach than a scientific theory. Phenomenological psychologists aren't interested in reaching general conclusions about humanity, preferring to work with each person as a unique individual whose problems require a unique approach. Rather than perceiving basic physical instincts as the primary motivating force in human behavior like psychoanalysts do, humanistic psychologists see humans as motivated by an innate drive toward growth, ultimately toward what Abraham Maslow called self-actualization; essentially, becoming the best "you" that you can be. Since each person interprets the world in his or her own unique way and therefore defines self-actualization differently, helping a person to achieve it will always be different.

Several other basic assumptions run through most humanistic/phenomenological psychology.

- Treatment is an encounter between equals, intended to help clients with their own natural growth. The therapist is *not* there as an expert to provide a cure.
- Under the right conditions, people will get better on their own. The therapist's job is to create those conditions.
- Ideal conditions require making the client feel accepted and welcomed as a human being without any judgment, no matter how undesirable or problematic the client's behavior may be. Carl Rogers, one of the best-known humanistic psychologists, called this *unconditional positive regard*.
- The therapist is not there to tell the client what to do. It is ultimately up to the client to decide how to think and behave. Rogers called this client-centered

therapy. It requires empathy, trying to develop an emotional understanding of what the client is thinking and feeling. Rogers advocated active listening—making eye contact, nodding, giving other signs of attentiveness—to accomplish this. It also often involves reflection, paraphrasing what the client has said in order to confirm what the client has said and to express interest in it.

Like psychoanalysis, humanistic therapy can be very time-consuming, and little evidence exists of its actually helping anyone with serious psychological problems, but it is an interesting tool of self-discovery for those with the time and money to devote to it.

Further Reading: Rogers, C. R. *On Becoming a Person: A Therapist's View of Psychotherapy*. New York: Houghton Mifflin (Mariner), 1972.

HYPNOSIS Phrases like "you are getting very sleepy" are central to the popular image of hypnosis as an altered state of consciousness, in which the subject falls into a sleeplike trance. The popular image also includes a charismatic hypnotist with a powerful yet soothing voice, who may make mysterious motions in the air while producing the trance. Some parts of this image certainly date back to late eighteenth-century Vienna, where physician Franz Anton Mesmer first discovered the hypnotic treatment of various ailments via mesmerism. His induction procedure was very elaborate, involving magnetized rods extending from tubs filled with iron filings, but the key element was his own physical touch. He believed that he possessed a high degree of what he called animal magnetism, which could influence the magnetic fluid that flows through all human beings. Upon receiving his touch after relaxing, his patients would fall into a trance, and upon coming out they would be cured. In modern hypnosis, the induction ritual is usually much simpler, involving staring at an object—a swinging pocket watch is in fact sometimes used—while receiving instructions to relax.

Under hypnosis, the subject will experience a loss of volition and become very willing to follow suggestions, along with becoming highly susceptible to hallucinations and delusions. While in the hypnotic state, a person may be able to remember things that were not remembered prior to hypnosis. MEMORY of what went on during the session may be gone afterwards as well, along with memories and physical urges that the subject wished to be rid of. After the hypnotic session, if the person has been given a post-hypnotic suggestion, he or she may still respond to the suggestion of the hypnotist.

The foregoing view of hypnosis is still widely accepted by the general public, but the academic and clinical communities have distanced themselves from it over the last several decades. Although some psychologists still refer to hypnosis as an altered state of consciousness, others view the hypnotic state as simply the enactment of a social role. This is often referred to as the state/non-state debate. The most popular state theory, which insists that hypnosis involves an altered state of consciousness, is Ernest Hilgard's "neodissociation" theory.

According to Hilgard, the mind contains multiple parts that are not all conscious at the same time, and which are ordinarily influenced by a centralized control structure. Under hypnosis, a dissociation, or split in consciousness, occurs in which subjects surrender to the hypnotist some of their usual control over voluntary actions, while gaining some control over normally involuntary processes, such as sensitivity to pain.

In a classic study intended to demonstrate dissociation, Hilgard had hypnotized subjects immerse one hand in ice water following a hypnotic suggestion that they would feel no pain. They were asked to press a key with the other hand if they felt any pain. Verbally, subjects typically reported almost no pain, but their key pressing indicated a substantial amount of pain. Hilgard explains that a "hidden observer" was reporting on the pain, while no pain was experienced by the part of the mind that had conscious awareness. Whether a hidden observer is involved or not, there is little question that hypnosis is sometimes useful in reducing pain, and it has been used successfully in surgery, amputations, and childbirth, as well as with chronic pain such as arthritis, nerve damage, migraines, and cancer. Some researchers have even claimed success with reduction of post-surgical bleeding.

Hilgard's state theory, however, is rapidly being eclipsed by a non-state view variously called role theory, the cognitive-behavioral view, or the sociocognitive view. According to non-state advocates, the view of hypnosis as an altered state is simply unnecessary and somewhat misleading. Role theory maintains that hypnotic phenomena can be explained in terms of compliance with social demands and acting in accordance with a special social role. The hypnotized person does behave differently from non-hypnotized people, but this is because he or she has agreed to act out an established role, with certain expectations and rules. The hypnotized person does feel less in control and becomes far more suggestible, but it is done voluntarily, as part of a social ritual. Furthermore, there is no evidence of any changes in neurophysiological responses during hypnosis, unlike what is seen in actual altered states of consciousness, such as sleep or the effects of psychedelic drugs. Indeed, in studies where some people are hypnotized and given suggestions and other, non-hypnotized people are asked to do the same things, a typical finding is that motivated but unhypnotized volunteers can duplicate most classic hypnotic effects, including such things as limb rigidity and pain insensitivity. Non-state theorists maintain that hypnotic behaviors and experiences represent no change in cognitive processes but merely reflect normal cognitive processes in a special social situation.

Within psychology, the myth about hypnosis most in need of debunking is certainly the idea that it is helpful in recovering lost memories. Sometimes, for example, age-regression is used to help people recover lost memories by having the hypnotized subject return to a childhood mentality and think and behave like a child. Such age-regression is often quite dramatic, with the adult subject adopting a childlike voice and demeanor and producing childlike drawings. On closer examination, however, the drawings typically resemble what adults expect a child's drawing to look like rather than actual children's drawings, and the adults tend to use that childlike voice to say things in a way that an actual child wouldn't. Furthermore, memories produced under hypnosis are less accurate than those produced by the same subjects without hypnosis; a key component of hypnosis is an increased susceptibility to suggestion and fantasy, thus making it an inappropriate tool for recovering accurate memories. Unfortunately, people who have recalled an incident under hypnosis tend to be more confident about that memory than about ordinary memories. This combination of factors has led to a huge scandal in the therapeutic world, involving a large number of criminal cases in which people have been accused of child sexual abuse solely on the basis of memories "recovered" under hypnosis (*see also* MEMORY).

Further Reading: Wagstaff, G. F. "Hypnosis." In Della Sala, S., ed. *Mind Myths: Exploring Popular Assumptions about the Brain and the Mind*. New York: Wiley, 1999.

IMPRINTING Immediately after hatching, if baby ducklings see a large object move past them, they will follow the object as though it were their mother, regardless of what the object actually is. It could be a duck, a cardboard box pulled by a string, or even, in the most famous case, Austrian zoologist and ethologist Konrad Lorenz (1903–1989). Lorenz discovered that ducklings come into the world with an instinctive drive to follow the first thing that passes by. When a large object or creature appears before them, it triggers this instinctive response, known as imprinting. Imprinting more generally occurs when an animal learns something very fast because a certain event occurring at the right time triggers the learning process.

Lorenz was the originator of the science of ethology, or the study of genetic sources of group and individual behavior patterns, for which he won a Nobel Prize in Physiology. Imprinting is a special case of a more general category of instinctive responses that he discovered, called innate release mechanisms. In his studies of fish and birds, he found that organisms are often genetically predisposed to be especially responsive to certain stimuli. The duck's tendency to follow any large moving object that happens by at the right moment is just one well-documented example of this. Another is the behavior of the male stickleback, a small fighting fish. A male stickleback will attack any other male stickleback that approaches his nest in a manner identical to the way every stickleback attacks. Furthermore, it will attack anything that resembles another male stickleback, even a paper model, as long as it displays the distinctive red spot that all male sticklebacks bear. In the case of both the ducks and the sticklebacks, the advantage of this mechanism to the animal is fairly clear. A complex behavior pattern occurs without any learning.

Further Reading: Lorenz, K. *The Foundations of Ethology*. New York: Springer-Verlag, 1981.

INSANITY DEFENSE Insanity is neither a medical term nor a psychiatric diagnosis; it has a specific meaning only in the legal arena. In U.S. courtrooms where a defendant may plead "not guilty by reason of insanity," or NGRI, insanity is defined as a state of mind in which the defendants were either not aware of the nature of what they were doing, or they did not know that the action was wrong. Technically this determination is referred to as Mental State at the time of the Offense, or MSO.

The definition of insanity given above is based on what is known as the M'Naughten rule, which derives its name from a case heard in England in 1843. M'Naughten, the defendant, suffered paranoid delusions, including a conspiracy against himself involving the prime minister. M'Naughten, believing himself to be acting in self-defense, went out with a gun to preemptively strike against the conspirators, but he accidentally shot the prime minister's secretary instead. This was the first case in history in which a plea of not guilty by reason of insanity was successfully used.

In the United States, only half of the states still follow the M'Naughten rule, and some have attached to it the idea of "irresistible impulse" as an additional condition of insanity. This clause is not often invoked, since even the best attorneys experience some difficulty explaining the subtle distinction between an impulse that was "irresistible" and one that was simply "unresisted."

The M'Naughten rule was supplanted in many jurisdictions in 1954 by the Durham rule, which was established by the District of Columbia Federal Court of Appeals. According to the Durham rule, the insanity defense can be used if the criminal act was a product of a mental disease or defect. Proving this turned out to be just as challenging as it sounds, and both the M'Naughten rule and the Durham rule were refined further by the 1972 Model Penal Code rule, now used by twenty U.S. states, which declares that "a person is not responsible for his conduct if at the time of such conduct, as a result of mental disease or defect, he lacks substantial capacity either to appreciate the criminality of his conduct or to conform his conduct to the requirements of the law." This differs from the M'Naughten rule in that the words "substantial capacity" and "appreciate" add an emotional, volitional side to the whole thing. A person can understand cognitively that an act is wrong and still be emotionally unable to appreciate its criminality.

The newest wrinkle in insanity defenses is the verdict of "guilty but mentally ill" (GBMI). About twelve states allow this verdict when an insanity plea has been entered. This means the defendant receives the same sentence that would accompany a guilty verdict, but time is served initially in a psychiatric hospital or similar setting. Post-treatment time is served in prison. It was a popular idea at first, but hasn't caught on very widely because juries find it very confusing to be asked to distinguish between mental illness that led to insanity and mental illness that didn't. The scarcity of GBMI verdicts may actually be a good thing, as research shows that offenders who succeed in getting a GBMI verdict only rarely receive adequate treatment and are often actually given harsher sentences than those who are simply found guilty. Some defendants have even received GBMI death sentences. Following treatment in a hospital setting, they have death row to look forward to.

Another legal issue that often involves psychologists is the determination of competency to stand trial. This is defined as the defendant's capacity to understand the criminal process and to consult with an attorney in preparation of a defense. Unlike an insanity defense, this involves present functioning rather than the mental state at the time of the offense. IQ tests play an important role in this process, because most courts will rule that a person with MENTAL RETARDATION at the moderate or more severe levels is incompetent to stand trial. For other types of incompetence, trials can be delayed while defendants undergo treatment. When they have recovered sufficiently to be found competent, the trial proceeds.

In recent years the insanity plea has become a controversial topic among politicians, who sometimes argue against it to appear tough on crime. Typically an emotional appeal is made to the voters based on the idea that the plea is being used too often, allowing murderers to walk the streets who should be in prison. Such appeals to the voters are often successful, and several states have now abolished the insanity defense. All too often missing in the political debate are statistics on the actual incidence of NGRI verdicts. Insanity is actually invoked as a complicating factor in fewer than 1 in 1,000 of all trials for violent crimes, and the NGRI plea is actually successful in less than one quarter of those. Also contrary to popular belief, recidivism rates among those found not guilty by reason of insanity are lower than among those actually convicted of similar crimes, suggesting that those defendants did receive the correct verdict.

Further Reading: Walker, L. E. A., and Shapiro, D. L. *Introduction to Forensic Psychology: Clinical and Social Psychological Perspectives*. New York: Plenum, 2003.

INTELLIGENCE   What is intelligence? That is hard to say. It seems to depend very much on who is asked. The subject has engaged thinkers for at least as long as people have been writing down their thoughts, and possibly for much longer. Intelligence-related terms are used all the time. If someone mentions a friend who is very smart, for example, the listener will surely have some general idea of what is meant. The concept of stupidity is equally intuitive. Coming to a real agreement on all the different things that entails, however, may prove much harder. Does being intelligent mean knowing a lot of facts? Does it mean being able to solve math problems quickly? Is fast reaction time important? Does a high score on an IQ insure survival for a week in the jungle with just a spear? Most introductory psychology textbooks attempt to provide a quick theoretical definition. Here's a favorite: intelligence is "the capacity to understand the world and the resourcefulness to cope with its challenges."

In psychological science it is very important to come up with an operational definition of a construct before studying it empirically. To operationally define something (or operationalize it) means to define it in a way that will allow its measurement. This principle has allowed psychologists to sidestep all the sticky philosophical arguments about the nature of intelligence by defining it thusly: intelligence is what intelligence tests measure. That is the definition most research on intelligence that actually involves measurement has used, at any rate. This introduces both an elegant simplicity and an infuriating circularity to the argument, however. Consider the next logical question: what do intelligence tests measure? Intelligence, of course. What's intelligence again? And so on.

Clearly, a better answer is needed to the question: What do intelligence tests *really* measure? Answering it may first require a digression about psychological tests and how they work. A basic definition: a psychological test is an objective, standardized measure of a sample of behavior. Each portion of that definition is important, if intelligence tests are to be properly understood.

First, the term *standardized*: a standardized measure is a procedure that is carried out in exactly the same way every time somebody takes the test. This means that the instructions given must be the same, and all other test conditions such as time limit and type of location, as well as such subtleties as ambient temperature and lighting, should be kept constant to whatever extent that it is possible.

To say that it is *objective* means that scoring is just as standardized as the rest of the test conditions. Personal opinions and feelings of the person scoring the test must not be allowed to influence the score that is given. This means that the manual for administering the test has to be very specific about which answers are correct and which are not, so no personal judgment is involved.

The third part of the definition is probably the most important, and the most frequently forgotten: a test score is simply a *sample* of behavior. It is not a measure, in other words, of the person's overall ability in all things, but rather it is just a measure of how that person was able to perform on a particular occasion, at a particular place and time. Anyone who has ever taken an exam with insufficient sleep or under really noisy conditions is aware that a test may not always give a true measure of a person's ability.

Given this definition, it seems as though a psychological test should be easy to devise; people try all the time. A few things separate the Wechsler Intelligence Scale for Children, Fourth Edition (WISC-IV), from the *Cosmopolitan* magazine's "What kind of lover are you?" quiz, however. In addition to the criteria described above, to qualify as a good psychological test, an assessment instrument needs to establish reliability, validity, and adequate norms.

Test reliability actually means much the same thing as it does with people—consistency or dependability. If a person takes a test today that shows them to be well adjusted and normal, and the same test a week later reveals that person to be a likely serial killer, there is a reliability problem. Test-retest reliability is the most common measure, and it is just what it sounds like. It's the mathematical CORRELATION between the results of a test taken by a group of subjects at two different times. If a strong positive relationship exists between the two sets of scores, that means that people tended to do about the same both times, and therefore the test is reliable. Sometimes reliability is established using alternate forms instead: two different but equivalent versions of a test are constructed, and subjects then take both tests. If they perform about the same on both, the test is reliable. This one is actually fairly challenging to use, since it requires designing two versions of a test that really are just like each other. One other kind of reliability measure is widely used: split-half reliability. This is measured by dividing a test in half after people take it and comparing the score on the first half of the items to the score on the second half. This one is also very tricky to use, and it is only useful with tests that are only trying to measure one thing, otherwise there would be many different and non-equivalent ways to split the test into two sets of items.

Another important gauge of a test's usefulness is validity. This is often defined as the extent to which a test measures what it claims to measure. A slightly more complex, yet far more precise definition comes from the *Standards for Educational and Psychological Testing* (a joint venture of the AMERICAN PSYCHOLOGICAL ASSOCIATION, the American Educational Research Association, and the National Council on Measurement in Education): "A test is valid to the extent that inferences made from it are appropriate, meaningful, and useful." This definition is important because the primary purpose of psychological tests, especially intelligence tests, is to make inferences about people.

Several different kinds of validity are important for intelligence tests. Predictive validity refers to the extent to which a test can predict future behaviors. This is measured by examining the correlation between the test and a future criterion; for example, SAT scores are used to predict college grade point averages. This is also sometimes called criterion-related validity, and the criterion used is often the score on another test of the same construct. A new IQ test, for example, will not be taken it seriously if it is not shown that performance on the new test correlates highly with performance on a better-established test, like the WISC or Stanford-Binet. Content validity is the extent to which a test adequately samples the behaviors being measured. Consider a math class in which multiplication and long division have been the primary focus. Would a cumulative final exam that only covers subtraction be a valid measure of whether students have learned the material?

Finally, construct validity refers to the extent to which scores on the test actually represent the desired theoretical construct. A construct is just a broad, vague psychological concept, such as leadership ability or intelligence; generally speaking, something too complex to really be measured by a single number. Construct validity can be established in a variety of ways, including research to determine whether intervention effects or developmental changes have effects on test scores that are consistent with theory. For example, if there is a new measure of depression and a group of depressed people takes the test both before and after a treatment that is already well established as effective, then depression scores on the test had better go down. If the scores don't, it clearly isn't measuring what it was meant to measure. Similarly, every major IQ test has a vocabulary subtest. If the same test is given to a group of second-graders and a group of sixth-graders, the older children should certainly get higher scores. If they do not, clearly something other than vocabulary is being measured.

Now, assume a person has just taken a new intelligence test, and the score is a 50. What does that mean? Until further information about the test is available, it means nothing at all. The only way to know what a 50 means is to give the test to a whole lot of people and make up a frequency distribution to see how most people do. If the mean (average) on the test is a 30, the person who scored 50 did extremely well. If the mean is a 70, that person has done rather poorly. The results from giving the test to a lot of people to give meaning to scores are called norms. Based on norms, the average score on both of the major intelligence tests for children is 100, and all other scores are judged accordingly.

Intelligence tests have been around for about a century. Alfred Binet (1857–1911) created the first modern intelligence test in 1905, along with Herbert Simon. His reason for doing so is important to know: the Paris school system wanted to identify students who required remedial classes. At the time, special education (indeed, the idea of MENTAL RETARDATION itself) was very new, and France was far more proactive in seeking to help these children than the United States was during the same period. As French law came to require that children in need of special help should receive it, it became clear that an objective way of identifying those children was necessary (more objective, at least, than asking teachers to select the children and remove them to a different classroom). To put it more crudely, the test was designed to identify people of low intelligence, not to identify people of normal or high intelligence.

By 1916, however, there was an American version, the Stanford-Binet, written by Lewis Terman. From the original version to the present, the test has always yielded a single score, which is considered a measure of what is sometimes called g, or general intelligence. This is the famous IQ, and it stands for intelligence quotient. It used to really be a quotient: mental age over chronological age. For example, a five-year-old child with a mental age of five would have an IQ of 5/5, or 1. A five year old with a mental age of three would have an IQ of 3/5, or .6. To remove those pesky decimals and make the numbers easier to deal with, it became standard practice to multiply the result times 100, so the two foregoing examples would have IQs of 100 and 60, respectively. The Stanford-Binet no longer estimates mental age, but the term IQ is still widely used, despite being highly inaccurate. Also, the modern test produces more than just one score.

The Stanford-Binet test is now in its fifth edition, and it follows a fairly complicated model of intelligence. The test is structured to measure five separate factors of intelligence in both verbal and nonverbal domains, making for a total of ten subtests. The five factors are: fluid reasoning, knowledge, quantitative reasoning, visual-spatial processing, and working memory. In addition to ten subtest scores, therefore, the test provides five factor scores and the familiar Full Scale IQ, as well as separate verbal and nonverbal IQ scores. Whereas the original test was intended for children, the current Stanford-Binet is normed on a sample ranging from two-year-old children all the way up to eighty-five-year-old adults.

The Stanford-Binet is the modern descendant of the original test, but the most frequently given of all psychological tests is its chief rival, the WAIS-III (Wechsler Adult Intelligence Scales, Third Edition). The WAIS originated in David Wechsler's belief that the Stanford-Binet, having been designed for children, was not the best test for adults. Wechsler was working with adult psychiatric patients at Bellevue hospital, and he quickly realized that the scoring system for the Binet test (and the early Stanford-Binet) simply made no sense with an adult population. While it may make sense to say that a seven-year-old has a mental age of five, for example, it would be meaningless to say that a thirty-eight-year-old patient has a mental age of only thirty-five. Wechsler therefore published his own test in 1939, designed for adults and scored using what he called a deviation IQ rather than a calculated mental/chronological ratio.

Scores were compared to a set of norms for the person's age, and the score was assigned according to where that person stood in comparison to other adults his or her own age. The WAIS is normed on a sample ranging in age from sixteen to eighty-nine. It's appropriate for ages sixteen through seventy-two. Its eleven subtests are organized into two scales, verbal and performance. When it is scored, it produces, in addition to a full-scale IQ, a verbal IQ and a performance IQ.

Following the success of the WAIS, Wechsler designed his own child tests as well, producing the WISC (Wechsler Intelligence Scales for Children, now in its fourth edition) and the WPPSI (Wechsler Preschool and Primary Scales of Intelligence, now revised and known as WPPSI-R). The WISC-IV is meant for ages six to sixteen, and the WPPSI covers the age range from three to seven years. Both the WISC-IV and WPPSI-R are very similar structurally to the WAIS, with a few differences among the subtests to reflect the ability differences between the age groups; and they produce the same pattern of IQ scores: full scale, verbal, and performance.

In addition to the Stanford-Binet and Wechsler tests, there are many others, but they are used a small fraction of the number of times that those two are used each year. Some fairly solid intelligence tests assess infants, the best of which is probably the Bayley Scales of Infant Development-II. The Bayley can be used with extremely young children, with norm tables that begin with the age of one month and range up to forty-two months. It is an ingenious test that mostly consists of engaging the child in age-appropriate play and carefully observing the child for a wide range of developmental milestones. IQ is actually quite unstable in the first few years of life, and although high scores on the Bayley are no guarantee of anything, unusually low scores can accurately predict later test scores or school performance; for instance, the test does an excellent job of detecting children who will test in the mentally retarded range of IQ scores later in life.

Although these tests are all clearly based in a particular theoretical notion of intelligence involving multiple factors, they still primarily serve to produce a single number, usually still called IQ, that is intended to provide a global measure of general ability. In this way they largely fail, at least in how the scores are used, to reflect the wide diversity of opinions visible in the work of various intelligence theorists over the years. They do, however, reflect the views of one influential thinker, Charles Spearman, who proposed that intelligence consisted largely of a single underlying general ability that he called g. Beyond Spearman's influential view lie many other points of view.

The very first attempts to measure intelligence, predating Binet, come from the late nineteenth century, a period sometimes called the Brass Instruments era of psychology, named for the serious machine-shop skills necessary among psychologists who had to build all their own apparatus rather than purchase products that didn't exist yet. The period was also when Sir Francis GALTON and his American disciple, James McKeen Cattell, believed intelligence required keen sensory abilities and a fast reaction time, and they sought to measure intelligence indirectly by taking various physical measurements, especially reaction time.

This sensory keenness approach to intelligence largely died out around the time that Binet published his first test, but it still has some modern adherents such as Arthur Jensen, who uses a device called the Reaction-Time/Movement-Time (RT-MT) apparatus in his attempts at culture-reduced study of intelligence. The device consists of a set of small buttons with lights next to them, arrayed in a fan shape on a console, with a single button at the base of the fan. The subject rests a hand on the button at the bottom and waits. When a light comes on, the subject moves that hand to strike the button adjacent to the light as rapidly as possible. The device measures both reaction time (how long the subject takes to remove the hand from the first button) and movement time (the interval between taking the hand off the first button and pressing the second one). Jensen claims fairly high correlations between these measurements and traditional measures of intelligence, but this technique has not caught on widely.

Raymond Cattell produced an influential intelligence theory in the 1940s by proposing that, rather than a single g factor, there are two major kinds of intelligence, which he called fluid and crystallized intelligence. Fluid intelligence is nonverbal and fairly immune to cultural bias, consisting primarily of a person's inherent capacity to learn and solve problems. This is the kind of intelligence required when a task calls for adaptation to a new situation. Crystallized intelligence consists of what a person has learned, and thus consists of knowledge rather than problem-solving skills (though fluid intelligence is required to increase crystallized intelligence). Much of the research inspired by Cattell's theory is concerned with the alleged decline of intelligence in old age. A large number of studies suggest that, while fluid intelligence may decline with age, crystallized intelligence does not.

The Russian psychologist A. R. Luria proposed a very different theory that also relied on the concept of two different kinds of mental processing. Based on his studies of brain-injured soldiers, he decided there were two different kinds of mental activity reflected in intelligence tests: simultaneous and successive processing. Simultaneous processing is what occurs when a task requires the execution of several different mental operations at the same time. Spatial tasks are a good example. When drawing, a person has to grasp the overall shape of what is being drawn, while also drawing its components individually. Successive processing, in which only one mental operation is carried out at a time, makes sense for solving math problems, but would be a disaster as an approach to drawing even a simple shape like a triangle. The person would have to draw lines of predetermined specific lengths, at certain angles to each other, and simply hope that they lined up.

Some theories have been somewhat more complicated, however. In the 1930s, Thurstone proposed a set of seven primary mental abilities (PMAs), and Guilford in the late 1960s proposed his structure-of-intellect model, which could have as many as 150 distinct factors. Theories proposing multiple types of intelligence to replace the single general-factor approach have enjoyed a renaissance of sorts in recent years with Robert Sternberg's triarchic model of intelligence. The triarchic model proposes the existence of three independent kinds of intelligence: analytical, creative, and practical. Analytical intelligence is the stuff tested by standard IQ tests that present clearly defined problems with a single acceptable "right" answer. Creative intelligence concerns whether a person reacts adaptively in novel situations and generates new ideas. Sternberg has criticized the standard tests for completely failing to test this at all. Practical intelligence, the other area neglected by the usual tests, is the intelligence used in dealing with everyday problems, which often have no single right answer; but rather a multitude of possible solutions, some better than others.

In 1983 Howard GARDNER decided to outdo Sternberg by increasing the number of kinds of intelligence further in his theory of multiple intelligences. According to Gardner, there are at least seven relatively independent kinds of human intelligence: linguistic, logical-mathematical, spatial, musical, bodily kinesthetic, interpersonal, and intrapersonal. He further states that the number has not been definitively established, and there may be more. He has recently proposed several additional candidates: naturalistic, spiritual, and existential intelligence. While these have so far proved very difficult to measure, Gardner's ideas have proven quite popular with educators, because they represent an escape from reliance on single test scores that may fail to value some of the very real skills and aptitudes that distinguish one human being from another (*see also* BRAIN).

Further Reading: Fancher, R. E. *The Intelligence Men: Makers of the IQ Controversy.* New York: W. W. Norton, 1985.

INTELLIGENCE TESTS   *See* INTELLIGENCE

J

JAMES, WILLIAM (1842–1910)   Born into a wealthy family of intellectual giants (the novelist Henry James was his brother) and educated both in Europe and at Harvard, William James is regarded as the founding father of American psychology. He introduced experimental psychology to America in a laboratory founded at about the same time as Wilhelm Wundt's, and was the first professor of psychology in the United States. He began teaching the subject in 1875, having no educational background in psychology himself, since no such courses were available in America until he started teaching them. He famously joked, "The first lecture in psychology that I ever heard was the first I ever gave."

From these humble beginnings, the field grew rapidly, and by 1895, more than twenty American universities were teaching psychology, the AMERICAN PSYCHOLOGICAL ASSOCIATION had been founded, and at least three academic journals were being published. A large measure of the credit for this rapid growth belongs to William James. Because the field barely existed before his work, his influence has been profound. He published dozens of articles, and the first crop of American psychologists studied under him; but his greatest and most influential achievement was undoubtedly the publication of *Principles of Psychology* (1890), a 1,400-page, two-volume compendium of the sum total of psychological knowledge of the time, infused throughout with wit, humor, and intellectual rigor. The book has been widely credited with transforming the dry, sterile, esoteric laboratory discipline of psychology into a vibrant, widely discussed, practical subject that is highly regarded outside the narrow hallways of academia. The book was originally intended as a textbook, a use that its length rendered impractical, so James went to work on an abridged textbook version, which appeared within two years. In U.S. academic circles, the unabridged version was usually referred to as "James," while the shorter edition went by "Jimmy."

Like Wundt and other structuralists, James used introspection to study consciousness, but he disagreed with their theoretical approach. Rather than attempting to break down the conscious experience into its component parts, James emphasized the unitary, unbroken flow of conscious thought, likening it to a stream and pointing out that it is a continuous process rather than a thing to be measured. James also emphasized the function of consciousness rather than its structure; adopting a Darwinian perspective, he argued that consciousness, like all other human traits, must have evolved to serve a particular function. The mind's complex processes, in other words, exist because of their adaptive value in ensuring survival, both of the individual and the species. For this reason, the label usually applied to Jamesian psychology is functionalism.

Further Reading: James, William. *Principles of Psychology.* New York: Henry Holt, 1890.

JOHN HENRY EFFECT   *See* HAWTHORN EFFECT

JOHNSON, VIRGINIA E.   *See* MASTERS, WILLIAM H. (1915–), AND JOHNSON, VIRGINIA E. (1925–)

JUNG, CARL GUSTAF (1875–1961)   One of Sigmund FREUD's early disciples, Carl Jung, accompanied him on his historic first visit to the United States in 1908 and was the first president of the International Psychoanalytic Society. Like many of Freud's followers, however, Jung eventually came to disagree with and criticize certain portions of psychoanalytic theory, in response to which Freud cut off all communication with him. Following his break with psychoanalysis, Jung developed his own theoretical and therapeutic approach, which he called analytic psychology.

A central disagreement between Freud and Jung involved Freud's emphasis on the role of early childhood trauma on the development of later neuroses, which Jung instead saw as manifestations of current maladjustment. Jung also

Carl Jung. © Bettmann/CORBIS.

was strongly critical of Freud's emphasis on sexuality both as a source of neuroses and as the primary source of unconscious drives and instinctive behavior. Like such other psychoanalysts as Karen Horney and Alfred Adler (*see* NEO-FREUDIANS), Jung believed nonsexual problems played a far greater role in maladjustment.

Jung also broke with Freud on the nature of the unconscious mind. Jung felt that, in addition to the individual unconscious, all humans possess a collective unconscious, containing symbols and images shared by all. These symbols and images, known as archetypes, emerge as common elements in dreams and myths, such as mother as a symbol of nurturance, or creation stories that include a great flood; and their presence in the collective unconscious explains why so many myths and stories appear repeatedly, with minor variations, in widely separated areas of the world.

Like Freud, Jung believed that conflict between the unconscious and conscious minds was the source of adult personality and neurosis, but he focused on a different sort of conflict, one between complementary opposite tendencies in personality such as introversion and extraversion. He also saw tension arising between sensing and intuiting, as well as between feeling and thinking. Jung believed that exaggeration of any of these tendencies in the conscious mind would be met by an increase in its opposite in the unconscious mind. Achieving psychological health requires their creative synthesis and reconciliation; therefore, Jungian analytic therapy focuses on exploration and discovery of the unconscious, as psychoanalysis also does.

Also like Freud, Jung has had a large impact on literary criticism and popular culture, but has experienced a steadily diminishing reputation within the field of psychology, for very similar reasons: his ideas, while interesting, are not especially scientific, because they are largely untestable. His impact on the study of world mythologies has been large, especially via the work of Joseph Campbell, author of many books on the cultural and psychological significance of mythology and folktales, but psychologists tend to be wary of some of his more outlandish notions, such as the concept of synchronicity, a vaguely defined "connecting principle" through which coincidences are meaningful and all events are ultimately related in more than a casual way. Most psychologists will respond to that last sentence in the same way as most readers: they will be unsure they've understood it, and they'll see no way to prove it wrong, and therefore no way to prove it right either.

Further Reading: Campbell, J., ed. *The Portable Jung.* New York: Viking, 1981.

K

KAVA Kava (*Piper methysticum*) or kavakava is a flowering shrub related to the common black pepper plant, indigenous to Polynesia, the Sandwich Islands, and various other island groups in the South Pacific and Indian Oceans. Its root has been used by island natives for thousands of years to prepare an intoxicating tea used before important religious ceremonies. Traditional preparation involves chewing the root and then spitting it out into a bowl fashioned from a coconut half, where it is combined with water. The resulting infusion acts as a mild stimulant, but also has a soporific and narcotic effect. This results in the user feeling both mild euphoria and tranquility. The muscles relax, but the user remains alert and fully in control. The plant resin is also sometimes used as a local anesthetic and in the treatment of urinary-tract infections and gonorrhea.

Kava became popular among herbal medicine enthusiasts in the United States and Europe in the 1990s as an alternative to prescription anti-anxiety medications and tranquilizers. Multiple clinical trials appeared to support kava's superiority to a placebo in reducing anxiety and promoting relaxation, and it became widely available in drugstores and supermarkets. By 2002, however, some troubling cases of liver damage, including hepatitis, cirrhosis, and total liver failure, led previously silent regulatory agencies, including the FDA, to warn that there may be some risks associated with its use, especially for people who already have liver problems or are taking drugs that can affect the liver. The action was prompted by over twenty-five adverse event reports in various countries, including at least five cases in which liver transplantation was necessary. Though such problems are rare, they are severe enough that some countries, including the United Kingdom, have ended the sale of kava products. Kava remains widely available in the United States (*see also* GINGKO BILOBA).

Further Reading: FDA/CFSAN. "Consumer Advisory: Kava-containing Food Supplements May Be Associated with Severe Liver Injury." http://vm.cfsan.fda.gov/~dms/addskava.html, 2002.

KINSEY, ALFRED (1894–1956) In one of the more bizarre mid-career shifts in scientific history, an entomologist previously known for his decades-long study of the little-known gall wasp became, in 1948, the man who changed how America looked at sexuality. A number of observers have gone so far as to divide sex in America into two eras: Before Kinsey and After Kinsey. The book that created the furor, *Sexual Behavior in the Human Male*, was published on April 5, 1948, and had within a few a months sold over 200,000 hardcover copies in the United States alone. Five years later, women got their turn, when *Sexual Behavior in the Human Female* was published. The sensational reception was largely due to novelty. Kinsey wrote about previously taboo subjects with the same dry scientific detachment he applied to his research on insect taxonomy, and so people who would ordinarily be wary of purchasing, much less publicly reading, a big book about sex, could simply tell others and themselves that this one, since it was scientific, was different.

Kinsey's results were startling to many readers, revealing that Americans were more sexually active, and engaged in a wider variety of sexual practices, than anyone had previously acknowledged. Furthermore, people were regularly breaking a range of both taboos and laws in the process. Some of Kinsey's most enduring and surprising findings concern the prevalence of homosexuality, previously assumed to be rare by most writers on the subject. In addition to reporting that over one-third of the men surveyed had had at least one homosexual experience between early adolescence and old age, the Kinsey team claimed that 10 percent of the male population is exclusively homosexual, a figure still widely quoted by activists today; more recent surveys conducted with larger, more-representative samples, put the figure at about 3 percent.

Kinsey also reported that marital infidelity was more widespread than most readers had believed and that it followed different patterns depending on socioeconomic status. Blue-collar men tended to stray widely in the early years of marriage before settling down and being faithful to their wives, whereas the white-collar executives tended toward monogamy early on with extramarital affairs coming later in the marriage. Despite its generally taboo status, masturbation was also far more common than generally reported.

A proper understanding of Kinsey's work requires careful examination of his methodology. Both Kinsey reports were based entirely on self-report data, with all the usual problems attendant on that method (people do not always tell the truth, for example). Over a decade of research, Kinsey and his assistants interviewed approximately 12,000 men and women. The questionnaire they used had more than 200 items, all concerning the individual's sexual history.

To encourage people to feel comfortable talking about such personal information, the interviewers were trained to appear completely indifferent to what they were told, no matter what was said, an approach that might have actually seemed strange to some of the interview subjects.

To the general public, Kinsey's presentation of his data as scientific was convincing, as both books' ready acceptance and incorporation into popular culture amply demonstrate. It helped that the research had been funded by the prestigious and extremely well known Rockefeller Foundation. Within the scientific community, however, Kinsey's findings were greeted in some quarters with a fair amount of skepticism right from the start. Beyond the basic problem of self-report data, a larger problem concerns the representativeness of the sample. Although Kinsey presented his data as broadly representative of the American male population, a substantial chunk of his sample consisted of prisoners and sex offenders, a fact widely criticized by scientists at the time. Like many scientists, Kinsey simply worked with a population that was cooperative and easy to find.

Kinsey's results may also have been biased by the wording of the interview questions. Rather than asking whether a person had ever engaged in a particular activity, the interviewer would ask when it had last occurred. "Never" was therefore not an acceptable reply. Also, when the time came to conduct the interviews for his book on women, his interviewers encountered more difficulty in getting women to talk to them than they had encountered with the men, which led to the loosening of some of the demographic categories used to distinguish the subjects. The "married" portion of the sample included all women who had lived with a man for more than a year, for example, as well as numerous prostitutes.

A more serious problem, which has been unaccountably overlooked by most of his readers over the decades, concerns his inclusion of data on sexual arousal in children, and his odd indifference to the moral questions raised by this part of his research. The chapter called "Early Sexual Growth and Activity," includes charts for which "trained persons" measured occurrences of "orgasm" in children as young as two months old. This appears to have required including pedophiles among his research subjects and ignoring both the legal and moral issues associated with their admissions. Indeed, a recent biography reveals that most of the data on preadolescent sexuality came from interviews with a single man who acknowledged having molested hundreds of children, and who had kept thorough notes on his activities. Far from being appalled, Kinsey seems to have regarded "Mr. Green," as he refers to him in his notes, as a bit of a scientific pioneer. In 1998 the British newspaper *The Telegraph* revealed the identity of Mr. Green after examining his diaries, used by Kinsey as research data. According to the diaries, he had molested over 800 children. A 1998 British documentary followed the story further, revealing that Kinsey was engaged in regular correspondence with a German pedophile during his trial for the rape and murder of a child.

Although there are clearly major problems with the data reported by Kinsey, it is undeniable that he single-handedly inspired the modern field of sexological research. Some influential major players in the field since Kinsey have followed in his footsteps with survey and interview research. One of the most widely read authors among them is Shere Hite, who wrote a series, the *Hite Reports on Sexuality*, which sold millions of copies. For one of her best-selling books, *Women and Love*, she mailed out 100,000 surveys to a highly non-random sample of members of women's organizations. Of these, she only got a return rate of 4.5 percent. The women who took the time to respond to the complex multi-page survey seemed to be angry and unhappy, which didn't stop *Time* magazine from turning her findings into a cover story reporting that 70 percent of women married five or more years were having extramarital affairs, and that an overwhelming 95 percent of women felt emotionally harassed by the men they loved. As with Kinsey's work, there was widespread criticism in the scientific community, but the general public and mainstream media have eagerly consumed Hite's research.

Some researchers, however, have set out to attempt a more scientific approach to sexual research, complete with laboratory observation and experimentation. The most famous of these researchers are William Masters and Virginia Johnson (*see* MASTERS, WILLIAM H., AND JOHNSON, VIRGINIA E.). Rather than content themselves with accepting self-reports at face value, they designed a variety of laboratory devices and techniques to allow them to measure all aspects of the human sexual response in over 700 subjects whom they observed in the laboratory. Like Kinsey's work, however, their research raises questions about representation and generalization, as their observations are based on people who are willing to perform sex acts in front of strangers in a laboratory while connected to a variety of monitoring devices.

Further Reading: Hite, Shere. *Women and Love*. New York: St. Martin's, 1989; Jones, James. *Alfred C. Kinsey: A Public/Private Life*. New York: W. W. Norton, 1997.

L

LEARNING DISABILITY The most widely accepted definition of a learning disability in the United States has for decades been based on language that appears in federal law. It first appeared in 1975 when Congress passed Public Law 94-142, the EDUCATION FOR ALL HANDICAPPED CHILDREN ACT. To require a free public education for children with learning disabilities, the law had to define them first, which it did in this way:

> The term "specific learning disability" means a disorder in one or more of the basic psychological processes involved in understanding or in using language, spoken or written, which may manifest itself in imperfect ability to listen, speak, read, write, spell, or to do mathematical calculations. . . . The term does not include children who have learning disabilities, which are primarily the result of visual, hearing, or motor handicaps, of mental retardation, or emotional disturbance, or of environmental, cultural, or economic disadvantage. (U.S. Department of Education, 1977, p. 65, 083)

The definition was refined further in the 1990 revision of the law, the Individuals with Disabilities Education Act (IDEA). IDEA clarifies and codifies an additional element of the definition: to be diagnosed with a learning disability, a student must demonstrate a severe discrepancy between general ability (usually defined as INTELLIGENCE) and specific achievement in one or more of seven academic areas: oral expression, listening comprehension, written expression, basic reading skill, reading comprehension, mathematics calculation, or mathematics reasoning.

The discrepancy requirement has resulted in a mandate for how children are to be tested for a learning disability. The assessment battery always includes a standard individual intelligence test, such as the WISC-III, and an individual achievement test. The individual achievement test is given one-on-one, unlike the usual school-based standardized achievement test administered in a group setting. This allows for much more diagnostic information to be collected regarding the kinds of errors being made, rather than simply knowing which items were wrong. A severe discrepancy is defined statistically as a difference of one standard deviation or more between the two scores, which in practice means a difference between the two scores of at least 15 points. What this means is that a child with a learning disability is performing at a lower level than would be expected based on his or her general intellectual ability.

This is not a rare problem. Between 4 and 5 percent of all U.S. schoolchildren are diagnosed with a learning disability. Boys are more likely to be diagnosed with learning disabilities than girls, by a ratio of about three to two.

Most learning disabilities belong to one of two broad categories: verbal or nonverbal. People with verbal learning disabilities, unsurprisingly, have difficulty with words. The most common form of verbal learning disability is dyslexia, which results in trouble recognizing or processing letters and the sounds they make. This causes people with dyslexia to have a great deal of difficulty with tasks that involve reading and writing. A common myth about dyslexia is that it causes people to reverse letters and numbers or to see them backwards, but those reversals are actually a normal part of language development, and are just as common in children without dyslexia. Though there are numerous forms of dyslexia, most people with dyslexia have special trouble recognizing phonemes (basic speech sounds) in print; for example, making the connection between the "ch" sound and the letter pair that produces it. Dyslexia used to be blamed on everything from laziness to innate stupidity to poor vision, but it is now fairly widely acknowledged to be a neurological problem with a probable genetic cause, as it clearly runs in families. This is supported by PET scan studies (*see* BRAIN IMAGING TECHNIQUES) that have shown that different parts of the brain are active when people with dyslexia read compared to people without dyslexia.

Dyslexia is not the only kind of verbal learning disability. Whereas dyslexia is a disorder that primarily affects ability to read, dysgraphia refers to learning disabilities that primarily affect writing ability. Like dyslexia, dysgraphia is now widely acknowledged to be a neurological disorder with a probable genetic component.

The nonverbal learning disabilities include all school problems fitting the federal definition that do not primarily involve verbal skills. Within that category, mathematical learning disabilities are often referred to as dyscalcula. Dyscalcula involves problems with learning fundamentals of math and one or more of the basic numerical skills. This may involve a variety of neurological underpinnings because mathematical skills depend on both the obvious (accurate visual processing and motor skills) and the not so obvious (memory, language comprehension, planning skills). Dyscalcula is often first diagnosed when a teacher notices the child transposing numbers, forgetting simple shape names, or apparently failing to understand simple spoken instructions. Although it doesn't fit the definition of a specific learning disability, as it doesn't impact a particular skill area, ATTENTION-DEFICIT/HYPERACTIVITY DISORDER (ADHD) is also frequently categorized by state laws as a learning disability.

The federal definition of a learning disability is now widely perceived among educational and psychological professionals as a failure, and other approaches are becoming increasingly popular. The main reason for this disenchantment with the discrepancy definition is the simple observation that great numbers of children who exhibit serious learning difficulties in school and who would certainly benefit from the services offered to those with learning disabilities cannot meet the discrepancy criterion. This occurs because a learning disability can easily have an adverse effect on both the achievement measures and the intelligence tests to which they are to be compared. Consider children with a nonverbal learning disability. There is no reason to expect that such children would consistently perform well on the nonverbal portions of the IQ test, yet if they perform poorly both on those and on the nonverbal measures of the achievement test, they will be judged not to have a learning disability by virtue of having performed poorly on both.

As a result of dissatisfaction with the federal definition, many psychologists and educators have begun to promote a new definition. It is the result of meetings by the National Joint Committee on Learning Disabilities (NJCLD), made up of representatives from eight national organizations interested in learning disabilities. The new definition is similar to the federal definition, but it differs in several important ways: it removes the severe discrepancy requirement, it acknowledges that a person may have a learning disability and other handicapping conditions, and it specifies that learning disabilities may continue into adulthood.

Further Reading: National Joint Committee on Learning Disabilities. "A Position Paper of the National Trust Committee on Learning Disabilities." *Journal of Learning Disabilities,* 21 (1988): 53–55; U. S. Department of Education. "Definition and Criteria for Defining Students as Learning Disabled." *Federal Register,* 42(250) (1977): 65083.

LEUCOTOMY   *See* PREFRONTAL LOBOTOMY

LINGUISTIC RELATIVITY   *See* SAPIR-WHORF HYPOTHESIS

LORENZ, KONRAD   *See* IMPRINTING

M

MAD COW DISEASE In the 1990s beef from the United Kingdom and several other countries was banned worldwide because of fears of bovine spongiform encephalopathy (BSE), a contagious progressive neurological disorder of cattle that is part of a group of diseases called transmissible spongiform encephalopathies, or TSEs. The disease results in dementia, uncoordinated movements, and other brain-related difficulties and therefore has become known as mad cow disease.

Rather than a traditional virus or bacterium, the culprit in TSEs is an abnormal form of a cell-surface protein, called a prion. The damaged prions are able to cause other proteins of the same type to change their shapes as well, and the misshapen protein molecules clump together and accumulate in brain tissue, much like the plaques characteristic of Alzheimer's disease.

The outbreak in the United Kingdom was serious, with more than 183,000 confirmed cases of BSE occurring in more than 35,000 herds by the end of November 2003. The outbreak has been widely attributed to the unnatural feeding methods that the worldwide demand for increased beef production has generated. Mad cow disease may be the result of cattle, which are herbivores in nature, being fed meat-and-bone meal derived from sheep. The problem was made far worse by feeding bovine meat-and-bone meal made from infected cattle to calves, essentially creating a population of cannibalistic cattle.

This is reminiscent of the spread of a similar disease in a human population earlier in the twentieth century. Kuru, a rare and fatal brain disorder also transmitted by prions, spread to epidemic levels during the 1950s and into the 1960s among the Fore people in the highlands of New Guinea. The disease was transmitted via ritualistic cannibalism among the Fore. In their funeral rites, relatives prepared and consumed the bodies, including the brain, of deceased family members. As with other TSEs, brain tissue of kuru victims was highly infectious, and kuru was also transmitted through contact with open sores and wounds. Kuru primarily affects the cerebellum, and so the early symptoms involved poor movement control. Victims would eventually become comatose and die within six months to a year of the first appearance of symptoms. Unlike the other TSEs, kuru does not appear to produce dementia. There is neither a cure nor any effective treatment for kuru—the only way to avoid it is to avoid cannibalism. The government of New Guinea began to actively discourage cannibalism in the 1960s, and the disease has now largely disappeared.

The main reason for the panic over the bovine disease is a concern that it may be possible for humans to develop a similar disease, Creutzfeldt-Jakob disease, through contact with infected meat. Evidence is strong that BSE can be transmitted to humans, where it develops into a variant form of Creutzfeldt-Jakob disease (called vCJD). As of December 2003, 143 cases of vCJD due to BSE exposure had been confirmed in the United Kingdom alone, but the beef supply in the United States appears to be completely safe, even though one case of BSE was identified in Oregon in 2003, in a cow purchased from Canada. This resulted in a temporary U.S. ban on Canadian beef, and no further cases have been reported here. We probably feel safer than we should at the moment, however, since the TSEs can have a very long incubation period. In the case of kuru, it was sometimes years or even decades after exposure that symptoms finally appeared.

Further Reading: Klitzman, R. *The Trembling Mountain: A Personal Account of Kuru, Cannibals, and Mad Cow Disease.* Boulder, CO: Perseus, 1998; Yam, P. *The Pathological Protein: Mad Cow, Chronic Wasting, and Other Deadly Prion Diseases.* New York: Copernicus Books, 2003.

MASTERS, WILLIAM H. (1915–) AND JOHNSON, VIRGINIA E.

(1925–) William Masters and Virginia Johnson were pioneers in the scientific study of human sexuality, as well as innovators in the therapeutic treatment of sexual dysfunction. Masters, a gynecologist, recognized that although Alfred Kinsey's work had made human sexuality a legitimate subject for scientific research, little was actually known about the physiological and psychological nature of the human sexual response. In his quest for an objective, scientific understanding of sexuality, he enlisted the help of psychologist Virginia Johnson in 1957 as a research assistant. Together, they went on to develop a wide range of clever and innovative tools to measure what happens to the bodies of men and women during sex. Despite the large amount of survey data turned out by Kinsey and others, almost no objective data existed, as no direct observation had actually been undertaken under scientific conditions.

Some of the devices Masters and Johnson created are quite inventive. For example, to measure various changes in the vagina during sexual arousal, they created a clear artificial penis containing sensors for temperature and blood flow, and which could also eventually be equipped with a small camera. To measure changes in penis girth during erection, as well as to time it, they invented the strain gauge: a flexible, mercury-filled rubber ring with wires attached, which could convert changes in size into electrical impulses to be read by a polygraph-like device.

By the time they published their book *Human Sexual Response* in 1966, they had observed over 700 men and women either having sex or masturbating in the laboratory, and they were able to turn these observations into a scientific description of the human sexual response cycle. According to Masters and Johnson, the response goes through four phases: excitement, plateau, orgasm, and resolution.

In the excitement phase, heart rate, blood pressure, and muscle tension all increase, and both sexes experience increased blood flow to the genitalia. In males, the penis becomes erect; and in females, the vagina becomes lubricated and the labia swell. In the plateau phase, physiological arousal increases further, along with both sexual pleasure and muscle tension. Orgasm is simply the conclusion of the plateau phase, with the release of sexual tension and rapid rhythmic muscle contractions in both men and women. During resolution, muscles relax, blood pressure and heart rate drop, and males experience a refractory period during which time must pass before orgasm can again be achieved.

The book became a best seller, and Masters and Johnson became household names. In 1970 they turned their attention to impotence, often referred to as erectile dysfunction, in the book *Human Sexual Inadequacy*. Based on their research, specifically the observation that many men experiencing impotence were nonetheless experiencing normal erections in their sleep, they argued that as many as 90 percent of the cases of impotence were due to psychological rather than physiological causes, and that the problem could therefore be overcome through psychological means, such as overcoming performance anxiety.

These two books together were largely responsible for the birth in the 1970s of the field of sex therapy, the clinical treatment of sexual problems. Masters and Johnson established a sex therapy practice in St. Louis that proceeded to train many sex therapists who then went out to establish their own practices in other parts of the country. For a time in the early 1970s, most of the country's sex therapists were either trained by Masters and Johnson or by their students.

For the next two decades Masters and Johnson continued their research and their string of successful books. In 1979 they published *Homosexuality in Perspective*, which described the sexual responses of gay men and women in the same detail as they had previously documented heterosexual behavior. This book devoted substantial space to debunking the notion that homosexuality is a psychological disorder (a position only abandoned by the American Psychiatric Association in 1973), but Masters and Johnson have drawn considerable fire, both from other sex researchers and from the gay community, for their claim to be able to change the sexual preferences of homosexuals who wished to change.

In fairness to Masters and Johnson, this claim was still a part of the psychiatric profession's diagnostic manual (*see DSM-IV*) at that time, listed as ego-dystonic homosexuality.

Masters and Johnson's collaboration ended with their divorce in 1993, but they have had an enormous influence on the way sexuality is viewed. Most widespread practices in sex therapy are based directly on their innovations. While better physiological measurement has shown that many cases of erectile dysfunction are in fact medical rather than psychological (hence the huge success of such drugs as Viagra and Cialis), for example, in the 40 to 50 percent of cases where psychological factors are involved, Masters and Johnson's treatment techniques are still widely applied.

One lingering concern about their original data should be addressed, however: it remains unclear how generalizable their findings are to the overall population, given how unrepresentative their research subjects may have been. After all, their data are based entirely on uninhibited people who volunteered to have sex under observation in a lab, attached to a variety of electrical monitoring devices.

Further Reading: Masters, W., and Johnson, V. *Human Sexual Response*. New York: Lippincott, Williams & Wilkins, 1966; Masters, W., and Johnson, V. *Human Sexual Inadequacy*. New York: Bantam, 1980 (reissue).

McGRAW, PHILLIP ("Dr. PHIL") (1950–) Dr. Phillip C. McGraw, known to his fans as "Dr. Phil," is currently one of America's top-selling authors, as well as a television star. He got his TV start by dispensing folksy advice during weekly appearances on Oprah Winfrey's daytime talk show, and he has starred on his own syndicated program since the fall of 2002. His frequent prodding of his audience to "get real" has clearly struck a chord; four of his books have occupied the number one spot on the *New York Times* best seller list, covering the usual range of self-help topics, including relationship improvement, strategies for improving one's own life, and weight loss. His books have little to say that is new, but his straightforward "tough love" style of presenting advice has won him many readers.

Prior to his ascent to stardom, Dr. Phil seems to have been involved in a variety of enterprises, including forensic psychology—he is president and co-founder of Courtroom Sciences, Inc., self-described as "the world's leading litigation consulting firm." It was in his capacity as a jury consultant in Winfrey's battle with the Texas beef industry (due to her on-camera references to MAD COW DISEASE) that he first became associated with her show. The company represents itself as involved in the legal affairs of most of the Fortune 500 companies, and Dr. Phil runs continuing-education seminars for lawyers on the subject of forecasting and influencing civil verdicts. His Web site represents him as having published "numerous scholarly articles"; however, a quick search through *Psychological Abstracts*, which indexes all scholarly psychological journals, turns up just one citation, a 1981 article on the treatment of rheumatoid arthritis by biofeedback and relaxation training.

Some of his fans in the media have turned on him regarding the new ventures that have followed in the wake of his latest best seller. With books like *Relationship Rescue*, he was following in the well-trodden footsteps of many other mass-media psychologists, but with *The Ultimate Weight Solution: The Seven Keys to Weight Loss Freedom*, he has moved beyond traditional psychological territory. Weight gain and loss can certainly have a psychological component, but it is his marketing deal with CSA Nutraceuticals that has drawn criticism and questions about his ethics. Through this deal, his name and likeness grace the packaging of nutritional supplements, including vitamin packets and meal-replacement drinks and bars sold under the brand name *Shape Up*. The book and the introduction of the products tied in directly with the contents of his television show, marking out previously unexplored territory in the gray area connecting entertainment, marketing, and health. Many TV hosts have sold books and videos, but Dr. Phil is endorsing products that could affect his audience's health, and the constant attachment of "Dr." to his name may cause people to trust his judgment on this matter more than they should. It may not be clear to all his viewers that he is trained as a psychologist, not a medical doctor.

Further Reading: McGraw, P. C. *The Ultimate Weight Solution: The Seven Keys to Weight Loss Freedom.* New York: The Free Press, 2003.

MEDIA VIOLENCE AND ITS EFFECTS ON CHILDREN It has been estimated that the average child in the United States spends more time each week watching television than attending school. This is of great concern, as a surprisingly large proportion of what children watch is violent. Saturday morning cartoons, for example, present as many as twenty violent acts per hour. One research team estimated that the average child in the United States will see at least 8,000 murders and more than 100,000 other acts of violence before finishing elementary school, simply by watching TV. Concern over the amount of violence being seen by children led to the law requiring a V-chip to block out programs containing violence in every new television set sold, as well as a system of television ratings, in the mid-1990s, yet the producers of violent programming have often continued to protest that children will not imitate what they see in those programs.

This last claim has sounded disingenuous to psychologists ever since Albert Bandura's classic "Bobo doll" studies in the early 1960s. Bandura showed preschoolers a film of an adult playing with a new toy, known at the time as a Bobo doll. It was an inflatable, four-foot-tall clown with a weighted base, designed to pop back up if knocked over. The toy has remained sporadically popular, usually in the shape of a currently popular cartoon character. At the time, the toy had just come on the market and was thus unfamiliar to the children. The adult in the film heaped abuse on the toy in various ways, punching it, kicking it, striking its head with a hammer, and throwing other toys at it, all the while clearly enjoying herself. The children were then led into a room with various toys in it, including the Bobo doll. Children who had seen the film were far more likely to beat up the doll than children who had not. This prompted Bandura to describe a new type of learning theory (beyond what was covered by B. F. SKINNER's operant conditioning, which requires that an action be reinforced to be learned); this theory is known as *social learning* or *modeling*.

Subsequent experiments revealed an interesting pattern: if the adult was praised for her behavior, the children became far more aggressive than the children who saw her scolded instead. Bandura called these phenomena vicarious reinforcement and vicarious punishment. Ever since Bandura's initial work in this area, psychological research indicating a clear link between children's television viewing and their subsequent actions has poured in, some of it rather frightening. In the famous Rip van Winkle study (so named because it was a longitudinal study that followed a group of children for two decades), psychologists Leonard Eron and E. Rowell Huesmann found that the amount of violent television watched at age eight was not linked to aggression at age eight, but it was predictive of long-term effects instead, including likelihood of arrest by age thirty.

In another study, a unique opportunity arose to examine the effect of American television on a population that had not previously been allowed to see it: the population of South Africa. In the days of apartheid, South Africa's repressive segregation of blacks, American and most European broadcasts were banned, as it was believed that seeing the state of race relations on those programs would incite rebellion. After the collapse of apartheid, American television shows were allowed and became quite popular. A comparison of white-on-white (the only kind looked at, in order to control for any rise in racial violence accompanying the large-scale societal change) murder rates before and after the introduction of American television shows a very clear increase, a pattern that has been observed in several other previously remote places as well (*see* CORRELATION).

The consensus among most psychologists is fairly clear. A recent comprehensive review of all research on media violence and aggression, commissioned by the AMERICAN PSYCHOLOGICAL SOCIETY, concludes that "research on violent television and films, video games, and music reveals *unequivocal* evidence that media violence increases the likelihood of aggressive and violent behavior in both immediate and long-term contexts."

This is no longer a matter of serious debate among psychologists. Television and video game violence and music with violent lyrics are definitely risk factors for aggressive and violent behavior.

It is important, however, to consider what that actually means. *Risk factor* does not mean the same thing as *cause*, a fact that is really not as well understood as it should be by many people. Consider the relationship between frequent sun exposure and skin cancer, for example. Frequent sun exposure elevates a person's chances of getting skin cancer, but it does not guarantee it. To the contrary, most people who are exposed to the sun frequently do not develop cancer. This is because many other factors intrude as well, including

This boy may be watching one of the 8,000 or more murders he will see on TV before finishing elementary school.

skin pigmentation, family history, and general health, to name just three. In the same way, violent television is a risk factor but nothing more. Most people who watch a lot of violent TV, or even play violent computer games, will not become violent offenders. Violent television has an effect on behavior, but it is often a very weak effect, because a person's likelihood of becoming violent is affected by a great many other factors as well.

In the Eron and Huesmann study described above, for example, the long-term effects of watching violent television were moderated by a variety of other things, including whether or not parents watched television with their children. Violent television definitely has an effect on aggression and violent behavior, and parents should be cautious about how much television children watch, but the effect is at best a weak one and interacts with many other variables.

Further Reading: Anderson, C. A., Berkowitz, L., Donnerstein, E., Huesmann, L. R., Johnson, J. D., Linz, D., Malamuth, N. M., and Wartella, E. "The Influence of Media Violence on Youth." *Psychological Science in the Public Interest*, 4(3) (2003).

MEMORY One estimate of the capacity of human memory is that over the course of a lifetime, a person will store more than 500 times as much information as appears in the entire *Encyclopedia Britannica*. Somehow, with all that information in there, a lot of it is immediately available on a moment's notice, with no apparent effort involved in the retrieval of it. For instance, if a person is asked, "What's your mother's middle name?" if it's a piece of information that the person knows at all, it will have just popped into their head when asked, with no deliberation necessary.

The three essential processes involved in memory are acquisition, storage, and retrieval. For information to go into memory, it must come from somewhere (acquisition). It must then be stored, sometimes for a long time. It hasn't truly been remembered, however, until it is retrieved. There are several competing models of how the human memory system works—the most popular one, known variously as the information-processing model or by the alliterative name of modal model, is presented here.

The memory system can be seen as consisting of three different storage systems, which differ from each other in capacity as well as in the duration of the memory. When information first enters the system (coming in from the senses when reading a book or listening to a conversation, for example), it is held in the sensory buffer, or sensory memory. The capacity of this store is quite large, as everything detected by the senses at any given moment is present there, but its duration is very brief (less than one second). If information held there is not attended to and perceived, it fades away almost instantly. If it is perceived, however, it enters into the next stage, short-term memory. The term *working memory* has largely supplanted short-term memory among cognitive psychologists, to reflect the growing recognition that it contains everything that is currently being attended to, both sensory information and information retrieved from long-term storage. In fact, some writers are even equating working memory with the conscious self. Everything we are thinking about at any given moment is in working memory.

Short-term memory (STM) has a fairly brief duration and a fairly small capacity, and whatever a person is currently paying attention to is held in it. Once information enters into it, it will remain for twenty seconds or less unless it is processed further. Keeping information in working memory involves a process known as maintenance rehearsal, which is familiar to anyone who has ever been told to call a particular telephone number right away and hasn't written the number down. The tendency is to repeat the number over and over until dialed, and it is completely forgotten once the phone conversation begins, and the number is no longer rehearsed. This idea of repeating the number to oneself, even with the mouth shut, is actually a very accurate representation of what is actually going on. People store things in STM using an auditory code. When people are interrupted while rehearsing a list of letters, for example, the resulting errors tend to involve sound-alike letters rather than letters that resemble the correct ones physically. Other laboratory evidence shows that hearing a separate list of letters while trying to rehearse another will interfere with memory, while seeing the new list on a screen will not. This is because rehearsal actually involves listening to the items in one's head.

The capacity of STM is approximately seven chunks, give or take two (ranging, in other words, from five to nine chunks). A chunk is simply a meaningful unit of information; it can be a digit, a word, a letter, or an entire sentence, depending on the task. When a person is rehearsing a seven-digit telephone number, and somebody interrupts them ("Hey, did you want eight or twelve of these?"), the number is lost immediately, because the capacity of STM was exceeded. People can easily use larger chunks than one digit, however. Consider a social security number. Most people think of it in three discrete chunks (three digits, two digits, and four digits) rather than as nine separate pieces of information.

Maintenance rehearsal is good for keeping information active in STM, but deeper processing is required to move it into long-term memory (LTM). Although some information enters LTM automatically, deliberate placement of information into it requires elaborative rehearsal. That term is a bit of a misnomer, as no rehearsal is involved, at least not in the sense of repeating the information. What is actually involved is making connections between the new information and information that is already in LTM. The moment such a relationship is established, the information is in long-term memory.

There are actually at least three basic kinds of long-term memory. Episodic memory is any memory of an episode in life, any specific event at which one was present. This kind of memory is also known as autobiographical memory. Semantic memory is general knowledge of the world that can be described in words and doesn't involve recollection of a particular event. Knowledge of a complex series of actions, or of how to do something, that cannot be adequately described in words, constitutes procedural memory. So, answering the question, "What is a bicycle?" involves semantic memory, recalling the long-distance bicycle race you rode last week is an episodic memory, and knowing how to ride a bicycle is a procedural memory. Neurologically, procedural memories seem to involve different brain mechanisms than other kinds of long-term memory. Brain damage that destroys a person's ability to form new semantic and episodic memories may leave the ability to form new procedural memories intact. In other words, it may be possible to learn how to do a new task without any explicit memory of having learned it (see AMNESIA).

The capacity of LTM is widely believed by psychologists to be unlimited. There is no real way to test this, but available evidence shows that people do store truly vast amounts of information for a very long time. One classic study using yearbooks showed that people were amazingly good at recognizing the faces of their high school classmates after not having seen them for over twenty-five years. This study found that a fair amount of information was lost within the first five years, but that anything that was remembered for those five years was still remembered after another twenty, forming part of what has been called the permastore. Another study found that people do surprisingly well on tests of a foreign language or high school algebra some fifty years after having formally studied the subject.

Long-term memory is not always as accurate as we expect it to be, however. People often have extremely vivid memories of highly emotional events (known as flashbulb memories), and the vividness leads us to believe more in the accuracy of these memories than in that of less-sharp memories. This may be a mistake, as a landmark study by Neisser and Harsch demonstrated. The day after the space shuttle *Challenger* exploded on liftoff, shocking the nation, they surveyed a large sample of college freshmen, asking them where they were when they found out about it, who was with them, and how they found out about it. They then re-interviewed the students three years later, and their results were fascinating: compared to what they recalled one day later, a large majority remembered things incorrectly three years later, and their memories often included surprisingly large errors such as failing to remember the correct location, or remembering a friend's presence even though they hadn't known that person at the time. This is especially notable given that almost everyone in the sample was sure, when asked, that they remembered it very accurately.

A similar study of flashbulb memories involved the reading of the verdict in the O. J. Simpson murder trial. A group of college students was asked to describe what they were doing at the moment when they heard the verdict, and they reported their recollections on three separate occasions: just three days later, after fifteen months, and after thirty-two months. At the last interview, almost all of them were sure that they still remembered it quite accurately, but more than 70 percent of their memories were distorted and inaccurate. As in the *Challenger* study, the most important thing to learn from this study is that the students were completely unaware that their memories had become distorted.

Many factors can influence the extent to which we are able to retrieve accurate memories, and some of them can be used by students to improve their likelihood of success on tests. A common piece of advice given to students who are struggling is to find an opportunity to study in the room in which the test will be given. Based on memory research, this turns out to be good advice, as memory retrieval is sometimes context-dependent. When a memory is first encoded and stored, other information present at the same time may also be encoded along with it, so that almost any feature of the environment present at the time of learning can also serve as a retrieval cue. One of the most intriguing studies of this effect was carried out by cognitive psychologists Baddeley and Hitch, along with a group of scuba-trained student volunteers. The students were divided into two groups to learn some information. Half of them learned it on a boat, while the other half were underwater, in full scuba gear, when they learned it. The groups were then divided again to be tested on the material, with half of each group being tested on the boat and the other half getting evaluated on the ocean floor (special boards that could be written on underwater were used). The results showed that people performed best when the context of retrieval matched the context in which the material was learned, even when that context was the bottom of the sea.

The external environment isn't the only one that matters, however; sometimes people also encode information about how they were *feeling* at the time the information was learned. This is known as state-dependent memory, as emotional state can also act as a retrieval cue. If a person is happy and peaceful at the time of learning, for example, he will perform better on a test if he is also happy and peaceful then. Conversely, if a person is extremely angry when learning something, she should enlist a friend to enrage her right before the test.

In a rather extreme test of this effect, people were taught new information after smoking marijuana, and they tended to do somewhat better on a test of the material if they were also under the influence of marijuana at the time of testing. Similar effects have been documented for caffeine, alcohol, and various other psychoactive drugs. Please note that this is not an endorsement of alcohol or drug use. In all cases, the best performance was shown by those who did not indulge in the substances on either occasion.

Even with context properly matched, of course, people sometimes forget things. Much forgetting is simply a failure to retrieve information correctly, though some is certainly due to simple decay: over time, some information is simply lost. A lot of forgetting, however, is due to interference, meaning that some information in memory interferes with the ability to retrieve other information. There are two kinds of interference, proactive and retroactive. In proactive interference, older information interferes with the ability to recall what was learned more recently. If a student who already knows Spanish takes a French class, for example, she or he may occasionally make errors in class by using a Spanish verb known for years rather than the French verb learned last week. Retroactive interference, on the other hand, is what happens when new learning interferes with retrieval of older memories. If that same student, in speaking with a grandparent who speaks only Spanish confuses her or him by inadvertently using a French expression, retroactive interference is to blame.

Contrary to the common impression people have of their memories as fairly accurate representations of how things really were, many factors actually can cause our memories to be inaccurate or even completely false. The human mind seeks regularity and predictability, and it works to provide it even where it doesn't exist. Inevitably, any event or situation has elements to which a person does not pay attention, and so they do not encode them in memory. Where such gaps occur, memory is constructive; so rather than consciously realize that the gaps are there, they are filled in from generalized knowledge of the world, as well as expectations and beliefs. People have schemas in their heads for various common situations, based on experiences, and they fill in the details they missed according to these schemas.

Consider your kitchen schema, for example: What are the things one would expect to see in a kitchen? For most Americans, and for the college student research participants in the next example, a sink was in the list somewhere. A group of students was made to wait in a small kitchen before being led into a lab for the experiment they had signed up for. Upon entering the lab, they found that the experiment had already begun, as they were asked a series of questions about what they had observed in the kitchen while they waited. Most students endorsed the statement that a sink had been present, and were then quite surprised to hear that the room didn't contain one. In a similar study, students waited for several minutes in a room that they had been told was a graduate student's office and were later asked to recall everything that was in the office. Most of them specifically remembered seeing books, despite the fact that the room did not contain a single book. Their expectations of what belongs in an academic office overruled the actual evidence of their senses. Again, note that the process of filling in these gaps is unconscious, and the only reason these people would ever know that their memories were inaccurate was because the researchers told them so.

The constructive nature of memory is an especially important (and dangerous) issue where eyewitness testimony in a courtroom is concerned. The use of eyewitnesses is predicated on two notions: that they will testify truthfully and honestly, and that their memories of what they witnessed will be accurate. Leaving aside the issue of whether witnesses tell the truth as they know it, witnesses can sometimes make serious mistakes without being aware of it, and these errors can have serious consequences. As of late September 2004, 151 death-row inmates in the United States have been released based on DNA evidence that showed they were not guilty of the crime of which they were convicted. In the vast majority of cases, the conviction was based primarily on eyewitness testimony. Like everyone else, an eyewitness can only remember what was perceived and can only perceive what was attended to. There are limits, imposed by the existence of memory gaps, to how accurate their testimony can possibly be, and a large body of evidence shows that those gaps may be filled in by new information about the crime, and a witness's memory can even be altered by the wording of a lawyer's question.

In a classic experiment by cognitive psychologist Elizabeth Loftus that has been widely replicated, subjects saw a film of a minor traffic accident and were then asked a question about how fast the cars were traveling when they made contact. The only difference between the groups of subjects was the verb used in the question. People who were asked how fast the cars were traveling when they *smashed* into each other estimated a significantly higher speed than those who were asked how fast the cars were traveling when they *hit* each other. When interviewed a week later, people who had heard the word *smashed* also provided a more violent description of the accident than the others. Loftus calls this the misinformation effect. In one variation on this experiment, the filmed accident was a very gentle collision, with no visible physical damage to either car, but at the delayed interview, people in the *smashed* group frequently recalled seeing broken glass on the pavement, although none was visible on the actual film. In another variation, a stop sign was visible in the film, but some of the subjects were asked questions that mentioned a yield sign instead at the delayed interview. These subjects frequently included the nonexistent yield sign in their recollections.

The use of young children's eyewitness testimony is especially problematic, given what is known about their memory and how susceptible it is to distortion. In the 1980s, several high-profile trials showed just how serious these problems can be. The McMartin family, who ran a preschool/day care center in California, became the defendants in the longest and costliest criminal proceeding in U.S. history, when well over 100 counts of child physical and sexual abuse were levied against them. The accusations included a number of fantastical allegations, including a secret room children were taken to through hidden tunnels to be abused, but no secret room or tunnels were ever found. Other children testified that they had arrived at the secret room by being flushed through the toilets, but were cleaned up upon their return. In a similar case involving the Little Rascals day care center in Edenton, North Carolina, accusations included a secret basement aquarium filled with trained sharks, used for disciplinary purposes. At one point in the trial, a child alleged that the entire class had been taken on a boat out into the ocean, where a child may or may not have been thrown to these trained sharks, which had been released for this purpose. There were also allegations about the disciplining of a child by hanging him upside down from a tree and setting him on fire. This child later testified, absent any evidence of burns.

In a New Jersey trial, a young teacher named Kelly Michaels was accused of, among other things, playing the piano naked, having children eat feces and drink urine, having children lick peanut butter off her naked body, and of amputating several boys' penises (presumably this last claim would have been fairly easy to dispel with physical evidence), as well as occasionally killing babies and having the children drink their blood (again, this would presumably have left some physical evidence, not to mention reports of missing babies).

What the above cases all have in common (other than the patent absurdity of many of the charges) is that all resulted in convictions, which were only overturned on appeal years later. The defendant in a similar case, Gerald Amirault, who was accused of raping children with kitchen knives (again, no physical evidence of the "crimes" was ever introduced), was finally released on parole by the state of Massachusetts in April 2004, a full eighteen years after first going to jail. One reason that he wasn't released sooner was his refusal to undergo sex-offender counseling while in prison, since he wasn't actually a sex offender. The state Board of Pardons had actually recognized the flaws in his prosecution and recommended his immediate release years earlier, but the governor at the time refused to endorse the pardon.

How could sensible judges, prosecutors, and juries have let things go this far? In each case, a major part of the prosecutor's argument was a question about the children: Why would they lie about this? The unspoken assumption was that if the children were not lying, then everything they were saying must really have happened, and the absence of physical evidence simply meant that child rapists are unusually clever at covering up their misdeeds. The truth is of course subtler: the children did not lie, but what they alleged in court was not true either. To the person doing the remembering, false memories do not differ from real ones, except that the false ones are often a bit "fuzzier." The children were telling the truth as they understood it, rather than either lying or telling the objective truth. Research on young children's ability to remember a traumatic event is especially relevant here. Obviously, it would be highly unethical to conduct an experiment in which children were randomly assigned to be abused, but there is another experience that preschoolers normally go through that involves an unfamiliar adult making them take off their clothes, touching them in uncomfortable ways, and sometimes causing pain: a trip to the doctor's office.

In a research design that has now been replicated numerous times, a pediatrician and a nurse fill out a checklist for each child who comes for an examination, listing everything that was actually done during the examination. Meanwhile, the children are interviewed immediately after the examination, and again after two to six weeks. An interesting pattern of results has emerged in these studies: younger children are far more prone to memory errors than older children, and the type of question asked matters a great deal. When they are asked open-ended questions, like "What did the doctor do?" preschool-aged children provide very little information spontaneously, but what they say tends to be accurate. When specific, yes/no questions are asked about their experiences, however, their accuracy drops to chance levels (a 50/50 shot at answering correctly, in other words) both for questions about what really happened and for questions about things that did not happen, even when the interview occurs immediately after the examination.

Another factor in the questioning of children that is known to influence children's testimony, present in all of the cases described above, is repeated questioning. When a very young child is asked the same question repeatedly, even when the answer is a firm "No," that child will eventually change his answer to satisfy the adult, because the adult is conveying quite clearly that the answer is wrong. The misinformation effect was also a factor in all of the cases. Most of the bizarre details came originally from the adults, and the children eventually incorporated them into their own testimony after hearing them repeatedly, with their own imaginations taking over to fill in gaps.

Another factor in the trials was stereotype induction, which is what happens when children are repeatedly given prejudicial information about a person ("He's a bad man") and later incorporate it into their memories of that person. In a classic study by Stephen Ceci and his colleagues, a guest visited a preschool classroom several times and told stories about his clumsy, accident-prone friend named Sam Stone. After several weeks of this, another guest visited the classroom. Introducing himself as Sam Stone, he simply greeted the class, stayed a while, and then left. The next day, the teacher drew the children's attention to a broken toy and a damaged book and asked them who had done it. When the children were later interviewed and asked what happened when Sam came to visit, many of them described his breaking of the toys, often accompanied by comments like, "He's so clumsy!"

Stereotype induction and the misinformation effect are examples of a larger problem that is often a factor in adult false memories as well: source misattribution. When a piece of information is stored in memory, information about the source of the information is also often encoded, but that piece of the memory is often not encoded well, so it fades much faster. The result is that a piece of information may sound familiar, but we no longer remember where we heard it. This is a familiar experience to anyone who has ever known an answer in a trivia game or on a test without any idea of why they know it. As with other memory gaps, people tend to fill these unconsciously with a likely source, rather than realizing that they don't know where the information came from.

A famous example of this comes from a speech in which President Ronald Reagan told a "true" story he had heard from a World War II veteran, in which the tail gunner in a damaged bomber was hit and couldn't eject with the rest of the men, so an officer remained on the plane so the gunner wouldn't die alone. The story seemed vaguely familiar to many listeners, which may be because it is a scene from the war movie *On a Wing and a Prayer*. Although cynics have accused Reagan of simply lying, it actually seems likely that he knew the story but no longer remembered where it came from, and he simply followed the usual human tendency to fill in the gap. When a person no longer recalls the source of a piece of information, they often attribute it to a source anyway. In the misinformation studies described above, subjects associated the vague impression that something was "smashed" with the film they had seen, but didn't remember that it came from the question rather than the film.

Adults are just as susceptible to these effects as children, with the added disadvantage of great confidence in the accuracy of their own memories. In the 1980s, during the same period as the assorted multiple-offender/multiple-victim child abuse cases described above, came a near-epidemic of cases in which adults accused others of child abuse that had allegedly occurred long before, sometimes decades earlier, and which had never previously been reported. In these cases, the memories had allegedly been repressed and had only been recovered after many sessions with a therapist (*see* FREUD). The therapists frequently used HYPNOSIS and guided imagery, along with other suggestive techniques, and after weeks or months of treatment, the patients began to believe in the reality of things that they had never previously remembered or reported. Based on such testimony, and in the absence of any corroborating evidence at all, a number of cases made it to trial, and some resulted in convictions. The problem became so widespread that a group of psychologists founded an organization, called the False Memory Syndrome Foundation, to bring together resources for families who had been falsely accused. On their Web site, they give the following definition of false memory syndrome: "[A] condition in which a person's identity and interpersonal relationships are centered around a memory of traumatic experience which is objectively false but in which the person strongly believes" (www.fmsonline.com/fmsffaq.html).

The foundation has been instrumental in changing public attitudes (and the behavior of judges) where such cases are concerned, and has inevitably suffered a backlash from those clinicians who believe strongly in the Freudian construct of repressed memory. Cognitive psychologists in general, and Loftus in particular, have been accused of lacking sympathy for the victims of abuse, as well as of ignoring the evidence for repression of memories. Childhood sexual abuse is a serious problem, and it is widely recognized that the problem has long remained underreported. People who have been sexually abused deserve our sympathy and any help that we can give them, and nobody associated with the False Memory Syndrome Foundation disagrees with that.

It is important to note that this has become a political controversy rather than a scientific one, as the scientific consensus on repression is fairly clear. A review of more than sixty years of research on repression concluded that there is no scientific evidence for the phenomenon to date, and, as the APA (1995) states, "the reality is that most people who are victims of childhood sexual abuse remember all or part of what happened to them" (*see also* BRAIN).

Further Reading: American Psychological Association. *Questions and Answers about Memories of Childhood Abuse.* Washington, DC: American Psychological Association, 1995; Bruck, M., Ceci, S. J., et al. "External and Internal Sources of Variation in the Creation of False Reports in Children." *Learning and Individual Differences,* 9(4) (1997): 289–317; Ceci, S. J., and Bruck, M. *Jeopardy in the Courtroom.* Washington, DC: American Psychological Association, 1995; Schacter, D. L. *The Seven Sins of Memory: How the Mind Forgets and Remembers.* New York: Houghton Mifflin Mariner Books, 2002.

MENTAL RETARDATION (MR) Mental retardation (MR) is a disorder characterized primarily by intellectual functioning that is markedly below average, as well as a general deficit in social and self-care skills. Most people's understanding of MR begins and ends with IQ scores, but there is substantially more to the disorder than an unusually low IQ (*see* INTELLIGENCE). Poor intellectual functioning is only one of three major components of the standard definition produced by the American Association on Mental Retardation (now echoed in both the *DSM-IV* and federal law).

- Significantly subaverage intellectual functioning (indicated by an IQ of 70 or less on a standard, individually administered test).
- A deficit in adaptive behavior. This means that in two or more of the following areas, the patient has more trouble functioning than would be expected for age and cultural group: communication, self-care, home living, social and interpersonal skills, using community resources, self-direction, academic ability, work, free time, health, and safety.
- Origin in the developmental period. This means that the signs of mental retardation are evident in childhood, or before age eighteen.

The second requirement is in the definition to clarify MR's status as a psychological disorder. Many reasons exist as to why a person might score poorly on an intelligence test, but that person has no disorder if that does not interfere with his or her functioning otherwise. The third requirement is there as a recognition that other circumstances, such as a serious head injury or disease affecting the brain, can lead to both a low IQ score and a loss of independent self-care skills. If such an incident occurs to an adult, mental retardation is an inappropriate label.

U.S. federal law, again reflecting the standards of the AAMR and the *DSM-IV*, further recognizes four distinct levels of mental retardation, classified according to IQ level: mild (IQ range 55–70), moderate (IQ range 40–54), severe (IQ range 25–39), and profound (IQ below 25). The prevalence of mental retardation in the U.S. population has been estimated at between 1 and 3 percent.

The large majority of cases of mental retardation fall in the mild range and have no clear physiological cause. These cases are sometimes referred to as cultural-familial or sociocultural retardation, as the primary cause appears to be a severely deprived and understimulated childhood. In cases where an organic cause exists, the most common causes appear to be DOWN SYNDROME, Fragile X syndrome (a chromosomal anomaly involving damage to the X chromosome), and Fetal Alcohol Syndrome (FAS).

As the leading identified cause of mental retardation, FAS merits special attention, because unlike genetic anomalies, it is completely preventable. Negative effects of binge drinking on developing fetuses have been documented for much of human history, but the syndrome was only formally identified and named in 1973. In addition to mental retardation, individuals with FAS have a distinct pattern of facial abnormalities, growth deficiency and evidence of central nervous system dysfunction. They may also have other neurological deficits such as poor motor skills and hand-eye coordination, as well as behavioral and learning problems, including difficulties with memory, attention, and judgment. Although most cases are associated with binge drinking by the mother, there is no completely safe known level of alcohol consumption during pregnancy. Prevention of FAS is simple, and it is one of the great medical success stories of the late twentieth century: simply advising pregnant women to avoid drinking alcohol has resulted in a substantial drop in the number of FAS cases.

The terminology used to refer to persons with mental retardation has changed dramatically over the last 150 years, as our understanding of the disorder has improved and become more refined. As recently as the mid-nineteenth century, people who would today be considered mentally retarded received no treatment other than to be locked away in asylums, with the only diagnosis being to occasionally distinguish the "idiots" from the "lunatics."

The first book devoted to treatment methods specifically intended for the "feeble-minded" (another popular nineteenth and early-twentieth century label), Seguín's *Idiocy and Its Treatment by Physiological Methods*, only appeared in 1866. By the late-nineteenth century, recognition was growing that feeble-mindedness could occur at differing levels of severity, and "idiot" was joined by the higher-functioning "imbecile." In the United States, H. H. Goddard added an additional level, corresponding to those mildly retarded persons whose disability was not as obvious to the casual observer: he called them "morons." Due to their widespread use as pejorative terms, all of these are obsolete, long since replaced by the four levels of mental retardation described above. In the early 1990s, the AAMR attempted to again change the diagnostic labels, partly in recognition of the extent to which "retarded" has joined the older terms as a stigma. They proposed replacing the four levels of retardation with terms describing the degree of services required: mild, moderate, severe, and profound became intermittent, limited, extensive, and pervasive. These terms have now been used in two different editions of the AAMR diagnostic manual, but they have failed to catch on among most professionals in the field or among textbook authors, who continue largely to use the older terms.

Further Reading: American Association on Mental Retardation. *Mental Retardation: Definition, Classification, and Systems of Supports.* 9th ed. Washington, DC: AAMR, 1992; American Association on Mental Retardation. *Mental Retardation: Definition, Classification, and Systems of Supports.* 10th ed. Washington, DC: AAMR, 2002; Beirne-Smith, M., Patton, J. R., and Ittenbach, R. *Mental Retardation.* 4th ed. New York: Merrill, 1994.

MESMERISM *See* HYPNOSIS

MILGRAM, STANLEY *See* OBEDIENCE TO AUTHORITY

MINNESOTA MULTIPHASIC PERSONALITY INVENTORY (MMPI) The MMPI-2, the latest version of the Minnesota Multiphasic Personality Inventory, is currently the world's most widely used instrument for diagnosis of psychopathology. Originally published in 1943, the MMPI is a 567-item, true-false test that was designed as an aid to psychiatric diagnosis. It produces scores on ten clinical scales, and elevated scores on these scales are then examined to produce a diagnosis. Descriptions of the scales appear in the table below:

Scale # and Abbreviation	Scale Name	Standard Interpretation of an Elevated Score
1. Hs	Hypochondriasis	Excessive preoccupation with the body and physical symptoms
2. D	Depression	Sadness, discomfort, and dissatisfaction with life
3. Hy	Hysteria	Feeling overwhelmed by stress
4. Pd	Psychopathic Deviance	Rebellion, difficulty adhering to standards of society
5. Mf	Masculinity-femininity	Lack of stereotypic masculine interests (in men—high scores are rare among women)
6. Pa	Paranoia	Excessive sensitivity, hostility, suspiciousness (very high scores indicate psychotic behavior)
7. Pt	Psychasthenia	Anxiety, tension, worry. Obsessive-compulsive disorder tends to score high
8. Sc	Schizophrenia	Confusion, disorganization, unusual thought processes
9. Ma	Hypomania	High energy and agitation, overactivity, unrealistic self-appraisal. Mania
10. Si	Social Introversion	Shy, insecure, timid, introverted

Scoring and interpretation of the MMPI often involves classifying the profile as belonging to a code type, consisting of a combination of two or more clinical scales elevated beyond a certain level. Many code types have been identified with particular disorders and extensively studied. The 49 code type, consisting of elevations on 4 (psychopathic deviance) and 9 (hypomania), for example, has been found to be highly characteristic of antisocial personality disorder. Code type 12 (elevations on 1, hypochondriasis, and 2, depression) is typical of the classic hypochondriac. Such types have been identified for most common disorders.

In addition to the clinical scales, the MMPI also features four validity scales, which allow the examiner to detect people who are faking or malingering, as well as those who may not be able to read or understand the test sufficiently. The L scale, for example, was designed to catch people who are answering dishonestly and evasively. It consists of fifteen items, which, if answered "False," indicate a very unlikely level of personal virtue (e.g., they never get angry, they like everybody they've ever met, they never lie, and they would rather lose than win).

Unlike most psychological tests that are usually grounded at least somewhat in a theory, the MMPI was created through an approach called criterion-keying. The designers of the test gave thousands of test items both to well-defined clinical samples that included a group of depressed patients, a group of schizophrenics, and so on, and to a control group made up of non-patients. They then examined the results for items that were endorsed by the clinical samples significantly more or significantly less frequently than the control group. All items that didn't reliably distinguish the controls from the other subjects were thrown out, leaving the final pool of items used in the test. For example, questions do not appear in the schizophrenia scale because they express thoughts characteristic of schizophrenia; to the contrary, they appear there only because schizophrenic patients usually answer them differently than people who are not mentally ill.

The current version of the test is known as the MMPI-2 because of a major overhaul and revision that was published in 1989, after nearly a decade of work. There were several reasons why the revision was necessary, but a major concern involved the representativeness of the original standardization sample. The test was originally devised at the University of Minnesota Hospital, and the control group consisted primarily of relatives and visitors of the patients who made up the clinical samples. This being Minnesota in the 1940s, all of the control subjects were white, married, from a small town or rural area, and had an average of eight years of formal education, and were therefore not an especially good representation of the U.S. population.

Item content was also troubling, because many items contained archaic references (to such things as sleeping powders and playing "drop the handkerchief"), which rendered them incomprehensible to modern readers. Some items were simply offensive, including sexist language, references to bowel and bladder function, and references to religious belief, which so offended some test-takers that they filed lawsuits over them. Furthermore, the method by which the test was created involved little editorial oversight, and many items therefore included poor grammar and inappropriate punctuation.

Concern also had arisen that the MMPI items were inadequate to assess the various disorders that had entered the lexicon of psychology and psychiatry since the test was first published. The test lacked items about drug abuse other than alcohol, for example, and failed to address suicide attempts. The MMPI-2 takes care of all of these concerns and was standardized on a sample that is far more representative of the U.S. population at large in terms of ethnicity, education level, income, and age. The MMPI should therefore continue as the premier psychodiagnostic tool for a long time to come (*see also* INTELLIGENCE).

Further Reading: Butcher, J. N. *A Beginner's Guide to the MMPI-2.* Washington, DC: American Psychological Association, 1999.

MMPI *See* MINNESOTA MULTIPHASIC PERSONALITY INVENTORY (MMPI)

MOOD DISORDERS Mood disorders are characterized primarily by marked changes in mood that interfere with the person's ability to function. Mood disorders fall into two categories: unipolar (also known as depressive), which involves depression only; and bipolar, which involves episodes of elevated mood (mania or hypomania) in addition to depression. Bipolar disorder was previously known and is still often popularly referred to as manic depression. Unipolar depression is fairly common, affecting about 20 percent of women and 10 percent of men, while bipolar disorder occurs far less frequently, affecting only 1 to 2 percent of the population and afflicting both genders equally.

The gender disparity in depression may be an illusion, however, reflecting gender differences in willingness to seek help, rather than an actual gender difference in the incidence of depression. This may be related to the apparently higher rate of alcoholism among men. Women who are depressed are more likely to seek help; depressed men are more likely to start drinking more. The difference also reflects the existence of certain forms of atypical depression that cannot affect men, such as postpartum depression.

Most patients experience multiple episodes, and mood disorders are often chronic. Even minimal symptoms are associated with increased risk for subsequent episodes and serious impairment. Suicide is a major concern, as depression accounts for a majority of suicides, and 15 percent of individuals with mood disorders will commit suicide.

Depression is characterized primarily by negative affect (emotional state), along with a loss of interest in activities that were once enjoyed. This is usually accompanied by a loss of energy and productivity, social withdrawal, pessimism, negative feelings about the self, and possibly suicidal ideation. Sleep disturbances are common and may involve either insomnia or excessive sleep. Depression may also be accompanied by disturbances in eating habits, which may involve either loss of appetite or excessive eating, as well as loss of interest in sex. Mania involves opposite changes in the same signs and symptoms. Mood is elevated or even euphoric, happiness replaces sadness, new interests and ventures are recklessly taken on, self-esteem is inflated to nearly delusional proportions, need for sleep is reduced, appetites and spending increase, and sexual indiscretions are also common.

The *DSM-IV* currently recognizes the following types of depressive and bipolar disorders:

	Type of Disorder	Description
Depressive Disorders (Unipolar)	Major Depressive Disorder	More severe; recurrent or chronic
	Dysthymic Disorder	Less severe; lasts at least 2 years
	Depressive Disorder Not Otherwise Specified (NOS)	
Bipolar Disorders (one or more manic episode)	Bipolar I Disorder	More severe; one or more fully manic episodes
	Bipolar II Disorder	Less severe; one or more hypomanic but no manic episodes
	Cyclothymic Disorder	Less severe, with mood deflections in both directions
	Bipolar Disorder NOS	
Mood Disorder Due to General Medical Condition		
Substance-Induced Mood Disorder		

Depression and mania both tend to occur in episodes that are often self-limiting (meaning they clear up on their own, with or without treatment). It is the recurrent nature of these episodes that causes treatment to be necessary. Also, depression can be chronic, though mania tends not to be.

Recent surveys have suggested that as many as 75 percent or more of depressed adults receive no treatment for their disorder. Even among those with bipolar disorders, which tend to be more severe and therefore more likely to be noticed by doctors than unipolar depression, nearly half do not receive appropriate treatment. Given the impact of mood disorders on quality of life, and the hugely elevated risk of suicide compared to the general population, this is tragic, especially in light of the availability of remarkably effective treatments. Antidepressant medications, for example, are very effective in many cases, and the newer generation of medications has largely eliminated the side effects associated with older drugs.

The newest antidepressant drugs provide some clear insights as to the causes of depression. As with other disorders, a variety of explanations of depression and bipolar disorder have been put forth over the years, including psychoanalytic explanations based on the idea of hatred for one's parents being turned inward, but most evidence is currently converging on a primarily physiological explanation for the syndrome. While it may not actually be the cause of the syndrome in all cases, there is a clear pattern of brain chemistry associated with depression. Variations in the available quantity of two neurotransmitters, serotonin and dopamine, are associated with feelings of well-being. Many psychoactive drugs, including cocaine and other stimulants, induce manic states by increasing the total level of serotonin and dopamine released in the brain, often by blocking the reuptake process which removes the neurotransmitters from the synapses, thus prolonging the feelings associated with the higher levels (*see* NERVOUS SYSTEM). Widely used antidepressants such as fluoxetine (sold under the trade name Prozac) work in exactly the same way. This is why the drugs are known as Selective Serotonin Reuptake Inhibitors (SSRIs).

The same chemical processes are also involved in the cycling between mania and depression that characterizes the bipolar disorders. The manic phase is associated with elevated levels of serotonin and dopamine, but production of excess amounts is something the neurons can only do for a limited time; the consequent drop in neurotransmitter levels which follows involves a drop to below-normal levels, thus returning the person to a depressed state. The same correlation between mood state and neurotransmitter levels may also be the reason for the effectiveness of ELECTROCONVULSIVE THERAPY (ECT) in cases of severe depression, as the electrical shock may disrupt current patterns and return neurotransmitters to normal levels.

The changes in neurotransmitter levels associated with depression and mania may also be caused by changes in state of mind, however, which is why non-pharmacological therapies, used either alone or in combination with drugs, can be very effective as well. Antidepressant medications are very effective for many patients and are relatively safe, but there is no evidence that they lower the risk of recurrence once their use is terminated. They treat the current episode of depression or mania, but they do not change the patterns in the patient's life that brought about the depression in the first place.

COGNITIVE-BEHAVIOR THERAPY (CBT) is especially promising as a treatment for depression, because it seems not only to be able to relieve distress even in severe depression, but it also seems to greatly reduce the risk of the return of symptoms as long as it is continued or maintained. It also reduces the risk of relapse long after treatment is over. This may be because rather than simply treating the symptoms, CBT involves learning techniques to prevent falling back into a depressed state again. Purely behavioral techniques haven't been studied as thoroughly as CBT, but they also appear to be quite effective for similar reasons. Meanwhile, there continues to be little or no evidence of the efficacy of psychodynamically based therapies.

Bipolar disorder can also be treated effectively with medications. In addition to antidepressants, treatment of bipolar disorder usually includes mood-stabilizer drugs, primarily lithium compounds or anticonvulsants, to prevent manic episodes. The use of psychotherapy with bipolar disorder has received much less attention from researchers than it has for depression, but what little research has been done suggests similar promise for a drugs plus therapy approach.

Further Reading: American Psychiatric Association. *DSM-IV-TR: Diagnostic and Statistical Manual of Mental Disorders*. 4th ed. Text revision. Washington, DC: American Psychiatric Association, 2000.

MORAL DEVELOPMENT   In trying to describe the stages through which children achieve cognitive development, a number of theorists have recognized that, since not all reasoning involves the sort of school-derived tasks that frequently drive research on child cognition, they should attempt to describe the development of reasoning about moral dilemmas as well. The best known of these theorists is Lawrence Kohlberg. Kohlberg based his theory on the work of Jean PIAGET, and like Piaget, he believed that a person's level of moral reasoning depended on that person's level of cognitive development. To study the processes of moral reasoning, Kohlberg presented his research participants with a series of moral dilemmas. One of the most famous is below:

> In Europe, a woman was near death from a special kind of cancer. There was one drug that the doctors thought might save her. It was a rare form of radium that a druggist in the same town had recently discovered. The drug was expensive to make, but the druggist was charging ten times what the drug cost him to make. He paid $200 for the radium and charged $2,000 for a small dose of the drug. The sick woman's husband, Heinz, went to everyone he knew to borrow the money, but he could only get together about $1,000, which is half of what it cost. He told the druggist that his wife was dying, and asked him to sell it cheaper or let him pay later. But the druggist said, "No, I discovered the drug and I'm going to make money from it." So Heinz got desperate and broke into the man's store to steal the drug for his wife. (Kohlberg and Elfenbein, 1975)

Participants would then be asked whether or not Heinz should have stolen the drug, followed by a series of additional probing questions. Kohlberg was less interested in whether the answer was "yes" or "no" than he was in the reasoning the subject followed to arrive at an answer.

Based on the responses his subjects gave to the dilemmas, Kohlberg concluded that people progress through three broad levels of moral reasoning, each of which he further subdivided into two specific stages (see table on following page). A convention is a standard rule or practice agreed to by a society. Kohlberg's levels are distinguished from each other in terms of the role of conventionality in moral reasoning. The preconventional child has not yet internalized conventions as the source of right and wrong, whereas the conventional child (or adult) bases decisions on what is or isn't expected, either by legal authorities (Stage 4) or by friends and family (Stage 3). In the postconventional level, the person has moved beyond social conventions as a source of morality, basing decisions on personal conscience rather than the expectations of others. In Kohlberg's theory, these stages are universal and invariant, meaning that all

---

Kohlberg's Levels and Stages of Moral Development:

Level 1 **Preconventional**

Stage 1   Punishment and obedience orientation: The physical consequences of an action are the only determinant of whether it is good or bad. In other words, the child obeys out of fear of punishment only.

At this stage a child may say that Heinz shouldn't steal the drug because he'll go to jail if he's caught.

Stage 2   Individualism, instrumental relativism: What's in it for me? The child does whatever serves his own interests, without regard for the interests of others. If it gets him what he wants, it's the right thing to do.

Heinz should steal the drug because then he'll get to keep his wife.

Level 2 **Conventional**

Stage 3   Interpersonal expectations and relationships: sometimes called the "good boy/good girl" orientation. What pleases or helps others, or what lives up to their expectations, is good. What disappoints others is bad.

Heinz should steal the drug because his wife and his family will be happier if she gets better, and they'll be very disappointed if he fails to obtain it.

Stage 4   Social norms/"Law and order" orientation. Right is defined as whatever conforms to the social order and doing one's duty according to the rules.

Heinz shouldn't steal the drug because stealing is wrong and illegal.

Level 3 **Postconventional**

Stage 5   Social contract orientation: Values and rules are relative and can be changed—some values are nonrelative and should be upheld regardless of the laws.

Stealing is legally and morally wrong, but preservation of life is more important, so he should steal the drug.

Stage 6   Universal ethical principles: What is right is a matter of conscience, derived from self-chosen ethical ideals that are above either the law or social custom. When laws violate these, the person's actions will be consistent with these principles instead.

Saving his wife is the only consistent moral action possible, and laws that allow the druggist's greed to prevent this should be disobeyed.

---

children should move through the same stages in the same order. The timing of the stages is not invariant, however: people move through them at a different pace, and the final stage achieved will differ from person to person as well.

A major criticism of Kohlberg's theory has been that his data, based on male subjects, produced a theory that focuses on and rewards a traditionally male perspective on morality. There may be some truth to this, as his original research was conducted using a sample of upper-class males, and so Carol Gilligan is correct in pointing out that female perspectives were missing from his theory. In 1982 Gilligan proposed that Kohlberg's higher stages at the conventional and postconventional levels reward a justice ethic, which she saw as primarily masculine, whereas a care ethic emphasizing concern for others and the maintenance of relationships, which Gilligan considered the source of women's moral reasoning, was regarded in Kohlberg's theory as less moral. Gilligan went so far as to propose a separate sequence of stages for women, based on a test that considered actual behavior in real-world moral dilemmas rather than hypothetical Kohlberg-style dilemmas that didn't resemble anything the participants had actually been through.

The problem with Gilligan's approach is that it may be unnecessary. Large-scale tests of Kohlberg's stage theory mostly fail to find any consistent gender differences, because both men and women can and do follow both the care orientation and the justice orientation, and neither approach is consistently scored at a lower level.

A bigger problem with the universal applicability of Kohlberg's stages involves cultural differences rather than gender differences. Cross-cultural studies have found that people in more rural, less technological cultures progress through the stages more slowly, and achieve a lower end-stage, than the American samples on which the theory was based. Kohlberg rewards reasoning based on justice and autonomy, but in some societies community and duty are considered more important.

Within the United States, however, data have provided remarkably consistent support for Kohlberg's sequence of stages and their universality, though the usual rate of progress through the stages is slower than Kohlberg envisioned. In a twenty-year follow-up of Kohlberg's original research participants, Stage 1 reasoning wasn't found in anyone after age sixteen, but some subjects remained at Stage 2 well into adulthood. Stage 3 and Stage 4 reasoning were frequently used in adulthood, but only 10 percent of subjects in their early thirties used Stage 5 reasoning, and not a single one of Kohlberg's original participants ever reached Stage 6. While this last fact has been the basis of some criticism of Kohlberg, it can also be seen as evidence that his theory provides a reasonably accurate description of human morality. A cursory glance at human history, and at the present state of the world, will suffice to demonstrate that the highest levels of moral development probably *should* be regarded as fairly rare.

Further Reading: Gilligan, C. *In a Different Voice: Psychological Theory and Women's Development.* Cambridge, MA: Harvard University Press, 1982; Kohlberg, L., and Elfenbein, D. "The Development of Moral Judgments Concerning Capital Punishment." *American Journal of Orthopsychiatry*, 45 (1975): 614–639.

MOZART EFFECT   One of the most widely disseminated fad ideas in the history of psychology, the Mozart effect is a term for the improvement in brain development that allegedly occurs in children when they are exposed to the music of Wolfgang Amadeus Mozart prior to the age of three. This idea has become so widely accepted that the governors of Tennessee and Georgia have both sponsored programs to provide a free Mozart CD to every newborn baby in their respective states. The National Academy of Recording Arts and Sciences (the organization that sponsors the Grammy awards), not to be outdone, has also given away free recordings of classical music to hundreds of hospitals.

Given the expense involved in these acts of philanthropy, and the attendant publicity the idea has received, the average new parent might be forgiven for believing that the Mozart effect is a real, well-documented scientific phenomenon. As so often happens with widely known psychological ideas, the consumer would be mistaken. The origin of the idea lies in a study conducted in 1993 by Gordon Shaw, a physicist, and Frances Rauscher, a developmental psychologist and former concert cellist. A small sample of college students listened to the first ten minutes of Mozart's *Sonata for Two Pianos in D major (K.448)* and experienced a temporary improvement in spatial-temporal reasoning, as compared to students who listened to nothing or who listened to a relaxation tape. This result has been misreported in many ways, probably most egregiously as the claim that Shaw and Rauscher produced a fifty-one-point improvement in SAT scores. In fact, the task they used involved folding and cutting paper, most certainly not the SAT. Although they agree that their work has been misrepresented, Shaw and Rauscher recognized that their work had spawned an industry, and have joined the flood of entrepreneurs seeking to spread the Mozart effect message. Their Music Intelligence Neural Development Institute (M.I.N.D.) sells software intended to improve children's spatial-temporal reasoning, for example.

The business enterprises of Shaw and Rauscher are small-time efforts, however, compared with the work of online entrepreneur Don Campbell. Campbell has actually trademarked the phrase "the Mozart Effect" and operates many business enterprises built around it, including Mozarteffect.com, where concerned parents may purchase a wide range of books and CDs, including many multi-volume series. Rather than limit his market to concerned parents with disposable income, however, Campbell also claims that "*The Mozart Effect* shows how music can be used to improve memory and learning, boost productivity, soothe jangled nerves, strengthen endurance, unlock creative impulses, sound away pain, and heal the body from a host of ailments" (Mozarteffect.com).

The scientific reliability of Campbell's ideas may be best assessed by considering his claim that he caused a blood clot in his brain to disappear via a treatment consisting of listening to classical and sacred music, humming, and the use of imagery. Despite the lack of evidence for the Mozart effect (or any of the related phenomena that Campbell writes about), millions of people now believe it to be scientific fact rather than the myth that it is, and Campbell has become widely known as an "expert" on the effect, with frequent speaking engagements and interview requests in the mainstream media.

Further Reading: Campbell, R. T. "Mozart Effect." In *The Skeptic's Dictionary.* Hoboken, NJ: Wiley, 2003, pp. 233–235, also see www.skepdic.com; Mozart Effect Resource Center. "Don Campbell's organization." www.MozartEffect.com, 2004.

MPD *See* MULTIPLE PERSONALITY DISORDER (MPD)

MR *See* MENTAL RETARDATION (MR)

MRI *See* BRAIN IMAGING TECHNIQUES

MSBP *See* MUNCHAUSEN SYNDROME

MULTIPLE INTELLIGENCES *See* GARDNER, HOWARD (1943–)

MULTIPLE PERSONALITY DISORDER (MPD) Probably the most controversial of all psychiatric diagnoses, multiple personality disorder (MPD) has as its primary symptom the presence of two or more conscious identities in the same person, although only one is conscious at a time. Each identity is capable of controlling behavior. These other personalities are commonly referred to in the MPD literature as "alters," and they are said to function independently of and usually without awareness of each other. The disorder also involves significant AMNESIA without apparent BRAIN damage, as the primary personality is usually unaware of the existence and activities of the alters. The number of alters varies in reported cases from as few as one to as many as several thousand.

Such an extreme dissociation requires fairly unusual circumstances to occur, and the consensus of the MPD treatment community is that severe, horrific child abuse is usually involved, frequently involving cult ritual activities or sexual victimization. As a defense against such trauma, the child goes into hiding in his or her own mind, creating new personalities who are stronger and better able to cope with the stress and pain. All of this occurs unconsciously, of course, and the person is unaware of the existence of both the alters and the abuse until a therapist helps him or her to recover memories of both (*see* FREUD). This is the explanation of the disorder endorsed by the MPD community, but another, very different, explanation has entered the mainstream psychological research community: that MPD is an iatrogenic condition.

An iatrogenic (from Greek, literally meaning physician-induced) condition is one that exists as a result of treatment, unlike conditions that exist independently and require treatment. This is a strong claim, made in its most potent form by Nicholas Spanos in his book *Multiple Identities & False Memories: A Sociocognitive Perspective*. Spanos argues that MPD is "created by therapists with the cooperation of their patients and the rest of society." There are several compelling reasons to accept this argument, among them the strong similarities between MPD cases and other cases of false memory syndrome: the clients typically have no memories of abuse when first consulting the therapist, and only "recover" them following extensive therapy, which involves such controversial techniques as HYPNOSIS and guided imagery. Once recovered, the memories usually prove impossible to corroborate and often contradict known information regarding the dates and alleged perpetrators. The typical patient also has no record of either reporting or manifesting alters prior to entering therapy. Most psychiatrists and clinical psychologists never see a single case of MPD, but a small handful see hundreds each in a single year. If a disorder is never seen in anyone who hasn't sought therapy, and whether it appears depends on the therapist's pre-existing ideas about the disorder, the iatrogenic explanation seems quite reasonable.

In addition to the therapist, Spanos also blames the cultural context. Indeed, the birth of MPD as currently understood can be traced back to a single successful book and television movie: *Sybil*. The book, by Flora Rheta Schreiber, appeared in 1973, followed by a very successful TV movie starring Sally Field in 1975. Prior to the book, a total of fifty to seventy-five cases suggestive of multiple personalities had been reported by psychiatrists worldwide. Since the movie, there have been about 40,000 cases, almost all in North America. The woman known as Sybil (not her real name) died in 1998 at age 75, and since then a number of people involved with the case have come forward to reveal further details. When she first approached her therapist Cornelia Wilbur, Sybil showed no symptoms of MPD and had reported no memories of abuse. In sessions that involved use of both hypnosis and sodium pentothal (film buffs may recall its frequent appearance in old spy movies as "truth serum"—just the thing for enhancing suggestibility), Wilbur suggested giving names to her various emotional states to deal with her problems more directly. Some of this information comes from Herbert Spiegel, a therapist who met with Sybil as a substitute when Wilbur went out of town. He further reports a conversation with Schreiber as she prepared the book, in which he told her all of this and Schreiber responded that if she didn't say that Sybil had multiple personalities, the book wouldn't sell. All of this information is important in light of the fact that Sybil's case was the one that established the currently accepted pattern of both symptoms and etiology, including the notion that severe abuse was involved, and it is still frequently cited as the classic case of the disorder.

Sybil was not the first successful book or movie about MPD. That honor goes to *The Three Faces of Eve*, written by Corbett Thigpen and filmed with Joanne Woodward as Eve. That book/film combination was much less influential on the therapy community and the public, perhaps because of its failure to provide a clear-cut and dramatic explanation for Eve's disorder. Sexual abuse was not part of the story, and so it doesn't fit what has now become the classic profile. The problems with the evidence for MPD, and with the therapeutic techniques involved in uncovering it, are severe enough that the *DSM-IV* changed the name of the disorder from MPD to Dissociative Identity Disorder (DID). This partly reflects the absence of a clear definition of what an alter is, and it partly reflects the skepticism in the psychological/psychiatric community regarding the existence of multiple personalities. Note that this is not meant in any way to ignore or dismiss the suffering of the clients with DID—the disorder is real and quite traumatic. The controversy is over how the disorder develops in the first place, not over whether they now have a condition in need of attention (*see also* MEMORY; SATANIC RITUAL ABUSE).

Further Reading: Borch-Jakkobsen, M. "Sybil: The Making of a Disease? An Interview with Dr. Herbert Spiegel." *The New York Review of Books*, April 24, 1997; Spanos, N. P. *Multiple Identities and False Memories: A Sociocognitive Perspective*. Washington, DC: American Psychological Association, 1996.

MUNCHAUSEN SYNDROME Munchausen syndrome is the most severe and chronic form of the factitious disorders, in which a person feigns, exaggerates, or even self-induces illness, with the apparent goal of winning attention and nurturance that has otherwise been unavailable. This is technically different from "malingering," in which the illness is faked for external gains such as drugs or disability payments. The fabricated illness tends to be dramatic and convincing. Munchausen patients frequently have scars from multiple surgeries, genuine fevers (often due to infection of self-induced abscesses), or even amputated limbs. Patients tend to be intelligent and well informed regarding medical practices, diagnoses, and treatments.

Like malingerers, they are aware of their deceit; unlike malingerers, their motives seem to be at least partially unconscious. This syndrome, though dramatic, is extremely rare, and its cause is unknown. Patients with Munchausen syndrome have, however, been observed to have associated personality disorders (e.g., poor impulse control, self-destructive behavior, borderline or passive-aggressive personality trait or disorder). Some clinicians have also suggested that the Munchausen patient tends to have a history of abuse or neglect, coupled with an experience at some point of having become ill and consequently having received far better and more nurturing treatment than was customary for him or her. Also, most Munchausen patients are male.

The syndrome is named for Baron von Munchausen (1720–1797), a notorious traveler and liar, known for his wildly extravagant, yet utterly untruthful, accounts of distant lands and events. The name is appropriate, as he used these fantasies to seek attention that his relatively unexciting experiences were unlikely to attract.

Munchausen syndrome should not be confused with an odd variation on the disease, Munchausen syndrome by proxy (MSBP), which is an unusual form of child abuse. In MSBP, a parent, usually the mother, fakes symptoms of illness in her child and seeks frequent, and often intrusive, medical attention on the child's behalf. In the hospital setting, the mother is very helpful and is seen by staff as unusually devoted and self-sacrificing. Her frequent visits, of course, give her easy access to the child to create more symptoms. The motivation is believed to be much the same as in Munchausen syndrome: the mother receives a lot of positive attention as a result of her efforts on the child's behalf.

MSBP has been a source of much controversy. The general consensus is that MSBP, like the classical Munchausen syndrome, is extremely rare, but the rate at which it is diagnosed is rising rather rapidly. The impact of the rising popularity of MSBP accusations is perhaps best illustrated by the first two "hits" to appear in a recent internet search on Munchausen syndrome. The first was the Web site of a large law firm, promising that "our criminal defense lawyers know how to defend Munchausen cases in any court in America"; the second was the home of Mothers Against Munchausen Allegations (M.A.M.A.), an advocacy group for mothers who have been falsely accused of harming their chronically ill children.

Further Reading: Feldman, M. D. *Playing Sick: Untangling the Web of Munchausen Syndrome, Munchausen by Proxy, Malingering, and Factitious Disorder.* New York: Brunner-Routledge, 2004.

MUNCHAUSEN SYNDROME BY PROXY (MSBP) *See* MUNCHAUSEN SYNDROME

N

NARCOLEPSY Narcolepsy is a sleep disorder in which a person in an active waking state shifts abruptly into several minutes of REM sleep, usually with no warning at all. As REM is the sleep stage in which most dreaming occurs, the disorder may be thought of as a sudden intrusion of dreaming sleep into the consciousness of a person who was awake a moment earlier. In addition to excessive daytime sleepiness, the classic symptoms of narcolepsy include cataplexy, a dramatic and sudden loss of muscle tone, often accompanied by paralysis, that is usually brought on by a strong emotion like fear, surprise, anxiety, or even excessive laughter. As narcolepsy involves the onset of REM sleep, this is unsurprising, as REM sleep is usually accompanied by sleep paralysis, or the disinhibition of muscle movement that prevents us from acting out our dreams as they happen.

Narcoleptic episodes are also frequently accompanied by hypnagogic hallucinations, extremely vivid dreamlike images that occur at the onset of sleep, before a person is fully asleep. This little-known phenomenon is actually fairly common in people without sleep disorders, and provides a possible explanatory mechanism for such unusual phenomena as ALIEN ABDUCTION experiences, among others. Disturbances of nighttime sleep, including nightmares, leg jerks, tossing and turning, and frequent awakening, are also very common in people with narcolepsy and may explain some of the daytime sleepiness associated with the disorder. Unrelenting daytime sleepiness is usually the first symptom of the disorder noticed, and it leads to irresistible "sleep attacks," also sometimes called microsleeps, which can last anywhere from thirty seconds or less to more than thirty minutes, and which can occur anytime, no matter how inappropriate. The sleep attacks can occur at work or social events, while eating, or even while driving or doing hazardous work with machinery.

Currently, no cure for narcolepsy is known, but both drug treatment and behavioral treatment have been found helpful. Drug treatment has usually consisted of amphetamines and similar stimulants, but in 1999 the Food and Drug Administration (FDA) approved a new drug, modafinil (brand name Provigil), for treatment of narcolepsy. While also a stimulant, it is notably different chemically from amphetamines, and it is said to be far less likely to cause jitteriness and difficulty sleeping at night, as well as possessing some mood-enhancing effects. Antidepressant medications are sometimes prescribed as well, to reduce cataplexy and sleep paralysis. Medications only alleviate symptoms, however, while doing nothing to eliminate the underlying problem. Behavioral treatments focused on lifestyle change, such as adjusting sleep schedules, scheduling regular naptimes, and avoiding the excessive emotional stimulation that can trigger cataplexy, have also shown promise.

Ultimately, the prognosis for narcolepsy sufferers will improve further as the causes of the disorder become better understood. In 1999 a team of Stanford University researchers working with dogs identified a defective gene that appeared to cause the disorder. More recently, this finding has been extended to humans, providing both a possible etiology for the disorder and potential new directions in treatment. The Stanford team found that a small peptide, hypocretin, which naturally occurs in the brains of people without narcolepsy, was absent in every narcoleptic brain studied. The cells that manufacture hypocretin, of which a normal brain contains between 10,000 and 15,000, appear to be completely absent from the brains of narcoleptic patients. If a drug can be synthesized which replaces hypocretin, or at least duplicates its action in the brain, a more permanent treatment, or even a cure, for narcolepsy may become possible (*see also* SLEEP AND DREAMING).

Further Reading: Scammell, Thomas E. "The Neurobiology, Diagnosis, and Treatment of Narcolepsy." *Annals of Neurology*, *53*(2) (2003): 154–166.

NEO-FREUDIANS Neo-Freudians is the term sometimes used to collectively describe the students and followers of Sigmund FREUD who subsequently broke ranks with him and produced their own variations on psychoanalysis instead. The member of this group who is best known and most highly regarded by the general public is Carl JUNG, but others have also had a lasting impact on psychology.

Alfred Adler (1870–1937) agreed with Freud that childhood experiences are important, but he focused his attention on social, rather than sexual, tensions as a source of personality development. Adler believed that such things as BIRTH ORDER and parents' child-rearing practices could produce childhood feelings of inferiority, and this inferiority complex led to behaviors characterized by a striving for superiority and power. Adler was especially critical of Freud's concept of penis envy, arguing that what shapes a woman's character is not an unconscious desire to obtain a penis, but rather the envy of the social advantages that accompany being male.

Karen Horney (1885–1952), who although German-born spent her career in the United States, also parted ways with Freud over his excessive emphasis on sexuality as the source of all problems. While practicing in Chicago during the Great Depression, she realized that the people who were coming to see her had problems associated with their present status, not deep-seated traumas rooted in early childhood. Her clients had no use for discussions of Oedipal feelings for their mothers; they were far more concerned about the fact that they'd lost their savings and couldn't feed their families. Horney also felt that Freud's theory was too narrowly deterministic, whereas she saw many different possible paths that the mother-child relationship could take other than the Oedipal conflict. Like Adler, she also found penis envy unconvincing, and she went so far as to argue that a reversal of the pattern occurs in men, who envy women's ability to create life within them.

Otto Rank (1884–1939) remained a close associate and follower of Freud for much of his professional life, but like the others, he too eventually diverged enough from Freudian orthodoxy that his relationship with Freud came to an end. Unlike the others, Rank did not fault Freud for his focus on sexuality, but his own thinking on the matter eventually struck even Freud as unlikely. Rank saw birth trauma as the chief source of anxiety and interpreted the male sexual urge as primarily a desire to return to the peace and safety of the womb.

Like Freud, the neo-Freudians have contributed enduring concepts and vocabulary (inferiority complex, birth trauma, and return to the womb, for example) to Western culture. Also like Freud, their impact on current psychology is rather limited, due to the untestable, and therefore unscientific, nature of their ideas.

Further Reading: Adler, A. *Individual Psychology of Alfred Adler.* New York: Perennial, 1964; Paris, B. J. *Karen Horney: A Psychoanalyst's Search for Self-Understanding.* New Haven, CT: Yale University Press, 1996.

NERVOUS BREAKDOWN Not a diagnosis so much as a euphemism, nervous breakdown is a term that was once widely used by the general public and the mass media, but rarely mentioned by psychiatrists or clinical psychologists, at least among themselves. It is an inexact term that has been popular since the early days of clinical practice, primarily as a term for patients to use so as not to stigmatize themselves with a psychiatric label. People simply prefer to be thought of as having a physical illness, a problem with the nervous system, rather than a psychological illness. In the early days of neurology and psychology, the diagnosis—often called neurasthenia, spinal irritation, neuralgic disease, or even "the vapors"—was believed to be a legitimate one, until it became clear that mental disorders were conditions of the mind rather than malfunctions of the nerves.

The term *nervous breakdown* survives today in its capacity as a nonspecific euphemism for psychological problems, especially among celebrities, with whom its set of possible meanings has expanded to include treatment for substance abuse. Other possible definitions also include various anxiety disorders, major depression, and even psychotic episodes. Nervous breakdown is currently losing ground as the favored euphemism, however, to something even more vague and physical sounding: exhaustion (*see also* BRAIN).

Further Reading: Barke, M., Fribush, R., and Stearns, P. N. "Nervous Breakdown in 20th-Century American Culture." *Journal of Social History,* 33(3) (2000): 565–585.

NERVOUS SYSTEM   The major biological determinant of human behavior is the nervous system, which is made up of two different kinds of cells: glial cells and neurons. Both types are very important, but the neurons tend to get most of the attention, because they are the cells that actually transmit information. Glial cells, or simply glia (the name means glue) exist to provide support for the neurons, by holding them in place, providing nourishment, destroying old and damaged neurons, and disposing of waste materials. Glia also provide myelin, an important insulating material for proper nervous transmission. Neurons are the cells that actually transmit information, making possible everything from higher-order thought processes to simple reflexes and movements. The body contains approximately one trillion neurons, with a large portion of them making up the BRAIN.

Neurons come in a variety of shapes and sizes, from a microscopic scale to several feet long—there are single neurons that extend from the spinal column to the foot, for example. Despite these disparities, most neurons share a basic configuration. This configuration may be roughly divided into three parts: cell body, dendrites, and axon. The cell body is essentially a life-support center for the rest of the cell, and like most cell bodies it includes a nucleus, which is where the cell DNA is located. The dendrites, which may number in the hundreds on a single neuron, are fingerlike projections (the name means fingers) with the task of receiving information from other neurons. The axon is the extended arm of the neuron, ending in more branching projections (these are called terminal buttons) through which information is passed along to other neurons. On many neurons, especially the longer ones, the axon is wrapped in a sheet of a waxy, fatty substance called myelin, which serves to enable much faster neural transmission than is possible in unmyelinated neurons. Many elementary psychology textbooks compare the myelin sheath to the rubber insulation on the outside of a wire, but this analogy is fairly inaccurate, because transmission of electrical impulses along neurons is quite different from how wires work.

The process of neural transmission is more accurately called an electrochemical process than a purely electrical one, and its complexity makes the speed at which it occurs especially impressive. Like in all cells of the body, a neuron's mass is made up largely of water, and the cell is surrounded by fluid as well. Suspended in that fluid are ions (atoms with a positive or a negative charge) of sodium (Na) and potassium (K), among other elements. These are the *electrolytes* that coaches worry will be lost through excessive sweating, and a major reason why dehydration is dangerous. Without the proper concentrations of these particles (too many or too few is bad), the cells that run things in the body cannot function properly.

Ordinarily, in its resting state, the inside of the cell has an excess of negatively charged ions, while the area surrounding it has an excess of positively charged ions. This balance, called a resting potential, is made possible by the cell membrane, which is selectively permeable, meaning it has "gates" through which positive ions cannot pass but negative ions can.

When a signal is received by the dendrites from another neuron or neurons telling the neuron to fire (transmit a message to the next neuron), the membrane flips open those gates at the first bit of the axon, allowing the positive ions to flood in. They are strongly attracted by the negative ions on the inside, rather like opposite poles on magnets. This flooding *depolarizes* that part of the axon, which causes the next section of membrane to do the same thing, and then the next, and so on, and thus an electrical impulse (known as an action potential) travels the length of the axon.

After a section of the membrane has depolarized, it pumps the positive ions back out and gets ready to do it all again. While the membrane does this, it is in the refractory period, and incapable of firing again until the resetting process is complete. Complex though this process sounds, some neurons can perform this set of functions 100 times in a single second.

The process is actually considerably more complex, considering the fact that each neuron can have dendritic connections to hundreds or even thousands of other neurons, all of which may be sending it signals at the same time. A neuron can transmit only two kinds of signal, excitatory and inhibitory. An excitatory signal encourages the cell to fire, whereas an inhibitory signal tells it not to. The cell body takes all the different signals into account and determines whether excitatory signals outnumber inhibitory signals to a large enough degree (the threshold). Think of it as a small political gathering: if the *yeas* exceed the *nays*, the resolution passes and an action potential is sent along. Each neuron is only capable of firing in a particular way, however; and firing is an all-or-nothing response. A neuron either fires or it doesn't, and a greater degree of excitation will not produce a more intense response.

Once that action potential reaches the terminal buttons at the other end of the axon, things get a bit more complicated. Although a cell's terminal buttons and dendrites can make connections to thousands of other neurons, no actual physical contact occurs between neurons. They are separated by an open, fluid-filled gap known as the synapse, or synaptic cleft. When the action potential reaches the terminal button, it triggers the release of messenger chemicals, called neurotransmitters, into the synapse. They cross the gap and attach to receptor sites on the dendrites of the next neuron, triggering slight changes (excitatory or inhibitory) in the cell membrane. Any neurotransmitter molecules that do not bind to receptor sites are reabsorbed by the terminal buttons that released them, in a process called reuptake. All of this takes about 1/10,000 of a second to occur. Many drugs, including the antidepressants known as SSRIs (selective serotonin reuptake inhibitors), work by preventing reuptake, thus making more neurotransmitter molecules available to the neurons in the brain.

There are dozens of different neurotransmitters, and particular pathways in the brain may only make use of one or two of them, thus giving certain neurotransmitters very particular effects on behavior, emotions, and cognitions:

- *Dopamine*—is involved in movement, learning, attention, and emotion. Insufficient dopamine is a major factor in Parkinson's disease, in which the primary symptom is difficulty coordinating movement, while excess activity at dopamine receptors is often seen in schizophrenia.

- *Serotonin*—is involved in regulating mood, hunger, sleep/waking cycles, and arousal. Prozac and several other popular antidepressants act primarily by maintaining high serotonin levels. LSD and other psychedelic drugs also act on serotonin levels, as do cocaine and other stimulants.

- *Acetylcholine*—is used by neurons involved in muscle action as well as learning and memory. In persons with Alzheimer's disease, levels of acetylcholine are unusually low.

- *Gamma-aminobutyric acid (GABA)*—serves primarily in inhibitory pathways and is involved in sleep disorders and eating disorders.

- *Norephinephrine*—is involved in control of alertness and arousal.

- *Endorphins*—these neurotransmitters are chemically similar to morphine and other opiates (the name is short for endogenous morphine). They are released in response to pain and vigorous exercise—hence the widely known "runner's high."

Most psychoactive drugs act by either fitting the receptor sites for neurotransmitters, thus mimicking their actions (drugs known as *agonists*); or by blocking the receptor sites, thus preventing the neurotransmitter from doing its job (*antagonists*).

The nervous system, where all those neurons do their work, can actually be thought of as several systems that work together. Traditionally, the nervous system has been divided into two main divisions, the central nervous system (CNS) and the peripheral nervous system. The central nervous system is made up of the brain and spinal cord, and the peripheral nervous system is made up of all the rest. The peripheral nervous system is further broken down into the somatic and the autonomic nervous systems. Another helpful way to think of these two systems is as the voluntary and involuntary systems. The somatic nervous system consists of all those neurons that are involved in bringing sensory information to the BRAIN, and is also responsible for the production of voluntary movements and actions, whereas the autonomic nervous system is made up of neurons involved in producing involuntary reactions.

One example of an autonomic nervous system response with which everyone should be familiar is the fight-or-flight response, the set of involuntary physiological reactions that is often activated by stress. Assume, for example, that a leisurely, pleasant hike in the woods is suddenly interrupted by coming face-to-face with a hungry Bengal tiger. Without any need for conscious thought to motivate it, the body goes into action, getting ready to either run away very fast or to give that tiger a walloping he won't soon forget (one of these is a more advisable plan of action than the other, considering the hiker's unarmed state). Symptoms are likely to include the following: faster, shallower breathing (to get more oxygen to your cells more rapidly), elevated pulse and blood pressure (same reason), rush of blood to the face (evolutionarily speaking, this is probably to intimidate the tiger, but it isn't likely to be effective), profuse perspiration (to cool off the fighting-or-fleeing body), dilated pupils (so the hiker can see his fate more clearly), and, under great stress, release of bladder and/or bowel control (probably for purposes of dropping ballast and lightening the load—this one made sense biologically before clothing).

The autonomic nervous system is also subdivided into two parts: the sympathetic nervous system and the parasympathetic nervous system. The sympathetic system is the one that produces the fight-or-flight response, but that state (fast heart rate, high blood pressure, etc.) isn't a healthy one to remain in for very long, so a separate system (the parasympathetic) exists simply to slow things back down to normal once the danger is past. In most (less dangerous than an encounter with a tiger) anxiety-producing circumstances, a lesser version of the response may occur (sweaty palms when about to meet someone important, discomfort in the stomach upon hearing a scary sound late at night), but the autonomic nervous system is still responsible.

Further Reading: Sylwester, R. *A Celebration of Neurons: An Educator's Guide to the Human Brain.* Association for Supervision and Curriculum Development, 1995.

NEUROIMAGING TECHNIQUES   *See* BRAIN IMAGING TECHNIQUES

NONSPECIFIC EFFECTS   Potential clients and students of psychology often ask a very good question: "Which therapy works best or, at least, does one work better than others?" Unfortunately, the answer, at least according to a famous meta-analysis (Smith et al., 1977, 1980), may be that all therapeutic approaches are equally effective (or ineffective, depending on how one interprets the data). This is due to a variety of factors known as nonspecific effects of treatment—nonspecific because they occur in all therapeutic settings, rather than being specific to a particular type.

Although all therapies have advocates who claim that theirs is clearly the superior product, Smith's comparison yielded no winner. Furthermore, the type of therapy, the context (individual or group), and the level of training and experience of the therapist were all equally useless in discerning relative effectiveness of therapies. Note, however, that this analysis was based on studies in which clients in treatment were compared to a control group of people who were not undergoing treatment. The real conclusion to be drawn, therefore, is that receiving treatment is generally more likely to be helpful than not receiving treatment.

These nonspecific effects involve elements that are common to all therapeutic settings. These include, but are not limited to, the following:

- Hope for improvement—Simply seeking out therapy indicates an expectation that improvement is possible, and so the person who seeks out treatment is motivated by hope in a way that somebody who does not seek it out clearly is not. In other words, they expect to get better, and so they do.

- A trusting relationship with a caring person—In seeking therapy, the client is establishing a trusting relationship with another person who also believes improvement can happen, and who is dedicated to helping the client. The mere fact that someone is paying attention to the client may produce improvement.

- Most illnesses, both mental and physical, are self-limiting—When a person has a cold and gets proper medical treatment, that person may feel much better within a week. Another person who does not seek treatment, however, may take as long as seven days to improve. Most physical illnesses go away on their own. What is missing from many discussions of Smith and his colleagues' findings, however, is that most of the untreated people in those studies of different therapies also got better over time.

It is because these effects are well known that studies of treatment efficacy must be designed in such a way as to distinguish real treatment effects from nonspecific effects.

One way that this is accomplished is through the use of placebos. A placebo is simply a fake treatment. In medical studies, a placebo is frequently a pill containing only an inert substance, often sugar, rather than any medically active ingredient. In this way, people receiving the actual drug can be compared to people who have experienced all aspects of treatment except for the drug. In psychological treatment studies, placebo treatments are often used in which the placebo control group is treated in the same way as the group receiving the experimental treatment except that they do not receive the elements of the treatment that are expected to actually produce improvement. One example of this would be a recent study of EYE MOVEMENT DESENSITIZATION AND REPROCESSING (EMDR). The control group received treatment without the eye movements that give the therapy its name. A common finding in such studies is that participants receiving a placebo almost always show significantly greater improvement than untreated control subjects. This well documented pattern of results is known as the *placebo effect* and is clearly due primarily to nonspecific effects.

Further Reading: Perlman, L. M. "Nonspecific, Unintended, and Serendipitous Effects in Psychotherapy." *Professional Psychology: Research & Practice,* 32(3) (2001): 283–289; Smith, M. L., and Glass, G. V. "Meta-Analysis of Psychotherapy Outcome Studies." *American Psychologist,* 32(9) (1977): 752–760; Smith, M. L., Glass, G. V., and Miller, R. L. *The Benefits of Psychotherapy.* Baltimore: Johns Hopkins, 1980.

O

OBEDIENCE TO AUTHORITY   Probably no single event in world history has distressed psychologists so much as the Nazi Holocaust. How could apparently normal, civilized members of a modern society treat their fellow human beings with such unparalleled cruelty and savagery? Early attempts to explain the Holocaust tended towards a psychoanalytic approach, in which bigotry and ethnic hatred are due to the authoritarian personality that resulted from poor parenting practices and traumatic childhood experiences. Unsurprisingly, this sort of simplistic explanation failed to satisfy many psychologists. In the early 1960s, Yale social psychologist Stanley Milgram decided to test an alternative explanation: there was something about the special social situation in which the Germans found themselves that could cause ordinary people to commit atrocities they would never consider committing under ordinary circumstances.

Milgram conducted a series of twenty experiments to test his hypothesis that strong social influences could cause people to behave in uncharacteristically cruel ways. In the first experiment, forty men ranging in age from twenty to fifty years old answered a newspaper ad and were selected to come to separate appointments at Milgram's laboratory. At the laboratory, each participant was met by the "researcher" (actually a local high school science teacher, playing a role), who introduced him to another volunteer (a middle-aged accountant *pretending* to be another "volunteer"). The volunteer and the other "volunteer" were told that they would be participating in a study of the role of punishment in learning. They drew slips of paper to find out who would be the teacher and who would be the student. Actually, both slips said "teacher," but the confederate discarded his without revealing it.

The "student" was then led into an adjoining room and strapped into a chair, and electrodes were strapped to his wrists, from which wires ran through the wall into the next room. The wires apparently connected the chair to a box described as an electric shock machine. It was a shiny metal box with a row of thirty switches on it, labeled with voltages in an ascending order from left to right. The numbers ranged from 15 to 450 and were supplemented by descriptive labels, from "slight shock" through "moderate shock" to "Danger: Severe Shock" at 435. The last two switches were simply marked "XXX."

The teacher was given a list of word pairs to read to the student, to be followed by a multiple-choice memory test. In the test, the teacher would read the first word of a pair, followed by four choices for the second word of the pair. The student would indicate his choice by pushing one of four buttons, which corresponded to four light bulbs on the top of the shock machine. Whenever a wrong answer was given, the teacher was to administer a shock, starting with the lowest voltage and working his way up as the test progressed. The device was of course fake, and no shocks were delivered, but the volunteers were unaware of this.

At first the test proceeded uneventfully, with some right answers and some wrong answers, and mild shocks following the wrong answers. At seventy-five volts, however, the learner made an audible sound of distress, and at 120 he shouted that the shock was painful. At 150, the learner shouted "Get me out of here! I refuse to go on!" At this point, the researcher merely said, "Please continue." The student's responses would eventually escalate to screams of agony, and he went completely silent at the 330-volt level, answering no further questions and making no sounds. At all stages, the researcher continued to sternly advise the teacher to continue, even saying, as the highest voltages approached, "You have no other choice; you must go on."

Milgram was hoping to better understand the role of authority figures in obedience of unreasonable orders, but the pattern of results he found was astonishing even to him. Sixty-three percent of the teachers went on despite the student's protests, all the way to the highest switch. Believing that perhaps the student's protests had simply not been convincing enough, he added something to the next experiment. This time the student mentioned a slight heart condition while being strapped to the chair. Under these conditions, 65 percent went all the way. In follow-up studies, Milgram made subtle variations in the experimental social situation, and found that under different conditions, the proportion of fully compliant subjects who went all the way to the highest voltage varied from none to 93 percent.

Obedience was highest when the person giving the orders was both close at hand and was perceived to be a legitimate authority figure, supported by a prestigious institution. When he took his experiments off-campus, so that the experimenter was no longer seen as representing Yale, compliance went down. High levels of compliance also required that the victim be depersonalized or at a distance, as compliance was much lower if he was in the same room. This is a well-known phenomenon in wartime, as many soldiers will not fire their rifles, or will not aim them properly, at an enemy they can clearly see. No such problem arises with those who operate large artillery pieces. Finally, high levels of compliance only occurred when no role models for defiance were present. If they saw another volunteer (actually, a confederate) disobeying the experimenter, subjects were far more likely to do so themselves. Milgram's findings have been replicated in over 100 other studies in multiple countries.

It is important to note that Milgram's subjects were not sadists, and while many of them followed instructions to the point of giving what they believed were potentially fatal shocks, the experience was not at all a pleasant one for them. Milgram observed participants "sweat, tremble, stutter, bit their lips, groan, and dig their fingernails into their flesh." A confident, smiling business-man "was reduced to a twitching, stuttering wreck who was rapidly approach-ing a point of nervous collapse." Although Milgram defended his experiments to the end, the ethical standards adopted by the AMERICAN PSYCHOLOGICAL ASSOCIATION in 1973 were heavily influenced by reaction to his accounts of his volunteers' experiences. Because of those standards, it would be virtually im-possible to receive institutional approval for his experiments at any U.S. univer-sity today. Among other things, APA standards require that subjects be allowed to stop, without penalty, at any time.

Some fundamental lessons about obedience to authority and its relationship to evil arose from this research. In Milgram's words, "The most fundamental lesson of our study is that ordinary people, simply doing their jobs, and without any particular hostility on their part, can become agents in a terrible destructive process." Indeed, his subjects did not behave according to their own moral beliefs or expectations. When Milgram described his experiment in detail to a wide range of audiences and asked them at what level they would stop giving shocks, the average answer was 150 volts. When Milgram's own subjects were asked at what level they should stop, the answer was again 150 volts. What people did in the experimental situation had nothing to do with either their expectations of their own behavior or their moral views. Milgram accomplished this by using a "foot-in-the-door" technique (*see* BRAINWASHING). He did not get his subjects to simply come into the lab and flip a switch that they believed might kill a man—that would not have worked. Instead, he had them start with very small acts. Having done those and feeling they were justified, they then moved on to greater and greater acts. The Nazi leaders used very similar tactics. Suspecting that most German government workers would refuse to directly take part in the killing of Jews, gypsies, homosexuals, and other "undesirables," they found them nonetheless willing and able to handle the bureaucratic paper-work involved. The single most famous statement made by any of the Nazi leaders during the Nuremberg war crimes trials comes from Adolf Eichmann, who was in charge of deportation of people to the concentration camps: "I was only following orders." The same justification was offered by some of the par-ticipants in the humiliation of Iraqi captives by American soldiers at Abu Ghraib prison, in 2004.

Further Reading: Milgram, S. "Behavioral Study of Obedience." *Journal of Abnormal and Social Psychology*, 67 (1963): 371–378; Milgram, S. *Obedience to Authority*. New York: Harper and Row, 1974.

OPIOIDS (OPIATES) Opioids (opiates) are also known as painkillers because of their analgesic, or pain-relieving, properties. This class of medications, also widely referred to as narcotics, is made up primarily of substances derived from opium, or artificially created analogs, and includes morphine, codeine, heroin, and related drugs. Morphine is frequently used before or after surgery to alleviate severe pain. Codeine, less effective than morphine, is prescribed for milder pain. Other widely prescribed opioids include oxycodone (recently in the news owing to abuse of its time-release form, OxyContin), propoxyphene (best known as Darvon), hydrocodone (best known as Vicodin), and meperidine (Demerol), which is used less often than the others because of its side effects. Codeine is also frequently used to treat coughs and is sometimes prescribed for serious diarrhea as well (all the opioids have constipating properties). The best-known illegal opiate, heroin, is actually the result of a failed experiment to produce a better medicine. It was introduced in 1896 by the Bayer Company, as a purer form of morphine that produced fewer side effects.

Opioids act by mimicking the actions of endorphins, naturally occurring neurotransmitters with just one job: inhibiting the transmittal of pain signals within the central NERVOUS SYSTEM. Because of the existence of endorphins, neurons in the brain and spinal cord (and, curiously, in the digestive tract) have specialized receptor sites for opioids. Opioid drugs simply attach to those receptors, thus halting the transmission of pain messages. In addition to pain relief, however, opiates can also produce constipation; cause drowsiness; and produce feelings of euphoria—this, more than pain relief, contributes to psychological dependence. When taken to excess, however, they can also act on brainstem areas that regulate respiration, depressing that function.

It is this ability to depress breathing that makes long-term abuse of opioids so dangerous. The fatal dose, the amount that will completely arrest respiration, remains fairly constant for each individual. As tolerance for the drug builds, larger and larger amounts are required to achieve the desired effect, but the fatal dose remains the same as the effective dose increases. Eventually, an addict will reach a point at which the effective dose exceeds the fatal dose. This is how accidental overdoses occur. In abusers of prescription opiates, accidental overdoses can also occur, but sometimes they happen after fairly short-term use, because the users simply take too much in their attempt to get high. This especially became a problem with the recent popularity of Oxycontin, which is used to treat severe chronic pain. Since the drug is intended to be released slowly into the bloodstream over a long period of time, each individual pill contains a much larger dose than typical painkiller tablets. Abusers frequently crush the pills and take it all at once, or even dissolve and inject it (this has led to the nickname "hillbilly heroin"), thus administering an unpredictably high dose that may be too much for them.

In addition to tolerance, long-term use of opioids also produces withdrawal symptoms if use of the drug is reduced or stopped. Opiate withdrawal can be severe, including insomnia, diarrhea, vomiting, pain, and cold flashes—the poultry-like appearance of the resulting goose bumps may be the source of the term "cold turkey." The sickness is severe enough to make quitting heroin very difficult, even when the user is highly motivated to quit. For this reason, quitting heroin is often accompanied by administration of methadone, intended to be a less potent opioid, to reduce the severity of the withdrawal symptoms. Unfortunately, some addicts simply become addicted to the methadone instead, and withdrawal from it can be fairly unpleasant, too. It bears mentioning, however, that a large body of research has shown that when prescribed narcotics are managed and monitored properly, their use is safe and rarely results in addiction. This is good news, as opioids remain by far the most effective way to manage serious pain (*see also* DEPRESSANTS; PSYCHEDELIC DRUGS; STIMULANTS).

Further Reading: Stimmel, B. *Opiate Receptors, Neurotransmitters, and Drug Dependence: Basic Science-Clinical Correlates*. Binghamton, NY: Haworth Press, 1981.

P

PARAPHILIAS The paraphilias are a set of sexual disorders that share a pattern of recurrent, intensely arousing fantasies, sexual urges, or behaviors involving either nonhuman objects, suffering and/or humiliation either of one's self or one's partner, or nonconsenting persons. The pattern must occur over a period of at least six months, and it must cause clinically significant distress or impairment in functioning. The person with a paraphilia is typically aware that the symptoms are negatively affecting his or her life, but feels unable to control them. In some cases, the fantasies or objects are always necessary for erotic arousal, whereas for others, the paraphiliac fantasies and behaviors may only occur episodically, such as in times of great stress. With the exception of sexual masochism, which occurs in twenty men for every woman who has it, the paraphilias are almost never diagnosed in women.

The *DSM-IV* identifies nine distinct categories of paraphilia, including the broad category Paraphilia Not Otherwise Specified, which brings together several rare types. They are defined as follows:

- *Exhibitionism*—This is the classic "flasher" syndrome; its primary symptom is the exposure of the genitals to strangers. Sometimes masturbation in the full view of strangers is involved as well.

- *Fetishism*—As the name suggests, the focus of sexual arousal is a fetish, or an inanimate object. The most frequently encountered fetishes are various women's undergarments, shoes, or other apparel. The person with fetishism frequently becomes sexually aroused by touching or smelling the fetish object, or may ask a sexual partner to do so during a sexual encounter.

The fetish is usually required for sexual arousal, and its absence may cause erectile dysfunction.

- *Frotteurism*—Frotteurism involves rubbing against or touching a nonconsenting person, usually in a crowded public place. The crowded location is preferred because the individual with frotteurism is aware that his or her acts, called frottage in the *DSM-IV*, are illegal and can more easily escape detection and arrest in this way.

- *Pedophilia*—Pedophilia involves sexual activity with a prepubescent child, usually defined as someone thirteen years old or younger, by a person who is age sixteen or older and at least five years older than the child (although no age difference is specified for late-adolescent pedophiles). There are two broad types of pedophile. The exclusive type is attracted only to children, whereas the nonexclusive type is sometimes attracted to adults as well. Some prefer females and some males; those attracted to females generally prefer eight- to ten-year-olds, and those attracted to males tend to prefer slightly older children. The pedophile usually does not see his or her behavior as wrong. Instead he or she rationalizes the activity in terms of its "educational value" for the child, or provision of pleasure to the child, or claims that the child behaved in a sexually provocative way. Most pedophiles limit their activities to children they know, including their own children, stepchildren, relatives, and neighbors. The sexual abduction by a stranger that parents have come to fear so much, due partly to extensive media coverage of a few isolated cases, is actually extremely rare. Pedophilia is usually chronic, and it is especially so in those who prefer male children: their recidivism rate is roughly twice what it is for those who prefer females.

- *Sexual Masochism*—In masochism, the source of arousal is humiliation and suffering. Some individuals are disturbed by their masochistic urges and act on them while alone, sticking themselves with pins, cutting themselves, or self-administering electrical shocks, while others seek help from a sexual partner. Common masochistic acts include physical restraint and bondage, paddling, spanking, beating, electrical shocks, piercing, cutting, and humiliation, including such things as being subjected to verbal abuse, as well as being urinated or defecated upon. An unusually dangerous form of sexual masochism is hypoxyphilia, in which the person is sexually aroused by oxygen deprivation, often achieved by the use of a noose or other tight ligature around the neck. The occasional accidental death is inevitable, with several such deaths documented in the United States each year. Like other paraphilias, sexual masochism is chronic, and many individuals simply find a particular masochistic act they like and stick with it in relative safety for many years. Some, however, increase the severity of the acts over time, especially in periods of stress, and may eventually suffer injury or death as a result.

- *Sexual Sadism*—Sexual masochism's opposite number, sexual sadism focuses on deriving sexual arousal from the psychological or physical suffering of a victim, frequently an individual with sexual masochism. Some individuals with this disorder, however, prefer the suffering of unconsenting victims, and as the paraphilia is chronic, they are likely to repeat the activity until they are apprehended. The sadistic fantasies have usually been present since childhood. Although not true in all cases, the severity of the sadistic acts tends to increase over time. In severe cases, especially when sadism is associated as it sometimes is with antisocial personality disorder, serious injury or death of the victim may result.

- *Transvestic Fetishism*—The source of sexual arousal here is cross-dressing. While dressed in women's clothing, the man with transvestic fetishism masturbates while fantasizing that he is both the male and female partner in the sex act. This disorder occurs exclusively in heterosexual males (in part, perhaps, because Western norms include the wearing of traditionally male clothing by women, but not the reverse), and it is different from the cross-dressing that occurs in Gender Identity Disorder. The degree of cross-dressing varies dramatically, with some men dressing entirely as females and wearing makeup, while others will wear a solitary item of women's clothing under their regular attire. Although it is not usually a feature, gender dysphoria (dissatisfaction and discomfort with one's gender identity) may also occur, and is listed in the *DSM-IV* as transvestic fetishism with gender dysphoria.

- *Voyeurism*—Voyeurism is the technical term for what is commonly known as being a "peeping tom." In voyeurism, the individual becomes sexually aroused by watching unsuspecting individuals, usually strangers, as they undress or as they engage in sexual activity. A fantasy involving sexual activity with the observed person is fairly common, but no actual sexual activity with the observed person is usually sought. Like all paraphilias, it is chronic, and it usually begins before age fifteen.

- *Paraphilia Not Otherwise Specified*—This category encompasses other paraphilias, usually quite rare, that do not meet the criteria for any of the other categories. A selected sampling, along with what the person is aroused by, follows:
  - Necrophilia—dead bodies
  - Zoophilia—animals (this one is often incorrectly called bestiality)
  - Coprophilia—feces
  - Urophilia—urine
  - Klismaphilia—enemas
  - Partialism—a single body part/area
  - Telephone scatologia—obscene phone calls

Individuals with paraphilias will often select a hobby or a job that brings them into closer contact with the arousing stimulus. A fetishist may work in a lingerie shop or a shoe store, for example, or a pedophile might get a job in a school setting. As with all psychological disorders, paraphilias must cause distress and impair functioning to be diagnosed. A man who finds women's shoes arousing, but does not require their presence to become aroused, may be a bit unusual, but he does not have a disorder (*see also* Phobias).

Further Reading: American Psychiatric Association. *DSM-IV-TR: Diagnostic and Statistical Manual of Mental Disorders*. 4th ed. Text revision. Washington, DC: American Psychiatric Association, 2000.

PARAPSYCHOLOGY   The field of parapsychology, or the scientific study of scientifically paranormal claims, dates back to the creation of the Society for Psychical Research in London in 1882 (the American Society for Psychical Research, today called the Parapsychological Association, followed in 1885). Belief in the phenomena they attempt to study appears to be as old as humanity itself. Most believers in the paranormal, including the scientists who study it, have become convinced through distinctly nonscientific evidence, including anomalous personal experiences, anecdotes, and folklore, along with credulous television coverage and books. The ultimate goal of parapsychologists is to establish credible, replicable evidence that such phenomena are real and to describe the conditions under which they occur, through application of the scientific method.

The set of phenomena of interest is referred to by many names, including psi powers, psychic phenomena, paranormal abilities, and the most popular of all, extrasensory perception (ESP). This last one is of special interest to psychologists, as perception is typically defined as the BRAIN's cognitive processing of information received from the senses. Perception is therefore sensory by definition. Ordinarily, the only circumstances under which perception occurs in the absence of sensory input would involve either hallucination or direct stimulation of the brain. This is one of the things that makes psychic research both fascinating and frustrating: if parapsychologists are able to establish convincingly that these phenomena occur, then much of what is known about how the human brain functions (to say nothing of the rest of the physical world, including the basic laws of physics) must be, at best, incomplete and obsolete and, at worst, just plain wrong.

The alleged phenomena include the following:

- *Telepathy*—The ability to send or receive information without using the usual sensory apparatus (speaking, hearing, seeing, etc.). Also colloquially referred to as mind reading. Anecdotal evidence abounds for telepathy, as when one "knows" who is calling when the telephone rings, or two close friends or relatives say the same thing at the exact same time (more parsimonious, but far less exciting, explanations exist for these situations). A demonstration used by self-proclaimed psychics that has been repeatedly tested by parapsychologists involves remote viewing, in which the "sender" travels to a remote (and unknown to the receiver) location and proceeds to concentrate on a landmark, picture, or other stimulus. The "receiver" attempts to form a mental impression of what the sender is seeing, then draws or describes it. Under loose testing conditions, remote viewing demonstrations are often successful; under conditions that have been set up to exclude various other ways of accomplishing the feat (several are well known among stage magicians), success is quite rare.

- *Clairvoyance*—Knowing information without resorting to ordinary perception, memory, or inference. Again, anecdotes abound about this sort of thing, and it is what dowsers claim to be able to do: detect water or minerals underground, often guided by a gently held stick or other device. Many laboratory experiments have attempted to demonstrate clairvoyance, usually requiring the subjects to detect the identity of a hidden target object, frequently a card.

- *Psychokinesis*—Sometimes referred to as "mind over matter," this is the ability to use the mind to cause physical movement or changes in other objects. Previously known as telekinesis, the term fell into such disrepute in the early days of psychic research, thanks to the many fraudulent manifestations produced by spirit mediums, that psychokinesis is now the preferred term.

- *Precognition*—Knowledge of events in advance of their occurrence, again without the usual means of acquisition. Stories of prophecy abound in religion, mythology, and folklore, and so many people are certainly prepared to believe that such a phenomenon exists. As with other psychic gifts, this one has not been reliably manifested by anyone under controlled conditions.

- *Spirit Mediumship*—Some practitioners, known as mediums, claim to obtain their extrasensory knowledge from the spirits of the deceased. In the early days of the practice, in the late nineteenth century, this information—often spoken by the medium in an eerie voice—was often accompanied by physical manifestations, such as odd sounds, mysteriously floating objects, ectoplasm, and so on (more information follows below), but most current mediums have completely abandoned this approach in favor of a fully vocal approach (*see* COLD READING).

The initial burst of interest in scientific study of the paranormal was a direct result of the explosion in popularity of spiritualism, also called spiritism, in late nineteenth-century America and Europe. In spiritualism, which eventually became an organized church based in New England, people interested in communicating with the spirits of the dead would hold séances, in which they would gather about a table in a darkened room, holding hands, and ask the spirits to communicate with them. The response would usually come in the form of mysterious rapping noises. Over time, the phenomena involved in séances grew to include such things as trumpets floating and mysteriously playing in the air, the table rising briefly off the floor, and the production of ectoplasm, or ghost substance, a mysterious shimmering product that the medium would pull from thin air, or sometimes from various body parts, and wave about.

The precise origin of the spiritualist movement, and thus of all subsequent efforts to demonstrate its authenticity, is actually quite well documented. The first séances were held in 1848, in the Hydesville, New York, home of the teenage Fox sisters, Margaret and Kate, who decided to have a bit of fun at their parents' expense. Margaret had developed the ability to produce loud rapping sounds with her toes, which seemed to be mysterious communications from beyond when performed in a dark room with everyone holding hands on the tabletop. Very soon the Fox sisters were performing séances with a wide range of people, and others followed their lead until people all over Europe and America were communicating with the dead and performing ever more elaborate variations on their initial deception.

Within a few years, some eminent men of science, believing the phenomena to be real, began to investigate the conditions under which they occurred. At the same time, these men also became interested in investigating the claims of mind readers, hypnotists, and fortune tellers. Soon they had formed formal organizations, and their "psychical research" was a respectable and rapidly growing enterprise. Early in their investigations, they began to document a few things about the conditions under which such phenomena seemed more likely to occur. A successful séance, for example, required darkness—the materializations would not occur in a well-lit room, and the spirits would often not communicate at all. The presence of very skeptical people, who might watch very closely, also seemed to make the spirits less likely to turn up.

Over several decades following the Fox sisters' initial breakthrough, several "superstar" mediums emerged, among them D. D. Home and Eusapia Palladino. These people were very skilled and were thus instrumental in attracting the interest of scientists. They were also frequently caught cheating by such prominent magicians as Houdini, people who tricked others into believing in the improbable for a living, who began to take notice of these competitors who claimed their miracles were real. Houdini made a whole second career of attending séances and exposing fraud therein. He eventually wrote the book *A Magician among the Spirits*, in which he revealed many of the most widely used tricks. Ectoplasm, for example, was usually cheesecloth coated with luminous paint.

The impact of such exposures on the popularity of the mediums was quite minimal. A common reaction was: "The spirits don't always respond, so of course they have to cheat sometimes, that doesn't mean it isn't real on the other occasions!" This justification continues as a major part of the arsenal of certain psychic performers today. Popularity didn't wane even when the originator of the movement admitted her fraud. In 1888, forty years after getting it all started, Margaret Fox, by this time a widow, told her story and gave public demonstrations of how the effects were achieved. Nevertheless, the Spiritualist church still exists today and still holds séances, and there are entertainers (such as John Edward and James Van Praagh, *see* COLD READING) who have become wealthy by claiming to communicate with the dead, although they have entirely eliminated physical manifestations from their repertoire. Further testament to the continuing popularity of the séance even today is the perennial sales success of the Ouija board, a do-it-yourself spiritualist board game that has been in continuous production since its introduction in 1890.

By the early twentieth century, psychical researchers had largely tired of the mediums and had turned their attention to telepaths and clairvoyants. As their methods became more rigorous and quantitative, and psychologists began to take over a field previously dominated by physical scientists, the new science began to find a home at major universities. Most prominent among the new American researchers was J. B. Rhine, cofounder (in 1934) and director of the Parapsychology Laboratory at Duke University, located in North Carolina. It was Rhine who shook off the phrase "psychical research," with its attendant baggage and coined the new, more scientific-sounding *parapsychology* to replace it. He also introduced the terms *extrasensory perception* and *psychokinesis*, and was easily the most influential of all parapsychologists, both in his methods and in his ability to popularize the field in his books, articles, and lectures.

Rhine founded the *Journal of Parapsychology* in 1937, thus providing American parapsychologists with a respectable peer-reviewed journal in which to publish their findings. Twenty years later, he was instrumental in founding the Parapsychological Association. He also developed, with his colleague Karl Zener, the most widely used piece of equipment in parapsychology, the Zener cards. The Zener cards are a deck made up of five simple symbols, one on each card: star, circle, square, cross, and wavy lines. The Zener cards were widely used in ESP experiments, in which the participant was required to identify a hidden target card from a set of five known possible targets. In a telepathy experiment, the cards were viewed by a remote person (the sender) who attempted to "transmit" the information to the participant. In a clairvoyance experiment, the participant would simply attempt to identify the order of the cards, without anyone looking at them first.

In 1962, with several decades of research having failed to conclusively demonstrate the existence of any paranormal phenomena, Duke University followed the lead of most other major institutions and quietly distanced itself from parapsychological research. Without the university's continuing support, Rhine simply moved off campus and founded the Parapsychological Laboratory's successor, the Foundation for Research on the Nature of Man, a short distance away in Durham, North Carolina. Although parapsychological research has continued unabated, it has remained marginalized, with very few degree programs in parapsychology still in existence. This has not halted innovation, however— parapsychology has come a long way from card-guessing experiments.

The most highly touted recent parapsychological paradigm is the ganzfeld experiment, pioneered by Charles Honorton in the 1970s, and widely regarded by parapsychologists as the best evidence for paranormal ability so far. The word *ganzfeld* means "total field" in German, and is used to refer to a technique of sensory deprivation that creates an absolutely uniform visual field. The usual procedure involves taping halves of ping-pong balls over the experimental subject's eyes. A bright light is then pointed at the eyes, creating a visual field without

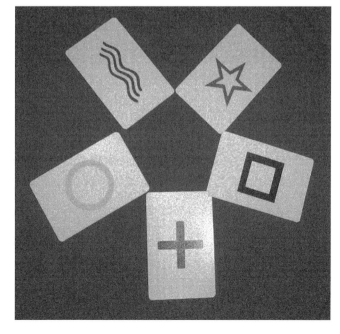

The Zener cards, made famous in J. B. Rhine's ESP experiments. Photo by author.

discontinuities. In addition to the bright light, the subject usually wears headphones playing pleasant noise, such as the sound of surf. Parapsychologists believe the pleasant, relaxed state thus produced is highly conducive to the reception of psychic signals. After the subject (receiver) has spent about fifteen minutes in this state, a sender is given a target image, randomly selected from four possible pictures, which were in turn randomly selected from a larger pool of possibilities.

The sender concentrates on the picture for a prearranged interval, while the receiver, in a soundproof room, freely describes all mental impressions that occur during this period. At the end of the session the receiver selects from the four the picture that best matches his impressions. Over a large number of trials, the receiver could expect to get 25 percent correct by chance. An actual rate of correct responses significantly above this level is assumed to be evidence of ESP. Honorton and others have claimed success rates in some experiments as high as 55 percent, but various psychologists (most notably Ray Hyman) have written extensive critiques faulting both the methodology and the statistical techniques involved. Similar experiments on psychokinesis, involving attempts to influence the activity of random number generators, have met with a similarly chilly reception.

The essential problem is that a large portion of the scientific community, including most research psychologists, regards parapsychology as a PSEUDOSCIENCE, due largely to its failure to move on beyond null results in the way science usually does. Ordinarily, when experimental evidence fails repeatedly to support a hypothesis, that hypothesis is abandoned. Within parapsychology, however, more than a century of experimentation has failed even to conclusively demonstrate the mere existence of paranormal phenomena, yet parapsychologists continue to pursue that elusive goal (*see also* MEMORY, PAST-LIFE REGRESSION).

Further Reading: Hyman, R. *The Elusive Quarry: A Scientific Appraisal of Psychical Research.* Buffalo, NY: Prometheus, 1989; Wolman, B. B., ed. *Handbook of Parapsychology.* New York: Van Nostrand Reinhold, 1977.

PARENTING STYLES In 1967, Diana Baumrind claimed, based on her research with a sample of California professors and their children, that the child-rearing methods adopted by parents had a profound influence on those children later in life. She identified three different parenting styles, which differ from each other on two dimensions, warmth and control, as follows:

- *Authoritarian*—These parents are low in warmth and high in control. They present children with clear rules and expectations and enforce them strictly. These parents are more likely to use physical punishment than the other two kinds, and they tend not to discuss the reasons for rules or punishments with the children. If they do, the reasons given are unlikely to extend much beyond "Because I said so."
- *Permissive*—These parents are high in warmth and low in control. They set few rules and are rather lax in enforcing them, but they give their children lots of support and love. They tend to believe that the children should be allowed to make their own mistakes and learn from them.

- *Authoritative*—These parents are high in both warmth and control. They set clear rules and expect them to be followed, but they are also affectionate and flexible and are willing to discuss the reasons behind their decisions and respect their children's opinions, so negotiation is possible.

These names do become confusing; in a famous critique of this research, Judith Rich Harris somewhat derisively, but less confusingly, renames them Too Hard, Too Soft, and Just Right. Baumrind argued that, of the three, the authoritative parenting style produces the best outcomes for children. Those children tend to perform better academically, and to get along better both with adults and with other children. They also appear to be less likely to fall into delinquency in adolescence.

Other research has not always supported Baumrind's findings, however. Cross-cultural research, for example, suggests that while the authoritative style might be the preferred style among middle-class white Americans, the same is not necessarily true of other ethnic groups, even within the same country. Asian American children, for example, perform better in school and are more successful as a group in later life than other minorities within the United States, yet their parents are the most likely to use the authoritarian style. African American and Hispanic cultures favor the authoritarian style, and within those groups, the parents of successful children are more likely to use those styles, therefore one might conclude that authoritative parenting is just a prototypically White middle-class American approach to successful parenting.

Actually, it isn't that simple. Baumrind's classification of parenting styles and the expected child outcomes seem to assume three things that may often be untrue: first, that a parent will consistently adhere to a single style; second, that the parent will use the same style with all children; and third, that both parents in a family will use the same style. In Baumrind's original research, only one parent from each family participated, and so data on consistency was unavailable. Other research on parenting styles suggests strongly that parents typically tailor their approach to a particular child's temperament and needs, and that this is what constitutes good parenting. It is also fairly evident that a parent often has a spouse who adopts a different style. Parenting behaviors will certainly have an effect on child outcomes, but so will many other variables, and to expect one small piece of the puzzle to significantly predict a child's future success may be too simplistic.

Further Reading: Baumrind, D. "Rearing Competent Children." In W. Damon, ed. *Child Development Today and Tomorrow*. San Francisco: Jossey-Bass, 1989, pp. 349–378; Harris, J. R. *The Nurture Assumption: Why Children Turn Out the Way They Do*. New York: The Free Press, 1998.

PAST-LIFE REGRESSION Of the many questionable uses to which HYPNOSIS has been applied, probably none is more absurd than past-life regression (PLR). In PLR, the hypnotized person is alleged to journey back into the past, to lives she or he lived before the present one. It is beyond dispute that some patients do in fact recall past lives; the source of the memories, however, is very much open to debate. Such memories have been taken by some to be evidence of reincarnation; in fact, they are very likely to be false memories, probably a combination of experiences from the current life, pure imagination, confabulations, and suggestions from the hypnotist.

The problem is that some therapists, frequently those with little or no scientific training in either hypnosis or the working of human MEMORY, sincerely believe that hypnosis provides access to the unconscious mind, where memories are stored that are inaccessible to the conscious mind. Frequently this is due to repression, the deliberate forgetting that FREUD proposed as the mind's way of dealing with memories that are too traumatic to confront directly. Although research on memory has consistently failed to support the theory of repression, and research on hypnosis shows that it is far more likely to result in new, false memories, some therapists have suggested that memories of past lives are also locked away in the subconscious. It is unclear, and usually unstated, how such past-life memories would have become repressed in the first place, since most such therapists adhere, however loosely, to some sort of doctrine of reincarnation. Traditions that incorporate reincarnation, however, such as Hinduism, do not include repressed memories of past lives among their beliefs.

Like all false memories, memories of past lives created under hypnosis are indistinguishable from "real" memories, at least from the point of view of the person remembering them, and they can be very vivid. Defenders of past-life therapy often point out, as proof that the memories are real, that people have remembered things they can't possibly have known otherwise. In fact, remembering information while having no idea where it came from is extremely common, and the phenomenon is quite well known among memory researchers, who sometimes call it *cryptomnesia*. The case that started the whole past-life regression boom, the case of Bridey Murphy, illustrates this phenomenon extremely well. In 1956, Morey Bernstein published *The Search for Bridey Murphy*, his account of his many hypnotic sessions with housewife Virginia Tighe, who under hypnosis recalled being a nineteenth-century woman in Ireland. Under hypnosis, she spoke in a thick brogue, sang Irish songs, told Irish stories that she didn't seem to know prior to hypnosis, and revealed various details about Ireland that the author said she couldn't have otherwise known. In addition to the book, Bernstein released tapes of these sessions, which also sold well. The case received so much attention that reporters were actually dispatched to Ireland to find out if a red-headed woman named Bridey Murphy had existed.

Unfortunately for Bernstein, one newspaper did find her. When Tighe was a small child, her neighbor across the street was an Irish woman. Her name? Bridie Murphy Corkell. Tighe was digging up old memories, but they dated back to her early childhood, not to a previous life. The rest was simply the combination of imagination and confabulation that often results from hypnosis. Some of the "astounding" details of Irish life that she recalled were actually the sort of things that are common knowledge, not just to any tourist who has been to Ireland, but even to those who have merely read about it. For example, Bernstein emphasized that she knew that kissing the Blarney Stone requires the help of a friend to hold one's legs while one leans over backwards. Despite these fifty-year-old revelations, the book remains in print today and continues to influence believers.

Past-life regression could be easily dismissed as just another relatively harmless pop-culture fad, were it not for the existence of therapists who represent it as a tool for healing psychological problems. Just as some therapists have claimed that most psychological disorders are the result of repressed memories of sexual abuse, past-life therapists suggest that adjustment difficulties in the present life require confronting things that happened in previous lives. Any therapy that requires the patient to create delusions is potentially quite dangerous and should be avoided. The same cautions apply here as with other types of false memories: although some false memories can be harmless and silly, others can increase the patient's suffering while also creating new suffering for the patient's loved ones or destroying family relationships. The damage is difficult to undo, as the memories are experienced by the patient as completely real, as real as things that actually happened (*see also* ALIEN ABDUCTION).

Further Reading: Bernstein, M. *The Search for Bridey Murphy.* Rev. ed. New York: Doubleday, 1965; Spanos, N. "Past-Life Hypnotic Regression." *Skeptical Inquirer,* 12(2) (1988): 174–180.

PAVLOV, IVAN (1849–1936)   As a physiologist who was actively hostile to psychology, which he viewed as an intellectual dead end, believing that the study of physical processes was the proper path to a better understanding of human nature, Ivan Pavlov might be amused to see that he has had such a profound impact on the field. Pavlov was the discoverer of classical conditioning, also known as respondent conditioning, one of the basic learning mechanisms. He won a Nobel Prize in 1904 for his work on the digestive processes of dogs, during which his discovery of classical conditioning occurred as a fortunate accident.

Pavlov was engaged in the study of salivation. He had surgically implanted a tube into his dogs' salivary glands to measure the amount of saliva secreted in response to the presence of food. He noticed that sometimes, however, the dogs would salivate even when no food was present, such as upon the arrival of the assistant who ordinarily fed the dogs. This was interesting because salivation was seen as a reflexive response to the food. Barring a taste for human flesh, there was no good reason for a dog to salivate at the sight of a lab assistant. Pavlov reasoned that the salivation reflex had somehow been transformed into a new response, by the frequent pairing of the stimulus that naturally produced the salivation response (food) with a neutral stimulus (the lab assistant), creating a brand-new learned response.

He conducted a series of famous experiments to test the learning process, which he called conditioning ("classical" was added later, to distinguish it from B. F. SKINNER's operant conditioning). He first selected a new neutral stimulus that should produce no particular response in a dog, a musical tone sounded by a tuning fork, in this case, and made the sound repeatedly, so the dog would become habituated to the sound and would no longer look over when he heard it. At this point, before conditioning has occurred, there are two stimulus-response pairs: the dog food is the unconditioned stimulus (UCS) and salivation is the unconditioned response (UCR), so-called because the connection between them is a natural reflex that requires no learning. The neutral stimulus (musical tone), henceforth to be referred to as the conditioned stimulus (CS), meanwhile, produces no salivation. The next step is to conduct a series of trials in which the CS is paired with the UCS. After a sufficient number of such trials, the CS by itself will produce salivation, now called the conditioned response (CR), to reflect the fact that it is now a learned response to a new stimulus:

- *Phase 1*—Unconditioned reflex: UCS (food) produces UCR (salivation)
- *Phase 2*—Conditioning trials: CS (tone) paired with UCS (food) produces UCR (salivation)
- *Phase 3*—Conditioning has occurred: CS (tone) produces CR (salivation)

If the food is later phased out, however, the salivation response to the tone will gradually disappear. This is called *extinction*. If the tone is again paired with the food, however, the salivation response will be relearned far more quickly than the first time around. Once extinction has occurred, moreover, the conditioned response may suddenly reappear if, after some time has passed, the conditioned stimulus occurs again unexpectedly. This is *spontaneous recovery*. Furthermore, after a conditioned response has been acquired, stimuli which are similar to the CS may also produce the response, through a process called stimulus generalization. A dog trained to salivate to a musical tone may also salivate in response to other tones, for example. This process is balanced by stimulus discrimination, however; as experience teaches the dog that those other tones don't precede the arrival of food, he will come to only respond to the original one.

Not all UCS-CS connections are equally easy to learn—we seem to be biologically more "ready" to learn some associations than others, a factor known as biopreparedness. For example, people are far more likely to develop fears of snakes or dogs than fears of compact discs or air fresheners. Conditioned taste aversions, also known as the Garcia effect, after the person whose research documented them, are an especially vivid example of *biopreparedness*. Most classical conditioning requires multiple pairings of the two stimuli for the learning to occur, as was the case with Pavlov's dogs, and the unconditioned stimulus has to occur right after the conditioned stimulus. Poisons may not produce their effects for several minutes, or possibly even several hours, after they are consumed, and yet people (and animals) who experience food poisoning may never wish to eat the food that made them sick again.

Unlike most classical conditioning, taste-aversion learning occurs in one trial, with a wide gap between the stimuli. A classic taste-aversion study involved cancer patients, chemotherapy, and ice cream. A group of cancer patients ate a particular flavor of ice cream one hour before receiving chemotherapy, which is notorious for producing tremendous nausea. A second group ate the same distinctive flavor on a day when they did not receive chemotherapy, and a third group ate no ice cream. A full five months later, the patients were asked to taste several ice cream flavors. The flavor that was eaten five months earlier was chosen as the favorite by the no-chemotherapy and the no ice-cream groups, but the chemotherapy group found that flavor of ice cream repulsive. This occurred despite a single exposure to the CS, hours before the UCS.

Biopreparedness is also a factor in the development of PHOBIAS, which are now widely regarded as a result of classical conditioning. Developing a fear of dogs, for example, requires only a single frightening experience with a dog. Consider fear as a UCS and distress and anxiety as the UCR—when the fear is preceded by the presence of a dog, distress and anxiety can easily become a CR in the presence of dogs. Phobias are so difficult to get rid of because the person with a phobia will avoid the stimulus that produces the fear. Extinction requires one to experience the CS while not paired with the UCS—as long as the CS is entirely avoided, the event that needs to happen to produce extinction doesn't occur.

Further Reading: Bouton, M., Mineka, S., and Barlow, D. "A Modern Learning Theory Perspective on the Etiology of Panic Disorder." *Psychological Review*, 108(1) (2001): 4–32; Garcia, J., Lasiter, P. S., and Bermudez-Rattoni, F. "A General Theory of Aversion Learning." *Annals of the New York Academy of Sciences*, 443 (1985): 8–21.

PDD *See* PERVASIVE DEVELOPMENTAL DISORDERS

PEDOPHILIA *See* PARAPHILIAS

PERVASIVE DEVELOPMENTAL DISORDERS This is a *DSM-IV* category of childhood disorders characterized by severe deficits in communication, impaired social skills, repetitive, stereotyped movements, and unusual preoccupations and interests. These are also known as the autism spectrum disorders, and they occur in ten to twenty children per 10,000 births. Of those, about half have autistic disorder (AUTISM), which is the most severe form of the disorder. These disorders usually manifest during the first several years of life, and are often associated with some degree of MENTAL RETARDATION.

In addition to autism and ASPERGER SYNDROME, this category also includes Rett's disorder (also known as Rett's syndrome), which is usually comorbid with severe or profound mental retardation. Rett's disorder is characterized by the development of multiple deficits by a child who was previously functioning normally since birth. Psychological and motor development are normal for at least the first five months, but between that age and thirty months, there is a loss of previously acquired hand skills, accompanied by stereotyped hand-wringing movements. In the first few years, interest in the social environment will also decrease steadily, and this is usually accompanied by a severe impairment in language development and motor coordination. Unlike other developmental disorders, this one occurs only in females. This may be for genetic reasons—a large proportion of girls with this syndrome have a mutation in the X chromosome.

Also in the Pervasive Developmental Disorder category is childhood disintegrative disorder, so called because the affected child begins life with at least two years of apparently normal development, including verbal and nonverbal communication, social and adaptive skills, and play habits. Before the age of ten, however, the child experiences a significant loss of skills in at least two areas, including language, social skills, adaptive behavior, bowel/bladder control, play, or motor skills, with the result that the child appears to be autistic. When a child has a severe, pervasive impairment in social interaction, verbal/nonverbal communication, or shows stereotyped behavior, but doesn't meet the diagnostic criteria for any of the other disorders in this category, the diagnosis given is "pervasive developmental disorder not otherwise specified."

Further Reading: American Psychiatric Association. *DSM-IV-TR: Diagnostic and Statistical Manual of Mental Disorders.* 4th ed. Text revision. Washington, DC: American Psychiatric Association, 2000.

PET SCAN *See* BRAIN IMAGING TECHNIQUES

PHENOMENOLOGICAL PSYCHOLOGY *See* HUMANISTIC PSYCHOLOGY

PHOBIAS A phobia, or phobic disorder, is an irrational or excessive fear of a particular object or situation. The *DSM-IV* lists three varieties of phobic disorder: social phobia, specific phobias, and agoraphobia, all of which are classified as anxiety disorders. People with social phobia have intense fears of social interactions, such as meeting others, dating, or public speaking. People with agoraphobia (literally "fear of the marketplace") fear venturing out into open spaces or going out in public. Specific phobias, the kind most people associate with the term, are fears of specific situations or objects. Phobias affect people of all ages, from all walks of life, and in every part of the country. The National Institutes of Mental Health report that 5.1 to 12.5 percent of Americans have phobias. They are the most common psychiatric illness among women of all ages and are the second most common among men older than twenty-five.

Phobias are manifested as emotional and physical reactions that can interfere with going about a daily routine. Symptoms include feelings of panic and dread, rapid heartbeat, shortness of breath, trembling, and an overwhelming desire to flee the situation. Fear of this reaction leads to avoidance of the feared situation or object, which can interfere with the ability to work, socialize, or care for one's personal needs.

People with agoraphobia avoid public places, especially busy streets or crowded places such as theatres, shopping malls, or churches. Some people with agoraphobia become so fearful that they remain housebound, leaving their homes only with great distress or when accompanied by a trusted friend or family member. Two-thirds of those with agoraphobia are women, and most develop the disorder as a result of suffering from one or more spontaneous panic attacks. Thus the prognosis for panic disorders often includes the development of agoraphobia. These sudden attacks of fear and physical discomfort seem to occur without warning, making it impossible for a person to predict what situation will trigger such a reaction. This unpredictability causes individuals to fear entering any situation in which such an attack might occur, as it seems that another attack may occur at any time. Symptoms usually develop between the ages of eighteen and thirty-five.

A person with social phobia fears being humiliated while doing something in public, and she or he will avoid any situation in which such activity may be required. The most common manifestation of social phobia involves public speaking, but the feared activity may be something as ordinary as signing a check, eating in a restaurant, or talking to a customer service representative on the telephone. An affected person with the generalized form of social phobia fears, and therefore avoids, interpersonal interaction in general. This is disabling, as it makes going to work or school, or indeed socializing, all but impossible. Social phobias are common in both men and women, and generally develop after puberty and peak after the age of thirty.

People with a specific phobia have an irrational fear of a specific object or situation. As the usual response to a phobia is avoidance of the feared object or situation, specific phobias can be seriously disabling if the feared object or situation is sufficiently common. The most common specific phobias involve animals, particularly dogs, snakes, insects, and mice. Other common specific phobias are fear of closed spaces (claustrophobia) and fear of heights (acrophobia). For a more extensive list, see the table below. Specific phobias are quite common in childhood, but they usually disappear. Those that persist into adulthood rarely go away on their own, however, and can be quite disabling without treatment.

Unlike many other psychological disorders, phobias are very easy to treat, and most people who seek treatment completely overcome their fears for life. The most popular treatment involves systematic desensitization, a type of behavior therapy. This treatment is based on the idea that phobias are created by a process of respondent conditioning and can be eliminated by creating a new response to the stimulus that elicits the fear. The idea is simple: the body's fight-or-flight response, which is the source of the physical sensations and dread associated with the phobia, is incompatible with a state of total relaxation, and so teaching a person to relax in the presence of the feared object or situation eliminates the fear reaction by replacing it. The first step in systematic desensitization is therefore teaching the patient to relax. This usually involves a series of training sessions on progressive relaxation, in which the patient learns to relax his or her entire body on demand. Once this skill is mastered, the desensitization sessions can begin. These involve presenting a series of non-threatening situations that progressively begin to approximate the feared situation more and more closely.

A Selection of Specific Phobias:

Acrophobia	Fear of heights
Agyrophobia	Fear of crossing streets
Aichmophobia	Fear of pointed objects
Ailurophobia	Fear of cats
Androphobia	Fear of men
Arachnophobia	Fear of spiders
Batrachophobia	Fear of frogs and toads
Claustrophobia	Fear of enclosed spaces
Coprophobia	Fear of excrement/feces
Cynophobia	Fear of dogs
Doraphobia	Fear of contact with animal fur or skin
Emetophobia	Fear of vomiting
Entomophobia	Fear of insects
Gynephobia	Fear or hatred of women
Hematophobia	Fear of the sight of blood
Herpetophobia	Fear of reptiles
Hippophobia	Fear of horses
Homophobia	Fear of homosexuality (the political use of this term is not always scientifically accurate)
Hydrophobia	Fear of water
Ichthyophobia	Fear of fish
Ophidiophobia	Fear of snakes (compare herpetophobia)
Ornithophobia	Fear of birds
Scotophobia	Fear of the dark
Taurophobia	Fear of bulls
Thanatophobia	Fear of death
Trichophobia	Fear of hair
Triskaidekaphobia	Fear of the number 13
Vermiphobia	Fear of earthworms
Xenophobia	Fear or hatred of foreigners and strange things
Zoophobia	Fear of animals

Consider, for example, the treatment used for Megan, a young woman with a fear of dogs. After she has learned the relaxation response, the therapist introduces a series of photographs of dogs. As she sees each one, she is cued to relax. When she is consistently able to relax in the presence of the photos, the recorded sound of barking on tape is added. When she can consistently relax in the presence of the photos and barking, a real dog is introduced into the room, but is kept in a cage across the room. When she can consistently relax in the caged dog's presence, the dog is brought closer but kept on a leash. Eventually, she will be able to relax fully while touching the dog, and her fear is therefore gone. By confronting the object of fear in this way rather than fleeing, the person becomes accustomed to it and no longer feels panic and dread in its presence.

A more controversial treatment for phobias, flooding, would dispense with the gradual nature of systematic desensitization by instead helping Megan get over her fear by immediately placing her in a room with one or more dogs and requiring that she stay there, and hopefully come to understand that there is no danger. The relaxation component of systematic desensitization is also sometimes replaced by a shortcut: antianxiety drugs are used to cause the person to relax in the presence of the feared object or situation. Such medications are also the favored treatment for social phobia and agoraphobia (*see also* PARAPHILIAS).

Further Reading: American Psychiatric Association. *DSM-IV-TR: Diagnostic and Statistical Manual of Mental Disorders.* 4th ed. Text revision. Washington, DC: American Psychiatric Association, 2000; U.S. Department of Health and Human Services, Substance Abuse and Mental Health Services Administration (USDHHS). *Mental Health: A Report of the Surgeon General.* Rockville, MD: USDHHS, 1999.

PHYSIOGNOMY *See* BODY TYPE

PIAGET, JEAN (1896–1980)

Among child psychologists who have attempted to track the dramatic shifts in cognition, knowledge, and memory that distinguish infants from adults, Jean Piaget has had the greatest influence. Based on intensive observations of a small sample of infants, including his own children, as well as extensive interviews with older children, the Swiss psychologist proposed a theory in which developmental change is qualitative rather than merely quantitative. In other words, an older child thinks differently than an infant, and a teenager thinks differently than an older child, and an adult thinks differently than all of them. Children don't just know less, remember less, and have less experience than adults, they actually think in completely different ways at different ages. Piaget's developmental theory, which he referred to as genetic epistemology, proposes that cognitive development proceeds through a series of distinct stages, or periods, and that all children pass through the same stages, in the same order, in a universal and invariant sequence. The start of each stage is marked by a qualitative change from what preceded it.

So what changes from stage to stage? Piaget saw the mind as made up of cognitive structures he called schemas, which are mental images or generalizations based on our experience of the world. We use schemas both to organize past experience and to provide a framework for organizing and understanding future experiences. The newborn infant has very little experience, thus very few schemas. Piaget saw infant reflexes, such as the sucking reflex, which allows the newborn to feed immediately, as the earliest schemas. The infant immediately begins gaining experience with the outside world, however, which causes the schemas to begin changing almost at once. The sucking schema will rapidly change to accommodate the fact that a range of objects may be sucked, but not all sucking will produce food, for example.

Two processes guide the development of ever more complex schemas: assimilation and accommodation. Assimilation is the process by which new information is placed into existing schemas. A child who has a cat at home, for example, will have no difficulty recognizing the nature of a new cat since the child already has a schema for what a cat is. Real cognitive change, however, comes from the challenges to our existing schemas that the world is always ready to provide. This process is known as accommodation. For example, when that same child encounters his or her first dog, the child will first try to fit this new creature into what is already known ("Kitty?" he or she says tentatively). Fairly brief experience will show that this creature doesn't fit the schema, however, and so the schemas must change to reflect the new state of the world. A new "doggie" schema, along with a more general "pet" or "animal" schema may be the result.

Piaget called the first stage of cognitive development, from birth to about age two, the *sensorimotor* period, as the child's development in this stage is largely confined to schemas about sensory functions and motor skills. Piaget believed that during this stage, infants can form schemas only about objects and actions that are actually present. If an object is not currently in sight or within grasp, the child cannot think about it. He based this belief largely on the observation that if an adult covers or hides a toy that the infant is currently reaching for, the child will immediately appear to lose all interest in the toy, without trying to find it. For the infant, out of sight is out of mind. The sensorimotor period ends when the child is able to form mental representations of objects despite being unable to see them, an ability Piaget called *object permanence*.

From about age two to around age seven, children are in the *preoperational* stage, in which they can think in images and symbols, able to represent something with something else. Unsurprisingly, this is the stage in which language use and pretend play become common. Piaget believed that children at this stage are highly egocentric, meaning they are unable to appreciate the perspectives of others or understand that there is any way to see a situation other than their own. He based this belief on a task in which the child walks around a three-dimensional model of three mountains and is then asked what someone (usually a doll) would see from a particular position. Preoperational children typically select the view that corresponds to their own current perspective, rather than the correct one. The name of the stage, however, comes from children's performance on tasks requiring conservation: recognition that important properties of a substance remain constant despite changes in shape or appearance. In the classic test of conservation, children watch as water or juice from two identical glasses is poured into two new glasses, one tall and thin and the other short and wide. When asked if one glass contains more than the other, preoperational children typically choose the taller glass. Children at this stage do not understand the mental operations of reversibility (if they poured the water back into the original glasses, they would clearly hold the same amount again) and complementarity (one glass is taller, but the other makes up for that difference by being wider), thus their thinking is preoperational.

In the concrete operations stage, ages seven to about twelve, the child becomes able to understand and apply logical principles, thus conservation is no longer a challenge, and the ability to apply such logic to number and amount makes mathematics learning possible. According to Piaget, however, the child's ability to perform logical operations is limited to real, concrete objects within their experience. The ability to think logically about abstract ideas awaits the development of formal operations, the developmental period that begins with adolescence, and the final stage proposed by Piaget. The fact that Piaget's developmental sequence ends with adolescence has prompted other theorists to propose several variations on an additional stage of postformal reasoning, to allow for recognition that the adult mind often works differently than that of a twelve-year-old child.

The basic elements of Piaget's theory remain very influential today, especially the insight that adult thinking differs qualitatively from that of young children, along with the recognition that various cognitive milestones are achieved in the same order by all children. Piaget has also been widely criticized, however, especially for underestimating the cognitive abilities of young children by frequently using tasks that the children didn't understand. A large body of research on infant memory, for example, indicates that children are capable of using mental representations at much younger ages than Piaget believed.

Conservation may also appear a lot earlier than Piaget suggested, an insight that requires altering Piaget's favorite tasks a bit. When the children do the pouring in the liquid conservation task, rather than watching an adult do it, preoperational children frequently answer correctly. Preoperational children are also less egocentric than Piaget imagined, as when the three-mountain task is redesigned a bit to more closely resemble a game children might actually play. Instead of mountains, children look in on a simple maze in which some walls contain windows and some don't. A doll dressed as a policeman is then placed in the model, as is a doll dressed as a thief. Children are asked to take the perspective of the policeman and decide whether he can see, and therefore catch, the thief. Preoperational children answer correctly at much higher rates than they did on Piaget's task, perhaps because the task is more relevant to the children's experience.

Furthermore, many psychologists question the wisdom of thinking in terms of rigidly bounded stages, rather than recognizing that children reach some concrete-operational milestones before others. It makes more sense, therefore, to think in terms of individual mental abilities developing rather the whole mind changing at once. Still, Piaget continues to cast a large shadow on the field of study that he created (*see also* VYGOTSKY, LEV).

Further Reading: Donaldson, Margaret. *Children's Minds.* New York: W. W. Norton & Co., 1979.

PLACEBO EFFECT *See* NONSPECIFIC EFFECTS

P.L. 94–142 *See* EDUCATION FOR ALL HANDICAPPED CHILDREN ACT (P. L. 94–142)

PLR *See* PAST-LIFE REGRESSION

PMDD   *See* PREMENSTRUAL DYSPHORIC DISORDER (PMDD)

PMS   *See* PREMENSTRUAL DYSPHORIC DISORDER (PMDD)

POSTTRAUMATIC STRESS DISORDER   Posttraumatic stress disorder (PTSD) is a disorder in which the survivor of a traumatic or severely stressful event re-experiences the traumatic event exactly as it happened, both in nightmares and in daytime flashbacks. Unlike dreams, these flashbacks can seem completely real, as though the event is actually occurring again. In addition to recurrent, intrusive thoughts, symptoms of PTSD also include increased physiological arousal and anxiety, which result in insomnia, irritability, difficulty concentrating, and loss of interest in familiar activities. These symptoms may recur for months, years, or even decades, and it may be years after the trauma before the first appearance of symptoms.

PTSD was first documented among combat veterans, who appear to be especially vulnerable to the disorder. According to one estimate, more than one-third of men who engaged in heavy combat in Vietnam have shown signs of PTSD. Although the disorder is closely identified in the public eye with Viet Nam, it has been known to doctors who work with soldiers since World War I. At that time it was called shell shock, the idea being that the men had been affected by shells exploding at such close proximity to them that the explosion literally rattled their brains. Veterans of World War II have also experienced PTSD, and many reported waking up shaking and sweating from nightmares, more than half a century later. The magnitude of the problem among WWII veterans took a long time to become apparent: one recent study reports that some veterans who functioned normally throughout their postwar lives have been developing PTSD symptoms upon retirement.

Although the syndrome was first identified in combat veterans, PTSD can strike anyone who has experienced a severe trauma, including natural disasters, automobile accidents, sexual abuse, and violent crimes, among other experiences. Most people who experience trauma, however, do not develop PTSD, and so research has been driven by the question of why some people do. Several factors, both physiological and psychological, have been found to distinguish trauma survivors with PTSD from those who did not develop it. People with PTSD tend to be more likely than more resilient survivors to have a relatively small hippocampus (a small subcortical BRAIN structure involved in MEMORY), below-average intelligence, and an elevated level of the personality trait neuroticism (*see* "BIG FIVE" PERSONALITY FACTORS).

As with all correlational data, it is possible that these differences could all be caused by having PTSD, rather than the other way around, but that hypothesis has been refuted by recent research using magnetic resonance imaging (MRI)—at least where the hippocampus is concerned. A research team located a sample of sets of identical twins in which one twin was a Viet Nam veteran and the other was not and used MRIs to examine the size of their respective hippocampi. If hippocampus size is affected by combat, then the veterans with PTSD should have had smaller hippocampi than their identical twins. Instead, they found that twins with smaller hippocampi but no military service did not develop PTSD, nor did those with combat experience but normal-sized hippocampi. In their sample, developing PTSD required both combat experience and a relatively small hippocampus. Like many disorders, PTSD appears to develop as a result of the combination of a physiological predisposition and the right environmental triggers.

Various treatment approaches to PTSD exist, but the most effective ones seem to center on a cognitive-behavioral approach, in which thinking and talking about the trauma in a safe environment is the major ingredient. Over time the patient learns to relax while thinking about the trauma, and so the learned response of extreme anxiety eventually disappears. Some rather unusual therapies, including EYE MOVEMENT DESENSITIZATION AND REPROCESSING (EMDR), have claimed remarkable success with PTSD, but upon closer examination the key ingredient of the treatment always seems to be thinking through the trauma in a safe environment, rather than added elements (*see also* BRAIN IMAGING TECHNIQUES).

Further Reading: Gelman, D. "Reliving the Painful Past." *Newsweek*, June 13, 1994, 20–22; Gilbertson, M. W., Shenton, M. E., and Ciszewski, A. "Hippocampal Volume Predicts Pathologic Vulnerability to Psychological Trauma." *Nature Neuroscience*, 5 (2002): 1242–1247.

PRECOGNITION *See* PARAPSYCHOLOGY

PREFRONTAL LOBOTOMY In 1949, Antonio Egas Moniz shared the Nobel Prize in Physiology or Medicine "for his discovery of the therapeutic value of frontal leucotomy." Frontal leucotomy is better known by its more common name, prefrontal lobotomy. The procedure, which involves severing the connection between the most anterior portions of the frontal lobes and the rest of the BRAIN, was hugely popular as a way of relieving the symptoms of psychotic patients in the United States, where between 40,000 and 50,000 lobotomies were performed by the late 1950s, primarily on patients with schizophrenia and depression. Moniz, a Portuguese neurologist, got the idea from research showing that bilateral frontal lobectomy, severing both frontal lobes, caused excitable chimpanzees to become docile and timid. It seemed that a similar procedure might have similar results in overly excitable (i.e., psychotic) humans. He performed the first prefrontal lobotomy in 1936, using alcohol injection to sever the connections. He later used surgical procedures to accomplish the same goals.

Encouraged by Moniz's early experiments, the American neurosurgeon Walter Freeman also began performing the procedure on human patients in 1936, and it is through his efforts that the procedure became widespread in the United States. Freeman traveled around the country performing the procedure, at which he had become so efficient that he would frequently lobotomize multiple patients in sequence in hospital hallways. He accomplished this by

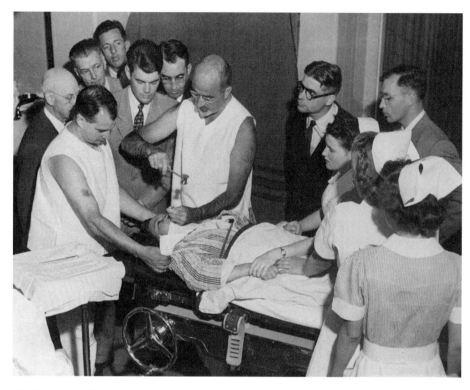

Working in a hallway, Walter Freeman demonstrates his technique for performing a lobotomy, while hospital employees and other curiosity-seekers look on. © Bettmann/CORBIS.

performing the surgery without an incision. He would first render the patient unconscious with several jolts from an electroshock therapy machine (*see* ELEC-TROCONVULSIVE THERAPY). The rest of the procedure involved an icepick-like instrument called a leucotome, which he would insert through a tear duct (after lifting the eyelid out of the way), breaking through the orbital bone by tapping the instrument with a hammer. He would then push the very sharp tip a short distance into the patient's frontal lobe and wiggle it back and forth a few times. The procedure would then be repeated in the other eye socket.

Horrendous though this treatment sounds to modern sensibilities, Freeman acted out of a genuine concern for the lives he saw wasted in mental asylums that could be salvaged, if the patients could become capable of living outside the hospital walls without posing a danger to themselves or others. In the days before effective antipsychotic medications, lobotomy seemed a reasonable alternative to what was essentially lifetime incarceration.

Clear data on the actual effectiveness of the procedure are difficult to come by, but even Freeman, the procedure's most zealous promoter, only claimed good results for 52 percent of his patients, and he provided no clear standard for what constituted an improvement. Along with inducing violent behavior and hallucinations among some patients, the indiscriminate and imprecise cutting would also damage memory, personality, motivation, language use, and many other functions. Patients often had to relearn basic adaptive skills, such as how to eat or use the bathroom. Obesity and epilepsy would sometimes result, and as many as 3 percent died of the procedure. The most high-profile failure among Freeman's patients was Rosemary Kennedy, sister of the U.S. president, who since her lobotomy in 1941 has required full-time care—although prior to the procedure, she was considered to be only mildly retarded. By the late 1950s, the advent of new, highly effective antipsychotic medications (*see* Schizophrenia) had begun to render lobotomies obsolete, but Freeman continued to perform the procedure until 1967. His final patient died within three days.

Although prefrontal lobotomies are no longer commonly performed, psychosurgery has begun to make a bit of a comeback, based on remarkably similar reasoning to that which prompted the first wave of popularity. Freeman believed the lobotomy procedure separated the frontal lobes, where judgment and decision-making are localized, from the thalamus, which was believed to be the seat of emotion, of which psychotic patients appeared to have an overabundance. Although his neurological speculations are now known to be wrong in their particulars, a newer procedure that accomplishes essentially what Freeman was attempting is gaining popularity—the cingulotomy.

In a cingulotomy, the cingulate gyrus, which is part of the pathway between the frontal lobes and deeper limbic system structures that govern emotional reactions, is severed. Both obsessive-compulsive disorder (OCD) and depression appear to involve abnormal passage of neurotransmitters along this pathway, and the cingulotomy appears to relieve or even eliminate symptoms. Although the reasons for this are not perfectly understood, the surgery is performed in dramatically different ways from Freeman's procedure. Modern brain imaging techniques and the use of very precise lasers allow destruction of only the targeted tissue, for example, with no collateral damage of surrounding healthy tissue.

Psychosurgery is still considered primarily a last-resort approach, but this is in part because the modern, vastly more precise version is still burdened by the public perception of Freeman's legacy. Such popular films as *Frances*, which traces the effects of a lobotomy on movie star Frances Farmer, have ensured that horrific images of destroyed minds accompany the idea of psychosurgery for many people.

Further Reading: El-Hai, J. "The Lobotomist." *Washington Post*, January 4, 2001: W16; Todkill, A. M. "The Leucotome." *Canadian Medical Association Journal*, 160(6) (1999): 871–874; Wray, H. "Psychosurgery Redux." *U.S. News and World Report*, 123(17) (1997): 63–64.

PREMENSTRUAL DYSPHORIC DISORDER (PMDD) Premenstrual dysphoric disorder, or PMDD, has been one of the more controversial additions to the disorders listed in the *DSM-IV* (it appeared in the *DSM-III-R* as Late Luteal Phase Dysphoric Disorder), not least because the distinctions between it and premenstrual syndrome (PMS), a perfectly normal, biological part of the menstrual cycle for most women, remain unclear to many people. PMS is a term that has come into common use since the early 1980s to refer to the mood changes, poor concentration, and physical discomfort that frequently precede the start of menstruation by several days. Some studies have suggested that up to 80 percent of women experience these kinds of cyclic symptoms, and so many women were upset to hear that something sounding very much like PMS, widely considered a medical condition, was now to be listed as a psychiatric disorder worthy of treatment.

What ultimately distinguishes many psychological disorders from most people's ordinary experiences is the severity of the symptoms and the degree to which they interfere with their ability to function. Anxiety, for example, is experienced by everyone, but only a few have anxiety disorders. In much the same way, most women experience PMS occasionally, but it has been estimated that only about 3 to 5 percent have symptoms so severe that their ability to function socially or at work is significantly impaired. In PMDD, the mood changes that occur are comparable in severity to a major depressive episode and may even be accompanied by suicidal thoughts. An actual diagnosis of PMDD requires that five or more of the following symptoms, including at least one of the first four, were present for most of the last week of most menstrual cycles in the past year, and that they were absent in the week following menstruation (adapted from *DSM-IV*):

- Markedly depressed mood, feelings of hopelessness, or self-deprecating thoughts
- Marked anxiety, tension, feelings of being "keyed up" or "on edge"
- Marked sudden emotional changes and increased sensitivity
- Persistent and marked anger or irritability or increased interpersonal conflicts
- Decreased interest in usual activities
- Difficulty in concentrating
- Lethargy, fatigue
- Changes in appetite
- Sleeping too much or too little
- Feeling overwhelmed or out of control
- Physical symptoms including bloating, headaches, weight gain, joint or muscle pain, breast tenderness

Note that, apart from the physical symptoms characteristic of PMS, the entire list strongly resembles the criteria for Major Depression.

Many feminist psychologists, including the membership of both the APA's Committee on Women and the National Coalition for Women's Mental Health, strongly objected to the inclusion of this disorder in the *DSM-III-R*. They felt that including PMDD stigmatizes women, since menstruation is a normal female bodily function, and thus psychological changes that occur as a result of this function are also a normal part of being female. Furthermore, no parallel diagnosis exists for men, such as post-football loss psychosis, nor are there any gender-neutral diagnostic categories for dysphoria caused by hormonal changes. This is therefore a psychiatric diagnosis that can only be made for women.

Since definitive criteria do not exist for distinguishing normal from abnormal changes in estrogen levels, the diagnostic criteria for distinguishing between PMS and PMDD are necessarily quite subjective, and women have also objected to treating something caused by normal physical changes as a psychiatric disorder rather than a physical one. The controversy over this disorder was so heated that the committee originally assigned to determine whether it should be included in the *DSM-IV* was unable to come to an agreement, and the disorder was ultimately put to a vote of the APA's legislative assembly. This is an unusual way to decide on whether something is an illness or not.

A larger problem with PMDD stems from its resemblance to depression, which has led to similar treatment recommendations. The U.S. Food and Drug Administration has approved the drug Serafem specifically for the treatment of PMDD, based on two double-blind trials in which it was shown to be effective in relieving the symptoms of the disorder. This is problematic because the Serafem brand is simply a relabeling of fluoxetine, better known as Prozac, already the most widely prescribed antidepressant. This is also problematic because fluoxetine is a selective serotonin reuptake inhibitor (SSRI), meaning it acts selectively on serotonin, a neurotransmitter found in the brain (*see* NERVOUS SYSTEM). It is not known, however, to have any impact whatsoever on levels of estrogen, the hormone that is presumed responsible for the symptoms of PMDD. Since depression is one of the symptoms of PMDD, it is not surprising that Prozac (under the other name) may relieve the symptoms, but it raises questions about what is really causing the symptoms. If the cause of PMDD is elevated estrogen levels, a drug that has no effect on those levels is an odd first-choice treatment for the disorder.

Further Reading: Kutchins, H., and Kirk, S. A. *Making Us Crazy: DSM: The Psychiatric Bible and the Creation of Mental Disorders*. Chicago: Free Press, 1997.

PREMENSTRUAL SYNDROME   *See* PREMENSTRUAL DYSPHORIC DISORDER (PMDD)

PRIMAL THERAPY   Primal therapy (also known as primal scream) is the brainchild of Arthur Janov. It is a psychodynamic therapeutic technique that claims to cure psychological disorders by encouraging people to feel deeply, and release, the feelings of pain and anger that have been within them since early childhood. Janov teaches that all neuroses are built upon primal pains, which are present in the person at every moment despite not being consciously felt. Some of the "Pain" actually predates childhood. Janov teaches that prenatal experiences, including trauma associated with the moment of conception, as well as birth trauma, influence our functioning and the later direction of our lives (this is very similar to one of the central tenets of DIANETICS). In Janov's own words, "Primal Therapy is aimed at eradicating these Pains. It is revolutionary because it involves overthrowing the neurotic system by a forceful upheaval. Nothing short of that will eliminate neurosis, in my opinion" (www.primaltherapy.com).

This violent overthrow of the so-called Pain usually takes the form of a long, loud, drawn-out scream (the "primal scream" for which the therapy is justly famous), after which the client feels much better and is healthier both physically and mentally. Since early traumatic experiences are believed to manifest themselves both in maladaptive behavior and in physical problems, Janov claims that primal therapy reduces or eliminates a wide range of physical and psychological ailments, including many serious medical problems such as high blood pressure, cancer, drug and alcohol addiction, and sexual difficulties, among others. Furthermore, claims have also been made of more bizarre physical changes, including size increases of patients' feet, breasts, and penises, as well as growth of facial hair in men whose puberty previously appeared arrested. Unfortunately, no scientific evidence has turned up to support these claims other than uncontrolled case histories and personal observations.

Given the questionable theoretical underpinning of primal therapy, the absence of controlled scientific evidence is unsurprising. Consider, for example, the claim that trauma associated with conception can be a major source of Pain in adulthood. Primal therapists teach that if a child is conceived through rape, the egg and sperm are imprinted with specific feelings about the incident and pass this memory along to all cells of the child's body. This will of course cause lifelong pain and anxiety, until the patient learns, with the help of primal therapy, of course, to release those feelings (again, this sounds remarkably like some of the teachings of DIANETICS/SCIENTOLOGY). The idea that individual cells, especially gametes, possess either feelings or memories and are able to pass those feelings along to subsequent cells, thus leading to psychological trauma felt by the organism as a whole, is completely incompatible with what is known about MEMORY and feelings, to say nothing of cellular biology.

Janov has more recently attempted (in his latest book, *The Biology of Love*) to connect his ideas to more conventional knowledge in neuroscience, in the hope of gaining greater scientific legitimacy. In agreeing with neurochemists that becoming emotionally upset and screaming can cause a release of endorphins, which produces a feeling of well-being, he actually harms his case more than he helps it. This phenomenon is also well known among athletes, after all, and there is no reason to believe that the "runner's high" is associated with the release of repressed trauma. The strenuous activity provides a complete explanation of the phenomenon.

The Primal Scream was published more than thirty years ago, and primal therapy is essentially unaltered from its earliest state. While undeniably an inventive and intriguing approach to psychotherapy, it lacks the scientific validation that potential clients ought to be able to expect at this point in our history (*see also* BRAIN; DIANETICS/SCIENTOLOGY; FREUD, SIGMUND; NERVOUS SYSTEM).

Further Reading: Janov, A. *The Primal Scream; Primal Therapy: The Cure for Neurosis.* New York: Putnam, 1970; Janov, A. *The Biology of Love.* Amherst, MA: Prometheus Books, 2001; Rosen, R. D. *Psychobabble: Fast Talk and Quick Cure in the Era of Feeling.* New York: Atheneum, 1978.

PRODIGIES   *See* SAVANTS AND PRODIGIES

PROJECTIVE TESTS OF PERSONALITY   In a projective test, the examiner presents unstructured, vague, or ambiguous stimuli (such as the inkblots of the Rorschach test) with the belief that responses to the test represent revelations about the unconscious mental processes of the respondent. As of the mid-1990s, five of the fifteen most frequently used psychological tests were projective techniques. This is somewhat surprising, given that the psychoanalytic approach in which the tests are based has been out of favor in the mainstream of American psychology for more than fifty years (*see* FREUD), yet the tests demand just such an approach in scoring and interpretation. The popularity of the tests is even more surprising given the lack of solid proof that they are even capable of providing any useful diagnostic information, along with a substantial body of evidence indicating that the tests lack reliability and validity—this is sometimes referred to as the "projective paradox." Validity is the extent to which a test is actually measuring what it claims to measure, as well as its ability to predict behavior. Reliability simply refers to the extent to which a person taking the same test more than once will obtain the same results each time, as well as the extent to which the test will yield similar results regardless of who scores it.

Certainly the best-known projective test is the Rorschach test, introduced in the 1920s by the Swiss psychiatrist Hermann Rorschach, in which people are asked to describe what they see in a series of ten inkblots. It is far and away the most popular projective technique, even now given to many hundreds of thousands of people annually. It came under harsh attack as long ago as the 1950s, due to its lack of standardized procedures and norms—averaged results from a representative sample of the population, used as a reference point. Without them it is impossible to determine whether an individual's results are "normal" or not. Standardization is important because apparently minor differences in how a test is given can strongly influence a person's responses.

Since the 1970s Rorschach users have felt protected against such criticism by John Exner's Comprehensive System, which provides detailed procedures for standardized administration of the test as well as norms for both children and adults. Unfortunately, the test continues to have major problems with reliability and validity, largely because of the continuing subjective nature of many of the scoring criteria. The person scoring the test rates the subject's responses on more than 100 characteristics, including such things as whether the person described the whole blot or just parts, whether the response was typical or

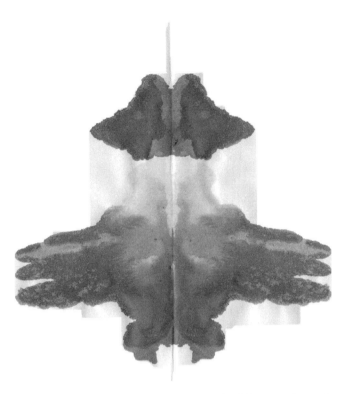

The Rorschach test consists of symmetrical inkblots similar to the one shown here, which was produced by the author (the actual Rorschach stimuli may not be reproduced). Photo by author.

unusual, whether the response was based on shape or color or both, whether the person focused on the dark portions or the white spaces, and many other details. As a result, two well-trained examiners may come up with strikingly different interpretations of a single person's responses.

The result of this lack of reliability is a remarkable lack of validity. The Rorschach is quite poor as a diagnostic tool for most psychiatric conditions, with the possible exception of schizophrenia and other thought disturbances, and even then the evidence is mixed. Quite clearly false, however, are the claims by some Rorschach proponents that the method can reliably detect depression, anxiety disorders, sexual abuse in children, antisocial personality disorder, tendencies towards violence, impulsivity, and criminal behavior. Furthermore, the norms that exist for the test are unrepresentative of the U.S. population, and their use results in substantial overestimation of maladjustment. In one California study of blood donors, for example, one in six appeared to have schizophrenia, according to their Rorschach scores.

The test also is remarkably susceptible to faking, an important consideration for a test so frequently introduced as evidence in court. A 1980 study is typical: Rorschach responses of twenty-four people were submitted to a panel of experts for diagnosis. The profiles actually came from the following four groups: six actual mental patients with a diagnosis of paranoid schizophrenia, six "uninformed" fakers instructed to try to fake the responses of a paranoid schizophrenic, six "informed" fakers who listened to a detailed tape about schizophrenia first, and six normal control subjects who simply took the test under standard conditions. Each test taker was rated by six to nine judges. The informed fakers were diagnosed as psychotic 72 percent of the time, versus only 48 percent for the actual psychotics. The uninformed fakers were also diagnosed as psychotic almost half of the time, and even the normal controls were diagnosed 24 percent of the time.

The reliability and validity of other projective tests also raise serious doubts. The Thematic Apperception Test (TAT), almost as widely used as the Rorschach, has neither standardized administration procedures nor an established scoring procedure. In the TAT, respondents are shown a series of ambiguous scenes drawn on large cards. For each picture, the respondent must make up a story. One card takes the projective approach to an extreme: it is totally blank. Individual clinicians choose the number of cards to show, up to thirty-one, as well as which particular cards are used. Although many standardized scoring systems have been created for the TAT, a survey of North American psychologists practicing in juvenile and family courts found that only 3 percent used any of them. Research suggests that using them would not help in any case. The systems show poor reliability and are unable to differentiate normal individuals from people who are either psychotic or depressed. Furthermore, these scoring systems provide no norms.

A third projective approach in wide use, again mostly by the courts, asks the person to draw a picture. The most widely used drawing test is the rather self-explanatory Draw-a-Person test. Interpretation proceeds in what has been called a "clinical-intuitive" manner, based on "signs" (features of the body or clothing, for example), usually guided by rather tentative psychodynamically based hypotheses. Large eyes might indicate paranoia and long ties might suggest sexual aggression, for example. A house with no windows might indicate feeling trapped. A person whose genitalia, or hands, or knees, or other features, depending on the interpretive guide used, are prominently visible might indicate a history of sexual abuse or latent homosexuality. There is no evidence, however, supporting the validity of this approach. Clinicians, in other words, have no grounds for believing any particular signs indicate any particular problem, other than their own prejudices and those of whoever trained them. Furthermore, studies suggest that clinicians will often attribute mental illness to many normal individuals who simply don't draw very well.

At this point, it is clear that projective tests fail to meet even the most basic standards of reliability and validity. In fact, a recent review of projective tests commissioned by the AMERICAN PSYCHOLOGICAL SOCIETY (APS) concluded "that, as usually administered, the Rorschach, TAT and human figure drawings are useful *only in very limited circumstances*" (author emphasis). Given this, how shall we interpret the projective paradox? Why are they still among the most popular tests? Of the various possible explanations, two seem especially important here. As human beings, clinicians are as susceptible as anyone to confirmation bias, or the tendency to take into account evidence that supports one's own beliefs and expectations while failing to consider evidence which fails to do so. A clinician who believes large eyes indicate paranoia, for example, will place great importance on the single client who drew large eyes and actually was paranoid, while remaining unmoved by (and possibly not even having noticed) the many large-eyed pictures drawn by clients who were not paranoid.

A second, more positive possibility to consider is the fact that many clinicians who use projective methods do not use them as tests or diagnostic tools at all, but rather as auxiliary tools in clinical interviews. They help the clinician to form initial, tentative hypotheses about the client, to be tested by closer examination with better tools. This use of the tests seems more appropriate, given the apparent uselessness of projectives where diagnosis is concerned. Unfortunately, surveys suggest that many clinicians, despite the clear evidence to the contrary, continue to believe in the diagnostic efficacy of projective tests.

Further Reading: Gregory, R. J. *Psychological Testing: History, Principles, and Applications.* 3rd ed. Boston: Allyn & Bacon, 2000; Lilienfeld, S. O., Wood, J. M., and Garb, H. N. "The Scientific Status of Projective Techniques." *Psychological Science in the Public Interest,* 1(2) (2000).

PSEUDOSCIENCE   Pseudoscience is simply false science. That is, anything that superficially resembles science, yet isn't science, is pseudoscience. The difference between them is one of degree rather than of kind, with no single clear boundary demarcating the essential difference. Although the boundaries are fuzzy, however, the distinction is a very important one, especially in the field of psychology. As a relatively young science, which unlike physics or chemistry has yet to enumerate a set of fixed principles that operate nearly universally, psychology is a discipline in which the distinction between real and false science is often unclear, especially to people outside the field.

One major distinction between science and pseudoscience lies in the concept of falsifiability. A central feature (possibly *the* defining characteristic) of science is the susceptibility of our hypotheses to refutation. In other words, for an idea to be considered scientific, it must be possible to conceive of evidence that could prove it wrong. An idea that cannot possibly be shown to be false is not scientific. It may be metaphysical, religious, or philosophical, but science is concerned with empirical testing of hypotheses, and testing an idea that cannot possibly be proven false is simply a waste of everyone's time.

For example, the idea that colds are caused by microscopic organisms is easily falsifiable (or has been, at least, since the invention of good reliable microscopes). All that is necessary to prove this is to examine mucus from both sick and healthy individuals. If there is no difference in the number and kind of microorganisms found in the secretions of the two groups, the hypothesis was wrong. This begs several questions. What about the idea that disease is caused by mischievous invisible demons that have no physical substance? What evidence could prove it wrong? Well, scientists could argue that the demons don't exist, because they don't see them, but the retort is fairly obvious: "Of course you don't see them, they're invisible." Ultimately, believing in them will come down to faith, not scientific physical evidence. The demon hypothesis is unfalsifiable because there is no way to demonstrate their existence, but also no way to prove their nonexistence, and it is therefore unscientific. This hypothesis is remarkably similar to the real-life argument made by sellers of SUBLIMINAL PERCEPTION self-help tapes. "Of course you can't hear (or detect, with sensitive laboratory equipment) the hidden messages. They're too quiet for you to hear." The obvious question, then, is how can we establish that they are even there? If the answer is, "You can't," then we are dealing with pseudoscience rather than science.

Beyond the lack of falsifiability, there is a set of characteristics typically found in pseudoscience that may help you to identify it (with a thank you to Bunge, 1984).

- *Reversed Burden of Proof*—In science, the burden of proof is on the claimant. If a person proclaims that something is true, then they must produce evidence to support that claim. Without evidence, there is no expectation that anyone will believe the claim. In pseudoscience, this burden is shifted to the critic. Rather than providing compelling evidence that he can actually communicate with the dead (*see* COLD READING), a medium may demand proof that he can't. This puts the scientific critic in a difficult position, because the scientific method cannot prove a negative.

This counterintuitive idea is well illustrated by an example that James Randi has frequently used to demonstrate the absurdity of a reversed burden of proof. First, assume that millions of people have come to believe that once a year, in the dead of winter, a large man in a red suit pilots a flying sleigh around the world, pulled by eight caribou or reindeer. The skeptical reader, may say, "But that's absurd! Reindeer can't fly!" The response from the true believer? "Prove it!" So, the skeptic sets out to prove that reindeer can't fly. This will require taking some reindeer into the air, either aboard an aircraft of some sort or to the top of a tall building, maybe Rockefeller Center in New York City. On the roof, the first animal is led up to the edge and given a good push. Sadly, it fails to fly. How many more reindeer carcasses would have to pile up on the ice rink below before the point was considered proven? Unfortunately, all that has been demonstrated is that *those* reindeer couldn't fly, or chose not to fly for reasons unknown, or were depressed and suicidal and welcomed the chance to end it all. For the Santa-supporters to prove their side of the argument, all they would have to do is produce, for public examination, one actual flying reindeer.

- *Overreliance on Testimonials and Anecdotal Evidence*—Real science uses controlled experimental designs, with results that are reproducible by other experimenters, not biased reports of individual people's uncontrolled personal experiences.

Right now, for example, there are clinics in California and Mexico that claim to prevent or cure cancer via the regular administration of coffee enemas. No controlled clinical trials have ever even hinted at the possibility that such a treatment might be effective, nor is there any good reason to believe that it would be, but the clinics are happy to provide evidence when asked. Unfortunately, the evidence consists of personal statements from people who believe the treatment worked for them. Missing is any medical evidence that these people ever had a proper medical diagnosis of cancer or have actually been cured of anything. The use of testimonials in television advertising is often taken to an absurd degree. One memorable ad for headache medicine, for example, featured treatment recommendations from a soap opera actor who presented his credentials thusly: "I'm not a doctor, but I play one on TV." To confuse this approach with scientific evidence is inappropriate.

- *Emphasis on Confirmation Rather Than Refutation*—Experimental design and statistical analysis in psychology are built around asking the question, "If I am wrong, could I have gotten these data anyway?" If other plausible alternative explanations for our results can be ruled out, only then can a hypothesis be accepted.

The true mark of a pseudoscientist, on the other hand, is the willful ignoring of evidence that fails to support a hypothesis, while clinging to any bit of evidence that seems to support it. Psychic investigators (*see* Parapsychology) have sometimes ignored famous psychics' complete failure to produce their claimed effects (blaming the failure on other factors), while emphasizing the testimonials of witnesses to the effects under less controlled conditions.

- *Overuse of Ad Hoc Hypotheses to Escape Refutation*—An ad hoc hypothesis is simply one that gets invented on the spot, rather than one that was already part of the theory.

Speaking of psychics, the list of excuses provided to explain away their failures (the hypothesis that their powers don't exist is rarely considered) is nearly endless—here are a few of the more popular ones: "The skeptical people present are sending out negative vibrations that interfere with the powers, gifts, spirits, etc." For some reason, being watched very closely by people who might spot cheating tends to shut the psychic powers down; "Of course he cheated this time, the powers weren't working properly, and he didn't want to disappoint you. But he usually doesn't cheat, and his powers are real"; "He got more wrong than we would expect by chance, that means *negative* psi is at work here, which is just as impressive as the positive kind."

- *Absence of Self-Correction*—No amount of evidence ever seems to get rid of a theory. True science is self-correcting over time. Theories that turn out not to be true tend to be dropped in favor of theories that are better supported by evidence.

In medicine, for example, the accumulation of evidence on the actions of microorganisms eventually led to the disappearance of the humoral theory of disease (that disease is caused by an excess of blood or bile, for example) in favor of the germ theory of disease. Within psychology, for example, some psychoanalysts have continued to view autism as a response to poor parenting in early childhood, despite the solid evidence that the disorder has physiological underpinnings and a genetic component.

- *Use of Obscurantist Language*—This simply refers to the pseudoscientist's tendency to use hazy, scientific-sounding language, that doesn't necessarily make any sense, to sound rigorous and complicated.

L. Ron Hubbard's *Dianetics* (1950) is filled with classic examples. Here's a favorite:

The scientific fact, observed and tested, is that the organism, in the presence of physical pain, lets the analyzer get knocked out of circuit so that there is a limited quantity or no quantity at all of personal awareness as a unit organism.

One can read and reread the section of the book in which it appears and still have no idea what it means.

- *Absence of Connectivity with Other Disciplines*—In pseudoscience, it is not unusual for a claim to require that a large area of human knowledge be wrong in order for the claim to be true.

Uri Geller, an Israeli psychic famous in the 1970s, claimed that he could bend metal objects using only the power of his mind. This can only be true if modern physics, chemistry, psychophysiology, and metallurgy are simply flat-out wrong about how the world works, and yet books celebrating his "gifts" remain in print and continue to be written.

As psychologists, we should be very concerned about the influx of pseudoscience into our field, especially in the clinical realm. A gulf has developed between psychological scientists and clinicians, with a number of therapies being widely promoted despite a lack of empirical support, and sometimes despite not especially making any sense (*see also* CORRELATION; CRANIOSACRAL THERAPY; DIANETICS/SCIENTOLOGY; EYE MOVEMENT DESENSITIZATION AND REPROCESSING (EMDR); KAVA; PAST-LIFE REGRESSION (PLR); PRIMAL THERAPY; PSYCHOLOGY, RESEARCH METHODS IN; ST. JOHN'S WORT; SUBLIMINAL PERCEPTION; THOUGHT FIELD THERAPY (TFT); and all the entries under Pseudoscience in the Guide to Related Topics).

Further Reading: Bunge, M. "What Is Pseudoscience?" *Skeptical Inquirer*, 9 (1984): 36–46; Lilienfeld, S. O. "Pseudoscience in Contemporary Clinical Psychology: What It Is and What We Can Do about It." *The Clinical Psychologist*, 51(4) (1998): 3–9.

PSI *See* PARAPSYCHOLOGY

PSYCHEDELIC DRUGS The word psychedelic is formed from Greek roots meaning "mind-manifesting," an appropriate name for psychoactive (hallucinogenic) drugs that can severely distort perceptions and evoke vivid hallucinations. A hallucination is simply a sensory experience that occurs in the absence of sensory input; in other words, seeing, hearing, feeling, or smelling something which is not, objectively speaking, there. Hallucinogens are often divided into two categories: major hallucinogens and marijuana (usually the only member listed in the "minor" category).

Marijuana—The hemp plant (*Cannabis sativa*) has been cultivated for over 5 millennia for its fiber, which has historically been very important in shipping, used primarily for rope and sailcloth. For approximately as long, its leaves and flowers (marijuana) and its concentrated resin (hashish) have been used both medicinally and recreationally. The primary active ingredient is delta-9-tetrahydrocannabinol (THC), but the plant also contains over eighty other cannabinoids, complex organic molecules found only in cannabis, many of which also contribute to the drug experience. THC produces a wide range of effects depending on the individual using the drug and the mode of use, thus making the drug difficult to classify. For example, some chemicals are active when smoked but not when ingested in food. Because of this, many references list marijuana as a separate drug category unto itself rather than including it among the hallucinogens. When marijuana is smoked, THC reaches the brain in about seven seconds, producing a stronger and more immediate effect than does ingesting it in food, which causes the peak concentration to be reached more slowly and unpredictably.

As with other hallucinogens, the marijuana user's experience will vary according to the situation in which the drug is taken and the individual user's state of mind at the time. When a person who feels happy takes the drug, the result will usually be an intensification of euphoric feelings; but when an anxious or depressed person takes the drug, those feelings too may be intensified. Standard effects of taking marijuana include the following:

- *Altered Sensory-Perceptual Experiences*—Vision, hearing, taste, and touch are changed. A commonly reported experience, for example, is that users hear things in music that they haven't heard before. Intriguingly, studies using objective measures of sensation and perception not only fail to find any evidence of enhancement during marijuana intoxication, but they actually tend to report the opposite.

- *Impaired Attention and Reaction Time*—On tasks requiring either sustained concentration or divided attention, performance is significantly disrupted, as is reaction time.

- *Memory Loss*—Disruption of short-term MEMORY is one of the best-known effects of marijuana. The marijuana user may be unable to keep up a conversation due to having forgotten what the other person just said, or may even forget what he or she is saying in mid-sentence. Reading comprehension is also disrupted, for the same reason. Marijuana also interferes with the transfer of information from short-term to long-term memory, which is why many college students have discovered to their sorrow that studying while stoned is a remarkably bad idea.

- *Distorted Subjective Experience of Time*—Marijuana causes serious distortions of the internal clock, in that time appears to pass more slowly.

- *Motivation Reduction*—Marijuana appears to reduce motivation to perform on cognitive tasks, in addition to its effects on ability to do so.

- *Altered Levels of Creativity*—Marijuana users frequently report that they are more creative and inspired while stoned. Research evidence tends not to support this. A common experience among marijuana users involves writing down one's thoughts while stoned, and then discovering while sober that the "profound and creative" thoughts are actually either very ordinary or downright incomprehensible.

- *Altered Social Skills*—Another common subjective experience while under the influence of marijuana is a sense of improved insight into others and enhanced interpersonal communication skills. This is also not supported by research, which tends instead to show diminished social perception.

- *Psychiatric Symptoms*—Contrary to long-standing myth (exacerbated by such classic films as *Reefer Madness*), marijuana use does not cause psychiatric disturbances in normal people using typical amounts. In people who already have tendencies towards psychosis (such as pre-existing paranoid or schizophrenic tendencies), however, marijuana use may trigger psychotic episodes.

- *"Coming Down"*—Marijuana users frequently express a belief that they can will themselves back to sobriety to carry out complex tasks such as driving a car. Again, evidence suggests that this is not the case.

- *"The Munchies"*—Marijuana frequently triggers ravenous hunger, usually referred to by users as "the munchies." This effect may have legitimate medical applications (see below).

The effects described above are mostly temporary, occurring only while the person is still "high," but marijuana also has some longer-term effects. Chronic use is associated with difficulties in attention, memory, and motivation, even when the drug is not currently in use. Unlike alcohol, which is eliminated from the body within a few hours, THC is stored in fatty tissues of the body and may remain present for a month or more. Research also suggests that marijuana may suppress testosterone production and reduce sperm counts. Studies also show that chronic marijuana smoking may damage the lungs more than tobacco smoking does.

Although marijuana is primarily used recreationally, its potential medical applications have led to powerful grass-roots movements supporting its legalization in the United States and Canada. Marijuana has long been a favored treatment for glaucoma, and other legitimate uses have become widely known more recently. Marijuana is far more effective than other drugs for many patients in relieving the nausea caused by chemotherapy. It also is effective in relieving the nausea and pain experienced by AIDS patients, and getting the munchies helps prevent the severe weight loss often seen in such patients. Knowledge of these uses is best accompanied, however, by an understanding of the ways in which the toxicity of marijuana smoke compromises the benefits provided by THC. Unfortunately, many glaucoma and chemotherapy patients report that THC in pill form is not as effective in providing relief as smoked marijuana.

Major Hallucinogens—Some hallucinogens are naturally occurring substances, but the best-known and best-documented drug in this category is LSD (lysergic acid diethylamide). The drug was created in 1943 by chemist Albert Hofmann, who also inadvertently took the first "acid trip" after accidentally ingesting a miniscule quantity of the chemical. LSD is effective in extremely small doses: where the effective doses of other drugs, including other hallucinogens, are measured in milligrams, LSD requires measurement in micrograms. LSD's effects on the user, which include vivid hallucinations, participation in dreamlike scenes, and powerful emotional states, appear to be highly dependent on the individual's mood and state of mind at the time of ingestion. Consequently, the emotions and images experienced may cover the whole range from euphoria and deep peace to terror and panic. Users also frequently experience synaesthesia, or the transformation of sensory experiences in one modality into experiences in another modality. In plain English, that means they hear colors and shapes and see sounds.

LSD appears to primarily mimic the action of the neurotransmitter serotonin in various parts of the brain, thus causing areas of the brain to communicate with each other which shouldn't (thus producing synaesthesia) and causing other areas to communicate when they shouldn't (some studies show that nerve pathways which are ordinarily active during dreaming are also highly active during an LSD trip). Some of LSD's effects may last long after the drug is no longer present. A well documented after-effect of LSD is the flashback, in which the user may re-experience portions of the trip weeks, months, or even years later. It has been suggested that this may be a result of actual physical changes to neurons that occur in the presence of LSD. Results of physiological studies remain inconclusive on this.

Although LSD was synthesized in 1943, the effects of similar drugs have been known for centuries, thanks to several naturally occurring plant substances that have been used ceremonially by Native Americans since long before the arrival of European settlers. Psilocybin is a hallucinogen found in several species of wild mushrooms, commonly referred to as "magic mushrooms" or simply "shrooms." The mushrooms were considered sacred by the pre-Columbian civilizations in Mexico and Central America, where the Aztec word for them was *teonanacatl*, or "flesh of God." They are still used by certain tribal groups in the Yucatán peninsula area of Mexico and Guatemala, and their effects are virtually identical to those described above for LSD. Since the hallucinogenic effects rely so profoundly on the user's emotional state, the tribesman who has prepared for a deep religious experience will generally have one, whereas bad trips are extremely rare under such conditions.

Mexican and Plains Indian tribal groups have also long used peyote, a spineless desert cactus that grows in Northern Mexico and the Southwestern United States. The top of the cactus is sliced into pieces known as buttons, which are then dried in the sun. In ceremonial use, the buttons are softened in the mouth and then chewed and swallowed. At first, the effects of the active ingredient, mescaline, include nausea, tremors, and vomiting. Once these feelings end, the hallucinogenic effects may take an hour to manifest themselves, at which time they may last for several hours.

Like the other hallucinogens, the effects of mescaline depend heavily on the mood and expectations of the user, and so the religious structure of the experience tends to produce very positive, ecstatic trips. Because it is used in the religious ceremonies of Native Americans, peyote is the only hallucinogen described here which is legal for use in the United States, but only when taken as part of a religious ceremony. This is a result of the government's reluctance to interfere in religious practices and was formalized by an act of Congress in 1970. A similar attempt by Rastafarians seeking to use marijuana legally as part of their religion, however, has failed (*see also* BRAIN; DEPRESSANTS; NERVOUS SYSTEM; STIMULANTS).

Further Reading: Stafford, P., Bigwood, J., and Orfali, S. J. *Psychedelics Encyclopedia*. Berkeley, CA: Ronin, 1992.

PSYCHIATRY   Psychiatry is the medical specialty that concerns itself with the diagnosis, treatment, and prevention of psychological disorders. A psychiatrist is, first and foremost, a physician, complete with M.D. degree. In addition to the usual medical training, however, a psychiatrist receives additional special training and clinical experience in the psychiatric specialty. In the public mind, psychiatrists and clinical psychologists often appear to be the same thing, but there are crucial differences in their areas of expertise and practice. A clinical psychologist relies on various psychotherapeutic techniques to treat a client, whereas a psychiatrist, adopting a medical model of mental illness instead, is far more likely to suggest and implement a pharmaceutical treatment approach. As a medical doctor, a psychiatrist can prescribe appropriate medication to deal with a disorder, while a psychologist lacks either the expertise or the legal right to do so (*see also* PSYCHOLOGY, RESEARCH METHODS IN).

Further Reading: Storey, P. *Psychological Medicine: An Introduction to Psychiatry*. 10th ed. London: Churchill Livingstone, 1986.

PSYCHIC MEDIUMSHIP   *See* COLD READING

PSYCHIC PHENOMENA   *See* PARAPSYCHOLOGY

PSYCHOANALYSIS   *See* FREUD, SIGMUND (1856–1939)

PSYCHOKINESIS   *See* PARAPSYCHOLOGY

PSYCHOLOGY, RESEARCH METHODS IN   As a scientific enterprise, psychology follows the methods of science, meaning that it uses data to generate testable hypotheses and constructs theories to explain the results of those tests. Research efforts are largely devoted to trying to describe people but also attempt to construct explanations. A theory is an explanatory framework, based on the observations. It suggests certain additional testable questions, known as hypotheses, which are tested by further research. Theories are always open to further refinement, but to become widely accepted in the first place, they must be based on replicable evidence. In the popular imagination, however, "theory" and "hypothesis" are often mixed up with each other, with theories dismissed as tentative guesses. One often hears evolution dismissed in this manner by religious fundamentalists, "It's only a theory!"

Actually, it's a whole range of theories, as there is much disagreement among biologists as to how exactly the processes involved in natural selection work. What they do not disagree on, however, is the question of whether it occurs. Mountains of data support it, and the general theoretical framework is the basis of all modern biology. Consider a problem in physics: gravity is only a theory, after all. There are actually some very different interpretations of how it operates, with Newtonian physics favoring the idea of a force that draws things towards objects as a function of their mass, while Einsteinian theory favors the idea that large objects actually warp space-time around them, causing objects to move towards them (note to any physicists who may be reading: Yes, I recognize that this is a very highly simplified explanation). Either way, however, loads of evidence suggests that if I drop an object, it will fall. We may have different theories about why it falls, but whether or not it will isn't a question anymore.

Psychology is a young science—people have observed selective breeding and the gravity of falling objects for thousands of years, and reaction time to subliminally presented stimuli has been measured for only a few decades. The theories aren't so well established, and they're all still looking for supportive evidence.

Psychological scientists seek evidence in several ways, but the ideal method for determining cause-and-effect relationships is the experimental method. In an experiment, a variable (a variable is anything at all that can have more than one value and can be measured—favorites in psychology include gender, age, and INTELLIGENCE, among many others) is manipulated by the experimenter, and changes in another variable are looked for as a result of the manipulation. For example, if the experimenter wants to see if the MOZART EFFECT actually works, he or she might take a group of people and give them a math test. After the math test, the experimenter will have them listen to some Mozart, and then give them the math test again. If they improve in their performance on the math test, it might be tempting to give Mozart credit, but it isn't a true experiment yet. How does the experimenter know that they wouldn't have done better on the second test even without the Mozart? The only way to find out is to take a second group of people (the control group) and have them take both tests at the same times as the first group (the experimental group), but without having them listen to Mozart. If the two groups perform differently from each other, then it may be assumed that Mozart was the cause, because there was control over that variable. In any experiment, the condition that the experimenter controls and varies (in this case, whether or not the subjects listened to Mozart) is called the independent variable, and the variable that is used to determine whether that manipulation had an effect (in this case, the math test) is the dependent variable.

For this experiment to serve as a definitive test of the hypothesis that listening to Mozart will improve math skills, however, there are some other variables that must also be dealt with, as they might affect the outcome. What about musical taste, for example? Some students may be big Mozart fans, but others might hate all music other than country or Swedish death metal. Such variables that are not part of the experimental design but that may provide alternative explanations of the data, are called confounding variables. A quick, efficient way of dealing with such things is random assignment to the experimental condition. Assuming that various musical tastes are distributed somewhat randomly among the participants, randomly picking who goes into the experimental group and who goes into the control group is a good way to get those Swedish death metal fans evenly distributed among the two groups, thus ensuring that they don't have a disproportionate impact on one group or the other (*see also* HAWTHORN EFFECT; NONSPECIFIC EFFECTS).

Sometimes it isn't possible or ethical to use random assignment to groups, even though the research question is an important one. Consider the question of the effects of cocaine exposure on prenatal development. The ideal way to investigate this question would be to conduct an experiment, in which half of a sample of pregnant women is randomly assigned to smoke crack during their pregnancy … the ethical and legal problems in this example are clear. Because people in the world already perform this type of behavior, it is still possible to study the effects, and even to use the same dependent variables, by simply recruiting a sample of women who are already using cocaine and comparing them to a carefully matched control group of women who aren't. Since the independent variable (cocaine use) wasn't manipulated by the experimenter, this isn't a true experiment. This kind of design is a quasi-experiment. It doesn't allow the same degree of causal inference as an experiment, because of the lack of manipulation, but it allows us to study problems that can't be looked at experimentally.

Less rigorous than experimental or quasi-experimental research is correlational research, in which multiple variables are measured, without any experimental manipulation, and the degree of relationship between the variables is measured (*see* CORRELATION). Most survey research is of this type. From a questionnaire, one might find, for example, that men who drive large SUVs are more likely to own basketballs than men who drive compact gas/electric hybrids. Cause-and-effect conclusions can't be drawn from this sort of data. How the two variables are related is impossible to discern from the data. This sort of research is very good for suggesting relationships between variables that may or not be causal, but which can then be examined more closely in experimental research. Before the experimental research (animal studies, mostly) that showed a causal link between smoking and lung cancer, the two were known to be correlated, but the causal inference could only be drawn after experiments were carried out (inspired by the correlational data).

Some of the questions that are of interest to psychologists involve very rare circumstances: the effects of having parents killed by terrorists on a child's school adjustment, for example. In these cases, traditional group research, be it experimental, quasi-experimental, or correlational, isn't appropriate. If there is only one person with the problem under study, or only a handful, it may be better to just observe that person in great depth to see what can be found out.

213

Such an in-depth examination of a single person is a case study, and while generalization of findings may be problematic (after all, one person can't be representative of the whole population), such research is invaluable in discovering more about rare clinical syndromes (*see also* PSYCHIATRY).

Further Reading: Mook, D. G. *Psychological Research: The Ideas behind the Methods.* New York: W. W. Norton, 2001.

PTSD   *See* POSTTRAUMATIC STRESS DISORDER

R

RANDI, JAMES (1928–) Canadian-born magician and escape artist James Randi had a highly successful career as a stage performer from the 1950s into the 1970s, but since the early 1960s, he has been primarily known as the world's leading skeptical investigator of paranormal, occult, and supernatural claims. In the beginning of this phase of his career, he carried around a blank check for $10,000, which he promised to anyone who could show, under proper conditions of observation, evidence of any of those claims. With inflation and the participation of some generous donors, the prize is up to over $1 million today and has yet to be given away.

He achieved his greatest notoriety with his ongoing battle with Israeli psychic superstar Uri Geller, who in 1972 convinced a pair of scientists at Stanford Research International (not a unit of Stanford University) that his paranormal gifts were genuine, chief among them clairvoyance and his ability to bend metal objects, usually silverware, with his mind. Randi next consulted with the *Tonight Show's* then-host, Johnny Carson, a skeptical ex-magician, on ways to prevent Geller from cheating. The result was an embarrassing twenty-two-minute *Tonight Show* appearance during which Geller was unable to perform any of his usual feats. From this experience, Randi went on to write an entire book detailing ways to duplicate many of Geller's "psychic" feats without resorting to any paranormal gifts.

Randi's mantra is a simple one: extraordinary claims require extraordinary evidence. If a person is claiming something that is not possible given our current understanding of the world, then it is unlikely to be true, and substantial scientific evidence should be required of that person before his claim is believed.

James Randi demonstrates Uri Geller–style spoon-bending. Photo courtesy of the James Randi Educational Foundation.

His devotion to the pursuit of truth against a rising tide of nonsense and PSEUDOSCIENCE earned him a MacArthur Foundation "genius" grant, a prize usually given to people pursuing groundbreaking academic research, in the 1980s. He put the funds toward his efforts to expose the tricks of phony faith healers. In 1976, he was a founding fellow of the Committee for the Scientific Investigation of Claims of the Paranormal (CSICOP), made up of leading scientists and thinkers in a variety of disciplines, and he has more recently left CSICOP behind, in part as a result of their being named as co-defendants in lawsuits filed against Randi by Geller and others, forming his own organization, the James Randi Educational Foundation (JREF). The JREF serves as a clearinghouse of information on pseudoscience, skepticism, and the paranormal, and it also hosts annual conferences devoted to those topics (*see also* COLD READING, PARAPSYCHOLOGY, PSEUDOSCIENCE).

Further Reading: Randi, J. *The Truth about Uri Geller.* Buffalo, NY: Prometheus, 1982; Randi, J. *Flim-Flam!* Buffalo, NY: Prometheus, 1987.

RANK, OTTO *See* NEO-FREUDIANS

RATIONAL-EMOTIVE BEHAVIOR THERAPY (REBT) *See* COGNITIVE-BEHAVIOR THERAPY

REBIRTHING Yet another example of therapeutic PSEUDOSCIENCE, rebirthing consists of a series of deep-breathing techniques intended to reduce stress, increase energy, and bring ease and pleasure to one's life and relationships. This sounds fairly innocuous so far; the problem lies in the reasons given for the technique's alleged effectiveness. The method is called rebirthing because it is intended to help people remember their own births. Apparently, they may have made some wrong decisions at birth, which have affected their lives and relationships, and current psychological problems may date back to those early decisions. By re-experiencing their birth, people can achieve a fresh start and resolve their problems. Rebirthers also teach that deep breathing cleanses the body of toxins, which leave when we exhale properly, resulting in a healthier self physically as well as mentally.

With some practitioners, the method includes activities intended to help the client remember being born by actually re-experiencing it, but most sources on the technique currently downplay the importance of this or completely fail to mention it. This may be due to the sentencing of two rebirthing therapists in Colorado, on June 18, 2001, to sixteen years of prison on charges of reckless child abuse resulting in death, along with lesser charges of criminal impersonation and unlawful practice of psychotherapy. The deceased patient, only ten years old, was allegedly being helped to bond with her adoptive mother, who was present at the time of the fatal therapy. The therapists felt that if she re-experienced the birth process, she and her adoptive mother could have a fresh start together, and her behavior problems would be left behind. This resulted in the girl being wrapped in a flannel blanket and covered with pillows, and then being sat upon by several adults, who did everything they could to prevent her from emerging. Their activities included shouting, "Go ahead and die!" in response to her anguished cries that she could not breathe. One result of her death was the passage of Colorado House Bill 1238, which prohibits reenactment of the birth process when accompanied by any sort of restraint. Clearly, rebirthing therapists have good reason to de-emphasize that part of the technique and focus instead on the breathing method.

The scientific ground under the breathing method of rebirthing, however, is nearly as shaky. Due to developmental changes in both brain physiology and strategy use, most adults remember little or nothing prior to about the age of four, and certainly nothing before two years, a phenomenon known as infantile AMNESIA. The idea, therefore, that they can resolve all adult problems by re-experiencing a MEMORY that they don't have to begin with, seems absurd. There is no evidence for either of the two central tenets of rebirthing: that an adult has a memory of his or her birth or that reliving the experience will somehow help to repair psychological damage that has occurred in the interim. Of course, the same applies to the secondary idea that a baby makes decisions during birth that affect the entire subsequent life course (*see also* DIANETICS, FREUD).

Further Reading: Ray, S., and Orr, L. *Rebirthing in the New Age.* Berkeley, CA: Celestial Arts, 1983; Sarner, L. "'Rebirthers' Who Killed Child Receive 16-Year Prison Terms." www.quackwatch.org/04ConsumerEducation/News/rebirthing.html, 2001; Taylor, K. *The Breathwork Experience: Exploration and Healing in Nonordinary States of Consciousness.* Santa Cruz, CA: Hanford Mead Publishers, 1994.

RESEARCH METHODS *See* PSYCHOLOGY, RESEARCH METHODS IN

ROLFING In the 1930s, Ida P. Rolf (1896–1979), an organic chemist who had also dabbled in yoga and chiropractic, introduced a form of massage that she believed would relieve people of stress caused by past traumatic experience.

According to Rolfing theory, memories of traumatic experiences are stored in various parts of the body (as "muscle memory"), blocking the free flow of "vital energy," and the proper sort of massage can release them, thus restoring the proper flow and integrating mind and body. Rolf also proposed that traditional ideas of good posture (shoulders back, back straight, head held high) are actually very unhealthy, as they misalign the spine and deform the body. Furthermore, past traumatic experiences can make posture even worse, and most people would be psychologically healthier if they realigned their bodies so that the earth's gravitational field could reinforce the body's energy field.

Rolfers, as practitioners call themselves, seek out areas of "energy imbalance" while performing the massage and adjust what they are doing when they detect these areas, to release the energy. The explicit goal of Rolfing is to reposition connective tissue, and so the massage can frequently be quite painful. Clients learn to see the pain as a good thing, however, as it represents the release of traumatic muscle memory. This is important, as Rolfing treatment involves a series of ten weekly sessions.

The idea of vital energy becoming blocked in various areas of the body and requiring outside help to be released is fairly popular in alternative-medicine circles (*see* ACUPUNCTURE; THOUGHT FIELD THERAPY), but it does not correspond to known facts of how the human body operates. Similarly, there is absolutely no support in psychological literature for the idea of traumatic experiences being repressed in the form of muscle memory, and so the basic ideas of Rolfing certainly fall into the category of PSEUDOSCIENCE. On the other hand, there is plenty of evidence that regular weekly massages can make some people feel much better, so Rolfing is not without merit.

Further Reading: Rolf, I. P. *Rolfing: Reestablishing the Natural Alignment and Structural Integration of the Human Body for Vitality and Well-Being.* Rochester, VT: Healing Arts Press, 1990.

RORSCHACH TEST *See* PROJECTIVE TESTS OF PERSONALITY

S

SAD   *See* SEASONAL AFFECTIVE DISORDER (SAD)

ST. JOHN'S WORT   St. John's wort (*Hypericum perforatum*) is a plant that has been widely claimed to be an effective natural antidepressant and has thus gained enormous popularity in the United States and Europe. Hypericin, one of many compounds found in the plant, is generally believed to be primarily responsible for the antidepressant action. Several studies of standardized hypericin extracts have found it to be twice as effective as a placebo, and a few European studies have found it somewhat more effective than a standard antidepressant in treating mild to moderate depression. The majority of the studies, however, used small sample sizes, inconsistent classification of depression, a wide range of dosages and hypericin concentrations, and only lasted a few weeks. In the absence of research that would establish either long-term effectiveness or long-term safety, the herb has nonetheless become very popular, with annual sales of about $55 million.

With so many people self-medicating, sometimes for major clinical depression, the National Institutes of Health launched a large-scale, multi-site randomized double-blind trial comparing a standardized hypericin extract to both a placebo and the widely prescribed antidepressant Zoloft (a selective serotonin reuptake inhibitor, or SSRI). The rather large sample consisted of 340 people with moderate to moderately severe major depression. The study concluded that St. John's wort was no more effective in relieving the symptoms of depression than a placebo. Intriguingly, neither was Zoloft on some measures, though it was more effective on others.

Unprocessed *Hypericum perforatum* (St. John's wort). Is it an effective antidepressant?

Having examined the effectiveness of St. John's wort, the National Institute of Mental Health has also recently addressed the herb's safety. Due to the side effects often associated with pharmaceutical antidepressants, many people are drawn to products such as St. John's wort in the belief that an herbal supplement will be safer than a drug. These people would do well to read the NIMH "Public Alert on St. John's Wort." In it, the agency reports that adverse interactions have been discovered between St. John's wort and indinavir, a protease inhibitor used to treat HIV-positive patients, as well as cyclosporine, a drug used to prevent organ rejection in transplant patients. So far, the effectiveness of St. John's wort has not been established for mild depression, but it is clearly unlikely to be effective for major depression, and it can be dangerous in combination with certain other drugs.

Further Reading: National Center for Complementary and Alternative Medicine. "Study Shows St. John's Wort Ineffective for Major Depression of Moderate Severity." www.nccam.nih.gov/news/2002/stjohnswort/pressrelease.htm, 2002; National Institute of Mental Health. "Public Alert on St. John's Wort." www.nimh.nih.gov/events/stjohnwort.cfm, 2001.

SAPIR-WHORF HYPOTHESIS The linguistic relativity principle, formulated by Edward Sapir (1884–1936) and refined by his student, Benjamin Lee Whorf (1897–1941), states that human thinking is highly dependent on the language spoken by the individual thinker. As language is our main tool for organizing our experiences, the argument goes, the language that we use imposes limits both on what is experienced and on how it is expressed. The structure of the language spoken by a social group, in other words, influences their understanding of reality and therefore how they behave with respect to it.

Whorf was influenced by his study of the Hopi language, which does not contain any words or grammatical structures corresponding to notions of time; the language makes no reference to past, present, or future. From this, Whorf argues that the metaphysics embodied in the Hopi language is fundamentally different from that encoded in Western European languages such as English. This suggests that the fundamental worldview of the Hopi, and therefore their underlying thought processes, must be different from ours. Another favorite piece of evidence for the hypothesis involves the observation that the Inuit language has many different words for snow, depending on such characteristics as color, density, etc., whereas we in temperate climates merely call it by one word.

This hypothesis has been a favorite among opponents of Noam CHOMSKY's ideas of a universal, deep structure to human languages and an innate language acquisition device; if different languages reflect or even determine different understandings of the world, then there is no underlying universal grammar. Evidence for this argument (also known as *linguistic determinism*—the idea that what we are capable of thinking is actually determined by the structure of our native language), however, is rather sparse, while countervailing evidence is all around. Consider the ability to learn foreign languages, for example. If the thought processes involved in the foreign languages were in fact alien to the mind of a speaker of another language, such learning should present almost insurmountable difficulties.

More difficult for Sapir-Whorf supporters, however, is the fact that their favorite pieces of evidence turn out simply not to be true. Ekkehart Malotki, an anthropologist who has studied the Hopi extensively, has shown that, contrary to Whorf's claims, their language contains multiple tenses and words for units of time. Additionally, far from having no concept of time, they actually have fairly sophisticated methods for recording events. Regarding the Inuits, as far as anthropologists have been able to determine, there may be as many as a dozen words for snow, around the same number as in English: slush, melted snow, light powder, wet snow, dirty snow, or any of the other terms regularly heard during a New England winter. Outdoor enthusiasts may of course have more, as their activities may require them to distinguish among more varieties. Rather than suggesting that a cultural group's language determines their worldview, the available evidence instead supports a weaker version of the Whorfian hypothesis: language does influence the way people perceive and remember their environment, and so it may predispose humans to look at the world in a certain way.

Further Reading: Hunter, E, and Agnoli, F. "The Whorfian Hypothesis: A Cognitive Psychology Perspective." *Psychological Review*, 98(3) (1991): 377–390; Malotki, E. *The Making of an Icon.* Lincoln: University of Nebraska Press, 2000.

SATANIC RITUAL ABUSE Under HYPNOSIS and during various other types of suggestive therapy, many individuals have eventually "recovered" memories of prolonged sexual, psychological, or physical abuse at the hands of devil-worshipping adults. Often these memories date from an age of less than two years old, a time from which most MEMORY experts agree that nothing can be remembered. This abuse often includes such elements as butchered infants, the breeding of babies for later sacrifice, ritual sexual abuse of children, drinking of blood, cannibalism, and sex orgies. This sort of recollection is nearly universal in victims of Dissociative Identity Disorder (also known as MULTIPLE PERSONALITY DISORDER), so as apparent victims of that disorder grew in number, so did belief in satanic ritual abuse. In November 1987 Geraldo Rivera, then an ABC and now a Fox News correspondent, hosted a syndicated TV special on which he claimed that there are over 1 million devil worshippers in this country, most of them part of a highly organized, secretive network involved nationwide in ritual child abuse and grisly murders.

In fact, the Federal Bureau of Investigation (FBI) has uncovered no evidence whatsoever of such a network, and whether Satanic ritual abuse (SRA) actually even exists has been a controversial topic since about 1980. Thanks to media attention, most people in the United States and Canada believed during the late 1980s and early 1990s that SRA was widespread. Some promoters of the notion of SRA have estimated the number of Satanic murders annually in the United States to be as high as 60,000. If that is true, then it is a very serious problem on our hands, albeit an extremely well kept secret, because that is about three times the total homicide rate for the entire country in most years. Also, despite the many recovered memories of thousands of sacrificed babies, nobody seems to have reported any of them missing, and no remains have turned up. There is, however, a near consensus among police and other investigators that it doesn't exist at all.

Although this was a big story in the early 1990s, not much is heard about it anymore. Lack of evidence and the growth in awareness of how easily false memories are created have today convinced most people that SRA is not occurring. Even Geraldo Rivera, who once fanned the flames of sensationalism so successfully, admitted on the air in December 1995 that he had been duped.

Further Reading: Victor, J. S. *Satanic Panic: The Creation of a Contemporary Legend.* Chicago: Open Court, 1993.

SAVANTS AND PRODIGIES The people known today as savants were previously known by the somewhat less-sensitive term *idiot* savants, reflecting the terminology that was once used with reference to mental retardation. A savant is a person in whom severe mental handicap, usually MENTAL RETARDATION or AUTISM, coexists with exceptional talent in a discrete skill or ability.

Some autistic savants, for example, cannot dress themselves or perform basic self-care, yet they can instantly tell the correct the day of the week on which any date in history fell. Others can perform multiple-digit multiplication in their heads, while lacking the ability to read. Savants can show exceptional performance in a wide range of abilities, the most common of which are called splinter skills. Frequently seen splinter skills include a preoccupation with, and huge memory for, music and sports trivia, license plate numbers, calendars, maps, and historical facts; as well as more unusual niche categories such as the many different models of vacuum tubes, and the appliances they were used in. A common feature of all savants, regardless of the particular skill area in which they excel, is clearly an extremely deep and detailed memory, though only for a very narrow range of information.

Some rare savants, referred to as prodigious savants, develop a skill to such a high level that it would be extremely impressive and outstanding even in a non-handicapped person. Some doctors estimate that as many as one in ten autistic patients have some degree of savant skill; and about one in 2,000 persons with mental retardation have it, although, owing to the much higher incidence of mental retardation, only about 50 percent of savants are autistic. It has been estimated that there are fewer than fifty prodigious savants in the world. Tony DeBlois, an autistic savant in Massachusetts, is an excellent example of this highly unusual combination of ability and disability. He is a musician who can play a repertoire of over 8,000 songs on twenty different instruments. His huge repertoire owes its existence in part to his ability to play on a piano, from memory, any piece of music after hearing it only once. Despite this prodigious level of musical skill, however, the blind musician only learned to buckle his own belt around age thirty. Other prodigious savants possess the ability to draw extremely detailed and life-like scenes or portraits from memory of people or places only seen once, and briefly, while lacking even the most rudimentary verbal skills.

Prodigies are similar to savants in that they have a single area of exceptional ability, but they differ in that their cognitive functioning is otherwise fairly ordinary, rather than subaverage. Although they excel in their particular area of skill, for example, prodigies tend not to achieve unusually high scores on general intelligence tests. The other defining feature of a prodigy is that the syndrome is apparent in early childhood—definitions tend to include the stipulation that prodigies are identified as such prior to age ten. These are unusual children: they tend to develop their particular interest well before reaching school age and possess a remarkable drive to learn more and do even better. Chess prodigies, for example, tend to begin playing by age three, and Wolfgang Amadeus Mozart, probably history's most famous prodigy, was performing complex pieces of music publicly at age four and composing them at age six.

Some very recent evidence, obtained through such BRAIN IMAGING TECHNIQUES as fMRI, suggests that the differences between prodigies and other children are qualitative, not just quantitative. Michael O'Boyle has discovered, for example, that right-hemisphere metabolic activity is six to seven times higher in math prodigies than in average children. More intriguing, however, is the fact that frontal lobe areas associated with executive functions, such as concentration and coordination of tasks, are also active in such children while doing math tasks, despite being mostly inactive in average children doing the same problems.

Spectacular though the achievements of prodigies can be, however, another facet of the syndrome is often overlooked: most child prodigies do not make major contributions to their fields once they reach adulthood. Some disappear from their field entirely, perhaps developing psychological problems along the way, as in the case of American chess prodigy Bobby Fischer.

Many carry on their specialties quite competently in adulthood, but without performing at the same spectacular levels or earning the acclaim that accompanied their childhood accomplishments, as seems to occur with most celebrated music prodigies. This may be due in part to the nature of the adult skill areas that tend to produce prodigies: highly structured, formal, rule-bound areas such as music, mathematics, and chess. Their precocious drive and skill level are outstanding in childhood, but intuition and creativity are necessary to make lasting adult contributions, and outstanding adult musicians have the necessary drive and skill level that they didn't possess as children. Perhaps the late bloomers catch up with the prodigies, so that what appeared to be precocious genius in childhood becomes merely a high level of competence in adulthood. Indeed, many genuinely world-changing geniuses were late bloomers, thoroughly undistinguished in childhood—Darwin and Einstein both come to mind (*see also* WILLIAMS SYNDROME).

Further Reading: Feldman, D. H. and Goldsmith, L. T. *Nature's Gambit: Child Prodigies and the Development of Human Potential.* New York: Teacher's College Press, 1991; Treffert, D. A. "Extraordinary People: Understanding Savant Syndrome." IUniverse.com, 2000.

SCHIZOPHRENIA Schizophrenia is one of the most severe psychological disorders, as well as one of the more common, and possibly the most widely misunderstood. The disorder's name is partly responsible for the confusion. It is not unusual to find people confusing schizophrenia with dissociative identity disorder (MULTIPLE PERSONALITY DISORDER), perhaps because the word schizophrenia comes from Greek roots meaning "split brain." The split in this term is actually a reference to the fragmented thinking and emotions experienced by victims of the disorder, not a split personality.

Schizophrenia strikes about one adult in 100 and is slightly more common in men than in women. The disorder also tends to develop earlier and to follow a more severe course in men than in women. The disorder tends to develop in adolescence or early adulthood (almost always before age forty-five), which lent it the name German psychiatrist Emil Kraepelin first gave the disorder, *dementia praecox*, meaning "youthful insanity." In the United States, schizophrenia accounts for 75 percent of mental health expenditures.

According to the *DSM-IV*, schizophrenia is a group of disorders rather than a single syndrome, characterized by disturbances in thought, perception, affect, behavior, and communication, and lasting longer than six months. Common psychotic symptoms include the following:

- *Catatonic behavior*—bizarre motor behavior marked by a decrease in reactivity to the environment, or hyperactivity that is unrelated to external stimuli.

- *Delusions*—unfounded beliefs that are thought to be true even in the face of contradictory evidence.

- *Hallucinations*—a sensory experience in the absence of external stimuli (may affect hearing, taste, vision, smell, or sense of touch).

- *Loose associations*—disordered thoughts, which seem to follow one upon another without logical connection. In conversation, this produces a pattern of incomprehensible speech sometimes called word salad.

- *Flat affect or inappropriate affect*—Emotional reactions are either absent, blunted, or inappropriate to the situation (laughing at tragic news, for example).

There are five recognized types of schizophrenia, showing the above symptoms in varying degrees: catatonic, paranoid, disorganized, undifferentiated, and residual. People with the catatonic subtype sometimes persist in a motionless, stuporous state for hours before abruptly shifting to an agitated, hyperactive state. They may hold a fixed posture for hours without responding to the environment. Less common is the phenomenon of *waxy flexibility*, in which body position can be molded by others into unusual and uncomfortable positions that will be held for hours. The catatonic type is a rare form.

The paranoid type, conversely, is the most common form of schizophrenia. It is characterized by delusions accompanied by auditory hallucinations. Delusions of grandeur (e.g., believing oneself to be Napoleon or Cleopatra) are common, as are delusions of persecution (believing one is being pursued by the Mafia or the CIA, or that the government is reading one's thoughts electronically, for example) and jealousy (e.g., believing one's spouse is unfaithful despite a complete lack of evidence).

The disorganized type (formerly known as hebephrenic schizophrenia) involves confused behavior, incoherent speech, frequent vivid hallucinations, inappropriate affect, and disorganized delusions (the delusions of the paranoid subtype, by comparison, tend to be well-organized and consistent), which often have sexual or religious themes. These symptoms are often accompanied by a neglect of personal hygiene, incontinence, and difficulty relating to others.

The undifferentiated and residual subtypes may be more properly considered transitional forms than actual subtypes of the disorder. In the undifferentiated type, signs of more than one type of schizophrenia are seen in the same individual. The residual type actually refers to a person in whom some recovery has occurred: the symptoms have largely abated but are not completely gone, with the occasional hallucination or delusional thought still occurring.

Opinion on the causes of schizophrenia has changed fairly dramatically over time. In the first half of the twentieth century, schizophrenia was seen as a *reactive* disorder, with symptoms that resulted from environmental influences. During the heyday of psychoanalysis, one influence towered above the others: the mother. Specifically, the disorder was caused by the poor parenting provided by a *schizophrenogenic* mother. Such a mother produced schizophrenia by being cold, dominant, overprotective, rejecting, moralistic, and fearful of intimacy.

Seemingly odd in modern eyes, but perfectly in keeping with psychoanalytic theory and tradition (*see* Freud, Sigmund), the fathers in these families receive no blame, nor indeed any attention at all from the psychoanalysts.

A growing body of evidence indicates that while schizophrenia may in fact run in families, it is for genetic rather than behavioral reasons. The closer the genetic relationship a person shares with a person with schizophrenia, the greater the likelihood that that person will also develop schizophrenia. For example, whereas the likelihood of anyone having schizophrenia is about 1 percent, the tendency for non-twin siblings of a person with schizophrenia jumps up to about 15 percent. The tendency for a monozygotic (identical) twin to develop the disorder if the other twin has it jumps up to anywhere from 30 to 50 percent, depending on the study. Clearly, then, there is a genetic factor involved in schizophrenia. Just as clearly, however, given the fact that 50 to 70 percent of identical twins of schizophrenics do not develop the disorder, genetic influences cannot be the only causal factor. What is inherited is a tendency to develop schizophrenia, not the disorder itself. A popular theory regarding the causes of schizophrenia is known as the diathesis-stress model, which suggests that schizophrenia results from the interaction between an inherited predisposition and severe environmental stress.

In addition to the genetic data, the evidence that schizophrenia is best seen as a physiological disease of the brain rather than as a purely psychological problem is fairly overwhelming. The most effective treatment for the symptoms of the disorder, for example, often involves antipsychotic drugs that work by blocking brain receptor sites for dopamine, a major neurotransmitter. Brain imaging techniques such as MRI and CT scans show evidence of abnormal brain development in many schizophrenia patients. The areas that seem to be most affected are the prefrontal cortex and the limbic system. This is unsurprising given the symptoms. The prefrontal cortex is the area responsible for organizing thoughts and behavior and is also involved in judgment and planning, while the limbic system is important in the processing of emotional experiences and memory. (Recognition of the involvement of these areas led to the widespread use of an earlier treatment for psychotic disorders, the prefrontal lobotomy).

Although antipsychotic drugs have rendered such earlier tools as surgery and restraints obsolete, they are not without drawbacks. Long-term use of antipsychotic drugs can lead to a wide range of unpleasant side effects, including weight gain, skin problems, restlessness, Parkinson's disease-like symptoms, dystonia (involuntary contraction of muscles), and tardive dyskinesia. Tardive dyskinesia is a loss of voluntary muscle control, especially in the face, where it takes the form of involuntary chewing, tongue movements, and lip smacking. About 25 to 40 percent of patients who take antipsychotic medications for at least several years develop tardive dyskinesia. Because of these side effects, the major public health issue facing professionals who work with schizophrenics today is the fact that many schizophrenic patients stop taking their medication and experience a return of symptoms, which of course makes it very difficult for them to function in society. One way to combat this problem is slowly appearing on the market, in the form of longer-lasting, time-released forms of antipsychotic medication. These do not have to be taken as frequently, and are associated with a lower incidence of side effects (*see also* MOOD DISORDERS).

Further Reading: Fowles, D. C. "Schizophrenia: Diathesis-Stress Revisited." *Annual Review of Psychology,* 43 (1992): 303–336; World Health Organization. *Schizophrenia: An International Follow-Up Study.* Chichester, U.K.: Wiley, 1979.

SCIENTOLOGY *See* DIANETICS/SCIENTOLOGY

SEASONAL AFFECTIVE DISORDER (SAD) Seasonal Affective Disorder (SAD) is a pattern, experienced by about 15 percent of people diagnosed with depression, in which depressive symptoms occur as a function of the calendar. In SAD a period of severe depression, accompanied by irritability and excessive sleeping, coincides with the months of shorter daylight that occur in winter. For obvious reasons, the disorder is far more common in temperate zones than in tropical areas. The depression tends to lift as daylight hours grow longer with the approach of spring, suggesting that disruptions in the body's circadian rhythms are responsible. For a diagnosis of SAD to be made, there should therefore be a full remission from depressed symptoms during the spring and summer months. Though poets have noted the debilitating effects of winter's darkness for centuries, and researchers have long puzzled over the high suicide rates in countries near the Arctic Circle, the disorder was only formally described and given its current name in the 1980s.

The body's internal clock is largely governed by the secretion of melatonin, a hormone, by the pineal gland. Melatonin is involved in governing our wake/sleep cycle and overall levels of arousal in the brain. Higher levels of melatonin are associated with reduced arousal and increased lethargy, which is why melatonin is sometimes sold as a sleep aid. The pineal gland's location near the optic chiasm, where the optic nerves, coming directly from the eyes, cross over each other, allows the secretion of melatonin to be governed by ambient light levels, and so more melatonin is released in periods with less sunlight. Since melatonin levels influence the levels of such neurotransmitters as norepinephrine, serotonin, and dopamine, all of which are known to be involved in depression, it follows that in certain individuals, the absence of sunlight may lead to neurotransmitter level changes sufficient to cause depression.

The standard treatment for SAD, phototherapy, has a fairly short history. In phototherapy the individual is exposed daily to bright, full-spectrum light for anywhere from half an hour to several hours. Usually this exposure comes in the form of a specially constructed light box, which contains several fluorescent tubes and a reflector to help focus the light, though research suggests that a half-hour walk outdoors in winter sunlight may be as helpful as two hours with an indoor light box. As with all psychotherapy, compliance can be a problem, especially in a disorder for which difficulty getting up in the morning is a defining symptom. It is therefore fairly common for light boxes to be set up as dawn simulators, coming on in the early morning according to a timer and gradually increasing in brightness so that they reach full intensity at the time the person wishes to awaken (*see also* BRAIN, NERVOUS SYSTEM).

Further Reading: Faedda, G., Tondo, L., Teicher, M., Baldessarini, R., Gelbard, H., and Floris, G. "Seasonal Mood Disorders: Patterns of Seasonal Recurrence in Mania and Depression." *Archives of General Psychiatry*, 50 (1993): 17–23.

SELF-ESTEEM Self-esteem has become a very widely used term over the last thirty years as teachers, parents, and therapists have expended enormous effort and expense on increasing it, on the assumption that raising self-esteem will provide benefits and improve outcomes in many areas of life, including school performance, relationships, discipline, and general quality of life. First, a definition: self-esteem is generally used to refer to how much value people place on themselves. High self-esteem would, therefore, refer to a highly favorable evaluation of the overall self, whereas low self-esteem refers to an unfavorable evaluation of the self. It is important to note, however, that measures of self-esteem carry with them no promise of accuracy: self-esteem represents perception rather than reality. High self-esteem may be the result of an accurate, justified measure of one's successes and abilities, but it may also indicate an arrogant, narcissistic, conceited, and thoroughly unwarranted self-impression. Low self-esteem may represent a well-founded dissection of one's shortcomings, or it may indicate an undeserved and inaccurate sense of inferiority and insecurity.

It is not unreasonable to expect increased self-esteem to bring some benefits or for reduced self-esteem to create problems. Classic psychological research has shown repeatedly that inaccurate beliefs about the self or about others can become self-fulfilling prophecies, influencing both the opportunities for success that arise and how those opportunities are received. It has become widely accepted among researchers, clinicians, parents, and school officials that high self-esteem will produce positive outcomes, a belief which has been based almost entirely on anecdotal evidence rather than any sort of solid research. This idea became so popular that in 1986, the California legislature funded a task force to increase the self-esteem of the people of California, with the idea that reductions in welfare dependency, school failure, crime, drug abuse, homelessness, and many other social problems would surely follow. This is based on the idea that too many people have low self-esteem, so raising it should improve many people's outlook. Empirical evidence casts some doubt on this assumption, however. When self-esteem scales are given to large numbers of Americans, most people's scores fall at the upper end of the distribution. In other words, self-esteem in America is, if anything, excessively high. The average American regards himself or herself as above average. This pattern holds regardless of race, gender, and socioeconomic status.

A recent large-scale review of available research on self-esteem, published by the AMERICAN PSYCHOLOGICAL SOCIETY, calls into question a number of the other standard assumptions about self-esteem's benefits. The relationship between self-esteem and school performance, for example, is modest at best, and it suggests that high self-esteem is partly the *result* of good school performance, rather than indicating that high self-esteem leads to good school performance. The relationship between self-esteem and occupational success is just as problematic: success in a job increases self-esteem, but higher self-esteem does not necessarily improve job performance.

Objective measures also shoot down the notion that higher self-esteem improves the quality or duration of relationships. Unsurprisingly, however, people in high-quality, long-term relationships do lean toward higher self-esteem than people whose relationships have failed. As for the relationship between self-esteem and crime or disciplinary problems, successful bullies and thieves often have high self-esteem, whereas their victims often do not. Furthermore, high self-esteem does not appear to prevent children from engaging in substance abuse or sexual activity. In fact, though the effect is a very small one, higher self-esteem may actually lead to more experimentation.

Self-esteem is associated with greater happiness, confidence, and initiative; but the causal direction is not clear. High self-esteem may well be a consequence of those things rather than a cause of them. There is little or no evidence that efforts aimed specifically at increasing self-esteem will actually produce improved outcomes. High self-esteem is not a bad thing; it just may not be the most important thing on which to focus intervention efforts (*see also* CORRELATION).

Further Reading: Baumeister, R. F., Campbell, J. D., Krueger, J. I., and Vohs, K. D. "Does High Self-Esteem Cause Better Performance, Interpersonal Success, Happiness, or Healthier Lifestyles?" *Psychological Science in the Public Interest,* 4(1) (2003).

SEPARATION ANXIETY *See* ATTACHMENT

SEXUAL MASOCHISM *See* PARAPHILIAS

SEXUAL SADISM *See* PARAPHILIAS

SHELL SHOCK *See* POSTTRAUMATIC STRESS DISORDER

SKINNER, B. F. (1904–1990)   Though John B. WATSON was the originator of behaviorism, it is through the efforts of Burrhus Frederic (B. F.) Skinner that behaviorist principles have found widespread practical application, through the therapeutic approach known as behavior modification, or applied behavior analysis. Like Watson, Skinner envisioned psychology free of mentalistic principles, focused only on observable, overt behavior. As mental phenomena cannot be directly observed, the behaviorists did not see them as a proper subject for scientific study. Skinner eventually came to embrace the study of

B. F. Skinner. © Bettmann/CORBIS

thought processes, though he regarded the object of study as thinking behavior, subject to the same learning principles as other behaviors.

Skinner's greatest contribution is probably the distinction he drew between classical (respondent) conditioning (*see* PAVLOV, IVAN), which was Watson's primary mechanism for explaining human behavior, and operant conditioning. Classical conditioning involves the study of how behaviors, such as a dog's reflexive salivation, are elicited by stimulus conditions such as the presence of dog food. Operant conditioning instead involves the role of the *consequences* of a behavior in determining the likelihood of that behavior occurring again. Two different categories of consequences determine behavior: reinforcement and punishment.

Reinforcement is any consequence that increases the frequency of the response that precedes it, whereas punishment is any consequence that decreases the frequency of the behavior. For example, praising a young child for saying a particular word (i.e., "Daddy") will make the child more likely to say it again, but yelling at the same child after saying a particular word will make the child less likely to say it again. Although most people think of reinforcers as rewards, *anything* that serves to strengthen a behavior is a reinforcer.

There are actually two different kinds of reinforcement: positive and negative. Positive reinforcement involves presenting a positive stimulus (such as food, attention, approval, money, etc.) after a behavior, whereas negative reinforcement involves removal of an aversive stimulus after the behavior. For example, the warning buzzer in a car is turned off in response to putting on a seatbelt; pain goes away in response to taking a pill. In common usage, negative reinforcement is often confused with punishment, but the difference between them is quite straightforward: punishment reduces a behavior by *applying* an aversive stimulus, and negative reinforcement increases a behavior by *removing* an aversive stimulus. If a parent yells at a child in response to a bad behavior, and the behavior stops, punishment of the child has occurred. If a child throws a tantrum in a store because he wants candy, and the parent stops the tantrum by giving the child candy, the candy-giving behavior has been produced by negative reinforcement for the parent. An aversive stimulus (the tantrum) stopped as a consequence of the behavior and that behavior is now more likely to occur again under similar circumstances.

Skinner further distinguished between primary and secondary reinforcers. Primary reinforcers, such as food, water, or relief from pain, are innately reinforcing, as they satisfy a biological need and do not have to be learned. Secondary reinforcers, also called conditioned reinforcers, are learned, as they only acquire power through their association with primary reinforcers. Money is a powerful reinforcer for humans, despite the fact that it is not edible and possesses no healing power. It does allow us to obtain primary reinforcers, however—though we cannot eat money, we can certainly use it to buy food.

Skinner explored the principles of operant conditioning through the use of a specialized cage called an operant chamber, popularly known as a Skinner Box (a name Skinner himself disliked). The glass-and-metal chamber is typically large enough for a rat or pigeon, Skinner's preferred experimental subjects, to walk around in comfortably, and is equipped with a bar or key that the animal can peck or press, a small chute near the bar through which edible reinforcers can be dropped, and a device that records bar-press responses.

Using the chamber, Skinner discovered that he could produce remarkably complicated behavior patterns through a process he called shaping. In shaping, a behavior which is not already occurring, such as pressing a bar by a rat, can be produced by reinforcing successive approximations of the desired behavior, until the target behavior occurs on its own, at which time it becomes the only behavior reinforced. Upon entering the chamber, a rat will typically explore his surroundings, walking around the entire chamber and sniffing all surfaces. In this exploration, he will eventually come into contact with the wall into which the bar is set. The moment this contact occurs, a food pellet is dropped down the chute. If the wall is touched again, reinforcement will immediately occur again. This will result in the rat spending more time against the front wall. In his movements, the rat will occasionally raise his body up and reach up the wall with his front paws. The first time this occurs (a closer approximation of the desired bar-press than simply touching the wall), immediate reinforcement will occur as well, while reinforcement for other behaviors stops. Soon the rat will be reaching up frequently, and so only reaching up, which occurs near the bar, will be reinforced. Eventually, the rat will press the bar—at this point only bar pressing will be reinforced. Through shaping, the rat is now engaging in a behavior that was not previously in his repertoire. The shaping procedure can be remarkably powerful, as shown by a famous film Skinner shot of two pigeons playing a lively game of table tennis.

All the examples above assume continuous reinforcement—reinforcement occurs every time the desired response occurs. This pattern of reinforcement has a built-in weakness, however—when reinforcement stops, extinction (the response dies out) occurs rapidly. If the experimenter stops providing food pellets, the rat stops pressing the bar, just as when the soda machine fails to provide a drink, we immediately stop putting money into it. This is interesting, because real life usually does not provide continuous reinforcement—the sales associate does not make a sale to every customer, nor does the fisherman always bring home a catch. Skinner observed that, in the lab as in real life, intermittent reinforcement, in which some responses are reinforced and some are not, produces behaviors that are far more resistant to extinction. How else to explain the behavior of gamblers in casinos, who despite rarely winning, will continue to pump money into slot machines? The soda machine, which reinforces continuously, loses the customer the first time no drink comes out, but the slot machine only reinforces occasionally, so the behavior of putting in money and pushing a button is far more persistent. The most common intermittent schedules of reinforcement are ratio schedules and interval schedules.

In a fixed-ratio schedule, behavior is reinforced after a set number of responses, as in a clothing factory where a worker is paid a set amount for every ten shirts produced. A variable-ratio schedule provides reinforcement after an unpredictable number of responses, and it produces behaviors that are difficult to extinguish. This is the schedule followed by slot machines: because an unknown number of responses will be required before reinforcement occurs, the schedule produces high rates of responding, since that is the only way to increase the frequency of reinforcement.

Interval schedules are based on elapsed time rather than number of responses. In a fixed-interval schedule, the first response after a fixed time period is reinforced, but responses that occur prior to the end of the interval are not reinforced. This leads to an increased frequency of responses as the end of the interval approaches, with very low responding at the beginning of the interval. An example would be checking more frequently for the mail as the delivery time approaches, but not checking at all when the usual time is still a long way off. If a consistently high rate of response is desired, this is clearly not an ideal schedule. A solution to the problem of inconsistent responding is the variable-interval schedule, in which the time interval prior to reinforcement is varied unpredictably. This results in slow, steady responding, which is resistant to extinction.

Much of the controversy over Skinner stems from his willingness to explore the philosophical implications of his ideas in books such as *Beyond Freedom and Dignity* and the novel *Walden Two*. Since his theory ignores mental phenomena and proposes that all behavior is under the control of external contingencies, it leaves no room for such notions as free will and personal freedom. His critics see him as dehumanizing people, both by denying free will and by suggesting that our behavior can be explained by the same mechanisms as that of animals. All controversy aside, however, Skinner's legacy is a set of principles which have found much broader, and more effective, application than the theories of any other psychologist. Behaviorist principles are now a major influence on educational practice; childrearing, where his terminology is now as ubiquitous as Freud's used to be; and highly effective therapeutic approaches for many psychological disorders.

Further Reading: Bjork, D. W. *B. F. Skinner: A Life.* Washington, DC: American Psychological Association, 1997; Skinner, B. F. *About Behaviorism.* New York: Vintage, 1976.

SLEEP AND DREAMING   Sleep is the most common altered state of consciousness, as most people spend a substantial fraction of every day engaged in it. Researchers who study sleep have made tremendous use of a device known as the electroencephalograph (EEG), which has in a few short decades provided far more insight into what actually happens during sleep than thousands of years of common sense. The EEG is a device that takes information from a set of electrodes attached to the scalp and converts it into a graphic representation of the overall pattern of electrical activity in the brain. The depiction of activity, also known as brain waves, changes as behavior and mental processes change. The brain waves of an awake, alert person have high frequency (speed) and low amplitude (height), appearing as small, closely spaced, irregularly sized spikes on the graph.

Careful observation of the EEG recordings of many sleepers reveals that the roughly ninety-minute sleep cycle, repeated several times a night, can be divided into stages. When the sleeper's eyes first close and relaxation begins, his or her EEG immediately becomes more regular, showing a pattern of slower, rhythmic waves at speeds of eight to twelve cycles per second (cps). These are called alpha waves, and this initial, relaxed state is sometimes called stage 0. Upon actually falling asleep, the person enters Stage 1, which lasts about five minutes. In Stage 1, people sometimes experience vivid images and sensations, including weightless floating, or perhaps a sensation of falling that may cause the sleeper to jerk awake. These experiences are called hypnagogic hallucinations. A person in Stage 1 is very easy to wake up. stage 1 is followed by the deeper relaxation of Stage 2, which lasts about twenty minutes. The Stage 2 EEG is characterized by occasional sleep spindles: short bursts of rapid, rhythmic brainwave activity. The person can still be awakened easily, but is now clearly asleep.

For just a few minutes after Stage 2, the EEG begins to show large, slow delta waves, which characterize both the transitional Stage 3 and Stage 4, which are together known as slow-wave sleep. Together they last about thirty minutes, during which the sleeper is extremely difficult to awaken. At this point a rather strange thing happens on the EEG—it shows a rapid passage back through Stages 3 and 2, and into a phase that looks, on the graph, almost exactly like being fully awake. This is Rapid Eye Movement (REM) sleep, named for the momentary bursts of eye activity that occur behind closed lids during this stage. Like the EEG, which shows levels of brain activity comparable to those of a fully awake and alert individual, the heart rate and breathing of a person in REM sleep return nearly to waking levels. Another unusual feature of REM sleep is genital arousal. Males typically have erections during REM sleep, and they typically outlast REM periods, taking from thirty to forty-five minutes to subside. Less is known about female genital arousal in this stage, as the phenomenon is much more easily measured in men.

The high levels of brain activity signal the most important feature of REM sleep; this is when dreams occur. Unlike the rapidly fading images of Stage 1 sleep, REM dreams are emotional and story-like, involving the same cognitive processes that operate while awake. This is why dreams often incorporate both old memories and current worries. Thus, another feature of REM sleep is especially important: sleep paralysis. During REM sleep, messages from the cortex are stopped at the brainstem, so that all skeletal muscles are relaxed and the body cannot act on anything that occurs in the dream. Even snoring usually occurs only in the other stages of sleep, stopping when REM begins. Contrary to popular belief, the eye movements are not related to dream content.

Although the full sleep cycle repeats itself, it changes somewhat over time. As the night wears on, Stage 4 sleep becomes briefer, while the REM sleep period becomes longer. In an average night, 20 to 25 percent of our sleep is REM sleep, and in infancy it is about 50 percent. Furthermore, when people are deliberately deprived of REM sleep in a laboratory setting, they experience much more REM sleep than usual, and enter the REM stage much faster, as soon as they are allowed to sleep uninterrupted. This is known as REM rebound. Clearly REM sleep must be important, but opinions and theories differ as to why.

FREUD, as is well known, focused on the role of dreams in allowing the expression of the otherwise unacceptable thoughts and impulses in the unconscious mind; this has largely given way to other theories. REM sleep may play a major role in memory consolidation, for example. REM sleep deprivation reduces laboratory subjects' ability to remember material learned just before falling asleep, and research also reveals that REM sleep increases following intense learning periods. The large amount of REM sleep observed in babies suggests that REM sleep also serves an important physiological function in brain development. Psychologists have long known that animals raised in impoverished environments, with less sensory stimulation, have less well-developed neural pathways in the brain. Perhaps the periodic high levels of brain stimulation in REM sleep occur to further develop and preserve those neural pathways. This would explain both the larger amount of REM sleep in infants, whose brains are rapidly developing and growing, and the memory effects on REM-deprived adults, whose brains haven't had the chance to stimulate and strengthen the connections formed by the previous day's learning.

As for the content of the dreams themselves, the most widely favored current account is known as the activation-synthesis theory. According to the activation-synthesis model, the brainstem increases the overall arousal level of the brain to waking levels during REM sleep, but this neural activation is generalized and fairly random. This spreading activation stimulates various areas of the cortex to produce what would be, in a waking state, hallucinations, along with stimulation of various areas involved in memory and thinking. Activation also spreads to various areas of the limbic system involved in emotion. Given this widespread, random, and ultimately meaningless activity, the brain's cognitive mechanisms do what they usually do with meaningless stimuli—try to make sense of it. The activation-synthesis theory simply suggests that dreams result from the brain's interpretation of its own random activity.

In addition to REM rebound, overall sleep deprivation also has clearly negative effects. Extensive research shows that regular loss of an hour or two of sleep nightly will accumulate over time (this is known as a "sleep debt"), resulting in slower reaction time, difficulty paying attention, memory problems, and impaired decision-making and judgment. The consequences of this can be fairly serious on tasks that require quick reactions, sustained attention, and clear judgment, such as driving a car. According to some estimates, sleep deprivation is a contributing factor in 200,000 to 400,000 automobile accidents annually in the United States alone, resulting in about 1,500 deaths. One study found that in both Canada and the United States, auto accidents increase immediately after the spring time change, losing an hour to daylight savings time, and decrease significantly on the Monday after the fall time change, when everyone gets an extra hour of sleep. Sleep deprivation is also widely recognized as a major factor in airline accidents and hospital errors. Several states have now shortened the shifts worked by hospital residents, and the FAA has restricted the number of hours a pilot may fly without taking time off to sleep. It is worth noting that the *Exxon Valdez* oil spill, the Chernobyl and Three Mile Island nuclear accidents, and the Union Carbide chemical accident in Bhopal, India, all occurred after midnight.

One effect of sleep deprivation is subtler, but hardly less dangerous: suppression of the immune system. Specifically, sleep deprivation increases levels of pathogens that would normally be suppressed by the immune system, while decreasing the levels of immune cells that fight off viral infections and cancer. This may be one reason why people who are chronically sleep-deprived tend not to live as long as people who sleep eight hours a night. Clearly, sleep, the state in which we spend nearly one-third of our lives, is of vital importance.

One possible reason for the many problems sleep deprivation causes today is the extent to which modern Western society ignores the importance of circadian rhythms, the daily sleep-wake cycles that are controlled by a combination of physiological and environmental factors, but certainly not by the force of will. In earlier times and in primitive societies, in other words, for the majority of human history, these cycles were synchronized with day-night cycles. In modern times, most of us synchronize our sleep periods with the clock instead, staying up well into the night as well as waking before sunrise. If synchronization with an external sign (the clock or the sun) was all that were involved, the process would be fairly easy and problem-free. Unfortunately, we also have an internal, biological clock to contend with, which evolved over hundreds of thousands of years of human experience before alarm clocks, graveyard shifts, and jet lag came along. When people are removed from the influence of external cues, perhaps by being placed in a windowless laboratory with no clocks or watches for several weeks, they continue to follow a steady sleep-wake cycle, but oddly enough, it is a twenty-five-hour cycle rather than a twenty-four-hour cycle, in which they fall asleep 1 hour later each night. The external cue (the sun) is used by the brain to reset its clock each day, and in its absence, the clock gets further and further off.

How this works is fairly straightforward: circadian rhythms are largely governed by blood levels of the hormone melatonin, secreted by the pineal gland. The pineal gland is located near the optic chiasm, the place where the optic nerves, bringing sensory information from the eyes, cross over one another, and it receives information about light levels from those nerves. When light levels indicate that the time to sleep is approaching, more melatonin is secreted, and when daylight returns, melatonin levels drop. In the absence of external light cues, this system cannot function properly. Nor can it function properly in the presence of the wrong light cues. When people travel across several time zones in a short period of time, the fatigue of jet lag can take from a few days to several weeks to wear off, as the internal clock becomes synchronized with the new day-night cycle. The same problem occurs when people who have been working during the day are assigned to a night shift, sometimes in such high-risk areas as hospitals, airline cockpits, and factories. If people would then stay on the new schedule for several weeks, they might be able to adjust fully, but research suggests that most workers never make a complete adjustment to night shifts, sleeping poorly during the day and remaining overtired and sleepy at night. The problem is due in part to these workers' tendency to revert to a normal day-night schedule on weekends, so that they can spend time with their family and friends. Another problem is employers' tendency to rotate people in and out of night shifts on a regular basis, so that they are switched back to a daytime schedule just as they are getting acclimated to the night schedule.

One other quirk of the average human's circadian rhythm is ignored by modern Western societies: the daily cycle has two high points (most awake and alert) and two low points (least alert). One of these lows is experienced in the early a.m. hours by most people, when they are usually asleep anyway, but the other is twelve hours away, which puts it in the early- to mid-afternoon for most people. Throughout Latin America, this fact is an intrinsic part of the culture, enshrined in the custom of the siesta. In the United States, however, napping is generally regarded as something small children need but as a sign of laziness in adults. This is unfortunate, since many sleep-deprived teens and adults would function much better if they had a small amount of sleep in the early afternoon. That feeling of overpowering sleepiness with which so many of us are familiar is the body's way of sending an important message. We continue to ignore it at our peril (*see also* MEMORY; NARCOLEPSY).

Further Reading: Coren, Stanley. *Sleep Thieves*. New York: Free Press, 1997.

SOMATOTYPE   *See* BODY TYPE

SPIRIT MEDIUMSHIP   *See* PARAPSYCHOLOGY

SPIRITUALISM/SPIRITISM   *See* PARAPSYCHOLOGY

SPLIT-BRAIN SURGERY   Much of what is known about hemispheric specialization in the BRAIN (that is, the distribution of various functions between the two sides) comes from the in-depth study, mostly by Roger Sperry and Michael Gazzaniga, of three patients who endured a very drastic and controversial surgical procedure. The split-brain operation, as it has become known, involved the complete severing of the corpus callosum, the thick bundle of nerve fibers that connects the two cerebral hemispheres to each other. The patients all suffered from severe EPILEPSY in the days before effective medications were available to help them.

In an epileptic seizure, a set of neurons in the brain, the focus of the seizure, begins to fire randomly, and the random activation spreads to surrounding brain areas. If the affected area is fairly small, only a very minor, petit mal seizure occurs. If the activation spreads widely, however, the result can be a grand mal seizure, in which the person can be in real danger. The split-brain patients represented a sort of worst-case scenario among epileptics: their seizures, having spread to involve an entire hemisphere, would then jump across the corpus callosum and involve most of the brain. Due to their failure to respond to lesser treatments, the radical split-brain surgery was regarded as their last hope. By removing all connections between the hemispheres, the surgery prevented a seizure from affecting the entire brain.

Following the surgery, the patients were able to live surprisingly normal lives, with intelligence and personality largely unaffected. Sperry and his colleagues knew that functioning must have been affected, however, and undertook a series of experiments to reveal the subtle ways in which the patients' functioning had been changed. One of their early successes involved simply confirming Paul Broca's identification, a century earlier, of an area in the left hemisphere as the seat of language production. Sperry and Gazzaniga found that these patients could not identify an unseen object placed in the left hand. Perceptual information was sent from the hand to the right hemisphere, and without a corpus callosum, the right hemisphere couldn't let the left hemisphere, where the ability to answer verbally resides, know what the object was. More extraordinary results emerged when they experimented with the visual field (simply the entire area taken in by your eyes at any given time).

Ordinarily, the left half of the visual field is represented in the right occipital lobe, and the right half of the visual field sends information to the left occipital lobe. In people with intact connections between the hemispheres, information cannot be presented to only one hemisphere or the other, as it is quickly sent across to the other. If a split-brain patient is presented with a visual stimulus that is only "seen" by one hemisphere while the other "sees" a different stimulus, and the hemispheres are then quizzed separately, however, something very intriguing happens, with implications not just for our knowledge of perception but also for how we conceive of consciousness itself. Consider an experiment in which the subject is told to stare straight ahead at a dot on a screen. Now suppose a compound word ("cowboy," for example) is flashed on the screen, just long enough to be read, and is positioned in such a way that a vertical line through the dot would divide it between the two words that make it up, as follows:

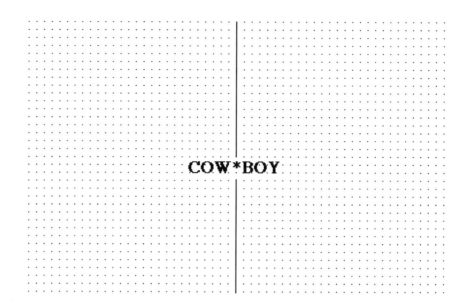

If asked to say what they saw, split-brain patients would say "Boy." They would then be startled when they saw their own left hands point to "Cow" on a nearby poster. Given the chance to express itself, each hemisphere reports only on what it saw, with no idea of what the other hemisphere saw.

Another experiment involves showing a picture of an object (a spoon, for example) to the left visual field, so that only the right hemisphere perceives it. When asked to say what they saw, the patients are unable to do so. When asked to identify the object by feeling an assortment of items behind a screen with the left hand, however, they quickly and efficiently select the spoon. When the experimenter says "Right!" the patient may respond with irritation and confusion rather than pleasure, since the speaking part of the brain has no idea what the right answer is. Another phenomenon documented by Sperry and Gazzaniga involves the left hand attempting to stop the right hand from selecting a particular answer to an experimental task. Outside the laboratory, the split-brain patients encountered similar phenomena while doing everyday tasks. The right hand may unbutton a shirt that the left has just buttoned, for example, or one hand may remove from a grocery cart the items that the other hand just placed there (this phenomenon has been dubbed "the alien hand").

In short, severing the corpus callosum seems to leave patients with two separate conscious minds occupying the same skull, and they are often at odds with each other. Under most ordinary circumstances, the hemispheres can use other mechanisms to determine each other's state, including input from the various senses (i.e., the right hemisphere can hear what the left hemisphere causes the person to say and infer what that half is thinking accordingly), or the simple expedient of turning the head frequently so both hemispheres are receiving the entire visual field. Because of these adaptations, unusual Sperry-led experiments were necessary to reveal the full extent of what was happening. The amount of information about hemispheric specialization that has emerged from the study of this small handful of patients is huge and has profoundly changed how we see consciousness as well as the separation of functions within the brain, to such an extent that Roger Sperry received the 1981 Nobel Prize in Medicine for his work.

The most recent area of psychology to be affected by split-brain research has to do with a possible explanation for the emergence of false memories: They're the left hemisphere's fault. Early signs of this were clear in experiments in which the right hemisphere was given an order to do something (get up and walk into the next room, for example), and the person was then asked, "Why did you do that?" The left hemisphere would unhesitatingly make up an explanation (e.g., "I decided I needed to stretch my legs," or "I'm thirsty, so I was on my way to the kitchen"), despite having absolutely no idea what was actually going on. Gazzaniga dubbed this the *interpreter function* of the left hemisphere. He has examined this notion further by looking at PET scans of patients as they relate both a false MEMORY and a true one. In both cases, they are asked about the explanation recently given for an action as in the above examples, with the left hemisphere unaware of the true explanation. When the false memory is recalled, areas in both the left and right hemispheres are activated, whereas when the true one is recalled, only the right-hemisphere area is activated. This is a fairly new, and highly speculative, perspective on false memories and their sources, but quite intriguing (*see also* BRAIN IMAGING TECHNIQUES).

Further Reading: Gazzaniga, M. S. *The Mind's Past*. Los Angeles: University of California Press, 1998; Penrose, R. *The Emperor's New Mind*. New York: Oxford University Press, 1989.

SRA   *See* SATANIC RITUAL ABUSE

STIMULANTS   Stimulants are a class of drugs that increase BRAIN activity, producing gains in alertness, attention, and overall arousal, accompanied by elevations in blood pressure and heart rate. The most widely used stimulant in the world is caffeine, followed closely by nicotine. Stimulant drugs have been prescribed for a wide variety of problems, including asthma, obesity (as an appetite suppressant), and a range of other disorders, including narcolepsy, attention-deficit/hyperactivity disorder, and even depression.

Most prescription stimulants belong to the category known as amphetamines, including dextroamphetamine (Dexedrine) and methylphenidate (Ritalin and Concerta are the best-known brands). In the world of illegal stimulants, methamphetamine (also called crystal meth) and cocaine are the most popular. All work by mimicking the action of the neurotransmitters known as monoamines, especially norepinephrine and dopamine, and by preventing reuptake (the process by which excess neurotransmitter molecules are reabsorbed into the neurons until they are needed again). In addition to the basic stimulant effect of increasing

CENTRAL NERVOUS SYSTEM (CNS) arousal and increasing blood pressure and heart rate, the elevation of dopamine levels is associated with a sense of euphoria—cocaine is especially good at this.

Stimulants are not associated with physical dependence and withdrawal to the same degree as OPIOIDS and DEPRESSANTS, but they can produce psychological dependence very quickly. In addition to the good feelings produced by the elevated dopamine levels, stimulants can also produce feelings of hostility and paranoia (the brain areas associated with these feelings are also stimulated). High doses of stimulants are also associated with heart arrhythmias and elevated body temperature, in addition to the obvious risks associated with elevated blood pressure.

Because of these well-established risks, stimulants are not prescribed very often anymore, with one odd exception: most stimulant prescriptions written today are for children with a diagnosis of ATTENTION-DEFICIT/HYPERACTIVITY DISORDER (ADHD). Most of these are for methylphenidate, but prescriptions for stronger amphetamines, including Dexedrine and Adderall, are rising steadily for children whose ADHD hasn't responded well to methylphenidate. This is a curious development, since all of the side effects produced by amphetamines in adults are also potentially problematic for children. Other treatments for ADHD are effective, especially behavioral treatments, but they are expensive and time-consuming to implement.

Since stimulants work for about two-thirds of children with ADHD and are much easier and cheaper to use, they have become overwhelmingly popular, to the point that ADHD is probably being overdiagnosed in this country. This is supported by recent figures comparing U.S. consumption of stimulants to that of other countries. As of 1998, for example, the United States was consuming more than 350 million single doses of methylphenidate a year, as compared to less than 100 million in the rest of the world *combined*. It should be noted additionally that in the same year, about 40 percent of all methylphenidate prescriptions were written for children between three and nine years of age, with over 4,000 written for children two years of age or younger. This is important because the safety and efficacy of the drug has not been established for children under the age of six, nor has the Food and Drug Administration (FDA) approved it. Because of its addiction potential, methylphenidate is listed by the U.S. Drug Enforcement Agency (DEA) as a controlled substance, and a thriving black market in methylphenidate has sprung up in many cities, as it has effects virtually identical to those of cocaine when similar quantities are consumed.

Further Reading: MTA Cooperative Group. "National Institute of Mental Health Multimodal Treatment Study of ADHD Follow-Up: 24-Month Outcomes of Treatment Strategies for Attention-Deficit/Hyperactivity Disorder." *Pediatrics*, 113(4) (2004): 754–762.

STOCKHOLM SYNDROME   On August 23, 1973, two ex-convicts armed with machine guns, explosives, and blasting caps entered one of Sweden's largest banks and took four hostages. For the next 131 hours, these hostages, whose captors had strapped explosives to them, were held in the bank vault. When rescuers arrived six days later, the captives surprised them by resisting rescue and defending their captors. They subsequently refused to testify against their captors and even raised money for their legal defense. Sources vary, but it has been widely reported that at least one (some sources say two) of the three female hostages eventually became engaged to one of the bank robbers.

Subsequent incidents, combined with a re-examination of many hostage situations by social scientists, suggested that this bizarre pattern of behavior was actually so common as to merit a name, and so it became widely known as the Stockholm syndrome. Psychologists have actually documented similar behavior patterns in many disparate situations, including concentration camps, cults, incest, the relationship between prostitutes and their pimps, prisoners of war, hijackings, spousal abuse, and of course kidnappings and hostage situations. Development of Stockholm syndrome seems to require that four conditions be met:

- The captive perceives both a threat to survival *and* a willingness by the captor to act on that threat.
- The captive perceives that he or she is unable to escape.
- The captive is isolated from perspectives other than those of the captor.
- The captor commits acts of kindness towards the captive. These can range from deciding not to kill the captive and informing him or her of that, to removing restraints, to simply speaking more gently.

Perhaps the best-known example of Stockholm-like behavior in America is the case of Patty Hearst. Hearst was kidnapped, confined, raped, and tortured by the Symbionese Liberation Army (SLA), a small radical outfit that gained some notoriety in the early 1970s (they were not an army, and their nationality was not Symbionese—indeed, that nationality is an invented word derived from "symbiosis"). After her ordeal Ms. Hearst, the heiress to an immense publishing fortune, was filmed by bank security cameras participating in a robbery along with members of the SLA under the new name "Tania."

Irrational as this behavior may seem to observers, the Stockholm syndrome is actually a survival mechanism, since more cooperative hostages are less likely to be shot, and is actually encouraged in some hostage situations. Unfortunately, it also improves the odds that the hostages will not be cooperative during either rescue or prosecution. A similar phenomenon has long been observed by police who arrest men for spousal battery. Women will frequently physically attack police officers who are called in to rescue them from a violent assault, and they will then bail the husband or boyfriend out of jail and subsequently fail to press charges.

At least one feminist psychologist, Dee Graham, has expanded this idea into a controversial theory: she maintains that, as our culture is patriarchal, all women suffer from what she calls Societal Stockholm Syndrome, to varying degrees. This idea has not caught on widely among psychologists, but her book on the subject sold in robust numbers, in part because it was seen by many feminists as an antidote to the ideas of JOHN GRAY. Whereas Gray presents the differences between men and women as innate, immutable differences that people must learn to live with, Graham suggests that the differences represent survival strategies in a world in which women are the "hostages" of dominant men, and thus it might be possible to overcome and eliminate those differences. It has become a very popular perspective in pop-psychology publishing—a search for "Stockholm syndrome" on the Internet mostly produces books on male-female relationships. While certainly an interesting perspective, this seems to have little to do with Stockholm syndrome as it is generally understood.

Further Reading: Graham, D. L. R. *Loving to Survive: Sexual Terror, Men's Violence, and Women's Lives.* New York: New York University Press, 1995.

STRANGE SITUATION   *See* ATTACHMENT

STROKE   A stroke happens when the blood supply to a particular area of the BRAIN is interrupted, thus depriving neurons of oxygen. There are two ways this can occur: in a hemorrhagic stroke, a blood vessel bursts, spilling blood into the space around the brain cells, causing damage. In an ischemic stroke, blood flow is interrupted but the blood vessel is undamaged. The deprived neurons suffer damage through deprivation of oxygen and nutrients, and this is reflected in whatever function the damaged brain region controlled.

Symptoms appear suddenly and often include numbness or weakness, usually affecting only one side of the body; some muscle paralysis on the same side; confusion; APHASIA (trouble speaking or understanding speech); trouble seeing in one or both eyes; difficulty walking; loss of balance or coordination; and dizziness. The cell damage doesn't kill the neurons immediately, however; treatment within several hours can often save them. In addition to the initial damage caused by the death of neurons, some of the brain damage that results from stroke appears to be a result of a toxic reaction to the primary damage. This reaction is poorly understood, but researchers are currently studying the mechanics of it and looking for ways to prevent this secondary injury, perhaps by developing drugs to protect the neurons from this damage.

Several other areas of research show promise for prevention of both strokes and the secondary damage that occurs after them. Vasodilators, substances that dilate blood vessels, thereby increasing the blood flow to the brain, show some promise for improving the flow of oxygen and nutrients to the affected area. Another interesting and unexpected area of promising research involves the study of hibernation processes. During hibernation, there is a very substantial decrease of blood flow to the brain, so much so that it would result in brain death for a non-hibernating animal (or, by extension, a human). Much of the damage in stroke victims is caused by a far less dramatic decrease in blood flow, so if researchers can work out how animals can hibernate without incurring serious brain damage, it may be possible to duplicate the processes involved to prevent neurological damage in stroke victims.

Another related phenomenon that may provide clues is hypothermia. People who have experienced hypothermia (dangerously reduced body temperature) have often gone without sufficient oxygen for extended periods without serious brain damage. Understanding how this occurs may lead to new ways to handle the reduced blood flow in strokes. Of course, the ideal treatment for stroke would be to discover a way to allow the brain to repair itself, since ordinarily, seriously damaged neurons are simply lost forever. Some evidence suggests that transcranial magnetic stimulation (TMS) may be that treatment.

In TMS, a rapidly changing magnetic field is applied to the brain. A magnet by itself will have no effect on the brain at all. A pulsed magnetic field, however, will induce any charged particles in its path (like the potassium and sodium ions in and around neurons, for example) to flow, thus inducing an electric current. This has been experimented with as a treatment for depression, as well, as it is much more precise and easy to control than the electrical current used in ELECTROCONVULSIVE THERAPY (ECT). Results have been promising, especially since traditional ECT requires anesthesia and TMS does not. Some research with stroke victims suggests that TMS might possibly increase the brain's flexibility of function, thus speeding up recovery of functions after a stroke. Research on this treatment is still tentative, but quite promising.

Diagnosis of strokes is often accomplished through brief neurological examinations and blood tests, though CT and MRI scans and ultrasound have revolutionized the process. There are multiple known risk factors for stroke, including genetics (strokes seem to run in families), hypertension (high blood pressure), heart disease, diabetes, heavy alcohol consumption, high blood cholesterol levels, illicit drug use, and smoking. Additionally, pregnancy, childbirth, and menopause all elevate risk of stroke as well. None of these risk factors will inevitably lead to stroke, but prevention efforts have largely centered on getting people to reduce the risk by changing what they can from this list. Predicting who will have a stroke cannot be done with any certainty, but it may become possible, through the treatments described above, to greatly reduce the damage it causes in many cases (*see also* BRAIN IMAGING TECHNIQUES).

Further Reading: Delvaux, V., Alagona, G., and Gerard, P. "Post-Stroke Reorganization of Hand Motor Area: A 1-Year Prospective Follow-Up with Focal Transcranial Magnetic Stimulation." *Clinical Neurophysiology*, 114(7) (2003): 1217–1225; Mills, K. R. *Magnetic Stimulation of the Human Nervous System*. New York: Oxford University Press, 2000.

SUBLIMINAL PERCEPTION A subliminal stimulus is, by definition, below the sensory threshold, and therefore cannot be perceived at all. The word is used by psychologists to refer instead to a stimulus that is presented in such a way that it is not *consciously* perceived, and few concepts in psychology have generated quite so much use in PSEUDOSCIENCE, as well as an enduring urban legend.

First, the legend. In 1957 a New Jersey movie theater flashed messages reading "drink Coke" and "eat popcorn" on the screen for a single frame's duration (1/24 of a second) during a feature presentation. The customers were unaware of having seen the messages, but popcorn sales increased by 58 percent, although Coca-Cola sales increased a comparatively disappointing 15 percent. Although the account of this phenomenon, provided by an advertising man (of course) turned out to be a hoax, the idea that such hidden messages can influence behavior is an enduring one. Numerous companies, for example, sell self-help audiotapes containing subliminal messages which are alleged to help the listener lose weight, quit smoking, become more confident, become a better lover, find one's mate, overcome stage fright, make smarter investments, and nearly anything else a person might wish to improve upon. Despite the nearly total lack of evidence that such a product could work as advertised, these tapes are a $50 million-a-year business. Furthermore, large retailers have shelled out hefty licensing fees for in-store music loaded with messages urging customers not to shoplift (and to buy something).

Belief in subliminal appeals to consumers also led to one of the more interesting conspiracy theories of our time in the late 1970s and early 1980s, with a series of books by Wilson Bryan Key (titles included *Subliminal Seduction* and *The Clam-Plate Orgy*) in which he claimed that advertisers were concealing graphic sexual images in all sorts of ads, to increase sales to people who had no idea they were being manipulated in this way. The title of *The Clam-Plate Orgy*, for example, refers to a photo on a restaurant menu in which fried clams were arranged to resemble a large-scale sexual orgy, involving numerous men and women, as well as a donkey. Oddly, nobody noticed this until Key suggested they look for it. He also saw the word "sex" in many places, including in the ice cubes in a glass of gin and in the salt crystals on the surface of a Ritz cracker.

Surely the most absurd manifestation of belief in subliminals, however, came in the late 1970s and early 1980s when rock musicians, especially heavy-metal bands, were accused of hiding paeans to sex, drugs, and Satan in the grooves of their vinyl record albums. Not only were the messages often subliminal, but also they were supposedly recorded backwards. They could be discovered only by the deliberate process of stopping the turntable and slowly turning it backwards by hand. How their discoverers happened to find themselves doing this, especially with records they considered immoral and inappropriate to purchase or listen to in the first place, usually remained unexplained. Many of the top names in rock were targeted, including Led Zeppelin (whose "Stairway to Heaven" allegedly says "a child is born for Satan, my sweet Satan"), Queen ("Another One Bites the Dust" backwards sounds, with a large helping of imagination, like it says "I want to smoke marijuana, marijuana"), and Ozzy Osbourne and Judas Priest (both of whom were accused of causing teenage suicides with their subliminal messages, though both seemed equally surprised to hear that their music contained them). The most absurd thing about the backward-masking frenzy is the suggestion, even if subliminal audio messages work, that they could work backwards. There is no evidence whatsoever that the human brain is capable of perceiving, consciously or otherwise, anything that is played backwards. Some bands, including Pink Floyd, Iron Maiden, and Electric Light Orchestra (ELO), responded to it all by actually placing clearly audible, humorous backward messages on their albums. ELO's *Fire on High* features the funniest: "The music is reversible! Turn back, Turn back!" in a deep, serious voice. Still, like most pseudosciences, the widespread belief in the influence of subliminals begins with a small grain of truth.

Subliminal perception, in the sense of getting experimental subjects to perceive stimuli without any awareness of having done so, has actually been central to cognitive research for decades. In studies of priming, subjects sit at a computer screen and are shown images (pictures, letters, or words) for very brief durations, measured in tens of milliseconds, to determine how long an exposure is necessary for the subject to detect the image and identify it. A common finding is that subjects will respond more rapidly and accurately to stimuli they have already seen, even when they were unaware of having seen them the first time. Clearly subliminal perception has a slight impact on MEMORY.

Some researchers have taken things a step further, attempting to influence subjects' emotional states with subliminal images. In one typical study, subjects were shown a series of photos of an ordinary woman going about her daily chores, always with a fairly neutral expression, and were asked immediately after the slide show to answer a series of questions about her, including whether she seems happy with her life. What they didn't know was that they had also seen other pictures, presented for fractions of a second. Some subjects saw "happy" pictures, such as puppies and kittens. Other subjects saw scary pictures, including spiders, snakes, and skulls. The result was a small but significant difference in how happy the experimental subjects judged the woman to be. When subjects were tested even a few minutes later, rather than immediately upon the end of the slide show, no effect was found. Subliminal images can have an effect, but the effect is very subtle and very fleeting. Absent is any evidence that actual behavior can be impacted. These studies concern only visual subliminals, however.

Where subliminal audiotapes are concerned, no evidence exists to suggest they will work, and the combination of simple logic and the design of the visual research suggests strongly that they *should* not work. For a visual image to be presented subliminally, it must be presented very briefly. For it to be perceived, even subliminally, however, it must be bright enough and clear enough for the eye to detect it—as bright and clear as the images the person is aware of seeing. The claim made by the marketers of audio subliminals is quite straightforward—the messages are recorded so quietly, relative to the other content of the tapes, that they are inaudible. Consider this in comparison to the research on visual subliminals—no researcher claims that a very dim or blurry image will result in anything being perceived at all. The messages on the tapes, on the other hand, are by definition too quiet to be heard. No evidence whatsoever exists to show that an *unheard* message can have any impact on behavior.

Finally, mention should be made of the fact that, in 1974, despite the absence of any empirical evidence supporting the notion that subliminal messages can change behavior, the Federal Communications Commission (FCC) issued a regulation specifically forbidding the broadcast of subliminal messages. This rule actually became relevant during the 2000 presidential campaign, when two Democratic senators complained to the FCC about a Republican television ad that flashed the word "RATS" for 1/30 of a second. Despite the absence of evidence that such an ad could have any effect other than to waste the money of those who paid for it, our government clearly continues to take the threat of subliminal seduction very seriously.

Further Reading: Pratkanis, A. R. "The Cargo-Cult Science of Subliminal Persuasion." *Skeptical Inquirer,* 16(3) (1997): 260–272; Pratkanis, A. R., Eskenazi, J., Greenwald, A. G. "What You Expect Is What You Believe (But Not Necessarily What You Get): A Test of the Effectiveness of Subliminal Self-Help Audiotapes." *Basic & Applied Social Psychology,* 15(3) (1994): 251–276.

T

TELEKINESIS *See* PARAPSYCHOLOGY

TELEPATHY *See* PARAPSYCHOLOGY

TEN PERCENT MYTH One of the most persistent brain-related myths confronted by frustrated psychology professors is the notion that humans only use 10 percent of the BRAIN. This idea is frequently accompanied by the notion that, if we could only tap into the vast unused portions, we would develop amazing powers of telepathy, clairvoyance, and psychokinesis; be able to levitate, heal disease, and solve humanity's social problems; achieve perfect recall or instantaneous learning; achieve voluntary control of our bodies' involuntary functions; achieve world peace; or bend spoons (trivial compared to the others, but quite popular all the same, *see* PARAPSYCHOLOGY and RANDI, JAMES).

This urban legend is now quite widespread, but its origins are shrouded in mystery. What is clear is that it was already widely believed a century ago, and ads for various organizations promising self-improvement were already treating the 10 percent figure as commonplace knowledge by the 1920s. As often happens with PSEUDOSCIENCE, appeals to authority have helped to spread this notion. In the 1950s, for example, the 10 percent myth appeared in editions of Dale Carnegie's books, which continue to cast a large shadow over the motivational-seminar industry and thus on corporate America. It is also not unusual to see the myth attributed to William JAMES, the father of American psychology. Another frequently credited source is Albert Einstein—why a physicist should be thought an expert on brain matters is unclear. There is no evidence that either of these two men ever addressed the idea at all, however. The myth is kept alive in an official capacity today by the TRANSCENDENTAL MEDITATION (TM) organization and Scientology (*see* DIANETICS/SCIENTOLOGY), both of which promise that their adherents will learn to tap this vast unused potential.

One possible source of the myth is a simple misunderstanding of neurological research carried out in the 1930s, when electrical stimulation of the exposed cortex of animal brains became a popular way of discovering the specific function of various brain areas. When a particular area of a dog's cortex is stimulated, for example, there is usually a visible motor response. Similar studies of human brains revealed a different pattern, however. Large areas of cortex did not evoke obvious responses, leading researchers to refer to these areas as "silent cortex." Others may have then taken this to mean that those areas—not 90 percent, but certainly a large proportion of the available tissue—were unused or inactive. No psychologist or neurologist would have interpreted it this way, of course. Far from being silent, those areas not involved in sensation and motor activity are responsible for such things as language, memory, perception, reasoning, and abstract thought.

The myth is easily refuted by modern BRAIN IMAGING TECHNIQUES, which show plainly that all the brain is active, all the time. Various tasks that engage particular brain structures may produce a temporary increase in the activity level of those areas, but even in sleep, no area is completely inactive, barring severe tissue damage. Simply put, neurons that show no activity are dead. If 90 percent of the brain were inactive, the tissue would degenerate rapidly. Therefore, techniques that promise to make inactive portions of the brain active are promising, Frankenstein-like, to reanimate dead cells.

Another line of evidence against this myth comes from the study of people who actually do have inactive areas of brain tissue. In STROKE victims, the loss of very small areas of tissue, often less than 1 percent of total brain mass, can produce catastrophic loss of function. The almost total loss of memory and sense of self which accompanies advanced cases of ALZHEIMER'S DISEASE, meanwhile, usually involves damage to 10 to 20 percent or less of the cortex. Damage to relatively small areas of the brain, as one can imagine, can usually be counted on to produce fairly serious damage. In other words, good scientific reasons exist for this bit of dialogue never being overheard in a hospital emergency room: "Thank God, the bullet passed through the 90 percent of the brain that the victim wasn't using!"

Further Reading: Beyerstein, B. L. "Whence Cometh the Myth That We Only Use 10% of Our Brains?" In S. Della Sala, ed. *Mind Myths: Exploring Popular Assumptions about the Mind and Brain*. New York: Wiley, 1999, pp. 3–24.

TFT   *See* THOUGHT FIELD THERAPY

THERAPEUTIC TOUCH   A classic example of PSEUDOSCIENCE, therapeutic touch (TT) was invented in the early 1970s by Dolores Krieger, R.N., a professor of nursing. It was originally based on the Hindu idea of prana, the vital force that flows around and through the body and keeps it alive, focused in various chakras, or energy centers, throughout the body. After various critiques focused on the unscientific nature of this, Krieger quietly moved to an explanation centered on the more scientific-sounding *human energy field*, which essentially sounds the same as an aura. The central assumption of TT is that this field surrounds and envelops the entire body and that physical and mental illness is caused by disturbances and imbalances in this field. Trained TT practitioners can detect and manipulate these imbalances using their hands, thus treating the problem. Oddly, practitioners can't seem to agree on how they detect these imbalances, variously describing them as feeling like pressure, tingling, pulling, hot or cold areas, or "spikes" of energy. Also, despite the name, therapeutic touch has evolved from its beginnings to a practice that doesn't actually involve touching the patient at all. Instead the practitioner moves his or her hands through the energy field, several inches away from the patient's body.

A standard session begins with a centering exercise, during which the practitioner meditates and focuses on the intent to heal. This is followed by the assessment phase, during which the practitioner waves her or his hands over the patient's entire body at a distance of a few inches, as a way of detecting "imbalances" (although it is difficult to discover a clear definition of what an imbalance is) in the patient's human energy field. This is followed by *unruffling*, a process of redistributing energy that has become congested, and sweeping away the excess negative energy, usually accompanied by a wringing of the hands that resembles shaking off excess water.

After nearly thirty years, no scientific evidence whatsoever exists that TT practitioners can actually do what they say they can, or for that matter, any evidence of the existence of the energy field that they claim to manipulate. Despite this, the practice has become enormously popular in the nursing profession, as well as with independent practitioners. As many as 100,000 people have been trained in TT, and training centers have existed at more than 100 colleges and universities. The North American Nursing Diagnosis Association was even persuaded to include "Energy Field Disturbance" as an official nursing diagnosis, for which TT is the recommended intervention.

Big money is to be made here: initial certification in TT costs up to $400 to obtain, making this a multimillion-dollar enterprise. Furthermore, the Nursing Diagnosis Association includes the requirement that TT should only be performed by persons who have obtained certification, with a minimum of twelve hours of instruction, and that the practitioner should be supervised by a nurse with a master's degree, who has thirty hours of instruction in TT theory and an additional thirty hours of supervised TT practice (this of course adds significantly to the amount of money involved). When big money becomes a factor, the pseudoscientific dragon can be difficult to slay, but a clever sixth-grader did more than anyone else has thus far to raise doubts about TT in the public mind.

Emily Rosa was preparing a project for her science fair, originally focused on using a bowl of candy to demonstrate probability, but she changed her direction when her skeptical nurse mother showed her a videotape about TT. For her science project, Emily conducted a simple, elegant empirical test of therapeutic touch practitioners. Where James RANDI has had great difficulty getting anyone to submit to a controlled test of TT abilities, even with a one million-dollar prize on the line, Emily Rosa convinced twenty-one therapeutic touch practitioners to participate in her test. The design was extremely simple: she set up a wall with two holes in it, and had the TT practitioners stick their hands through the holes. Her hand was positioned over one of their hands; their task was to indicate which one. Each practitioner got twenty trials. In the end, they were only able to "detect" Emily's hand 44 percent of the time, less often than the 50 percent hit rate that could be expected from random guessing. Some of these test subjects were quite well known and had even published articles on therapeutic touch. In April 1998, Emily's data were published in the *Journal of the American Medical Association*, making her the youngest author ever to publish in that prestigious journal.

Reaction to that study from TT practitioners and advocates has been predictably hostile, with many ad hoc hypotheses put forward to explain away the sometimes bizarre results. These hypotheses include the following:

- *The experiment was not double-blind.* There's no reason why it should have been. It was important that the practitioners be uninformed about which hand she was targeting, but there's no reason why Emily should have been unaware of it, as that knowledge couldn't logically influence the outcome. To the contrary, in order to place her hand near one or the other, Emily *had* to know which one she was targeting.

- *Expecting the practitioners to get most of the trials right was unreasonable.* They either can detect the human energy field or they can't. If they can, *100 percent correct* would be a reasonable expectation.

- *Emily's energy field was wrong for such a test.* It was a wild pubescent field, or it was too perfect or too unhealthy, or it had too short a range, or it was so large it surrounded both hands, making a single hand impossible to detect, or she somehow was able to suppress her field. This might be a good place to mention that all practitioners got to examine her hands and "sense" her field ahead of time, and they also got to pick which of her hands had the easier field to detect.

- *A practitioner doesn't actually have to be able to feel the Human Energy Field.* Since practitioners have used their ability to do so as the justification for the practice since its inception, this argument is especially bizarre.

- *It doesn't matter if it works or not—so what if it is a placebo effect? If it makes people feel better, let's keep doing it.* If it is a placebo effect, why is costly certification and oversight required to practice?

- *JAMA published the results because TT is cheap and doesn't require the services of doctors or pharmaceutical companies—they'd never publish studies critical of them.* The best retort to this criticism is to simply look at an index of articles published by *JAMA* over the years. If a treatment is found ineffective or harmful, that gets published too.

This last criticism may contain a small kernel of the truth about the open embrace of TT by the nursing profession. In the medical field, most of the patient care is done by nurses, while most of the power rests with doctors. This is a treatment carried out by nurses without any help from doctors, using specialized training that the doctors haven't had. It has served the purpose of giving many nurses a sense of power in patient care, an ability to heal that only they have. It is true that nurses should probably have more influence over patient care than they often do, but this is the wrong way to go about wielding it. When *JAMA* published Emily Rosa's study, the article included the following statement:

> To our knowledge, no other objective, quantitative study involving more than a few TT practitioners has been published, and no well-designed study demonstrates any health benefit from TT. These facts, together with our experimental findings, suggest that TT claims are groundless and that further use of TT by health professionals is unjustified.

At the moment, scientifically speaking, that is the last word on therapeutic touch (*see also* ACUPUNCTURE; PSYCHOLOGY, RESEARCH METHODS IN; THOUGHT FIELD THERAPY).

Further Reading: Rosa, L., Rosa, E., Sarner, L., and Barrett, S. "A Close Look at Therapeutic Touch." *Journal of the American Medical Association*, 279(13) (1998): 1005–1011; Sarner, L. "The 'Emily Event.'" *Skeptic*, 6(2) (1998): 32–38.

THOUGHT FIELD THERAPY

Thought Field Therapy (TFT) is a relatively new therapy, of somewhat dubious value, invented and promoted by Dr. Roger J. Callahan, clinical psychologist and author of *The Five Minute Phobia Cure* and (with Richard Turbo) *Tapping the Healer Within: Using Thought Field Therapy to Instantly Conquer Your Fears, Anxieties, and Emotional Distress.* To see the source of the skepticism towards TFT within the psychological community, one need not look beyond the use of the words "five minute" and "instantly" in those book titles. Psychological disorders, especially such difficult and intractable conditions as major depression and posttraumatic stress disorder, are difficult to treat and often take a long time to improve; and cure rates in the 50 percent or lower range are not unusual, even for relatively effective treatments. The suggestion that a 97 percent cure rate for "almost all psychological and some physical problems" is possible, often in a single session (www.thoughtfieldtherapy.co.uk), seems a bit difficult to take seriously.

More challenging still to the reader well-read in the psychotherapy literature is the claim that through Dr. Callahan's Voice Technology, "all the required information for diagnosis is contained in the voice, [thus] it is possible for treatment to be completed in the course of a telephone call from anywhere in the world."

These are truly remarkable claims, and TFT is a truly remarkable therapy. It is based loosely on the ideas underlying traditional Chinese ACUPUNCTURE— that is, that good and bad energies flow through a set of invisible meridians in the body, and health problems are due to insufficient or blocked flow of energy through these. In traditional acupuncture, these blockages and imbalances are corrected through the insertion of very thin needles into the body. In TFT, emotional and psychological disturbances are also seen as due to the impeded flow of energy, and the therapy consists largely of sequences of finger tapping on acupuncture (acupressure) points, along with other activities such as repeating statements, counting, rolling the eyes, or humming a tune, all while thinking of the distressing situation.

Callahan's promotional books and Web sites assert, among other oddities, that large quantities of extremely well documented and widely accepted neurological knowledge are simply wrong. The amygdala, a structure deep within the BRAIN, for example, is not involved in production of emotional states after all (despite what every introductory psychology or neurology text teaches)—that job is carried out entirely by the human energy field (*see* THERAPEUTIC TOUCH). The flow of energy around and through the body is a vital part of Callahan's approach, and so evidence that such a flow exists would seem an important component of any argument in favor of Callahan.

In contrast to the claims of TFT, however, no research has confirmed the existence of human energy fields related either to illness or to response to treatment. To the contrary, recent reviews plainly show that there is insufficient evidence to justify seeking treatments based on the existence of such energies (Basser, 1998; Richardson, 1986; Prance, 1988; Skrabanek, 1984). Furthermore, the lack of evidence for traditional acupuncture meridians renders it a bit difficult to take seriously the suggestion that, contrary to modern scientific psychology research, they are the source of all psychological disorders.

Further Reading: Basser, S. "Acupuncture: The Facts." *The Skeptic*, 13(2) (1998): 27; Callahan, R. J., and Callahan, J. *Thought Field Therapy (TFT) and Trauma: Treatment and Theory.* Indian Wells, CA: The Callahan Techniques, 1996; Callahan, R. J., and Turbo, R. *Tapping the Healer Within: Using Thought Field Therapy to Instantly Conquer Your Fears, Anxieties, and Emotional Distress.* New York: McGraw-Hill/Contemporary Books, 2000; Prance, S. E. (1988). "Research on Traditional Acupuncture—Science or Myth? A Review." *Journal of The Royal Society of Medicine*, 81(10) (1988): 588–590; Skrabanek, P. "Acupuncture and the Age of Unreason." *Lancet*, 1(8387) (1984): 1169–1171.

TM *See* TRANSCENDENTAL MEDITATION

TOURETTE SYNDROME Tourette syndrome, also known as Tourette's syndrome, is a neurological disorder characterized by both muscle tics (repeated, involuntary movements) and verbal tics (uncontrollable vocalizations). Central to the public image of the disorder, outbursts of vulgar and inappropriate language (technically known as coprolalia—literally, "talking about feces") actually occur in a minority of cases, possibly in as few as 15 percent. Typical tics include eye blinking, involuntary facial muscle twitching, kicking, shoulder shrugging, frequent throat clearing, and sniffing.

The disorder was first described by French physician Georges Gilles de la Tourette, in a paper published in 1885. The disorder's cause remains unknown, but the dominant theory concerns a genetic defect resulting in abnormal functioning of at least one neurotransmitter reuptake system in the brain (*see* NERVOUS SYSTEM). This theory is supported by the success of selective serotonin reuptake inhibitors (SSRIs, a category of antidepressant medications) in treating some cases of Tourette syndrome. Symptoms usually emerge in childhood or adolescence, and Tourette syndrome occurs in three to four times as many boys than girls. For a diagnosis of Tourette syndrome to be made, both verbal tics and multiple motor tics must be present, and they must occur many times a day over a span of at least one year. The most common first symptom is a minor facial tic, such as a mouth twitch or eye blink. The syndrome actually can involve a wide spectrum of symptom patterns, with no typical set of tics, but most cases are considered mild rather than severe.

Tourette syndrome and other tic disorders rarely occur alone but rather tend to be comorbid with other problems, including but not limited to depression, anxiety disorders, obsessive-compulsive disorder, ATTENTION-DEFICIT/HYPERACTIVITY DISORDER (ADHD), and SLEEP disorders. Treatment is complicated, consequently, by the need to treat the symptoms of the other disorders as well. Fortunately, the majority of persons with Tourette syndrome are not sufficiently disabled by their tics to require treatment. In cases of greater severity, antidepressants and antiseizure medicines (including clonidine and haloperidol) have been widely used to reduce symptoms. Methylphenidate (Ritalin) has also been used in cases where Tourette syndrome is comorbid with ADHD, but its use in Tourette syndrome is otherwise uncommon, as its properties as a stimulant can exacerbate tics rather than reduce them.

Further Reading: *The Tourette Syndrome Association Web site*, www.tsa-usa.org, The Tourette Syndrome Association, 2004.

TRADITIONAL CHINESE MEDICINE *See* ACUPUNCTURE

TRANSCENDENTAL MEDITATION Transcendental Meditation (TM) is a cult-like organization built around the Maharishi Mahesh Yogi and his Hindu meditation techniques. He began the organization in 1956, but it first became widely known in the 1960s, thanks to his ability to attract celebrities to his ashram (the Beatles were his followers for a while). TM involves chanting a mantra, a special word or phrase allegedly chosen especially for the individual meditator, and for which the meditator pays hundreds of dollars. Proper meditation will bring the meditator to a special union with "universal consciousness" known as bliss or enlightenment.

TM promotional materials, including an array of Web sites and a university (Maharishi University of Management, formerly Maharishi International University, in Fairfield, Iowa), represent TM as a scientifically validated way, based, apparently, on the *Science of Creative Intelligence*, to improve health, eliminate stress, increase creativity and intelligence, and achieve inner happiness and fulfillment. These claims of scientific validation are fascinating, given the nature of what advocates claim that the practice can do. Take yogic flying, for example. Since the early days, transcendental meditators (TMers) have claimed that, with sufficient experience at meditation, levitation would be possible. They've gone so far as to allow themselves to be filmed flying. The practice, however, looks to the untrained eye as though the TMers are simply hopping around on the well-cushioned floor while in a lotus position. Most advocates have now distanced themselves from this claim, but the claim has been replaced

Relaxation is always a good thing; however, levitation is probably not one of its side benefits.

by others that are both more ludicrous and more difficult to disprove. Some TMers, for example, now claim to be able to make themselves invisible.

Another widely made TM claim is the existence of something called the "Maharishi effect." They claim to have demonstrated scientifically that collective meditation, defined as a large group of people meditating together, reduced crime while increasing crop production in the area of Iowa immediately surrounding the Maharishi University of Management. The data used to back this claim appear to have been wholly invented, as they don't match up with what either the Fairfield Police Department or the Iowa Department of Agriculture have been able to find out. In one of the most cynically capitalistic responses to the terrorist events of September 11, 2001, the TM organization sought to raise 1 billion dollars to set up a group of 40,000 young men in India to meditate in unison, claiming that this would bring about world peace and prevent future terrorism.

Plenty of research shows that relaxing more provides various health benefits, and this evidence is widely touted by TM as proof that their practice is the best way to achieve those benefits. However, no scientific research actually shows that the physiological results obtainable through TM are any different from those obtained by simply learning to relax more effectively. Relaxation can be learned fairly cheaply, however, and the mantras turn out to be not so special after all. They are assigned from tables, based on age and sometimes, depending on the instructor, gender, that can be found online at www.minet.org/mantras.html.

TM's health claims have actually moved well beyond those associated only with relaxation, as the group has also moved into the world of medicine. Ayurvedic medicine is a Maharishi invention, and Deepak CHOPRA, its best-known advocate, is a former Maharishi employee. As if this were not enough, the TMers have also moved their agenda into the political arena. The Natural Law Party, which has mysteriously appeared on many U.S. ballots in the last decade or so, including presidential ballots in a number of states, is TM's thinly veiled attempt to work its ideas into the American mainstream, with official policies on the usual things like health, education, energy, the environment , as well as policies on more unusual areas like health foods (and, yes, the benefits of widespread meditation).

Further Reading: Randi, J. *Flim-Flam! The Truth about Psychics, ESP, Unicorns, and Other Delusions.* Buffalo, NY: Prometheus, 1988; Roth, R. *TM—Transcendental Meditation: A New Introduction to Maharishi's Easy, Effective and Scientifically Proven Technique for Promoting Better Health, Unfolding Your Creative Potential, and Creating Peace in the World.* New York: Donald I. Fine, 1994.

TRANSVESTIC FETISHISM   *See* PARAPHILIAS

TT   *See* THERAPEUTIC TOUCH

V

VOYEURISM *See* PARAPHILIAS

VYGOTSKY, LEV SEMENOVICH (1896–1934) Lev Vygotsky was a Russian psychologist who began his professional career just after the Bolshevik Revolution. Like all successful Soviet scholars of the time, he was a committed Marxist, and his theory of child development provides an excellent example of the influence of politics and society on scientific progress. In Western Europe and the United States, Jean PIAGET, whose theory emphasizes the role of the child's own independent action on his environment, has long been the dominant voice in child development. When Vygotsky first became well known among American psychologists in the late 1970s, it was largely because his approach, which emphasizes the interaction between the child and other people as the source of cognitive development, was seen as an alternative to Piaget.

Because of his goal of creating a psychology consistent with Marxism's emphasis on collective action over individualism, Vygotsky inevitably produced a very different theory than Piaget. In *The Communist Manifesto*, for example, Marx argues that the development of language made cooperation among people, and therefore the development of civilization, possible. In his two best-known works, *Thinking and Speech* and *Mind in Society*, Vygotsky lays out the basics of his theoretical approach, in which the development of language precedes the development of most higher mental functions, and the role of interaction between adults and children is emphasized far more than the role of the individual child.

According to Vygotsky, all cognitive functions originate in social interaction and are eventually internalized as the child becomes more competent. This includes language, which begins as a means of communicating with others before it evolves into what Vygotsky calls private speech (Piaget's term for the same thing was egocentric speech), easily seen in young children talking to themselves as they play. Where Piaget saw private speech as something that eventually stops as children outgrow it, Vygotsky instead argued that it never goes away—it simply goes underground, continuing silently rather than out loud. Through this mechanism, the child goes from requiring external instructions to self-regulating via internal ones. As has occurred often in the history of psychology, the two theorists agree on the existence of the phenomenon, but disagree as to its function.

Vygotsky's greatest impact on American psychologists came with the concept of the Zone of Proximal Development (ZPD). Vygotsky felt that the way we test students, focusing on what they already know rather than what they are capable of learning, an approach now known among educational psychologists as static testing, should be replaced by a more dynamic approach, in which we measure how much more the children are capable of doing when provided with supportive help. The gap between what the children can do on their own and what they can accomplish with help is the ZPD, and Vygotsky believed that measuring it would yield far more useful information than the static tests currently in use. These ideas have become very popular among educational psychologists in America today, some seventy years after Vygotsky's death, in part because it is viewed as both a radical departure from Piaget, which is not entirely true (since as with most dichotomies, there is actually much about which they agree), and as a more realistic description of what actually occurs in child development.

Vygotsky's work was unknown in the West until 1958, largely due to the Cold War between the United States and the Soviet Union, and didn't really become popular until several decades later. What many of Vygotsky's followers today fail to realize, however, is that his work was also largely unknown within the Soviet Union as well, as his version of Marxist psychology was, ironically, too Western European for Stalin, and his works were suppressed for many years.

Further Reading: Vygotsky, L. S. *Mind in Society.* Cambridge, MA: Harvard University Press, 1930; Vygotsky, L. S. *Thinking and Speech.* Cambridge, MA: MIT Press, 1934. U.S. publication in 1962.

W

WATSON, JOHN B. (1878–1958)   Born in Greenville, South Carolina, in 1878, John Broadus Watson eventually became one of the most influential figures in American psychology, despite a relatively short academic career and very little significant research. His influence comes as a result of an idea, most fully expressed in his 1913 paper, "Psychology as the Behaviorist Views It."

In this paper, Watson argued that the proper subject matter of psychology is overt, observable behavior, whereas mental and emotional phenomena, which cannot be directly and objectively observed, should form no part of the new science. Indeed, he suggested that psychologists' preoccupation with consciousness might prevent psychology from truly becoming a science. Instead, the behaviorist should concern himself only with stimulus-response connections. Watson believed that human behavior was entirely predictable, given sufficient knowledge of the individual's history of stimuli and responses. He famously expressed this by claiming that, given full charge of a dozen healthy infants, he could provide the learning experiences necessary to produce any sort of person desired—doctor, lawyer, even criminal.

His most famous experiment was his demonstration that emotional experiences could be produced through classical conditioning (also known as respondent conditioning, *see* PAVLOV, IVAN). This demonstration involved a baby (forever known in the psychological literature as Little Albert), a loud noise, and a white rat. Albert enjoyed playing with the laboratory rat, looking at it and touching it with obvious pleasure, which made it the ideal object for Watson to turn into a source of fear. A series of trials was conducted in which, as Albert reached for the rat, a large metal bar behind him was struck with a hammer, producing a loud noise, which startled and frightened him. Soon, he began to show a fear response at the sight of the rat, demonstrating that emotional states could be produced as conditioned responses.

Watson's career at Johns Hopkins University, where he edited the *Psychological Review* and founded the *Journal of Experimental Psychology*, lasted only from 1908 to 1920. The reason for this was an ill-advised affair with his graduate assistant on the Little Albert study, which resulted in a highly publicized, scandalous divorce (after which he married the graduate student), followed by an administration request for his resignation. Watson went on to great success in the advertising world, where he has been credited with, among other things, inventing the concept of the "coffee break" in a series of magazine ads. He also continued to write books and articles for popular magazines, but he never taught or published in academic journals again. Behaviorism went on to become a dominant perspective in American psychology through much of the twentieth century, largely due to the efforts of B. F. SKINNER, who refined and expanded on Watson's ideas to such a degree that his name is now far more widely associated with behaviorism than Watson's.

Further Reading: Buckley, K. W. *Mechanical Man: John B. Watson and the Beginnings of Behaviorism.* New York: Guilford, 1989; Watson, J. B. "Psychology as the Behaviorist Sees It." *Psychological Review*, 20 (1913): 158–177.

WHORFIAN HYPOTHESIS   *See* SAPIR-WHORF HYPOTHESIS

WILLIAMS SYNDROME   Williams syndrome is a rare genetic disorder with a rate of incidence of approximately 1 in 20,000 births. This usually results in mild to moderate MENTAL RETARDATION, although this is frequently accompanied by behavior patterns and abilities reminiscent of those of autistic SAVANTS. The literature on Williams syndrome is filled with cases such as Gloria Lenhoff, a forty-six-year-old lyric soprano who has performed with both the San Diego Master Chorale and members of the rock group Aerosmith. She is said to know almost 2,500 songs in more than twenty-five languages, which she sings with perfect pitch and in the correct accents. She also has an IQ of about 55, the borderline between mild and moderate mental retardation.

Typically, the individual with Williams syndrome has difficulty with all but the simplest mental and physical tasks; but certain abilities, including both verbal and musical skills, appear to be unaffected. Indeed, virtually everyone with this syndrome who has been studied thus far appears to have an exceptional affinity for music. The incidence of perfect pitch is reported to be unusually high, and a very fine-tuned sense of rhythm is also quite common. Exceptional social skills are also widely reported by those who work with children with Williams syndrome.

The cause of Williams syndrome appears to be an abnormality in the seventh pair of chromosomes. Specifically, one chromosome in the pair is missing some genetic material, including the gene that codes for the production of elastin. Elastin is a vital protein in the human body, responsible for lending flexibility both to internal organs and to blood vessels. Unsurprisingly, heart and circulatory problems are common in people with Williams syndrome, as is a higher than normal incidence of other problems involving internal organs. What remains unclear is what, if any, relationship exists between the absence of elastin and the other problems (and advantages) associated with Williams syndrome. The elastin gene is not the only deletion on the seventh chromosome, but very little is known about what else has been affected. Research on Williams syndrome is in its infancy, but it will surely become much better understood over time.

Further Reading: *The Williams Syndrome Foundation Official Web Site*, www.wsf.org, Williams Syndrome Foundation, 2003.

WUNDT, WILHELM (1832–1920)   Textbook authors frequently refer to Wundt as the father of modern, scientific psychology. This is due to his establishment at Leipzig, Germany, of the world's first psychological laboratory. Other scientists had begun to study the mind and the nervous system prior to this, but Wundt's program, begun in 1879, was the first degree-granting laboratory science program devoted exclusively to psychology. Some authors make a case for William JAMES (1842–1910) as the real founder of psychology, as he also established a psychology lab in 1879, but his was used primarily for classroom demonstrations rather than as part of a degree program in psychological research, so Wundt generally gets the credit.

In his lab Wundt devoted himself to the study of conscious experience, through the use of introspection. Introspection was approached very formally at Leipzig, with extensive training in self-observation and self-report required before a subject participated in Wundt's experiments. The early psychologists were inspired by nineteenth-century progress in chemistry and the physical sciences, and so Wundt hoped to train his subjects to analyze their own conscious experiences into more basic elements. Wundt believed that once these elements were identified and the processes by which they were related and integrated became understood, the structure of conscious experience would no longer be a mystery. Because of this philosophical underpinning, Wundt's approach to psychology became known as structuralism. Structuralist methods were applied primarily to the study of sensation and perception.

Wundt's greatest contribution to psychology may be through the ideas and research he inspired in those who disagreed with him. His methods came to America with his student, E. B. Titchener, where they immediately came under fire from James, who insisted that to break down conscious experience into its component parts was to remove the continuous, flowing nature that is a defining feature of consciousness. Meanwhile, back in Germany, a group of psychologists who became known as the GESTALT school made a similar argument, pointing out that the whole conscious experience was more than just the sum of its component parts. In Vienna, Sigmund FREUD (1856–1939) went in a different direction a few years later. Believing that much of what goes on in the human mind and motivates us to action is below the level of consciousness, Freud saw the method of introspection as incapable of truly illuminating the human mind, as it assumes that the subject is aware of his or her own thoughts and feelings and is able to articulate them.

Wundt's ideas and methods have long since faded from psychology, but his status in the history of the discipline remains secure, thanks to his major contribution towards establishing psychology as a legitimate scientific discipline.

Further Reading: Rieber, R. W., and Robinson, D. K., eds. *Wilhelm Wundt in History: The Making of a Scientific Psychology*. New York: Kluwer, 2001.

Annotated Bibliography

The resources listed below will help readers delve more deeply into the topics covered in this book. This is a listing of books and other sources that were especially useful in putting this book together; and, unlike most psychological literature, most are written at a level that won't require a postgraduate education to keep up.

General Psychological Reading

American Psychiatric Association. *DSM-IV-TR: Diagnostic and Statistical Manual of Mental Disorders*. 4th ed. Text revision. Washington, DC: American Psychiatric Association, 2000.

   All "official," or at least widely accepted, diagnostic criteria for all mental disorders that you've heard of, and many that you haven't, are in this book. Highly technical, but fascinating.

Della Sala, S., ed. *Mind Myths: Exploring Popular Assumptions about the Brain and the Mind*. New York: Wiley, 1999.

   This collection of essays tackles a wide range of topics on which people are often wrong, yet adamant, including hemispheric dominance, the ten percent myth, brain tonics, near-death experiences, false memories, hypnosis, and age-related decline. Fairly scholarly, but readable.

History of Psychology

Fancher, R. *The Intelligence Men: Makers of the IQ Controversy*. New York: W.W. Norton & Company, 1985.

This is an excellent history of IQ tests and their uses but also an interesting exploration of the personalities who created them.

Gould, S. J. *The Mismeasure of Man*. Rev. ed. New York: W.W. Norton & Company, 1996.

Although he is primarily known for his musings on evolution and natural history, the late Stephen Jay Gould's real masterpiece is this history of the use of psychometric pseudoscience to promote racism and sexism. His revelations about the role of American scientists in providing the theoretical underpinnings of the Nazi Holocaust are especially eye opening.

Hunt, M. *The Story of Psychology*. New York: Doubleday Anchor, 1993.

Unlike most books on the history of psychology, this 762-page volume is actually written for a lay audience and is remarkably entertaining.

Pseudoscience

Bunge, M. "What Is Pseudoscience?" *Skeptical Inquirer*, 9 (1984): 36–46.

This article clearly explains the difference between science and pseudoscience.

Gardner, Martin. *Fads and Fallacies in the Name of Science*. New York: Dover, 1952.

After more than fifty years in print, this little volume remains the best book ever written about current trends in pseudoscience. Actually, the fact that about two-thirds of the movements Gardner debunks are still current trends also says a lot about the attraction of pseudoscience.

Gardner, Martin. *The New Age: Notes of a Fringe Watcher*. Buffalo, NY: Prometheus, 1988.

Gardner, Martin. *Weird Water and Fuzzy Logic: More Notes of a Fringe Watcher*. Buffalo, NY: Prometheus, 1996.

Decades later, Gardner's collected columns from the *Skeptical Inquirer* pick up where *Fads and Fallacies* left off, covering all the pseudoscience that has developed since the early 1950s. These two volumes are entertaining and funny, while also very informative.

Lilienfeld, S. O. "Pseudoscience in Contemporary Clinical Psychology: What It Is and What We Can Do about It." *The Clinical Psychologist*, 51(4) (1998): 3–9.

Like the Bunge article above, this journal article lays out, with great clarity, the differences between science and pseudoscience.

Randi, James. *Flim-Flam! Psychics, ESP, and Other Delusions*. Buffalo, NY: Prometheus, 1987.

The best book by the world's leading crusader against nonsense.

Shermer, Michael. *Why People Believe Weird Things*: Pseudoscience, *Superstition, and Other Confusions of Our Time*. New York: W. H. Freeman, 1997.

The title is self-explanatory. Shermer, the publisher of *Skeptic* magazine and head of the Skeptics Society, tackles near-death experiences, false-memory witch hunts, daytime talk shows, and Holocaust deniers, among other things.

Wynn, C. M., and Wiggins, A. W. *Quantum Leaps in the Wrong Direction: Where Real Science Ends . . . and Pseudoscience Begins*. Washington, DC: Joseph Henry Press, 2001.

Astrology, alien abduction, out-of-body experiences, ESP, and creationism all come under entertaining attack in this well-illustrated (cartoons by Sidney Harris) volume.

Web Sites

www.csicop.org

This is the official Web site of the Committee for Scientific Investigation of Claims of the Paranormal (CSICOP), publishers of another essential source, the *Skeptical Inquirer.*

www.quackwatch.org

This Web site, run by Dr. Stephen Barrett, keeps an eye on questionable treatments of all kinds, including both medical and psychological. The amount of content here is simply enormous.

www.randi.org

This site is the home of the James Randi Educational Foundation, and a great place to learn more about what's going on in the world of pseudoscience. Randi's weekly commentary should be required reading.

www.skepdic.com

The Skeptic's Dictionary, a site run by Robert Todd Carroll, a philosophy professor, receives more than half a million hits a month. This is because it is the best online compendium of all things pseudoscientific.

Biographies and Seminal Works of Major Figures

Bjork, D. W. *B. F. Skinner: A Life.* Washington, DC: American Psychological Association, 1997.

Buckley, K. W. *Mechanical Man: John B. Watson and the Beginnings of Behaviorism.* New York: Guilford, 1989.

Campbell, J., ed. *The Portable Jung.* New York: Viking, 1981.

Gay, P. *Freud: A Life for Our Time.* New York: W. W. Norton, 1988.

James, William. *Principles of Psychology.* New York: Henry Holt, 1890.

Jones, James. *Alfred C. Kinsey: A Public/Private Life.* New York: W. W. Norton, 1997.

Rieber, R. W., and Robinson, D. K., eds. *Wilhelm Wundt in History: The Making of a Scientific Psychology.* New York: Kluwer, 2001.

Vygotsky, L. S. *Mind in Society.* Cambridge, MA: Harvard University Press, 1930.

Specific Topics within Psychology

American Association on Mental Retardation. *Mental Retardation: Definition, Classification, and Systems of Supports.* 10th ed. Washington, DC: Author, 2002.

This document provides the most widely accepted current definition of mental retardation.

Anderson, C. A., Berkowitz, L., Donnerstein, E., Huesmann, L. R., Johnson, J. D., Linz, D., Malamuth, N. M., and Wartella, E. "The Influence of Media Violence on Youth." *Psychological Science in the Public Interest,* 4(3) (2003).

A thorough American Psychological Society (APS) monograph that reviews all research to date on the influence of media violence.

Baumeister, R. F., Campbell, J. D., Krueger, J. I., and Vohs, K. D. "Does High Self-Esteem Cause Better Performance, Interpersonal Success, Happiness, or Healthier Lifestyles?" *Psychological Science in the Public Interest,* 4(1) (2003).

Another APS monograph, this one debunks the alleged importance of self-esteem.

Coren, Stanley. *Sleep Thieves.* New York: Free Press, 1997.

An excellent book-length exploration of the problems associated with sleep deprivation.

Hyman, R. "Cold Reading: How to Convince Strangers That You Know All about Them." *Skeptical Inquirer,* 2(1) (1977): 18–37.

Without exaggerating, I can say that almost every psychologist who understands cold reading learned about it from Ray Hyman, either directly or indirectly.

Lilienfeld, S. O., Wood, J. M., and Garb, H. N. "The Scientific Status of Projective Techniques." *Psychological Science in the Public Interest*, 1(2) (2000).

An APS monograph that thoroughly explores the usefulness and psychometric properties of the Rorschach and other projective tests.

Mook, D. G. *Psychological Research: The Ideas behind the Methods*. New York: W. W. Norton, 2001.

An excellent introduction to the ways in which psychological research is conducted.

Index

Index

Birth order, 38–39
Bovine spongiform encephalopathy.
　See Mad cow disease
Bowlby, John, 22
Brain, 41–45, 164–166, 195–197
Brain imaging, 45–46, 226, 248
Brainwashing, 46–47
Breuer, Josef, 86
Bridey Murphy, 185
Broca, Paul, 14–16, 237
Buck vs. Bell, 93
Bystander effect, 64

Callahan, Roger J., 251–252
Campbell, Don, 156
Cannibalism, 132
Case study, 214
Cataplexy, 161–162
Catatonic schizophrenia, 225
Cattell, Raymond, 116
Ceci, Stephen, 144
Central nervous system, 147, 166, 172
Cerebellum, 41
"Chemical imbalance," 49–50
Chi, 1
Childhood disintegrative disorder, 188
Children's testimony, 144
Chomsky, Noam, 50–51
Chopra, Deepak, 51–53
Cingulotomy, 197
Circadian rhythms, 235–236
Clairvoyance, 178
Classical conditioning, 185–187, 189–190
Cocaine, 239–240
Coercive persuasion, 46–47
Cognitive-behavior therapy, 53–54
Cognitive dissonance, 54–55
Cold reading, 55–56
Collective unconscious, 121
Colliculi, superior and inferior, 43
Committee for the Scientific Investigation
　of Claims of the Paranormal (CSICOP),
　20–22, 216
Context-dependent memory, 140
Contralaterality, 42
Conventional morality 153
Coprolalia, 252
Coprophilia, 177

Corpus callosum, 44, 236–239
Correlation, 56–58, 91, 194, 213
Cortex, 43–45, 195–197, 226
Craniosacral therapy, 58, 207
Creutzfeldt-Jakob disease, 10, 132.
　See Mad cow disease
Criterion-keying, 149
CT scans, 45–46
Cult Awareness Network, 63

Declarative memory, 14, 139
Delta-9-tetrahydrocannabinol (THC),
　208–209
Dementia, 9–11
Dendrites, 164–165
Depressants, 59–60
Depression, 49–50, 53, 150–153, 195, 197,
　198–199, 219–220, 227–228, 243, 251–252
Dianetics, 60–63
Diffusion of responsibility, 63–65
Disorganized schizophrenia, 225
Displacement, 87
Dissociative amnesia, 14
Dissociative identity disorder, 157–158
Dopamine, 152, 166, 226, 227
Down syndrome, 10–11, 65–67, 147
Draw-a-Person test, 203
Dream interpretation, 87–88
Dreams, 87–88, 233–234
DSM-IV, 68–71
Dyscalcula, 128
Dyslexia, 128

Echinacea, 58
Ectomorph, 40
Ego, 86–87
Electroconvulsive shock therapy (ECT),
　73–75
Electroencephalograph (EEG), 233
Electrolytes, 165
Ellis, Albert, 54
Emotional intelligence (EQ), 75–76
Endomorph, 40
Endorphins, 166, 172
Engram, 61
Epilepsy, 76–77, 237
Episodic memory, 139
Erikson, Erik, 77–80

270

Index

Index

About the Author

LUIS A. CORDÓN is Associate Professor and Chairperson, Psychology, Eastern Connecticut State University, Willimantic. He has published in the *Journal of Research and Development in Education* and the *Journal of Educational Psychology*.

HOTSPUR

RITA MAE BROWN

BALLANTINE BOOKS
NEW YORK

A Ballantine Book
Published by The Ballantine Publishing Group

Copyright © 2002 by American Artists, Inc.

Title page illustrations copyright © 2002 by Lee Gildea Jr.

All rights reserved under International and Pan-American Copyright
Conventions. Published in the United States by The Ballantine Publishing
Group, a division of Random House, Inc., New York, and simultaneously in
Canada by Random House of Canada Limited, Toronto.

Ballantine and colophon are registered trademarks of Random House, Inc.

www.ballantinebooks.com

Library of Congress Cataloging-in-Publication Data
is available from the publisher upon request.

ISBN 0-345-42822-6

Manufactured in the United States of America

First Edition: December 2002

2   4   6   8   10   9   7   5   3   1

Dedicated with admiration to
Mrs. Paul D. Summers, Jr., M.F.H.
Her hounds sing her praise.

C H A P T E R 1

Awind devil swirled upward, sending tiny bits of stone
dust glittering in the sunlight.

Even though it was the fourteenth of July, the morning
proved breezy and quite pleasant at sixty-one degrees.

The staff and friends of the Jefferson Hunt were walking
out hounds. Since it was seven-thirty in the morning, "dedicated friends" was perhaps a more accurate term, Sister thought
to herself. The master, Jane Arnold, called Sister by all, walked
behind her pack. The huntsman, Shaker Crown, a medium-build
fellow, strode in front of the hounds.

Two whippers-in, Doug Kinser and Betty Franklin, flanked
either side of the pack, and the dedicated friends, two this
morning, tagged behind the master.

This two-mile walk down a crushed gravel road served to
exercise hounds and to introduce the young entry, those

hounds that would be hunting this fall for the first time, to the ways of the pack. As the summer progressed and the length of the walks became longer, fat melted off the human bodies. People looked healthier, more fit.

It amused Sister that millions of Americans, overweight and overfed, emptied their pockets on one fad diet after another. If they'd only make it a habit to walk out hounds they'd lose the pounds, save their money, and experience the most beautiful time of the day.

On any given morning, Sister saw bluebirds, indigo buntings, goldfinches, cardinals, robins, ravens, and hawks roaring over in search of breakfast—or maybe just a good time.

Rabbits, moles, shrews, even wild little sleek minks rustled in the meadows off the roadside.

Safe in the trees, cicadas, their Winston Churchill eyes surveying all, sang with deafening exuberance.

Clouds of black-and-yellow butterflies swirled up from the cow patties and horse patties dotting the verdant pastures of After All Farm, the glorious estate of Theodora and Edward Bancroft. Gleaming white fences, painted every two years, divided the pastures, and each fence line boasted a lovely coop or stone jump. Theodora, called Tedi, delighted in designing jumps and set them perfectly. Building the jumps seemed to give the wealthy but directionless woman something like a purpose in life.

As the small group walked briskly past the western pastures of After All, three old pensioners lifted their wise heads. Peppermint, the oldest at thirty-four, had taught two generations of Bancrofts to hunt.

From the other side of the pasture he nickered in acknowledgment of the humans and hounds he knew so well. Behind him Domino and Merry Andrew also stopped munching for a moment. In the background a pristine covered bridge crossed over Snake Creek. Tedi had built it in the heat of one of her architectural enthusiasms back in 1981.

"Hello, old man," Sister called, waving to the gray horse.

"Good to see you, too," Peppermint answered before turning to drink deeply from the creek.

"Good horse never forgets the pack or the master," Shaker called over his shoulder.

"Indeed," Betty Franklin agreed with a smile. She was the happiest she'd ever been in her life. She'd lost twenty-five pounds and felt like a teenager again.

Cora, the head bitch, gaily walked in front, and the young entry following tried to imitate their leader. The second-year hounds acted like the sophomores they were. Truly "wise idiots," they at least knew better than to float out of the pack.

As they walked, the hounds kicked up little puffs of gravel dust. Inquisitive grasshoppers flew tantalizingly close to their black moist noses, darting away in the nick of time.

Raleigh, Sister's devoted Doberman, flattened his ears to block out the din of the hounds. He considered himself hunt staff and if a youngster strayed from the group Raleigh pushed him back in before a human could react. Hounds, like humans, thought the better of getting into an argument with a Doberman.

Dr. Walter Lungrun, young, blond, and athletic, was walking next to Bobby Franklin, who was huffing and puffing.

"Goddamn that Betty," Bobby said, cursing his wife loudly. "Told me if I don't do hound walk and lose fifty pounds she's going to divorce me."

"She won't have to divorce you, you'll die first!" Sister called back to him.

"Probably why she wants you on these morning jaunts,

Bobby. She'll inherit your enormous wealth," Walter added, knowing quite well that Bobby and Betty both worked like dogs at Franklin Printing and weren't amassing any great fortune for it.

"You notice I only drag my ass out when I know you're going to be here, Doc. If I grab my chest, you'll know what to do." Bobby winked.

Sister noticed a hound's head come up, drawn by an enticing aroma lifting off the meadows.

"Nellie, settle," Sister quietly said, and Nellie dispelled her brief notion of making a wild break for the rising fox scent.

They walked and chatted for another half mile, then returned home by the route they had come.

At the covered bridge, Shaker noticed Peppermint stretched out by the creekside. Eyes sharp, he turned to face his pack. "Hold up."

The hounds stopped.

"What's up?" Betty asked as she pushed a stray lock of blonde hair off her forehead.

"Walter, go over there and check on Peppermint, will you?" Shaker called back to the physician.

Walter, a former star halfback at Cornell, put one hand on the top rail of the fence and gracefully vaulted over it. He loped to the unmoving horse, who was being watched over by his two old friends.

Walter called to Peppermint. No response. When he reached the aged animal he knelt down and felt Peppermint's neck for a pulse.

"Oh, Pepper, what a good horse you were." He gently patted the dead animal's neck, then rose and recrossed the green meadow back to the waiting group.

He leaned over the fence and simply said, "Gone."

Sister lowered her head for several moments as the news

sank in. She'd known this horse for more than three decades. As sad as she was, Tedi would be devastated.

"Shaker, Bobby, take the hounds back to the kennels," she instructed. "Betty and Walter, if you can spare the time, stay with me. We need to bury this fellow before Tedi comes out and finds him. She loved him so." Sister paused. "A last link with Nola."

"And it is July, he'll blow up fast," Shaker said under his breath. Then he called to the hounds in a singsong voice, "Come along."

The hounds followed after him, though Cora couldn't help a glance over her shoulder at the horse she remembered well.

"Walter, do you mind finding one of Tedi's men? Just ask him to meet us at the bridge with the backhoe. Button his lip. I'll tell Tedi once we've properly buried Peppermint."

Walter jogged across the bridge as Betty and Sister went to the carcass at creek's edge.

Betty knelt down to touch the large shoulder. "What a great one he was. Godspeed, Peppermint. You had a wonderful life."

Sister, with Raleigh at her side, consoled Domino and Merry Andrew before sitting down beside Peppermint. "Jesus, Betty, I'm getting old. I remember Pepper when he was steel gray. He's pure white now." She referred to the fact that gray horses, born dark, lighten in color as they age.

"Remember the time Tedi hit every fence perfectly in the hunter trials? Tedi couldn't find her distance if you gave her measuring tape. But by God, she won the blue ribbon that year. I think it was one of the happiest moments of her life." Betty continued stroking the animal's beautiful gray head. "He did it for her. Pepper didn't much like showing. He liked hunting." Betty smiled, marveling at the capacity of animals to love humans, creatures who so often failed to reciprocate.

"God, I hope we can pull this off before Tedi finds out. I mean, I hope she's not up there in the barn or gardening or something. If she sees the backhoe rumble out of the equipment shed, she'll be curious." Sister plucked a blade of grass, sucking out the sweetness. "Peppermint was the last horse Nola hunted. Tedi is going to be upset."

"That's why you sent Walter—in case the news has to be broken now."

"Yes, I did, didn't I?" Sister grinned, an appealing, girlish grin for a seventy-one-year-old woman, thin as a blade and just as sharp.

"Poor Tedi, not that I wouldn't cry my eyes out if Outlaw died, mind you." Betty referred to her adored and sturdily built horse.

"We all would. Even that asshole Crawford Howard would cry if Czapaka died." Crawford was a rich, blowhard member of the Hunt, and his horse, Czapaka, endured him with only occasional moments of justified rebellion. Sister and Betty had known each other for all of Betty's forty-odd years, so Sister spoke with complete candor to her. Had it been anyone but an old friend she would never have openly criticized Crawford.

"Tedi's such a dear soul." Betty sighed.

"Strange life."

"I don't wish inherited wealth on anyone. It's a real curse," Betty declared. "It's one thing to earn a pile of money, it's another to never work for anything at all."

"I agree. I've known very few people who weren't scalded by it in one way or t'other." She pronounced "another" the old Virginia way.

"Tedi has surely had her share of suffering."

"That she has."

They halted their conversation, rising as a large backhoe

chugged over the hill, down the farm road, then rattled through the covered bridge. Walter stood behind the driver, Jimmy Chirios, an industrious, cheerful young man only two years in the Bancrofts' employ.

Jimmy cut the motor and looked down at Peppermint. "Just like that?"

"A peaceful death." Sister had to shade her eyes to look up at him in the morning sun.

Walter hopped off the equipment. "Jimmy, we can't bury him here. The creek floods wicked bad every couple of years. Higher ground."

Domino and Merry Andrew, having moved away when the backhoe arrived, now returned to stand near their fallen friend.

"This side of the bridge is anchored on high ground. You wouldn't have to drag him but a hundred yards. Did you bring a chain?" Sister inquired.

"Yep." Jimmy handed the thick chain to Walter, who looped it around Peppermint's hind legs, then snapped the heavy hook around another loop of chain on the back of the big yellow machine.

"Slow," Walter ordered as the two women walked up to what they concluded would be the ideal spot above the abutment.

As Peppermint was dragged to his final resting place, Domino, his bay head bowed, and Merry Andrew, curious as always, followed behind, somewhat obscuring the mark Peppermint's body made. Walter unhitched the chain, then unwrapped it from Peppermint. Jimmy started digging.

The rise, just above the bridge abutment, was a good place. Rain had softened the earth two days earlier, and the clawed jaw of the backhoe easily bit into it. Jimmy rapidly dug out a seven-foot-deep trench, then squared the sides, forming a tidy rectangle. As they were all country people, they knew that animals could smell decay under the earth. A good six feet or more for a grave was mandatory or, sure enough, whatever was buried would be resurrected by scavengers. And much as one might have missed the deceased, one did not wish the return of a hoof or a leg.

"Looks good," Walter hollered through hands cupped to his mouth.

But Jimmy decided the side of the grave closest to the bridge needed more tidying.

He lowered the jaws into the earth. A crumble of rich alluvial deposit rolled down into the bottom as he swung the captured earth over the side of the grave.

"Stop!" Sister cried. She astonished them all by leaping into the grave.

"What the hell are you doing?" Betty said as Walter leaned over the grave. Then he, too, jumped right in.

At the bottom edge of the freshly dug hole, Walter and Sister stared at the whitened bones of what looked like an elbow.

"Human?" Sister asked.

"I think so." Walter carefully brushed away the earth until more bone was revealed. Unable to resist, Betty joined them. Jimmy clambered down from the cab of the backhoe and knelt down at the edge of the gaping hole.

"I can't believe this," Betty gasped.

Walter kept brushing. More arm bones. Then a hand. Definitely human.

The long rays of the morning sun crept into the tomb, causing the royal blue of a huge sapphire flanked by two diamonds to glitter in the light.

"The Hapsburg sapphire," Betty whispered.

"Sweet Jesus." Sister's hands shook as she reached to touch the sapphire, then pulled back.

CHAPTER 2

Creamy suds of disinfectant swirled down the large kennel drain as Shaker washed the feed room. The female hounds, called bitches or gyps, drowsy after their exercise and breakfast, lounged on the benches on their side of the kennels. The dog hounds on their side, separate from the girls, did likewise as well as being scattered throughout the runs like so many canine statues.

A few hound ears perked up, then dropped back as Sister Jane and Betty hurried into the kennels.

Shaker turned off the power washer. "Sad job putting old Pepper in the ground." He hung the washer nozzle on a wall hook, then glanced over at his boss and dear friend. "Janie, you look like you've seen a ghost."

Ashen-faced, still a little shaky, she replied, "I have."

The three repaired to Shaker's office next to the kennels.

The open windows let in the breeze carrying the tang of hound scent.

"Here, you'd better sit down." He pulled out his desk chair for Sister. "You, too, Betty." He moved over the spartan extra chair for Betty Franklin, who dropped into it. Betty kept swallowing.

"We have seen a ghost. We have." Tears welled up in Betty's expressive eyes.

Shaker, always a bit awkward in emotional situations but a feeling man nonetheless, patted Betty on the back. "On Hangman's Ridge?" They hadn't walked out that way, but it was the first thing that popped into his mind. The ridge was reputed to have been haunted since Lawrence Pollard had swung from the oak for having masterminded a land speculation deal that had impoverished all who had invested in it in 1702.

Sister shook her silver head. "Nola Bancroft."

He perched his spare frame on the edge of the desk, a flicker of disbelief on his sunburnt features. "What are you talking about?"

Sister closed her eyes, inhaled deeply. "After you took hounds back, Walter got Jimmy to bury Peppermint. We couldn't put him by Snake Creek, so Betty and I thought just above the abutment by the covered bridge would be high enough." She took a deep breath. "Well, Jimmy did a fine job, but I saw bones. I jumped in, Walter after me——"

"Me too," Betty chimed in. "It was an elbow."

"Walter brushed away the earth, and the arm bones appeared and then the hand. The Hapsburg sapphire was still on her finger. . . ."

Raleigh wedged himself tightly next to Sister's leg since he could tell she was upset.

"My God, I don't believe it! After all these years."

"Twenty-one years," Betty added. "Just a pile of whitened bones and that ring. The little metal belt buckle from her dress was there, too. Remember when Paul Ramy kept asking each of us what Nola was wearing the last time we saw her? Well, we'd all just seen her at Sorrel Buruss's party."

"She had on a blue flowered sundress," Sister recalled. "Everyone teased her that she bought the dress because the blue matched her eyes and she sassed back that she bought it because it showed off her cleavage." Sister smiled, remembering the impossibly beautiful younger daughter of Tedi and Edward Bancroft.

Nola had been twenty-four years old when she'd disappeared more than two decades earlier.

"Uh, is she still in the grave?" Shaker lowered his voice.

"I don't know." Betty shifted in her seat. "The sheriff showed up with Gaston Marshall, the coroner. Ben took statements from each of us and told us we could leave."

Ben Sidell was the sheriff. Betty, like many county residents, often called him by his first name.

"What did Gaston do?" Shaker asked.

"He made the sheriff's assistant take pictures and then he got down in the grave and they started cleaning off the dirt. They were very careful. We were excused before they'd finished the job. Maybe there will be clues left."

"What a pity old Sheriff Ramy isn't still alive for this," Betty said.

"I always thought Sheriff Ramy pretty much died the day his son Guy disappeared. His body just kept on for a while longer," Sister added.

Guy Ramy had been courting Nola. The Bancrofts did not consider the sheriff's son a suitable match for their daughter. They offered strong resistance, which only made Guy more attractive to the headstrong Nola. And he wasn't bad-looking to begin with. He disappeared when Nola did, so at first people naturally figured they'd run off to get married without parental blessing. But as days passed, then weeks, no one heard a peep. Even Sybil, Nola's older sister, didn't hear from Nola, and the two sisters were close. Sybil, married but a year to Ken Fawkes, plunged into a depression. In a sense, the whole family did as the weeks passed into months. As Sybil had married beneath her, to use Tedi's phrase, she felt guilty because she thought her marriage had put even more pressure on Nola to marry a Randolph, a Valentine, a Venable, a DeJarnette, names considered suitable in Virginia.

No one ever saw or heard from Nola Bancroft or Guy Ramy again after Saturday, September 5, 1981.

"Walter's still there. As a medical man, Ben asked him to stay. The worst was what to do about telling Tedi. We all agreed she couldn't find her daughter and Peppermint together. The sheriff allowed Jimmy to haul Peppermint up on the ridge and bury him there so Tedi won't have to see that. And he said he wouldn't fetch Tedi and Edward until Nola's body is completely free of its tomb. Well, I guess it isn't a tomb, but you know what I mean. Oh, it's just awful, Shaker."

The thought of Tedi Bancroft viewing the skeletal remains of her beloved daughter made Shaker grimace. "Can't someone else identify her?"

"Actually none of us can. Not even Tedi. We assume it's Nola because of the sapphire. The coroner will have to go by dental records."

"Assuming the skull is there." Betty furrowed her eyebrows.

"Betty," Sister said, looking at her sternly.

"Well, we don't know how she died. Killers do really strange things. I mean, some of them are fascinated with death.

They keep coming back. And who knows but what they might find Guy right there with her. Maybe he killed her and then shot himself."

"He'd never kill Nola. He loved that girl," Shaker said with conviction.

"Furthermore, how could he bury himself?" Sister sensibly added.

"Well, I am shook up. I'm not being very logical. But I can't help it. The sight of that big ring on that bony finger will stay with me forever."

"Yes, me too." Sister sighed, dropping her hand to pet Raleigh's sleek head. "Let's pray that Walter can talk Ben out of fetching Tedi. Edward can come down. Or Ken, or Sybil, or anyone but Tedi. Anyway, I think the only reason Ben would subject them to this is to see if he can jolt something out of them," Sister said shrewdly.

"None of them did it," Betty flatly stated.

"But people suppress things, Betty. Maybe the grisly sight will force out a memory that will help put the pieces of the puzzle together. I don't know about you, but I'm sure I've suppressed plenty in my own life."

"Haven't we all." Betty cracked her knuckles, a nervous gesture.

"You know what my memory of Nola is?" Shaker asked. "I see this beautiful girl just flying her fences on Peppermint. Like that great big old stone wall down there at Duelling Grounds." Shaker mentioned a farm where they hunted. "Everyone takes the low end, but she'd put him right to the four-foot section and sail over, hands forward, eyes up, big smile on her face."

"Girl could ride," Betty agreed as she smiled in remembrance.

In these parts, indeed in most of Virginia, the ability to ride was considered one of the social graces. It had nothing to do with money and a lot to do with talent. Or at least determination, should one lack talent. Nola had it all: talent, determination, and money.

Sybil, a very good rider herself, pitted herself against Nola or rode with her as her partner in hunter pairs at hunter trials and hunter paces, outdoor competitions. They were fun to watch.

Golliwog, a large calico, sauntered into the kennel. She'd been waiting up at the house for Sister to return and she was quite irritated about her delay. Not only was Sister overdue, but Golliwog had artfully arranged a large field mouse on the back porch for Sister's delectation. But the heat was rising, the mouse ripening with it. Golly did not like such unsavory things, although Raleigh did, of course. This was just one more reason that dogs were inferior to cats in Golly's mind.

"*I am sick and tired of waiting for everyone!*" she complained.

"Pipe down, Golly!" Sister ordered the cat, a useless order, of course.

"*We found Nola Bancroft's body,*" Raleigh informed the imperious creature.

Nola had disappeared long before Golly was born—the cat was now in the prime of life—but she had heard odd snippets over the years concerning the Bancroft girl who could have been a movie star. Not that she paid much attention, since she always preferred to be the topic of conversation herself.

"*What, she just popped up somewhere?*"

"*Peppermint died this morning and we found her when Jimmy Chirios dug the grave with the backhoe.*"

As the dog and cat considered the morning's events, Sister stood up. "Well, we've got to do something, but I don't know exactly what."

"Pay a call," Betty suggested.

"Yes, I know that. We've got to let the club members know. She was a member of Jefferson Hunt, after all."

"You're right. I'll get the telephone tree going," Betty said. Shaker pulled the club directory from his long middle desk drawer, handing it to Betty.

"I suggest you don't," he said.

"Why?" Both women stared at him.

"Wait until you talk again to the sheriff. He might not want the news out quite that fast."

"Shaker, this is Jefferson County. Gossip travels faster than light," Sister truthfully stated. "Even now the phones are ringing throughout the county."

"But it shouldn't be on our heads. He's going to want to talk to anyone who remembers Nola, which is anyone in our club over twenty-five, and that's most everyone."

"He's right." Betty handed back the directory.

Sister, usually politically astute, considered the wisdom of Shaker's suggestion and realized she'd been more rattled by the discovery than she'd thought. "Right." She rubbed her temples a moment. "Do you know what keeps running through my mind? It's Peppermint. He loved her. He would do anything for Nola. He carried all the Bancrofts at one time or another, but he loved Nola best of all and now he's led us back to her."

"In death," Betty said, sounding a trifle morbid even to herself.

"Fate." Shaker reached for his old briarwood Dunhill pipe, his father's.

"Aren't death and fate the same thing?" Betty wondered.

"No, ma'am, not by a long shot." Shaker leaned against the desk. "Not by a long shot."

CHAPTER 3

As the last human left the grave site, a tremendous clap of thunder shook the earth.

Inky, a member of the gray fox clan who happened to be black, had been watching the activity at the grave site so intently that she jumped at the thunder. She looked toward the west. Roiling low clouds would be directly overhead in fifteen minutes or less.

Her curiosity, overcome by the weather, gave way to a mad dash for her den, a tidy place two miles west of After All Farm. Inky lived on Sister Jane's place, Roughneck Farm, at the edge of the cornfield, near a mighty old walnut, on high ground above a small tributary feeding into Broad Creek. She lived very well and at one and a half years of age she was a sleek, healthy creature with unusually bright eyes.

The first huge raindrops splattered around her just as she

reached the border of Roughneck Farm. Another few minutes and she'd be home. The sky, dark now, seemed close enough to touch. Sister pulled out onto the farm road in her new red GMC truck. Her headlights caught Inky for a moment, but the fox did not stop to give the older woman the pleasure of her company. She raced for her den, shooting in as thunder rumbled overhead and lightning momentarily turned the sky lavender green.

Inky hated getting wet. She nestled in her sweet-smelling hay bed, which she'd carried home after the last cutting.

Like all foxes, reds and grays, Inky was a highly intelligent, adaptable creature. Part of this adaptability derived from being omnivorous like humans. Whenever that insufferable cat, Golliwog, would fuss at Inky for visiting the kennels where she liked to chat with Diana, a young gyp, Inky would remind her as she left that Golliwog was an obligate carnivore.

This would infuriate Golly, who in retaliation would stir up the hounds. Then Shaker would open the front door of his clapboard cottage and speak to the hounds to quiet them. Golly could be vengeful, but she was smart. Inky had to give her that.

As Inky dried herself she wondered who was in that grave. The human emotions had cast a strong scent that carried up to her. As soon as the storm was over she thought she'd go out again and visit her parents, who lived deeper in the woods near strong-running Broad Creek. Perhaps they would know something. And she wanted to tell her family that Peppermint had passed on. He had loved chatting with his former adversaries, as he'd dubbed the foxes. Peppermint had always had a quaint turn of phrase like the older gentleman he was.

Inky knew that when humans were feeling wretched the shock waves would vibrate over the countryside. Her curiosity was thus more than a mental exercise; it was key to survival.

"Hello, Inky," Sister said, noting the lovely animal racing beside the road.

"I worry that she's getting too tame." Shaker pressed two fingers around the knot of his tie.

Never comfortable in a coat and tie, he was a proper fellow. Given the circumstances, he would not cross the Bancroft threshold unless respectfully dressed. Lean and wiry, Shaker exuded a toughness that belied his kindly nature.

Both Shaker and Sister had hurried to clean up after Betty had hopped into her car. She'd pick up Bobby, fill him in, clean up herself, and meet the master and huntsman at After All.

"The legend of the black fox."

"Bull. We've always had black foxes." He half snorted. "We just don't always see them."

"I know that." She turned the windshield wipers to a higher speed. She wasn't 100 percent familiar with her new truck yet, so she had to fiddle with the stick on the steering column.

"Be nice when you learn to drive this thing."

"Be nice when you learn to treat me with respect."

"Oh la." He half sang. "Janie, none of this bodes well, does it?"

"No, it doesn't. And I know I'm using Inky as an excuse, but you will recall a black fox gave us a hell of a run just before Ray died, and then again before Raymond died." Ray, her son, was killed in a freak harvesting accident in 1974. Her husband, Raymond, died of emphysema in 1991. "And Raymond's grandmother would always rattle on about how her mother swore that in 1860 all they hunted was black foxes."

"Hunted Yankees after that." Shaker, born and bred in Mount Sidney, Virginia, half smiled as he said it.

"Jesus, think we'll ever get over it?"

"The Jews built Pharaoh's pyramids five thousand years

ago and they're still talking about it. The Irish still fuss about Elizabeth the First like she just left the throne. People have to have something to bitch and moan about." He caught his breath for a moment. "If you ask me, people can't do without their tragedies. Makes them feel important."

"You might be right. The Bancrofts aren't like that, thank God. Shaker, I can't exactly fathom it. Not to know where your child is for all those years and then to find out she's been buried on your own property all along. A ring on a bony hand."

"Horrible." Although he wasn't a father, he could sympathize as could most anybody with a heart.

"When I lost Ray, well, you were there. Yes, it was dreadful. Yes, I wanted to die with him. But at least I knew. I could say good-bye. I could grieve. All those years that Tedi and Edward hoped and prayed and then settled into a dull ache of a life. And now, to finally know where Nola is. Where she's been all along . . ."

"I think Tedi knew."

"In her heart—yes, I think she knew Nola was dead the night she went missing. But Edward could never give up."

"Alice Ramy broke bad."

"Wonder who's going to tell her?"

Alice Ramy, the mother of Guy Ramy, turned bitter and disruptive after her son's disappearance. Her only positive outlets seemed to be the prize chickens she bred and her gardens. But even these activities led to frustration. At least once a year her dahlias would be shredded when the prize chickens escaped into her gardens for a feast.

Shaker shifted nervously in his seat as they drove through the majestic wrought-iron gates, the serried spearpoints gilded, of After All Farm's main entrance. "Ben Sidell will tell Alice."

"There are plenty of people who still believe Guy killed her and then disappeared. Some ass would come back from a vacation in Paris and declare, 'Saw Guy Ramy on the Left Bank. He's bald now.' You know perfectly well they never saw a goddamned thing." Sister's knuckles were white on the steering wheel. She, too, was nervous.

"Guy Ramy might have killed someone over Nola, but he would have never killed Nola," Shaker said.

They peered out their windows through the streaming rain. Half the hunt club members were already there. A tightly knit community, the Jefferson Hunt Club supported one another instantly through every crisis—but felt free to gossip about one another with equal alacrity.

A red Mercedes S500 was parked closest to the front walk, trailed by a silver Jaguar, a 1987 Ford pickup, a hunter green Explorer, and a Tahoe. The number of trucks suggested people had walked away from their farm chores to hasten to the Bancrofts'. A Toyota Land Cruiser announced that Ralph Assumptio was there. He was a cousin on his mother's side to Guy Ramy.

Sister had to park halfway down to the barns.

Shaker picked up the golf umbrella resting slantways across his feet. "You stay there. I'll come 'round to your side."

He opened the door and the rain slashed down.

When the arc of the red and yellow umbrella loomed outside, Sister opened her door and stepped down, ducking under cover.

She clutched Shaker's strong forearm. "Well, let's do what we can."

A huge hanging glass lantern, supported by four heavy chains, cast diffuse light into the rainy night. The white columns glistened as did the slate roof of this magnificent Palladian triumph.

The fan window above the oversized black door was handblown glass, as were all the paned windows.

After All, one of the great mansions of the early eighteenth century, had received many visitors in both joy and sorrow.

As they reached the front door, Walter Lungrun opened it before the harried butler could get to it. For a moment, with the light framing his face, Sister felt an odd sense of comfort— something akin to homecoming. She shook off the unexpected feeling, deciding that all her nerve endings were on red alert. Of course she was glad to see him. She'd known Walter, at a distance, since his childhood.

"Sister, thank God you're here." Walter bent down to kiss her cheek. "You, too, Shaker. Tedi and Edward are in the living room. Ken and Sybil, too."

A servant hung their dripping raincoats in the coat closet. They heard Betty and Bobby come through the door as well as other people behind them.

Walter took Sister's hand and led her to the living room, crowded with people. Shaker walked on her other side. People parted for Sister. They usually did.

Tedi sat perched on the edge of her Sheraton sofa, the cost of which alone could buy most Americans a lovely home. When she looked up to see one of her oldest friends and her master, she burst into tears again and stood up, throwing her arms around Sister. "Janie."

Edward, whose eyes also were wet, stood up next to his wife and embraced Sister when Tedi relinquished her. Then Tedi hugged Shaker, and Edward shook his hand.

"Thank you for coming, Shaker."

"Mr. Bancroft, I'm terribly sorry for the circumstances." Shaker, always correct as a hunt servant, addressed Edward, a member, by his surname.

"Yes, yes." Edward's lip began to quiver and Shaker reached for his hand again, holding it in both of his.

"Janie, sit with us." Tedi pulled her down on the sofa.

A servant in livery—the Bancrofts, wonderful though they were, had pretensions—offered refreshments on a tray. Perhaps they weren't pretentious. It was the world into which both had been raised. This was part of life.

"You knew it was Nola." Tedi wiped her eyes.

"The ring." Sister draped her arm around Tedi's thin shoulders.

"Edward went to see. I couldn't go. I just couldn't." Tedi choked, then composed herself. "I don't know how Edward did it."

Sister looked up at the tall man, severely handsome with a full head of closely cropped white hair and a trim military mustache. He greeted guests and shepherded them away from Tedi so she could talk to Sister for a moment. "He's a strong man."

"Guess he had to be." Tedi leaned into Sister. "You can't run a business like his without people trying to tear you into little pieces."

"Tedi, I don't know if something like today's discovery can bring good. But—maybe it can bring peace."

Tedi shook her head. "I don't know. I don't know about peace, but I must find out what happened to my—baby."

A chill touched Sister at the base of her neck just as a blazing bolt of lightning hit close to the house. Sparks flew, pink sparks widened into a halo of fireworks, and then the room went dark.

Ken Fawkes, the Bancrofts' son-in-law, said, "Dad, it must have hit the transformer. I'll crank up the generator."

Ken had fallen into the habit of calling his father-in-law "Dad."

The servants glided into the room, lighting candles, carrying hurricane lamps. Being plunged into darkness was not an uncommon experience in the country.

Sister wondered whether she should tell Tedi what she felt, felt so strongly that it was as if she'd been hit by that bolt of lightning. "Tedi, you *will* find out."

Tedi turned to look directly into her friend's warm eyes. "Yes, I think I will. I don't think I'm going to like it."

Sister kissed her friend again. "So many people want to see you, Tedi. I'll come by tomorrow."

"No, no, let me come to you. I want out of this place."

"Good." Tedi embraced her one more time, holding her tightly, then released her.

Sister nodded to people, shaking hands as she made her way over to Sybil, Nola's older sister. Sybil, an attractive forty-six years old, was red-eyed from crying. The sisters had resembled each other, but in Nola, Sybil's features had found perfection. Sybil's jaw was a trifle too long, her eyes a light blue, whereas Nola's were electric blue just like Tedi's.

Scattered throughout the house were family photographs. If Nola had not been in those photographs your eye would have focused on Sybil, a pretty girl. But Nola was there and you couldn't take your eyes off her.

On a few occasions, Sybil's resentment of her sister would explode. Everyone understood, even Sybil's own peers when they were children. It was damned hard to be outshone by your bratty little sister, and yet Sybil did love her. The two of them could fall into transports of giggles, pulling pranks, riding first flight in the hunt field. Both were good students, both were good with people, and both clung to each other as the children of the very rich often do once they discover they are very rich.

"Sister—" Sybil didn't finish her sentence as the tears came.

Sister took her in her arms. "Be strong. Grab mane. Eyes up." She told her the same thing she used to tell her when Sybil faced a big fence as a small child. And Sybil had been good to Ray Junior. Sister loved her for that. Sybil was a few years older than her son, yet always paid attention to him and rode with him. Both of them could ride like banshees.

Nola, while always friendly to Ray Junior, was too busy conquering men even as a fourteen-year-old to pay much attention to the boy. Nola had discovered her powers early and was determined to use them.

"I will." Sybil sniffed.

Ken joined them. "Thank you for coming." He embraced Sister.

"I'm just so glad you and the children are here."

"We haven't told the children all of it. Only that their Aunt Nola was finally found. What do you tell a ten-year-old and a six-year-old in a situation like this?" Ken shrugged.

"The truth—as gently as you can, because if you don't, someone else will," Sister forthrightly replied. "They're strong."

"Mother wants us to move back into the big house, but we can't. We're staying at Hunter's Rest, but I'll be with Mother every day," Sybil said.

Hunter's Rest, a two-story frame house, was located at the southernmost border of the large estate. It once housed the farm manager.

"If you need to get the children away, drop them with me. The S litter"—Sister mentioned a robust litter of foxhound puppies whelped in mid-May—"need walking out and handling. And you know they're always as welcome as you are."

"Thank you." Ken placed his large hand on her shoulder. Apart from a slight paunch, he was holding his own against middle age. A few strands of gray appeared in his sandy hair and eyebrows. A small bald spot like a tonsure bore testimony to the encroaching years, but one had to be taller than Ken to see it.

Later, as Sister and Shaker drove back through the continuing rain, Shaker loosened his dark blue tie. "Had the damndest feeling."

"What?"

"Well"—he paused, then sheepishly looked over at Sister— "I think I've seen too many TV mysteries."

"What?" she persisted, knowing he'd have to work up to anything that couldn't be proven by logic.

"Well, I felt that somebody in that room knew—knew what had really happened to Nola."

CHAPTER 4

The windshield wipers on the Mercedes S500 flipped at their highest speed as Crawford Howard and his wife, Marty, drove back toward town. They had met and married at the University of Indiana, made a fortune in strip malls, moved to central Virginia, divorced, and remarried, all before age forty-seven. Surprisingly, neither of them appeared exhausted by this process.

"Honey, slow down." Marty involuntarily shrank back as the water from puddles splashed against her side window.

"This machine can handle everything."

"This machine must still obey the laws of physics," she wryly replied. But knowing how he loathed being corrected, she hastened to add, "Edward was glad to see you. I know you've had a long day, but thank you for making the effort."

He slowed to forty-five miles an hour. "That girl must have been something. Those photographs of her all over the house—really something."

The Howards had moved to Jefferson Hunt Country after Nola's disappearance.

"Don't you think people are jumping to conclusions?" Marty's voice rose.

"What? That she was murdered?"

"Right."

"Honey, people don't commit suicide and bury themselves. If they commit suicide, sooner or later the body is found. And she disappeared in September, so you know she would have been found quick enough."

"Betty Franklin said the last time anyone saw her alive was at a party Sorrel Buruss gave for the first day of cubbing. But you're right. It's still hot in September."

"A first-day-of-cubbing party. That's a good idea."

Foxhunting rarely opened with a home run, more like a base hit. Cubbing introduced young entry, those hounds hunting for their first year, to the young foxes, being hunted for the first time. The older hounds and hunt staff helped steady the youngsters, keeping them running between the bases instead of straying off into center field. The young foxes, with a bit of luck, learned the rules from the older foxes, but in case a youngster was caught unawares, many a huntsman would steer his pack away to save the fox. If the pack couldn't be deterred, if scent was just flaming, a whipper-in would do his or her best to warn the fox. If hounds were far enough away, the whipper-in would speak to the fox. The sound of a human voice usually set the fox to running. If hounds were close, the whipper-in would smack his or her boot with their crop. The sound alerted the fox. The whipper-in didn't want to use his or her voice, if possible, in those circumstances, for the hounds would know the human's voice.

No one wanted to kill a fox under any circumstances, whether in cubbing or later in formal hunting. American fox-hunting was purely about the thrill of the chase—the joy of good hound work and hard riding. Unfortunately, most Americans formed their concept of foxhunting from the English traditions. This was a misunderstanding American foxhunters fretted over continually.

"Wonder why we don't have a party like that anymore?"

"Bad organization." Crawford rarely let slip the opportunity to criticize, implicitly suggesting he could do better.

Foxhunting clubs, like all volunteer organizations, rolled with the ebb and flow of individual enthusiasm. One member might host an annual breakfast or party for years, then grow weary of it. The master might suggest that someone else pick up the slack, but she or he couldn't exactly give orders. Orders usually attend paychecks.

"Well, darling, perhaps we should host one. Bring back a lovely tradition."

He braked sharply as a deer shot across the road. "Big rats, that's what they are." Then he returned his attentions to his recently remarried wife. "Wouldn't hurt. And let's do it properly. None of this platter of ham biscuits and a pile of doughnuts. Mumm de Cramant." He mentioned a champagne of which he was particularly fond.

"Cristal." She loved Louis Roederer.

"I'm not serving $270 bottles of champagne. As it is, the de Cramant is running about $70, although if I order a few cases from Sherry-Lehmann I can get the price down. Don't worry, sweetie, they'll be damned impressed when they taste it."

"I'm sure you're right." She noticed the sign to the entrance of the Franklins' small farm swinging wildly in the increasing wind. "Turning into a filthy night. Almost as if Nola's ghost has stirred up the winds."

"Now, Marty." He laughed.

"I believe in spirits. What about the ghosts at Hangman's Ridge? People have seen them, and people who aren't"—she weighed her next word—"flighty."

"Pure bunk. Anyway, this will all blow over, forgive the pun. If there's any evidence left on the body at all, I guarantee you it will lead back to Guy Ramy. It just figures. So the real work is finally tracking him down. You know someone around here knows where he is or helped him get out of town. Boy's father was the sheriff. Man might have been the sheriff, but I'll bet you he protected his own."

"But honey, everyone who knew them said Guy loved her."

"Men kill the women they say they love every day."

"Makes me wonder why the compliment isn't reciprocated."

"Women are more moral."

"Do you really believe that?"

"I do. I know you're my moral superior. And I wished when we were younger I'd asked you about things, deals, people. But I didn't." He shifted in his seat. "Although I still think you can't make an omelette without breaking eggs. Not that I'm condoning smashing people to bits, but competition is the lifeblood of trade, it's the lifeblood of this country. Someone has to win and someone has to lose."

"I guess Nola lost."

"Don't worry over it, Marty. This will get settled now that the body has surfaced. Really. And there's nothing we can do about it except do whatever the Bancrofts need done." He slowed for the entrance to their farm, Beasley Hall. It was named long before they bought it. It was named for Tobias

Beasley, the original holder of the land grant from Charles II. "Wonder if Edward Bancroft has more money than I do? If I'd inherited what he inherited I'd have turned it into four or five billion dollars by now. You know, these people who inherit fortunes let gentlemen investors manage their money. The investments return maybe three percent or four percent a year. I can't understand anyone being that passive about their money."

"I don't know if Edward has as much as you do, honey, but he's not passive. He ran the Bancroft empire until a few years ago when he retired."

"Coffee."

"What, dear?"

"Their money started in coffee, of all the damn things. I'd never put my money in anything where Mother Nature was my partner. But I guess it was a different time. Early nineteenth century. That ancestor of his had to be pretty damned smart."

"Now they just seem damned, don't they?"

"The Bancrofts? No. Marty, don't let this Nola thing affect you. The Bancrofts made whatever adjustment they had to twenty years ago. Sybil married a decent enough fellow, they have two grandchildren, and sure, you never forget a child, but I don't think you can say they're damned." He pulled into the new garage attached to the original main house, an addition Crawford had commissioned.

The new wing was tastefully done and didn't resemble a garage. If anything, it was the tiniest bit overdone.

The garage doors rolled down behind the red Mercedes.

The first building on this site was a log cabin built in 1730 by Tobias Beasley's grandson. Over the years it had been replaced with a handsome brick structure boasting a huge center hall and four-over-four windows. Each generation that made money added to the main house. This meant about every thirty or forty years a ballroom would be built or more bedrooms with sleeping porches. Whatever excited the owners' fancy was added, which gave Beasley Hall true character.

Crawford opened the door into the mudroom and ushered his wife through.

"Thank you, dear."

"Nightcap?"

"How about a small brandy with a rind of orange on the rim."

He laughed at her but made her the drink and brought it upstairs to their huge bedroom, decorated by Colefax and Fowler. Crawford could have hired Parish Hadley out of New York, but no, he had to go to London. The woman who put the English country house look on the map, Nancy Lancaster, whose mother, Lizzie, had been born a Langhorne of Virginia, was influenced by Mirador, the Langhorne seat in Albemarle County. Crawford liked telling people he and Marty were simply bringing her talent back home. Nancy Lancaster, born in 1897, had been dead since 1994, but her decorating firm soldiered on.

The simple truth was that Crawford was a dreadful snob.

They slipped into their scarlet cashmere bathrobes from Woods and Falon, another English firm, and nestled into an overstuffed sofa suffocating with chintz-covered pillows.

Marty enjoyed unwinding on this sofa before retiring to bed. When she and Howard had separated and Crawford's lawyers had played the old starve-the-wife routine, she'd had ample time to consider the financial impact of divorce on middle-aged women. She realized she could not make a graceful transition into the ranks of the *nouveau pauvre.*

"When *is* the first day of cubbing this year?" Crawford put his arm around her.

"September seventh, I think."

"Time to leg up the horses."

"Time to leg up ourselves."

"Oh, honey, you look fantastic. In fact, you look better than when I married you."

"Liar."

"It's true."

"You can thank the business—and yourself."

One of her demands for returning to Crawford, who had been unfaithful to her, was that he buy her the landscaping firm where she had been working to make ends meet. She'd fallen in love with the business. When the owner, Fontaine Buruss, died an untimely death in the hunt field, Crawford made a handsome settlement upon Fontaine's widow. Marty had never been happier now that she was running her own business. She had a real purpose of her own.

He kissed her. "Funny how things work out."

"You look pretty fantastic yourself." She winked at him.

He'd lost his paunch, changed his diet, and worked with a personal trainer. He'd also endured liposuction, but he wasn't advertising that fact.

The rain slashed at the windowpanes, and Crawford's heart beat right along with it. When Marty winked it meant she wanted sex.

Crawford, like most people with business drive, also had a high sex drive. He adored making love on a rainy night, too.

He reached up and rubbed her neck. "Did I tell you how crazy I am about you?"

What he didn't tell her was that he had not given up his long-standing goal of becoming joint-master of the Jefferson Hunt and that that very day he had put his plan in motion. By God, he would be joint-master whether Jane Arnold wanted him or not.

CHAPTER 5

L arge, overhead industrial fans set high in the ceiling
swirled, their flat blades pushing the air downward, and
window fans also sucked in air from the outside and sent it over
the sleeping hounds. This arrangement kept flies out of the
kennels as well.

It was late afternoon, the day after Nola had been discovered. The rains had been followed by the oppressive heat typical of the South.

The Jefferson Hunt Club Kennels, built in the 1950s, were
simple and graceful. The building's exterior was brick, much
too expensive to use now thanks to higher taxes and higher labor costs. The large square structure housed the office, the
feed rooms, and an examination room where a hound could
be isolated for worming or the administration of medicines. At
the back of this was a 150-foot-square courtyard of poured

concrete sloping down to a central drain. The roofline from the main building gracefully extended over one side of this courtyard by about eight feet. Lovely arches much like those underneath the walkways at Monticello supported the overhang.

Open archways bounded the courtyard, again like the ones at Monticello. The dog hounds lived on the right side and the gyps on the left. Each gender had its own runs and kennel houses with raised beds and little porches. The puppies lived at the rear with their own courtyard and special house. A small, separate sick bay nestled under trees far to the right.

The design—simple, functional—was pleasing to the eye. Doorways into the sleeping quarters were covered with tin to discourage chewing. The center sections of the doors to the runs were cut out and covered with a swinging heavy rubber flat, like a large mud flap on a truck, so the hounds could come and go as they wished. Eventually someone would get the bright idea to chew the flap, but a large square of rubber was easier to replace than an entire door.

All sleeping quarters were washed down every morning and evening. Painted cinder-block walls discouraged insect infestation. The floors sloped to central drains.

Many hounds slept in their raised beds, the wash of refreshing air keeping them cool. Others were dreaming in the huge runs, a quarter of an acre each, filled with large deciduous and fir trees. Some hounds felt the only proper response to blistering weather was to dig a crater in the earth, curling up in it. Fans whirling over kennel beds was sissy stuff.

Two such tough characters, Diana and Cora, faced each other from their shallow earthen holes now muddy, which pleased them.

"Hate summer," Cora grumbled.

"It's not so bad," the beautiful tricolor replied, her head resting on the edge of her crater.

"You're still young. Heat gets harder to handle as you get older," Cora said. She had recently turned six.

Six, while not old, gave Cora maturity. She was the strike hound, the hound who pushes forward. She sensed she was slowing just the tiniest bit and knew Dragon, Diana's litter-mate, would jostle for her position.

Cora hated Dragon as much as she loved his sister. Quite a few hounds loathed the talented, arrogant Dragon.

Being the strike hound didn't mean that Cora always found the scent first. But she worked a bit ahead of the rest—not much, perhaps only five yards in front, but she was first and she wanted to keep it that way.

If another hound, say a flanker, a hound on the sides of the pack, found scent before she did, Cora would slow, listening for the anchor hound, the quarterback, to speak. If the anchor said the scent was valid, then Cora would swing around to the new line, racing up front again. She had to be first.

If the anchor hound said nothing, then Cora would wait for a moment to listen for someone else whom she trusted. All she waited for was *"It is good."* If she didn't hear it soon, then she'd push on.

For years the anchor hound of the Jefferson Hunt had been Archie, a great American hound of substance, bone, deep voice, and reliable nose. Archie, a true leader, knew when to knock a smart-ass youngster silly, when to encourage, when to chide the whole pack, and when to urge them on. He died a fighting death against a bear, ensuring his glory among the pack as well as among the humans. They all missed him.

Diana, though young, possessed the brains to be an

anchor hound. No one else exhibited that subtle combination of leadership, drive, nose, and identifiable cry. Cora knew Diana would become a wonderful anchor, but her youth would cause some problems this season. Like a young, talented quarterback, Diana would misread some signals and get blitzed. But the girl had it, she definitely had it.

In fact, the whole D litter, named for the first letter of their mother's name as is the custom among foxhunters, oozed talent. And in Dragon's case, overweening conceit.

Puppies taunted one another, their high-pitched voices carrying over the yards drenched in late-afternoon sunshine.

"Pipe down, you worthless rats," Cora yelled at them.

They quieted.

"Too bad Archie can't see this litter. He was their grandfather. They're beauties." Diana watched one chubby puppy waddle to the chain-link fence between the yards, where he studied a mockingbird staring right back at him from the other side.

"Babblers." Cora laughed. *"They are beautiful. But the proof is in the pudding. We'll see what they can really do two seasons from now. And don't forget"*—she lowered her voice because gossip travels fast in close quarters— *"Sweetpea just isn't brilliant. Steady, God bless her, steady as a rock, but not an A student."*

Sweetpea was the mother of this litter.

"I wish it were the first day of cubbing." Diana sighed.

"Don't we all. I don't mind the walking out. Really. The exercise is good, and each week the walks get longer. You know next week we'll start with the horses again, which I enjoy, but still—not the same."

"Heard the boys in the pasture yesterday." Diana meant the horses. *"They're excited about starting back to work so long as Sister, Shaker, and Doug go out early, really early."* Diana sniffed the air. A familiar light odor announced the presence of Golly grandly

picking her way through the freshly mowed grass toward the outdoor run.

Diana rose, shaking the dirt off.

Cora, too, smelled Golly. *"Insufferable shit."*

Diana laughed. *"Cora, you're crabby today."*

"It's the heat. But that doesn't change the fact that that cat is a holy horror." Cora curled farther into her cool mud crater. She wasn't going to talk to the calico.

Golly reached the chain-link fence. *"Good afternoon, Diana. Your nose is dirty."*

Diana sat down at the chain-link fence. *"Keeps the bugs off."*

"I wouldn't know. I don't get bugs."

"Liar," Cora called out.

"Tick hotel," Golly fired right back.

"Flea bait. You hallucinate. I've seen you chase the ghosts of fleas," Cora replied, giggling.

"I have never hallucinated in my life, Cora. And you can't get my goat, ha," she said, *"because you're a lower life-form and I'm not letting you needle me."*

"Oh, if you aren't hallucinating, then what are you doing when you, for no reason, leap straight into the air, twist around, race to a tree, climb up, drop down, and do it all over again? You're mental."

"Spoken like the unimaginative canine you are." Golly raised her chin, half closing her eyes. *"I'm being visited by The Muse on those occasions."*

"I'm going to throw up," Cora said, and made a gagging sound.

"Worms!" Golly triumphantly decreed.

Diana, thoroughly enjoying the hostilities, said, *"Just got wormed Monday."*

"Well, I walked down here in the heat of the day to give you girls

some news, but since you're insulting me I think I'll go hiss at the puppies, teach them who's boss around here."

"You can tell me." Diana lowered her voice and her head, her dirt-encrusted nose touching the fence.

"You're a sensible girl," the cat replied.

In truth, Diana was sensible and also quite sweet. She loved everybody.

Cora, upright now, walked over. *"Well?"*

"Who said I was talking to you?" Golly opened her eyes wide.

"Oh come on, Golliwog, you know we're dying to hear it," Cora coaxed, buttering her up.

The luxurious calico leaned forward, her nose on the chain-link fence now. *"It was Nola. The family dentist identified her not an hour ago."*

Cora thought for a moment. *"This will stir up a hornet's nest."*

"If only we had known her . . . we hear and smell things." Diana frowned. *"We might have been able to help find out something useful."*

"The last hound that knew Nola Bancroft would have been Archie's grandmother. She lived to be eighteen, you know," Cora said. *"It was a long, long time ago."*

"You'd think if any of us had known about the murder, or if any of the horses over at After All Farm knew, they would have told. We'd know. We pass those things down," Diana said.

"Undomesticated." Cora meant that undomesticated animals might have witnessed something at the time.

"Who lives that long?" Diana wondered.

"Turtles. That snapping turtle at After All Farm, the huge one in the back pond, he's got to be forty years old, I swear it," Cora said.

"Amphibians aren't terribly smart, you know. Their brain moves at about the same speed they do," Golly said with a laugh. Then she thought again. *"But they do remember everything."*

"*How old is Athena?*" Diana asked, thinking of the great horned owl. "*They live a long time, don't they?*"

"*Don't know,*" the cat and hound said in unison.

Diana lay down, her head on her paws, her face now level with Golly's face, almost. "*Why does it matter? To us, I mean?*"

"*Because it really will stir up a hornet's nest, Diana. People start buzzing. Old dirt will get turned over, and I promise you, ladies, I promise you, this will all come back to the Jefferson Hunt Club. Sooner or later, everything in this part of the world does,*" Cora said.

"*Think Sister knows that?*" Diana asked. She loved Sister.

"*She knows. Sister has lived almost six hound lifetimes. Think of what she knows,*" Cora said, shaking her head in wonder.

"*Well, exactly how do you think this will affect us? Will people not pay their dues or something like that?*" Diana asked.

"*No. People drop out when it's a bad season. No hunt club has control over the weather, but people act as though they do, the fair-weather hunters, I mean.*" Cora observed human behavior closely. "*Or when there's a club blowup, which happens about every seven years. Archie always said humans do things in seven-year cycles. They just don't recognize it.*"

"*Crawford Howard.*" Golly curled her upper lip as she said his name.

"*Up to his old tricks?*" Cora snapped at a low-flying dragonfly.

"*Cat intuition.*" Golly smiled. "*I have an idea. Whatever happened to Nola in 1981 was well done, if you will. When you're hunting you all go places humans don't. Sometimes even Shaker can't keep up with you when territory's rough. You might find something or smell something out there that could help solve this mess. After all, the best noses in the world are*"—she paused for effect—"*bloodhounds, but you all are second.*"

"*Second to none!*" Cora's voice rose, which caused a few sleepers to open one eye and grumble.

Humans ranked the noses of bloodhounds first, followed by bassets second and foxhounds third, with all other canines following. Foxhounds thought this an outrage. Of course they were best. Besides, who in the world could hunt behind a bloodhound? The poor horse would die of boredom. This was a pure article of foxhound faith.

"This has to do with hunting? Is that what you're really thinking, Golly?" Diana noticed a few of the boys in the kennel were quarreling over a stick. How they had the energy to even growl in this heat mystified her. One of the troublemakers, of course, was her brother, Dragon.

"Yes, think about it. Cubbing starts September seventh. It's the end of July. Stuff happens when you're hunting. Everything speeds up. People reveal themselves out there."

"We sure hear them scream for Jesus." Diana giggled as she recalled a few of the oaths elicited by a stiff fence.

"I have never figured that out. The horse jumps the fence, not them," Cora said, laughing.

"Oh, but that's just it, Cora. Sometimes the human takes the fence and the horse doesn't."

They all laughed at that.

"We'll keep our nose to the ground," Cora promised.

"I have the strangest feeling that Guy Ramy will be coming back." Golly lowered her voice again. *"More cat intuition."*

In a way, Golly was right.

CHAPTER 6

The Hapsburg sapphire glittered on the small glass-topped table. Outside, the long summer twilight cloaked the grand old trees surrounding Roughneck Farm, and scarlet tendrils of sunset seemed to ensnare the wisteria that climbed all over the back porch. The rose and gold light reflected off the windowpanes of the neat gardening shed, casting intricate designs across the emerald lawn.

Tedi and Sister sat on the screened-in back porch. The humidity was particularly oppressive this evening. Sister drank dark hot tea while Tedi nursed a martini as well as a glass of iced green tea. The mercury was dropping with evening's approach. The humidity seemed determined to hang on. Sister believed drinking a hot drink on a hot day kept you healthier. No one else could stand anything hot.

Raleigh and Golliwog were curled up together in Raleigh's

Black Watch plaid dog bed. Rooster, Peter Wheeler's lovely harrier, was stretched out in his own bed, covered in the Wallace tartan, next to Raleigh. Peter, an ex-lover of Sister's, had bequeathed his handsome hound to her and his entire estate to the Jefferson Hunt to be administered solely by the master—not the Board of Directors. Peter's eight decades on this earth had taught him a benign dictatorship was infinitely preferable to democracy. He died peacefully last year, a quiet end to a productive life.

Both Sister and Tedi now knew Nola had not died peacefully, a fact they were currently grappling with.

The animals listened intently, even Golly, who under normal circumstances would have told Raleigh how lucky he was to have her in his special porch bed.

"I knew. I always knew. So did you," Tedi said sadly.

Sister heard a squirrel clamber up the wisteria on her way to her nest in the attic. "We hoped. We always hoped."

"I'm done crying. I know, Janie, that I can be all over the map, as you say." She held up her hand to quell the protest. "I am a little different. I was never able to think the way you do. You think in sequences, you see patterns. Edward's like that. I don't. I gather it all up in one big basket, then dump it on the table and start sorting. But I eventually find what I'm looking for even if I drive everyone crazy doing it. It's just the way my mind works."

"You are an original," Sister said, smiling. "I'm lucky to know you."

"Do you realize we've known each other all our lives? But it seems like a split second. I don't understand it. We're seventy-one years old and I don't feel old, I don't act old, at least I don't think I do. I don't know where the years are. Are they hiding in my pocket? Are they wherever Nola is? What happened?"

Sister shrugged. "Wherever they are we sure packed a lot into them." She sipped her tea.

"Yes, we did." Tedi inhaled, her bright blue eyes flickering for a moment. "I'm not avoiding the subject."

"I didn't think you were."

"I know Nola was murdered. I didn't need the dental chart to prove those bones were Nola's any more than I needed Ben Sidell to tell me her skull had been crushed. A blunt instrument, he said, or a large rock. They aren't going to find the answers to this under a microscope, it's been too long. Too long."

"Well, he has to go by the book. Otherwise he won't stay sheriff for long."

"I know that. I just want to know who killed her. I still think it was Guy Ramy. Dog in a manger. I can't have her, so no one else can have her."

"But Nola was perfectly capable of running off with Guy and he was madly in love with her."

"They all were. And she wouldn't have run off with Guy. Headstrong as she was, Janie, Nola loved money. I think she might have allowed herself a flaming affair. And enjoy it all the more knowing I did not approve nor did her father. But marry Guy?" She shook her head. "No."

"I think she would."

"Why?"

"She knew in time you and Edward would forgive her. You'd have made a settlement on her with the appearance of the first grandchild. After all, you acquiesced to Ken in time."

A silence followed this.

"Maybe."

"No maybe about it. Nola could play her father like a harp,

and eventually you'd have given in as well. So long as she was happy."

"He wouldn't have made her happy." Tedi's voice dropped a quarter of an octave.

"Tedi, there's ripe disagreement on that subject. People started talking about it in 1980, when Nola and Guy first fell in love. Opening Hunt. You could feel the electricity."

"Odd. They'd known each other all their lives."

"Not so odd. He went away to college, graduated, put in two years in the service. She hadn't seen him, hardly, for six years."

"I don't understand it."

"No one does. That's why love is love." Sister smiled. "Freshen your drink?"

"I'll do it." Tedi rose, walking to the small bar in the pantry just off the kitchen, the wide, uneven heart pine planks creaking underfoot.

A larger bar, more elaborate, still stood ready between the living room and the dining room. Raymond had loved to throw big parties. Sister had gotten out of the habit after his death in 1991; she figured hunting was her form of throwing a big party. Although she did always have the Opening Hunt from her farm, with a huge breakfast following at the house. Raymond and Ray both had gloried in these occasions. She rather more endured them and hoped she was a gracious hostess. The glitter on the table held her eye. Two diamonds of two karats each flanked the eleven-karat sapphire and picked up all available light, throwing it back on the large square-cut blue stone. Sapphires are usually too muddy or too pale. This one was a perfect royal blue—like a strip of startling water in the Caribbean.

Tedi called from the pantry, "You could pour me more tea, please."

Sister poured tea from a graceful cut-glass pitcher, ice cubes tinkling inside, into Tedi's frosted glass.

Tedi rejoined her. "Are you surprised I'm not crying? I'm not on the floor frothing at the mouth? It's not that I don't care. I do. I care passionately, but I don't have one tear left in my body. And I don't trust my emotions."

"What do you mean?"

"When Nola disappeared I went to pieces. There's really no other way to put it. Fragments of Tedi Prescott"—she used her maiden name—"were scattered from here to Washington and back. I wore out the road driving up there to the FBI. I just knew Paul Ramy wasn't up to the task. Especially when Guy went missing. I was a total wreck. I regret that."

"Honey, any mother would have been torn to shreds inside."

"Yes, but I missed things. If I could have kept my wits about me, especially in those early days, I believe I might have picked up information, clues, nuances. I didn't. All I felt was pain. I believe we were very close to the killer, to finding out who the killer was, and he slipped through our fingers to land God knows where."

"We were all distraught."

"Which works to a killer's advantage."

"Can you go over it again? Will it upset you?"

"No. I mean, I have been over it. I last saw Nola at Sorrel Buruss's party. I think that's the last time any of us saw her alive. We'd patched things up in the stable before hunting that day. She apologized and so did I. Had a whopping fight the night before over Guy. Anyway, she was in high spirits, I was in neutral spirits. Edward was grumpy but putting a good face on it since we were at Sorrel's. Fontaine was an ass, as usual." She mentioned the handsome husband of Sorrel. "Since Nola wouldn't go to bed with him, he thought Sybil might be honored at his attentions. She slapped him square in the face. Sorrel, accustomed to his outrages, simply flipped him an ice cube to hold to his face. Nola laughed and laughed. Fontaine's face grew redder and redder. I was furious when I saw Fontaine pressure Sybil. She's a bit retiring and perhaps too anxious to please. I remember being very proud of her that she stopped that insufferable womanizer. Do you remember?"

"I do. And Peter Wheeler made a toast to Sybil. Let's see, 'Here's to Sybil, beloved of Apollo. Let her be an example to all women.'"

"Everyone was pretty well lubricated except you. I used to wish you'd drink with us, and now I'm glad you never did. You were smarter than all of us, and you look better for it, too. Ah well, then." Tedi sipped some martini, chased it with green tea. "Nola left without saying good-bye. The last time I saw her."

Sister raised her index finger. "I overheard Sybil saying that she and Ken would meet Nola at the C&O downstairs. Some band was playing they wanted to hear. But I was talking to everyone and I can't say I was paying particular attention to Nola."

The C&O was and remained a popular restaurant and nightspot over in Albemarle County.

"And I didn't know until the next morning that Nola never showed up. It wasn't that unusual for her to say she'd be somewhere and not show. Nola was always open to a better offer, her words." Tedi's memories, bittersweet, haunted her. "I didn't know until I saw Sybil at church. I was furious that Nola had stayed out all night but, well, it wasn't the first time. I didn't start to worry until Sunday supper."

Leaning back in her chair, Sister glanced outside at the sky, darkening from turquoise to cobalt, then back at Tedi.

"Here's what I think, knowing what we now know. Nola was killed sometime between seven in the evening and early the next morning. You and Edward were building the covered bridge. The earth was still soft around it, remember? She had to have been killed in that time frame, because people don't go burying their victims in broad daylight. Whoever killed her had to have known about the bridge work. That was a drought summer. The earth was hard as rock. Thanks to the bulldozers, the embankment and the base for the bridge weren't packed tight yet. You were just putting the roof on the bridge. So whoever killed Nola knew that."

"That's right," Tedi whispered.

"And we'd hunted through there Saturday morning. I've checked my hunt records." Sister, like many masters, kept a detailed hunt diary. "We had forty-one people the first day of cubbing."

"Everyone in the county knew about the bridge work," Tedi said, a wave of hopelessness washing over her. She fought it off. "A lot of people knew, anyway." Tedi reached for the ring. "I should have never given this ring to Nola. For her it was the Hapless sapphire, just as it was for its first owner."

"Old sorrows," Sister said.

"It was made for the Empress of the Austro-Hungarian Empire, Elizabeth. She had dark hair, was a wonderful, wonderful horsewoman like Nola. Loved foxhunting. Rented hunting boxes in England and flew her fences. But hers was not a happy life. Her son committed suicide, and she was assassinated. I often wonder, if she'd lived, would Franz Josef have signed the Declaration of War of 1918?"

As a foxhunter, Sister had always found the empress's story irresistible. "As I recall, the Bancrofts bought this right after the First World War," she said. "Nolan couldn't have worried too much about the history of the stone if he gave it to his wife. She lived a long, happy life." Nolan was Edward's grandfather, who had lived through the terrifying action at Belleau Wood during the Great War.

Tedi held the ring up to the light; bits of rainbow struck off the diamonds, little dots splashing the walls. She slipped the ring on the middle finger of her left hand. "This was on my baby's finger when she died. Now I'm wearing it. Every time I look at it I'll remember her laughter. I'll remember how much I loved her. I've not spent one day that I haven't missed her, felt that ache. It's kind of like my tongue going back to the site of a missing tooth. I swore I would find out what happened to her but never did. Now—this. Sister, I will find Nola's killer even if it kills me."

"That makes two of us."

CHAPTER 7

Jesus Christ, Doug, watch what you're doing." Shaker rubbed the back of his elbow where a heavy oak board had smacked him from behind.

"Sorry," the handsome young man apologized. "It's this heat. I can't think today."

Sticky, clammy humidity added to the discomfort this Monday, July twenty-second.

Shaker put down his hammer, tilting his head to direct Doug's attention across the road.

Doug followed Shaker's eyes. Wearing a torn tank top and equally torn jeans, an old red bandanna tied around her forehead, Sister toiled on the other side of the dirt farm road building a new coop, a jump resembling a chicken coop, with Walter Lungrun's help.

The old hunt club truck, Peter Wheeler's 1974 Chevy with the 454 engine, was parked off to the side of the road.

"Can't slow down," Doug pretended to whisper, "she'll cuss us."

"I heard that."

"I thought you were working, not eavesdropping," Shaker said.

"Women can do two or three things at the same time. Unlike men," Sister said, laughing.

"Doc, are you going to let her get away with that kind of abuse?" Shaker looked to the blond doctor for help.

"I suggest you call the state employment commission and register a complaint of sexism," Walter solemnly intoned.

"Oh, do make it a complaint of sexual assault. At my age, I'll be a heroine."

They all laughed at that and decided spontaneously to take a break and sit under a huge chestnut tree.

This particular tree was much studied by Virginia Tech students motoring up from Blacksburg, as it was one of the few original chestnuts to survive the horrible blight that almost entirely killed this most beautiful of species. The disease had started in New York State in 1904, spread west to Michigan, north to the border, and south to Alabama. Within a few decades most every native American chestnut, many over one hundred feet high, was dead.

This tree had survived because it was alone.

They were working at Foxglove Farm, a tidy farm north of Sister's farm. You could see the long, flat top of Hangman's Ridge to the south from high spots on Foxglove.

The staff and dedicated members of a hunt club worked harder during the summers than during hunt season. Puppies were whelped. Young entry had to be taught their lessons.

Foxes would be carefully watched, wormer and other medicines put out for them to ensure their health. Seasoned hounds might need a few reminders of their tasks. The hunt horses would be turned out for vacation time. Young horses, called green, would be trained to see if they could become staff horses, a harder task than being a field hunter. Neighboring landowners would be visited, always a pleasure. Old jumps would be repaired or replaced, and new jumps would be built in new territory to be opened if the club was lucky enough to secure new territory.

Foxglove had been part of the Jefferson Hunt territory from the late nineteenth century, when a group of farmer friends had merged their small packs of hounds together into one communal pack. Many of these men had been veterans of the War Between the States. Their sons and grandsons were destined to be shipped overseas to the horrors of the First World War.

Out of this raggle-taggle mess of hounds, a systematic breeding program emerged under the visionary second master, Major H. H. Joubert, called Double H by all. He blended his tough local Bywaters hounds from northern Virginia with a little Skinker blood from Orange County Hunt. Then he folded in a lacing of English blood. Whether by guess or by God, Double H's system worked. He was a smart master, he bred for the territory, and he studied other packs of hounds, ever eager to improve his pack and his methods.

Hound men had been bragging about their animals since the early seventeenth century and a few very wealthy colonists imported hounds from England, products of a line that could be traced to a single source.

In 1670, the Duke of Buckingham fell from favor at Charles II's court. In his disgrace, he retired to North Riding in

Yorkshire and established a pack of hounds solely devoted to hunt fox. If the vigorous, robust duke offended His Majesty the King, he pleased subsequent generations of foxhunters, all of whom owe him a debt. Until Buckingham's time, packs hunted stag, otter, and hare somewhat indiscriminately.

The Duke of Buckingham, a fashionable man as most Buckinghams were and still are, prompted his contemporaries Lord Monmouth and Lord Grey to specialize in foxhunting down in Sussex. These gentlemen began to study their quarry and to consider, intelligently, the best type of hound to hunt such a wily foe.

Thomas, Sixth Lord Fairfax, born in 1693, drew inspiration from this older generation of Englishmen. He lived a long life, dying in 1781, and he kept good records concerning his hounds. Lord Fairfax also had the wit to repair to Virginia in 1748, where he had been granted an estate of 5 million acres— the Northern Neck. The entire Northern Neck between the Potomac and Rappahannock Rivers was his backyard. And he brought his passion for foxhounds with him. Young George Washington hunted with Fairfax, his cousin Col. William Fairfax, and the Colonel's son, George William Fairfax. When George William Fairfax married the enchanting Sally Fairfax, young Washington fell in love with her, an unrequited love. But foxhunting repaid his passion by giving Washington a lifetime of pleasure.

Then, as now, foxhunting imparted a certain social cachet, and men eager to rise found a good pack of hounds was one way to do so. Ripe arguments continually erupted about who had the best hounds. Some argued for the French Bleu hound; others said the large Kerry beagle was best for the New World. The black and tan had many admirers, and any white hound was always claimed to go back to the medieval kennels of King Louis of France.

Out of this mix came an American hound much like the American human: tough, quick, filled with remarkable drive to succeed. The American hound was of lighter weight than his English and French brothers. His clear voice could be heard in the virgin forests covering Virginia and Maryland even if he couldn't be seen, and this remains a prime virtue of the American hound.

The Revolutionary War slowed down the remarkable progress that had been made up to that point. After 1781, foxhunters returned to their passion—a passion undimmed even at the dawn of the twenty-first century.

When Sister took over as the fifth master in the hunt's history she was grateful that she inherited a great pack and she didn't have to start from scratch. She knew her hound history. She simply had to be reasonably intelligent so as not to screw up Double H's original plan.

The home fixtures—Roughneck Farm, Foxglove, Mill Ruins, After All, and Beveridge Hundred—nourished the diverse creatures who had been living there since before the white man settled in Virginia in 1607. Decent soil, a wealth of underground and overground water, and the protection of the Blue Ridge Mountains a few miles west conspired to make this a kind of heaven on earth.

Not even a hot, muggy, buggy day like today diminished the glory of the place. Each and every resident believed that she or he lived in God's country. To make it even sweeter, most of them liked one another. And those few who qualified as flaming assholes were appreciated for providing ripe comment and amusement for the others.

As Sister's mother used to say, "Nobody's worthless. They can always serve as a horrible example."

One such specimen was just puttering down the road.

Alice Ramy stopped her Isuzu truck with a lurch. The four workers sitting under the chestnut tree looked up, composing their features so as not to look discomfited at the lady's arrival.

Alice's unhappiness seeped through every pore, marring her pleasant features.

"Sister, if you or your hounds come near my chickens I am taking out a warrant!"

Alice delivered this message at least twice a year. It was usually the pretext for something else.

"Now Alice, my hounds have never so much as glanced at your fine chickens."

"No, but that damned dog of Peter Wheeler's killed three of them. Dog should have followed Peter to the grave."

Rooster, Peter's harrier, had chased Aunt Netty, an especially fast and sneaky fox, into and then out of Alice's chicken pen. But poor Rooster—the pen door slammed shut and he was stuck with the corpses of two Australorp chickens. Netty, a small fox, dragged off the other one. No easy task since the beautiful black chickens were quite plump.

"Hello, Mrs. Ramy." Shaker smiled.

"Mrs. Ramy." Doug touched his head with his forefinger in greeting.

Doug, skin color that of coffee with cream, was experimenting with long, thick sideburns.

"Alice, good to see you," Walter lied convincingly.

"Hmmph." Alice's reply sounded like a balloon deflating.

"You know, Alice, we're building coops here. We could build one for you." Sister's eyes brightened.

"Ha! Don't you dare set one foot on my land."

"How about a hoof?" Sister felt mischievous.

"Never."

"Well, Alice, I know you've lost more chickens and I know Peter's harrier hasn't been off my farm. Now just what or who do you think is dispatching your chickens?"

Alice generally ignored what she didn't wish to hear, and she did so now. Unbeknownst to her, Aunt Netty was sauntering through the hayfield at that very moment. When she heard Alice's strident voice she stopped to listen.

Aunt Netty thought Alice a pluperfect fool because she shut her chicken yard gate but she never poured concrete along the edges of the pen. Digging under was a cinch. Netty considered the Ramy residence one big supermarket.

Strolling down the fence line from the opposite direction was Comet, a gray fox, Inky's brother. He, too, stopped when he caught a whiff of the nearby humans.

"You'll say anything to hunt!" Alice curled her lip, heavily impacted with hot pink lipstick.

"Of course, Alice, I'm a master." Sister laughed, but good-naturedly.

She'd known Alice most of her life and while she had never really liked the woman, she'd grown accustomed to her.

Alice put her hands on her rounded hips. "I know what you all are thinking. I know what everyone is thinking. You think Guy killed Nola. He didn't."

"I don't think that for a minute, Alice. Sit down here on the grass with us and have a Co-Cola." Sister reached into the cooler and handed an ice-cold can to Alice, who accepted the Coke but not the seat.

Aunt Netty's ears swept forward when she heard the pop of the can's pull tab. She liked sweets, considering Coke a sweet. She wondered if she could open the cooler when the humans returned to their coops. Might even be doughnuts or brownies in that cooler. Wouldn't hurt to look.

"Well, a lot of people did." Alice's voice softened. "But you didn't. I remember, you didn't."

A slight breeze rolled down over the mountainside, causing the leaves to sway. The old chestnut tree was so huge, Alice was sheltered in its shade even standing yards away from the workers.

Walter spoke in his most soothing baritone, which could be hypnotic. "Mrs. Ramy, finding Nola has shocked everyone. With the advancements of forensic science, we might learn more now."

"What good does it do?" Alice betrayed more anguish than she wanted.

"I don't know." Sister stood up and put her arm around Alice's shoulder, patting her. "Maybe it will bring peace to Tedi and Edward."

"Well, it won't bring peace to me. No one will believe me unless Guy is found. People think he's in"—she shook her head—"Berlin or Quito or"—her tone darkened—"in this county I hear everything. And I know plenty of people think Paul covered up for Guy. If Guy had killed her, Paul would have brought him in. His own son." Alice finally decided to sit down.

"I believe he would," Sister replied.

"Has Ben Sidell visited you?" Walter asked.

"Yes. Impertinent. Ohio." She uttered "Ohio" as if it were a communicable disease.

"Good farms there." Sister wished she could think of something to say to make Alice feel better and to go away.

"If they're so damned good, then let those people go back to them. He accused me of covering for my son. Oh, not in so many words, but that's what he meant. I should have knocked him down." She drank her Coke in five big gulps.

Comet crouched down, slinking through the hay, and nearly bumped right into Aunt Netty.

He giggled.

"Hush." Aunt Netty glared at him.

Comet did stop giggling, but he still had a silly grin on his face. Reds thought they were superior to grays. Comet, a gray, couldn't have cared less but he did respect Aunt Netty. Her speed and tricks were legendary among foxes.

"He's been calling on all of us, even people who were children back in '81," Sister said.

"I don't know any more today than I did that September. I never saw Guy again after that Saturday. Never." She breathed in deeply. "Why can't the past stay in the past?"

"Never does," Sister simply said.

"You lost a son and a husband. We're both all alone." Alice blurted this out. "Nobody cares what happens to old women."

"Now, now, Mrs. Ramy, people do care. They do." Walter was gallant. "And raking up the past, well, it sets teeth on edge. Don't worry about what people say. They love to talk, don't they? And the sillier they are, the more they gossip. And furthermore, Mrs. Ramy, you don't look your age. Don't call yourself an old lady." His voice conveyed sympathy and warmth.

"Damn right!" Alice stood up, brushed off the back of her khaki Bermuda shorts. "You know, Jane Arnold, I could never for the life of me imagine why you'd want to be master of the hunt. Too much work and too much danger. But now I know why you do it." She walked away a step. "You're surrounded by such handsome men." With that she climbed over the fence and drove off.

Shaker ran his hand through his auburn curls. "Her elevator doesn't go all the way to the top."

"I'd better call on her in a day or two," Sister said.

"Why?" Doug asked, feeling that Sister had been kind enough.

"Because she's alone."

"She brought it on herself, poor thing," Walter quietly said, and without rancor.

"We all pretty much make the bed we lie in. Or is it lay in?" Sister held up her hand. "Isn't grammar a bitch? Anyway, she is a neighbor. This is awful for her, too. And who knows, maybe I'll get us the right to pass through her farm."

"Spoken like a true master," Walter said, laughing as he headed back to the coop.

The two coops faced each other from opposite sides of the dirt farm road. During a hunt it was great fun to jump one, canter across the road, and sail over the other. However, some horses would jump out of the hayfield, their hooves would touch the dirt road, and they'd suck back. If the rider didn't squeeze hard with his or her legs, the horse might refuse the next coop, which meant horses behind would stack up with dolorous results.

Some would fuss because they were ready to jump and the nervous humans messed up their rhythm. Others would think to themselves that this must be quite a scary situation if Old Paint up front had chickened out.

Sister, who also being field master led the field, could never resist slowing a bit to look over her shoulder to see who made it and who didn't. The results would provoke a stream of laughter back in the tack room or in the kennel as she, Shaker, and Doug finished up the chores of the day. Not that the master herself hadn't supplied laughter and comment over the years. That's part of the appeal of foxhunting. Sooner or later, you'll make a spectacle of yourself.

As the humans returned to their task, Aunt Netty and Comet crept over to the cooler. Netty used her nose to pop the lid right up. Both foxes peered into the ice-filled container.

"*No brownies,*" Aunt Netty mourned.

"*Pack of Nabs.*" Comet spied the little pack of orange crackers beloved by Southerners and loathed by everyone else.

"*What's wrong with people?*" Aunt Netty moaned. "*This should be full of sandwiches, brownies, chocolate chip cookies!*"

"*Lazy. They're getting lazy as sin,*" the young gray concurred with her negative assessment.

"*I don't know what this world is coming to. Why, there used to be a time, young one, when those two-legged idiots would charge off on the hunt, we'd send someone to keep them busy, while the rest of us would raid their trailers. Hamper baskets full of ham biscuits, corn bread, cinnamon buns, fried chicken.*"

"*Aren't things still like that when they have tailgates?*" Comet inquired.

"*Sometimes. But, you see, women work now. In the old days more stayed home, so the food was better. That's my analysis of the situation. Actually it's my husband's, who as you know is inclined to theorize.*" She eyed the pack of Nabs. "*I'm not eating those things.*"

"*I will.*" Comet reached in and flipped out the cellophane-wrapped crackers.

Walter, nailing the last board in place, a top board over the peak of the coop, looked up. He whispered, "Tallyho."

Sister stopped and turned to look. "Aha. Aunt Netty. That gray with her is out of last year's litter on my farm."

"*They see us.*" Comet picked up the crackers.

"*Let them look all they want. Can't very well chase us. I'm telling you, a praying mantis can run faster than a human being. My God they are slow. Makes you wonder how they survived."* She slapped the cracker pack out of Comet's mouth. *"Open that pack and eat it. Give them a show."*

"Okay." Comet tore open the crackers and gobbled them down.

"Aunt Netty, I know that's you." Sister shook her finger at the red fox.

"So?" Aunt Netty laughed.

"I'm going to chase you this fall," Sister promised.

Shaker and Doug stopped work to watch the two foxes.

"Reds and grays don't much fraternize, means the game's good. Plenty for them to eat, so they might as well be friends," Shaker noted.

"You can chase me until the Second Coming. You will never catch me, Sister Jane," Netty taunted.

Comet swallowed the last of the Nabs. *"Jeez, these things are salty. And I can't open a can."*

"Me neither. Put an ice cube in your mouth and let it melt. That will help. Now you see what I mean—a cheap old pack of Nabs when it could have been fried chicken. Just terrible. Standards have fallen."

Comet did as he was told.

"I'm going closer. Give them a thrill."

Comet couldn't talk because he had an ice cube in his mouth, but he watched as Aunt Netty sashayed to within twenty yards of Sister and Walter. She stared at them for a moment, then leapt straight up in the air as though catching a bird. When she landed she rolled over and scooted back into the hay. Comet, too, disappeared into the hay and headed back to his den above Broad Creek, which traversed many farms on its way to spilling into the Rockfish River.

"She's a pistol," Walter said, slapping his leg.

"Fastest damned fox. Not the prettiest. That pathetic brush of hers looks more like a bottlebrush," Sister said, laughing, too.

"When I first started hunting with you, I didn't really believe you could identify the foxes. But you can. They're all different from one another."

"And she's sassy. She's not happy unless she has people flying off horses like pinballs spinning out of a pinball machine. She likes to hear them hit the ground." Sister giggled.

Shaker was picking up the leftover wood bits. "Well, we recognize them as individuals and they recognize us. She came right on up to you to give you a show." He tossed the wood fragments in a five-gallon kelly green plastic bucket.

"That she did." Sister picked up the wood bits at her coop. "The gray looked healthy."

"Lot of people don't like running a gray," Doug said.

"I love getting on a gray. Love to start my puppies on a gray," Sister enthusiastically said, her voice rising a little. "They'll give you a good run—but in circles or figure eights. More contained. For the young ones, that's a help." She thought for a moment. "You know, cubbing is harder than formal hunting in the sense that you've got to give the youngsters, hounds, and foxes positive experiences. The leaves are on trees and shrubs. It's difficult to see. More to handle, I guess is what I'm trying to say. Kind of like the preseason in football."

"Still can't believe she came up here like that."

"Alice?" Doug spoke.

"No, Aunt Netty." Walter took the extra planks, unplaned oak, heavy, and slipped them on the back of the pickup.

"A lot more pleasant than Alice." Shaker dropped his hammer into his tool belt. "Alice never was strong on social skills and they're really rusty now."

A loud moo and the appearance of a large Holstein heifer, her calf in tow, captured their attention.

"That damned cow." Shaker took off his ball cap, wiping his brow with his forearm.

"I'll walk them back." Sister reached in the bed of the pickup, retrieving a small bucket of grain kept there for just such events.

"I'll walk with you," Walter eagerly volunteered.

"Best offer I've had in years." She smiled.

"When you two are done flirting, tell me, boss, how do you propose to get home?"

"You're going to pick us up at Cindy's barn in a half hour."

Shaker nodded in agreement as he and Doug climbed into the old Chevy pickup.

"Come on, Clytemnestra. Come on, Orestes," Sister called, shaking the bucket enticingly.

Clytemnestra followed and kept pushing Sister for the bucket. Once on the woody path, Walter broke off a thin branch and used it as a switch. Orestes stuck with his fat mother. Both were terribly spoiled and mischievous.

Out of the woods, they passed the lovely schoolhouse that Foxglove Farm's owner, Cindy Chandler, had restored.

"Can't keep this cow in. She opens gates, crashes fences. Bovine wanderlust." Sister slapped Clytemnestra's wet nose as the cow nudged her again.

"Picture of health."

"Raymond and I used to run cattle. Very cyclical business. Don't know if I'll ever go back to it."

They walked in silence for a while, punctuated only by Clytemnestra's mooish comments, the loud swish of her tail.

"Do you think Guy killed Nola?" Walter asked. He'd been in his teens at the time and remembered little of it.

"No."

"It's strange. On the one hand I'm glad Nola was found and on the other I'm not." Walter took the bucket from Sister, handing her the switch.

"I think we all feel that way. I try not to trouble myself with things out of my control," Sister said. "I can't do anything about the past, but maybe I'll be able to do something to help."

"Count me in." Walter growled at Clytemnestra, who balked at going back through her pasture gate.

"I do count on you, Walter. I do."

CHAPTER 8

Roger's Corner, a white frame convenience store, commanded the crossroads of Soldier Road, the road heading west from town, and White Cat Road, an old wagon road heading north and south. Far in the distance, a thin turquoise line rimmed the mountains. A first-quarter moon accompanied by a red star hovered above the last bright strip of twilight.

Roger, now in his middle forties, ate too much of his own pizza heated in a revolving infrared glass case. On the shelves, Snickers, Cheez-Its, Little Debbie cakes, and Entenmann's chocolate-covered doughnuts vied with bags of charcoal, ammunition, hunting knives. In the coolers, handmade sandwiches—including Roger's famous olive cream cheese on whole wheat—enticed folks to stop. If they hadn't tanked up in town, they pretty much had to stop at Roger's, because gas was hard to find in these parts. The next pump was over the Blue Ridge Mountains in Waynesboro.

The outside floodlights hummed in the night air accompanied by the flutter of saturniid moths and the buzz of many bugs, a few zapped by the lights themselves. A long sign, ROGER'S CORNER, white with well-proportioned red block letters, ran almost the entire length of the roof. Roger might never achieve his fifteen minutes of Warholian fame in the world at large, but his sign announced his presence emphatically in these parts.

Shaker Crown, his Orioles baseball cap pulled up off his forehead, worn out from the day's work and not much of a cook, leaned over the counter.

Henry Xavier, owner of the largest insurance company in town, had stopped by on his way home as had Ralph Assumptio, owner of the John Deere tractor dealership. Both men had farms on this west side of the county that were part of Jefferson Hunt territory and both men hunted with Sister. Most members didn't say they hunted with the Jefferson Hunt. They'd simply say, "I hunt with Sister Jane."

By so doing, they found out instantly if the person to whom they were talking knew anything about local society. If they were met with a blank they would graciously add, "the Jefferson Hunt." It was one of those little pride things like the way members of Green Springs Valley Hounds outside of Baltimore never discussed how big their jumps were. They shrugged and would say about their horse, "Oh, he got over nicely." Green Springs Valley Hounds, founded in 1892, boasted some stiff fences. It was not a hunt for the fainthearted, but such details were never explained, simply announced.

All groups cherish their ceremonies of togetherness, rituals that prove them set apart and special.

"Where's your chew?" Roger was ringing up Shaker's sandwich.

"Um . . ."

"Here it is. You left it on top of the Twinkies." Henry Xavier, known only as Xavier, picked up the neat round tin of Copenhagen Black and handed it to Shaker.

"Ah, thanks." Shaker tapped his head. "Vapor lock."

Ralph joined them, banging on the counter the gallon of milk his wife had told him to pick up. "Day wasn't fit for man nor beast."

"We built new coops over there at Foxglove. And it was hateful."

"Thank God." Ralph lovingly stared at the round can of chew in Shaker's hand. "Damn, I wish I hadn't promised Frances I'd give that up."

"Guess who showed up to bitch out Sister?" Shaker asked as he pulled soggy bills out of his pocket, gently peeling a fiver off the wad.

"Crawford," Xavier offered.

"On a mission," Roger simply said.

"Mission impossible." Xavier smiled as the others laughed.

"That jumped-up jackass really believes we'll elect him joint-master." Ralph put his milk back in the cooler because he sensed this might be a ripening chat.

"Hey, if he dumps enough money into the club, who knows?" Xavier's heavy brows, black with some gray, shot upward. "Money papers over many sins."

"Sins I can handle. But he lacks the imagination to be a sinner. He's just a Yankee jackass," Ralph said as he walked back from the cooler.

"Aren't they all?" Shaker winked.

"I was born in Connecticut." Xavier smiled. He was a genial man becoming portly. In this heat he favored seersucker shirts, which somehow made him look fatter, not thinner.

"Oh, Xavier, you were raised here. Don't turn P.C. on us." Roger slapped at him over the counter.

"Well, do you guys want to know who rolled down the road or not?"

"Shoot," Xavier said.

"Alice Ramy."

"What did she want?" Ralph couldn't stand it any longer; he grabbed a tin of Skoal menthol chew, pulled the string around it, and with delight placed a pinch between his lip and his gum. He closed his teeth in contentment.

"Oh, the usual. Got up in Janie's face and said we couldn't hunt there and she'd loose the hounds of hell on us"—Shaker enjoyed his little reference to hounds—"and that Peter's harrier better stay out of her chicken coop, wait, make that her golden chicken coop."

"And Sister smiled through it all," Ralph said.

"And that's why Crawford Howard can't ever be a joint-master. His ego would be in the way. He'd fire back at the old battle-ax or buy up all the land around her and choke her out. Son of a bitch." Xavier knew a good deal about Crawford's local business dealings since he insured many of them. He hated Crawford, but business was business.

"True." Roger clasped his hands. "But you guys need a joint-master so Sister can train him to her ways. She can't live forever."

"She might come close," Shaker said with a laugh. "She was throwing around oak boards today like a thirty-year-old. Tough as nails, the old girl is."

"Don't make 'em like that anymore." Xavier admired Sister. After all, he'd hunted in the field with her when he was a boy. She'd been in her forties then.

"I kind of felt sorry for Alice," Shaker continued. "Guess Ben Sidell got her knickers in a knot. She felt he accused her of covering up for Guy, and you know, the whole ugly mess is flaring up all over again. Sister was real good about it. Said she'd call on her. I couldn't take it that far, but I do feel kind of bad for Alice."

"Alice doesn't make it any easier, and I should know," Ralph said, and shook his head. He was Alice's nephew; his mother was Alice's sister. "Everything has to be her way. If you take a can of beer out of her refrigerator, she opens the door behind you to make sure you didn't disturb the other cans lined up inside. You can't smoke a whole cigarette but what she whisks the ashtray and dumps the ashes. Jesus, Mary, and Joseph, she'll run you crazy. And now she's out of control. At least when Paul was alive he'd make fun of her and snap her out of it."

"Women dry up," Xavier simply stated.

"And men get sentimental," Roger, a sharp observer of folks, said. He reached for a brew. "Anyone? On me?"

"Thanks." Xavier accepted a cold can of Bud while Roger reached for an import, Sol.

"People dry up if they aren't tended to. I'm kind of worried about myself," Shaker joked.

"I don't want to hear, 'There are no women out there.' " Xavier punched him. "Clean up, get out, and start looking."

"Did Ben call on you?" Ralph asked Roger.

"Sure."

"Me too." Xavier sighed.

"Hasn't gotten to me yet," Shaker added. "I was hired on as a whipper-in that year. What a year."

"Give Ben credit. He's going over the file and questioning every name he finds in there. I talked to him." Roger liked the aftertaste the crisp Sol beer left in his mouth. He liked Mexican beers. "Guy stopped by here that last night. Bought something. I don't remember what. Dad was behind the counter. I was helping to unload the Coca-Cola truck."

"You had muscles then," Xavier teased him.

"Still do. They're protected by this layer of fat."

"You'll never have that problem," Xavier, also a bit heftier than in his running days, commented to Shaker.

"Most huntsmen stay pretty lean, takes a lean hound for a long race and a lean huntsman, too. Although I know one or two fat huntsmen. Pity the horse."

"Ever notice how a lot of fat people are really light on their feet?" Xavier thought about a copy of *Men's Health* magazine he'd seen on the rack at Barnes & Noble. A fellow in swim trunks was on the cover, his abs rippled like the proverbial six-packs. Xavier made a mental note to buy the magazine. He was standing around looking at his buddies, and except for Shaker they looked like overweight middle-aged men.

"I don't want to see it," Ralph blurted out.

"See what?" Xavier asked.

"The grave. The grave over at After All."

"Ralph, what made you think of that?" Shaker noticed how white Ralph's face had turned.

"First day of cubbing. We'll probably leave from the kennels, and if the fox heads east we could wind up over there, and I don't want to see that grave. Every time I think about Nola I get sick. I mean it."

A silence followed.

Roger broke it. "Me too."

"Ditto," Xavier sighed.

"I guess when the sheriff is done with the bones, he'll give them back to the Bancrofts," Shaker said.

"And that's another thing—all this bullshit about forensic

science," Ralph exploded. "Nola's been in that dirt tomb for twenty-one years. They aren't going to find squat. You know why you hear so much about pathology and this miracle and that miracle? Because any law enforcement officer can tell you, murder is damned easy to pull off. So if you create this propaganda about how you can be convicted from one strand of hair, people believe it. I suppose it deters the weak-willed. I don't know much, but I can tell you those lab coat dudes aren't going to find much."

"They know her head was crushed," Xavier said. "Ben told me."

"Oh, come on. If we'd dug her up we'd know that, too," Ralph practically spit out. "Do you think he cares? The killer? People kill every day and never give it a second thought. They don't have a conscience. It would eat you or me up alive. But whoever killed Nola"—Ralph pointed his forefinger for emphasis—"walked away and thought he was right, or rid of her, or whatever he thought, but he didn't give a damn."

"I don't believe that," Shaker argued.

"Me neither. Killing a beautiful woman like that would haunt him for the rest of his days," Roger agreed with Shaker.

Xavier tapped his lips with his forefinger, a little stream of air escaping, then he said, "Maybe. Maybe not. If it was Guy, we will never know. Apologies to you, Ralph. I know he was your cousin, but let's just look at this from every angle. If it was Guy, it's done and he's gone. Maybe he'll return someday in old age, confess, repent. I don't know. Stranger things have happened, but if it wasn't Guy, I don't think the man who smashed in the side of her head cares that he killed her. He just cares that he doesn't get caught."

CHAPTER 9

The vents whooshed out cooling air. As Sister plumped up pillows behind her so she could read, she was grateful she'd installed central air-conditioning ten years ago and she wondered why she'd been so stubborn about having it before.

Raleigh slept stretched out on the floor and Rooster was curled up in a nearby doggie bed. Doggie beds liberally dotted the house. Golliwog thought she'd read with Sister, so she sat next to her as Sister opened a recently published history of the Hapsburg Empire. She didn't expect to find a mention of the sapphire, but she used the index to find the times Elizabeth's name appeared. As this was a scholarly work the tone was dry. She picked up the notebook she always kept beside her bed on the nightstand and wrote down to find a good biography of the last empress of the Austro-Hungarian Empire.

The phone rang at nine-fifteen, which meant it was an old

friend. No one else dared call after nine in the evening since Sister retired early and rose before sunup.

It was Shaker, and he told her about Ralph's squeamishness about seeing Nola's grave while cubbing.

"Actually, Shaker, it probably isn't a good idea to go over there. I'm glad you called my attention to it. How was Ralph?"

"Seemed a little jumpy."

"He loved Nola."

"I remember that was how I figured out Ron Haslip was gay—he didn't have a crush on Nola." Shaker laughed, mentioning a hunt club member they all liked who, after years of pretending otherwise, finally came out.

"Guess you're right. A man would have to have been homosexual or dead not to have responded to her."

"Xavier warned me that Crawford's up to his tricks."

"I'll just bet he is." She pressed her lips together. "Hey, it's supposed to be bloody hot again tomorrow. Let's not walk out hounds with horses. Tell Doug. We can start up day after tomorrow—six, six-thirty in the morning. Let's try to beat the heat. Anyway, I could use tomorrow to catch up on my errands."

Doug, as professional whipper-in, was responsible for the staff horses, so he needed to know the schedule change.

"One more day won't hurt them." Shaker meant the horses. "Do you want to walk out on foot in the evening?"

"Tell you what, let's just give everyone a rest. I'll call Betty. We could all use a day off."

She hung up, then dialed Betty, who was madly clicking away on her channel surfer, furious that she and Bobby paid money for a satellite dish with 128 channels and there wasn't one damn thing worth watching. Betty, too, was glad for a day off.

Sister then picked up her book again, but the pages soon blurred. She hadn't realized how tired she was from working in the blistering heat all day. She turned out the light as Golly artfully arranged herself around Sister's head.

"Golly, will you settle down."

"Then stop hogging the pillow," the cat complained, but she did stop wiggling.

The memory of Aunt Netty cutting a shine made Sister giggle. Then she thought about Alice's distress and a pang of guilt shot through her for disliking Alice. She remembered that Guy's nickname was Hotspur. She thought of Henry Hotspur, Sir Henry Percy, the bold supporter of Henry IV of England.

She opened her eyes. "Damn."

"Now what's the matter?" Golly shifted.

"Golly, will you stop crabbing?" Raleigh rolled over onto his other side.

Rooster, snoring, missed the exchange.

"When something pops into my head like that, it's leading somewhere." She sat upright, which irritated Golly. "Am I trolling the depths of my subconscious? Do I even have one? I ask you animals, is there a subconscious or is it a human invention? And if I have one, you have one. We aren't that far apart."

"Glad you recognize that." Golly moved to the other pillow. She knew when Sister's brain clicked on she'd be up and down half the night writing notes in her book.

"Gang, I don't know about a subconscious, but I do know about memories. You either remember something or you don't. Repressed memories are something lawyers use to get criminals off scot-free. But there is imagination. Indeed. And Henry Hotspur is riding right at me, right out of Shakespeare's imagination and my own. I think he's got a message. I hope I can figure it out." She clicked on the light, making a few notes.

"Why do humans read?" Raleigh asked.

"To cure insomnia," Golly replied.

CHAPTER 10

As Sister settled in for the night, Athena started hunting. *Bubo virginianus,* great horned owl, her scientific and English name, cared little what she was called.

She was the queen of the night, and all other creatures need listen to her. If anyone challenged her supremacy she'd fly away as though in a huff, her wingspan seeming to cast a shadow even at night. Athena would then turn and silently strike the offender from behind; her balled-up talons could crack a skull. She feared no one. All feared her.

At two feet tall and nearly five pounds in weight, she could vanish in the blink of one of her golden eyes. How such a large creature could do this mystified other creatures. Like the goddess to whom she was sacred, Athena could appear and disappear at will.

Her cry, easily identified, was a deep, musical hoo, hoo-hoo,

hoo-hoo. Sometimes she would vary the sequence and send out three low hoos. But her cry was distinctive and bore little resemblance to the barred owl's or the long-eared owl's, other hoo singers. Humans close to nature could tell the difference. Country people knew her song and her value to them. Athena rid them of raiders, rodents. Her worth was beyond rubies.

Other owls admired her and many wished they had her song. The short-eared owl emitted a little squeak. The barn owl, thick in these parts and also a friend to farmers, hissed or snapped her bill.

The only owl not intimidated by Athena's sonorous voice was the screech owl, who would sing to her heart's content and the misery of all around her. Only ten inches high, this reddish or gray little thing could crank out a volume that was most impressive. And she hardly limited herself to a bloodcurdling screech that scared the urine right out of city folks visiting the country. No, she could purr, trill, pitch high, then run down the scale to a lower register. When feeling marvelous—"mahvalous," as she might say—she even provided tremolo.

Her sturdy ego meant that she, too, had no fear. In fact, a sly delight filled her when "visitors," meaning city folk, shivered at her concert. She'd then fly close to them, putting on a display of fierceness that usually made one of these two-legged twits cry, "Rabies."

As if she would ever get rabies. Puh-lease!

Already full from hunting, the screech owl sat in the old orchard by Roughneck Farm and hollered to her heart's content. The hounds couldn't shut her up.

Shaker and Doug, secure in air-conditioning in their separate quarters, could hear an occasional high note.

Bitsy, as she was known, rather hoped she could entice the hounds to sing with her. Sometimes one would lift his head and start a note, one or two others would follow or honor, the correct term, and within a minute the entire kennel would join her in ribald chorus.

They were really saying, *"Bitsy, shut up, for God's sake."* But the little brown owl thought she was the diva and they were her chorus in this great opera of life.

"Bitsy, do shut up."

Bitsy complied this time as this request came from Athena, who had landed on a branch opposite her. The screech owl knew in her heart that Athena was jealous—after all, the other owls never challenged her in song contests—but Athena was Athena, so Bitsy shut up. *"Hello. I didn't hear you."*

"Of course not, you idiot. You make such a racket." Athena fluffed out her feathers, appearing even more grand.

"It's such a beautiful night. And I have dined on delicious mice this evening. Full of corn they were, raiding the barns. So sweet and crunchy."

"Me too," Athena replied. She smoothed out her feathers. *"Come with me."*

Bitsy, thrilled to be asked to accompany the queen herself, spread her strong little wings and lifted off, flying just to Athena's right.

Both birds noiselessly soared through the sky, passing through the fragrant orchard where the apples hung gathering sweetness for a fall harvest. Beneath them a large pasture bisected by the dusty farm road appeared, the grasses swaying in the light breeze. They climbed upward, heading north over copses hugging the creek beds below. Within ten minutes of leisurely flying they passed over the fearsome tree on Hangman's Ridge, then descended to the low, narrow fertile valley that ran east to west. A two-lane paved road, Soldier Road, ran through this valley. Sister owned the land south of Soldier Road.

Foxglove Farm, the land north of Soldier Road, had been in the Chandler family since 1803.

The animals knew where the human boundaries were, but they looked at the land in geological terms. The long, thin valley, cultivated fields, on which Soldier Road was built, was the pinkie finger of a tiny glacier splinter that had veered off from the main push so long ago, humans weren't even around here to write about it.

Parked along the side of the road, facing west, not two miles from Roger's Corner, Ralph Assumptio sat in his Toyota Land Cruiser. The motor was cut off.

Athena and Bitsy landed in a poplar by Broad Creek. Steep and fed by runoff from the Blue Ridge Mountains, the creek crossed the road below Hangman's Ridge at a diagonal. During hard, persistent rains, it often jumped its bed, spreading muddy waters over the low areas and in the worst of rains rising to drown the roadbed.

Ralph, his head in his hands, elbows on the steering wheel, was sobbing his heart out.

"It's never good when a man cries," Bitsy murmured.

"Mmm." Athena's gorgeous eyes opened wider, movement in the creek bed making her alert.

Inky, having eaten an early supper, was on her way to play at the kennels. Her den was by the walnut at cornfield's edge, a mile from the kennel if one could fly. Inky liked chatting with Diana and she liked sitting under the apple trees, too.

She noticed the Land Cruiser. SUVs reminded her of large hercules beetles. Curiosity aroused, she walked closer, then stopped when she saw the two owls in the poplar. She softly padded over to them instead. She could hear Ralph's sobs.

"Does he need help?" the glossy young fox asked.

"Not that we can supply," Athena said.

"Should we wait until he leaves, just to make sure?" Inky, a kindhearted animal, wondered.

"Let's examine the situation." Athena puffed out her chest. *"A man, alone, is pulled off to the side of the road, a road not heavily traveled except on the way to work and when they come home. He's not drunk and he's not sick. I can always smell sickness."* This was uttered with great authority.

"Wife left him," Bitsy said.

"Could be, but he's reputed to have a good marriage," Athena said.

"And it's not money. Ralph's smart that way," Inky said.

Indeed, Ralph was smart that way. He had graduated from Hamilton College in New York, then come back to Virginia to the university's Darden School of Business. He took a job at the local John Deere dealership and wound up buying it in his mid-thirties. Now in his forties, he owned dealerships throughout Virginia. He was rumored to have a silent partner, but no one knew who that might be. Some people thought the silent partner concept was jealousy, because Ralph came up on his own. A small percentage of people can't stand to be shown up by anyone. Ralph was a handy target for the stupid or lazy. He let them talk while he kept working—and making money.

"Maybe he's received some kind of bad news, a friend is ill or someone that he loved died." Bitsy turned her head nearly upside down thinking about it.

"Nola," Athena said.

"Ah, all the men his age loved her, didn't they? That's what I hear." And Bitsy heard quite a lot sitting in trees or on a crossbeam in a hayloft.

Ralph coughed, snuffled loudly, coughed again, and wiped his eyes. He spit out the open car window. He wiped his eyes again, then reached into the glove compartment, pulling out a white aspirin bottle. He popped three into his mouth, swallowing them without water. He turned on the engine and drove off.

"Been almost a week since she was found. Why is he crying now?" Inky thought it strange.

"Maybe it's just hitting him," Bitsy opined.

"No," Athena crisply replied. *"It's worse than that."*

They sat there for another fifteen minutes chatting, then the two owls flew toward the Chandler barn.

Inky crossed the road, trotted up Hangman's Ridge, and walked along the flat ridge toward the huge old tree, well over three hundred years old.

A whisper drew her eyes to the tree.

Inky thought she saw a ghost, a man in his mid-thirties dressed in fine clothes although his neck had been unnaturally stretched and his tongue hung out.

" 'For I do not do the good I want, but the evil I do not want is what I do.' Romans, chapter twelve, verse nine." His anguish was palpable.

Inky knew spirits existed. Just like Hamlet told Horatio, there were more things in heaven and earth than we knew, but that didn't mean she wanted any part of them.

She raced back toward her den, deciding not to visit Diana tonight. A whippoorwill disturbed by her passing let out its characteristic call.

She dashed into her den, snuggling in the fresh hay she'd lined there.

"How sad humans are," she thought to herself. *"They hurt others and they hurt themselves and their misery flows down through the centuries. Maybe there really is original sin for them."* She closed her eyes and prayed to God, who, for her, looked like a beautiful gray fox. *"Thank you, dear God, thank you for making me a fox."*

CHAPTER 11

I've always loved this spot, but now . . ." Sybil's voice trailed off. Tears rolled down her cheek.

"Honey, try not to think about it." Ken Fawkes thought that idea comforting, but it was impossible for either of them not to stare at the newly packed earth and not think about where Nola had lain for two decades and one year.

"When we were little girls, we'd sit up there, where Peppermint is buried now, and we'd look back over the creek and the meadows. I loved this time of year because it was cooler here and the cornflowers bloomed. Nola's eyes were cornflower blue. She said I had iris eyes. Most times they're pale blue, so that was nice of her." Sybil sobbed harder.

Ken wrapped his arms around her, resting his chin on her head. "You have lavender eyes. The most beautiful eyes I've ever seen."

"Ken, what do we do now?"

He couldn't answer right off. "Well, we keep on keeping on."

"Did you notice Mother wearing the sapphire?"

"Yes."

"I asked her why. She said she'd made a promise. The sapphire would remind her to keep it."

A horsefly buzzed near Ken's head, then moved away as he slapped at it, releasing his grasp on his wife. "Bad luck, that ring."

Sybil smoothed her glossy hair. "I wonder. Maybe we just invest objects with our emotions. They're neutral."

"Well, don't you wear that goddamned ring."

"Don't worry. I won't." She noticed color coming up on his cheeks.

Ken stuck his boot toe in the turf, scuffing at it like a petulant child. "Talked to this new sheriff guy who hardly inspires confidence. I'm starting to think if his brains were BBs they'd be rolling around a six-lane highway."

"Paul Ramy must have had one BB, then," Sybil ruefully replied.

"A good ol' boy in the good old days. Shit." Ken grimaced. "Things are supposed to be different. I don't know if this Sidell is able to investigate roadside kill, much less this. The questions he asked me were pointless."

"Twenty-one years. I guess from his standpoint it's not pressing. No one else is in danger. If they were, more blood would have been spilled back in 1981."

"You're right." Ken slapped at another fly. "Biting. Must be rain coming up." He smiled. "Tuesday's a good day for rain. Better now than the weekend."

Domino and Merry Andrew trotted up from the other

side of the hill. After nuzzlings and pats on the neck, they left the two humans.

"Ken, I don't think we should let Mom or Dad collect Nola. What's left of her." A dark note of bitterness and loss crept into Sybil's well-modulated voice. "They've been through enough. You and I should go get her. I didn't ask Sidell when they'd release her remains to us."

"Shouldn't be much longer. They photographed the grave, her position in the earth. They'll measure the bones. Scrape whatever they can scrape and send it to the lab. Guess it will tell them something. I'm not a scientist."

"She was healthy as a horse." Sybil scanned the western sky; a few gray cumulus tops were peeping over the mountains. "The horseflies watched the weather report."

"They always bite before rain." Ken checked his expensive watch, tapping the crystal, a habit. "Still time to call the sheriff today. I'll see if I can make arrangements to get her."

"I think you'd better call the funeral director first."

"Why?"

"I don't think family members can pick up corpses. I think the law is, a funeral director or employee has to do it. I'm pretty sure. You can't just carry her out in a bag."

"No." Ken's voice became a bit indignant. "I was going to get a proper coffin and put her in that. There's nothing but bones. It's not, well, you know . . ."

Sybil acknowledged with a nod that she did know. One doesn't grow up in the country without a good sense of the disintegration of dead things. She knew, intellectually, that buzzards, worms, and beetles had their work to do. Without them the whole earth would be piled miles high with corpses. But why couldn't the Lord have made it a tidier process? The stench alone was horrible. To think of her sister's body decaying in the earth . . . she couldn't. She just couldn't. She struggled to remember her sister's staccato laugh, to snatch at something lovely.

The backfire of an engine drew their attention to the farm lane leading to the covered bridge. Jimmy Chirios coasted over the small rise, the farm truck emitting small puffs of dark smoke.

"That truck burns too much oil." Sybil was glad to switch to another subject.

"Your father refuses to buy a new one."

Edward, despite his wealth, was no more sensible about personal expenditures than the rest of humanity. He would squander money on some things, yet he was tight as a tick about others.

The dark green Dodge rattled across the bridge.

Jimmy pulled up to the couple. "Storm's coming. Heard on the radio. Coming fast. Flash floods."

The minute they hopped into the cab the wind shifted gears. The willows by the creek swayed like geishas.

"You did a good job filling in that . . . the grave," Ken awkwardly thanked the young man.

"Oh." Jimmy couldn't muster a smile even though he was being complimented. The thought of that whole mess upset him deeply. "Why'd they make me wait a week? Nothing else there."

"Can't be too careful." Ken drummed on the edge of the door, his elbow on the armrest. "Cops, I mean."

"Yeah." Jimmy drove them back to the big house. No sooner had Sybil and Ken reached the front door than the first big raindrops splattered across the immaculate lawn.

Sybil called out, "Mom."

"In the den."

They walked into the richly paneled den, a glowing cherry

wood, its patina enhanced by age. Moroccan leather-bound volumes—dark blue, red with gold, green, black, saddle-leather tan—filled the shelves. Photographs, some among the very first made in the nineteenth century, also dotted the shelves, each sepia-toned image encased in either its original filigree frame or a plain, sterling silver one. There was so much silver at After All, it could have filled one of the legendary Nevada mines.

Tedi was seated on the chintz sofa, an album spread out before her on the coffee table. Images of Nola in her Christmas dress, her senior year at Madeira; images of Nola in ratcatcher, reins in hand, Peppermint, young and handsome, by her side; images of Nola at twenty-two, accepting her diploma from Mount Holyoke, where she distinguished herself on the show-jumping team but not in the classroom; images of Nola as maid of honor at Sybil's wedding, and even a photograph of Nola at Opening Hunt in 1980, Guy Ramy in the background staring at her with a big grin on his face. Maybe he did love her. Tedi smiled back from those photographs, too. She was in her twenties, then thirties, forties, fifties, sixties. She remained thin, well groomed, and youngish thanks to excellent plastic surgery.

"Oh, Momma, don't."

Tedi, with steely resolve, said, "I know I missed something. The pictures help. Sit down, both of you."

"I'm all sweaty. Would either of you girls like a drink?" Ken, fearful of a possible emotional outburst, inquired.

"Sweet iced tea and my martini."

Sybil, next to her mother, squeezed her hand. "I remember when I used to think you were so uncool drinking martinis. Now they're all the rage again."

"Cycles. By the time you're my age, you've seen them all."

Within minutes, Ken and Edward joined them, each man handing his wife a drink.

Sybil gratefully tasted her daiquiri, the perfect summer drink, as the rain ramped up to a true downpour. "Mercy. It's really coming down."

Edward, tall and patrician with an aquiline nose, seemed a forbidding presence, yet he was a kind man, a good man. He stared out the window, then back at his remaining daughter. He smiled, taking a sip of his scotch on the rocks. "Feast or famine. It's either drought or a gully washer."

"True," Ken agreed from where he still stood.

"Honey, will you sit down. It's not like there's never been a sweaty man in this room before," Sybil ordered.

He perched on the edge of one of the oversized chairs. "Dad, how about eighteen holes tomorrow? David Wheeler and Pat Butterfield need us to clean out their wallets."

A flicker lit in Edward's eyes. "The money in David's wallet has mold on it."

"You're right. That money needs to see the light of day. Capitalism depends on the circulation of cash. We can take them." Ken's voice was a bit too hearty. "Greens will be slow, too."

"We should. Will you call them?"

"Already did," Ken replied, happy that his father-in-law was evidencing some interest in the outside world.

Privilege and the Fawkes name were not accustomed to each other. Fawkes was the surname of many poor whites in these parts. A few over the centuries had risen, but the name clung to them like a digger bee, wouldn't let go.

Ken's people, hardworking, all attended the Baptist church. The Bancrofts had never and would never set foot in a Baptist church.

Ken had worked his way through North Carolina State, made the football team as a walk-on. He proved so ferocious as outside linebacker that he won a scholarship for his junior and senior years. He majored in business, making respectable grades. He didn't know what he would do exactly. He just wanted to find some type of work he liked and make a decent living. But then he met Sybil and his compass shifted. Making do wouldn't be good enough.

Jealous folks said, "That Ken Fawkes landed in the honey pot."

And he did, no doubt about it. But he was reasonably intelligent. Edward created a niche for him through the Bancroft real estate business in a small local company. Ken started learning the business. He studied the roads, bought near crossroads, and developed subdivisions. Of course, some people said the hardest way to make money was to marry it. Ken never said that.

He exuded an air of masculinity. Women found him very attractive indeed, even though he couldn't be described as classically handsome.

Sybil bent closer to the photo album. "Amazing."

"What, dear?" Tedi thought her tea could use another hit of sugar, although her martini was perfect. "Ken, be a darling and put another spoonful in there for me. I'm having my late-afternoon sinking spell."

"Of course." Ken stood up, took her glass, and left the room for a moment.

"Twenty-five years ago this picture, and Sister looks the same. Her hair's silver now, that's all."

"The outdoor life," Tedi said.

"And you look fabulous yourself, my love." Edward, unlike many men, learned very early in life that you can never compliment a woman—especially your wife—too many times.

"Thank you, dear." Tedi smiled. "But I feel old. I feel, well, let's just say I comprehend vulnerability."

Ken returned with her tea. "Here's your sugar buzz." He looked outside. "Black as the devil's eyebrows."

"Nothing like a summer thunderstorm to make you glad you're inside," Edward said, savoring the distinctive deep sweetness of the scotch.

"I've been thinking." Tedi leaned back on the sofa. "A ceremony is in order, a commemoration and celebration of Nola's life. We never had one—"

Ken quickly said, "We always hoped."

"Yes." Tedi never liked being interrupted. "That's over now. A service is in order. I've spoken to Reverend Thigpin and I've considered where Nola should have her final resting place."

Edward cleared his throat, waiting. Would Tedi pick the Prescott plot on the Northern Neck near Warsaw, the seat of the first Prescotts, or would she choose the Bancroft private cemetery, here on After All?

"And what have you decided, dear?"

"Let's make a special place, let's build low stone walls around it, plant white lilacs there, too. Love. It must be a place filled with love. Nola loved Peppermint. More than any man, she loved Pepper. I like to think they're hunting now with Ikey Bell carrying the horn." Ikey Bell was a famous huntsman of the early twentieth century.

No one knew what to say.

Finally Sybil broached the subject. "Mom, it's awfully close to where she was found."

"I know. But she had no peace there. She couldn't. She'll have peace with Peppermint. He loved her in life, he'll be with her in death. It's fitting, you see."

Edward stared out at the rain. His hand touched his Adam's apple. "Whatever you want. You know better about these things."

"And let's do all the things that Nola loved. Yes. Let's plant huge blue hydrangeas, and the dwarf kind, too. I say fiddle to snotty gardeners and snotty gardens. Isn't that a nasty word?" She brightened as though a burden had been lifted from her. "Red poppies next to purple iris and mounds of something snowy white. Let's use all the colors Nola loved."

"Cornflower blue." Sybil had tears in her eyes.

"Yes. And you know what she loved more than anything in the world?" The family hung expectantly on Tedi's next word. "Foxhunting!"

CHAPTER 12

The creamy coral of Crawford's Paul Stuart polo shirt reflected warmth on his face. Crawford liked the best. Paul Stuart was an exclusive men's shop on Madison Avenue. If he wasn't shopping there or at Sulka up on Park, he thought nothing of picking up the phone and ordering a dozen shirts from Turnbull and Asser in London, shoes and boots from Lobb, luxurious cashmeres and silks from a dealer in Turin. To his credit, he always looked splendid.

The morning, hazy, promised a muggy day. This July 28, the anniversary of the day Elizabeth's bold men dispersed the Spanish Armada in 1588 and Arthur Wellesley knocked the stuffing out of the French at Talavera in 1809. A student of history and business, he remembered odd dates.

He and Marty had attended early service at Saint Luke's and now he puttered happily in the tack room of his sumptuous stable with its fittings of polished brass, PavSafe floors that cost a fortune, impeccable doors and stall fronts painted deep navy blue, all made by Lucas Equine in Cythiana, Kentucky. His stable colors were navy and red. Many in these parts painted their vehicles in stable colors, or painted a small symbol or name in those colors on the driver's door. Crawford's red Mercedes had BEASLEY HALL in one-inch script, navy blue, painted on the driver's door, plus the car was pin-striped in navy blue.

His cell phone, perched on custom-made tack trunks also in his colors, jingled.

"Crawford here."

"Haslip," came the terse, mocking reply.

Crawford missed that Ronnie Haslip was making fun of him. "How are you?"

"Fine. Two things." Ronnie knew that with Crawford you got the best result by being brief and direct, most emphatically not the Virginia Way. "The hunt club is sponsoring a class at the Fall Classic Horse Show, Thanksgiving weekend this year. We'd like a perpetual trophy—silver, I think. It will cost quite a bit."

"How much?"

"Seven thousand."

"My God, Ronnie, how big is this thing?"

"Well, it's huge. Sterling silver. The kind of stuff they used to do in the 1800s."

"Why is Sister being so grand? Not like her, really."

"It's a secret. She wants us to do it in honor of Nola. The Nola Bancroft Perpetual Trophy, Ladies Over Fences."

"Oh." Crawford thought a moment. "Put me down for three thousand five hundred. That ought to get the ball rolling."

"That is exceedingly generous, Crawford. Not only will Sister be grateful, the Bancrofts will be thrilled, once they know, of course."

"Awful thing."

"Yes. Oh, I just heard that Tedi intends to bury her August tenth at the farm. The club will be attending en masse."

"Naturally." He found this news depressing even though he never knew Nola. Funerals were not Crawford's preferred social activity, but one must play one's part. And he was not an unfeeling man, simply an overreaching one. "Ronnie, you grew up with Nola. Was she what everyone says?"

"And more." Ronnie laughed. "There was a capriciousness about Nola that was divine, really, unless you were in love with her. Then she'd run you crazy or break your heart."

"Was she aware of what she was doing to people?"

"I always thought she was like those Indian warriors collecting scalps. She'd keep four, five, who knows how many, on a string."

"Sleeping with them?"

"Well . . ." Ronnie didn't want to cast aspersions on any lady, but how could he put this? "Let's just say that Nola was a high-spirited animal with prodigious energy."

"For Christ's sake, Ronnie!"

"She'd have lunch with one fellow, go to a party with another, and home with a third. She was heartless." Ronnie laughed.

"You weren't in love with her?" Crawford couldn't resist this little dig.

"I wasn't rich enough for Nola," came the even reply, as Ronnie refused to rise to the bait.

"Neither was Guy Ramy, from what I hear."

"But he was as beautiful as Nola was. Jet-black curly hair,

ice blue eyes, shoulders as wide as Atlas himself. Fearless on a horse. Not the best rider, but fearless."

"That's how he got the nickname Hotspur?"

"Yes and no. I'm assuming you know the life of Sir Henry Percy."

"Of course I do, Ronnie." A note of indignation darkened Crawford's voice. "I graduated Phi Beta Kappa."

Bold, impetuous, strong, Henry Percy was the eldest son of the 1st Earl of Northumberland. Henry was born on May 20, 1364. He was taught to fight like all noble-born boys, displaying a true gift for it. In his early twenties he harried the Scots, who gave him the name Hotspur for his vigorous border patrols.

When Richard II began to show clear signs that he wasn't up to the demands of being king, unrest grew throughout England. Many giggled that Richard would make a better queen than king. Hotspur and his father helped put Henry Boling-broke on the throne in 1399, who then called himself Henry IV.

Hotspur's daring brought him fame and admiration that perhaps incited a certain jealousy in the king. But Henry IV was no fool. He rewarded Hotspur with lands and offices in northern England and Wales, two places where a strong military leader was necessary.

The Percys demolished the Scots at Humbleton Hill in Durham on September 14, 1402. Henry IV, who was vainly try-ing to suppress the Welsh, paled by comparison. Henry's ego clouded his usually calculating judgment. He wouldn't allow Hotspur to ransom the Scottish nobles he had captured, a common policy that would have fattened Hotspur's pocket-book as well as the crown's.

To add insult to injury, Henry wouldn't pay the bill for Hotspur's border warfare. Not only was the king jealous, he was cheap.

Furious, Hotspur and his father raised a rebellion to depose the king in 1403. Henry, more clever than the Percys realized, intercepted Hotspur near Shrewsbury before he could join up with his father. Though outnumbered, Hotspur fought like the lion he was but in the end he was beaten, hanged, drawn, and quartered. His violent end came on July 21, at the age of thirty-nine.

"There was always a sense," Ronnie's bass voice intoned, "that Guy would draw his sword against the wrong man."

"Sword as in weapon or sword as in cock?"

"Both."

"So he ran around on Nola?"

"Oh no. No, he was totally in love with her. But while she might have been in love with him, that didn't prevent her from enjoying other men's attentions."

"But people say she would have married him." Crawford began to understand how complex this was and how reluctant people were to tell what they knew. Let sleeping dogs lie and all that. Except the dogs were now wide awake.

"Some people. I think that opinion reveals more about the romantic nature of the speaker than it does about Nola."

"Exactly what do you mean, Ronnie?" Crawford lacked the patience for linguistic subtlety as practiced in Virginia.

"Unearthly beauty, child of Midas, marries country boy. People love that sort of thing. She wouldn't have married him. She saw what Sybil endured when she married Ken Fawkes."

"He's done quite well. With the old man's help, of course."

"Yes," Ronnie inhaled, "but he'll never be one of them. He was set up, then propped up by Edward, so everyone wonders about Ken's abilities. And Sybil bears the Fawkes name, not Bancroft."

"So?"

"Crawford. This is Virginia. No one forgets a goddamned thing. No way in green hell would Nola be Nola Ramy."

"But Ken's no slouch. In time, Guy may have proved he possessed business acumen."

"At the time that Nola was flaming around with Guy, Ken was struggling not just to master the real estate business but to master the nuances of the life into which he had married. Scott Fitzgerald said the rich are different. And I know that you know they are. Old money, I mean. Really old money."

"Not like my money." Crawford's voice had an edge.

"I didn't say that." Ronnie didn't have to say it.

"You weren't in love with Nola but you did like her?" Crawford changed the subject.

A beat passed, then Ronnie honestly replied, "She was a vacuous, spoiled child who had no feelings for anyone but herself. But she was also fun, enormous fun."

Crawford knew that in this assessment Ronnie betrayed his own emotions. Perhaps he was once in love with Guy Ramy or one of the other men Nola had so easily vanquished. "Then maybe it's better that she always be young and beautiful in everyone's mind."

"She would have been an impossible middle-aged bitch. Women like Nola can't age. It kills them."

"In her case, someone else did the job."

Ronnie didn't respond; he waited a moment and then asked, "I also thought you might want to know given the discussion we had about hunt staff last week that David Headdon left Shenandoah Valley Hounds last night. Left them flat."

"Hmm." Crawford smiled. The huntsman David Headdon was known both for his brilliance and his temper. "Does Sister know?"

"Sister knows everything."

Crawford chuckled. "Almost, but she doesn't know who killed Nola Bancroft."

Ronnie respected Sister, even though many people might have interpreted his coziness with Crawford as a betrayal of her. He truly believed that Crawford needed to be joint-master of the Jefferson Hunt. Let him pour money into the club until a true hunting master could be found to succeed Sister should she step down or step up to heaven. At this point in the political development of looking for a joint-master, Ronnie kept his support of Crawford quiet.

"You know something, Crawford, if anyone can find out what really happened now that Nola has reappeared, it will be Jane Arnold."

"Ronnie, you've been most helpful."

"So have you. Thank you for the donation."

"If you didn't like Nola, why are you collecting for the trophy?"

Sometimes Ronnie couldn't believe that Crawford didn't get it. He'd lived here over a decade. "Because Sister gave me the job and because it's the proper thing to do."

Crawford snapped shut his tiny cell phone, hopped in his car, and drove west toward Roughneck Farm.

CHAPTER 13

I'm going. You'd better put a check by my name," Dragon, his handsome head held high, yelled over the other dog hounds.

"Pipe down," Dasher, his brother, growled.

Asa, Archie's relative, same breeding but one year later, sat in silent splendor. If young entry were going to foxpen, then he'd be there to steady them.

Shaker, clipboard in hand, wrote down the names Sister called out.

Sister would gladly have given Shaker Sundays off, but Shaker, like most hound men, wanted to be with his hounds. Sister was the same way. Covered with mud, red clay caked onto their work boots, both humans breathed in the heady odor of hound, shavings, and a hint of Penn-o-Pine disinfectant.

Doug had taken the day off, as he'd promised the new girl he was dating they'd canoe down the James River.

"If we have Asa, Cora, Delia, and Nellie for made hounds, then we can just take young ones. Those four will keep the freshman class in line." She rubbed her chin, unaware that she had mud on her hands.

"Supposed to rain again this afternoon." Shaker slipped the pen behind his ear.

"We're not sugar, we won't melt."

"Moisture will be good for scent." Shaker smiled.

"Last time we went to foxpen it was dust over there, but that's good for the youngsters. Every day they hunt isn't going to be a good scenting day, and I was proud of them. They pushed and pushed until they finally picked up a line. Took them forty-five minutes. That shows a lot of patience for youngsters."

The sound of a deep motor made all heads turn.

Raleigh left Sister's side, stood on his hind legs, and peered out the kennel window. *"Crawford Howard."*

"If only I were out of here, I'd pee on his leg," Dragon promised as the others laughed.

Shaker walked over, his head just above Raleigh's. It would have made a funny photograph. "Your favorite."

She laughed. "I have so many."

"This is your true favorite, Crawford." Shaker slapped the clipboard against his side.

She didn't reply, but her lip curled slightly upward.

"He's going to the house, Mom," Raleigh announced.

Sister figured as much. She called over her shoulder as she opened the kennel door, "Five-thirty tomorrow."

"Yes'um."

She was looking forward to the morrow. Foxpen delighted

her. A foxpen is a fenced-in area, often hundreds of acres. Foxes can't get out and deer can't get in. Man-made dens and natural dens cover the land. The purpose of a foxpen is to introduce young entry to fox scent, a lighter scent than deer.

A good hound wants to hunt, and on a miserable scenting day, deer scent becomes enticing. No foxhunter wants his or her hounds chasing deer, particularly since there are now so many of them. Introducing a youngster to fox scent in controlled conditions helped to guide them on the paths of righteousness.

Hounds can't harm the foxes at a foxpen since there are so many dens in which to escape, so everyone can rest easy, but most especially the foxes. Hounds hunt by scent not sight, and by the time they were cast, the foxes, being nocturnal hunters, were usually in their dens. If not, the foxes soon found one, the trail of scent leading to their secure den. All in all it was a perfect setup.

The foxes enjoyed good food, regular wormings, and regular exercise. The hounds enjoyed the run followed by praise and cookies.

Sister laughed to herself as she and Raleigh trudged up to the house. Crawford so desperately wanted to be joint-master, but she couldn't imagine him rousing himself to go to foxpen before dawn.

Then again, too many cooks spoil the broth. Crawford, if she could find no alternative, could swan about and be one of those fellows who is better at running his mouth than running the fox. Still, he could write checks better than anyone else. That's something.

"Crawford," she called out as he headed for the back porch door of the simple Federal house painted a soft yellow with white trim and Charleston green shutters.

"Good morning." He turned, smiling.

"Have you had your breakfast?"

"I have."

She opened the door. "Another cup of coffee and a bran muffin?"

"One of your bran muffins?" He wiped his feet on the rug just inside the porch door.

"Yes. I'm in my domestic goddess phase."

"All this time I thought you were the goddess of the hunt." He'd picked up a few Virginia ways, even though most folks didn't notice since they were too busy criticizing him. It never hurt to flatter a woman, a truth southern men imbibe with their mother's milk. Crawford still had to think about it, but he was practicing, which was a great step forward.

He sat down at the kitchen table while Sister made a pot of Jamaican coffee, the aroma filling the room. The bran muffins, under a mesh cover, were placed before him along with a plate, utensils, and country butter.

"Ever eat bran muffins with clotted cream? Sounds awful, but it's a step away from heaven." She poured his coffee into a mug bearing the symbol of the Jefferson Hunt, a fox mask.

"Too rich for me. I shouldn't even use this butter."

"You have lost weight. Look good." She sat next to him at the large old farmhouse table. "What can I do for you?"

"Mmm, this is wonderful." He took a sip of coffee. "You and I both like good coffee, too. Well, I guess you've heard about Shenandoah Valley Hounds. I suspect it was one of those 'You're fired.' 'I quit!' things." Crawford was fishing. He could have asked Sister directly. "The huntsman leaving, I mean."

"If a master is discharging a hunt servant or a hunt servant is leaving, notice must be given by January first. After that it's considered bad form. You leave either party hanging," Sister evenly replied.

"Shenandoah would have endured him for another year?"

"Of course. David is actually a good huntsman. He's an erratic person. That's the problem."

"Booze."

"With huntsmen it generally is booze or women. One often leads to the other." She laughed.

He drained his cup and she refilled it. Both drank their coffee black, which Sister called "barefoot."

"I'll get right to the point. Shaker will be our huntsman for many more years, barring injury. Am I correct?"

"You are."

"Doug's a young man, talented. He could carry the horn for Shenandoah." He held up his hand, even though she'd made no sign of protest. "Now give me a minute. I've thought about this. Five years with Shenandoah and he'd be ready to move up to a fancier, richer hunt or come back here should Shaker retire or become injured.

"Now I know that being left without your first whipper-in this late in the day might cause a ripple of discontent, but it can't be as bad as being without a huntsman."

"You're right about that." She listened intently, knowing other cards were stuffed up his sleeve.

"Do you think Shenandoah would hire him?"

"In a heartbeat."

"Do you think he would go?"

"This has been his home for years, but it would be a good opportunity, a step up. I don't think he would leave without my blessing."

"And would you give him that blessing?"

"I would, as would Shaker."

"I would be happy to pay the salary of the next professional whipper-in."

Her eyebrows raised. "Crawford, that's very generous. You must be in a giving mood today, because Ronnie Haslip told me what you just pledged to the Nola Bancroft Trophy."

"Ah." He wondered if Ronnie was calling to make him, Crawford, look good or if Ronnie had called to make Ronnie look good, boasting about what he'd managed to pry out of him. He wasn't sure about Ronnie. No matter. He was sure about himself. "You know I like the Bancrofts. And while I never knew their younger daughter, I'm happy to do this. Mostly, I enjoy supporting the club."

"And we are all grateful to you." Her smile was genuine.

When she smiled like that, Crawford could see her as a young woman. Odd.

"I'm sure there's a pool of people who might qualify for the job," Crawford said.

"I'd ask the Masters of Foxhounds Association director, Lieutenant Colonel Dennis Foster, if he knows anyone who is suitable. There are always people out there who might have the skills you need for the job, but the chemistry is wrong where they are." She wondered if he had a candidate who would then be his mole. She respected Crawford's intelligence but wished he didn't continue to think a hunt club could be run as a business. It was something quite different, halfway between a church and a charity perhaps. She was never sure.

"I'd be happy to help in the search."

She breathed a sigh of inner relief. He wasn't going to foist someone on her. "Crawford, would you still consider making the salary contribution if for this year I utilized an honorary whipper-in? I think Shaker and I can handle the kennels."

"Yes, but I thought the first whipper-in was responsible for keeping the hunt horses fit."

"True. But the hunt club could use that money. Desperately.

Our truck is on its last legs. It's twelve years old and has 180,000 miles on it. These one-ton Duallys are so expensive now. Forty thousand dollars."

"Who will take care of the horses?"

"If I had part-time help, Jennifer Franklin after school, perhaps, I think we could do it. You don't have to give me an answer now. Maybe this feels like a bait and switch."

"No, I held out the bait. The workload is overwhelming. Can you really do it with one less pair of hands?"

"Like I said, I think we can."

"What would you do with the cottage?"

"Rent it out as a hunting box or convert it into an office. We don't have an office. Papers are stuffed in Shaker's house and mine. I'm not sure yet. I'll have to think this through."

But the fact that she had ready answers for the whipper-in position told Crawford she'd already considered encouraging Doug to apply for the huntsman's job.

"Let me buy the truck. GM is making the best right now."

A pause followed; Raleigh put his head on Sister's knee. Her hand rested on his shiny black head.

Golliwog, sitting in the kitchen window over the sink, remarked, *"Rain coming. Be here in fifteen minutes. It's on top of the mountain."* As no one responded, she raised the decibel level. *"Isn't anyone listening to me?"*

"Golly, hush," Sister chided her.

"It must be raindrops, so many raindrops." The cat warbled the song she'd heard on the golden oldie radio station.

Sister didn't listen to oldies, but Shaker did.

As Golly's singing filled the room, Sister stood up and walked over to the window.

"You're just awful." Then she glanced out the window.

"Crawford, rain's sliding down the mountain. Are your car windows closed?"

"They are. This has been a wet summer."

"Compared to last one. I love the weather. Let me amend that. I love observing the weather. For instance, you'd think when raindrops are hanging from a branch, you know, hanging not dropping, that scent would be fabulous. My experience is that you can't find a damn thing."

Not schooled in the refinements of hunting or country life, Crawford was nonetheless interested. "Doesn't compute, does it?"

"No, but there it is." She sat back down as the cat preened in the window. "I am overwhelmed by your willingness to share your resources. And I'm not unmindful that you want to be my joint-master." She smiled. "I would hate for you to give us all this money and be disappointed down the road."

"If you told people you wanted me, I'd be joint-master," he bluntly replied, but in good humor.

"Don't feel that I don't value you. I do. But Crawford, you are not a hunting man. You're still new to it."

"Ten years." This came out in a puff of wind.

"For the first two or three years, you, like every other beginner, were just trying to hang on. It takes a long time to learn about foxhunting, and the truth is most people are out there to run and jump. Real hunting is an art, and I don't pretend to be Rembrandt, but I know it takes study, then more study, and the recognition that these animals are often far wiser than we are. I guess I'm saying it takes humility."

Crawford could not believe that any animal was superior to the human animal, but he did know her assessment of his early years was accurate. "I'm willing to learn."

"And I respect that. You must also realize, surely you know, that if you are elected joint-master there will be one whopping fight."

He looked up from his cup. "I know. I've stepped on toes."

"Let me throw this out to you. I don't expect you to be a hunting master, Crawford, but you can certainly learn what it takes to run a club. Money is a big part of it, but the medley of breeding, of seeing to the health of your foxes, of landowner relations, of relations with the Board of Governors, of opening new territory and maintaining the old, it's a great deal of work. One must treat people with a light touch."

"I'm not good at that," he honestly admitted.

"And you know nothing about hounds."

"That's true, too. One hound looks pretty much like the next to me. But I have ideas. I have resources. And if I do say so, Marty would be invaluable to our social members." He meant Marty would throw a lot of parties, a real plus.

"Promise me this: that this hunt season you will pay attention. Try to keep your ego in check. It will make a difference."

"So, you are considering me?"

"I am. And what about Bobby Franklin? He punched you and bodily threw you out of his shop last year. He's our president."

A club president ran the various committees. It, too, was a big job. The master was responsible for hunt staff, hounds, territory, and actual hunting in a subscription club—which the Jefferson Hunt was.

"Unusual circumstances." Crawford cleared his throat.

"Can you bring yourself to apologize?"

"Yes." This was hard.

"You have no children. People are blind about their own

children, and what you told him about Cody may have been one hundred percent on the money. But few fathers could hear it."

Cody, the Franklins' oldest daughter, was currently in jail. The beginning of this dismal reality was her infatuation with drugs.

"I understand." He paused. "Do you think you were blind to your son's faults?"

"I'd like to think I wasn't, but I'm sure I was. He was a beguiling boy." She smiled.

"Speaking of children, it's funny. I've asked people about Nola Bancroft and gotten some wildly different replies. Some men thought she was Venus, others thought she was a bitch."

"I expect there were more of the former than the latter."

"True."

"We're like chemicals. We react with one another differently."

"What did you think of her?"

"Oh, she was great fun. As a woman, I saw her differently than men did, obviously. She had a great sense of humor, loved practical jokes, had energy to burn. She had lots of girl friends, which is important. You need friends of your own sex. But I thought she was heading for a fall."

"Why?"

She folded her hands. "She was getting a little too wild. Enjoying her hold over men a little too much."

"And Tedi didn't see it?"

"No. Well, she was beginning to sense it, but as I said, parents are blind."

"Here it comes." The rain hit the windows and Golly moved off the sill.

"Back on track. Bobby Franklin will be our president for

as long as he can stand the job. He's good at it and we're lucky to have him. If you want to be a joint-master, you must work with Bobby. And Betty, too." Sister returned to what Crawford needed to do.

"You've never had a joint-master. Think you could do it?"

"If you or whoever stays out of the kennel, I can. I won't have anyone messing with my hounds or my breeding program."

"Well, what happens if you drop dead?"

"Crawford, I do make allowances for the fact that you are from Indiana, but for God's sake could you be a little less direct? Of course, I will drop dead one day, as you so bluntly put it. Who knows when?"

"Well, who will continue your breeding program?"

"Shaker."

"What if he's gone?"

"I've written it down. But you do point out a vulnerability. If you are chosen as a joint-master, I will need to be training someone to take my place when that time comes. A true hunting master."

"I understand that."

"Good."

They talked a bit more, then Crawford rose.

She accompanied him to the back door. "Would you like an umbrella?"

"No. I'll make a dash for it." He pecked her on the cheek. He'd grown fond of her even though she frustrated him. "Are you worried about this Nola thing?"

"The truth?" She took a deep breath. "I'm worried sick."

C H A P T E R   1 4

At six-thirty on the morning of Saturday, September 7, a light easterly wind carried a fresh tang in the air, a hint of changes to come.

A hardy band of twelve gathered at the kennels in these last moments before sunup. Sunrise was 6:38 on this day. The first day of cubbing excited the hard-core foxhunters, the ones who would follow hounds on horseback or on foot, in cars, in rickshaws if there was no other way. For this happy group, hunting with hounds was a passion right up there with the ecstasies of Saint Teresa of Avila.

Those hounds waiting in the draw run, a special pen to hold the hounds hunting that day, leapt up and down in excitement. Those not drawn wailed in abject misery.

Not to go out on the first day of cubbing was no disgrace to a hound. Only a foolish huntsman or master would stack the pack with young entry. Each day of cubbing, like each day of preseason football, different young hounds would be mixed with different mature hounds. By the end of cubbing, huntsman and master would have a solid sense of which youngsters had learned their lessons and which older hounds had become a step too slow.

The older, trusted hounds understood this training process, but that didn't mean they wanted to stay behind even if they knew perfectly well they'd be out next time. No good hound wants to sit in the kennel.

Atop her light bay with the blaze, Sybil Fawkes's quiet demeanor belied her inner nervousness. She had accepted the position of honorary first whipper-in, the honorary meaning no remuneration, with excitement and fear. She could ride hard, but she wasn't sure she could identify all the hounds even though she'd come to the kennel almost every day since the end of July. Doug had spent a lot of time with her before leaving to carry the horn at Shenandoah, but she was still nervous.

August had drained Sybil. It hadn't just been the heat. The ceremony at Nola's grave, although restrained, even beautiful, had hammered home her loss.

She found herself snapping at her boys. Ken, sensitive to her moods, kept the kids busy.

Sybil's restorative time proved to be with the hounds. Working with the animals, with Sister and Shaker, gave her some peace. Their focus on the pack was so intense, it crowded out her sadness over Nola.

When she worried that she wouldn't make a good whipper-in, Sister encouraged her, telling her she'd make mistakes but she'd learn from them.

"I've been hunting since I was six and I still make mistakes. Always will," Sister had said.

Betty Franklin, who had been second whipper-in for over a decade, could have filled the first's boots but she had to work for a living. There might be times when she couldn't show up. Also, Betty had limited resources and one daughter to get through college. She couldn't afford the horses. She owned two fabulous horses, Outlaw and Magellan, and Bobby owned a horse. They couldn't afford any more horses, which depressed Betty.

But she was anything but depressed this morning. Butterflies fluttered in her stomach just as the real things were awakening to soft light.

Sister, too, had butterflies. Opening Hunt would mean the beginning of the formal season, but this, this was the true beginning and she so wanted her young entry to do her proud.

As Crawford and others had predicted, nothing more was learned concerning Nola's death. The murder crept into conversations but not with the earlier frequency and intensity.

Tedi accepted the offer of a sip from Crawford's flask as she sat on Maid of Honor, her smallish chestnut mare, who possessed a fiery temper—but then, she was a redhead. Tedi's salt sack, an unbleached linen coat worn in hot weather, hung perfectly from her shoulders, a subtle nip in at the waist. Salt sacks usually hang like sacks, but Tedi, a fastidious woman, had hers hand-fitted.

Every stitch of clothing on her body had been tailored for her over forty years ago. Good hunting clothes pass from generation to generation. A few fads might appear—such as short hunting coats during the seventies and eighties—but hunters soon return to the tried and true. A longer skirt on a hunting jacket protects the thigh. Sensible. Everything must be sensible.

Cubbing granted the rider a greater latitude of personal

expression in matters of dress. One could wear a tweed jacket with or without a waistcoat depending on the temperature. It was already sixty degrees, so everyone there, seasoned hunters, knew by the time hounds were lifted they'd be boiling in a vest. Their vests hung back in their trailers.

People wore white, yellow, pink, or oxford blue shirts with ties. Their britches were beige or canary, as no one wore white in the field on an informal day.

Betty wore a pair of twenty-year-old oxblood boots; their patina glowed with the years. Her gloves were also oxblood and she wore a thin, thin navy jacket with a yellow shirt and a hunter green tie.

Bobby, after asking the master's permission, rode in a shirt only. It wasn't truly proper, but he was so overweight that the heat vexed him especially. He wore a lovely Egyptian cotton white shirt and a maroon tie with light blue rampant lions embroidered on it. He'd worn the same tie for the first day of cubbing for the last fourteen years. It brought luck.

Shaker wore a gray tweed so old, it was even thinner than Betty's navy coat. His brown field boots glistened. His well-worn brown hunting cap gave testimony to many a season. He carried the cap under his arm. Protocol decreed he could put on his cap only when the master said, "Hounds, please!"

While spanking-new clothes were beautiful, there was a quiet pride in the faded ones, proof of hard rides over the years.

Edward Bancroft, more reserved and preoccupied of late, roused himself to be convivial. Ken Fawkes, also wearing a salt sack, offered his flask to one and all. He beamed with pride at his wife and counseled her before they set off that morning that cubbing would be more difficult than the formal season because hounds weren't yet settled. If she could get through cubbing, why, the rest of the season would be a piece of cake.

Ronnie Haslip rivaled the impeccable Crawford in the splendor of his turnout. His gloves, butter-soft pale yellow, matched his breeches. He wore Newmarket boots, the height of fashion for warm days but rarely seen because they wear out much faster than all leather boots. The inside of the boot and the foot was either brown or oxblood leather, but the shank of the boot was made of a burlaplike fabric lined in microthin leather. A rolled rim of leather topped off these impressive boots. Ronnie even wore garters with his Newmarkets, something rarely seen now.

His shirt, a pale pink button-down, fit him just right as did the dark green hunting jacket he'd had made while visiting in Ireland. A deep violet tie secured by a narrow, unadorned gold bar was echoed by a woven belt the same color as his tie. His black velvet cap, tails up since he was neither a master nor a huntsman, had faded to a pleasing hue that declared he knew his business. He carried an expensive applewood knob end crop with a kangaroo thong.

All the riders carried crops. Usually they saved the staghorn crops for formal hunting, but in Betty's case that was all she had. It wasn't improper to carry the staghorn while cubbing, really, it was just that once formal hunting started, riders were locked into a more rigid sartorial system. Then you had to carry the staghorn crop or none at all. Though they were rarely used on the horses, they proved useful. One could lean out of the saddle and hook a gate or close it with the crop. The really dexterous might dangle the staghorn end over their horse's flank and pick up a dropped cap or glove. This was always met with approval.

Today, Sister carried a knob end crop, an old blackthorn,

perfectly balanced with a whopping eight-foot, twelve-plaited thong topped off by a cracker she made herself out of plastic baling twine. When she popped her whip it sounded like a rifle shot.

Her cheeks were flushed, her eyes bright; she couldn't wait to get going. As the wind came out of the east, there was no point in fiddle-faddling, she'd cast right into it. Hit a line fast and go.

The youngsters had shone at their foxpen outings. She wasn't worried that they needed to head downwind for a bit to settle. Anyway, the temperature would climb quickly. Off to a good start, a bracing run, then lift and bring everyone back to the kennels on a high note.

Positive reinforcement worked much better than negative, in Sister's opinion. Let the youngsters feel they've done well and they'd do even better next time.

Her old salt sack with its holes carefully patched, her boots repaired that summer by Dehner, a boot maker in Omaha, her mustard breeches and light blue shirt all suited her. She wore a bridle leather belt, matching her boots, peanut brittle in color. She looked exactly right, but she wasn't showing off.

Jane Arnold was a stickler for being correct. One intrepid soul mentioned to her that another hunt was allowing members to cub in chaps.

"Oh, how interesting," she replied, and uttered not another word.

That was the end of that.

Being superstitious, she pinned Raymond's grandfather's pocket watch to the inside of her coat pocket as she always did. John "Hap" Arnold, a hunting man, had a pocket watch devised wherein the cover had a round glass center so he could see the arms where they attached to the center of the watch.

The outside rim of the watch, gold, had the hours engraved on it. She could see enough of the slender blued hands to make out the time without popping open the top. This cover came in handy should Sister smack into a tree or take an involuntary dismount. And she never had to open the watch in rain. As Bobby had his good-luck tie, she had her good-luck watch.

On the right rear side of her saddle hung couple straps in case she had to bring back tuckered-out hounds early. However, on the High Holy Days—Opening Hunt, Thanksgiving, Christmas, and New Year's Hunts—she carried a ladies' sandwich case, instead of couple straps, with the rectangular glass flask inside the case. When visiting other hunts she also carried this case. A small silver flask filled with iced tea rested in her inside coat pocket.

It took years to conquer the minutiae of hunting attire, ever a fruitful source of discord. An elderly member might fume that few wore garters anymore. A younger member would respond that boots stayed up quite well by themselves when bespoke by Dehner, Vogel, Lobb, or Maxwell.

Someone else would be horrified if a lady wore a hunt cap rather than a derby, and no one really wanted to say what they thought of chin straps. No master could disallow them, but behind the users' backs they were always called "sissy straps."

Ladies had been known to tear one another's veils off during formal hunting when one disdained the concave of another lady's top hat. One of the worst arguments Nola ever got into the last year of her life occurred when she sniffed that Frances Gohanna, soon to be Frances Assumptio, had a dressage top hat perched on her head instead of a true hunting top hat. Exactly why these trifles inspired such emotion amused Sister, but then foxhunters were passionate by nature.

Even Golliwog, viewing the assembled from the vantage

point of the open stable door, was excited and took note of how the people were turned out. Once hounds were loosed she would take the precaution of repairing to the hayloft to watch the hunt. Occasionally an errant hound youngster would wander into the stable, and Golly loathed all that whining and slobber.

Sister, on Lafayette, rode over to Shaker. "Wind's picking up. I know we didn't want to run into After All, but we have two miles until their border. Best to cast east now."

Shaker, too, had noticed the shift. Their original plan was to strike north and hunt toward Foxglove Farm. Then he'd swing the pack around to the bottom of Hangman's Ridge and hunt through the woods on the west side of the old farm road right back to the kennels. Given their hound walks all summer this territory would be familiar to a youngster if he or she became separated from the pack. The last thing either of them wanted to do was have a young one lost and frantic first time out.

Three couple of young entry were in the pack. Six to watch. The veterans were pretty foolproof.

"East it is." His voice lowered.

Sister left him and rode to the small field. "Sun's up. What are we waiting for?" She beamed.

"Here's to a great season," Crawford called.

The others murmured their agreement.

"Hounds, please," Sister called to Shaker.

He slapped his cap on his head and Betty opened the gate. She then quickly swung herself onto Outlaw, as good a horse as was ever foaled if not the most beautiful.

"YAHOO," the hounds cried.

Thirty couple of hounds bounded out of the kennel, spirits high, then waited for Shaker to blow a low wiggly note followed by a high short one that meant, "We're on our way." This was blown as much for the humans as for the hounds. Humans have a tendency to dawdle.

Hounds gaily trotted behind their huntsman, Sybil to their left and Betty to their right. Sister followed forty yards behind, leading the field as the rim of the sun, shocking scarlet, inched over the horizon.

Beyond the apple orchard they passed an old peach orchard, filled with delicious Alberta peaches. Tempting though it was to cast in there, both huntsman and master wanted to reach the sheep's meadow between the farm road and the woods. That pasture's rich soil held scent. On a good day, hounds might tease a line into the woods or back toward the orchards and the pace picked up accordingly. Not that hitting a scorching scent right off wasn't a dream, it was, but sometimes, especially with young ones, a teasing scent helped organize their minds. You never knew with scent.

A black three-board fence marked off the meadow, a coop squatted in the best place to jump. Shaker on Gunpowder, a rangy gray formerly off the racetrack, effortlessly sailed over. His whippers-in had preceded him into the field. Sister could always push up a straggling hound.

"Noses down, young ones!" Cora commanded.

"I got something. I got something!" Trident, a first-year entry, squealed.

Asa ambled over, sniffled, *"Yes, you do, son. That's a groundhog."*

The other hounds laughed as Trident, ears dropping for a moment, accepted his chastisement, then decided he'd follow Asa. He couldn't go wrong then.

A sweetish, heavy, lingering line greeted Diana's sensitive nose as she probed a mossy patch amidst the timothy swaying in the east wind. *"Pay dirt."*

Although only in her second year, Diana, tremendously gifted, had earned the respect of the older hounds.

Just to be certain, Asa touched his nose to the spot. *"We're off."*

Both Diana and Asa pushed forward, Cora already ahead of them. Her nose, while not as extraordinary as Diana's, was plenty good enough. Yes, this line was perhaps fifteen minutes old and, on the dew, the temperature in the low sixties, it would hold for perhaps another five or ten minutes in the hay. Then the rising sun plus the wind would scatter it forever.

Trident inhaled the light fragrance. *"This is it! This is it! I'm really hunting. It's not foxpen. This is the real deal."* He was so overcome, he tripped and rolled over.

Trudy, his littermate, laughed as she moved past him, her nose on the ground. *"Showtime!"*

Archie used to say *"Showtime!"* when hounds would find. It made everyone laugh, relaxing yet energizing them.

Hearing their former anchor hound's phrase from this new kid made the others really laugh.

The scent grew stronger, snaking toward the woods. Who-ever left it was in no hurry.

Whoever left it happened to be dozing on a rock outcrop-ping about a quarter of a mile into the woods. Uncle Yancy, a red fox and the husband of Aunt Netty, filled with blackberries, peaches, and grain from Sister's stable, needed a nap to aid his digestion. Uncle Yancy would frequently sit on the window ledge and watch TV at either Shaker's or Doug's cottage. Now that Doug had taken the horn at Shenandoah Valley Hunt, he won-dered if anyone would be in there. He could see the picture bet-ter from Doug's window than from Shaker's. He liked to keep up with the world. Raleigh and Rooster never minded his curiosity, but that damned cat would torment him sometimes. She'd call out to the hounds, *"Look who's here, you lazy sots."* Then some offended creature would open his big mouth and Yancy'd push off.

He lifted his head from his delicate paws. *"Oh, bother."*

Bitsy, on her way home from a very successful night, screeched, *"They'll be fast, Uncle Yancy."*

"Ha! The foxhound isn't born that can keep up with me."

Bitsy landed on a low maple limb. *"Pride goeth before a fall."*

He stretched as the sound grew closer. *"Not pride. Simple fact. If you want a good time, fly with me as I send these young ones in the wrong direction. Might even unseat a few humans, too. Why any creature would want to totter around on two legs is beyond me."*

"That's why they ride horses. Then they have four," Bitsy sensibly concluded.

"I hadn't thought of that. Of course, some of them can't stay on those horses, now can they? A weak and vain species, the human, but a few are quite lovely. Oh well"—he shook himself—*"let's cause as much mayhem as possible."*

He left the rocks, walked down to Broad Creek, crossed it, then climbed out on the other side. He shook off the water.

"I'm telling you, Uncle Yancy, these young ones are fast."

"Bitsy, they aren't supposed to run in front of the pack. They're supposed to run as a pack."

"That's what cubbing is for, to teach them. And I wouldn't be so cocky if I were you. If St. Just is about, he'll make trouble."

St. Just, king of the crows, hated foxes, especially red foxes, because Target, Uncle Yancy's brother, had killed his mate. St. Just swore revenge on the whole fox nation and he had led one young red to his death last year.

Finally heeding the little owl, Uncle Yancy started trotting east.

"It's getting stronger!" Trudy yelped as she approached the rocks.

Sybil, up ahead, spied Uncle Yancy slipping through a thick stand of holly. "Tallyho!"

Yancy decided to run after that. He broke out of the holly, crossed an old rutted path, dove into a thick thorny underbrush, then slithered out of that and headed for the edge of the woods.

"*Over here.*" Dasher, a second-year dog hound, littermate to Diana, reached the edge of the creek the same time as Cora. He splashed across the creek, then began whining because he couldn't pick up the scent.

"*Don't be a nincompoop!*" Cora chided him. "*Do you really think a fox is going to walk straight across a creek? You go left, I'll go right. And who's to say he didn't double back? Trudy,*" she called to the youngster, "*you and your idiot brother work that side of the creek.*"

While hounds searched for the scent, Sister and the field quietly waited on the rutted wagon road.

Crawford had just unscrewed the top of his silver flask when Dasher hollered, "*Here.*"

"Drat." Crawford knocked back a hasty gulp, motioned for Marty to have a sip, which she declined. As they trotted off he screwed on the cap, its little silver hinge ensuring it wouldn't fall off. Not a drop sloshed on him even though he'd filled it to the brim. He was quite proud of himself.

"*Stronger!*" Cora, again ahead, spoke in her light, pretty voice.

Bitsy flew back to watch the hounds, then took off again to give Yancy a progress report. "*They just ran into the thorns.*"

"*Damn,*" Yancy cursed. These hounds were faster than he thought.

He broke out of the woods and into the easternmost meadow of Roughneck Farm, which was filled with black-eyed Susans, Queen Anne's lace, and cornflowers; it hadn't been weeded or overseeded in years. Sister thought of it as her wild-flower experiment and was loath to return it to timothy, alfalfa, or orchard grass.

A hog's-back jump loomed in the fence line. Sister and Lafayette sailed over it as the pace was picking up. She saw Betty, up ahead, already flying over the spanking-new coop that marked the westernmost border of After All Farm.

"This fox is a devil," she thought to herself.

The hounds, in full cry now, roared across the wildflower meadow. Even Trident was on, his concentration improving.

Walter Lungrun, riding Clemson, an older and wiser horse, steered clear of Crawford, whose horse, Czapaka, a big warm-blood, occasionally refused a jump when he'd had enough of Crawford sawing at the reins.

New coops, not having yet settled into the earth, looked bigger than normal. Fortunately, Tedi and Edward painted theirs black. Unpainted coops seemed to cause more trouble than painted ones. Sister never knew if the trouble was with the horses or with the people.

As she trusted Lafayette with her heart and soul, she didn't give this jump a second thought, landing just as she heard Shaker double the notes on the horn.

They were close, close to their fox, who must have tarried along the way.

Uncle Yancy, putting on the afterburners now, was shad-owed by Bitsy, who was quite worried about him. She wished she hadn't said *"Pride goeth before a fall,"* as she had no desire to see Uncle Yancy, everybody's uncle, perish. Rarely did Sister's hounds kill, but if a fox was ancient or sick, the hounds might dispatch it swiftly. In three seconds the quarry was dead, its neck snapped by the lead hound.

Bitsy tried to remember the last time there was a kill. It

had been three years ago; one of the red tribe at the edge of the territory came down with distemper. Either way he was going to die because he refused to eat the medicines put out for him; he refused to go into one of the Havahart traps that Sister and Shaker put out in an effort to save him. He knew other foxes had been taken to the vet, but he did not trust any human, not even Sister.

"At least he died fast," Bitsy thought to herself.

If she was worried, Uncle Yancy was not. Yes, the pack was faster. Sister had retired quite a few older hounds over the summer who now graced barns and hearths throughout the membership. These young ones had speed. Sister was breeding in more speed. He would have to tell the others.

In the meantime, he had to shake these damned hounds. He heard Cora's distinctive voice, then Asa's, both smart hounds.

"But not as smart as I am." He chuckled as he raced for the covered bridge and trotted across it, dragging his brush purposefully to leave a heavy, heavy scent. Then he started up the farm road, covered in brown pearock. The Bancrofts spared no expense on those items they considered aesthetically pleasing.

He whirled around, 180 degrees, backtracking in his own footprints, then launched himself at the edge of the covered bridge and down into the waters of Snake Creek, which were high, muddy, and fast from all the rain. Swimming to the opposite bank proved harder than he'd anticipated.

"Hurry!" Bitsy blinked from atop the covered bridge.

Uncle Yancy made it to the far side. The swim had cost him precious time and tired him. He heard the hounds not a third of a mile away, closing with blinding speed.

"Damn them," he cursed as he raced for the place where Nola and Peppermint were now buried.

The red fox with a little white tip on his tail leapt over the zigzag fence, crossed the twenty yards to the other side, and leapt over that. The earth, still soft from the digging and from the rains, showed distinct footprints marking his progress. Tedi had put up a zigzag fence until the stonemason, in high demand, could build stone walls around the graves.

A muddy trail followed him as he headed along the ridge, then turned in an arc back toward Roughneck Farm. He was more tired than he wanted to be. A groundhog hole, messy but under the circumstances better than nothing, had been dug right along the fence line between After All Farm and Sister's wildflower meadow. He wasn't going to be able to make the loop back to his den at this rate and he wished he'd paid more attention to Bitsy, faithfully flying overhead.

"Ouch!"

Uncle Yancy looked upward. St. Just had dive-bombed Bitsy, pecking her.

"You little creep!" St. Just pecked at Bitsy again, who was built for silent flight. She couldn't maneuver as handily as the blue-black bird, but she was smarter. She flew low to the ground, right over Uncle Yancy. If St. Just tried for her, Yancy could whirl around and possibly catch the hated bird in his jaws, or even with his front paws.

St. Just knew better than to get close to a fox. He cursed Bitsy for helping the fox and squawked loudly. If only he could turn the hounds before they reached the covered bridge, he could get them on Uncle Yancy fast. But his outburst and his bad language offended Athena, who had just stopped over between the two farms. A nest of baby copperheads, born late but with a good chance of survival thanks to the abundance of game, were close to the large rock where they lived. She thought one would make a tasty dessert, and St. Just spoiled everything by scaring them back under their rock.

He offended her in principle. He didn't know his place. Then, when she saw him go after Bitsy, her blood boiled. She lifted off the evergreen branch, her large wingspan impressive, and noiselessly, effortlessly came up behind the crow with four big flaps of her wings. She zoomed for him, talons down. He heard her a split second too late. As he turned to avoid the full impact of her blow, she caught him on the right wing. Enough to throw him off and enough to tear out feathers painfully.

"Out of my sight, peasant!"

Feathers flying, St. Just feared he might fall to earth with them. He pulled himself out of the dive, veering back toward the woods. Uncle Yancy, pursued though he was, would have made short work of this mortal enemy and then left the carcass to distract the hounds. Fresh blood was always distracting to a hound.

"Thank God you're here," Bitsy hollered, her high-pitched voice frightening four deer grazing below.

"Thank Athena." The large bird hooted low, mentioning her namesake, then with a few powerful blasts she was over the wildflower meadow, heading to her home high in a huge walnut by Sister's house.

Back at the creek, the hounds charged across the covered bridge in full cry.

Sister was about to lead the field across, knowing there'd be some fussing from the horses inside the bridge, when she heard a change in Diana's voice. Wisely, for she trusted her hounds, she paused.

People panted. Horses' ears pricked forward; they thought stopping pure folly, but they did as they were told.

Cora had overrun the line. Asa came up to Diana. He, too, changed his tune.

"*What's happening? What's happening?*" Trident thought he'd done something wrong.

"*Pipe down and listen.*" Dasher put his nose to the ground.

In a situation like this, Dragon was invaluable, for he was highly intelligent and had an incredible nose. But he'd been left back in the kennel since Shaker felt he had enough good hounds out and Dragon could be a handful. He thought the young ones, especially this T litter, might do better without Dragon today.

Little by little, Dasher, not as brilliant as his brother but methodical, worked his way back to the bridge. "*I think he's doubled back.*"

Hounds milled around, then Cora said, "*Well, there's only one way to be sure. Dasher, go through the bridge; be careful, because some fool human will say you are doubling back on the line, and then Sybil, who's new, remember, will rate you. But if he has doubled back, his scent will be stronger on the other side. Which direction, I don't know. Take Diana with you.*"

Both Dasher and Diana tore back across the bridge.

"Heel," Ronnie Haslip whispered to Crawford, who nodded knowingly.

Technically they were right, but Sister did not call out to her hounds to join the others. Diana and Dasher were terrific second-year entry.

Sybil, forward of the bridge, turned to head back. Shaker sat right on the far side of the bridge, close to his lead hounds.

Dasher said low to Diana, "*Here, I think this is fresher.*"

She put her nose down and inhaled. "*Yes, but we'd best be sure before we call them all back to us.*"

They ran top speed and then were quite certain that the fox had headed up the ridge. "*Yes! He's here. Come on.*"

Shaker, thrilled with these two, blew three doubling notes,

sending the others on to them, claws clicking on the wooden floor of the bridge.

They emerged, cut hard right, and flew up the ridge. They all jumped the newly installed zigzag fence, running hard over Nola's and Peppermint's graves, headstones not yet carved.

Sister hesitated one moment, waiting for her huntsman to get ahead of her. She then rode up the ridge but wide of the new grave sites. Ken Fawkes, usually a strong rider, lost control of his horse, who wanted to follow the hounds directly. The big dark horse, almost black, catapulted over the first line of the zigzag fence, took one giant stride, and was over the second. Deep hoofprints now mingled with Uncle Yancy's prints and those of the hounds.

The woods reverberated with the song of the hounds. Within minutes they were back over the fence line dividing After All Farm from Roughneck Farm.

Sister, knowing she had to head back to the new coop, turned and pressed Lafayette on. She cursed because the underbrush was thick. The leaves were still on the trees, and she couldn't see her hounds in the thick woods. This was another reason cubbing was harder than formal hunting. If she didn't hurry up she'd get thrown out and be way behind. She reached the new coop, got well over, then headed right on a diagonal across the open field. She could see the flowers and hay swaying and sterns swaying, too, where hounds pushed through, their voices in unison.

"He's close! He's close!"

And he was. Uncle Yancy slid into the groundhog hole, rolling right on top of the groundhog.

"I beg your pardon."

The groundhog, large and unkempt, but jolly, said, *"Care for some sweet grass?"*

"Thank you, no." Yancy couldn't understand how any animal could be as sloppy as this fellow. *"You know within a second those hounds will start digging at your main entrance."*

"Good. That will save me work."

"I shall assume you have other exits should it come to that."

"One of them right under a hanging hornet's nest. Three feet long it is." The groundhog, lying on his back, laughed just as Cora dove toward the hole and began digging frantically.

Uncle Yancy's scent was so strong, it drove her wild. Red, moist earth splattered up behind her paws. Diana joined her at the edges, as did Asa and Dasher.

Trident asked his sister, *"Are we supposed to do that?"*

"I think you have to be first. There isn't room for us to get in there, but I think we're supposed to sing really, really loud."

Trudy and Trident did just that and were joined by every hound there. Triumph!

Shaker arrived, hopped off Gunpowder, and blew the happy notes signifying that these wonderful hounds had denned their fox.

Sybil rode up, taking Gunpowder's reins.

"I know my job," the gray snapped, incensed that Sybil thought he might walk off.

Betty rode in from the opposite direction as the field pulled up not ten yards away.

Shaker took the horn from his lips. "He's in there. He's in there. What good hounds. Good hounds." He grabbed Cora's tail, pulling her out of there. She weighed seventy pounds of pure muscle. "You're quite the girl."

"I am!" Cora turned a circle of pure joy.

Then Shaker called each hound by name, praising their good work. He petted the puppies.

Sister rode up. "A fine beginning. Shall we call it a day?"

"Yes, ma'am." Shaker smiled. "And did you see how Dasher and Diana came back across the bridge? That's as nice a piece of work as I have ever seen in my life."

Sister looked down at the two tricolor hounds. "Diana and Dasher, you have made me very, very proud."

They wagged their whole bodies.

"Proud of you, proud of you." Shaker again blew the notes of victory, then, without a grunt, lifted himself back into the saddle.

As they rode back toward the kennels, Ken, ashen-faced, came alongside his mother-in-law. "I am terribly sorry. I couldn't hold him. I—"

She held up her hand. "Ken, to have the fox and hounds run across your grave is a good thing. No apology necessary. Nola would be laughing with the excitement of it."

No one else said a word about it while the Bancrofts were around.

Uncle Yancy thanked his host and stuck his head up to make sure there were no stragglers.

Bitsy, in a pawpaw tree, giggled. *"A near thing. And running over Nola and Peppermint like that."*

"That's an unquiet grave," the red fox said. Mask to the west, he headed for home.

CHAPTER 15

Crawford and Marty Howard hosted a First Day of Cubbing breakfast. Upon reflection they decided to pass on having an evening gathering. Instead they hired a local caterer who set up outdoor stoves outside Sister's stable. Crawford considered setting them up on the long rolling lawn overlooking Sister's fall gardens, but then he'd have to tell her. He wanted the breakfast to be a surprise, as did Marty. Having it back at the stable where the trailers were parked wouldn't disturb her lawn. As people often brought homemade breads, sandwiches, or drinks, sharing same at the trailers, Crawford and Marty thought they wouldn't need to ask permission and the surprise would be complete.

It was. People untacked and wiped down their horses to the scent of bacon crackling on the grill, succulent blond and regular sausages, and omelettes.

One gave the two chefs their omelette order and within minutes it was ready. Breads, jellies, fruits, cold cereals, and fresh milk along with sweets covered the long table to the side of the stoves.

The riders were thrilled, as were the hounds, who could smell the enticing medley of aromas. Whatever might be left over would be mixed into their kibble later.

"What a wonderful idea," Betty Franklin said to Sybil as they stood in line.

"I never realize how famished I am while I'm hunting, but the second I get back to the trailers my stomach makes as much noise as *The 1812 Overture.*" Sybil laughed at herself.

Marty Howard was whispering directions to the caterer's assistant, pouring coffee.

"Right away, madam." He handed her a large cup.

She carried the steaming coffee to Shaker, still in the kennels.

He looked up and smiled as she came through the door. "Mrs. Howard."

"Here. What a great day. Now come on over and get your piping hot omelette. The Boss said for me to tell you to come on, you can wash down the kennels on a full stomach better than on an empty one."

"Did she?" He smiled broadly. "What a good woman." He gratefully took a swallow. "Very good."

"Jamaican."

"High test."

"Ninety-three octane." Marty waited for him to toss a collar in the bucket hanging from the wall, a bucket used just for this purpose, as collars were removed from hounds when they returned from their labors.

As they walked back together to the festivities, Marty asked, "Did you always want to be a huntsman?"

"Yes, I did."

"How did you learn?"

"My parents allowed me to move up to Warrenton to live with my aunt. I was twelve and I begged because the huntsman at Warrenton, Fred Duncan, said he'd set me to work in the kennels. That's how I started. Fred was a fine huntsman. He'd whipped-in to Eddie Bywaters, the last huntsman of the great Bywaters clan. I learned so much from Fred, and I could go over and watch Melvin Poe hunt the Orange County hounds. Fred would take me up to watch the Piedmont hounds."

Marty loved hearing these stories and knew there was so much to learn not just about foxhunting itself but about the incredible people who had carried it forward throughout the generations. "When did you get your first job?"

"Here." He put his hand under Marty's elbow as she was about to step into a small depression. "Jefferson Hunt needed a first whipper-in, and even though I was young, Fred vouched for me. Raymond put me on every screwball horse he could beg, borrow, or steal before he'd hire me. He finally said, 'Kid can stick on a horse.' That was that. And I never want to leave. I love it here."

"Do you ever worry about the money? I mean, huntsmen make so little, and what if something were to happen?"

"I don't worry. Maybe I should, but I knew as a little kid that my life wasn't about money. This is what I've always wanted to do, and you know, Mrs. Howard, there isn't enough money in the world to get me to give it up."

"But what if you're hurt?" Marty belonged to the worrying class.

"The Boss will take care of me just like I'd take care of her. We've been though a lot together."

Marty thought about this, an attitude so different from the way she was raised and from the milieu in which she lived. "You're a lucky man."

Betty called out to Shaker, "How about those young entry?"

He gave her the thumbs-up sign.

Crawford, hoping to ingratiate himself with a person he considered a servant, and technically, Shaker was a servant, said, "Thank you."

"The hounds did all the work." Shaker smiled.

Sister, in line, observed the exchange as well as the high spirits of the group.

Bobby, in front of her, was chatting with Tedi. He noticed his wife. "Hey, hey there. I see you flirting with my wife."

Ken Fawkes, who was holding a plate for Betty, replied, "Bobby, I'll give you credit. You knew a good thing when you saw it."

Everyone laughed.

As Shaker moved through the line, people complimented him. He was their star. They watched him ahead, taking the jumps first, without a lead. They saw him traverse territory they could loop around thanks to the wisdom of Sister, and they watched him work patiently with the hounds.

"Well done." Bobby beamed as he passed Shaker.

"Can you eat all that?" Shaker looked at Bobby's full plate.

"I can. That's the problem."

Once everyone had a full plate, the caterer's assistant walked about refilling coffee cups, fetching hot tea or a cold Co-Cola.

People sat on their portable mounting blocks, hay bales, upturned buckets.

Sister, sitting next to Shaker, said to Ronnie Haslip, "Do you remember the day two years ago when Shaker had the flu so I took the horn?"

"Indeed, I do," Ronnie replied.

"I asked him for advice and he said, 'Well, I'll tell you what Fred Duncan told me: Hunt your hounds and don't look behind you.' So I did."

The horses hung their heads over the fence, observing the delighted people. The caterer gave them apples from the fruit basket.

"I like this guy," Keepsake commented.

Golly had positioned herself in the middle of the seated humans. She lay on her side, her tail lazily swishing up and down. Then she casually rolled on her back, her glittering eyes scanning the group. *"I'm here."*

Sybil laughed. "Sister, Golly is speaking to us."

Everyone focused on the cat, which encouraged her behavior. Raleigh and Rooster, seated by Sister, ignored the calico.

"Golly, come over here. I'll give you bacon," Tedi offered.

That fast, the cat sprang to her feet, zoomed over, and snatched the bacon from Tedi's fingers.

"Shameless," Marty commented.

The conversation bounced between everyone at once and then small fragments of people.

Tedi was mentioning to Sister her memories of a safari her parents had taken her on when she was a teenager. ". . . no one thought much about conservation back then. You know, I look back and I regret those tigers and giraffes my parents bagged. But I can't bring himself to throw out the hides. It seems sacrilegious somehow. And you know, too, Janie, I have much more fun foxhunting than I ever did or could on a safari. 'O, the blood more stirs,/ To rouse a lion than to start a hare!' Remember? Hotspur. He was wrong."

"Sir Henry Percy never hunted fox, he was too busy hunting the Scots." Crawford joined the conversation.

"Never hunted behind Ashland Bassets, either," Edward commented, mentioning a pack of bassets whose quarry was rabbit. Following them on foot could be very exciting.

"Hey, where's Ralph today?" Betty asked.

"Moline," Ken answered. "Conference."

Moline was the headquarters of John Deere.

"Poor Ralph. Had to miss the first day of cubbing because of business. Work interferes with the really important things in life," Bobby said, and laughed.

As the gathering broke up, Crawford was telling Ron why they chose a breakfast instead of a party. He kept his voice low. "... memories. Marty discreetly inquired around and found out that after Nola and Guy disappeared no one ever gave a First Day of Cubbing evening party again. We thought better of it, but then Marty suggested we do this. I think we'll make a tradition of it."

"I hope you do. Of course, that means next year you'll have one hundred people out on the first day."

Crawford shrugged. "Good. I'll just buy more eggs." He picked up his mounting block, placing it inside the tack room of his trailer. "As nothing else had turned up, comes as no surprise, I think we've heard the last of Nola and Guy. It's for the best."

Ron replied, voice even lower, "God, I hope so."

CHAPTER 16

A thin wisp of ground fog snaked over the pasture where Lafayette, Rickyroo, Keepsake, and Aztec munched and a family of raccoons crossed toward the garbage cans in the barn. Occasionally if Sister forgot to close the tack room door the raccoons would open the desk drawer and pull out bags of bite-sized Hershey's bars. They loved sweets, as did the possums who followed them at a discreet distance.

Lafayette lorded it over the Rickyroo and Aztec, both young horses at six and five respectively. He relayed the day's hunting, from the first moment the bit was in his mouth to his wash down with warm water in the wash stall, in colorful detail.

Keepsake, eight years old and a thoroughbred/quarter horse cross, thought Lafayette was laying it on a little thick. He nibbled twenty feet away from the three thoroughbreds. He liked them well enough but he felt he was more intelligent, or at least less gullible.

He noticed the downstairs lights in the house going off, the upstairs bedroom light switching on. The blue light of the television shone from Shaker's window. He noticed Showboat, Gunpowder, and Hojo, three former steeplechasers, dozing in the adjoining pasture. Each of them had been donated to the hunt for the huntsmen's use. Sometimes that meant the horses were orangutans; no one else could handle them, so this was the last stop unless the owner shipped them off to the killers. Few foxhunters wanted to put a horse in the knacker's trailer no matter how badly the animal behaved. But the Jefferson Hunt membership had a wide sweep of contacts. Gunpowder had even spent time competing on the flat track. Having run over timber in steeplechase meets, these three disdained the jumps in the hunt field and thought any equine who even glanced sideways at such a puny obstacle, the largest being three feet six inches, was a wimp.

Keepsake could and would jump anything, so he shrugged off their air of superiority.

The night was thankfully cool and pleasant, the breeze still easterly. Sister turned off the air-conditioning and opened the bedroom windows.

The horses and hounds could faintly hear Mozart's *A Little Night Music* floating from her bedroom. Then her phone rang.

She groaned, wondering what the problem was. A night call usually meant a problem. A master's work is endless, whether physical or political, putting out the brush fires flaring up within the hunt club, any hunt club. Some fool left a gate open, another printed up the trail riding schedule and one date was wrong. Someone else hated that cubbing started so early in the morning and they were sure this was a conspiracy to keep them home.

Any group of humans swirls about in a fog of gossip, misunderstanding, and good intentions. Political maneuvering makes for strange bedfellows—and in many an instance the bedfellows really are in bed together. Foxhunting seems to foster even more of that than other activities. The people, by nature, are hot-blooded just like their horses.

By the end of any given day, Sister's reserves of emotional restraint ebbed.

Not all humans depleted her. The ones she loved energized her: Betty Franklin, Shaker Crown, Tedi and Edward Bancroft, and she thought she could learn to love Dr. Walter Lungrun. Maybe it was because he rented Peter Wheeler's old place and she'd loved Peter, had even been his lover for years. In some ways, Walter reminded her of her husband, a curious resemblance, although socially Walter was more reserved than Raymond. Raymond had come to life in a group, his natural element.

Because of that, Raymond had made a fantastic field master. He'd understood the hounds, but he'd loved the people.

Sister felt her husband had been a better field master than she. She would occasionally forget about the people, so intense was her focus on the hounds. But she put her field in the right place time after time, which they greatly appreciated.

Ray Junior had taken after his father. She'd assumed he'd follow her as field master and then master someday.

She often thought of her husband and son at nighttime. The house, quiet, yielded up memories. Even Golly, a naturally mouthy cat, rested her voice at night.

Melancholy and Sister were never on good terms. She

wasn't one to dwell on her losses, on the sorrows that come to us all if we live long enough. They were part of life. If anything, she had learned to thank God for them. Her losses taught her about grace and true love. Her victories taught her to be generous and ultimately thankful.

Tonight as she listened to that most delicious of Mozart compositions, it occurred to her that the structure of music and literature were one and the same thing.

Then the damn phone rang just as this insight was unfolding.

"This better be good!" she growled into the receiver.

A muffled but queerly familiar voice said, "Master, look off the Norwood Bridge—the deep end."

"I beg your pardon." She sat bolt upright.

Both Raleigh and Rooster lifted their heads. Golly, on the pillow next to Sister, pricked forward her ears to better hear the voice on the other end of the line.

"A fifty-five-gallon drum."

"Who is this?"

"Hotspur." With a click, the call ended.

Her hand shaking, she called the sheriff. He'd once given her his cell phone and his home numbers, which she'd prudently placed by the kennel, stable, kitchen, and bedroom phones.

She reached Ben and related her bizarre phone call. Then she hung up, slipped on her moccasins, her white terry cloth robe with her initials, JOA, stitched on the left breast pocket, and hurried down the back stairs into the kitchen. She charged out the back door, running toward Shaker's.

All the horses trotted along with her in their paddocks.

Trident, gazing at the stars, still thrilled from his first hunt, saw her dash to the huntsman's cottage. *"What's Sister doing?"*

Asa, also outside for a walkabout, said, *"Go to sleep, son. You've had a big day."* But he knew something was coming down.

Sister knocked on Shaker's door knocker, a brass crown. "Shaker, Shaker, forgive me for disturbing you."

He opened the door, bare-chested, toothbrush in hand. "What's happened?"

"Oh, Shaker, I heard a voice from the dead."

CHAPTER 17

The Norwood Bridge curved out below a bluff above the Upper James River. Even this far from where its mouth poured into the Chesapeake Bay, the James proved a formidable river. Strong currents, sudden fluctuations in volume, and rough patches of rapids followed by successive small falls meant anyone navigating these waters best be wary.

At times the waters could become surprisingly clear; other times rains pulled down earth from the Blue Ridge Mountains, sending cascades of runoff flowing into the James, making it muddy for days, even weeks.

The village of Norwood, named for Norwood Plantation, still a working farm, clung to the bluff above the river, the source of transportation and commerce well into the 1840s when the bateaus were replaced by the railroads. A small redbrick former church, its steeple pleasingly proportionate to its base, served as the town's post office. While small homes perched along the river roads, larger dwellings sat grandly on the bluff itself, where they had been surveying the river and its passing traffic for three centuries.

Sheriff Ben Sidell watched divers, three of them, submerge then rise again. The Norwood Bridge connected Nelson County with Buckingham County. This was not the deepest part of the Upper James, but was, however, one of the most undisturbed parts of the river.

Few motorized vessels plied these waters. Tubers, rollicking along, would cascade by until they were stopped by the first set of rapids, if indeed they lasted that long. Canoers enjoyed this stretch as the river straightened out from its northern bend. They paddled past fishermen, quietly waiting in their rowboats.

Once a year the bateau festival filled the small town. Flatboats heading downriver and people in period costume drew droves of tourists to watch.

Although it was Sunday, August fourth, Ben acted immediately upon hearing about Sister Jane's mysterious phone call.

After a long talk with Shaker, she'd also called Walter, who agreed to spend the day with Ben Sidell. Sister wanted a hunt club person there and she felt Walter, both by training and temperament, was a good choice.

"If a body was tossed off this bridge, even if sufficiently weighted, it surely would have been carried downstream," Ben said, "be nothing left."

"Two hurricanes tore through here since 1981," Walter replied, "plus plenty of gully washers. But if you follow the direction of the current, a body would have eventually snagged on the shore, maybe there"—he pointed to an eddy on the Buckingham side—"or hung up farther down on the next big arc. Surely someone would have seen it."

"Well, there might only be old shoes to see. Nature's aquatic garbagemen work very efficiently." Ben sighed.

"The murder weapon might have been tossed off the bridge."

Ben pursed his lips. "Yes, but that would work its way downriver as well. Obviously, it's hard to say what killed Nola—a rock or a hammer or even the butt end of a revolver. The side of her skull was shattered. Almost like the murderer had snapped into a killing frenzy."

"The reptilian brain." Walter crossed his arms over his chest. "See it with animals. A few will go crazy with killing. That old part of our brain usually means violence."

The temperature was rising, the heavy river smell rising with it.

"I see a lot of strange things in my business," the sheriff said. "As the social controls have eroded, it seems self-control has eroded with it. We're becoming more violent, not less."

"Rwanda."

"Yugoslavia. Attacks on our country." The sheriff, a pleasant-looking man about the same age as Walter, in the prime of life, squinted as the reflection of the sun off the water temporarily blinded him. "People can usually find a reason to harm someone else. Mix religion into it like the Islamic terrorists and you've glamorized humankind's worst instincts."

Walter half smiled. "Whoever killed Nola didn't need an ideology or national cause."

"And given that she was buried with that huge sapphire on her finger, it sure wasn't robbery. No, her death was about rage or lust."

"Let's go back to the murder weapon for a minute. Assuming that Sister's caller is telling the truth, if whatever was tossed over this bridge was heavy enough, like a sledgehammer, isn't it possible it sank headfirst into the silt, stuck there, and has been covered and uncovered and probably covered again over the last two decades?" Walter put on his sunglasses, blue elliptical lenses.

"I suppose." Ben leaned against the bridge rail, back to the sun. "Walter, you're a member of the hunt. Why do you think Sister Jane got this call?"

"Trust."

"Huh?"

"He trusts her."

"Hmm." Ben turned this over in his mind. "If it was Guy Ramy he would call her instead of his own mother?"

"You don't know that he hasn't been in contact with Alice. She'd never tell."

"True." Ben nodded.

"If he's guilty, he wants us to find whatever is in this river."

"But he doesn't want us to find him."

"Not yet, anyway."

"I wonder if he'd tell Sister where he is."

"I don't know. But Guy would be about forty-eight now. That's a long time to carry around guilt. He may have killed her, but he also loved her."

"You were in junior high, right?" Ben had talked to a lot of people and his memory was good.

"Seventh grade."

"You didn't really know these people?"

"We lived in Louisa County. I saw them at horse shows. My mother and father knew the hunt club crowd. Dad owned a small tire company in Charlottesville. My mother worked there, too. Sooner or later, everyone would need their tires replaced on trucks or trailers."

"Funny, when I go out to question people, whatever the crime, I sweep up a lot of dust."

"Guess you do."

"In your line of work, I'm sure you pick up a lot, too."

"People usually talk to their doctors." Walter jingled the keys in his pocket.

"There's jockeying for power in the hunt club. Hey, maybe it was a crank call. People are worried about Sister getting too old," Ben said.

Walter took his hand out of his pocket, waving away this thought. "She'll outlive us all."

Ben laughed. "She just might."

One of the divers surfaced, flipped up his face mask, and clung to the side of the boat.

Carl Walsh, sitting at the oars, cupped his hand to his mouth and hollered, "Sheriff, found the top of a fifty-five-gallon drum. Can't see the rest of it, it's sunk all the way in the mud."

Ben crossed the bridge to the northerly side. "Well, see if they can get chains around it."

"Bet there's a stove and a refrigerator down there, too." Walter crossed over with him.

"Just one?" Ben hid his anticipation behind humor.

An hour later, a black fifty-five-gallon drum rested on the shore directly under the bridge. The label had long since washed away, but it appeared to be an old oil drum, maybe a paint drum. A few holes, tiny, had been punched into the metal by rocks or fast-moving debris.

What was curious about it was that the top was welded into

place. A rattle could be heard inside when the drum was jostled. And it was heavy, off balance.

"Must be someone in Norwood with an acetylene torch." Ben didn't want to move the drum any more if he could help it. "Carl, call in for a department photographer, too."

Another forty-five minutes passed before Frank Kinser, a distant relative of Doug's, was there with his torch. The photographer arrived, too.

Walter stood back as the blue sparks flew.

Within minutes the lid, cleanly cut, was lifted off.

"Jesus Christ!" Frank cut off his torch, his eyes wide.

A few scraps of cloth clung to a jumble of bones. In the bottom of the drum was a blacksmith's anvil.

The photographer clicked away. Ben carefully observed the remains but did not touch or remove them.

Walter felt that there would be hell to pay.

CHAPTER 18

Technology makes a good servant but a bad master. When the Internet first got rolling, Sister Jane hopped on the bandwagon. Her phone bills soon reached stratospheric proportions. She continued using e-mail only to send out notes to the Hunt's Board of Governors and dear friends. The research possibilities pleased her, but more often than not she found she'd much rather pull out her old *Encyclopaedia Britannica*s. The writing could be quite good, and pausing to peruse subjects other than the searched-for subject always provided unexpected delights.

Keeping expenses down was a struggle she shared with millions of Americans who were no longer driven by hunger or need but were victims of advertising and their own acquisitive natures. Wonderful as the Internet might be, it cost money. Before you knew it you were paying for services and technology you didn't really need.

One of these nonnecessities Sister still indulged was Caller I.D. When her mysterious phone call came in, the number appeared on the small telephone screen: 555-7644. Naturally, she gave the number to Ben Sidell, but she already knew it was the outside pay phone at Roger's Corner.

The sheriff called Roger, who dutifully looked out the window, but by then no one was standing at the pay phone. The last hour before Roger's ten P.M. closing time often proved hectic as people came by for a last pack of cigarettes or muffins for breakfast.

Roger's Corner stayed open on Sundays, but Roger himself took the day off. That Sunday morning, Sister drove down there and parked by the blue eggshell that housed the phone. Gone was the tall glass phone booth with the folding door. The replacement was a cheap small plastic egg offering no protection from the elements. She knew what it looked like, but still for some reason she wanted to check out the phone.

People waved to her as they strolled in and out of the store. Why she wanted to pick up the phone, she didn't know.

Kyle Dawson, Ronnie Haslip, and Dr. Tandy Zachs came and went, all of them riding or social members of the hunt. Finally, she realized she couldn't stand there all day, as no new thoughts were coming to her. She climbed back into the truck and drove to After All Farm.

The sheriff's car and Walter's truck, parked in the driveway, made her question if she should go in. She decided she would when Tedi, who had heard her drive up, opened the front door and waved her in. "Come on. Kitchen."

Seated in the cavernous kitchen she found Edward, Sybil,

Ken, Ben, and Walter. The men rose when Sister entered the room.

Edward pulled up a chair for her.

Ben smiled but gave her a look. She interpreted it to mean she should keep quiet. Walter sat beside her, draping his arm over the back of her chair. She liked that.

"I'm sorry to barge in."

"You could never barge in," Tedi replied.

"Mrs. Arnold, I was just informing the Bancrofts that I received a telephone tip, a voice that was unidentified, telling me to search off the Norwood Bridge." Ben kicked himself. He'd slipped up in his haste to gather together a team to rendezvous at the bridge at sunrise, and neglected to order Sister to keep her mouth shut.

Ben assumed gossip wasn't Sister's lifeblood, but she could have told a few friends. He'd talk to her afterward, but he was worried. He'd made a mistake. He didn't want Sister Jane to pay for it.

Sister understood Ben's intention when he said that he'd received the phone call.

"Sheriff, I take it you found something or you wouldn't be here," Edward surmised.

"Yes. I asked the Doc to be with me this morning." Again, Ben didn't round out the fact that Sister had called Walter's from Shaker's cottage. "A fifty-five-gallon drum mired in the silt and muck was discovered at seven-thirty this morning. Once we raised it, we cut off the top, as it was soldered shut." Everyone held their breath as Ben continued. "Upon opening it, we discovered it contained human remains. How long the body had been there I can't ascertain, but I would guess for years. We might have a positive I.D. later today."

"So soon?" Ken questioned.

"Larry Hund is meeting the coroner in about an hour." Larry was one of the area's best dentists, a man who had been practicing for twenty-five years.

Tedi folded her hands together on the table and it seemed to Sister that the sapphire burned brighter on her hand. "Ben, you think you know who that body is. That's why you're here. Who is it?"

"Like I said, Mrs. Bancroft, I think we'll have a positive I.D. in an hour or so."

"Was the body recognizable?" Sybil felt a rising panic.

"No flesh remained, a bit of clothing. We know it was a man," Ben replied.

"Oh God," Sybil whispered.

"Hotspur." Tedi Bancroft suddenly felt a wave of sympathy for Alice Ramy. "Does Alice know?"

"I have a deputy with her now and I'll be going over there after I leave here," Ben quietly answered. "Again, the I.D. isn't positive, but we are working from the standpoint that the body may be Guy Ramy because of circumstances."

"And you know that whoever killed Guy didn't dispose of the body alone. It would take a Hercules to stuff a man like Guy into a fifty-five-gallon drum, solder it, and then heave it over the bridge," Edward said with a grimace.

"Yes, we are working from that angle as well," Ben said. "Two or more people."

Ken, ashen-faced, simply said, "Horrible. This is horrible."

Ben had hurried to the Bancrofts' because bad news travels fast. He did not want them to receive a phone call from Mr. Kinser or an onlooker. He wished the I.D. could be 100 percent certain, but the feelings of the Bancrofts were important to him. Ben was a sensitive man in a rough line of work. And he knew the discovery of two bodies would have the killer or killers rattled. What they had thought was long buried had arisen from the dead. Feeling in danger, they might endanger others.

"Is there anything we can do to help you?" Edward inquired, his silver eyebrows raised, his face drawn in concern.

"Be alert," Ben replied simply. "And call me if anything occurs to you, no matter how trivial it might seem."

"Yes, of course," Tedi said.

"Let me be off to Mrs. Ramy's. Oh, Sister, walk out with me to the squad car, will you? Walter, too. Perhaps you two can give me an idea of how to handle Mrs. Ramy."

As Sister, Walter, and Ben walked outside, Sybil rubbed her eyes for a moment.

Tedi patted her daughter on the back. "It's sordid, isn't it?"

"You know, Mom, he was a beautiful thing, like some wild animal—just a beautiful thing."

"Not anymore," Ken said softly as he watched the three people outside.

Ben leaned against his brown squad car. "Sister, I apologize to you. I should have asked you last night not to tell anyone about the phone call. Did you talk to anyone else?"

"Walter"—she nodded at the handsome doctor—"and Shaker. Shaker won't tell anyone. He's not a talker unless it's about hounds."

"Nonetheless, remind him."

"I will."

"Walter?" Ben asked him.

Walter shrugged. "No one."

"Mrs. Arnold, do you have any idea why you were called?"

"No, Ben, I told you, I really don't and I wish I did." She

made a straight line in the brown pearock with the toe of her boot. "And please call me Sister or Jane, won't you?"

"I'll try." Ben liked this woman. "Look, this is what I know. Whoever called knows you, trusts you, and lives here. Everyone stops at Roger's Corner in these parts."

"It's one of us," Sister said with no surprise.

"Yes."

"I wish I could tell you more about the voice. A man's voice. I sort of recognized it. He was disguising it, of course, muffling it and speaking in a higher tone, but—" She shrugged.

"You may get another call. Whoever called you knows you called me, and whoever called you may be the murderer."

"After all these years?" Walter hooked his thumb in his belt loop.

"Guilt. Often they want to get caught."

"And more often they don't," Sister sensibly said. "My hunch is whoever called me helped the killer toss that drum over the deep end of the bridge all those years ago."

"I think your hunch is right," Ben agreed.

CHAPTER 19

There's no hope. I don't care if I live or die!" Alice Ramy cried, teetering on the brink of hysteria.

She'd held herself together when Ben Sidell visited her. Now Tedi, Edward, Sybil, and Ken had come by to express their sympathy. Sister Jane had also come with them after Tedi had asked her please to do so. Alice couldn't put a good face on it any longer.

Tedi, perched on the edge of the wing chair where Alice sat crumpled, said, "You do care. You must care."

"Why?"

"For Guy," Tedi responded.

"He's dead. Dead." She stared at Tedi with vacant eyes.

"You already knew that, didn't you?" Edward tried to be consoling, but this wasn't the path to take.

"No! I prayed he had run away. I didn't want him to be a murderer, but I didn't want him dead."

Sister, standing by the other side of the chair, said, "Alice, I believe Nola and Guy died together. If not at the same moment, then because of each other. I pray their souls rest in peace, but I know mine is in a state. I want to find their killer or killers."

"How?" A flash of life illuminated Alice's eyes; anger, too. "Especially now. Too much time, Sister, too much time."

Sybil, sitting across from Alice with Ken by her side, spoke up. "Fate. It's fate that they died and now it's fate that they have reappeared. We're supposed to find the killers."

"Fate is just an excuse not to do your homework." Alice smiled ruefully, tears in her eyes now. "When Guy brought home a D in geometry he said it was fate. I said fate is just an excuse not to do your homework. It stuck. There is no such thing as fate."

Resting a strong hand on Alice's shoulder, Sister leaned down. "Then let's do our homework. Try to remember—"

Alice interrupted, "I have!"

"Things can pop into your head at strange times. Come to some hunt breakfasts. Talk to the gang. Something might click," Sister encouraged her.

"Nobody wants to talk to me."

"Of course they do," Tedi said warmly.

"Xavier keeps chickens," Edward said, smiling.

"Fighting chickens," Tedi sniffed.

"Not illegal to keep them. Just illegal to fight and bet on them," Ken responded, trying to humor her, calm her. He didn't really know what to say.

"Guy used to come home from those cockfights plucked

cleaner than the chickens. I don't believe he ever won a red cent."

"He won sometimes," Ken said, trying surreptitiously to check the time. "I was there. You just never saw a penny, Alice, because he spent it on wine, women, and song."

"Guy could be very naughty." Alice couldn't conceal a note of pride. After all, how many women bear a son who is widely considered movie-star handsome?

Tedi, having a different take, said, "So could Nola, unfortunately."

"Oh, Tedi, she was high-spirited," Sister said.

"High-spirited with other women's husbands."

"Mother," Sybil exclaimed.

"You thought I didn't know. Nola was a bad girl. I loved her. I couldn't help but love her, but men were chess pieces to her. Every man a pawn and she the only queen."

A moment of embarrassing silence followed, broken when Alice surprisingly said, "She met her match in Guy. That's why they fell in love. Both of them wild as dogs in heat." She looked fleetingly at Edward, then Tedi. "Forgive me."

"It's the truth," Tedi agreed.

Edward, not knowing about all of Nola's amours, shifted uncomfortably in his chair. No father likes hearing these things about his daughter. Tedi certainly had never told him. Nola was the apple of his eye.

Ken, sensing Edward's pain, said, "Dad, she wasn't as bad as all that. Nola was a terrible flirt. She didn't, well, you know . . ."

Tedi knew that was a flat-out lie but decided to let it pass. No point going into the details in front of everyone. It wouldn't help Alice.

"Come to our hunt breakfasts. Reacquaint yourself with your neighbors and friends," Sister said, again extending the invitation. "We go out cubbing Tuesdays, Thursdays, and Saturdays. If weather's iffy, I change around the days, but call me up. Once formal hunting starts October twenty-sixth, I'll send you a fixture card."

"You're just trying to get me to let you hunt here. Guy used to beg me to let you do it, but I still won't. Poor little foxes."

"Those poor little foxes make fools of us all. But Alice, you know that's not why I'm here. I mean it. Come out and see us. You'll be surprised how friendly everyone is. All of Guy's friends are there. You know Ralph and Xavier. Ronnie Haslip, of course. Ken will be there on Saturdays; sometimes he can squeeze in a weekday. Oh, the Franklins. The boys in their mid-forties—they're all Guy's old running buddies."

"Maybe."

"Alice, excuse me, but I have to go. Richmond business calls." Ken stood up.

"Haven't been to Richmond since 1986." Alice noticed her mantel clock had stopped running. She'd forgotten to wind it.

"Downtown is a little sad. No Miller and Rhoads, no Thalheimer's." Ken mentioned the great department stores that used to draw shoppers like a magnet in the old days. "But it's much the same. What's changed is the West End. The shops, the businesses, Alice, they're all the way out to Manakin Sabot on Broad Street. You just wouldn't believe it."

"Don't want to see it." Her obstinacy was returning, which meant she felt better.

"If you change your mind, I'd be happy to take you down. Be fun to find some fall clothes," Sybil suggested.

Ken smiled. "Sybil, we need to build a new wing on the house for all your clothes."

"She always looks so nice," Alice said. "Thank you, Sybil, but I think I'll pass on Richmond."

Ken walked over, took both of Alice's hands in his, leaned down, and kissed her on the cheek. Sybil also leaned over to kiss her good-bye. Alice hadn't been kissed since Paul died in 1986. She craved human touch but didn't realize it.

"You take care now. And you call me if you need anything," Ken said warmly.

After Sybil and Ken left, the four contemporaries remained quiet for a few minutes.

"You've kept the place up," Edward complimented her.

"Full-time job. Wouldn't be so much work if it weren't for the chickens. I change their water every day. I scrub out their coop every day, too. Doesn't stink like chickens can, you know."

"That's wonderful." Edward nodded pleasantly.

"Edward, Tedi, were you afraid Nola would run off with Guy?"

"Yes," Tedi forthrightly answered for both herself and her husband.

"I was, too. I always assumed you didn't think my boy was good enough for her." An edge sharpened Alice's voice, not the most melodious in any circumstances.

"No, Alice, that wasn't it." Edward approached this with his usual tact. "A fire that flames that blazingly hot can turn to ashes in a heartbeat."

Tedi's eyes searched out her husband's. She had under-rated him. Like most women she felt she understood emotions far better than men. Edward might not choose to talk about emotions, but he understood them, a real victory.

"I thought of that, too." Alice glanced down at her crepe-soled shoes, then up again at Edward. "It scared me. For him, I mean. I don't think Guy had ever truly been in love until Nola."

"For what it's worth, I think she loved him," Sister said. She moved to sit opposite Alice.

"Did you?" Tedi genuinely inquired.

"I did. I didn't know what would come of it. They both had a history of being carefree, if you will, but there is something to be said about the changes that happen to you when you meet the right one. One does settle down eventually."

"I thought she'd throw him away." Alice didn't sound rancorous. If anything, she was grateful to finally be able to speak about this.

"I did, too," Tedi said. "It wasn't Guy. Don't get me wrong. It was money. Nola loved money. She might have married him, but it would have fizzled. And regardless of what you might think, we did not spoil either of our girls. Yes, they both went to the best schools, but they didn't get cars handed to them on their sixteenth birthdays. They had to earn the money. And every summer each one took a job. Oh, it might have been something fun like working on a ranch in Wyoming, but still, it was the beginning of responsibility. And, well, it's as clear as the nose on our faces, Sybil was by far the more prudent, the more sensible. Nola worked, but she spent it as fast as she made it. Then she'd run out and come begging. I certainly never made up her debts, but I think"—Tedi nodded at Edward—"her father may have."

"Once or twice, my dear, I didn't make it a habit."

"Oh, Edward." Tedi didn't believe a word of it.

"She wouldn't have had money with Guy," Alice argued. "Burned a hole in his pocket. He could have made money. He had the brains for it, but not the discipline. But he was only twenty-five when he died. Almost twenty-six. I'd like to think he would have found something to gainfully occupy him."

"I'm sure he would have," Sister said. She had seen Ralph, Ken, Ronnie, and Xavier each settle down and prosper. She thought Guy would have come 'round, too.

"Perhaps the fates are kind," Tedi said, smoothing her skirt. "Nola and Guy were killed at the height of love, the first blush. They never knew disillusionment."

"I told you I don't believe in fate," Alice stubbornly insisted. "And I don't see how dying at twenty-five can be considered kind. So they would have fought. Guy would have gotten drunk or picked up sticks and left for a while. He would have recovered. She would have, too. It's all stuff and nonsense, this love business."

"Not when you're young and maybe not when you're old. I might be seventy-one, but I tell you, let another woman go after Edward and I'll knock her sideways."

"You flatter me." Edward smiled. "I'm the one on guard here. I have a wife who looks thirty years younger than myself. It can be quite nerve-racking. Why, one of Ken's friends tried to woo her at a company gathering over the Fourth of July."

"Now who's the flatterer?" Tedi shook her head.

"Well, I'm the cynic. Year in and year out Paul Ramy brought me flowers on my birthday, chocolates on Valentine's Day, and usually a charm for my charm bracelet at Christmas. That was it. No variety and no spontaneity. I think Guy became romantic just because his father wasn't. Now, my son always brought me little presents, even as a child." She stopped herself and swallowed. "When Ben Sidell came here I thought it was more questions. I didn't think I'd find out what happened to Guy."

CHAPTER 20

Diminutive, intense, levelheaded, Gaston B. Marshall became a pathologist by default and county coroner by fiat. When Vee Jansen, the coroner since 1949, died of a heart attack in 1995, Gaston inherited the job.

In other counties, especially above the Mason-Dixon line, county commissioners might have grumbled at having such an ancient coroner as Vee Jansen performing autopsies. This would have been superseded by a new wave of grumbling as a much younger man assumed the duties. But in central Virginia, in this county, where everyone claimed everyone else as shirttail cousins, Gaston was readily accepted when he became coroner. He was a homeboy. Gaston B. Marshall, a professor of medicine at the university, now had two jobs. The extra stipend from the county was useful. Gaston was the father of three grade-school children. The university, for all its grandeur, paid poorly.

The other good thing about this job was Gaston was left to his own devices. If he wanted students to assist him, no one quibbled. If he wanted to utilize his findings in his lectures, names of the deceased changed, he could do it. Being county coroner proved a rich source of teaching material. His students could see things they might not see at the university hospital. During one autopsy of a drunken gentleman, well born but bone idle, when he attempted to lift out the liver it literally disintegrated in his hands. If nothing else, those students witnessing the diseased liver would think twice before drinking too much.

On the Sunday the body was recovered from the river, he had but one assistant, a female intern utterly enraptured by pathology, Mandy Collatos. Perhaps the appeal was you were always right but one day late. In the case of Guy Ramy their findings were twenty-one years late almost to the day.

Walter Lungrun stood in scrubs over the stainless-steel table, the channels on the side sloping downward for drainage.

Ben Sidell, a by-the-book man most times, wanted Gaston to see the drum, so he delivered that as well. It sat near the table. A large double sink, also stainless steel, ran along the wall.

All three physicians wore thin rubber gloves.

"You know if there hadn't been punctures in the drum I believe he would have been mummified." Mandy was proud that they had extracted the skeleton doing precious little damage to it, no easy task.

"Yes." Gaston finished placing the bones in their proper position. The major joint areas had come apart when the skeleton was removed, much as a joint pulls out of a chicken leg. Plus the anvil in the bottom of the drum had broken bones probably on the drop into the river. The drum had settled after that.

Walter watched intently.

"Dr. Marshall," Mandy said, pointing to two ribs, left side.

Gaston bent down, his upturned nose almost touching the graceful, thin rib bones. "Uh-huh. When a body has been out this long, you hope for the best. We were lucky Nola was buried in red clay. It preserved her longer."

"The methods of killing were different for these two," Walter said.

"Yes. Interesting . . ." Gaston noticed that Guy's right shinbone was shorter than the left and thicker. "Old break."

"Casanova Point-to-Point Races. Late seventies," Walter said. He marveled at the body's ability to knit itself back together.

"You were there?"

"Actually, I was. My mother took me. I was always crazy for horses. Guy crashed a timber fence. No fault of his own. The jockey in front of him bobbled in front of the jump, flew off, and Guy's horse braked hard." Walter smiled slightly. "He threw Guy straight into the timber. He was out foxhunting the next week in a cast. At least that's what I heard."

A knock on the door made Gaston pause in his examination. "Come in."

Larry Hund, the dentist, entered the room. He was carrying a folder. "Still has a jawbone."

"Larry, we see a lot of strange things in here—including one another." Gaston motioned for him to step up to the table.

Larry pulled out the dental charts and swiftly checked the teeth, most still in the jawbone. "Guy Ramy."

Gaston and Mandy, nothing if not thorough, finished up in another hour, obsessively checking and double-checking, measuring bones, making detailed notes.

Larry inspected the drum before leaving. "Boy, someone wanted him to stay put. Got an anvil in there."

"But he didn't stay put, did he?" Gaston yanked a paper towel off the dowel.

"I don't know how you can do your work." Larry smiled. "It's one thing when bare bones are on the table. But when you have to cut into a corpse that's been out there for days or weeks . . ."

"You get used to it, but I don't think any of us look forward to working on a body exposed for a few days. When it's hot, one day will do it. I can smoke cigars, shove Vicks Vapo-Rub up my nose or camphor oil, the damned stench still gets through. After they've been out a week, unless, of course, they're frozen, it actually begins to improve."

"What's the fascination?" Larry rarely had an opportunity to talk to Gaston like this.

"Answers. I can often get the answers and, in the case of wrongful death, clues to the killer."

"Well, I don't know about this one." Larry picked up his folder. "How will you ever find the killer?"

"I don't know." Gaston sighed.

Mandy put the body in a cooler drawer, slid it shut with a thunk, and inserted a paper card in the small slot in the front, with a number on it.

"Anyone else in here?" Larry was curious.

"No, it's been quiet." He finished toweling off. "You did a good job on Nola, by the way. I don't remember if I thanked you. So many teeth were missing. I don't know if her killer smashed her skull in first or hit her in the face first."

"Do you think it's weird—pathology?" Mandy asked Larry.

"In a sense," he honestly answered. "The typical response to death is aversion, even repulsion."

"True," Gaston agreed. "I had to overcome that myself in med school. But then, I remember it as clear as yesterday, we were in lab working on the circulatory system and I was lifting up the aorta, like rubber those cadavers, and I stepped back to look at the body. The arteries and the veins were a tracery of life. It was beautiful. I looked at bodies differently after that, and let's face it, I wasn't meant to be a plastic surgeon. No bedside manner."

"Yeah, you don't have to talk to your patients," Walter said, smiling. He regularly dealt with people in acute distress.

"Right," Larry laughed at Gaston and Mandy, "your patients don't talk back."

"Oh, but they do," Gaston countered, "they do."

CHAPTER 21

Aunt Netty, cross with Uncle Yancy, trotted over to Target's den. The last quarter of the moon, a thin melon slice in the Prussian blue sky, pulsated with feeble light.

Target, a hefty eight pounds if he was an ounce, sat near the main entrance. His mate, Charlene, was eating blackberries curling over the fence line near the edge of the woods about a quarter of a mile from the den. Just beyond that fence, rolling pastures swept up to the farm road and then on to the kennels.

Their three cubs this year, half grown, had left early to set up homes around Wheeler's Mill. Roughneck Farm, After All, and Foxglove, filled with reds and grays, were reaching the saturation point. Target and Charlene knew that the old, nasty red who had lived underneath the mill had succumbed to old age. The place needed foxes, and it was better to get their cubs established early before the reds farther south got the bright idea to move in.

Plentiful game meant the young ones would be fine for food. Also, Walter Lungrun occasionally put out dog food supplemented with liquid wormer as well as tasty bits of sweet feed. The molasses flavor was delicious.

"Netty, you've got on your mad face." Target laughed at his sister.

"Yancy's in one of his hoarding moods. He's burying dead crickets, which is the dumbest thing. Chicken, rabbit pieces, yes. But crickets? That run on the first day of cubbing has affected his mind."

"I thought it was being married to you," Target wryly said.

"What a pathetic attempt at humor. I wouldn't be sitting here laughing. Tuesday, Sister will take out more puppies and she'll have Dragon in the pack. He wasn't with them Saturday or Yancy would be a goner for sure."

"Sister ought to draft out that hound. He's too fast. He'll ruin the pack." Target knew for a pack of hounds to be good they should run together. Dragon pushed ahead too far.

"It's his second year. She'll give him the year to see if he improves. And you know she loves his blood, lot of Piedmont blood in her D line." Piedmont Fox Hounds, founded in northern Virginia in 1840, was the oldest organized hunt in America.

Henry Hudson brought hounds with him when he discovered the river that now bears his name. American settlers hunted with hounds almost from the founding of the first surviving colony in 1607. But Piedmont was the first hunt organized in the modern sense, and those who wore its colors, old gold, could be forgiven a bit of swagger.

"He's an arrogant hound," Netty said.

"I got my revenge last year when I lured him into a copperhead."

"He'll never forget it, which is why I'm here. To remind you that Tuesday, Sister will cast hounds this way and Dragon will be with them. I'd stay in my den if I were you."

"Ha! I'll break his neck yet."

"Unless he breaks yours. He's fast, Target, and he's seventy pounds of hard muscle to your eight. He can snap your neck in a split second if he bumps you and rolls you. He has that kind of drive."

"Netty," Target said, incensed, standing up. "I'm almost as fast as you are."

She wanted to say, "but not as smart." Instead, she cajoled him. "True enough. I'm just giving you a heads-up. The whole pack is faster, and if Bitsy hadn't been around it really would have been a near thing for Yancy, the damned fool."

"Wonder why Sister is breeding for more speed? They're already fast enough and I must commend her and them for their nose. Boy, she has really improved the way they track a scent." Target mentioned the ability of a hound to scent.

"She has, and let's not forget, we've had more moisture this year. That's going to help them, too. We'd better be on our paws. I know neither Sister nor Shaker wants to kill any of us, but accidents happen."

"If I have to die I'd rather die that way than from mange." Target flicked his tail. Netty's infernal and constant advice irritated him.

"Wouldn't we all. Here's to old age! But take your medicine. Sister spends good money on that stuff and now she's putting it on dog kibble instead of stuffing it inside dead chickens. It's easier to get at."

"I do eat the damned stuff, Netty!"

Before he could cuss her out and tell her to stop mothering him, Athena, talons spread, swooped over them. "Hoo hoo hoo." She laughed as they both flattened. She turned and landed on the lowest limb of the slippery elm. "Good evening."

"Athena, you scared the wits out of me," Netty grumbled as she dusted herself off.

"Why, Netty, I don't think that's possible."

Netty, somewhat mollified, said, *"You're looking well."*

"Shrews, I've been eating shrews. Does wonders for me. Well, Target, cat got your tongue?"

"No, it's good to see you. I hear you helped out Uncle Yancy the other morning."

"St. Just was calling the hounds on after they'd lost scent."

"I'll kill him if it's the last thing I do."

"You know, Target, that's what he says about you," Aunt Netty said, adding her two cents.

"I'm here with the news. Guy Ramy's body, sealed in a fifty-five-gallon drum, was dredged out of the James this morning. A red-winged blackbird watched the whole thing."

"Blackbirds, crows, ravens," Target snarled, *"can't believe a word they say."*

"Don't let your hostility to the species blind you to the truth," Athena sagely counseled.

"You're quite right," Aunt Netty agreed, and wanted to kick her brother hard with her hind leg. One needed to pay court to Athena. She stared crossly at Target.

Although full of himself, he wasn't stupid. *"You are right, Athena. I hear the name, St. Just, and my blood boils. He killed my son."*

"And you killed his wife. You're even. Be done with it." She raised herself to her full height, as she'd been leaning down to speak to the foxes. Athena, at two feet tall, was undeniably regal.

Target weighed his next words. *"Yes, but I think it's gone beyond that. I don't think he'll stop. After all, he called the hounds on Uncle Yancy."*

"I know. My concern is that you don't endanger other animals

with this blood feud. There's enough going on now. Finding Guy Ramy is not a good omen for any of us."

"The humans are already stirred up about Nola Bancroft." Aunt Netty moved over to sit beside her brother.

"The human who killed these two knew enough to put them where vultures couldn't get them or dogs dig them up. He or she knows a little something about animals. Right?"

"Yes." Aunt Netty nodded her head.

"And although none of us were born then, we know from the humans' incessant talking that Nola and Guy disappeared after the first day of cubbing in 1981. A full cycle. Cubbing has just begun." She leaned down toward them again. *"And if they turn up something or someone gets a notion, they'll start digging, literally. They'll disturb our dens and nests and flush game. They'll make a mess."*

"I'd better tell the cubs at Wheeler's Mill," Target thought out loud.

"I already did. And Bitsy is telling Butch, Mary Vey, Comet, and Inky." Athena mentioned the gray foxes.

"Do you really think it's that bad?" Target wondered, not wanting to challenge her, just wondering.

"Actually, I'm afraid one of them's going to snap." Athena's low voice dipped even lower. *"Bitsy, Inky, and I saw Ralph Assumptio, crying, parked by the side of the road."*

"That's it. He's the killer, then," Target declared.

"Maybe. Maybe not." The brown bird cast her golden eyes upward as a blue heron, late, headed for home. *"My point is they are all feeling the strain."*

"Do the hounds know?" Aunt Netty asked.

"Yes. Bitsy is telling them."

"Who cares if they know?" Target didn't dislike the hounds, but he felt them an inferior member of the canine family because they allowed themselves to be domesticated.

"Are you argumentative tonight or thickheaded?" Netty nudged him on his shoulder. *"The hounds are closer to the humans than we are."*

"And the killer is a foxhunter as surely as I am the Queen of the Night."

A little while after Athena had left, Charlene returned. Target and Netty filled her in, then they all discussed what Athena meant about the killer being a foxhunter. They weren't sure.

Athena had been figuring. There had been no reports of struggle. If there'd been a fight in a car or truck, someone would have noticed the blood and the damage to the vehicle. If someone had sold their vehicle immediately after the disappearance, someone would have noticed that, too. Both Nola and Guy willingly followed or climbed into the vehicle of their murderer. Nola's car was left at the Burusses'. Guy's was parked downtown on the street. Athena had gathered all this with Bitsy's help by listening to the humans talk on their porches or on the phone, windows open.

She had been just sharing all this with Bitsy, sitting on a crossbeam in Sister's barn. Bitsy nodded. *"Guy and Nola knew their killer."*

Athena added, *"And trusted him."*

CHAPTER 22

The humidity, suddenly oppressive, pressed down on the green pastures, the blazing white and deep pink crepe myrtle, the orange daylilies. Even the green metallic dragonflies, surprised by the rapid climb in temperatures and the dew point, sat motionless on lily pads in ponds. Rockfish dozed in deep creek eddies, frogs burrowed in cooling mud.

Lafayette, Rickyroo, Keepsake, and Aztec stood nose to tail under the enormous pin oak in their pasture. Showboat, Gunpowder, and Hojo did the same under a fiddle oak in their neighboring separate pasture.

Golliwog reposed on the library sofa. Raleigh and Rooster stretched out at Sister's feet beneath her desk.

The Louis XV desk, a wedding gift from Raymond's mother, was not an idle antique. Despite its great value, Sister worked at the desk much as the royal court secretary who had scribbled at it centuries ago.

The library, not a large room, housed Sister's most beloved books, especially her sporting library. Some of those volumes, precious to her as well as collectors, had been written and printed in the eighteenth century. She loved the pages themselves, crisp paper of such high quality, one would have to search the great libraries of Europe for its equivalent today. The type, velvet black, had been cut into the paper by metal, each letter set by hand. The typefaces, elegant yet simple, had been carefully selected by the bookmaker or possibly even the author.

Sister had observed that modern books, printed on cheap paper, thermographed print, disintegrated in decades. The author not only had nothing to do with the process but was actively kept from it.

Sister inhaled the special tang of her library as she worked. Old fires, leather bindings, a scented candle on the mantelpiece added to the allure of the room along with the Heather St. Claire Davis painting of herself on Lafayette leaping down an embankment over a creek bed, hounds in the near distance, the huntsman right up with them.

The twenty-first century, mass production having vulgarized just about every single human activity, still could not cheapen foxhunting. For this, the older woman was profoundly grateful. This pastime could never become a vehicle for mass merchandisers. Whippers-in would not be embroidering advertisements for tires, cars, or deodorant on their coat sleeves. Saddle pads would not bear a pharmaceutical logo. Velvet hunt caps, black derbies, glistening silk top hats would be spared a dotcom address.

Sister wasn't a snob, far from it. Nor was she especially rich. Raymond, to his eternal credit, had done well as a stockbroker, leaving her with a portfolio large enough to provide for her needs. Raymond figured life would never get cheaper, only more and more expensive, as Americans demanded ever more services, which meant ever more taxes. He knew the cities would always vote themselves more money. Country people would have to fight not only for their way of life but simply to have a life. He had invested wisely and died knowing that whatever his failings as a husband, he had been a good provider.

Sister was of that generation who expected men to provide for women and children. Indeed, it was a disgrace if a man's wife worked. Poor women had to work, so if a woman took a job it meant a man had failed. Through supporting a host of charitable organizations, well-to-do women did work. They just weren't paid for it. That was fine. It made the men feel better and perhaps some of the women, too.

She didn't think of herself as a rebel, but she'd taught geology at Mary Baldwin College even after marrying Raymond. He'd fussed, but she'd loved it so much. She stopped working when Ray Junior was born in 1960. When Ray was killed in 1974 she probably should have picked up teaching again, but somehow she couldn't seem to put one foot in front of the other for a year. The second year after her son died she functioned perfectly well but felt numb. The third year she came back to herself. Had it not been for her husband, foxhunting, her friends, and Peter Wheeler, she thought she might have disappeared into the hole the White Rabbit had vanished into. Maybe life was *Alice in Wonderland.*

There wasn't a day when she didn't think of Ray Junior and miss him. She missed her husband, too, who died in 1991, although missing a husband stirs emotions of a darker shade than missing a son. A husband left one with transgressions to forgive. A son left blasted promise. Then again, she'd transgressed enough herself to forgive Raymond his exuberance for life, which spilled over into an excessive appreciation for beautiful women. We were all human. Sister could forgive. It might take her time, but she could. She could never figure out if she was a good Christian or if exhaustion finally won out.

A photograph in a silver frame lit up the left corner of the desk. Raymond, herself, and a twelve-year-old Ray Junior, all in formal hunting attire, rode as a hunt team at the Washington International Horse Show. Raymond, resplendent in his scarlet weaselbelly and his white vest, grinned, his teeth sparkling white against his tanned face. Sister wore a black shadbelly, Continental blue colors on the collar, patent leather tops on her Spanish-cut boots so polished, they reflected the photographer's flashbulb. Ray wore a hunt cap, black melton, fawn-colored breeches, and butcher boots. He was properly dressed for a junior, the unspoken rule of thumb being that even if a child has earned his colors, he doesn't wear tails, called weaselbelly for a man, or a frock coat or tops on his boots until his voice changes and he shaves. For girls, whose voices change but not as dramatically, the rule was harder to interpret but by sixteen few masters would look amiss if a young lady rode out in a frock as opposed to a simple melton. A frock coat has two buttons on the back and a double vent, whereas the melton has a single vent on the back.

Sister, having grown up foxhunting, knew the sartorial rules, but sometimes even she had to consult the authorities from prior centuries in her library. If stymied she'd call Cindy Chandler at Foxglove Farm or Dr. Chuck Beegle at Brookhill Farm. Among the three of them they could usually find the definitive answer.

Nola had often caused feuds in the hunt field. For whatever reason, Nola appointed herself the fashion police, which did not go down with older members. The fight over Frances's veil was but one of many such eruptions. She pitched a fit when Gordie Tomlinson rode out in dark brown gloves. One should wear mustard-colored gloves or white knit gloves, depending on the weather and the formality of the occasion. Even a British tan deerskin pair would pass muster, but Gordie wore dark brown, which sent Nola into orbit.

Sister had to chastise Nola for her behavior and tell Gordie that while dark brown wasn't perfect, she was only too happy to accept it except for High Holy Days. Nola fumed for weeks after that, declaring that Sister was letting standards go to hell.

The most recent fuss had occurred the previous March when Ralph Assumptio carried a blackthorn knob end whip on a Saturday, a formal day. Ronnie Haslip snapped at Ralph over this lapse in taste.

Ralph should have properly carried his staghorn crop, thong attached. However, the broad fat loop at the end of the crop to which the thong attaches had torn clear through on a hard, long hunt two days before. Ralph left his crop with Betty Franklin to repair. Betty enjoyed doing leather repair, she said it was kind of like needlepoint only harder. So, he grabbed his blackthorn knob end.

Sister rode back, heard the explanation, then told Ralph naturally he could carry his knob end until repairs were completed. This had to be declared in front of the whole field to satisfy all parties. If Ralph had thought about it, he would have obtained Sister's permission for this variance before the hunt.

Knob ends, technically, can be carried during cubbing and during informal days after Opening Hunt. Most every hunt granted its members at least one informal day during the formal season. This allowed members time to repair torn jackets, dry out boots if they'd crossed high water, bleach stock ties, or do whatever needed to be done to restore their formal kit.

She glanced again at the photograph of the three of them. She used to grumble to big Raymond about the cost of outfitting a child. She wished she had shut up. He had been worth every penny. Many's the time she'd dragged that poor kid through the shops in Marshall and Middleburg where good used hunting attire was sold. He was an angel about it, especially since he'd really wanted to go to Horse Country in Warrenton.

He would have been forty-one in December.

Where does the time go? Where does the soul go?

Would she see him again when her time came?

She banished these ruminations from her mind. They served no purpose and would make her cry. She had a draw list to compose for Tuesday's hunt. She looked down at the sheet of paper, organized into bitches, dog hounds, second-year entry, first-year entry. Each hunt she kept a list of who participated. Then she'd take the sheet back to her desk and make a notation of who did what. A sharp pencil is worth more than a good memory.

Dragon had to go this time. Trident and Trudy had gone, so she'd take their littermates, Tinsel, Trinkle, and Trinity. Rassle and Ruthie, also first year, should go. She hated to leave Cora in the kennel because Dragon would then be the strike hound, but Cora had gone Saturday and she had a tendency to run weight right off herself. Sister wanted to start the season with her hounds a few pounds over their fighting weight so by Opening Hunt they'd be perfect. Then she and Shaker needed to watch them like hawks. A hound can easily run thirty or forty miles in one day, and on a screaming day, even sixty. They run much farther than the riders, for the hounds are running into coverts, coming back, going out again. The riders, confined to ground horses can navigate, cover fewer miles. Still, after a hard day many an experienced hunter would dismount only to find his legs like jelly.

If a hound was starting to get light, Shaker would feed her or him separately or leave the animal in the kennel until back up to sufficient weight. Sister would not hunt a hound whose weight had fallen too low for her liking.

Her kennel practices bordered on the obsessive, but no one could ever say this woman did not love her hounds or her horses.

Her fierce concentration prevented her from hearing a car roll up the driveway.

Raleigh lifted his head. *"Visitor."*

"Maybe it's an intruder." Rooster sprang up and raced for the back door.

"Yoo-hoo, Janie," Tedi called out.

"In the library."

Rooster greeted Tedi, then escorted her to the library, where Raleigh met her, too. Golliwog opened one eye; that was the extent of her greeting.

"Bills?" Tedi asked.

"Tuesday's draw list. I need to mix my steady Eddies with the youngsters. Can I get you anything?"

"No. Ken just left for Richmond much too late. Edward and Sybil went to the club. She had a bad spell, floods of tears, which is why Ken got off so late. I just had to get out of the house, which I suppose makes me some sort of chicken. I can't bear to see all those pictures of Nola right now. And I feel guilty because I should feel more compassion for Alice than I do."

"Join the club."

"She doesn't make it easy, does she?"

"You were kind to go to her."

"Who better to understand both the shock and the relief?" Tedi sat in the overstuffed club chair, tucking a needlepoint pillow behind her in the small of her back.

"It's been a grisly time, hasn't it?" agreed Sister, now sitting comfortably on the sofa.

"Don't jiggle the sofa," Golly complained.

Sister reached back to pet her.

"You ought to smack her," Rooster advised.

"I'd smack back. In fact, why don't you stick your wet nose here? I'll smack you, too," Golly threatened.

"Chatty, isn't she?" Tedi thought the long-haired calico an exceptionally beautiful cat. "Do you know I have had the most curious experience. These last three days I've noticed a little screech owl, she's no bigger than a minute, either in the barn or in the tree. She winks at me. I swear it. And I see her around. I feel as if this owl is following me. Sybil says, 'Mom, you're out there.' "

"She probably likes you. Just because an animal is undomesticated doesn't mean it can't take an interest in you."

"Do you really think so?"

"Sure, look at Inky or Aunt Netty." The two foxes were both well-known to hunt club members.

"I hope we don't hop Aunt Netty until it cools down. She'll run the legs right off of the hounds and us."

"That she will. You know, Inky will sit at a distance when I'm in the hound graveyard or when I'm gardening up here around the house. She'll sit and stare. She's a dear little thing."

"The black fox legend doesn't scare you?" Tedi brought up the legend that the appearance of a black fox presages upheaval.

"No, not really. It's not that uncommon a color variation.

On the other end of it, look at that cub over at Wheeler's Mill. So blond, he looks like a golden retriever and just as leggy. He's going to be an odd-looking creation."

"Let's go out to dinner, my treat," Tedi smiled. "In fact, let's take Shaker. Come on, you can finish your draw list later." She checked her watch. "You call Shaker. I'll call Keswick Hall."

"Oh, we'll have to get all dressed up."

"I mean the Sport Club. We can go in Bermuda shorts and sit at the little table by the bar. I don't want to get dressed up, either."

Within forty-five minutes all three of them were awaiting their appetizers. Sister sipped hot tea, Shaker drank iced tea, while Tedi indulged in a martini, the tiny corkscrew of lemon peel dancing around in the gin and vermouth. She said she wanted a twist instead of an olive because olives were for cool weather, lemons were for hot.

The three had also made a pact to not discuss Nola or Guy. One, it was too depressing. Two, they felt they were going around in circles about it. Three, Tedi especially needed to be distracted, which is exactly why she had left her daughter and husband at Farmington Country Club while she repaired to Keswick. Both country clubs also had hunt clubs bearing their names.

By the time the main courses arrived, all were in much more relaxed moods. Sister ordered sesame-crusted salmon; Tedi tried the pan-seared tuna, which she found delicious. Shaker stuck to chicken.

By the time they'd ordered their desserts they were telling old hunting stories and laughing.

Nancy Holt, the club tennis pro, came in and was hailed over to the table. She hunted with Keswick Hunt Club during the season on her day off Wednesday.

"And what are you doing at work?" Tedi asked the tall, attractive woman.

"Just finished a kids' tournament. Hey, I didn't know Crawford Howard paid an extra five thousand dollars so Doug would come over to Shenandoah."

"What?" All three stopped, forks filled with rich dessert poised in midair.

"Yes. Doakie Sproul was in the tournament. His mother told me they were surprised but grateful." Mrs. Georgianna Sproul, wife of the master of the Shenandoah Hunt, was Doakie's mother.

"That son of a bitch." Shaker put his fork down.

"Uh-oh. Did I say something wrong?" Nancy put her hand to her mouth.

"No, you did not. Sit here. Would you like dinner?" Tedi patted the seat.

"No, thank you, but I'll take a drink."

As the drink was ordered, Shaker's face grew redder. "That asshole. That total shit." He drank a sip of tea. "I'm sorry, ladies."

"I guess you didn't know." Nancy had no great love for Crawford since he kept running into her during joint meets. He'd use her for a bumper when he couldn't hold Czapaka.

"Who did?" Tedi wondered. "And how come Wyatt Sproul didn't tell you?" Wyatt was Shenandoah's master.

"Wy is a good man. He must have thought I already knew." Sister was putting two and two together.

"Doug would have told you. Means he doesn't know," Shaker said, his color returning to its normal ruddy shade. "Sister, do I have your permission to strangle Crawford?"

"No, dear, he's not worth going to jail over."

"We have to get even." Tedi, too, was disturbed at this underhanded ploy.

"Oh, Tedi, we will." Sister returned to her impossibly rich chocolate ice cream.

All four people realized Crawford had secretly paid to bump up Doug's salary. Not only would this make the huntsman's job more attractive but it would help Sister Jane accept that Doug should be at Shenandoah Hunt, not a particularly well-heeled club. Much as she wanted him to carry the horn, she didn't want him to starve doing it.

Sister realized Crawford wasn't motivated by a desire to help Doug, but rather one to weaken Jefferson Hunt. Doug was an inspired first whipper-in, and one reason for the club's success in the field. Crawford was betting on his substitute, like any rookie, making mistakes. If the season wasn't as good as it might be, if other clubs boasted better seasons, a certain amount of unrest would bubble up in the club. The hardened hunters knew better, but the fair-weather hunters and newcomers to the sport could be easily discouraged by a lackluster season. Especially if other clubs were having a good one.

Then he'd move in, and fan the unrest. As he was fanning, he would make certain everyone would become aware of the many fine things he could do if he were master, but you can't expect a man to spend his hard-earned cash in lavish amounts if he isn't going to carry the title of joint-master.

Tedi leaned back. "He'll stop at nothing."

"That idiot will be joint-master over my dead body." Shaker's eyes blazed.

"Don't say that—not under the circumstances," Sister gently corrected him.

CHAPTER 23

Spotty scent kept the hounds picking on the morning of September 10. They'd find a thread of enticement in the woods at Foxglove Farm, tease it toward the hayfields, then lose it in the middle of the hay, bent low under a steady wind slicing down off the Blue Ridge Mountains.

Days like this tested hounds, huntsman, and staff. During formal hunting, if the field was running and jumping, they usually paid little mind to the hard work of hounds, the conditions of soil and wind. But most of the souls who roused themselves to be at the fixture at seven-thirty in the morning knew hunting and were respectful of hound work. Cubbing brought out the best.

The tails, down, on Sister's old brown hunt cap flapped as she reined in one hundred yards from the huge chestnut in the middle of the hayfield. Two jumps beckoned enticingly in the fence line, but there was no telling if the hounds would head in that direction.

Walter took off work to hunt Thursday mornings, but as this was Tuesday, she found she missed him. Most wise employers in Virginia Horse Country will allow their employees one morning off, especially if the employee will work late another day. Beneficent as this sounds, it's a little bit like the schoolteacher who wishes everyone well on the first day of deer season and suspends classes. They're going to go, so you might as well make the best of it. City people frothed at the mouth over this when they moved to these parts to start a business. They often left declaring the eternal backwardness of Southerners.

Tuesdays and Thursdays, the numbers in the field remained low until Opening Hunt, perhaps ten to twenty depending on the weather. During formal hunting, Sister Jane averaged about twenty-five on weekdays and sixty on weekends.

Today, Tedi, Edward, Ralph, Xavier, Ronnie, Jennifer Franklin, Crawford, Marty, and Sari Rasmussen, a school friend of Jennifer's, waited with Sister in the hayfield.

The fox whose fading trail they'd been following, Grace, was a vixen from Target and Charlene's litter last year. Slender with a lot of black on her mask, she loved to fish in the ponds at Foxglove Farm. These two ponds on different levels had a waterwheel between them, moving water from one level to another, aerating the water. Grace's mother would shake her head and wonder why any child of hers preferred fishing to sauntering into the barn to eat grain and a few fat barn mice. Foxglove's house dog, a German shepherd, betrayed no interest in chasing foxes.

Once Grace heard Dragon's big mouth, she took off, running up the creek, over the rocks, and finally bursting into the hayfield. She knew hounds were far behind her and struggling with scent, so she doubled back on her track and slipped into her brother Reynard's old den. Reynard, killed last year by an act of human malice, had a roomy den that no other creature currently used. Grace's den was under one of the barns at Foxglove Farm. She could walk to work, as she put it.

She curled up for a well-earned snooze.

The field waited for ten minutes as the morning sun changed from scarlet to pink to gold.

Betty Franklin, on the left side today, stood at the edge of the hayfield. Sister figured Sybil was still in the woods to the right. Every now and then she heard Shaker's "Whoop."

He could blow a beautiful hunting horn but preferred to use his voice until hounds found scent, then he'd call other hounds to the line. When hounds burst out of the covert he'd blow "Gone Away."

The riders watched the hounds fan out over the field. Sister was very proud of her members, even Crawford, as they didn't automatically chatter and gossip at checks like this. Since he so desperately wanted to be joint-master, Crawford was now listening intently and making certain his behavior was unimpeachable in the field.

Target heard the hounds as he was heading home from the south side of Hangman's Ridge. He trotted across the sunken fields, crossed Soldier Road, then loped across the floodplain fields until the earth rose in front of him. He crossed under a three-board fence and entered the swaying hayfields directly across the farm road from where Sister waited.

Every now and then he'd catch a word or two in the distance from Dragon. He laughed to himself.

He walked through the hay, jumped on top of a coop, and sat, waiting for someone in the hayfield opposite to notice him. He was, at most, four football fields distant.

To add insult to injury, he groomed himself.

Edward had kicked his feet out of the stirrups to let his long legs dangle. When he picked up his stirrups again he looked across the field.

"Tallyho," he whispered.

Tedi passed it up to Sister. "Tallyho."

Sister's eyes followed the direction of Edward's cap. He'd taken off his hunt cap, pointed his arm straight toward the fox, and also pointed his horse's nose toward Target.

Crawford saw and foolishly bellowed, "Tallyho!"

He should have remained silent. Since hounds diligently kept their noses to the ground, he didn't spoil anything except he again demonstrated how slender his grasp was of both the necessities and proprieties of hunting.

"*Tallyho, yourselves,*" Target murmured, and continued grooming.

On ascertaining that Target, whom she recognized, was in no hurry to depart, Sister cupped her hands to her mouth, being certain to holler in the direction of her huntsman. She let out the rebel yell, "Yip yip yo-o-o-o."

That particular cry alerted Shaker that it was the master viewing and the master was unlikely to "tallyho" a groundhog, house cat, or fawn, each of which had been tallyho'd at one time or another by a member of the field.

He raised his voice to a high pitch. "Come to me. Whoop. Whoop."

Trinity, although on her very first hunt, knew she was being called back to the huntsman, so she obediently turned, as did her sister, Tinsel. Delia, the mother of Dragon, Diana, and Dasher, called out to the others. Delia, moving a step slow these days, proved invaluable in steadying young ones. If she ran at the back of the pack she didn't much mind. She'd had her day up front and she didn't straggle, she stayed with the pack. A hound like Delia is a godsend to a huntsman.

Even Dragon, who resented interference, as he saw it, from Shaker, wanted to chase a fox. If Shaker was calling them, something must be up.

As the hounds returned to the huntsman, Sybil, who had been shadowing the pack on the right side, swung back with them.

Shaker wished to speak to his hounds, not humans. Sybil knew enough to stay on the right, so he merely waved her forward a bit. He was sure she'd learn the ropes quickly, but he hadn't realized how much he had relied on Doug Kinser, who would have been across the farm road by now.

"Let's find a fox." Shaker smiled down at the upturned faces, then squeezed Hojo, a loud paint, his Tuesday horse, into an easy gallop. They moved smartly through the hayfield where the happy sight of the entire field, caps off, pointing to Target, poised on the far coop, greeted him.

Shaker slowed to a trot, let his hounds get up front of him, then urged them toward the farm road. The point was to give Target a chance to run; it would have been unsporting to do otherwise.

He let out a loud "whoop" to wake up the fox.

"*What an ugly sound.*" Target looked brightly at the huntsman.

Wind swept the golden hay where hounds were working toward him; he could see sterns aloft. Target knew his scent was being blown away from the hounds but, as they closed in, they'd pick up his scent when he moved off. His pads would leave a scentprint for hound noses.

Betty quietly moved forward on the left, at a walk, no need to make a show of it.

Sister held her breath. "What is Target doing?"

"*Dragon?*"

Dragon lifted his head at the sound of Target's voice.

Tinsel and Trinity lifted their heads, too. No one had told them about this part.

"*You couldn't find a fox with radar,*" Target taunted Dragon, then lifted off the far coop, swirled in midair, and ran flat out through the hay toward the sunken meadows. He figured he'd make a burst straight for his den, only zigging and zagging when he had to throw them off.

"*I'll break your neck!*" Dragon roared back, his deep voice sending shivers down the spines of the humans. "*Follow me,*" he called over his shoulder.

Target had vanished into the hay, but Dragon relied on his nose to find him. He knew he could be fooled by sight and his eyes weren't as good as a fox's or a cat's. But his nose—his nose was superb.

He leapt over the first coop. Why go under the fence line? Give everyone a show! He reached the second, cleared the coop without even touching it, put his nose right to ground on the other side, and let out a soul-stirring note in his rich baritone.

"*I'm on!*"

Shaker cheered the other hounds toward him. Delia double-checked Dragon's findings. Dragon was now about fifty yards ahead. "*Scorching!*"

The young ones got a nose full of burning scent and became so excited that they tumbled over themselves. They picked themselves back up, hoping no one noticed.

All voices lifted to celebrate the thrill of the chase.

Shaker and Hojo smartly sailed over the first coop, raced across the farm road, sunken perhaps a foot below the hayfields, then went up and over the second.

Sister, heart racing, a grin from ear to ear, rode Keepsake over both coops and was thankful they'd just rebuilt them. Behind her she heard the rap of hooves as someone got in too close. Mostly she heard the "oomph," "oomph," "oomph," of humans exhaling as they landed safely.

She kept about forty yards behind Shaker, fighting the urge to go right up with him.

"Squeeze him over," she heard Marty Howard calling behind her. Sister glanced back to see that Crawford had gotten stuck on the farm road between the two jumps.

Under these circumstances, a rider is supposed to circle and go to the rear or wait, if he can't circle, and let everyone else by. Crawford, however, bottled up the rest of the field. No one wanted to thunder past him for fear of spooking Czapaka or, worse, crashing into him. He didn't have sense to go down the road and get out of everyone's way.

Finally, with a terrific squeeze and smack of his crop, he lurched over the second coop. Ronnie Haslip, not deigning even to look at Crawford, effortlessly sailed over both coops, flying by Crawford perched on his big, beautiful warmblood. Ronnie was followed by the two high school seniors, Jennifer and Sari, who didn't want to get stuck behind Crawford again, just in case.

There was an old stone fence line on the south side of the hayfield. After that pretty jump it was open country, Soldier Road, more open country, and up Hangman's Ridge or the long way around it at the bottom.

Betty, thinking ahead, was already over the stone wall on Magellan, a horse who had a tendency to stand back and leave a half step earlier than her trusted and true Outlaw. She and Magellan were still getting accustomed to each other, but she was thrilled at having two horses to hunt.

The day was turning out to be so good, she felt half guilty about leaving Bobby at work—but not so guilty she wouldn't do it again.

Sybil didn't move fast enough, and Shaker preceded her over the stone wall at a low point where a few gray stones had fallen down. She swung in behind him, then tore out to his right side. He didn't criticize her since he knew she already understood she was not in the right position.

Keepsake, a handy fellow, thought the stone wall a lark. He liked taking different types of fences and he really liked having Sister on his back. She was much lighter than his former owner. Sister felt like a feather on his back.

This time Crawford took the jump last and cleared without incident.

Hounds streamed across the sunken meadow filled with the last of the black-eyed Susans and the first of the Jerusalem artichokes. Pendulous blackberries marked its eastern boundary.

Sister paused a moment at Soldier Road. She couldn't hear or see any motor traffic. She trotted over, jumped the old sagging coop—it needed replacing—and rode into the sunken meadow on the north side of the road. She galloped past more black-eyed Susans, Jerusalem artichokes, cornflowers, Queen Anne's lace, and white morning glories, their magenta throats pointing to the sun. Purple morning glories tangled through the grasses.

Hounds screamed. Their music gave her goose bumps.

Target, putting on the afterburners just to prove a point, shot straight up Hangman's Ridge, which at its summit was seven hundred feet above the watershed meadows below.

"Force those damned hounds to climb—and the people, too, if they're dumb enough," he thought.

Sister, however, wasn't going to push anyone that hard

quite this early in the season. If it had been December, the air cool, the horses 100 percent fit instead of 85 percent fit, she would have climbed up. Today she circled around to the old rutted wagon path. It cost her precious minutes and she'd have to hustle once she reached the ridge to make them up. This she did.

Target, for effect, had raced to the hanging tree, left a mark at its base, then charged straight down the other side. He could now hear Dragon behind him. The hound was fast. Target had indulged in too much chicken the previous evening. A straight shot to his den might not be the best plan after all.

So he hatched a diabolical new one. Once at the base of the ridge he crossed the farm road there and dashed through Sister's old apple orchard.

Sister, now on the ridge, saw the last of her hounds go by the hanging tree, then straight down the ridge. The wagon path on the other side of the ridge connected to her farm road. If she pushed Keepsake toward it, they'd have to cover a quarter mile to reach it.

The wind, always stronger on the ridge, whipped at her face. As she passed the ancient oak, its heavy branches moaned in the wind, as if the souls punished there were crying for release.

She banished that thought, slowed to account for the steeper grade down. The footing was slick in spots. At the bottom she pressed on into the apple orchard.

Target ran right up to the kennel. *"Wake up!"*

Diana lifted her head, as did Cora, Trinkle, Trudy, Trident, Asa, Dasher, and all the others.

"Target! Fox! Fox!" everyone screamed at once.

Golliwog, on her way to the kennel to remind the benighted canines there that they were lower life-forms, saw Target scurry around to the front of the kennel. She was between the stable and the kennel, and the big red ran straight for her.

Golly puffed up and jumped in the air as high as she could go. She looked like she'd sucked on an air hose, she was so big.

Target flew right under her, laughing.

As she came down she cursed, *"You stupid ass!"* As the hounds weren't far behind she considered it wiser to get out of their way than to continue to upbraid Target, who was never properly deferential to her. She did not like the attitude of the reds. She hurried to the bending hickory near the barn, unleashed her claws, and reached the lowest limb just as Dragon appeared by the kennel yards.

"Target! In the stable!" All the kenneled hounds ran back and forth, the hackles on their necks up, their sterns fluffed.

Dragon sped toward the stable. Target was already through it and could hear the hounds getting a little closer than he preferred. Well, he had other tricks up his sleeve.

The whole pack roared through the stable, knocking over buckets in the aisle, even slamming into the hay bales stacked at the aisle's end to be distributed for the evening's feedings.

Target reached Sister's colorful fall gardens, ran smack through them, then into the gardening shed, and leapt out the open window on the back wall.

No chance of turning back toward his den now. But there was a good hole with lots of entrances and exits just behind the hound cemetery. He sped through the cemetery.

Zinnias were squashed, red and yellow petals sprinkling the ground as the pack chased Target. Shaker trotted Hojo between the flower beds, cursing as he rode.

"Damn that sly son of a bitch!" Then he heard the crash of breaking glass and moved faster over the manicured lawn only to see the pack jammed into the gardening shed, howling their frustration.

Sister came up behind just in time to see Dragon jump through the window, followed by the others. They tore the window clear out of the jamb, the sound of tinkling glass a counterpoint to their cries.

Across more beautiful lawn, through an allée of locusts and hollies, curving through another allée of still-green scarlet maples into the usually peaceful hound cemetery bounded by a wrought-iron fence.

The gate, open as always, let hounds in. The line of the scent went out the other side, which had no such gate. Dragon in his fury turned and literally ran through and over the pack, out the gate again, and around the other side. With some confusion and cussing, the rest followed, running around the sculpture of a hound in the middle. It was as though the stone hound was running with them. Sister pulled up hard behind Shaker by the iron fence.

"Oh, thank God!" Marty exclaimed.

No one else said a word, they just panted for breath.

Hounds found the den, digging and claiming victory for all they were worth.

Target, safe inside, made a mental note that Dragon, in his second year, had learned a great deal from his first year's experiences. He wasn't going to be easy to fool anymore. The ferocious drive that misled him last year had become more disciplined. Target would need to take this fellow more seriously. He would have to be more clever and he would have to teach him a lesson. Today would only build the handsome hound's confidence. Dragon needed to be knocked down a peg or two. Aunt Netty had been right.

Target also thought he'd better tell his offspring, especially the youngest over at Mill Ruins.

Hojo stood quietly while Shaker walked to the den, stood, and blew the notes of triumph. He praised each hound, then led them away with Betty's and Sybil's help.

"Another excellent day," he said, reaching for the reins.

"I didn't think we'd do much today." Sister smiled and turned. The faces behind her, flushed with heat and excitement, radiated happiness as well as relief. Ralph breathed hard, laughing at himself for being a bit out of shape. Xavier huffed and puffed.

"Well, what do you think?" Shaker, back in the saddle, asked the master.

"I think we call it a day." She turned to Marty and asked, "And what were you thanking God for?"

"That you didn't jump the wrought-iron fence into the graveyard."

Tedi and Edward flanked Sister as they rode back across her lawn, the pathetic remains of her garden testifying to the fervor of the chase.

"Janie, winter is coming. You'll just prepare the new beds early." Tedi made light of it.

"You're right."

"You'll need a new window." Edward nodded toward the gardening shed. "I've got an extra. I'll have Jimmy bring it over and put it in for you."

"Thank you, Edward. You are the most generous soul."

"Well, he is, but don't be too impressed. You know we have the top of the old bank barn filled with Edward's treasures. Old windows, mantels, heart pine flooring. You name it, Edward's got it."

Edward smiled. He was a pack rat by nature, but he had

compromised early in their marriage by storing his finds outside the house. When he'd swear these items, such as cartons of old *Esquire* magazines, the large kind from the forties and fifties, would be worth something someday, Tedi would always reply, "Yes, dear."

Sybil had inherited the pack rat gene. Nola, on the other hand, never saved anything.

As people dismounted at the trailers, talking about the terrific run, sharing a thermos of coffee, a cold beer or a ham sandwich, Sister rode with Shaker, Sybil, and Betty to the kennels. Once the hounds were inside she turned toward her own stable. Shaker would be busy with the hounds, washing out cuts and scratches from the gardening shed episode.

Jennifer and Sari, with no prompting from Betty, met her as she dismounted. "Sister, we'll clean up your horses for you."

"Why, girls, thank you so much."

"And Mom says I can work here on weekends if that's okay with you." Jennifer wanted desperately to work with Sister. She wanted to learn everything about hunting.

"Jennifer, you'll be a big help to me." Sister could never refuse a young person in love with hunting.

Sari, her dark eyes almost black, timidly spoke up. "Master, I could work, too, if you need an extra hand."

"Why, yes. You can start right now. I'll pay you for the day."

"No, we'll clean the stable because we want to," Jennifer said just as her mother joined her. Magellan was now tied to the trailer.

"Tell you what, I'll accept your generous offer for today. And you can ride Rickyroo, Lafayette, and Aztec. Ask Shaker about Showboat and Gunpowder. At least a half hour of trotting for those guys."

"Okay." The two girls were thrilled.

"Ten dollars an hour."

"Sister, that's too much," Betty protested.

"Good help is hard to find. Ten dollars an hour." Sister, feeling fabulous, winked at them all.

Jennifer took Keepsake into the stable as Sister joined the gang at the trailers for an impromptu breakfast. She liked these tailgates better than the big affairs.

She complimented Sybil on her second day as first whipper-in.

"I got behind at the stone wall."

"You made up for it. Whipping-in is a lot different from riding in the field. You can never stop thinking, reaching." Sister popped a deviled egg into her mouth.

When she walked back to the barn later, the two girls were cleaning away. Tack was hanging from hooks. Keepsake, washed, was content in his stall, telling the other horses just what a fine day it was.

Sister loved having young people around. She walked outside, listening to the girls talking, laughing. She heard the big diesel engines of the vans fire up, detected the throaty roar of the pickup trucks for those pulling goosenecks. People called good-bye to one another, called "good night" to her, which was proper. One said "good night" to the master at the end of a hunt even if it was ten in the morning—which it was.

She walked across her desecrated lawn thinking the destruction was worth the fun. Golliwog, Raleigh, and Rooster sashayed alongside her. They had been very upset at the goings-on. Golly, of course, bragged about how she faced down Target just spitting at him, her claws unleashed.

They followed Sister under the hickories and hollies, past the scarlet maples that would turn flaming red in another month. They could smell the apples on the trees in the far orchard. Sister walked through the wrought-iron gate. Under the walnut tree in the middle of the graveyard was a graceful stone statue of a hound running. On the front was inscribed: REST, DEAR FRIENDS, WE'LL HUNT AGAIN SOMEDAY.

Bronze plaques, each bearing a hound's name, were attached to the base, representing forty years of Jefferson Hunt hounds. Although the hunt was founded at the end of the nineteenth century, the graveyard was only forty years old. Newer plaques were affixed to the wrought-iron fence. A special tombstone had been erected for Archie, her great anchor hound, a hound she had loved as no other.

"Archie, you missed quite a day. And that pup whom you hated, Dragon, actually did very well, very well indeed."

As they left, Rooster asked why Archie had his name on a plaque and a tombstone, too.

"Her fave," Raleigh answered.

"Will we be buried here?" Rooster asked.

"No, we'll be buried up under the pear trees behind the house." Raleigh liked the idea of being by the house close to Sister.

"Not me," Golly bragged. *"I'm going to be cremated and when Sister dies she'll be cremated, too. We'll go in the ground together."*

"You are so full of it." Raleigh laid his ears back.

Sister walked on over to the den. "Target, quite a show."

He stuck his nose out of the largest opening. *"I am the greatest."*

Raleigh and Rooster knew not to do anything or Sister would tell them, "Leave it." She always told them what to do, and since she didn't give a "whoop" they looked down at the fox, even larger than he was last year.

Golliwog huffed up and spit, and as they walked away she bragged, *"He's afraid of me."*

The two house dogs thought it better not to answer or a nasty fight would explode.

Sister stopped again at the hound graveyard. Leaning on the iron fence, she remembered something about the first day of cubbing in 1981. She just now recalled a check at a remote part of After All Farm. They'd had a good hard run and finally lost scent at the estate's easternmost border where an old, well-tended slave graveyard reposed, small, smooth worn tombstones standing out against deep green grass, the whole bounded by a low stone wall. Most old graveyards were marked off by stone walls or wrought-iron fences. This graveyard belonged to the Lorillards, an old central Virginia family, both black and white. These were the original black Lorillards.

She'd stepped a bit away from the field, listening for Shaker or a hound. The hounds were casting back into the covert by a narrow creek bed. She'd turned to look back at Nola, Sybil, Guy, Ken, Ralph, and Xavier, off from the others, a small group of the younger set. Now she remembered seeing Nola, radiant from the run, at the center, the object of all male eyes, while Sybil cast her gaze down, then looked back into the Lorillard graveyard.

She remembered thinking to herself at the time that that tableau moment said it all.

CHAPTER 24

A cool jet stream of Canadian air dipped over Virginia in the middle of the night, bringing with it a breath of fall.

At five-thirty in the morning, heavy fog like gray cotton candy wrapped the earth. Sister rose and felt the chill, for she had forgotten to turn on the heat in the upstairs section before going to bed. She threw on her heavy robe, slipped on her sheepskin slippers, and clicked the thermostat to seventy degrees.

The house was divided into zones, each with a separate thermostat. The intention, to save money, never panned out and the need to check all four thermostats irritated Sister.

By the time she reached the kitchen she was wide awake—which could not be said for Golly. Nestled deep in the pillow, she still snored lightly. Both Raleigh and Rooster dutifully followed their master downstairs.

Sister put down kibble for "the boys," as she called them,

then ground coffee beans and soon had a pot percolating. She couldn't see a thing from the kitchen window. The outdoor thermometer in the window read forty-nine degrees.

She poured coffee into a big mug, then hurried upstairs by the back stairway. She put on two pairs of socks, one thin, one heavier, jeans, and her work shoes with rust and yellow around the laces. Layers worked best in changing weather. She slipped on a thin undershirt, a T-shirt over that, and topped it off with an old navy pullover. Then she was down the stairs and out the back door with Raleigh and Rooster scampering to keep up.

The hounds would fuss if they heard her, so she gave the kennel a wide berth, moving slower than usual because of the fog. Blurry shapes would suddenly appear, then, as she neared, transform into the hay barn or an ornamental pear. She reached the farm road and headed without hesitation toward Hangman's Ridge, as though drawn there.

Inky, returning to her den at the edge of the cornfield, smelled the approaching human and two dogs, then heard their footfalls on the dirt road. She shadowed them, curious, keeping downwind.

Raleigh wouldn't chase her, but every now and then Rooster wanted to prove a harrier could hunt a fox as well as a foxhound. Sister would walk out with Rooster and let him hunt rabbits, making a big fuss over him. She'd call him back if he picked up fox scent, which was easy to tell since the fox covered more territory than the rabbit, but if the line was good and he was slow to obey she didn't get angry at him. Can't punish a hound for hunting.

Inky enjoyed being a few yards behind everyone. She could turn on a dime and give you a nickel's change. Even if the wind shifted and Rooster got a whiff of her, she could literally spin and run right under his belly. Hounds were agile as far as dogs go, but the only creature as quick and nimble as the fox was the cat. As they both hunted the same game this made sense. They had developed the same strategies for killing mice, moles, rabbits, and the occasional lazy bird.

A soft whoosh alerted Inky to Athena's presence. Another swoosh meant Bitsy. They passed low overhead.

Sister looked up but saw nothing through the fog. Rooster opened his mouth, but she swiftly put her hand around his muzzle, putting her finger to her own lips. All her pets knew the sign. Rooster said nothing.

The dampness of the fog made Sister wish she'd put on yet another layer. Rooster lifted his nose, then put it down on the farm road. Comet had passed that way, the dampness holding down scent. But he said nothing, keeping close to Sister.

They reached the base of Hangman's Ridge in twenty minutes. Mimosa trees near the farm road would appear and disappear in the fog, their beautiful pink-gold blossoms adding color to the gray mist.

The climb to the top, not as steep on this side of the ridge, proved steep enough to make them breathe heavily.

A soft light in the eastern sky, gunmetal gray underlined with dove gray, announced the sun would rise in another thirty to thirty-five minutes, but Sister knew fog this thick would not lift for hours after that. Only when the sun had sufficiently warmed the thick blanket wrapping the meadows, ridges, and mountains would it evaporate, leaving slivers lingering just above the creeks and rivers, tongues of silver gray.

Once on the ridge, Sister paused to catch her breath. Inky ducked off the dirt road, slinking under a clutch of mountain laurel, slick with dew.

The mild breeze on the ridge tousled Sister's hair. Ahead,

the huge outline of the hanging tree took shape, its massive silhouette mute testimony to its centuries of life. What a pity such a magnificent oak had been used to kill.

Hanging, not a pleasant way to die, could at least be quick if the length of rope was correct and the drop proper. But those criminals executed here were strung up to dangle and choke to death, which could take four or five minutes. Occasionally the convict's windpipe would be broken by the violence of the initial jerk and lift as the horse on which he sat was slapped out from underneath him. Death came with merciful swiftness then.

Lawrence Pollard, the first man ever to be hanged from the tree, had so enraged his enemies, they hauled him up without benefit of a horse in 1702. His executioners believed he had swindled them in land speculation—which he had. By all accounts a dark-haired, handsome man, a smooth talker, an elegant dresser, he seduced the few hardy families who had settled this far west, the Wild West at that time, into putting up money to purchase tens of thousands of acres in what is now Lewisburg, West Virginia.

He did buy thousands of acres in that area, but he also kept a portion of the money for dissolute living in Philadelphia, the largest city in the colonies. Word of his profligacy filtered back to the Tidewater and even there leached out to the farthest borders of civilization, this particular county at the base of the Blue Ridge Mountains. Through guile, the irate investors lured Lawrence back to his death.

The last man hanged in this spot was Gilliam Norris, a Confederate veteran, a brave and well-respected man who lost his mind, killing his mother, father, two sisters, and brother with his service revolver.

In between 1702 and 1875, eighteen men were hanged, all murderers with the exception of Lawrence.

Two shapes in the tree startled Sister until she drew closer and recognized Athena and Bitsy. Neither flew away as she approached them.

The sound of a moan stopped her in her tracks. Both Raleigh and Rooster swept their ears forward.

Inky, behind them, stepped out of the fog.

Sister saw her and said to Rooster, "Leave it."

But Rooster paid no attention to Inky, as something by the trunk of the tree had his full attention.

"I'm here to find something. I don't know what it is," she said as if to reassure the animals, but mainly to calm her own fears.

When the swirling fog momentarily parted in front of her, she thought she saw the form of a man by the tree, disfigured, wearing silk breeches and silk stockings, his neck horribly twisted.

She tried to blink the apparition away. This spot could arouse even the most phlegmatic person's imagination.

But then she heard a hoarse whisper and recognized a verse from Psalm 42:

"My tears have been my meat day and night, while they continually say unto me, Where is thy God? . . . all thy waves and thy billows are gone over me. My soul is bereft of peace."

Raleigh growled, putting himself right in front of Sister.

Shaking, she backed away. She might be crazy as that hoot owl in the tree, but whatever she was seeing looked real enough to her.

As the fog swallowed the form back up, it let out a howl of pure anguish. Wind swept over the ridge with a slashing gust.

Sister turned and ran through the fog, only able to see three feet in front of her in a good patch. She was glad she lived a physically active life. She might be seventy-one years old, but she could run like the devil.

Skidding, slipping, sliding down the ridge, she didn't stop until she reached the base.

"Goddamn, I swear that really was Lawrence Pollard's ghost!"

"It was," Inky said. *"I've seen him before. There are a couple up there. They can't go to ground."* She meant they couldn't go to their den, her concept of home.

Sweat rolled down Sister's forehead, between her breasts, down the small of her back. She hadn't been so scared in years.

"His tongue was hanging out." Rooster, too, was a little shaken by the apparition.

Then Athena and Bitsy swooped by in the fog, and that startled Sister.

"Dammit!"

"Don't swear at me!" Athena laughed because she'd scared Sister.

To Sister it sounded like "hoo, hoo-hoo, hoo-hoo."

Of course, Bitsy had to let out one of her bloodcurdling shrieks, which nearly caused all of them to have heart attacks.

Bitsy thought she was singing "The Ride of the Valkyries."

Even Inky's ruff stood up on end.

"God, that's awful." Raleigh blinked.

Sister got hold of herself and started back toward home.

Inky headed for her own den. *"Sister, those spirits up there got what they deserved. They can't hurt you."*

"Why don't they leave?" Rooster asked.

Athena, her voice ghostly and deep in the fog, answered him. *"They can't let go. They can't find absolution or redemption. You know there's a stag like that. It's not just humans. He leads deer hunters to their death. He sets them up so they shoot each other. Kills two or three a year."*

"*They'd better not hurt Sister. Human or stag, I don't care. I'll kill them,*" Raleigh growled.

"*Can't,*" Bitsy shrieked. "*They're already dead.*"

Sister jumped at the sound of Bitsy's voice. "Good God, that bird could wake the dead." Then she realized what she'd said and she had to laugh.

By the time Sister reached her kitchen, she needed that second cup of coffee. She wondered if she also needed prayer, psychiatry, or a good knock on the head.

Instead, there was a knock on the back door.

She opened the door and was happy to see Shaker's familiar, placid face.

"Morning, Boss," he said as he walked in.

At seven in the morning, it was not too early to call.

"Thick as pea soup out there," she said. She wanted so badly to tell him what she thought she saw.

"Yes it is. Patty's ready. I called Tony over at Keswick and he said I could bring her by." Patty was a gyp who was at the right time in her cycle for breeding. The huntsman at Keswick Hunt had a hound, Mischief, whose pedigree and conformation, hopefully, would match up well with Patty.

"Mmm, fine. Here, have a cup of coffee. I make better coffee than you do."

"You look a little peaked. You all right?"

"Well, I had a scare."

"I have them every month when my bills come due."

She smiled. "I have those, too. Next board meeting, I'll bring up the subject of a raise once again. And you know, if they don't vote it through I'm going to Crawford."

"I don't want his money!"

"If he wants to throw it around, I say we take it. I can handle him."

"I can't."

"You won't have to—but don't worry. I'll get this past the board. It's been four years since you've had a raise, and it's not right. I'm tired of it. He offered to buy a Dually for the club. Much as we need the truck, this is more important."

Sister Jane was in charge of hunting and everything to do with the hunting, but the board of governors was in charge of the purse strings and the social direction of the club. It could make for friction.

"That's not why I came over. Really it was about Patty." He sipped the delicious coffee, a perfect mixture of blends to start the day.

"Now that we don't have Doug's salary to pay, I know I have the ammunition to get this through." She paused. "Do you believe in ghosts?"

"I'm Irish. Of course I believe in ghosts." He laughed. "I remember the time you thought you saw the Grim Reaper. And he held someone's claim ticket, didn't he?"

"But you didn't believe me at the time, Shaker. You accused me of drinking."

Sheepishly he put his mug down. "I did." He glanced out the window. "Too bad we aren't hunting this morning."

"We'd need fog lights on our bridles."

He laughed again. "That we would, but I love casting on a foggy morning."

"Shaker, I walked up to Hangman's Ridge this morning. Before sunup. I don't know why. I felt like something was calling me up there. And I thought I saw a ghost. Actually, I won't be wishy-washy about it. I did see a ghost. He quoted from

Psalms. All about misery. Scared me half to death. Then that damned little screech owl flew by and let out a hoot. I don't know why my heart is still beating."

He roared at this. "She's scarier than the ghost."

"Ah, so you do think there's a ghost up there?"

"More'n one. Earth's full of spirits, I think. Don't know why, although my mother would say we have to pray them into Purgatory and then up to Heaven."

"Even the murderers?"

"God's grace."

"Yes, I guess forgiveness *is* His trade. I'm not sure it's mine. I wish I knew why I felt drawn to that tree. I've lived here for forty-eight years, Shaker. I know that old pin oak very well. But until this morning I never felt a call to go there."

"Maybe it's a warning, something to prepare you. You know, sometimes I have dreams. I think we get, uh, premonitions."

"I suppose. Yesterday after hunting I remembered something about the day Nola and Guy disappeared. Nola hunted. We pulled up at the Lorillard graveyard."

"My second season carrying the horn. Still a little nervous. Not at all anymore." He winked. Like any good athlete, Shaker always felt a twinge of nerves before an event.

"We'd run hard. Horses were blowing, people, too, and I stepped away from the field to listen for you. Anyway, Nola, Guy, Ralph, Xavier, Ron, Ken, and Sybil formed a small group a bit away from the others. Nola was the center of attention. It's not that they were coffeehousing, it was just the men's eyes. Sybil was staring into the graveyard. She knew she was invisible then. Even her husband couldn't take his eyes off Nola at that moment.

"When Nola disappeared and Guy didn't show up, my mind was focused on finding them. I didn't think of what I *felt*. I certainly didn't think of that moment at the Lorillard graveyard."

"And what was it you felt?"

"That Sybil would always be overshadowed by Nola even though she was the better woman. At least I think so."

"Me too."

"That Nola had conquered each of those men there, except Ken, I suppose. Maybe she slept with Ralph and Xavier, I don't know, but she could have had them had she wanted them. Even Ron. If she'd put her mind to it."

"Could have had Ken, too, I'll reckon."

"You think?"

He nodded, then got up and opened the bread box. "I'll owe you one." He took out a package of chocolate-covered doughnuts.

"Or two or three."

"Nola could have had most any man. Maybe not for life, but for a night. She was, I don't know, I can't think of the word, like some potion."

"You, too?"

He smiled, breaking the doughnut in two. "I was a young huntsman. She wouldn't have looked at me twice."

"Plenty of other women have. Huntsmen can pretty well have their pick of the litter." Sister stated one of those hunting facts that everybody knows but few people say out loud. Huntsmen are like rock stars to many female members of the field. It doesn't seem to work so strongly in reverse. If the huntsman is a female, the male members don't automatically fawn over her.

He shook his head. "Not me."

"By the end of the season maybe," Sister said, teasing him. "But you knew even then, young as you were, twenty-five or so, that Nola could be . . ."

"Cruel. Nola was cruel to men."

"Well, I don't know as that's the right word, but if you knew that about her, you would still have gone to bed with her?"

He straightened his back. "No, ma'am, I would not, but I would have wanted to."

"I don't get it."

"It's a guy thing. You can know a woman is pure poison and still want her. For some men, they only want her more."

"Women, a lot of them, anyway, always want the man who will hurt them. The Bad Boy. Maybe it's the same."

"Maybe. All I know is when she'd fix me with those blue eyes and start smiling, I could feel the blood in my body burn."

"She affected women, too. That kind of beauty is erotically charged for both sexes, but to different degrees."

"Guy kind of had that quality, too. He could have most any woman he wanted. Probably why Fontaine Buruss hated him. Fontaine thought they all belonged to him."

"Did men dislike him?" Sister asked.

"I think most men didn't trust him around their women. Or maybe they didn't trust their women around Guy," Shaker astutely commented.

"Do you think Guy was sleeping with other women when he was going with Nola?"

"No. Funny, I don't think he was."

"What about her?"

"Yes."

"Who?"

"Ralph Assumptio, for one."

"Who else?"

"Fontaine."

"Jesus." She paused. "Raymond?"

"No." Shaker would have lied, but it was true. Sister's

husband had not been sleeping with Nola. Raymond had slowed down a bit by then. Got caught too many times and made too many messes.

"That's a relief." Sister exhaled. "I would hate to think Raymond was mixed up in this. But he wasn't, I mean, he wouldn't."

"Raymond was a good man. He had a weakness."

"He did, God bless him." Sister had spent enough emotion on her deceased husband. She wasn't going to waste any time dwelling on the negative. "Do you think Ralph, Fontaine, or some jilted lover could have killed Nola?"

"I don't know. You think you know people, but they can surprise you."

She waited, lowered her voice. "Sybil?"

"Kill her own sister?" Shaker was genuinely shocked.

"She'd spent her life in Nola's shadow. And what if Nola decided to make a conquest of Ken?"

"Nola flirted with everyone. And Ken would have to be one of the dumbest men, dumber that snot, to kill the goose that laid the golden egg."

"Nola?"

"His marriage. He'd just married into the Bancroft family, and his people don't have doodly-squat."

"I thought that, too. Well, what about Xavier?"

"She was done with him before first day of cubbing."

"He held a grudge."

Shaker shrugged. "I don't know. Like I said, you think you know someone and then they fool you."

"You're a good huntsman. You trust your instincts. What's your instinct?"

"That the killer is going to break cover."

"And?"

He reached for his third doughnut. "I don't want to accuse a man of murder, but I remember that Ralph Assumptio was courting Frances that fall." She nodded that she remembered and he continued. "He married her at Christmas, and he wasn't especially happy at his own wedding."

"Everyone said he got loaded the night before."

"More. I think Ralph was still in love with Nola."

"Their marriage seems happy enough."

Shaker shrugged. "Who knows?"

"You're right. Who does know?"

"I'm not saying he killed her. I'm saying I think he was in love with her and I think her body being found has shaken him up."

"Did Guy know she was sleeping with other men?"

"It would have killed him. I don't think he knew, but time was coming when he would have found out. Too many of us knew her, I mean. Those of us in our twenties. It was bound to come out sooner or later."

"Would he have killed her?"

"I don't know."

Sister frowned. "Maybe he found out that last day."

Shaker refilled his and Sister's coffee cups, then sat back down. "Or maybe Nola really fell in love. It happens. Maybe she said good-bye to whoever else."

"I remember Guy bumped Ralph going over a jump that day. Caused a fuss."

"They were fixing to fight sooner or later."

She reached down to pat Raleigh's head. "Did you tell Paul Ramy what you thought about Ralph back then?"

Shaker shook his head. "No. First off, I couldn't prove it. Yes, I saw Nola kiss Ralph, oh, spring of '81, something like that. But that doesn't mean I could prove she slept with him. At the time I didn't think it served any purpose other than to upset Paul, who was already upset."

"Upset him because his son's girl wasn't faithful?"

"Uh-huh." He nodded in agreement.

"Well, have you told Ben Sidell?"

"I did. He's okay, Sidell."

"Yes, I think so, too. Why didn't you tell me?"

He put down his coffee mug. "When have we had time to talk? We've been working nonstop to get ready for cubbing, and now we're cubbing and," he paused, "I don't like saying things I can't prove, things that could hurt people, even to you, and I know you won't talk."

"I understand. Oh, before I forget, Jennifer Franklin and her friend Sari Rasmussen are going to work here on weekends, and I expect they'll show up after school sometimes, too, now that Jennifer's got her driver's license. Do you want them to work any of your horses?"

"No. Too hot for them. Especially Showboat."

"Okay." She looked out the window. "Fog hasn't lifted a bit. Well, let's clean the kennels." They stood up and took their cups to the sink.

"You know, when Nola first disappeared I figured she was cutting a shine," Shaker said. "Either she ran off with Guy or she dumped him and ran off with the Prince of Wales. I didn't worry until a week passed."

"I did. I figured she'd at least call her mother or sister to laugh about what she'd done," Sister replied.

"Women like Nola provoke people."

"This sounds suspiciously like blaming the victim."

His melodic tenor voice rose. "No. Anyone who lives above

the rules gets pulled down eventually. Might take a long time, but people will take their revenge."

"You're right." She washed the cups while he leaned on the counter. "Oh, to change subjects, you know Sari's mother, Lorraine, is a very attractive woman. She's been divorced for two years."

"And?"

"Just some information," she said, smiling.

"Cupid."

CHAPTER 25

The Board of Governors of the Jefferson Hunt met the third Wednesday of each month except for July. This month's meeting would be September 18, which gave Sister a little time to gather the votes for Shaker's pay raise. She hoped the discussion about when and where to locate the Hunter Trials would wear them out so the raise would slide through.

As Thursday's hunt and Saturday's hunt both produced bracing runs, the buzz around town was that this was going to be a good season. Sister knew the numbers in the cubbing field would swell and she could expect a sizable field on Saturday, the twenty-first. She was already wondering which young entry to subject to the increased numbers of people and had an evil moment where she thought about pushing up the first cast to six-thirty in the morning. They'd revolt. No, she'd keep it at seven-thirty but deliver a little lecture about cub-bing's purpose being for young entry, hounds first, last, and always.

Monday was her town day, meaning errands, including the most hated shopping for groceries. Well, she'd combine politicking with shopping. Her first stop was Ken Fawkes's of-fice, in a discreet modern building that blended into the land-scape. Unlike most of her contemporaries, Sister liked modern architecture so long as it was good. Perhaps she preferred Pal-ladian architecture, but something as beautiful as the Seagram Building in New York City deserved to be praised.

This was Ken Fawkes's first year on the board. She'd called ahead and was instantly ushered into his office, decorated in a minimalist style that was a total contrast to the way in which Sybil had decorated their home. She realized she'd never been in Ken's office and this reflected something new about him, an aesthetic sensibility all his own.

"How good of you to stop by," he greeted her, his white broadcloth shirt offset by a simple royal blue tie.

"Well, you're kind to let me barge in. I won't take much of your time."

They sat down facing each other over a coffee table of highly polished black marble with thin green veins snaking throughout.

"Coffee? Anything to drink?"

"No, thank you. Ken, I'll get right to the point. As you know, thanks to Doug leaving to take the horn at Shenandoah Valley, we have his salary in the till." He nodded and she con-tinued. "Shaker hasn't had a raise in four years, and that one was negligible, another thousand a year. We've just got to give this man more money."

"I agree." He folded his hands together, his elbows on his

knees, and leaned toward her with a grin. "Means you want to keep my wife as a whipper-in, does it? She's free."

"She has talent." Sister smiled. "Where would we be without your contributions, the contributions of the Bancrofts? I am grateful."

He demurred. "That's foxhunting. If you have it, you give. Like church."

"I find I'm closer to the Good Lord out there than with my butt parked in a pew."

"Me too."

"You know, I have this terrible confession." She leaned toward him, their heads closer over the exquisite marble. "I can tell you this because you're an Episcopalian, too. I've always thought of Episcopalians as junior varsity Catholics," she said, grinning mischievously.

He laughed, leaning back into his seat. "Wait until I tell that to Sybil."

"Ken, I may not get to Heaven with thoughts like that."

"You know, they say foxhunters don't go to Heaven because they have their Heaven on earth." He paused. "Of course, you have my full support for a raise. Would five thousand dollars be acceptable?"

"Yes, I think that would be." She beamed at him. "Now, one more thing. Ralph Assumptio has been a true-blue hunting member and I value him, but he is obsessed with money matters. I actually think that helps us on the board because he goes over every single thing with a fine-tooth comb." She cleared her throat. "I expect resistance from Ralph. He'll be swayed by you before he'll be swayed by me."

"Oh, I don't know about that, but I will talk to him."

What neither acknowledged was that Ken had sent Ralph

a lot of business over the years. Ralph could just keep quiet and come through on this one thing.

Sister thanked him and as she reached the door she asked one more question. "You know, I recalled a lovely picture of you and Sybil. Funny how things come into your mind. I was remembering that first day of cubbing back in 1981 for the obvious reason—well, we'd such a good run and we pulled up at Lorillard graveyard. Do you remember?"

"Vaguely."

"You, Sybil, Ralph, Nola, Xavier, Guy, all together, all so young, flushed from the run. It was a pleasant memory. Being up front, I can't see what goes on behind me on a run. Did you see Guy bump Ralph?"

"Oh, that long coop. Ralph was touchy. It wasn't that bad."

"Not bad enough to induce murder?"

His eyes widened. "Ralph never really liked Guy. He just hated that we called him Hotspur. Said it glamorized the bastard. Pardon my language." Ken cleared his throat. He'd been taught not to swear in front of a lady. "But kill Guy? No."

She left, stopped by Franklin Printing. Betty and Bobby offered their full support for the raise.

By noon she'd called on every board member except for Ralph. She'd give Ken the day to reach him and then she'd have a word with Ralph at tomorrow's cubbing.

She pulled up to the feed store. Given all the stops she needed to make, she'd left Raleigh and Rooster home. She missed having them in the truck with her. She enjoyed their "conversation," as she told friends. She'd chatter away to her dogs, who always seemed so interested in everything she had to say.

She bumped into Alice Ramy emerging with a dolly loaded with chicken feed.

"Alice, let me help you." Sister unloaded the fifty-pound sacks onto the back of Alice's pickup. Alice, although a few years younger than Sister, was frail with tiny, light bones.

"Thank you." Alice shut the tailgate. "Sister, I'm told I can have Guy back. I don't know what to do."

"Would you like me to make arrangements? It might be easier." Alice nodded as Sister put her arm around Alice's waist. "Tell you what. I'll follow you home and unload the feed. You make a cup of tea, or even better, a gin rickey. It's still warm enough for a gin rickey. I'll call Carl from your house." Carl Haslip, Ronnie's cousin, owned the best funeral home in the county.

An hour later, the feed safely stacked in the chicken coop, Sister called Carl, who lifted this burden off her shoulders.

Alice wanted Guy placed next to his father. She didn't want a service. Enough time had passed was how she put it.

The two women sat on Alice's back porch, where a canopy of wisteria draped over the crossbeams, for the back porch was under a huge pergola. Alice had taste in some things, plus she made a wickedly delicious gin rickey.

"Thank you, Jane."

"I was glad to help."

"I haven't been a good neighbor. Wasn't much of a neighbor to Peter, either." She mentioned Peter Wheeler, whose farm adjoined hers to the south. "I miss him. I don't know why. All I ever did was complain to him or about him."

"He was a good man. I miss his sense of humor."

"Guy adored him."

"Mutual, I think."

"You know that fellow who is in there now? Walter, the doctor? He puts me to mind of Raymond."

"Oh?"

"Different coloring, but same size and build, and even the

bone structure of his face." She sipped a deep draft. "A quieter man than Raymond."

"My husband liked being the center of attention."

"And how. Guy was like that, too. Don't know where he got it. Both Paul and I were quiet-living people even when we were young."

"He was beautiful. Beauty generates its own energy."

Alice watched her cat, Malarky, climb up the wisteria to nestle in a branch and gaze down at them. "Yes, he was beautiful. He took after my grandmother. Same eyes, same black curly hair. I always wished I looked like her. She was beautiful even in old age."

"Now, Alice, you're an attractive woman."

"Liar"—she stretched her legs out—"but I thank you all the same." Malarky shifted his weight, sending wisteria leaves twirling downward. "Fatty," she called up to him.

He ignored her.

"Won't be long before the leaves turn, even though it's seventy-four degrees today. The other morning I walked out in the fog and it was chilly."

"Lot of fog now. Earth's warmer than the air." She turned to face Sister. "Since they found Guy I've thought about things. I guess I knew he was gone. He would have found some way to reach me even if he had killed Nola. He wouldn't have killed her, but even if he had. I just don't know who killed him, but I think we'll find out."

"Yes, I think we will, too. Alice, did Paul ever tell you anything he'd discovered?"

"No. He said he could account for people's movements. I guess you'd say everyone had an alibi. He didn't really have suspects."

"Did Guy ever talk about someone he hated or who might have hated him?"

"Mmm, sometimes Ronnie Haslip would get on his nerves. Guy thought Ronnie was flirting with him. I just laughed at him. And he and Ralph started bickering. They'd got on well as children and all through high school. But those last months of Guy's life they were at odds."

"Did you know why?"

"No. You know, the night before he died, he stopped off home. I was watching an old movie, *Dark Victory,* with Bette Davis. He sat next to me on the sofa and said he was getting bored with everyone. He needed a change."

"Do you think he meant Nola?"

"I don't know. He wasn't very specific. But he said the time had come for him to do something with his life. He wasn't upset, just kind of sober. I can't think of a better word."

"Did Paul find out anything that upset you?"

"No. I knew Guy partied too much with all those rich people. I knew he had some growing up to do."

"Ronnie Haslip, Xavier, and Ralph weren't rich then."

"No. But the Bancrofts, the Taylors, the Jansens. Too much too soon. All of them."

"Yes."

"Did you ever worry that Ray would fall in with that crowd, or their younger sisters and brothers, when he became a little older?" Alice sipped her drink, held one of the ice cubes in her mouth, then released it on the next swallow of gin rickey.

"I did."

"Well, you and Raymond weren't poor. I suppose Little Ray could have kept up with the Joneses."

"That was Big Ray's department. But Alice, I don't think Raymond or I would have tolerated that behavior in our son even if we could have afforded it. This county is full of people who just suck off their trust funds."

"Most don't amount to a hill of beans."

"I don't begrudge them the money. What I can't stand is that they don't do anything for anybody else. They party, golf, hunt, travel, ricochet from one thing to another. They marry, have children, divorce, marry again, and think the world belongs to them. I have to tolerate the ones in the hunt club, but I sure don't have to socialize with them."

Alice smiled. "I've never heard you talk like that."

"Alice, you've never heard me talk," Sister bluntly replied.

A silence followed, then Alice spoke. "I haven't liked myself much since Guy disappeared. I lived for my family, and when they were gone I didn't have any friends. Well, you are right. I haven't heard you talk, really talk. I haven't heard anyone talk. And how much life do I have left? I don't want to live it like this. My son has come back to me. Not as I wished, but he's come back and, you know, he reproaches me. Guy wouldn't want me as his mother now."

Surprised by this outburst, Sister softly said, "Love never dies. His love is as real today as the day he died. He would want you as his mother. He wants you to be happy."

"Do you think so?"

"I do. I draw on Raymond's love every day. He wasn't perfect. Neither am I. But he loved me and so did my son. I live with that love."

Alice finished her drink. "I never thought of it that way. I only thought of what I'd lost. Well, I've cried through many a night. I cried when Ben Sidell told me they'd found Guy. The more I cried, the more I knew I had to do something. I can become someone my son would like to know."

"What are you going to do?"

"The first thing I'm going to do is take some classes at Virginia Tech. I'll have to commute, but I checked out the classes on the computer. I can take classes on Mondays and Wednesdays. I'm going to get a little apartment in Blacksburg, go down Sunday nights and return Wednesday afternoons. I heard that Lorraine Rasmussen wanted to get out in the country, money's tight for her, and I've rented her rooms upstairs. We'll share the kitchen, the living room. She'll take care of Malarky and my chickens."

"Well, Alice, that's wonderful."

"Do you want to know what I'm going to study?"

"Of course."

"Poultry science and cattle breeding. I've always wanted to breed high-quality cattle, but Paul wouldn't let me do it. He said the market was like a roller coaster. Well, he's gone. I'm going to do what I want to do."

"Good for you."

"And one other thing. You were always nice to me even when I wasn't nice to you. So if you want to go through here when you hunt, you go right ahead."

"Alice!" Sister leapt out of her chair and gave Alice a hug.

"See, I knew all this time you just wanted to hunt my land." Alice, her face red, laughed.

It wasn't until she was halfway up her own driveway that Sister realized she never did buy her groceries.

CHAPTER 26

Each board meeting rotated to a different board member's home. Ralph and Frances Assumptio hosted this one. Frances spent her time and energy cleaning and decorating. The place, farther west from Sister's down Soldier Road, had a warm feel to it full of handsomely worn oriental rugs, old silver, and overstuffed club chairs.

One of the rules of the Jefferson Hunt was that no food or liquor could be served until after the board meeting. Past experience proved the necessity of this rule.

As usual, the entire board showed up. Shaker's raise passed unanimously. When Ralph wasn't looking, Ken winked at Sister, who winked back.

They had checked off everything on the agenda when Bobby Franklin, as president, asked pro forma, "Are there any new items not on the agenda?"

Crawford, wearing a flattering turquoise shirt, spoke. "I'd like us to consider building a clubhouse and showgrounds. We lack a central meeting place—neutral territory, if you will—and showgrounds would help our horse show committee immeasurably. We'd have a permanent home for our activities."

"Wait a minute. This club has no debt. You're talking about running up mountains of debt," Ralph piped up, his eyebrows knit together in concern.

"One of the reasons we have no debt is because Raymond and Sister built the 'new' kennels on their farm at their own expense," Bobby said, quickly giving credit where credit was due. He knew perfectly well what Crawford was up to.

"What happens when Sister leaves us?" Crawford blurted out.

"I'm not leaving," Sister said, enjoying watching him squirm. "I would never willingly leave the Jefferson Hunt. You might vote me out, but I won't leave on my own."

"Never!" Betty vehemently spoke.

The rest rumbled their agreement.

"Well, what I meant to say is, what if you have to leave us, what if it's not your idea?" Crawford recognized his blunder and wished these damned Virginians weren't so subtle. And how they prized it, too. Made him sick. Everything took twice as long because of their damned subtlety.

"You mean if I died?" Her gray eyebrows raised quizzically.

"Well—yes," Crawford sheepishly replied.

"The kennels will still belong to the Jefferson Hunt Club, as will the rest of Roughneck Farm." She had dropped a bombshell.

No one knew what to say.

Betty started to cry.

Bobby also wiped away tears. "Now, we don't have to go into this. It's not our business."

"You know, I wasn't withholding it to be obstructionist." Sister folded her hands on the table. "It's just no one likes to think of their own demise. When Peter died, it shook me." Murmurs echoed this sentence, as it had upset all of them. "He'd had good, long innings. I never thought Peter would die. He was made of iron, but the last year when he didn't ride anymore, I guess deep down, I knew. When a foxhunter stops riding, well?" She shrugged, and the others knew what she meant.

"You aren't going anytime soon. Only the good die young." Bobby recovered himself.

Everyone laughed.

"I should live forever, in that case. But I had to think about how I had arranged my effects. And I'd pretty much left everything as Raymond and I had once decided. But that time is past. I have no true physical heirs, but I have plenty of hound children and horse children—and your children." She smiled warmly. "The Jefferson Hunt will always have a home. I wish I could leave you more money. Who knows what the future will bring. But you have the physical plant."

"Hear! Hear!" Ken applauded.

The others followed his lead.

"So we don't need to go into debt." Ralph Assumptio's long face lit up.

"I rather wanted this to be a surprise, but Crawford, your concern, which is quite legitimate, forced my hand."

"I certainly had no idea. I didn't mean to." He truly meant it.

"And I agree with you, Crawford, that a showgrounds would help us," Sister said. "We might even be able to rent it out to other groups and make a bit of money. Imagine that, a hunt club more in the black than in the red."

Everyone laughed again.

"You have an idea about the showgrounds?" Crawford ran his forefinger and middle finger over his lips, an unconscious gesture of thoughtfulness.

"I think it's a good idea, but I really don't want it at Roughneck Farm while I'm alive. I couldn't stand the commotion."

"What if I bought a piece of property near your place?" Crawford suggested.

"I don't think that will be necessary," Ken said. His voice carried authority, an authority he didn't have in his youth. "Naturally, I'll need to discuss this with Tedi, Edward, and Sybil, but there is a triangle of land, those acres on our western border. The old logging road goes into it. Perhaps we could donate that to the club and start on the showgrounds next spring, if all goes well."

"Still taking on debt," Ralph grumbled, lowering his head like a bull. He'd been sullen lately. "Bulldozers, grading—why, just the preparation for a ring can easily cost thirty thousand dollars. It's the drainage that gets you. Now, I don't want to discourage your gift, Ken, assuming your wife, mother-in-law, and father-in-law agree, but a building program would still mean debt—a grandstand, fencing, fencing around the show ring, that cash register starts ringing up. And you need a sprinkler system, otherwise you've got a dust bowl in the summer. You need a tractor and harrow to drag the ring. You need night lights. You need P.A. equipment, otherwise no one will know what's going on, and I can tell you right now a bullhorn isn't going to cut it. That's for starters, folks. And how big do you want the ring? Big. Doesn't do you a bit of good to build a small one."

"Now, Ralph, we can figure these things out." At that moment Crawford wanted more than anything to strangle Ralph.

"He's right, though," Betty chimed in. "It's a long-term project, but if the land is donated, with effort and a lot of bake sales, hunter trials, and hunter paces, we could raise the money over the years and then build it." Betty feared debt, too. She and Bobby struggled to pay their mortgage sometimes.

The last thing Betty, Bobby, or Sister wanted to do was wear out the members by always trying to squeeze money or work out of them.

Ronnie Haslip, uncharacteristically silent for most of the meeting, said, "If you build a ring, you should build it three hundred feet by one hundred and fifty feet and board it solid so you can also play arena polo there. Could bring in a little more revenue. And you might want to think about stables, the kind that used to be at the Warrenton Fairgrounds. Then you've expanded your versatility." He held up his hand as Ralph opened his mouth. "And your budget, I know."

Bobby twiddled with his pencil, then spoke, a rather high voice from such a large body. "How can we do this without exhausting our members? This is a huge project. If we add more obligations like more shows, hunter trials, bake sales, you name it, we are going to plain wear out our people. Today, just about everybody works a real job and they don't have time."

"Well, what if I headed up an exploratory committee?" Crawford suggested. "Maybe we could float a bond so people aren't going crazy with these nickel-and-dime projects."

"My nickel-and-dime project brought in fourteen thousand dollars last year," Ralph reminded them. He was justifiably proud of his horse shows, one of which was A rated.

"No disrespect, Ralph, but those shows are a lot of work," Ronnie said. "If Claiborne and Tom Bishop didn't give us the use of the Barracks," Ronnie named their large indoor arena, "gratis, we'd be lucky to make a thousand dollars. And it takes just about everyone in the club to work that big show you do, the A one."

Shows were rated by the American Horse Shows Association. Tempting though it was to think of it as a report card, it usually reflected the level of competition, the courses, etc. A show rated B wasn't necessarily a bad show, it was just somewhat simpler and didn't attract many professional riders who wanted to gain points, rather like professional tennis players trying to keep their rankings on the computer.

Sister kept out of most board discussions unless they related to hounds, hunt staff, hunt territory. She kept out of this one but was listening intently.

"Crawford, do you have dollar figures in mind?" Ken short-circuited Ralph's indignation. "These horse shows are a godsend to us even if they are a lot of work. How much more could we bring in if we had this facility?"

"You could charge the polo club, homeless since the old fairgrounds were torn down, at least five thousand a summer. Other groups would be charged on a day rate. I can get figures from Expoland, Commonwealth Park, and the Virginia Horse Center."

"Those are big operations." Bobby tried not to let his personal animosity for Crawford cloud his judgment.

Crawford was struggling with the same problem in reverse. "I also thought I could see what the Albemarle County Fair brings in. And I will get a variety of construction figures based on different types of footing, ring sizes, stuff like that. I expect the exploratory process will take four to five months."

"The fair suffered the last two years, rained out," Betty flatly stated. "It's a huge problem."

"Which is why we also need an indoor arena if we're going to do this right," Ronnie said, gathering steam. "And I don't want to do this if we aren't going to do it right. Have any of you ever seen the Mercer County Fairgrounds in Kentucky or the Shelbyville Fairgrounds? They're beautiful. Right out of the 1890s. If we're going to do this, then we must do it properly and it should be a thing of beauty."

"And a joy forever." Ken laughed partly because Ronnie had turned so serious.

"He's right, though," Bobby said. "And I don't want to go into debt. Crawford, I am underlining that thought three times. But I agree with Ron. If we do it, we do it right."

"Well, would any of you care to serve on my exploratory committee?" Crawford threw down the gauntlet.

"I will," Ralph said. "To keep an eye on you!"

Everyone laughed.

"Me too," Ken agreed.

Betty nudged Bobby. He ignored her as she spoke up herself. "I'd be happy to do some research on this. It's exciting."

Sister said, "Might I suggest you ask Walter. He'd be invaluable in dealing with details like handicap access, sanitary facilities. And he's got a wealth of common sense, too."

"Good idea," Betty said. She liked Walter.

"All right, if there's no further discussion, will someone make a motion that we adjourn?"

"Wait. One more piece of hunting news," Sister said, and rolled her eyes heavenward as if announcing a miracle from Heaven. "Alice Ramy will let us hunt through her land." Just then an enormous thunderclap startled all of them. "Perfect timing." Sister laughed. The power wavered, then went out.

"I've got candles. Don't worry." Frances bustled in from the kitchen as Ralph lit the graceful hurricane lamps on the mantelpiece.

"How did you do it?" Betty was agape.

"You know, I didn't do a thing. If we give credit to anyone, let's give it to our former member, Guy Ramy. His memory changed his mother's mind."

A silence followed this.

Ken finally said, "Well, that's wonderful. I think each of us board members should make the effort to call on Alice and personally thank her."

"Hear. Hear!" Bobby lightly rapped the table with his gavel. "Excellent development. Excellent idea."

A flash of lightning, another thunderclap, and a torrent of rain dropped out of the sky.

"I don't ever remember this many thunderstorms. This year's been peculiar," Ralph said. He struck a safety match, lighting more candles.

Everyone talked about the weather, Alice, and local events while Betty and Sister helped Frances bring out the food. Ralph opened the bar.

After everyone had a drink in hand, Ralph pulled out a flask holder from behind the bar. "Would you look at what my lovely wife bought me?"

Bobby Franklin reached for it; the British tan leather was cool to his touch. He put his thumb under the small metal button knob, popping up the leather flap that secured the top. Carefully he lifted out the silver-topped flask. Holding the glass to the candlelight, he whistled and said, "Handblown."

"Let me see that." Ken took the flask. "Even got your initial on it."

"Frances thinks of everything," Ralph boasted.

"Wonderful woman," Ronnie agreed. "Only ever made one mistake."

"What's that?" Ralph's eyebrows knitted together.

"Married you," Ronnie said, and laughed.

As they ate, talked, joked with one another, Betty said to Sister, "Bet we don't hunt tomorrow."

"It will clear up."

"You always say that." Betty dabbed her mouth with a linen napkin. "That Frances makes the best deviled eggs. Guards the recipe with her life."

"Hounds are going out unless it's a monsoon."

And that's what it was. So hounds stayed in the kennels and Sister finally knocked off her overdue grocery shopping. She knew, given the moisture, that Saturday's hunt would be slick but that scent ought to hold. She couldn't wait.

CHAPTER 27

Aztec's ears swept forward and back. Although possessed of 360-degree vision, give or take a degree, Aztec couldn't see more than three feet in front of his well-shaped nostrils thanks to persistent fog. Relying on his hearing, he could tell hounds, on a light line in front of him, were working hard to stay with scent. He knew scent should have been glorious, but it wasn't. Foxhunting is a humbling sport, and Nature makes a volatile partner.

Sister listened for hounds, Shaker's voice, the horn, and for the horses behind her. She couldn't move out too quickly because the field, twenty-four strong this early morning, would be scattered like ninepins in the blanket of fog. Mostly they walked and trotted. If hounds hit a hot line, she'd need to use her knowledge of the territory to try to keep up without losing people or running into a barn.

The fog hung over them, refusing to lift. Foxes, knowing the night would bring a full moon, stayed in their dens resting up for what they hoped would be a party night. Lunacy didn't just apply to people.

Fortunately for the hunters, the trails of scent from the night before still lingered. Those late coming home, around sunup, left even fresher scent, but as yet the pack hadn't hit it.

Betty Franklin, on the left side, crept along Snake Creek's bank. The ground was soggy, but she knew where she was. If hounds really moved off she thought she could stay with them until they entered either the hayfield about four hundred yards to her right, or ran straight through the woods and came out into the cornfield bottom. Once in an open field, Betty knew she'd become disoriented. All she could do was ride to cry, but ultimately that's all any whipper-in can do under harsh conditions.

Sybil, feeling jittery, hoped she wouldn't get in the hounds' way. Hounds met at her parents' big house at After All. Under normal circumstances, Shaker and Sister together with Betty and Sybil would have met at the kennels and roaded them over. This would give hounds time to settle, horses and humans time to limber up, but the fog prevented that. Instead, they loaded everyone on the hound trailer and drove to After All, parking down at the barns.

Even though Sybil was born and raised on this land, the fog transformed the most ordinary things into the extraordinary.

She jumped, startled, as the covered bridge appeared before her like the gaping mouth of the mask of tragedy. Her fear made Marquise, her horse, leap sideways.

"Sorry, Sweetie."

They clip-clopped over the bridge. She thought Betty was up ahead. In a situation like this, Betty would go forward on the left side and Sybil would come behind on the right side.

Sybil could hear hounds ahead of her moving along the creek bed. She had no idea where the field was but reminded herself that Sister knew the land even better than she did. Sister had had twenty-five more years to study it.

She climbed the low ridge, sending small stones rolling down the slick mud behind her. She pulled up by her sister's and Peppermint's graves.

"Nola, you'd enjoy today."

Never having spoken to a grave or a dead person before, she felt slightly foolish, but there persisted deep within her the idea that Nola was near. Not just her remains, but her spirit. And that spirit loved her. Yes, when small they fought like banty roosters. As they became teenagers, Sybil swallowed her resentment of her sister's beauty, her extroverted personality. Alone upstairs at night, one or the other would slide down the polished hall floor, socks barely making a squeak. Then they'd sit together on the bed, compare their days, make fun of everyone else, study the models in *Seventeen* or *Vogue* magazine, and talk endlessly about horses.

When Ken Fawkes courted Sybil, Nola fought with Tedi and Edward right alongside her. She even told her father he was a snob. Ken might be poor, but he wasn't stupid and he made Sybil happy. She loved Nola for that. Somehow she hadn't even minded that at her wedding the maid of honor unintentionally outshone the bride.

A ripple of anguish washed over her as she wondered, yet again, what Nola's last moments were like. Was she terrified? Perhaps. Defiant? Most likely. Did she know she was about to die? Sybil prayed that she did not. Perhaps her murderer was merciful in that he didn't torture her. Maybe he killed swiftly and Nola never knew what was happening.

Ken told her not to dwell on it. They couldn't change the past. Focus on the present, on their life together and their sons.

He was right, but she couldn't keep her mind from playing Nola's last day over and over again. Nothing unusual ever stuck out like a red flag. The day's cubbing had put everyone in high spirits. The party that evening at the Burusses' filled them up with food and spirits of a different, more liquid sort. Nola didn't lean over and confess any "sins" to her. Actually, Nola confided in Sybil less once Sybil was married. She'd tease her by saying she didn't want to upset a proper matron.

She shook herself. Concentrate on today. Listen for the hounds.

She wondered where the field was. Ken was with them.

At that moment they were moving, creeping, really, up the right side of the creek, heading upstream. Even Athena and Bitsy, who often enjoyed shadowing them, stayed in the rafters of the stable. Why fly around in the fog when mice scampered right under your talons?

Ralph Assumptio and Ronnie Haslip rode side by side. Everyone out that day wanted to ride next to a buddy and in view of the riders in front, if possible. No one spoke.

Sari and Jennifer rode together; Walter and Ken, Crawford and Marty hung right behind Sister, which irritated Ken, who thought Crawford had no business being up front. Bobby and Xavier brought up the rear, doing their best to keep the twenty-four riders from fading into the fog. That's all they'd need today, someone out there riding around, turning foxes, getting in the way of hounds and finally hollering their damned head off because they were lost and scared.

Tedi and Edward, also furious at Crawford for his pushiness, stuck with Ken and Walter until the path narrowed as the creek forked sharply left, northwest. They scooted in front of the two men, who graciously nodded, "Go ahead."

"Whoop. Whoop." Shaker's cry faded away up front.

Sister knew they'd be in the cornfield soon enough. The corn was planted north to south because of the lay of the land. If she hugged the end row, which she'd have done even if she could see, she'd come out on the farm road leading up to Hangman's Ridge.

Cora and Dragon, brimming with drive, wanted to find a better line than the tattered trail they currently followed.

"If we could bolt Charlie, we'd have a run," Dragon said. Charlie was Target's son from last year's litter who had a den close by.

"You might be able to bait him," Cora said. She was glad that Asa, Diana, Dasher, and the others were close behind. The fog didn't bother her as much as the humans and the horses, because she relied on her nose even in the brightest of weather. Still, it's always reassuring to see one's surroundings.

Charlie's den had fresh earth scattered outside as he'd been housecleaning. It emitted the sweetish, skunky odor of fox. Charlie, an ego as big as his luxurious brush, wanted every male animal in the universe to respect his territory. He even intruded on Uncle Yancy's territory and marked that. A loud lecture followed this insult.

Not only did he hear Dragon coming, he smelled the sleek hound.

Dragon crawled halfway into the entranceway before his shoulders proved too broad for further movement. *"I know you're in there."*

"So does everyone else in this kingdom." Charlie thought of his territory as a kingdom. His mentality was truly feudal.

"Give us a run. I'll give you a head start. How about if I let you get to the other side of the cornfield?"

"I wouldn't trust you any farther than I could throw a dead mouse."

Charlie, who was full of himself and eager to make Dragon eat his words, slipped out his back exit. Dragon, butt still in the air, continued hollering down the front entrance. It took Dragon about five minutes before he realized he'd been had. Then he put his nose to the ground. *"Hot! Hot! I'm right."* His rich baritone reverberated throughout the woods, echoing deeper as the hound was engulfed in the thickening fog.

The rest of the hounds sped over to Charlie's den. Dasher could see Dragon's pawprints. He followed the prints as well as his nose to the exit hole.

His sister was right behind him. He spoke low, then she spoke louder. *"It's good!"*

Cora called to the others moving through the fog. *"Burning scent! Burning scent!"*

"Hurry hounds, hurry," Asa encouraged them. *"All on. We want to be all on."* Then under his breath he whispered to Diana, *"Especially in this pea soup."*

Within seconds the hounds converged on Charlie's den, picked up the escape route line, and flew on it. All could hear Dragon up ahead by perhaps a quarter of a mile, too far ahead.

Charlie, flying fast and low, wanted to put as much distance as possible between himself and Dragon.

Shaker couldn't see anything, but he blew "Gone Away" as he recognized Dragon's voice, then Cora's, Diana's, Asa's, and the young entry who yelped as much as sang. Sounded like the whole pack, to him. He heard no stragglers.

The first problem was to get through the woods, over the coop in the fence line, through the corn to get up with his hounds. Like most huntsmen, bravery came naturally to him, but he was old enough not to be stupid. This was a day to let

Gunpowder pick his way. He trusted his horse more than he trusted himself.

Betty, already in the cornfield, as she'd had the presence of mind to move forward while hounds were picking at the old line, cantered through a line of corn, the long green leaves swishing. She knew she couldn't get into too much trouble if she stayed in a row. Once out of the field, the old zigzag fence between the corn and the farm road was easy enough to jump even in the fog.

That couldn't be said of the coop between the woods and the cornfield. Shaker and Gunpowder found it and got over because Gunpowder, long-strided and with the élan of a thoroughbred, trotted two steps and arched over effortlessly.

Sister heard her hounds, then the horn. She'd fallen farther behind than she realized.

Sybil, too, was jolted out of her reverie. She pushed along the low ridge, leaving Nola's grave behind her, but she knew she'd gotten thrown out. Right now she was utterly useless to the huntsman. She cursed herself, then the fog as she tried to make up the ground without breaking her neck.

Sister hugged the creek bed and crossed where the smooth rocks led down into the creek and where Snake Creek fed into Broad Creek. The footing, still slick and deep, was better here. Aztec, his light bay coat oddly translucent in the strange muted light, reached the other side of this part of Broad Creek with no problem. When Sister looked back to see if the person behind her, now Tedi Bancroft, had made it across, she couldn't see anyone. And she could only hear her when Tedi appeared by her side.

"We've got to kick on, Tedi."

Edward charged out of the fog, then held hard, pulling sharply back on the reins. "Sorry, Master."

"Can't see the hand in front of your face. I was telling

Tedi, we've got to kick on and hope for the best." She cupped her hands. Normally she wouldn't speak much during a run, but the hounds were well ahead. She wasn't going to cause any hound heads to come up and she wasn't going to turn a fox, either. "If you can hear me, listen for hoofbeats. We've got to move out. If you can't hear the hoofbeats, ride to cry."

"All right," Walter called back.

Bobby, bringing up the rear, had visions of picking up people like scattered croquet balls. But he was a foxhunter, and foxhunters stay with hounds.

Sister trotted along, spied a rock outcropping, its red streak glistening like blood in the moisture-laden air. Curious. A narrow path forked off from the left of this rock, which would bring her near the coop much more quickly than if she stayed on the wider path. She decided to chance it.

She squeezed her legs, Aztec extending his trot; he had a lovely floating trot, easy on an old back. The club hadn't brushed back this trail, one of those jobs waiting to be knocked out before Opening Hunt. She crouched low, her face alongside Aztec's muscled neck.

"Take care of me, honey."

"Piece of cake," he snorted.

Ralph, Xavier, Walter, and Ronnie cut left by the rock, hoofbeats fading away in front of them. Wordlessly they moved out. Behind them came Ken, Jennifer, and Sari, excited at hounds in full cry and the wildness of the morning.

Bobby kept pushing up stragglers.

Enough people had slid by Crawford when they had the chance that he and Marty rode in the middle of the group, which he didn't like. He so wanted to be in the master's pocket on this day, but he couldn't hang in there. He wasn't quite enough of a rider. Czapaka, a big warmblood and not as nimble as some of the other smaller horses, bulled through the narrow path; a low-hanging pine bough smacked Crawford in the face, disturbing a squirrel up above.

"*Watch it,*" the squirrel chattered.

"*You're nothing but a rat with more fur,*" Czapaka called over his shoulder, which caused the squirrel to throw pinecones on following riders and scream at the top of his lungs. Squirrels aren't known for their emotional self-control.

Sister emerged from the overgrown path knowing the three-board fence should be twenty yards in front of her; Jimmy kept all the fence lines clear. This fence line was the dividing line between After All Farm and Roughneck Farm, with Broad Creek cutting through both properties as it flowed in a southerly direction. The old boundary had been set with squared-off stones back in 1791, when the original land grant was subdivided. The stones stood to this day.

Sister slowed. She didn't want to run into the fence, plus she knew Aztec, bursting with talent, would just lift off and clear the fence. She thought it unwise to ask some of the riders behind her to follow suit. The coop, once she found it, would be more prudent.

Off in the distance she heard Diana's voice, and Cora's bel canto. "*Fly! Fly! Fly!*" The other hounds in chorus, "*Yes.*"

"Where is that damned coop?" she whispered, eager to be with her hounds.

A blackened shape interrupted the fence line.

"*That's it.*" Aztec curved to the right, then swung to the left with long, fluid strides to hit the spot perfectly in front of the coop, the rain-soaked earth squishing underneath his hooves. He gave an extra surge of power because of the footing, clearing the coop with a foot to spare, which made Sister laugh as she hadn't expected Aztec to jump so big. He was still young, inclined to overjump.

"Good boy." She patted his neck.

Behind her she heard Tedi land, then Edward, both superbly mounted, as always. She headed left again, following the face of the corn.

Shaker was in the cornfield, behind his hounds. Betty sat now on the farm road, waiting for the hounds to emerge like small ghosts from between the straight-planted rows.

She heard Shaker's high-pitched "Whoop." If he was going to turn or call them back, she'd hear the horn, the three or four long, piercing notes of equal length.

Betty hoped Sybil was on the far side of the cornfield. She couldn't see a thing, contenting herself with the knowledge that no one else could, either.

The bulk of the pack now ran thirty paces behind Dragon. Delia, bringing up the rear, was fifty paces behind.

Charlie scampered over the zigzag fence, ran between Outlaw's legs for effect.

"Gotcha!" he shouted over his shoulder.

Both Betty and Outlaw, hearts in their mouths, had to settle themselves for a second, then Betty laughed. The gall of that fox.

"Outlaw," she whispered. *"Steady yourself. The whole pack is going to run right through us."*

He twitched his ears forward and back. *"Okay."*

Within two minutes they did just that, then Betty jumped over the fence on the opposite side of the farm road and was swallowed by the fog. She was heading for the orchard. Had she been able to see she would have spurred on Outlaw the minute Charlie ran between her legs, but she couldn't. She thought the wiser course was to let the hounds blow through her; she wouldn't hurt anyone that way and she could ride hard through the orchard, a kind of shortcut.

Sister, face wet from corn leaves, heard the flap, flap, flap behind her as other riders were getting it full in the face. There was no ducking the corn, the silken red tassels loaded with the moisture.

She felt clammy. The dew point was soggy to the max. Then Sister felt the first drops of a drizzle. She blasted out of the corn row, lifted over the zigzag fence, hooves sunk into the farm road, the red clay now viscous. She hooked left.

Shaker, ahead, blew them on.

Before she knew it, she'd jumped over the zigzag fence on the opposite side of the road and headed straight into the apple orchard. The scent of the apples, almost ready to be picked, filled the air.

The voices of the hounds suddenly stopped.

Trident whispered, *"What happened?"*

Diana said, *"We've lost the scent."*

Dragon, furious, growled, *"I was right behind him! He's got to be here!"*

Shaker rode up to his hounds. "Try on. Eee-lou."

Dutifully, all hounds put their noses to the ground, but nothing. A youngster wanted to run heel, but Cora put her right.

"But it's good here," Rassle whined.

"I know, but you're heading backwards. Must stay forward." Diana confirmed Cora's correction.

The field finally caught up. Betty stayed on the other side of the apple orchard since Shaker didn't blow her in.

Sybil was at the foot of Hangman's Ridge; having gotten

herself turned around, she finally found her way out by following first the creek bed, then emerging into the north side of
the cornfield. She followed a row in the fog and drizzle to the
farm road at the base of the ridge.

Sister rode up to Shaker. "You know, we'd better call it a
day."

"Damn, how could he give us the slip like that!"

"I don't know. He's got some kind of mojo, but the fog
isn't lifting. If anything, Shaker, it's thickening and my built-in
weather station"—she tapped her collarbone broken in the
seventies—"tells me this drizzle will be a downpour soon
enough."

"Okay." He put his horn to his lips, blowing in his
whippers-in.

"Thank God," Betty thought to herself as she picked her
way through the fog back down into the apple orchard.

Betty couldn't understand how Charlie could turn his
scent off. If he'd ducked into a den, they'd know. But he'd vanished. Not a trace.

Sister turned to face the field, huddled together, exhilarated that they'd survived the fog hunt, as it would come to be
known. "Folks, well done. This wasn't an easy task, but it was an
exciting one." She turned to Edward. "Do you mind leading
people home? Since I'm here I thought Aztec and I would road
hounds back to the kennels. We'll come back to pick up the
hound wagon."

"I'd be happy to take everyone back." Edward touched
the brim of his cap with his crop.

"Shaker, ready?"

"You read my mind."

"Sybil," Sister addressed a bedraggled Sybil, who had just

joined them, "Shaker, Betty, and I will put hounds up. You ride back with the others."

"Thank you."

After each field member said, "Good night, Master," and rode off, Sister turned to her hounds.

Edward took the riders back over the zigzag fences and followed the edge of the corn row. Tedi rode up front with him. Folks tried to stay within sight of one another.

The fog, pewter gray now, swirled droplets of moisture. People waited to jump the last coop into After All Farm, although you could barely see it until one stride in front of it.

Ralph Assumptio, boot to boot with Xavier, passed his old friend his flask.

"You know what? Let's walk the fence line and find the gate. This is stupid. We have the whole rest of the hunt season in front of us, and I, for one, don't want to buy real estate during cubbing."

Xavier savored the marvelous port in Ralph's flask. "You got that right, buddy."

"I agree," Ken called from in front of them, although they couldn't see him.

"Me too," Sybil chimed in.

The sound played tricks on them in the fog.

"Ron, you still with us?" Xavier asked.

"To your right." Ron gently squeezed his horse, who walked forward, the two of them appearing spectral in the swirling mists.

He handed Ron his flask, then turned to Xavier. "What do you have in yours?"

"Schnapps."

Ralph wrinkled his nose. "You carry that stuff so the rest of us won't drink it."

"I like it."

Ken's voice floated toward them. "Xavier, admit it."

"Admit what? I like schnapps. I like sweet stuff. My waist-line ought to prove that. Sybil, where the hell are you? Not with your husband, I hope. The entire point of foxhunting is to depart from one's spouse." He knocked back some of his schnapps. "Within limits, of course."

"I'm on your left," she called out.

Ken laughed. "Xavier, don't give my wife ideas."

They heard a rub up ahead at the jump. Someone's horse's hind hooves literally rubbed on the jump.

"If I recall, the hand gate is maybe two hundred yards down the line, wrong direction from the house, but we can follow the fence line back once we're through the gate." Ron handed Ralph his flask.

Rolling his shoulders, Ralph replied, "Well, let's do it. It's too damned raw out here."

Ken's voice again reached them. "I'll go first. Why don't we fall in line and try to keep the horse in front of you in view."

Ron moved toward the fence, or what he thought was the fence. "I don't hear anyone up ahead."

"Must all be over." Xavier picked up his reins.

"Or unconscious from missing that jump." Ron laughed.

"We'd have heard the screams," Ken called out, his voice moving farther and farther away.

"Sybil, where are you?" Ron asked.

"I'm the rear guard."

"I'll take your word for it." Ralph raised his voice so she could hear, but the fog carried sounds strangely; little sounds were magnified.

"I'm here," she called back reassuringly.

They walked along, silent for a few moments. The squish, squish of their horses' hooves accentuated the increasingly dismal day.

A soft whisper in his ear made Ralph sit up straight in his saddle. It sounded like "I'm going to kill you."

"What'd you say?" Xavier, too, heard the whisper.

"Nothing," Sybil replied, soaked and cold.

Ralph, the fence line to his right, now heard, "I know it was you." He couldn't quite recognize the voice. A knife edge of fear ripped at his stomach.

Ron turned in his saddle. "Where the hell is the gate?"

Xavier grumbled, "I don't know."

Ken called, "Keep up."

"We're behind you," Ron called back. "Just moving slower."

"Gate, please." Ken uttered the traditional foxhunting command that directed the last person to close the gate.

Ralph thought he was between Ron and Xavier, but he could no longer see them.

Ron reached the opened gate, passing through. "Sybil, gate please," he bellowed.

"Okay," she responded, her voice fading away.

The voice whispered in Ralph's ear again. "Time to join Hotspur."

Ralph pressed with his right leg, and his horse swerved left. He didn't pass through the gate, but instead he tore off through the cornfield.

Ron heard him take off. "What the shit is going on?"

Xavier clucked to his horse and caught up to Ron. "What's going on?"

"That's just what I said." Ron frowned. "Ralph!" No response. "Sybil."

"Here I am." She appeared out of the silver.

"What's going on?" Ron again asked.

"I don't know." Sybil shrugged.

"Well, Ralph's not here." Ron yelled, "Ken!"

"Yo," Ken called back, from an indeterminate distance.

Xavier leaned forward. "Look, we're going to get lost out here. Let's trot. The sooner we get back the better."

"Yeah, but where's Ralph?" Ron, truly worried now, pointed his crop at Xavier.

"I don't know." Xavier knocked his crop away with his own crop. "What are you so worried about? For all we know, he's ahead of us. Maybe he's ahead of Ken."

"We can't leave him."

"You two go back. I know this country. I'll look for him," Sybil calmly replied.

"Sybil, we can't leave a lady out here. I'm telling you, there's a storm coming up," Ron said sternly.

"Don't think of me as a lady. Think of me as a whipper-in and there's a lost hound. I'd be out then. Just tell Ken when you see him that I'll be late getting in and not to worry. If the weather turns nasty I'll put my horse up at Sister's." She disappeared into the fog.

"Sybil! Sybil!" Ron shouted.

Then they both heard a light rap on the coop.

"She's going the wrong way," Xavier exhaled, thoroughly tired of the whole thing. "Come on, Ron."

"Something is really wrong. I don't think we should leave them."

"Leave Ralph? We don't know where he is, and Sybil's right, she does know the territory even if she is heading in the wrong direction," Xavier said.

Ron's eyes narrowed. "How do you know it was Sybil who just took that jump?"

"Look, old buddy, I'll grant you that things have been

really crazy. But maybe Ralph got sick of crawling through the mist. Maybe he spurred on and he's halfway back to the trailers by now."

"He turned in the opposite direction. I heard him hit the corn."

"What do you mean?"

Ron shook his helmet as a raindrop hit the velvet top. "I heard the stalks, the leaves, you know, the long leaves. I heard them hitting him."

Xavier sat silent, then spoke. "Hear anything else?"

"Just that rub on the fence when Sybil jumped in. She should have headed back toward Sister's."

"We have to go in. We do. We can't do anything to help. It's going to rain. It's already raining." Xavier peered up into the deepening gray as the drizzle slicked his face. "If they aren't there, then we can worry. Come on."

With reluctance, Ron passed through the gate, waited for Xavier to walk through, then he leaned over from atop his kind, patient horse and closed the gate, dropping the metal kiwi latch, shaped like a comma, through the steel circle.

Ralph galloped through the corn. His face wet, broad flat corn leaves were hitting him. He thought he heard hoofbeats behind him. He reached the farm road as the first raindrop splattered. If he had been in better command of himself he would have prudently turned left, jumped into the orchard, and ridden to Sister's barn, perhaps a fifteen-minute trot. But panic had overtaken him, and he turned his horse right, pushing toward Hangman's Ridge.

Inky heard him pass as she snuggled in her den. Five minutes later she heard a second set of hoofbeats, only this horse wasn't running. This horse moved at a deliberate trot. As the weather was filthy, her curiosity was dimmed. She wasn't going out to see what was going on.

Ralph, breathing heavily, eyes wide, transmitted his terror to his horse as he urged the animal up to the right. They reached the flat plateau of Hangman's Ridge.

"Oh shit." Ralph shook his head. He hadn't wanted to come up here, but his mind was fuzzy. Hands shaking, he reached down for his flask, flipped open the leather case, now slippery, and pulled out the heavy, handblown flask. He unscrewed the top and emptied the entire contents. The fire wiggled down his throat, into his belly. He took a deep breath.

Clutching the flask, he moved toward the giant oak, ignoring the warning snorts of his horse, a far better judge of danger than Ralph.

"Trooper, get a grip," commanded Ralph, whose spirits were now stronger thanks to those he had imbibed.

The enormous glistening tree loomed out of the fog. A shrieking sound so unnerved Trooper that he shied, all four feet off the ground. Ralph hit with a thud, his flask rolling across the wet grass.

Trooper turned and fled back toward the farm road. The horse smelled another horse moving up through the narrow deer paths on the side of the ridge. He didn't bother to whinny. He lowered his head and ran as if his life depended on it, the stirrup irons banging at his sides.

Ralph, cursing, picked himself up. Only then did he see, or think he saw, the hanging corpse of Lawrence Pollard, the fine lace of his sleeves drooping in the wet.

"And being found in fashion as a man, he humbled himself and became obedient unto death, even the death of the cross,"

Lawrence quoted Philippians, chapter two, verse eight. Then he moaned, "Obedient unto death, even death on a hanging tree." The wind that always blew on the ridge carried his voice away.

Ralph, sweat running down his face, his hands wet with sweat, backed away from the tree. He turned to follow his horse in flight. Running, slipping, sliding, falling, picking himself up—only to run smack into another horror.

"Oh God," Ralph sobbed.

"You'll see Him before I do."

Down in the kennels, Sister and Shaker were removing collars from hounds who had hunted. The boys were then released to go to their side of the kennel, the girls to the other side. This allowed the master and huntsman to inspect each hound, making sure no one's pads had been cut, no ears sliced by deadly Virginia thorns.

A crack brought hound and human heads up.

"What was that?"

"No one's sighting a rifle today," Shaker said, hands fallen to his sides. He looked toward the north.

"Sound plays tricks in this weather. Could have been a backfire on Soldier Road," Sister said halfheartedly.

"*Small caliber,*" Asa told them.

"*Handgun,*" Diana added, her ears lifted, her nose in the air. Although there was nothing to smell inside the draw pen, she still trusted her nose above all other senses.

"All right, boys." Shaker led the boys to their door.

"Come on, girls." Sister did the same for the gyps.

Once the hounds were in their proper kennels, both humans, without speaking to each other, walked out the front door of the main kennel to listen.

Far away they heard hoofbeats, trotting. As the sound came closer, they walked through the intensifying rain to the stable.

The girls inside had finished cleaning the tack.

"Can't see a bloody thing." Shaker felt uneasy.

"We came in in the nick of time." As Sister reached for a towel hanging on a tack hook, Sybil materialized out of the fog, leading Trooper.

"Sybil?"

"Sister, I found him wandering through the orchard. Guess he jumped the fence by himself."

A shaking Trooper stared wild-eyed at the people. The other horses, munching hay in their stalls, stopped.

"Girls, gently, gently, put him in the end stall, take his tack off, and wipe him down."

As Trooper passed the others, he rolled his eyes. *"I saw the ghost. Ralph wouldn't listen,"* he kept babbling.

Keepsake, hoping to calm him, said, *"There are a couple up there."*

Sybil dismounted as Jennifer took her reins. "Somehow Ralph became separated from the group, so I went out to look for him. Can't find anything in this."

Sister, worried, said, "He could be walking back here or to your farm. No telling."

"Or he could be hurt." Shaker said what she was thinking.

"Girls, take care of Sybil's horse, too, please."

"Yes, ma'am. Then can we help you look?" Sari asked.

She waited a moment, her mind racing. "Yes. Take care of Trooper and Marquise first." Then, voice lower, as if speaking to herself, she murmured, "Trooper is a sensible horse."

Shaker, his shirt soggy against his skin, touched Sybil's elbow. "When did you last see Ralph?"

"At the gate between the cornfield and our line. The hand gate. Of course, couldn't see anything, but that's where I heard him last. Ken, Xavier, Ron, Ralph, and I decided to go through the gate to get back home. You couldn't even see the coop anymore until you were right up on it. No sense getting hurt. But we got strung out."

"The first thing to do is call your mother. It could be that everyone is back safe and sound."

Sister hurried into the tack room, knowing in her bones that all was most emphatically not safe and sound.

CHAPTER 28

Aand why weren't you out hunting today?" Tedi, steaming cup of hot chocolate in hand, asked Cindy Chandler, the owner of Foxglove Farm.

The pretty blonde smiled. "I was going to go."

"Sure, Weenie," Betty Franklin, nursing roped coffee, teased. She'd roaded hounds back to the kennel and left her horse there. As a whipper-in, her concern was the hounds. And Sister never minded Betty putting her horse up in Sister's barn. She'd driven Jennifer's car to After All since Sister asked her to go on ahead and be her stand-in while she and Shaker removed collars.

"I really was. Cat Dancing and I are ready," she mentioned her beloved mare, "but Clytemnestra and her calf, Orestes, broke down the back side of the fencing and escaped. Still haven't found them."

"Cindy, can't you call that damned cow Bessie? Does it have to be Clytemnestra?" Betty checked her watch. "God, it's terrible to have to work for a living. I'd better roll on."

Tedi scanned her living room. "Sybil's still not back."

Betty frowned a moment. "Maybe she's at the barn."

Members had carried cakes, biscuits, and sandwiches they'd packed for a small tailgate into Tedi's dining room. As with most spontaneous gatherings, it proved much more fun than the arduously planned variety.

Edward had shepherded the field back to his barns. Not often acting as field master, he had neglected to make a head count.

"Have any idea where the cow headed? Tracks?" Betty returned to the case of the missing cow and calf.

"I tracked her across Soldier Road but lost her trail in the wildflower meadows. This fog is unbelievable. Don't know how you all were out there without getting lost."

"Well, that's another story." Betty laughed.

"We were never lost. No, not the trusty Jefferson Hunt Club." Ken sipped his coffee, a shot of Irish Mist adding immeasurably to his pleasure since he was wet and chilled.

"Rain dropped buckets on me, like the heavens had unzipped, so I went back home, took a hot shower, and then came over to ask Tedi and Edward to keep an eye out for Cly and Orestes. I'd better alert Sister, too," Cindy thought out loud.

"Once this fog lifts, we'll find her. She's hard to miss," Tedi said.

Clytemnestra, the black and white Holstein cow, was quite flashy. Her pastures, rich in redbud clover and alfalfa, should give the cow no reason for complaint, but Cly liked the excitement of escape. Also, she was nosy and wanted to see what was happening on other farms. She was teaching her offspring her tricks. Although still a little fellow, he eagerly absorbed his mother's lessons. Their jailbreak over the summer when Sister, Walter, Shaker, and Doug built the new in and out jumps only inflamed them to further adventures.

People slowly began to head home. They checked on their horses in their trailers, then drove away.

"Hey," Betty said, poking her head back inside the living room. She had left, gone to Jennifer's car, then returned. "Ralph Assumptio's trailer is down at the barn, but he wasn't at the breakfast."

"Edward," Tedi called, and her husband came in from the library.

"What, dear?"

"Did you see Ralph at breakfast?"

"No, don't think so."

"Ken?" Tedi asked her son-in-law, who wanted to change clothes and head for the office.

He shook his head. "No."

"Good God, he must still be out there." Tedi blanched.

"Bobby brought up the rear," Betty said. "We might reach him in the truck." She walked into the kitchen to use the phone. Tedi followed. "Oh, Bobby, glad I got you. I'm still at the Bancrofts'. We can't find Ralph."

"What?"

"His trailer is here but he's not, and no one remembers seeing him at breakfast." Betty's eyes met Tedi's.

"The last time I saw Ralph was at the coop between the cornfields and the woods. A couple of guys were back there," Bobby recalled.

"Let me talk to him." Ken took the phone from Betty. "Hey, Bobby. Ronnie, Xavier, Ralph, and I had a drink while everyone was negotiating the coop. Sybil was back there with us, too. That's the last time I saw him. You're sure he didn't come in and go home with someone else? Maybe put his horse on their trailer?"

"No." Bobby felt terrible. His job was to bring up the rear.

Edward felt responsible, too.

"Ralph wouldn't leave his trailer here without asking," Tedi said, truly worried now.

As Ken talked to Bobby, the other line rang. Ken put Bobby on hold and heard Sister's voice.

"Is Ralph there?" she inquired.

"No. We just noticed. I'm on the other line with Bobby."

"We need to look for him. I'm sending Sybil to where Snake Creek feeds into Broad. She'll follow the creek back to your covered bridge. Ralph's smart enough to use the creek. Put Betty on."

"Let me say good-bye to Bobby."

"Tell him to stay at work. We have enough people to find Ralph. Okay?"

Ken relayed her message to Bobby, pressed the flashing button, and handed the phone to Betty.

"Boss?" Betty's voice rose.

"Take Edward. Go to the Bleeding Rock. Retrace our steps that way. You'll come out at the coop. Maybe he came a cropper at the coop."

"Okay."

"Ask Ken and Tedi to drive along Soldier Road. He might be walking on the road."

"Where are you going?"

"Cornfield and all around the base of Hangman's Ridge. If we don't find him in an hour I'm calling Ben Sidell. In fact, tell the others to take their cell phones. If no one finds Ralph, call me on my cell in one hour."

"Roger."

"Oh. Jennifer and Sari want to help. Do you mind?"

"No."

"Good. I'll put them in the orchard and tell them to follow hound tracks backward to the cornfield in case Ralph tracked hounds." She hoped the tracks hadn't completely washed away.

"Okay."

"One hour."

"Right." Betty hung up and gave the others Sister's orders.

They threw on Barbour coats or Gore-Tex jackets and hurried out of the house.

Sister scribbled her cell phone number on a pad and handed it to Jennifer. "Call us. We'll be in the cornfields and then around the bottom of Hangman's Ridge. If you don't find anything when you finally reach the cornfield, come straight back to the barn. Don't leave the barn until you hear from me."

"Yes, ma'am," Jennifer said.

With that, Sister and Shaker hopped into the truck. They parked and combed the cornfields, rain pouring down, fog as dense as ever, but found nothing unusual.

Then they climbed back into the truck, mud caked on their boots, every new step seemingly heavier than the last, and they checked the base of the ridge. The rain had washed away any tracks.

"We might as well go to the top of the ridge. At least we can drive up," Sister said, water running off her coat and onto the floor.

"Why would he go up there? Even in the fog he'd know Hangman's Ridge. He'd have to have climbed up," Shaker sensibly said.

"That's true, but maybe he rode up to get his bearings and

try to find the farm road. We don't know where he parted company with Trooper. He could have covered a lot of ground and he could have suffered a concussion and been disoriented."

"We've tried everything else," Shaker agreed. He kept the headlights on low since high beams would only reflect back off the fog, making vision even worse. "Can't see a bloody thing!"

"Drive along the flat part. At least to the tree."

"Christ, in this stuff we'll probably run into it." He crept ahead.

The great gnarled shape hove into view, silvery fog sliding over branches.

Not until they were almost right up to the tree did they see Ralph flat on his back.

Shaker braked. Both he and Sister bolted out of the truck.

"Oh no." Sister covered her face for a second. Ralph had been shot right between the eyes.

Shaker knelt down to feel for a pulse. Sister knelt on the other side of Ralph's body. She, too, touched his neck.

"Warm. He can't have been dead long," she said.

"We heard the shot."

"Oh, Shaker, if only we knew what he knew."

"If we knew what he knew, we'd be dead, too."

Sister, a surge of fury running through her, cried, "Why didn't he tell us!"

"Because he knew he'd be killed." Shaker held up his hands in a gesture of defeat.

She stood up. "Goddamn whoever killed him!"

CHAPTER 29

The horses calling over the pastures told the hounds what had happened. The news passed from animal to animal. Domesticated animals wished to protect their humans.

The wild animals, with the exception of the foxes, generally didn't care what humans did to one another. Sister took care of the foxes, and they wished no harm to come to her.

Athena, Bitsy, and Inky sat protected under a heavy canopy of oak leaves.

"The killer's come out of his lair," Bitsy said. She had grown fond of some of the humans.

"Bad enough Nola was killed. Bad enough," Inky repeated to herself.

Athena turned her head upside down, then right side up. *"Cold-blooded. If we hadn't sheltered in the Bancrofts' barn we'd know who shot Ralph."*

"The humans won't figure it out, will they?" Bitsy worried.

Athena breathed in, her huge chest expanding outward, parting her feathers enough to show the beautiful shaded variations underneath. *"This is bad. Very bad. When a killer breaks cover like this he's both ruthless and now reckless."*

"What about Sister? Is she safe?"

"Who knows?" Bitsy shrugged. *"Any human who gets in the way is in danger, I would guess."*

"Pity you foxes can't lead the killer to his death. It would be a fitting end," Athena said.

"A lot of things happen during a hunt. Maybe we will get our chance," Inky said, *"if we can find out who it is."*

"Well, this is certainly a hunt. If a mouse sits stock-still, I might miss him. But if he moves, then I've got a chance. This human is moving." Athena blinked. *"He really has broken cover."*

"But he's foiling his scent," Inky said.

"He'll make a mistake. He'll come into view. I just hope the next human who flushes him out is ready."

CHAPTER 30

For some people, Ralph's end came as a relief. Eager for tidy answers, they assumed he had killed Nola and Guy and had finally, undone by the unearthing of the dead, shot himself. The fact that no gun had been found did not disturb their desire for an easy answer. Then, too, most suicides don't shoot themselves between the eyes.

Others, no less eager for answers but less inclined to take the easy way out, wondered what Ralph could have done to provoke such a violent end.

Sister felt a sense of foreboding; an evil had been unleashed. Then she realized the evil had always been with them, they'd just chosen not to notice.

She and Shaker sat on that ridge for two full hours. First came the sheriff and his crew, then the Rescue Squad to remove the body once it had been photographed, examined, and finally released.

The kids waited back at the stable as they were told. Sister informed them they'd found Ralph. She spared them the details. When she and Shaker finally returned to the farm, they discovered the girls had done all their chores.

Raleigh and Rooster stuck to Sister's side likes burrs.

The rain continued, but the fog started thinning out. An oppressive mugginess made it hard to breathe, and even though the temperature remained tolerable, the closeness of the air felt like a shroud.

As they lacked a kennelman, Sister and Shaker were responsible for the job of cleaning the kennels after a hunt. Tired but usually happy from the day's hunt, they tackled this with the help of a couple of cups of black coffee. Today the girls had given them an unexpected respite. When Betty returned to pick up Jennifer and Sari, Sister insisted on giving the girls each a fifty-dollar bonus. Betty didn't protest. She was too shaken up by Ralph's murder.

The outdoor runs glistened in the downpour. The indoor runs and pens had been powerwashed. Each of the raised sleeping beds was filled with fresh, soft sawdust chips.

The hounds were snuggled down in their cozy beds, sleeping after a good hunt. They had enjoyed having the two young women fuss over them.

After the girls left, Sister and Shaker sat down in the kennel office. They'd told everything they could think of to Ben Sidell, but they hadn't had a chance to talk to each other. Given the swift shock of it, they found they hadn't much to say to each other immediately.

"Hell of a note." Shaker wiped his face with a towel.

"It's not a sight I'll soon forget." She took the towel from him and wiped her own face and hands. "If only I'd led the field back to the Bancrofts'."

"Sister, you couldn't have seen any more than Edward did. Fog was thick. Cut it with a knife."

"My ears are more educated."

"True, but you'd have been up ahead. Ralph was in the back. Once it stops raining we can go back to the coop. Maybe we'll find something on the ground, but it would appear he left the coop and rode to the ridge."

"I've been thinking. He didn't go alone. And someone who really knew the territory, despite the fog or maybe even because of it, could have taken him up there, shot him, flown down the back side of the ridge, and been at the trailers not long after everyone else came in."

"True."

They sat there on the beat-up wooden chairs that had been donated to the kennel office almost thirty years ago.

He drummed his fingers on the metal desktop. "Why would Ralph willingly ride with his killer?"

"Maybe he didn't know he was going to be killed. Maybe the killer said he needed help or he knew a shortcut—"

"Ralph knew Hangman's Ridge. He had to know he was going wrong."

"He still could have been bamboozled in some fashion."

"Killer could have forced him up there." Shaker wiped his hands on his thighs. "And somewhere along the way he made Ralph dismount."

"Sybil was out there." Sister shifted uneasily in her chair.

"Easy to slip away in the fog." He poured himself more coffee. "I'm drinking too much of this stuff. So are you."

"What if whatever the killer knew about Ralph was enough to ensure his cooperation?" Sister ignored his coffee comment.

"I wonder if we'll ever know."

She said with weariness, "Shaker, I believe it was Ralph who called me about looking in the river off Norwood Bridge."

"Jesus." Shaker sat up straight because some pieces were falling into place.

"Just hear me out. I don't think Ralph killed Nola. He might have killed Guy; he couldn't stand him because of Nola. But I don't think he killed her. I think he accepted that he'd lost her. That romance was busted, and he was already courting Frances. On the rebound maybe, but people are like that."

"They are."

"But somehow he was connected with those murders. There is no doubt in my mind he helped the killer lift that fifty-five-gallon drum and toss it into the James."

"But over all these years you'd think he'd have told, or the guilt would have gotten to him."

"Well, I couldn't live with it. You couldn't live with it. But obviously he could. And maybe, just maybe, he stood to gain by his actions."

"I suppose he gained his life." Shaker shrugged.

"Why?"

"Well, he knew the killer might kill him if he didn't help."

"Possibly. I think, though, that he came out ahead in some other way."

"Was Ralph a vengeful enough man to want to see Nola dead?"

Sister turned this over in her mind. "No, but he might have wanted to see her suffer. You know, to see her finally get dumped by someone. But you're right, I don't think Ralph could have helped her killer. Which leads us to—what?"

Shaker's thick auburn eyebrows jerked upward. "The killer might have told him Guy killed Nola. Ralph exploded and killed Guy. Or Nola's killer had already done the deed and needed help disposing Guy's body. He'd be plenty tired from digging Nola's grave, not that Ralph would know that."

She shook her head. "If Ralph had known Nola was killed or thought she was killed by Guy, then he would have told Tedi and Edward."

"I don't think so. Look, we can never know what goes through someone's head, but maybe Ralph thought, 'done is done.' He can't bring her back. Maybe he had a special sympathy for the murderer. Or maybe the killer could somehow pin it on him? How could Ralph prove he was innocent?"

"That's a good point." She didn't know if too much coffee was making her jittery or if she was jittery anyway. "Either way, he was vulnerable."

Shaker slapped the table. "And who stood to gain more than Sybil? She'd get Nola's part of the Bancroft fortune. Millions upon millions upon millions. Right?"

"We know one thing for certain we'd only suspected before."

"What?"

"The killer really is in our hunt field."

C H A P T E R   3 1

The rain stopped Sunday morning, revealing skies of robin's egg blue and temperatures in the middle sixties.

Sister, Shaker, and Walter met Ben Sidell at the mailbox for Roughneck Farm. They drove in two four-wheel-drive trucks to the cornfield, then parked off the farm road to walk to the coop between the cornfield and the Bancroft woods.

Impressed by Walter's attention to detail at Norwood Bridge, the sheriff was glad the doctor accompanied them. Sister just felt better when Walter was around, although she didn't really know why. The same was true for Shaker. He grounded her.

The mud sucked on their work boots. The ends of their pants' legs were sopping wet from the grass.

Raleigh and Rooster bounded along with them. At first Ben resisted, but Sister convinced him their superior senses might turn up something helpful.

A half-moon puddle glistened before the coop, the depression the result of many hooves digging in before the jump.

Ben crouched down. The rains had washed away hoofprints. He stood up, leaning his hands on the top kickboard as he studied what had been the landing side of the coop on the way home from Saturday's hunt. All he had found near the body was Ralph's new flask. He'd hoped he'd find more here.

"And this was the last place anyone saw Ralph?"

"Yes," Walter answered. "It was the last any of us saw him, those of us who stayed with Edward."

"Shaker, Betty, and I left him at the apple orchard," Sister reminded Ben.

"Right." He cupped his chin in his right hand. "And you couldn't see the hand in front of your face."

"Right," Walter again replied.

"Well, how'd you get over the coop?"

"Trusted my horse," Walter said.

"And you still jumped it?" Ben thought these foxhunters were crazy.

"Sheriff, you do things in the hunt field you'd never do anywhere else." Walter heard a caw as St. Just flew overhead.

"Over here," Raleigh barked at Sister.

Sister walked to where both the Doberman and the harrier stood. A sodden handkerchief lay in the cleared path between the cornfield and the fence line. "Sheriff, I don't want to touch this."

They hurried over, and Ben knelt down and peered at the handkerchief. He pulled on a thin latex glove, picked up the wet, muddy handkerchief, and dropped it in a plastic bag.

"Keep coming," Rooster, farther down the fence line, called out.

Shaker walked up to the hound. "Sheriff. A string glove."

The white woven glove lay in a puddle.

A few minutes later the other glove was found where the cornfield curled right toward a small tributary feeding into Broad Creek.

The four humans and two dogs, wet to the knees, ankle deep in mud, sloshed to the base of Hangman's Ridge.

"Hansel and Gretel," Sister sorrowfully said. "Maybe Ralph dropped or threw away his gloves and handkerchief on the way."

Shaker exhaled. "Anyone could have dropped gloves or a handkerchief. I just don't know why Ralph would have left the other people. It makes no sense to me even if he was nervous. Wouldn't there be protection in numbers?"

"Guilt—or he snapped. People do," Walter said. He jammed his hands into his jeans pockets, then asked Ben, "What do you think?"

"I try not to jump to conclusions."

"What can we do?" Walter asked.

"Wait for a crack in the armor," Ben evenly replied. "The morning newspaper, which I'm sure you read, reported he was shot, the weapon hadn't been found, and the sheriff is investigating." He smiled ruefully, folding his arms across his chest. "That's a nice way of saying we don't know a damned thing."

"You're a doctor, Walter. Do you think our killer is rational?" Sister asked as she knocked one shoe on the other. Mud fell off in red clumps.

"I'm a neurosurgeon, not a psychiatrist."

"For which we're all grateful." Sister half smiled at him. "But you see people in crisis daily. Surely you get a feeling about the real person. Do you have a sense of this person?"

"Well, yes, I think our killer is rational and opportunistic. The fog gave him—or her—a chance to do what he or she was ultimately planing to do. Sister, I think it was Ralph who called you," Walter said.

"Me too. Shaker and I thought of that. And I told the sheriff, too."

"Shock. It's a hell of a shock to see someone you know like that." Shaker wanted to get his hands on the killer. "Poor bastard, flat out in the rain."

"Which brings me back to why?" Sister said. "Why make a spectacle of Ralph? Why not kill him away from everyone? Why not dispose of his body and be done with it just like he thought he had done with Nola and Guy? I wonder if this isn't a warning."

"The hanging tree, a warning to all, the place of punishment." Shaker nodded up toward the ridge.

"Shaker's right. This was so dramatic. He's arrogant. He thinks he's invincible. He must have some incredible sense that he'd never be suspected."

"No one would think Sybil killed her sister," Shaker said quietly. He didn't want to think Sybil capable of such a deed, but she had the best motive that he could discern.

"Paul Ramy certainly fingered her for a suspect. But he couldn't make anything stick," Ben confided to them. "He thought if she killed her sister that her family would protect her."

"Tedi? Never!" Sister quickly responded.

"Sister's right. But Edward might cover for her," Shaker added. "He'd lost one daughter. What good would it do to have the other in jail? I assume that's what a father would think."

"I don't believe it. I know Edward is protective of his girls, well, fathers always are, aren't they?" Sister's voice rose quizzically. "But he's a man of principle. I don't know that he would provide an alibi for her. Even if he thought the original murders were an isolated incident, you know, if he was sure she'd never kill again, he wouldn't help her."

"Paul's reports say she stayed at the party, then went to the C&O with Ken. Other witnesses confirm seeing her there."

"The Bancrofts could pay off the entire county," Shaker said.

"Oh, come now, someone would talk. Keep a secret for two decades? Not here." Sister interlocked her fingers. "I agree that Sybil had a financial and perhaps even an emotional incentive, but I don't think she did it. Had Nola lived, Sybil's inheritance would still be beyond most people's wildest dreams."

"Never underestimate the greed of the rich," Ben Sidell said. "But you're right, Sister, that our killer feels we can't touch him. He's fooled everybody for twenty-one years. I doubt he's even that scared now."

"Pride goeth before a fall," Sister said quickly. Then she whirled around, as did Shaker, their senses sharper than either Ben's or Walter's.

A brush, brush in the cornfield alerted them.

Raleigh and Rooster charged down a row, the stalks bending deeply.

"It's Clytemnestra and Orestes," Raleigh informed them.

Encouraged by the canine companionship and hearing the human voices, the large Holstein cow and her calf walked out of the corn, making a squishy sound with each step.

"You two!" Sister was disgusted with them. "Raleigh, Rooster, let's herd them home with us. We'll get them over to Cindy's later."

"You bet." The dogs paced themselves behind the two bovines, keeping just out of reach of a cow kick.

"Guess we might as well walk you home, too," Ben said. "I'll take down the yellow tape tonight." He indicated the police tape used to cordon off Hangman's Ridge's. "Nothing else to find here."

CHAPTER 32

A Titleist golf ball, white, rolled to a stop next to a small grooming brush, bristles full of flaming red fur.

"You thought that golf ball was an egg when you brought it home, didn't you?" Inky mischievously batted the golf ball.

Charlie, a natural collector of all sorts of objects, replied, *"It's fun to play with, but I don't think the humans that play with them have much fun. They curse and throw their sticks. Why do they do it if they hate it so much?"*

"Human psychology." Inky observed the flat-faced species with great interest. For one thing, their curious locomotion intrigued her. She thought of human walking as a form of falling. They'd catch themselves just in time. It must be awful to totter around on two legs.

"They do like to suffer," Charlie noted. *"I believe they are the only species who willingly deny themselves food, sex, pleasure."*

"And they're so happy when they finally give in and enjoy themselves." Inky laughed.

Charlie's den used to belong to Aunt Netty, but she'd wanted to be closer to the orchard, so she had moved last year. Netty was like a perfectionist lady forever in search of the ideal apartment.

Charlie had enlarged the den. Given his penchant for toys, he needed more space.

"Look at this." He swept his face against the dandy brush. *"Feels really good."*

"Where'd you get that?"

"Cindy Chandler. She left it on the top of her tack trunk. When she forgets potato chips or crackers, that's the greatest. Not only does the stuff taste good, the bags crinkle!"

"Some sounds are so enticing. Sister's big wind chimes—I like to sit in the garden and listen to them ringing at night."

Inky and Charlie, the same age, belonged to two different species of fox. Inky, a gray, was slightly smaller. She could climb trees with dexterity, and in many ways she was more modest than the red fox, who had to live in a grand place, making a conspicuous mound so everyone would know how important he was.

The reds found this lack of show on the part of the grays proof that they were beneath the salt. Nice, yes, but not truly first class. And their conversational abilities missed the mark most times, as well. The reds enjoyed chattering, barking, even yodeling when the mood struck. Grays were more taciturn.

Both types of fox, raised in loving homes, went out into the world at about seven or eight months. The annual diaspora usually started in mid-September in central Virginia.

And both types of fox believed themselves the most intelligent of the land creatures. They allowed that cats could be rather smart, dogs less so. Humans, made foolish by their own delusions of superiority, delighted the foxes because they could outwit them with such ease. Nothing like a small battalion of humans on horseback and forty to sixty hounds, all bent on chasing a fox, to reaffirm the fox's sense of his own cleverness.

"Charlie, how did you disappear in the apple orchard?" Inky had heard from Diana how the red fox evaporated as if by magic, leaving not an atom of scent.

He puffed out his silky chest. *"Inky, there I was in the middle of the apple orchard, fog like blinders, I tell you, the heavy scent of ripe apples aiding me immeasurably. I'd intended to duck into that abandoned den at the edge of the orchard. You know the one?"* She nodded that she did, so he continued. *"But along came Clytemnestra and Orestes. And I thought to myself that those hounds, young entry, mind you, have denned a fox each time they've been cubbing. Getting too sure of themselves. If I simply vanish, they'll be bumping into one another running in circles, whimpering, 'Where'd he go?' I jumped on a big rock and up on Orestes's back. Up and away."* He flashed his devilish grin.

"You shook their confidence," she admiringly complimented him, *"for which every fox is grateful."*

"The T's and R's are going to be very good, I think. Trinity, Tinsel, Trudy, and Trident, Rassle and Ruthie. Good. And now that the D's are in their second season, well, we may have to pick up the pace. Aunt Netty was right."

"Usually is," Inky agreed.

Outside, the arrival of soft twilight announced the approaching night.

"Would you like a golf ball?"

"That would be fun." Inky liked to play.

"I know where she keeps them at Foxglove. It's a piece of cake to reach into the golf bag and filch one. And her house dog sleeps right through it."

"Charlie," Inky said and blinked, *"did you notice anything unusual in that fog when you were riding Orestes?"*

"I smelled Ralph. He sent off a strong, strong odor of fear. And I heard two other riders moving in different directions. They weren't together. I know one was Sybil, because I could smell. I couldn't get a whiff of the other rider. Too far away." He rolled upright. *"Don't you find it odd that humans kill one another? To kill for food, well, we must all survive, but to kill members of your own species? Very nasty."*

"You know, sometimes a vixen will go into a killing frenzy to teach her cubs how to kill," Inky soberly said. *"I think humans can go into killing frenzies, too, but for a different reason. I worry that this person might do that."*

"Possibly." Charlie swept forward his whiskers. *"You know that Cly and Orestes didn't see the killer or they would have blabbed to everyone. Cly can't keep a secret. Cows are dumb as posts."* He laughed.

As the two left the den, Inky wondered if murder was a pleasure for humans the way catching a mouse was a pleasure for her. If so, how could a killer ever stop killing?

CHAPTER 33

P lain pews of rich walnut accented the severe yet uplifting architecture of the local Episcopal church. When its first stone was laid in 1702 it was a rough affair. Few Christian people lived this far west, and those who did had little money. The native tribes of Virginia, divided into Iroquois-speaking peoples and Sioux-speaking peoples, warred against one another sporadically. The handful of whites found themselves in the middle, an uneasy place to be.

The small church proved a refuge from the unrelenting hostilities of the New World, a land devoid of familiar English nightingales yet filled with scarlet tanagers. For every animal left behind on England's shores, there appeared here some new, beautiful creature.

Stone or brick was necessary for buildings of any permanence since the Indians used fire when raiding settlers. The large church bell could be used to sound an alarm. Every farm also had a bell. Upon hearing it, people set free their livestock, hopped on their horses, and galloped to the church.

While it may not have been its most Christian feature, the church, like their homes, was built with a small room with gun slits in the walls. The settlers took aim at attackers through those narrow openings in the stone. A slate roof provided protection from fire.

Over time, truces were made, later broken by both sides. But as the Thirty Years War raged, followed by the English Civil War, the trickle of colonists swelled to a stream, then a river. The hardships of America were more alluring than the hatreds of Europe. A few adventurous souls pushed west toward the fall line.

The fall line was a series of rapids dividing the upland freshwaters from the saltier waters below. Above the fall line rolled the undulating, fertile hills of the Piedmont, which lapped to the very feet of the Blue Ridge Mountains.

Very few whites had reached the Blue Ridge. Those who did hung on for dear life. Building churches with rifle slits did not seem a Christian contradiction to them.

The early American experience was one of intense loneliness and backbreaking labor relieved by bouts of paralyzing danger. Church on Sundays meant seeing other people as much as prayer.

Once the Thirty Years War ended, the worst destruction that would befall Europe until the Great War, there was less reason for Europeans to flee. And after Charles II was restored to the English throne, he had the sense not to kill most of those who had overthrown his father, with a few exceptions. Even more Englishmen decided to stay home.

Hands were needed to work in Virginia, South Carolina,

New York, and Massachusetts. So as the seventeenth century became the eighteenth, Africans were forcibly hauled onto the shores of the New World in increasing numbers.

The parishioners of this isolated church had argued among themselves over slavery. Many noted that the Bible not only has numerous stories about slaves, it never actually says that one human being should not own another. Reason enough, many said, reason enough. And so an economic monstrosity found theological dress clothes to hide in.

If the Native tribes thought the slaves would turn on their masters during attacks, they discovered these new people fought against them as ferociously as the Europeans.

Slave and master, back to back in the fortress room, would shoot at the raiders, then emerge to clean up the mess, the vertical hierarchy again restored. If anyone perceived the irony in this arrangement, they tactfully kept it to themselves.

By the time of the Revolutionary War, the fortress room attached to the church was no longer needed but, as is the wont of Virginians, they kept it out of tradition.

Ralph Assumptio's body lay in this room, his casket on a kind of gurney that would be pushed into the sanctuary at the appropriate moment by two burly employees of the funeral parlor, flanked by two honorary pallbearers. The other pallbearers acted as ushers.

Frances sat in the first pew with her two daughters and two sons, grown now with families of their own.

The entire membership of the Jefferson Hunt attended, all 135 people. Sister Jane sat to the right of the Assumptios, three pews behind. The Bancrofts and Sybil Fawkes sat in front of her. Ken, being a pallbearer, remained in the fortress room.

Shaker escorted Sister while Walter sat with Alice Ramy,

who had driven all the way back from Blacksburg the minute she'd heard the news. This surprised some people, but Alice really had turned over a new leaf.

The closed casket was brought out. The service for the dead had begun.

For Sari Rasmussen, this was the first time she heard the priest read, "Out of the depths have I cried unto thee, O Lord."

Sister had heard Psalm 130 more times than she could count, but the profoundness of The Order for the Burial of the Dead never failed to move her. Some people hated funerals and wouldn't go. Sister called that selfishness. If ever there was a time when a person needed the sight of friends, words of sympathy, this was that time.

What always struck her about the service was the abiding sense of love. Love for the deceased, love for the survivors, love for God. At such a moment, there were those whose faith was shaken. Hers never was, not even when Ray Junior died. She'd heard her own heart crack, but she hadn't lost her faith. Had not women lost sons since the beginning of time? One bore one's losses with fortitude. Anything less was an insult to the dead.

Frances and her children may or may not have believed this way, but they held themselves with dignity.

As Sister sat there, she found it sad that Ralph himself could not hear the words intoned by the Episcopal priest, "Depart in peace, thou ransomed soul. May God the Father Almighty, Who created thee; and Jesus Christ, the Son of the Living God, Who redeemed thee; and the Holy Ghost, Who sanctified thee, preserve thy going out and thy coming in, from this time forth, even for evermore. Amen."

She recalled Raymond, at the end, sitting up on a hospital bed that they'd put in the living room so he could receive visitors and see the hounds and horses go by. The large windows afforded him a good view. She remembered every word they'd said to each other.

"I'm dying like an old man," he rasped.

"Well, dear, you are an old man," Sister teased him, hoping to keep his spirits up.

"You, of course, are still a nubile lovely." He coughed as he winked at her. "I don't mind being old, Janie, I mind dying like a candyass."

"You haven't lived like one."

He coughed again; the muscles in his chest and back ached from the continual spasms. "No. Didn't live like a saint, either. But I thought I'd die on my feet."

"Heart attack?"

"War. Or misjudging a fence. That sort of thing."

"I'm glad you stuck around as long as you have." She reached for his hand, cool and elegant. "We've had a good, long run. We took our fences in style. Maybe we crashed a few, but we were always game, Raymond. You most of all."

He leaned back on the plumped-up pillow. "Foxhunting is the closest we'll come to a cavalry charge."

"Without the bullets and cannonballs."

"Wouldn't have minded that as much as this. It's not fitting for a man to die like this, you know." He sat up again. "What I've always longed for is a release from safety. We're ruined by uniformity and tameness." His eyes blazed.

"I know," she simply said.

He tried to take a breath but couldn't. "You've done a good job breeding the hounds. I forget to tell you the good things you do."

"I inherited a good pack."

"We've both seen good packs go to ruin in the hands of an idiot, of which there are many. Christ, put M.F.H. behind a man's name and he thinks he's God."

"The fox has a way of humbling us all. Raymond, for what it's worth, I have been an imperfect wife, but I love you. I have always loved you."

He smiled. "It all does come down to love, doesn't it? And even if you've only loved for one day, then you've lived. Well, I love you. And as we both know, my feet are made of clay. But my love for you has always been true. Like the hunt, it takes me beyond safety, beyond tameness." He smiled more broadly. "Apart from this ignominious end, I am a most lucky fellow."

"Sounds like a Broadway play." She squeezed his hand.

He brought her hand to his lips and kissed it. "Oh, for a straight-necked fox and a curvaceous woman." He kissed her hand again. "Has to be hunting in heaven. I'll look up Tom Firr, Thomas Assheton Smith, the other Thomas Smith, Ikey Bell, oh, the list could go on." He cited famous masters and huntsmen from the past. "And I shall look for Ray, mounted on a small thoroughbred, and we'll ride together." He stopped talking because he couldn't fight back the tears.

Nor could Sister. And as she snapped out of her reverie she discovered her cheeks were wet but her heart was oddly full. As Raymond had said, it's all about love. And love remembered washed over her with a power beyond reason.

Poor Ralph had no such comfort at his death. As Father Banks continued the service, a still, white-hot anger began to fill Sister.

Did he beg for his life? Knowing Ralph, she thought he probably did not, even if he were terrified.

Did Nola? Or Guy? Sister prayed and prayed mightily for them all.

Three people snatched from life, not one of them feeling a tender hand on their brow, a kind voice offering all the love there was to offer.

Nola, Guy, and Ralph had not walked on water. Each could be foolish and, as Nola and Guy were so young when they died, they had never had the chance to learn wisdom. They never outgrew the behavior that must have infuriated their killer. It's possible both Nola and Guy would have remained wild, but unlikely. The duties and pains of this life fundamentally change all but the most dedicated to immaturity. And those duties are actually wonderful. It's duty that makes you who you are. Duty and honor.

Sister never thought of this as bending to the yoke; for her, it was rising to the occasion. Nola and Guy never had the time to recognize their duties, much less fulfill them. At least Ralph did. He made something of himself, proved a good husband and father.

The stupidity of these deaths, the casual evil of them, overwhelmed her.

She sat there, boiling, knowing the killer had to be in the church.

"Whoever he or she is, they're a consummate actor," she thought to herself.

As the service ended, the pallbearers, Ken, Ronnie, Xavier, Bobby, Roger, and Kevin McKenna, Ralph's college roommate, took their places around the polished mahogany casket. In one practiced motion they lifted Ralph on their shoulders and, in step, arms swinging in unison, carried him down the center aisle, then out into the glowing late-September light.

The congregation followed the family at a respectful distance and filed into the cemetery, home to three centuries of the departed.

The service ended with Shaker, standing at the head of the casket as it was lowered into the ground, blowing "Going Home." This mournful cry, the traditional signal of the end of the hunt, brought everyone to tears.

Afterward, Sybil walked alongside Sister. "Are you going to cancel Tuesday's hunt?" she asked.

"No. Ralph would be appalled if I did such a thing."

Shaker, on Sister's other side, added, "If the fox runs across his grave it will be a good omen."

"We sure need one," Sybil said, her eyes doleful.

CHAPTER 34

Tuesday and Thursday's hunts, sparsely attended, did little to lift Sister's spirits. Although hounds worked well together, two young ones rioted on deer. Betty pushed the two back, but the miniriot upset Sister even though she knew the youngsters might stray on a deer during cubbing. Diana was settling in as anchor hound with Asa's help, and that made up for the miniriot.

Saturday's hunt, on September twenty-eighth, started at seven-thirty in the morning from Mill Ruins, Peter Wheeler's old place. Walter lived there under a long lease arrangement of the sort usually seen in England. In essence, he owned the property even though Peter had willed it to the hunt club.

During the year he'd lived there, Walter had already made significant improvements. He'd fertilized all the pastures and replaced the collapsed fences with white three-board fencing. White paint, now lead-free, lasted two years if you were lucky. Walter said he didn't care, he'd paint the damn boards every two years. He loved white fences. Most folks switched to black, since that paint lasted five to seven years depending on the brand. Board fencing itself lasted fifteen years, give or take.

The horrendous expense of stone fencing was actually practical if you considered its life span. A stone fence might need a tap or two of repair over sixty or seventy years, but if properly built by a master stonesmason, stone fences ought to last for centuries.

One of Walter's secret dreams was, some fine day, to have the drive to the house lined with two-and-a-half-foot stone fences.

Today, Walter was living another of his dreams. This was the first hunt from Mill Ruins since Peter had lived there. It turned into a crackerjack.

Shaker cast down by the old mill, which was redolent of scent. So many generations of foxes had lived near or under the mill, great blocks of natural stone, wheel still intact, that the address among foxes had a certain cachet, say like Dumbarton Oaks in Washington, D.C., or East Sixty-eighth Street in New York.

Considered too tony for grays, the place was inhabited by reds.

Naturally, the hounds found scent at the mill, but they didn't get far with it since that particular fox had no desire for aerobic exercise.

The day, crystal clear, temperature in the middle fifties and climbing, wasn't the best day for scent. No frost had been on the ground, and the rains of last week were soaking in, although a deep puddle glistened here or there. The high-pressure system that produced those electric blue skies also sucked away moisture, hence scent.

Had Shaker been a lesser huntsman he might have returned to the mill to find another line. Shaker and Sister thought once you drew a cover, move on, don't dawdle. Occasionally they could blow over a fox clever enough to lie low as hounds moved through perhaps a trifle too quickly. But more often than not, moving along, especially if your pack had good noses, flushed more foxes than inching through every twig, holly bush, and scrap of moss.

He sat on Gunpowder and thought for a moment as hounds moved along the millrace and back to the strong running stream that fed it.

Gunpowder, wise in the ways of the sport, snorted, *"Draw an S. Move up higher and snake down. If you catch him high, he'll probably come back low. If you catch him low, unless he belongs on the other side of this fixture, I bet you he stays low."*

An English huntsman from the Shires will often draw a triangle just like Tom Firr, the great huntsman who perfected this maneuver back in the nineteenth century. And such a cast or draw worked beautifully if your country was neatly divided into squares and rectangles.

America, having been cultivated according to European methods only since the early seventeenth century, wasn't that neat, that geometric. Plus, the sheer boastful size of the country forced American foxhunters to devise their own methods for seducing foxes out to play.

Whole European nations could fit into one midsized state like Missouri. American foxes took full advantage of their land's scale as well as the rich woodlands blanketing the East Coast.

Virginia, enriched by the alluvial deposits of the Potomac, the Rappahannock, and the James, as well as their many feeders and tributaries, offered wondrous means of escape. A fox could dash over Davis loam, a kind of rich, sandy soil, scramble up on hard rock, a real scent killer, plunge into a forest carpeted with pine needles and pinecones, more scent killer, and then clop down a baked red clay farm road.

Huntsmen and hounds needed to be quick, to be problem solvers, and to respect those venerable English texts while finding their own way. The American way, like Americans themselves, was a little wilder.

Shaker was going to need that wildness.

Sister patiently waited forty yards behind him. Keepsake, very proud to be used instead of Lafayette, Sister's usual choice for Saturday, pranced. He desperately wanted to show how perfectly he jumped.

Sister liked a horse that knew how to use his or her body. Good conformation, good early training usually gave a horse confidence. A horse in this way is no different from a professional golfer. The golfer perfects the various strokes; the horse perfects the various gaits and also learns to jump with a human on his back. Any horse can jump without a human up there, but the two-legged riders shift their weight, fall up on one's ears, flop back behind the saddle, slip to the side, jerk the reins, and, worst of all, they yelp and blame the horse.

The horse needs more patience than the human.

Horses liked Sister. She rode lightly. She might make mistakes, but she always apologized. Mostly she stayed out of the horse's way, for which it was grateful.

And proud as Keepsake was of his form over fences, Sister tly liked that he didn't hang a jump. He gathered himself back on his haunches and sailed over, forelegs tucked up under his chin, neat as a pin.

As they hadn't yet jumped even a cigarette pack, Keepsake fretted.

The field behind her kept quiet. The Hilltoppers also remained silent. Bobby Franklin, that most genial man, ran a tight group. His Hilltoppers didn't jump fences, but they kept right up behind first flight, led by Sister. It would never do to let these two fields become strung out. No coffeehousing. No skylarking. No using the horse in front of you as a bumper. Bobby moved out, kept it fun, and the Hilltoppers often ran harder than the field because they needed to find ways around the jumps.

Immediately behind Sister rode Ken, Xavier, Tedi, Ron, Edward, and Walter. Thirty-two others filled out the first flight, with Jennifer and Sari riding tail. Being juniors, they pulled hard tasks, and riding tail was one of them. It was also a fabulous way to learn what to do and what not to do in the hunt field. Whoever rode tail usually picked up the pieces—loose horses, dismounted humans. In most hunts those in the rear were grooms, juniors, and riders on green horses. Often the riders on green horses were the first ones picked up.

Sister, unlike many masters, liked juniors up front, but they had to earn their stripes first. You earned them in the back.

Bobby used his juniors to go forward and open the gates. He figured he'd lose between three and five minutes on every gate, and this time had to be made up, otherwise he'd lose sight of Sister and the hounds. Not good.

There they all sat quiet as mice.

The noise came from St. Just, cawing overhead. *"I know where there's a fox with an infected paw. You could kill him."*

"*Don't listen to him,*" Dasher warned the young entry. "*He'll lead you to a fox, but he'll lead you to Hell, too.*"

The hounds heard a long, rising blast followed by two short toots.

Trident, still trying to memorize the calls, whispered to his sister, Trudy, "*What's that one?*"

"*Uh, he's not calling us back, he's kind of telling us to go right.*" Trudy watched as Asa walked toward the right and crossed the stream.

"*I don't know if I'll ever remember all the notes,*" Trident worried.

"*You will,*" Delia reassured him. "*Watch Asa and Diana. Don't worry about the strike hounds just yet. You keep your eye on the steady hounds.*"

"*Why is he moving us out of the streambed? Isn't scent better down here?*" Trinity asked, the white Y on his head distinctive.

"*Because the wind has shifted. He's pushing us into the wind,*" Delia answered.

"*Why don't we just go right down here by the water?*" Tinsel asked, a good question.

"*The trees, the underbrush are cutting the wind. But up there*"— Delia cocked her head toward higher ground—"*it's a little stiffer. And if we pick it up there, we'll follow it wherever it goes, and if we can't get anything heading into the wind we can always come back here where it will be cooler longer. Trust Shaker.*"

"*Do the other humans know this stuff?*" Trident asked.

Delia laughed. "*No, dear, they're just trying to stay on their horses.*"

"*Do the whippers-in know?*" Trudy crossed the stream, the clear water chilly.

"*Some understand. Others just ride hard,*" Delia said.

Asa, now with them, spoke, his voice deep. "*It's an article of faith that every whipper-in believes he or she can hunt hounds— until they have the horn to their lips.*"

"*Why?*" Trinity gracefully leapt an old log.

"*Kind of like the difference between a strike hound and an anchor hound. The anchor hound has to know where everyone is and what the fox and humans might do. Remember, they're always behind us. The strike hound pushes out to get the line. That's all that hound has to do, have a great nose and great drive. Doesn't have to have a brain in its head, which I am here to tell you Dragon does not. So don't imitate that ass.*"

The young ones giggled.

Delia added, "*But Cora is smart. She's got brains and athletic ability. What a nose that girl has.*"

Just then Cora found. "*Got one!*"

Dragon skidded up to her. "*Yo yo yo. It's good.*"

"*God, I just hate him,*" Asa grumbled as the youngsters flew up ahead, all excited.

Delia laughed as she ran with Asa.

Diana, nose down, figured the scent was about an hour old but holding. They'd better make the most of it. She didn't know who it was. Often she did.

They clambered up the banks, leaving the stream behind, and came into a huge hayfield, sixty acres of cut hay rolled up in huge round bales. This was galloping country.

Sister popped over the tiger trap jump that Walter had built in the fence line. The logs, upright, created a coop, but it looked formidable. In this case it was because Walter was over-zealous when he built it. The trap was three feet six inches but looked like four feet. A few people decided to join the Hilltoppers then and there. The rest squeezed hard, grabbed mane, and over they soared.

St. Just swooped overhead one more time, screaming about the fox with the sore paw, but no one was listening. Furious, he pooped on a brand-new velvet cap, then flew away.

Keepsake stretched out, head low, covering ground effortlessly. How he loved open fields, as did Sister. They moved so fast, she had tears in her eyes.

One of Ronnie Haslip's contact lenses blew out. He cursed but kept right up. He'd jump with that eye closed.

Betty, wisely using the territory, cleared a jump, three large logs lashed together with heavy rope, at the end of the big field. She listened intently. Shaker had blown "Gone Away" when the hounds all broke out of the covert on the line.

Now and then Shaker shouted encouragement. Why ruin the beautiful music of the hounds by blowing all the time?

The riders thundered across the field, took the three-log jump into another pasture, smaller, maybe twenty-five acres.

Hounds ran right out of it, crawling under the fence on the far side or just taking the triple-wide coop in the fence line. The jump, about three feet tall, was a glorious twenty-four feet long.

Shaker and Gunpowder glided over, as did Sister and Keepsake. Behind her, Sister could hear the sound of hooves hitting the earth, the slight jingle of curb chains on bits, the occasional sharp exhalation of breath. She never looked back. Her job was to stay behind the huntsman.

Ron and Xavier took the wide jump in tandem. Neither could resist a little warble of victory. A few people cheered behind them.

The fox, Prescott, one of Target and Charlene's new litter, hit top speed and hooked sharply left in the woods on the other side of the triple-wide jump.

He dashed over moss, rocks, then ducked into a den carefully placed under the roots of a massive walnut. Earth thrown out everywhere announced his abode.

Hounds marked him.

The T youngsters pushed right up front and Trident even dug in the den.

Shaker dismounted, blowing the triumphant notes of victory as the field rode up.

Within five minutes, after much praise, he was back up on Gunpowder.

"Thought I'd go back to the big meadow, hit the south side where Walter planted corn."

"Good enough," Sister answered, smiling.

They jumped back over the three logs, trotted over the smaller pasture, jumped the triple-wide coop. Others thought this a good opportunity to try jumping in tandem or even in threes, like a hunt team.

Since hounds weren't casting, Sister had pulled up to the side to watch the fun. As masters go, she was strict but not a killjoy. The attempts of the makeshift teams to hit the jump stride for stride was fun to watch. Ron and Xavier got their timing just right.

Ken, Tedi, and Edward almost managed it, and they received big smiles for their efforts.

Sister could hear the light chatter behind her. She knew they'd stop once hounds were cast.

"Remember when Nola and Guy took that jump holding hands?" Ron recalled, laughing.

"I think that was one of the few times I was really jealous," Ken said. "Sybil and I tried but couldn't do it."

Xavier handed his flask around. "Funny. You know what made me jealous? That Guy's nickname was Hotspur. Ralph and I hated that name. Ever notice how people have to live up or down to their names? Hotspur, impetuous valor. Went right to his head."

"Who first called him that?" Ken tried to remember.

"I think Nola started it." Ron licked his lips. Xavier put good stuff in his flask.

"She always had nicknames for everyone," Xavier said.

"Mustache. That was mine. Shaved it off once we knew she wasn't coming home."

A beat followed this.

"Mine was Zorro," Ron said with a slightly embarrassed grin.

"The Gay Blade?" Ken couldn't resist.

"I could die laughing." Ron, sarcastic, handed Xavier back his flask. "No. Because I got into a fistfight at the Phi Delt house and got two black eyes. She said it looked like I wore a mask. Zorro was okay by me."

"She called Sister 'Artemis,' " Ken remembered.

"And she called you Di Maggio," Xavier reminded him.

"Oh, she did not." Ken's face reddened.

"Big stick." Ron laughed.

"Like she would know." Ken really was embarrassed.

"Oh, those tight breeches." Ron rolled his eyes. "And I've only got one contact in, but Ken, the bulge is noticeable."

"See, I was right, Zorro, the Gay Blade." Ken laughed.

"Let's see, she called Sybil 'Puffin' when they were little, but I don't remember any nickname when they were older," Xavier recalled.

"Big Sis," Ken replied. "Not original, but it fit. You know, I've only glimpsed her once today. Hope she remembers the territory."

"Sybil? You kidding?" Ron adored Sybil.

"What do you know, Cyclops?" Ken teased him.

"Hey, I can jump better with one eye closed than you can with two open." Ron winked as he said it.

"Well, you'd better start squinting, buddy, because Sister

just took off." Ken clapped his leg on his horse and shot off after her.

"Damn, that's what we get for talking!" Ron knew he should have paid more attention to what was going on.

Hounds, now in the cornfield, pushed another fox. This run was brief but invigorating. Hounds, master, and huntsman were well pleased.

They gathered themselves up, riding back to the mill ruins and their trailers.

Sister chatted with Bobby as they walked back. He rode up to her and the Hilltoppers mingled in with the field, always a treat.

"Bobby, as I recall, your childhood nickname was Bruiser. Did it scar you for life?"

He laughed. "No. What made you think of that?"

"Nicknames. I overheard the Three Musketeers back there talking about nicknames. Ron said he thought Guy had to live up to the name Hotspur after Nola gave it to him. Do you really think it was inspired by Shakespeare?"

"I don't know."

"He was impulsive."

"Quick with his fists."

"Wonder if we're missing something?"

"Like premature ejaculation?"

"Bobby, that thought never crossed my mind!"

What did cross her mind was Shakespeare's Hotspur saying, "Why, what a candy deal of courtesy this fawning greyhound then did proffer me!" She felt the killer was handing her and everyone else a candy deal of courtesy.

CHAPTER 35

"Amputate. It's the only way to save her," Dr. Middleton gravely said.

Walter and Sister bent over the stainless-steel table where the anesthetized vixen lay. Using Sister's instructions and a Hava-hart trap, Walter had caught the red fox with the infected paw.

He'd watched her limping about down by the ruins. When she went off her feed he knew the infection was worsening.

"How much of her paw do you think you'll need to remove?" Walter stroked the animal's beautiful head.

"I won't really know until I get in there and see how far the infection has spread. It's in the bone, and that worries me. Her white cell count is hitting the stratosphere. I've got to do this now."

"Of course, we must save her. I'll pay all expenses," Sister said. She loved all foxes, and this perfect young vixen with her spotless white tip had to be one of Target's daughters.

"My concern is she won't be able to survive in the wild." Dr. Middleton removed his glasses.

A compassionate veterinarian and also a foxhunter, Chris Middleton was a trusted figure in the community.

"She'll have to live in a kennel, then," Walter replied. "I can build her a wonderful home with a doghouse, plus I'll dig a big den for her, too."

"You'll have to dig two feet down, lay in the chain-link fence. Even with one paw she's going to try to dig out."

"By the time she's ready to come home, she'll have everything she needs." Walter rubbed her ears.

"All right, then. I'll get to work."

"Do you mind if I stay?" Walter asked.

"No. Be glad to have you." Chris was already scrubbing up.

"Gentlemen, I'll leave you to it, much as I'd like to watch." Sister reached over and patted the vixen's side. "You'll get through this, miss. You're in good hands." She looked at Walter and smiled. "Maybe I should say a pair of good hands."

"He's smarter than I am." Walter smiled back. "I only had to learn one animal inside out. He had to learn dozens."

"Bird bones. Now, that's something." Chris pulled on a pair of thin latex gloves. "Walter, scrub up. I might need you."

"Okay, boys. Walter, call and give me a report." Sister opened the large, heavy swinging doors, passed down the short hall and back into the waiting room.

Sybil Fawkes, trying to get out the front door with her arms full of large bags of cat food, was surprised when Sister appeared to open the door for her. "Where'd you come from?"

"Operating room."

"Not a hound, I hope, or Raleigh?"

"No. Walter managed to trap that injured vixen at his place. Chris's working on her now." She flipped up the hatchback of Sybil's Mercedes wagon.

"Thank you. Usually the girl at the front desk will help me, but today everybody's busy." She exhaled heavily. The forty-pound bag of food seemed heavier than usual. She closed the hatch. "Sister, I wanted to tell you that I know I'm not Doug Kinser, but I'm learning a lot out there."

"I'm grateful for your help and I think you're doing very nicely."

"Thank you. I get nervous, you know."

"No one day is like any other. If you think about it, this is a sport that has no time-outs, no manicured playing field, no time limits. And when I watch other sports, you know how I love baseball and football, I watch man pitted against man. At least, usually it's men." She smiled. "But with us, it's man against fox. Guess who wins?"

"Humbling." Sybil noticed the dogwoods turning red. "Won't be long till Opening Hunt."

"No. I'd guess the first frost is two weeks away, max."

"Sister, thanks for all you've done for Mom and Dad. Me too."

"Your mother and father helped me get through Ray's death, and then Big Raymond's. That's what friends do, and I am so lucky to have you all for my friends. This is an odd time. Or maybe it's me. I hope everyone at After All is—"

"Coping?" Sybil filled in for her. "Horrible as it was to find Nola, in a way it was also an ending of sorts. Do you know what I mean?"

"Yes, I do."

"I called on Frances this morning. She's bearing up, but she hates that there are people who think Ralph brought this on himself somehow. Maybe it's easier to think that."

"Why?"

"Blame the victim. It eases the threat. People are always looking for easy answers, aren't they?"

"Do *you* feel threatened?"

Sybil paused, then looked Sister straight in the eye. "Yes."

"Has anyone verbally threatened you?"

"No, but"—she fumbled around for a moment—"I feel watched. I can't put my finger on it, but I feel a tension building."

"Yes." Sister knew exactly the feeling.

"And Ken said to me after Ralph's service, that night, he said this all gets back to Nola and Guy. And then he really upset me because he said some people might think I killed Nola for the inheritance." Her creamy complexion darkened. "I nearly slapped him, even though he doesn't believe it. I don't know when I've been that upset. Never."

"I would be, too."

"Have you heard that, Sister?"

She didn't lie. "Yes."

"You don't believe it—do you?" Sybil's voice rose, plaintive.

"No. If you were going to kill Nola you would have done it when you two were teenagers. Like normal siblings." She smiled, hoping to relieve Sybil.

Tears filled her light blue eyes. "The times I told her I hated her. That I wished she were dead. The time I threw a bottle of Coke at her head. God."

"You were kids. She gave as good as she got. What about the time she sewed shut the legs on all your breeches just before Opening Hunt?"

"Oh that!" Sybil smiled.

"The time she put ginger under your horse's tail. That was a rodeo show."

"I still don't know how I hung on." Sybil brightened. "I look at my two boys and wonder how I'll live through their teens."

"You will. Everyone lived through your teens and my teens, and well, that's just how it goes." She put her hand on Sybil's forearm. "You said you felt watched. Is there anyone in particular?"

"It's kind of a general feeling. I guess some people really do think I killed her. Maybe others wonder if I'll crack under the strain. They don't think I'm a murderer, or should I say murderess, but you know. Hard times and all that. And maybe I'm supersensitive. I'm jumpy. I can't help it. I feel this . . . this . . . awful creepy something. Like there's a monster hiding under my bed."

"Honey, I'm going to ask you a very offensive question. Under the circumstances, I hope you will forgive me."

"Go ahead." Sybil wondered what this lady could ever do to offend her.

"Did you ever sleep with Guy Ramy?"

Sybil blinked. "No. That doesn't offend me, but no. Why?"

"Revenge for all the beaux Nola took, so to speak."

"Oh that." Sybil shrugged. "She was beautiful. Kissed by the gods. I knew before first grade that I could never compare with Nola."

"That must have been very difficult."

"It hurt like hell. What could I do? She was my sister. I loved her."

"If it's any consolation, she loved you, too, and you are also a beautiful woman. But we all paled standing next to Nola. She was like Ava Gardner or Vivien Leigh. Otherworldly beautiful." She smiled. "Showing my age by my points of reference."

"Not at all. You'll never get old." She changed the subject. "You can tell Mother's feeling better because she visited the Tarot reader, Madame Pacholi. You know her real name has got to be Smith or Schwartz or something like that. Anyway, Mother had her cards read and a card came up that supposedly represented justice. So Mother feels certain justice will be done. Oh, and you'll love this. She asked about you, so Madame Pacholi read your cards in your absence. Let's see, I think some kind of queen came up, but the long and short of it is that you will be foxhunting when you are one hundred. Nifty, huh?"

"Tell that to Crawford Howard."

They both laughed.

"You know, speaking of being watched, there's this little screech owl who hangs around our place now and she doesn't seem to care if we see her. She blinks and winks. And sometimes the big one, the horned owl, will be with her. Maybe we have more mice than we thought."

"Every now and then I'll see the little one." Sister thought the little owl adorable, as long as she kept quiet. "I guess she's taken a shine to you and Tedi."

"Oh, she winks at Dad, too."

"The hussy."

"Why did you ask if I'd slept with Guy? There's more to it than revenge."

"Ken."

"What do you mean?"

"If Ken found out, he'd have killed Guy."

A kind of secret pride shot through Sybil, the thought that her husband would kill a man out of jealousy. This rapidly dissipated. "He's not the type. Ken's just not that passionate." She shrugged.

"It's a funny thing about men. We want them passionate

and out of control and then we don't. One of the great things about getting old is qualities like kindness, humor, reliability, compassion—oh, how sexy they become."

"Raymond had all those."

"Actually, he did. But he was a passionate man and rarely met a beauty he didn't try to conquer, within reason."

"God, you don't think he slept with Nola, do you?"

"No." Sister laughed. "He'd always consider a woman ten years younger, and then when he reached his sixties, twenty years younger, but Nola was always safe. However, I expect your mother had to slap him once or twice and always had the supreme good manners never to tell me."

"How did you stand it?"

"I loved him. You don't really know someone until you live with him, and every day Raymond exploded with energy, love of life. That's why I fell in love with him, and he never lost that energy."

"He was the most fun. He'd let us kids ride up front sometimes when he led the field. He'd make us feel important."

"Charm. Irresistible charm."

"Funny thing, you said you don't know a man until you live with him. But I think you can live with a man and not know him. I think any two people, whether it's husband and wife, or lovers, or parents and children, can miss seeing things. And sometimes they're things everyone else knows. It's peculiar." She paused a moment. "You say Ken could have killed Guy out of jealousy. What about Nola? Could she have killed Guy?"

"It's possible that two different people killed them," Sister replied.

"One. I believe it was one."

"I do, too, but I'm letting my mind go anywhere and everywhere."

"You know I would have never gone to bed with Guy Ramy even if he'd been attracted to me before I got serious about Ken. He was too—flash."

"That he was."

"Like a red Corvette. Nola ate that up."

"When she was sexually done with a man was she really done? She had an affair with Ralph. When it was over, did she leave him alone or would she come back just to exert power over him?"

"Done," Sybil simply said. "Poor Ralph. I loved him."

"Childhood friends. The best." Sister exhaled through her nose.

"And you know what else? I keep thinking about Peppermint, that Pepper led us to Nola. There's some kind of poetry to that, something I don't understand, I can't put it into words, but"—she closed her eyes—"God, I want this to be over!"

"It will be."

"Do you know something I don't?"

"No, but the discovery of Nola's and Guy's bodies certainly can't have added to their killer's tranquillity. He's arrogant and opportunistic, but stupid, too. His arrogance has made him stupid. Killing Ralph like that."

"Maybe he thought it was kill or be killed." She scuffed at the bluestone in the parking lot. "I hope I get to see him caught and punished."

"I think every person in our hunt field feels that except one."

"Who?"

"The killer."

CHAPTER 36

S he's going to be fine," Walker enthusiastically reported to Sister on the vixen's surgery.

"What good news! We could use a little good news around here," Sister, on the kennel phone, said warmly.

After more details on the recovery of the vixen, whom Walter had named Bessie, Sister hung up the phone and she gave Shaker a full report. When she was done, she told Shaker something that had been running around, unarticulated, in the back of her mind for quite some time. "You know, it's the most curious thing, Walter reminds me of Raymond. He even moves like Raymond. Same jaw, square shoulders. He's a touch shorter and quieter than Raymond, but it's uncanny. It's one of those realizations that's grown on me." She looked brightly at Shaker. "Have you noticed it?"

"Uh, well, I suppose," Shaker fumbled.

Sister knew in an instant that her huntsman knew more than she did. "Ah." A long silence followed. "Does Walter know?"

"No." Deeply embarrassed, he gave a small shrug.

"Shaker, don't fret. I should have figured it out. It's as plain as the nose on my face."

"Things happen."

"With Raymond they certainly did." She spoke with conviction, breathed, then smiled. "How did you know?"

"He confessed in a weak moment."

"Aided by scotch?"

"Scotch and emphysema. He asked me to watch out for Walter."

"I see. She was pretty, as I recall, Walter's mother."

"They were all pretty, but Janie, not one of them was as good a woman as you." Shaker's voice rose and he looked her straight in the eye.

"Thank you. But I have my failings." She glanced down at her hands, the red clay ground within. "I can't believe I've been so stupid."

"You weren't stupid."

"Not about that." She smiled sadly. "Not about that. But I think I've been half in love with Walter. Now it makes sense." She dismissed the notion with a wave of her hand. "Younger men don't look at older women. I guess I just realized how drawn I am to him." She sighed. "Love never dies."

"I don't know. I'm not good at those things."

She paused a moment. "Well, I've had my revelation. Love never dies." She fell quiet again, then suddenly sat up and said with much animation, "Shaker, that's it!"

"What?"

"Love never dies! The killer is still in love with Nola or with Guy."

CHAPTER 37

For the remainder of the day, Sister felt as though she had a red-hot marble rolling around in her brain. The mental discomfort was excruciating.

When troubled, the stable provided solace.

She brushed down Rickyroo, Lafayette, Keepsake, and Aztec and then turned them out. The horses calmed her, helped her organize her thoughts.

She cleaned out the brushes, hung up the wipe-down towels, inhaled the bracing mix of liniment, hay, and *eau de cheval*.

Golliwog nestled on a cooler, gray and gold, folded on the huge tack trunk that originally belonged to Raymond's grandfather, John "Hap" Arnold. Raleigh and Rooster flopped on their sides in a stall and snored, each exhale sending tiny motes of hay dust upward. The large wall clock above the tack room door read three-thirty.

Sister firmly believed the more horses were allowed to be horses the better they behaved. The animal is meant to graze and walk, graze and walk. Being cooped up in a stall, fed all manner of hopped-up grains, makes for a lunatic. She brought them in each morning, and fed them sweet feed in their individual stalls, because each of her boys needed time alone. She also added crimped oats and as much high-quality hay as they would eat. Then she'd go to the kennels to help Shaker feed and clean. By the time she returned, usually after about two hours, each horse had cleaned his plate. Then she turned them back out.

People complimented her on the condition of her horses, their glistening coats, their good hooves. Their eyes were bright, their attitudes cheery.

She replied that her methods were common sense. Avoid fads. Listen to the feed salesmen respectfully, but remember they're there to sell you a lot of stuff you don't need. Take excellent care of your pastures and your pastures will take excellent care of your horses. Keep your horses on a routine. Animals, including humans, like a routine, and this includes regular exercise. Be sure you work with the best equine dentist, vet, and blacksmith in the area. While you're at it, take yourself to the best dentist and doctor, too. You may skip the blacksmith.

Newcomers often asked questions, and Sister was glad when they did. Better to ask than to be taken to the cleaners by the guy who wants to put automatic waterers in your barn or the dealer who wants to sell you a fortune in vitamin supplements. Not that automatic waterers might not be useful for some people and vitamins useful for others, but if you didn't know horses, thousands of dollars would fly out the window.

One thing never changed. Over the forty years of her mastership she had watched new person after new person buy exactly the wrong horse. The only way to become a foxhunter is to buy a made horse, a seasoned veteran who can teach the human. He's better than an insurance policy. He *is* your insurance policy. But in all her years, she had only known a handful of people to exhibit such sense. Walter was one. His gelding, Clemson, lacked in the looks department, was a little clunky, even big-headed. He had age on him, but that horse knew his job. He was giving Walter tremendous confidence. Walter could hunt and listen for hounds instead of riding in terror.

The Clemsons of the world should be gold-plated. In their own way they are as much treasures as a Secretariat.

She watched Aztec, Lafayette, Rickyroo, and Keepsake play with one another in their pasture and thought of the people she had come to know through foxhunting. Any hunt club reflects the history of its region. She thought of the older people, her idols from her childhood, her own peers, and now the young ones coming up behind her. She had learned a lot from all those people; she was still learning.

Leaning over the fence, she sniffed the first tang of the odor of turning leaves. The fiery marble in her brain had stopped rolling. She had a plan.

She found Shaker walking puppies, a task requiring strong shoulders since they pulled and leapt about. He smiled as she fell in with him and took a leash from his hands.

"To what do I owe this unexpected pleasure?"

"Shaker, I have an idea. It's unorthodox, but I think I can bolt our killer from his den, flush him right out. We've been running over him, you know."

"Darby, boy, steady." Shaker's low voice quieted a yapping young fellow. "Well, he's been in the covert, that we know."

"It's going to take some work on our part and a little luck." She was nearly pulled off her feet by Doughboy.

"The luck part"—Shaker's bushy eyebrows rose—"that's interesting."

Before she could spin out her idea, Ben Sidell drove onto the farm. He cut the motor, stepped outside the squad car, and walked over to them. "Afternoon."

"Good afternoon, Ben. What can we do for you?" Sister set her feet wide so Doughboy couldn't yank her off balance again.

"Wanted you to know the gun that killed Ralph was a .38. Can't trace it, so it has to be an old gun sold before registrations or one sold on the black market."

"What about the used market?" Shaker knew you could buy a used side arm without going through the computer checks.

"Possible. Do you have people in your field who carry guns?"

"Yes. Both whippers-in carry a .22 filled with ratshot which, I am happy to say, they have not had occasion to use for years, and Bobby Franklin carries a .38 hidden in his jacket."

"Why?"

"We don't want to upset people," Sister forthrightly replied.

"No, I don't mean that." Ben stifled a smile as he folded his arms across his chest. "I mean, why would he carry that caliber? Why not a .22?"

"Should a horse break its neck, or a hound, we want to end its suffering as soon as possible. And again I'm happy to say the last time we had to do so was in 1984."

Shaker added, "And sometimes the deer hunters don't finish the job. They don't track their deer, or it gets away. We have to kill them."

"Very upsetting." Sister reached down to pat Doughboy, who sat quietly observing the sheriff. As he was only five months old, she was very proud of him.

"I see. Well, I would imagine that many of your members have old weapons."

"Probably." Sister's voice rose upward.

"You have members, older members, many of whom might have guns that they bought back in the fifties or sixties."

"I suppose. What would you like me to do?"

"Get them. I want to test them. I can go to each house and demand them, but I think the most efficient method is to have you ask for them."

"I'd be glad to do that. Did you drive the whole way out here to ask me that?"

"Uh, yes." He shifted his weight from one foot to the other. "And"—he paused a moment—"it's such a beautiful place here. I like visiting your farm. And I was wondering if you might advise me, which I will keep to myself because I realize the position you're in, I was kind of wondering if you could suggest someone I could ride with—take lessons, that is."

"Ah." She smiled, as did Shaker. "Lynne Beegle. Actually, I should ask what kind of riding."

"Foxhunting. The more I find out about this sport, the more it intrigues me. It's complicated."

"Oh, just keep the horse between your legs." Shaker laughed.

"There is that." Ben smiled.

"As I recall, Ben, you're from Ohio, and there are some good hunt clubs there. Rocky Fork Headley, Chagrin Valley, Miami Valley, Camargo, Grand River, and Gully Ridge. And they've been there for a long time. I think Chagrin Valley was founded in 1908."

"Camargo and Rocky Ford Headley were founded in 1925," Shaker added.

"How do you remember all that?"

"You tend to remember what you like. I just thought you might have seen hunting in Ohio."

"No. Not until I got here."

"Well, it's a way of life in Virginia."

"A way of death, too," Ben commented, a wry tone to his voice. "You don't need to hunt the fox, you're so busy hunting one another."

Sister exhaled, which brought Doughboy's ears up. He looked at her quizzically. "These truly are extraordinary circumstances."

Shaker murmured his agreement with that statement.

After Ben drove away, the two walked the puppies back to the puppy palace, as they called it.

"Want to hear my plan?"

"Can't wait."

CHAPTER 38

"Janie, are you sure?" Tedi's lovely blue eyes were sorrowful.

"Yes. But I can't prove a thing yet."

Tedi, Edward, Walter, Shaker, and Sister sat around Sister's kitchen table. She had thrown together a quick dinner for them. Each had come with the express instructions to tell no one where they were going that night. Not a soul.

Sister started the bowl of peas around to the left. "Tedi and Edward, I know this is most disquieting."

"We'll handle it." Edward spoke with authority.

"The killer has to be Sybil, Ken, Xavier, or Ron. If you think about each one, each has benefited since Nola's and Guy's deaths. When Ron first hung out his lawyer's shingle, you used him and you also switched insurance over to Xavier. Right?" Walter asked.

"Right." Edward nodded. "Ken encouraged us, and both men gave us very good service."

"They all ran around together," Tedi added. "Our support in the early stages of their business lives was beneficial."

"And would it be possible for Sybil to divert some of her monies to either Ron or Xavier without either of you knowing about it?" Sister added.

"Up to a point," Edward succinctly replied. "If the sums were excessive, I think I'd know."

"I've been thinking about Hotspur." Sister changed the subject. "The only way that Henry IV could defeat him was to divide and conquer. He picked Hotspur off before he could join up with his father. Had the two been united, Sir Henry Percy's father would have sat on the throne. They were much better soldiers than the king. I believe our killer separated Nola and Guy. She'd been unfaithful to Guy."

Edward interrupted, "But it's not like she was married to him!"

"No, but love isn't rational. It would seem to me that both Nola and the killer had something to lose. Nola would lose Guy, and she had finally fallen in love with Guy. What the killer would lose, I don't know. If we knew the answer to that I think we'd solve this." Sister looked at Walter; she couldn't stop staring at him, but she made sure he didn't see her doing it. "Well, perhaps I make too much of this Hotspur thing. My mind works in fits and starts. They don't all lead in the right direction, but they do fire me up."

"Me too." Shaker reached for the fried chicken, then handed the plate to Tedi on his left. "And I find the older I get the more wood I need to get fired up. Sister, let's get down to brass tacks here."

"Well, yes. I digress. I want Walter to grow a military mustache or paste one on and play a key part. And I want us to find two actors who can ride who resemble Guy and Nola."

"Have you lost your mind?" Edward sat up straight in his chair.

"Maybe there isn't much of it left to lose. Now hear me out before you become ruthlessly logical, Edward. I believe our killer is still in love with Nola or Guy. We've got to shake him or her out of the covert. Bolt our fox."

"Ah." Walter was getting it, as was Tedi.

"Perhaps you have noticed how much Walter resembles Raymond. With a mustache, the resemblance will be impossible to miss."

All eyes were on Walter, who blushed.

"Uncanny." Tedi blinked.

"Remember Raymond's big hunter, A. P. Hill? Found a horse who looks much like him and is very kind." She smiled at Walter. "We'll take care of you, Walter." She said to the others, "I want to place Walter far enough away so when he is glimpsed—and it will be just a glimpse—people won't really know if they've seen him or not. And I want Nola and Guy together down by Cindy's two ponds at Foxglove Farm. There's got to be someone we can use—call Central Casting, if we must. I want to blast this murderer into the open. Let us resurrect our dead. They'll beckon to the killer. However, we can't use a Ralph stand-in. We can't do that to Frances."

"It's lunacy."

"Edward, we have no hard evidence. I'd rather be a lunatic than do nothing," Tedi said, touching Nola's ring.

Sister softly said, a bit of humor in her voice as she hoped to defuse Edward's resistance, "I know, Edward, you won't overestimate my faculty for constructive thought. I've had to resort to imagination."

"Well, I'll do it," Walter said with determination.

"You lead the field. What are you going to do when people see these apparitions?" A note of sarcasm dripped into Edward's voice.

"Maybe I won't see these apparitions."

"Ah. You'll be up front. By the time someone tells you, they'll fade away." Tedi was catching on.

"Sybil will be whipping-in that day." Edward could not believe for one instant that his daughter was a killer.

"I'll put her in the field and let Jennifer whip. She doesn't know but so much, but she knows enough to keep the hounds between her and the huntsman. Can't ask for more than that. Will you all help me?" She touched Shaker's forearm as they had discussed it. She knew he would do it, and Walter had just agreed.

"I will. I'll do anything to get Nola's killer, and this will clear Sybil's name. I know people suspect her. The gossip eventually seeps under the door."

"Impossible! Sybil would never have killed Nola." Edward's face turned crimson. "I can't believe anyone would say something like that about Sybil."

"I'm willing to try anything." Tedi leaned toward Sister. "I'll help you find our Guy and Nola. I have all of Nola's clothes."

"And we can all pray," Sister breathed in. "A bit of mist. Just a bit."

CHAPTER 39

Sister and Tedi worked like demons.

Tedi, thanks to friends in the film business, found two physically appropriate actors who could ride a little. She flew them to Richmond. Her friend, senior master of the Deep Run Hunt, Mary Robertson, put them up so no one would see them back in Jefferson Hunt territory. She also, prudently, worked with them a bit on their riding.

Actors, eager for employment, regularly overstate their credentials. The young lady, Melissa Lords, had ridden once or twice in a Western saddle.

Mary had her work cut out for her. But she'd managed to get the beautiful Melissa somewhat comfortable at the trot.

When Tedi drove down to check on their progress, she burst into tears at the sight of Melissa.

The actor, Brandon Sullivan, had more riding experience. His fabulous looks kept the barn girls in a twitter.

Mary would deliver the horses, Melissa, and Brandon to Roughneck Farm early in the morning of the hunt. She'd ride as a guest that day. This would stir no suspicions, as Sister often drove down for a day's sport at Deep Run and Mary Robertson, Tom Mackell, Red Dog Covington, and Ginny Perrin, the joint-masters, returned the favor.

Walter would park in the hay shed to hide his truck that morning.

Sister chose the day by calling Robert Van Winkle, the weatherman, a local celebrity who had a genuine passion for studying weather.

He told her there might be a bit of ground cover October fourth or fifth. An edge of chilly air should be cutting into central Virginia then.

True to her word, she asked the membership to allow the sheriff to test their .38s. People complied with her request. Nothing came of it, which was no surprise.

She called Alice Ramy in Blacksburg and told her if any wild rumors reached her at Virginia Tech or back home, to dismiss them until they could talk.

By Thursday, October third, she felt they were as ready as they'd ever be. It was still warm with azure skies. She fretted over the weather.

That afternoon she and Shaker walked out puppies.

"Had a good look at Sari Rasmussen's mother yet?"

Shaker rolled his eyes. "A meddlesome woman."

"Me or Lorraine?"

"You." He laughed. "I've spoken to her a few times—when she comes by to pick up Sari. I'm starting to like the days when Jennifer's car breaks down."

"Good."

They walked along, praising the young ones. Clouds of butterflies whirled upward from the horse manure in the farm road. Small butterfly umbrellas of yellow, orange, milk white, and rust attracted the puppies' attention as they passed.

"Nervous?"

"Yes," Sister answered truthfully.

"I still think you should give Ben Sidell a heads-up."

"I don't know. He'd be wasting an entire morning. Nothing may happen."

"The problem is, if something does flare up, if we do rock the killer's world, it could get real ugly. You carry your gun."

"I will."

"Let's stroll through the orchard. Won't hurt these chillun' to smell apples."

The boughs of the old trees bent low, their bounty ready for picking. The Mexicans specializing in such small orchards were due next Monday. A young enterprising fellow, Concho, contracted with the small orchards, and his business was booming.

Puppies lifted their heads, nostrils wide open. The rich fragrance of apples greeted them as it did the humans. However, the hounds could also smell the different types of insects there as well as all the various types of bird droppings. Their experience of the orchard was richer than that of humans', whose senses were duller.

The hound pads pattered over the grass, creating a rhythm. Their light panting provided a counterpoint. The heavier tread of Sister and Shaker sounded like a backbeat.

Once out of the orchard they headed back toward the kennels.

"Occurs to me we are putting down a T cross." Shaker finally spoke.

"Uh-huh." Sister felt the warm sun on her back like a friend's hand, reassuring.

Sometimes, especially if the summer or fall lacked rainfall, the earth packed hard like brick. Getting a line of scent proved damnably difficult. Older hounds, having endured bad scenting conditions, stuck it out, kept trying. Younger hounds became frustrated more easily. Cubbing season coincided with rutting season for deer, so their odor was intensified and tempted young ones. If they couldn't find fox scent why not try this other heavy, powerful aroma, so powerful even humans could smell it.

Whippers-in would crack their whips, pushing back the "bad kids" if they could reach them. The thick coverts of Virginia sometimes delayed a whipper-in and hounds skedaddled.

Staff could forgive a hound breaking once and needing to be corrected. Touching a deer twice, the proper word being touching not chasing, called for other measures.

Sister and Shaker would get the whippers-in or two trusty members to lay a T cross of scent.

Early in the morning, the dew heavy on the meadows, one person would put down fox scent. The line ended up in a glorious pile of dog cookies.

Crossing this just like a T bar would be a line of deer scent. This line led directly to a thick covert. One or two persons hid in there with noisemakers and ratshot.

Deer scent and fox scent can be purchased at hunting stores. Whoever handled the potent little bottles needed to be careful or they'd reek for days.

If hounds broke at the cross of the T and headed to the covert, an unpleasant surprise awaited them. The humans hollered at them, fired ratshot in the air. If a hound occasioned to be particularly thickheaded, persisting in pushing the deer scent, a little peppering of ratshot on the nether regions cured him.

Usually, the cacophony startled the hounds and they turned tail quickly, joining their comrades who stuck to fox scent.

By the time the group reached the cookies they knew they had made the right decision.

The foxhound is a problem solver, a most intelligent creature. It remained the province of the human to make sure that the hound solved the problem correctly and was properly rewarded for it.

"If this works and the killer goes on the false scent, you'll be in high cotton." He opened the chain-link gate to the puppy run. " 'Course if that doesn't work you are going to have a lot of people spring-loaded in the pissed-off position."

"I know." She shut the gate as the last young one scooted in.

"Even if you don't see anything, by the time you get back to the trailers there will be questions. For all I know, these two actors will be back there waiting for their Oscars."

"Well, they're supposed to come back here."

"Boss, Murphy's Law."

"Oh, shut up. Don't you think I've gone over this until I'm dizzy? I don't know what's going to happen." She said this in a good-natured way.

He sighed. "Maybe it's a blessing we don't know the future."

CHAPTER 40

Hounds' voices pleased hounds and humans, but Golly thought them cacophonous. Her oh-so-sensitive ears could listen to Bach or to the sound of a can of cat food being opened but not to hounds. She avoided the kennels on hunt mornings. The hounds in the draw pen exuded a state of rare excitement. The ones left behind howled piteously.

Only after everyone settled down would she venture forth, pushing open her cat door, next to the much larger doggie door. She'd sit just outside looking left, right, up, and down with an air of studied superiority. Then, every move considered, she would daintily walk to her destination.

This morning, Saturday, October fifth, she sat outside despite the noise at the kennels. This was the day the Jefferson Hunt would hunt Foxglove Farm.

Walter, Melissa Lords, and Brandon Sullivan had arrived

at the barn at six-thirty A.M. Each person so resembled the deceased that the effect was startling even without a mist. And Robert Van Winkle's forecast had been on the money. A cold front nudged through, and thin fog hugged the creeks and swales. Walter, knowing the territory, led Melissa and Brandon to their places.

Raleigh and Rooster sat with Golly, watching the activity.

"Why don't you jump in the back of the pickup?" Rooster suggested to Raleigh, who could jump much higher than he could.

"She'd see me and make me get out." Raleigh sneezed as a whiff of goldenrod tickled his nose.

"Dirty pool. We get stuck here and hounds get to go—and on such an important morning," Rooster grumbled.

Golly knew her human. *"She'll put you in the tack room if you don't behave and you won't go anywhere. You sit tight. Once they move off you'll have to circle in the woods, but you can do it if you want to follow."*

Rooster looked at Raleigh, who lay down, putting his elegant head on his paws. *"I don't like one thing about this."*

Rooster grumbled, *"I bet those good-for-nothing red foxes won't run. On top of everything else, a blank day."* He closed his eyes on "blank."

Golly replied, *"You never know what a fox will do. But Sister needs you."*

"Thought you could take or leave humans," Raleigh wryly said.

Golly puffed out her chest, showing off her long, silky fur. She was vain about her coat, but then she was vain about everything. *"This is hardly the time to mock me, Raleigh. You know perfectly well that I love Sister. I just don't see the reason to fawn and slobber over her as you do."* Her ears twitched forward. *"There they go. Hurry!"*

The meet was at eight. It was now seven. As the light changed and the temperature dropped, the first cast time would be pushed from seven-thirty to eight and then finally to nine in the morning, except for the High Holy Days. People needed more time on those days since everyone and their horses had to be perfectly turned out. Braiding manes and tails took a long time on a frosty morning. Fingers ached.

Not that the members of the Jefferson Hunt didn't sparkle and shine even during cubbing, but braids were not called for, nor silk top hats. And even though it was probably a trick of the mind, brown boots always seemed to clean up faster than black ones.

As soon as the "party wagon" filled with hounds pulled out, followed by the horse trailer, Raleigh and Rooster took off for Foxglove Farm.

Sixty-three people gathered at Foxglove. As hounds were decanted from their trailer, the whippers-in, Betty and Jennifer, stood with them. Members and guests hurried to tighten girths, find hairnets, knock the dust off jackets.

By the time the hounds walked to Cindy Chandler's graceful stable—with its whiskey barrels filled with mums and baskets of hanging flowers outside, her turquoise and black stable colors painted on each outside beam—everyone was mounted.

Some hunts insisted that staff wear scarlet even during cubbing. At other hunts, staff wore red shirts. And there were those hunts whose staff turned out in tweeds. The Jefferson Hunt staff wore informal kit. After Opening Hunt they would ride exclusively in scarlet even on informal, also called rat-catcher, days.

Although many people erroneously believe there is an absolute standard for hunt attire, in truth, the standard is set by each individual hunt. There was a hunt in Florida, before

World War II, that rode in white. Considering the climate, a sensible choice.

As Sister trotted forward to greet the riders, the hounds looked up at her but dutifully stayed with Shaker.

Raleigh and Rooster, who had sped across the sunken meadows, lurked behind the hay barn. Both canines considered their early run just a romp. They were ready for more.

Sybil, curiously, wore an old jacket of Nola's, a dark blue fabric with rust windowpane woven through it. When her mother commented on it, Sybil said she'd left her lightweight cubbing jacket at her house so she'd grabbed one of her sister's. All extra coats, jackets, vests, and stock ties were kept in the stable closet at After All. Tedi wondered if Sybil had noticed a missing jacket and derby. Her darker question, of course, was just what did Sybil know?

Ken, too, commented on her attire. Both her mother's and her husband's questions irritated her. Half the field was too young to remember Nola's clothing and the other half had seen her in her sister's jackets before. She dismissed them and said everyone was too jittery. Ken soothed her by saying how happy he was to be riding in the field with his wife for a change.

"Good morning. Welcome, visitors. I see some friends from other hunts." Sister smiled. "I'm thrilled to have the senior master of Deep Run with us today, Mary Robertson."

Mary smiled. "Glad to be here." She, too, had butterflies.

"I see some friends from Rockbridge Hunt and Glenmore Hunt, Keswick and Farmington. Welcome." She turned to her hounds. "You children better find Mr. Fox and show everyone good sport."

"No problem," Dragon shot off his big mouth.

"God, I hate him!" Asa repeated his leitmotiv, voice low.

"I'd be remiss if I did not thank our hostess today. Cindy Chandler, thank you for allowing us to hunt Foxglove."

Cindy, immaculately turned out, replied, "My pleasure. Don't forget the breakfast afterward. There's fried okra."

Crawford involuntarily grimaced, which made Sister laugh. Most Northerners couldn't abide this particular southern specialty.

Tendrils of mist curled through the lowlands. The long rays of the rising sun painted the buildings with scarlet and gold. The temperature was a cool forty-five degrees. It was beginning to feel like hunt season!

Traditionally, the master decides on the first cast. In many hunts, the master isn't a true hound person and so agrees with whatever the huntsman suggests. Sister, loving her hounds beyond all measure, would sit down with Shaker the night before a hunt and plan the day's hunt.

Plan your hunt; hunt your plan.

The advantage of this over the years was that each person developed an appreciation for the other's mind. Sister might suggest going low on a windy day, and Shaker might remind her the muck on that particular bottom would be rough sledding. Try high first even with the wind. They'd bat ideas back and forth, they'd check the humidity, the wind, the temperature. They'd obsessively watch The Weather Channel, then sit down, grumbling that those people knew nothing about the weather hard by the mountains, which could change in the bat of an eye.

They'd devise their plan, rise early in the morning, open their window, or hurry out the front door to check the weather. Had there been a light frost? It would occur up here before it would in town. Did the wind change? What was the speed and direction? If Nature decided to change her clothes overnight, the two of them could alter their plan to suit. Both people were flexible and both were true hunters. They worked with Nature as their partner. People who slaved in air-conditioned offices, drove home in cars with air-conditioning or heated seats, had mostly forgotten that humans don't control Nature. If she shifts, you shift with her.

Today's plan was to cast eastward, over the rolling hay-fields, past the huge old chestnut. If scent held on the pastures it ought to be a hell of a day. If not, they'd comb through the woods, good trails throughout, and surely hit a line.

They'd go east to the one-room schoolhouse at the edge of Cindy's property. By then, people and horses would be re-laxed. Walter would appear then disappear in the swale before the schoolhouse. Then they would turn northward, making a semicircle until reaching the waterwheel at the twin ponds, one above the other. Mist ought to be thickest there. Melissa and Brandon would be the wraiths of the ponds.

The cast they'd devised kept the wind glancing at them at about a ninety-degree angle up to the schoolhouse. Turning there, hounds would be heading full into the breeze.

"*Think they'll hit?*" Raleigh deferred to Rooster, who as a harrier possessed more knowledge of hunting.

"*Shouldn't take long. This place is crawling with foxes.*" Rooster lifted his head. "*Crawling.*"

Inky, sitting in the hayloft, the top door open to keep the hay fresh, looked down. "*Didn't crawl. I climbed.*"

"*Inky, what are you doing here?*" Raleigh liked the black small vixen.

"*Well, it's not like I live that far away. Curiosity got the better of me.*"

"*Who will give them the first run?*" Raleigh asked.

"Yancy. If he poops out, Grace is fishing down by the waterwheel ponds."

The waterwheel ponds, built by Cindy for practicality and beauty, had a small waterwheel that kept the water moving between the two levels of the ponds. Grace, Charlie's sister, would fish there for hours.

Cindy would watch through her binoculars. Grace's Christmas present was a juicy salmon placed outside her den.

"Rooster, come on." Raleigh loped toward the sound of the horn. *"See you later, Inky."*

The two house dogs hurried past the stable, past the freshly painted outbuildings, down the fenced paddocks, and out into the larger pasture. They need not have hurried, for the hounds were drawing northward in a thin line of trees lining the creek, twenty yards at the widest point.

A heavy gray cloud cover began to creep over the Blue Ridge Mountains. This would help hold scent down—and the temperature.

Uncle Yancy heard them coming. He waited by the fence line at the chestnut tree pasture. He'd give them another five minutes, then he'd walk across the pasture, mark the chestnut tree, trot to the in and out jumps on the road, go over them, and then run all the way to the old schoolhouse. He'd dive into the den under the schoolhouse. That ought to get everyone's blood up.

Back in the covert, Ruthie wrinkled her nose. *"What's this?"* Tears filled her eyes.

Delia touched her nose to the spot. *"Skunk. Don't go there, dear."*

Her brother took a whiff and his eyes watered, too.

"Mmm." Cora inhaled the musky fox odor of Yancy.

Dasher ran past his brother, irritating him, put his nose down, then bellowed, *"Dog fox! Yippee."*

"Just wants to show off for the Saturday crowd," grumbled the king of show-offs, Dragon.

"You poor baby." Asa bumped him as he ran by, which only irritated Dragon more.

Seeing the handsome young hound snarl, Betty, on the left bank of the narrow creek, said quietly, "Dragon."

"I know. I know." He put his nose down and hollered in his pleasing voice, *"Good. Good. Good."*

Shaker blew three sharp "rat-ta-tats," which brought together the other hounds that had been fanning away from that spot. They all ran in, put their noses to the ground, then opened, honoring Dasher and Cora.

Dasher, now in the front, was quite proud. He usually deferred to his brother, a bully, but today the glory was his, and Cora let him have it. Even if she picked the line first, it was okay that he opened, it would build his confidence.

Shaker now blew "Gone Away," one of the happiest series of notes a human can blow on a horn. Each longish one-note blast is topped by doubled or tripled notes. Usually three such bars suffice, but in his excitement, a huntsman who is a true windbag can go on and on and on. You think they'd pass out from light-headedness.

The members of the field squared their shoulders. The Hilltoppers, right behind them, also put their heels down and lifted their chins.

Sister waited until the last hound, Tinsel, cleared the covert. Having somehow gotten turned around in the excitement, Tinsel finally went right and Sister then squeezed Lafayette. Off they flew.

Lafayette, her usual Saturday horse, earned that honor by virtue of his brains, his beauty, and his smooth gait. Aztec and Rickyroo were still young and learning their trade. Keepsake, at eight, was a wonderful horse who did whatever Sister asked of him. She took Keepsake to other hunts because he would ride in the field without fussing. Lafayette had to be first. He believed deep in his heart that everyone was there to see him.

Over the cut hay pasture, over the coop in the fence line, over the still uncut hayfield with the chestnut tree, over the in and out with the usual rubs and tumps and oomphs. Over the next field and over its jump and down into the thin, parked out woods, the underbrush cleared away, with another trickly creek. Splashing through the creek, cantering alongside the fence, then over the sliprail jump, a little airy, and down a steep incline to another jump at the bottom. This one usually scared the bejesus out of people since you approached at a slight drop and you landed on a bigger drop. It wasn't perfect, but it was the only way. Down and over Sister and Lafayette went. Oh, how Lafayette loved drop jumps, because they let him stay airborne longer. And on to another hayfield cut so trim, it looked like a front lawn. The three-board fence around it had a freshly painted black coop.

Sister could see Jennifer way at the other side of this field on her right. There was a coop there, and the girl took it in good form as she moved along with hounds but far out of their way. Jennifer was having the time of her life.

Shaker, in his element, screamed encouragement to the hounds, his horn tucked between the first and second button of his brown tweed jacket, his forest green tie a little bunched up behind the horn.

After Sister and Lafayette cleared the coop, she turned to

glance behind. Mary Robertson was right behind her. She thought to herself how good her field was. They put the visitors before themselves, and no one had to be told to do it.

As she approached the swale, frothing with mist, she slowed to trot along the edge before heading down into it.

As they had planned, Walter rode up out of the mist onto the far side of this low pasture.

She saw him out of the corner of her eye. On a horse like A. P. Hill, a stout handsome hunter, Walter looked so much like Raymond, she couldn't hold back a tear.

She pressed on. A murmur behind her swelled and she heard a gasp.

Xavier's voice came out of the mist. "Did you see that?"

Tedi simply replied, "I'm not sure. It's too strange."

By the time the field came up out of the swale, the schoolhouse now in view, a few riders were bug-eyed. Sybil came up alongside her mother, they were still cantering.

"Mother, did you—"

"Yes."

As the pace again increased, conversation decreased.

Uncle Yancy paused at the door to the schoolhouse long enough for everyone to admire him, then he ducked under the stone steps into the den.

"*Yo ho ho and a bottle of rum,*" he sang in his reedy voice.

Dragon, there first, started digging. "*Yancy, you push your luck.*"

"*Three blind hounds, three blind hounds, see how they run, see how they run—*" Yancy threw in vibrato for effect.

"*Come on out!*" Diana called in as she dug next to her brother.

"*When the deep purple falls over sleepy garden walls.*" Yancy loved the sound of his own voice.

"Good hounds, Good hounds." Shaker praised them, then blew "Gone to Ground."

Jennifer held Hojo's reins. Usually Shaker took Gunpowder on Saturdays, but he wanted to see how his younger horse would handle the crowd. Handled it just fine. Shaker scanned the field, saw a few of them whispering excitedly. A few wondering whether to speak to Sister about what they thought they'd seen.

"Dragon, come on, boy."

"Yancy! Yancy, you're a coward. Show your face."

"When I'm calling you-oo-oo-oo," Yancy imitated Nelson Eddy. It was not a success.

Dragon blinked as he heard the *"oo-oo-oo."*

Shaker pulled his tail. "Dragon, come on, fella. You're a good hound."

"Some of us don't agree," Asa barked.

Out came Dragon, dirt all over his face, to the cheers of the humans. He looked around at the other hounds, then at the humans. *"I am the greatest!"*

Shaker patted each head, sure to let the young entry know they could not have accomplished this victory without them. Then he nimbly vaulted up into the saddle, winked at Sister, called his charges, and headed northwest into the breeze, exactly as planned. By now, the cloud cover was overhead, but the eastern sky was still clear. The effect was dramatic.

As they rode across the beautiful pasture, rambling roses clambering over some of the fence, Bobby Franklin spied Raleigh and Rooster. Hearing the excitement, they'd come out into the pasture instead of staying in the woods. Bobby hadn't seen "Raymond," but the buzz reached him. He figured it was some type of illusion, but he did note that Walter was absent. Being an instinctual creature, he shut up. He sensed something was afoot. He became very alert.

As hounds weren't cast yet, Bobby gave the field over to Kitty English, a reliable person, and rode up to Sister.

"Sister, Raleigh and Rooster are here." He turned in the saddle and pointed to where the two house dogs, in their excitement, had revealed themselves.

The two culprits hurried back toward the woods, but too late.

"Those devils!" Sister fumed. "Well, there's nothing to do for it now. Thanks for telling me."

"And Sister," he whispered, "a few people think they saw, in the mists, Raymond on A. P. Hill."

"Trust me, Bobby. It's going to be a strange day."

"Okay." He touched his cap with his crop and rode back to the Hilltoppers.

Hounds moved on, a little scent here and there but picking.

Grace, down at the waterwheel ponds, heard them. She'd been fishing when Melissa and Brandon, led by Walter, took up their position on the far lip of the upper pond. The soft lap of the waterwheel had covered the sounds of their arrival, but Grace moved away before they reached the pond. She crept back because they didn't speak. Her experience with humans was they just had to yak.

As she silently circled them, Melissa's horse swept his ears forward and back. He snorted, stamping his foot. She made a little sound.

Brandon whispered, "Pat his neck."

They sat there in the swirling silver mists while the air danced over the ponds. Grace was astonished.

She stayed behind them until she heard hounds coming. Then she trotted over by the waterwheel and dipped down into the meadow heading back toward the stables, which were one mile away. Fishing was good and she wanted to get back to it, so she thought she'd run to the first den between the ponds and the stable, which was a large entrance on the creek embankment.

Grace usually didn't mind giving the foxhunters some fun, but today she preferred fishing. She tracked across the ponds pasture, swallowed in ground fog, rubbed against a fence post, and walked along the top of a fallen log. She put down so much scent that if one of the humans got down on all fours, he'd smell it, too.

Cora had reached the waterwheel, gently turning, each large cup of water spilling to the pond below. The sound alone was better than any tranquilizer. She smelled the two horses and riders, then saw them. They frightened her for a second. She let out a gruff little yelp.

Diana came right to her. *"Why aren't they riding?"*

"Don't know. But they rode past the kennels at seven. The lady is very nervous. Let's take the pack up ahead. I'm pretty sure we can pick up scent there. It's fresh." Cora put her nose down.

Melissa's horse had quieted, but she was so frightened, he began to worry and jig a little.

Brandon whispered, "Remember, smile. Pick up your reins a little. Our horses might want to join the others."

A smile froze on Melissa's gorgeous face, moist with mist.

Cora and Diana loped along the pond embankment, then tore down the side of it.

Shaker flanked the embankment. He said, as much for Melissa and Brandon as for his pack, "You'll get 'em!" He dipped deep into the cauldron of mist rising over the twin ponds, then he, too, dropped into the pasture, rivers of mist snaking through it, silver stripes next to green.

Within thirty seconds, horn blowing, hounds baying, the field reached the waterwheel ponds.

Edward, even though he knew Melissa and Brandon stood

in the mists, was shocked when he caught a glimpse of them. Melissa, the spitting image of Nola, stopped his heart. He sucked in his breath.

Tedi, all steely resolve, refused to cry.

Ron Haslip, overwhelmed, blurted out loud, "Guy! Guy and Nola!"

Xavier pitched forward on his horse.

Sybil screamed.

Ken stopped, so all the horses behind him had to stop, too.

Walter, hiding in the woods near the pond, imitated a mourning dove. That was the signal for Melissa and Brandon to evaporate into the shroud of silver.

Raleigh and Rooster stuck with Walter.

Just like remembering blocking on a stage, Melissa and Brandon turned their horses' heads. They disappeared as St. Just cawed overhead.

Chills ran down people's spines.

Although hounds were running, people couldn't help it. They started talking.

Sister, pretending not to see or know, said quite firmly, "Hark!"

The field shut up and followed her, but she and they could feel a force building, a long hidden emotion.

Hounds flew to the creek, which meandered into the pasture closest to the stables, finally feeding into Broad Creek not far from where Broad Creek crossed Soldier Road. Grace ducked into the den.

Clytemnestra and Orestes in the back pasture heard hounds moving closer.

"I'll crash this fence!" Clytemnestra loved any act of destruction.

With a moo of rapture, Clytemnestra lowered her head,

crashing through the three-board fence as though it were matchsticks. Then she frolicked past the stables, hind end higher than her front end; she even turned a circle. Orestes followed suit.

As the hounds and Shaker appeared out of the mists streaking toward the creek, Clytemnestra put on a tremendous show, mooing, bucking, prancing, a mockery of ballet.

"Bloody cow," Shaker said.

"Happy one." Delia, at the rear, giggled.

The field, close behind Shaker and the hounds, didn't laugh at Clytemnestra's antics. They'd seen too many strange sights.

As the field began to emerge from the mists, a commotion occurred at the rear.

Ken bumped Sybil hard as he turned his horse.

"Ken, what are you doing?" Sybil sharply reprimanded him. "Where are you going?"

Tedi cupped her hands to her mouth. "Sister! Ken, turning back to the waterwheel."

Sister whirled around in the saddle. "That son of a bitch!" She plunged back in the fog.

Mary Robertson, field master at Deep Run Hunt as well as MFH, calmly addressed the people riding up. "We're going back to the trailers. Please follow me."

Ken, hearing someone chasing him, clapped the spurs to his horse and flew south, toward the sunken meadows. He'd find Nola later.

Raleigh and Rooster, hearing Ken ride off, followed him.

"Mother! Mother, what's going on?" Sybil cried.

Edward grabbed Sybil's horse's bridle. "Honey, we've got to go in. Your mother and I must talk to you."

Tedi sandwiched her in by riding along her other side. "Just do as we say, honey. Please."

Betty Franklin trotted in from the left and saw Sister charge into the mist, then come out behind her, heading south. She pulled up, then obeyed the call of the horn. Jennifer, coming in from the right, saw nothing but came to the horn.

The field, in shock, watched as first Ken flew out of the ground fog and then Sister.

Clytemnestra, oblivious, kept bucking along, throwing her massive head to the right and the left. Orestes imitated his mother.

Cindy Chandler sat there knowing there'd be more fence to repair, as well as wondering what the hell was going on.

Sister pushed Lafayette. The wonderful older thoroughbred had no bottom, he'd not wear out. He'd catch that horse in front of him. He'd show him who was the best of the best.

Ken, on a good horse, jumped out of the pasture, heading for the sunken acres. He knew the territory. Knew if he crossed Soldier Road, he could get into the brush at the bottom if Sister pushed too hard. If he could keep his lead he could ride straight to Roughneck Farm, get in her truck, and get away. Just where he'd go wasn't in his mind at that moment.

A vision of twenty-one years ago was going through his mind. He wanted Nola.

Sister reached around and pulled out the .38 tucked in the small of her back. She fired a warning shot over her head.

Ken spurred on his horse.

Shaker, hearing the shot, knew it wasn't ratshot. "Jesus," he thought to himself. He told Betty and Jennifer to load up the hounds. He knew hounds would follow him, so he had to wait while they were hastily loaded. Then he was off.

Ken thought he could outride Sister, thought that because he was forty-eight and she was seventy-one he had the advantage. He should have known better. He'd ridden behind her for thirty years. She was tough as nails and always on fast horses.

He jumped into the sunken meadows and raced across, traces of rising mist all around him. He heard the two dogs behind him. Raleigh couldn't have been more than twenty yards behind. Rooster was only a few paces behind the Doberman.

He crossed Soldier Road, got across the wildflower meadows just as Sister and Lafayette crossed Soldier Road.

Shaker and Hojo cleared the fence into the sunken meadows. He looked up ahead in the distance and saw Sister leveling her gun on Ken. She fired and missed.

"Christ," he thought. "If she kills him she'll go to jail even though he deserves it." He laid his body low over Hojo, and the gelding knew just what to do. He put on the afterburners. They were over Soldier Road in no time.

Ken plunged into the wooded base of Hangman's Ridge. There was enough cover that Sister couldn't hit him. Raleigh and Rooster, however, were right behind him, giving tongue for all they were worth.

Ken cursed the fact that he didn't have a gun. He'd shoot them and he'd shoot that goddamned old woman riding hard on his tail. The bitch. If she'd come to him quietly he would have paid her off generously. And killed her later, of course.

Sister and Lafayette pulled up at the base of Hangman's Ridge for a moment, and she saw Shaker heading for her. She heard Raleigh and Rooster. She followed their voices. Like any good hunter she trusted her partners—in this case, one harrier, one Doberman, and one thoroughbred.

Warily she rode into the brush. She heard her dogs making a huge fuss and Ken cursing them. He was climbing. Well, it was faster than going around the ridge.

She pushed up the ridge. Shaker was now a third of a mile behind her.

While leading Melissa and Brandon home, Walter had heard Ken, then Sister, riding away. Now, hearing gunfire and a third set of hoofbeats, he urged the two actors to do their best and trot.

He nudged them toward Hangman's Ridge.

Ken finally reached the top of the ridge, his horse blowing hard. He pushed on, heading to the hanging tree. The mists from below, rising, dissipating, wove in and out of the branches like silvery silk ribbons. He looked up. There sat Athena and Bitsy, an unnerving sight, especially since Athena held her wings fully outstretched, spooking his horse, who jumped sideways as Ken kicked him on.

Sister was over the ridge now, and Lafayette was gaining on Ken's horse. Sister leveled her arm and fired. She hit Ken in the right shoulder. He didn't make a sound but he bobbled in the saddle.

Lafayette drew even closer. She fired again, and this time hit him in the left shoulder. Blood seeped out of the back of his coat.

He had no grip left in his hands. Ken fell off the horse, his spurs digging up the earth as he hit hard.

His horse, grateful, stopped, sides heaving, covered in lather.

Athena kept her wings spread. She looked spectral.

Sister pulled up Lafayette to stand over Ken. "I have three bullets left. I will put one through your head."

"I'll tear his throat out." Raleigh leapt on Ken.

"Off, Raleigh."

The Doberman obeyed but sat by the bleeding man, ready to strike.

Shaker came up alongside. He dismounted, whipped off his belt, and tied Ken's hands behind his back.

"Well done," Shaker said. "Jesus, I thought you were going to kill him."

"Day's not over. I just might." She stared down at Ken. "Why?"

He didn't answer, so Shaker kicked him in the kidney. "Speak when a lady speaks to you."

"I was going to lose everything."

"But you already had lost everything." Her face darkened.

He looked up at her through watery eyes.

"You lost your soul." She slipped the gun back into her belt as Athena folded her wings.

Just then Walter, with an exhausted Melissa and Brandon, rode up by the wagon road.

Ken saw Melissa. His head fell to his chest as he sobbed.

CHAPTER 41

The sordidness of it." Alice Ramy stared at a tendril of poison ivy, flaming red, twining around a walnut tree.

Sister, Alice, and Tedi Bancroft sat on the bench in the hound graveyard. The three women had gravitated there as they walked together Sunday afternoon. They found themselves bound by time, by losses and loves, and finally by the profound shock of Ken Fawkes's perfidy.

"You risked your life, Janie. I don't know how to thank you. Edward and I can never truly thank you."

"He didn't have a gun. I was safe." She grinned raffishly.

"He'd killed three people. He would have killed you if he could." Alice noticed the long rays of the sun, the changing light from summer's harshness to the soft, sweet light of winter.

"I don't know if Sybil will ever thank me."

"She will. Edward and I will get her through this. And the boys, she has to live for the boys now."

"Poor girl . . ." Alice's voice trailed off.

Alice put her arm around Tedi's shoulders. "At least we know. That's something."

Tedi's left hand fluttered to her face, the blue from Nola's sapphire pulsating. "I loved her. She was like the light on my face, but"—she struggled against her emotions—"she was wrong. Nola's capriciousness cost her life, Guy's life, Ralph's life, and her sister's happiness. She didn't deserve to die, but she was wrong, so very wrong."

Sister quietly said, "Tedi, when you're young and you have that kind of power, that power Nola had over men, maybe you just have to use it."

"I feel so guilty." Tedi choked up.

"Oh don't, Tedi. Don't." Alice hugged her. "I don't blame you. Those babies come out of the womb as who they are. We might help them or hurt them, but they're formed. You didn't make Nola the way she was. And maybe Sister's right—when you have that kind of power, you use it."

Tedi put her face in her hands. "If only I'd known!"

"Nobody knew except Ralph. And even he didn't know all of it." Sister leaned back on the bench. "I suppose we can be grateful that Ken confessed. We'd still be trying to put all the pieces together."

"To think that he'd been having an affair with Nola for six months and none of us knew. I guess they were better actors than we realized." Sister watched a small branch dip as a red-tailed hawk landed on it.

"What a fool." Tedi spat out the words.

"Well, that was it, wasn't it? She made fools of men? I don't know why Nola did it. It's one thing to exert your power, it's another thing to hurt men." Alice dropped her arm off Tedi's shoulder and held her hand. "We'll never really know what went on inside. I think at the end Guy knew. Maybe he sensed he'd never really have her. He was twenty-five. He was thinking about the future in a way he never had before. He wanted her to be part of it."

"You warned him." Tedi remembered Alice trying to steer Guy away from Nola.

"Children don't listen."

"Amen." Tedi sighed, wiping away her tears with her free hand.

Ken's confession stated that he had been sleeping with his sister-in-law. She'd grown bored, as Nola was wont to do with any man. She toyed with him while flaming around with Guy. But Ken wouldn't give up. He said he'd tell Guy. Then he said he'd kill Guy. Nola finally threatened to tell her sister, to tell her parents, if he wouldn't leave her alone.

Ken knew Sybil would divorce him. He loved being married to all that money. He couldn't expect to receive a settlement since he was the one having the affair. The Bancrofts would cast him out without a penny. He'd also grown fond of his new social position.

But Nola, being Nola, couldn't resist tantalizing him. She surreptitiously flirted with him during the first day of cubbing, even while she hung all over Guy. She brushed by Ken at Sorrell Buruss's party, pressing against his body. And she made sure he saw her every move with Guy, running her hands through Guy's black curly hair, kissing his cheek, leaning seductively against him at the bar.

Guy left the party early. He told Nola to meet him at the office. There was some paperwork he had to do, but then they could really party once he was done.

The party was wild. Ken lured Nola outside with the promise of great cocaine. They all did drugs back then, and Nola was never one to pass up a free toot.

He dangled his little vial in front of her, leading her ever farther away from the house. When he was sure no one could observe them, he tried to kiss her. She kissed him lightly, then wanted the coke. When she opened the vial to find only a few grains, she told him he was pathetic. She also told him Guy was a better lover. He lost it, grabbed her by the neck, and strangled the life right out of her. Just to make sure she was dead, he smashed her skull in with a rock, then dragged her body to the compost pile and covered her up. This took perhaps ten minutes.

He returned to the party, danced a few dances, then told his wife he would drive Ralph home in Ralph's car since their good friend was blotto. He'd be home by seven so they could go to the C&O.

Ralph, tipsy, didn't complain when Ken took him by the elbow and hustled him out. In the car, Ken spun a tale that Ralph was only too willing to believe: Guy had killed Nola because she was still in love with Ralph and that her affair with Guy was over. They drove to Guy's office and called to him. When he came outside, Ken surprised him and hit him over the head, stuffed him in Ralph's car, and drove toward After All, not five miles away. Ken pulled off the road and shot Guy before going to the house. They stuffed Guy into a big paint drum—the farm always had drums around because the fence painting never stopped. Ken dropped in the blacksmith's anvil and soldered shut the lid.

Ken promised Ralph he'd make this all worth his while. He'd give him business for the rest of his life. He'd help him buy the tractor dealership as a silent partner. Besides, he insisted Nola was dead in part because of her feelings for Ralph.

He was already implicated. In his slightly intoxicated state, it all made a strange sort of sense to Ralph.

Ken, Sybil, Ralph, and Frances met at the C&O. Later, back home when Sybil was asleep, he crawled out of bed, got a shovel, and dug a grave where the excavation work was finished for the covered bridge. Then he pushed his truck down the driveway, started it at the end so Sybil wouldn't hear, and drove back near Sorrell's. He parked off the road, walked back to the body, old canvas over his shoulder. He picked up Nola, who was cold and starting to go into rigor. She was twice as heavy. He drove back, dumped her in the grave, and filled it in. The final landscaping around the new bridge did the rest.

The next night, he prevailed upon Ralph again. They loaded the drum onto the truck in the middle of the night, drove to Norwood Bridge, and heaved Guy over the side, secure in the knowledge he would never surface.

Ralph, distressed over Nola's death and people's reaction to her disappearance, asked Ken to tell about her demise, but Ken said he'd go to jail for killing Guy. This way, cruel though it was that Tedi, Edward, and Sybil didn't know the truth of Nola's disappearance, at least Ken would be safe and Sybil would have a husband. Surely Ralph understood why Ken had to kill Guy. Nor would he tell Ralph where Guy had buried Nola's body. Ralph wanted to know, bursting into tears at the thought. Ken told him to get a grip, to get over it.

Ralph, if he figured out the truth, kept it to himself. He had a lot to lose. Ken was as good as his word about giving Ralph money for the business.

And so they prospered for twenty-one years until Nola returned. Ralph, consumed with guilt long kept at bay, called Sister. Ralph took his first step toward redemption, but he didn't have the opportunity to take any more.

Ken knew Ralph had tipped off somebody about the location of Guy's body. It was a matter of time until he killed him. The thick fog gave him an opportunity to strike before Ralph cracked, told the story.

He whispered to Ralph. No one could see him. He didn't expect Ralph to bolt. Ken had planned a more conventional end for Ralph, poison, but when Ralph ran off in the fog, Ken, who had been on the other side of the fence line, jumped the coop. He had no trouble hearing the terrified man crash through the cornfield. He tracked him up to Hangman's Ridge, shot him, hurried down the steep back way, risked all by galloping in the fog, slowing only as he neared the stables at After All. He put up his horse and reached the house shortly after the other returned riders.

Not only was he not upset by this murder, he was exhilarated by it.

Ken made his confession in great physical pain but with a clear mind and no appreciable awakening of conscience.

The only glimmer that there was something salvageable inside was when he told Ben Sidell he regretted the pain he would be causing his wife and children. Sybil had been a good wife and a good mother. He opened his mouth to say something more, but nothing came out.

As for Nola, when he spoke of her, all his suppressed rage, lust, and love boiled over with each word. Nor had twenty-one years dimmed his blind jealousy of Guy Ramy. Ken still believed they both got what they deserved.

As the three women sat there discussing what had transpired, it occurred to Sister that Tedi had seen more of the world than either she or Alice ever would. However, when you reached a certain age, even if you never left the county into which you were born, you'd usually seen most of what the human animal can do for good or evil. And you also realized that most humans were so busy defending themselves and their version of reality that they missed the nose on their own faces. They hadn't the energy to change or grow, diverting it into a lonely self-centeredness. Truly intelligent people learned from others and from history.

"It's so peaceful here," Alice said.

"Yes, I come here often. Sometimes Inky, the black fox, visits here. She sits and looks at me. I sit and look at her."

"Foxes," Tedi mused, then touched Sister's hand. "What went through your mind when you were chasing Ken?"

"I don't know exactly." She studied the hound sculpture. "Well, maybe in a way I do." Sister stopped, then smiled at Raleigh, Rooster, and Golly snoozing in the shade of the statue.

"Janie?" Tedi raised her eyebrows. "What were you thinking?"

"Just that I needed to catch him. But then once he was down I thought of Hotspur. You might remember his lines: 'And I can teach thee, coz, to shame the devil, / By telling truth: tell truth and shame the devil.' "

"Shakespeare and I aren't well acquainted." Alice smiled.

"Henry IV, Part I, Act III, Scene I," said Tedi, who recognized Sister's source. "I have to show off my expensive education from time to time."

"Well, it's over and we have to get on with our lives. I'd give anything to have Guy back, but what I do have is memories, and maybe a new way of looking at things. I intend to honor my son, not mourn him."

"Well said." Tedi felt the same way about her daughter.

"You know what I think? I've probably known it in the back of my mind, but not so I could say it." Sister gazed in wonder at tiny dancing particles suspended in a ray of light. "To wantonly destroy life is a sin, a stain, an affront to every one of us. I believe, with my heart and soul, that all life is sacred. That, it seems to me, is a truth that would shame any devil."

SOME USEFUL TERMS

AWAY—A fox has "gone away" when he has left the covert. Hounds are "away" when they have left the covert on the line of the fox.

BRUSH—The fox's tail.

BURNING SCENT—Scent so strong or hot that hounds pursue the line without hesitation.

BYE DAY—A day not regularly on the fixture card.

CAP—The fee nonmembers pay to a hunt for that day's sport.

CARRY A GOOD HEAD—When hounds run well together to a good scent, a scent spread wide enough for the whole pack to feel it.

CARRY A LINE—When hounds follow the scent. This is also called "working a line."

CAST—Hounds spread out in search of scent. They may cast themselves or be cast by the huntsman.

CHARLIE—A term for a fox. A fox may also be called Reynard.

CHECK—When hounds lose the scent and stop. The field must wait quietly while the hounds search for scent.

COLORS—A distinguishing color—usually worn on the collar but sometimes on the facings of a coat—that identifies a hunt. Colors can be awarded only by the master and can be won only in the field.

COUPLE STRAPS—Two-strap hound collars connected by a swivel link. Some members of staff will carry these on the right rear of the saddle. Since the Middle Ages hounds had been brought to the meets coupled. Hounds are always spoken of, counted, in couples. Today hounds walk or are driven to the meets. Rarely, if ever, are they coupled, but a whipper-in still carries couple straps should a hound need assistance.

COVERT—A patch of woods or bushes where a fox might hide. Pronounced *cover*.

CRY—How one hound tells another what is happening. The sound will differ according to the various stages of the chase. It's also called "giving tongue" and should occur when a hound is working a line.

CUB HUNTING—The informal hunting of young foxes in the late summer and early fall, before formal hunting. The main purpose is to enter young hounds into the pack. Until recently only the most knowledgeable members were invited to cub hunt since they would not interfere with young hounds.

DOG FOX—The male fox.

DOG HOUND—The male hound.

DOUBLE—A series of short, sharp notes blown on the horn to alert all that a fox is afoot. The "gone away" series of notes are a form of doubling the horn.

DRAFT—To acquire hounds from another hunt is to draft them.

DRAW—The plan by which a fox is hunted or searched for in a certain area, like a covert.

DRIVE—The desire to push the fox, to get up with the line. It's a very desirable trait in a hound, so long as they remain obedient.

DWELL—To hunt without getting forward. A hound that dwells is a bit of a putterer.

ENTER—Hounds are entered into the pack when they first hunt, usually during cubbing season.

FIELD—The group of people riding to hounds, exclusive of the master and hunt staff.

FIELD MASTER—The person appointed by the master to control the field. Often it is the master him- or herself.

FIXTURE—A card sent to all dues-paying members, stating when and where the hounds will meet. A fixture card properly received is an invitation to hunt. This means the card would be mailed or handed to you by the master.

GONE AWAY—The call on the horn when the fox leaves the covert.

GONE TO GROUND—A fox who has ducked into his den or some other refuge has gone to ground.

GOOD NIGHT—The traditional farewell to the master after the hunt, regardless of the time of day.

HILLTOPPER—A rider who follows the hunt but who does not jump. Hilltoppers are also called the "second field." The jumpers are called the "first flight."

HOICK—The huntsman's cheer to the hounds. It is derived from the Latin *hic haec hoc*, which means "here."

HOLD HARD—To stop immediately.

HUNTSMAN—The person in charge of the hounds in the field and in the kennel.

KENNELMAN—A hunt staff member who feeds the hounds and cleans the kennels. In wealthy hunts there may be a number of kennelmen. In hunts with a modest budget, the huntsman or even the master cleans the kennels and feeds hounds.

LARK—To jump fences unnecessarily when hounds aren't running. Masters frown on this since it is often an invitation to an accident.

LIFT—To take the hounds from a lost scent in the hopes of finding a better scent farther on.

LINE—The scent trail of the fox.

LIVERY—The uniform worn by the professional members of the hunt staff. Usually it is scarlet, but blue, yellow, brown, or gray are also used. The recent dominance of scarlet has to do with people buying coats off the rack as opposed to having tailors cut them. (When anything is mass-produced the choices usually dwindle, and such is the case with livery.)

MASK—The fox's head.

MEET—The site where the day's hunting begins.

MFH—The master of foxhounds; the individual in charge of the hunt: hiring, firing, landowner relations, opening territory (in large hunts this is the job of the hunt secretary), developing the pack of hounds, determining the first cast of each meet. As in any leadership position, the master is also the lightning rod for criticism. The master may hunt the hounds, although this is usually done by a professional huntsman, who is also responsible for the hounds in the field, at the kennels. A long relationship between a master and a huntsman allows the hunt to develop and grow.

NOSE—The scenting ability of a hound.

OVERRIDE—To press hounds too closely.

OVERRUN—When hounds shoot past the line of scent. Often the scent has been diverted or foiled by a clever fox.

RATCATCHER—The informal dress worn during cubbing season and bye days.

STERN—A hound's tail.

STIFF-NECKED FOX—One that runs in a straight line.

STRIKE HOUNDS—Those hounds who through keenness, nose, and often higher intelligence find the scent first and who press it.

TAIL HOUNDS—Those hounds running at the rear of the pack. This is not necessarily because they aren't keen; they may be older hounds.

TALLYHO—The cheer when the fox is viewed. Derived from the Norman *ty a hillaut*, thus coming into our language in 1066.

TONGUE—To vocally pursue the fox.

VIEW HALLOO (HALLOA)—The cry given by a staff member who views a fox. Staff may also say tallyho or tally back should the fox turn back. One reason a different cry may be used by staff, especially in territory where the huntsman can't see the staff, is that the field in their enthusiasm may cheer something other than a fox.

VIXEN—The female fox.

WALK—Puppies are "walked out" in the summer and fall of their first year. It's part of their education and a delight for puppies and staff.

WHIPPERS-IN—Also called whips, these are the staff members who assist the huntsman, who make sure the hounds "do right."

About the Author

Rita Mae Brown is the bestselling author of (among others) *Rubyfruit Jungle, Six of One, Southern Discomfort, Outfoxed*, and a memoir, *Rita Will.* She also collaborates with her tiger cat, Sneaky Pie, on the *New York Times* bestselling Mrs. Murphy mystery series. An Emmy-nominated screenwriter and a poet, she lives in Charlottesville, Virginia. She is master and huntsman of the Oak Ridge Foxhunt Club.